Interactive Computer Graphics

A Top-Down Approach with OpenGL™

Edward Angel
University of New Mexico

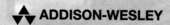

ADDISON-WESLEY

An imprint of Addison Wesley Longman, Inc.

Reading, Massachusetts • Harlow, England • Menlo Park, California
Berkeley, California • Don Mills, Ontario • Sydney
Bonn • Amsterdam • Tokyo • Mexico City

Reprinted with corrections, November 1997.

Library of Congress Cataloging-in-Publication Data

Angel, Edward.
    Interactive computer graphics : a top-down approach with OpenGL /
Edward Angel.
      p. cm.
    Includes bibliographical references and index.
    ISBN 0-201-85571-2
    1. Computer graphics.   2. OpenGL.   3. Interactive computer
systems.   I. Title.
T385.A514   1997
006.6'6—dc20   96-21656
                                                            CIP

Access the latest information about Addison-Wesley books from our World Wide Web
page: http://www.aw.com/cseng

  3 4 5 6 7 8 9 10–MA–00 99 98 97

To Rose Mary

Preface

This book is an introduction to computer graphics, with an emphasis on applications programming. Since I wrote my previous text,[1] the field has continued to experience enormous growth—a rate of growth that has exceeded most people's expectations, including my own. The recent release of the first feature-length computer-animated movie, the explosion of interest in graphical applications over the Internet, and the increase in graphics capabilities coupled with the reduced costs of both high- and low-end workstations are just a few of the exciting advances that have enhanced students' and professionals' interest in computer graphics.

A Top-Down Approach

These recent advances have reinforced my belief in a top-down, programming-oriented approach to introductory computer graphics. Although many computer-science and engineering departments now support more than one course in the subject, most students will take only a single course. Such a course is placed in the curriculum after students have already studied programming, data structures, algorithms, software engineering, and basic mathematics. A class in computer graphics allows the instructor to build on these topics in a way that can be both informative and fun. I want these students to be programming three-dimensional applications as soon as possible. Low-level algorithms, such as those that draw lines or fill polygons, can be dealt with later, after students are creating graphics.

John Kemeny, a pioneer in computer education, adapted a familiar automobile analogy to give computer literacy a programming slant: You don't have to

---

[1] *Computer Graphics*, Addison-Wesley, Reading, MA, 1990.

know what's under the hood to be literate, he agreed, but unless you know how to program, you'll be sitting in the back seat instead of driving. That same analogy applies to the way we teach computer graphics. One approach—the algorithmic approach—is to teach everything about what makes a car function: the engine, the transmission, the combustion process. A second approach—the survey approach—is to hire a chauffeur, to sit back, and to see the world as a spectator. The third approach—the programming approach that I have adopted here—is to teach you how to drive, and how to take yourself wherever you want to go. As the old auto-rental commercial used to say, "Let us put *you* in the driver's seat."

Programming with OpenGL™ and C

The greatest impediment to implementing a programming-oriented course, and to writing a textbook for that course, has been the lack of a widely accepted graphics library or application programmer's interface (API). Difficulties have included high cost, limited availability, lack of generality, and high complexity. The development of OpenGL appears to have resolved most of the difficulties many of us have experienced with other APIs (such as GKS and PHIGS), and with the alternative of using home-brewed software. OpenGL today is supported by most workstation suppliers and is available for most platforms through third-party vendors. It is bundled with Microsoft Windows NT, and both Microsoft and Silicon Graphics offer implementations for Windows 95. There is also available a free OpenGL version for most systems and an inexpensive LINUX version (see page 435 in Appendix A).

A graphics class teaches far more than the use of a particular API, but a good API makes it easier to teach key graphics topics, such as three-dimensional graphics, shading, client–server graphics, modeling, and implementation algorithms. I believe that OpenGL's extensive capabilities and well-defined architecture lead to a stronger foundation for teaching both theoretical and practical aspects of the field, and for teaching important new capabilities, such as texture mapping and compositing, that, until recently, were not supported in any API.

I switched my classes to OpenGL about 2 years ago, and the results astounded me. By the middle of the semester, *every* student was able to write a moderately complex three-dimensional program that required understanding of three-dimensional viewing and event-driven input. In 15 years of teaching computer graphics, I had never come even close to this result. That class led me to rewrite my previous book from scratch.

This book is a textbook on computer graphics; it is not an OpenGL manual. Consequently, I do not cover all aspects of the OpenGL API, but rather explain only what is necessary for mastering this book's contents. I present OpenGL at a level that should permit users of other APIs to have little difficulty with the material.

I have chosen to use the C programming language in this book, rather than C++ or another object-oriented language. There are two reasons for this decision. First, OpenGL is not object-oriented, so using C++ would not add significantly to the presentation, unless I were to insert an object-oriented geometric library between OpenGL and the user. I have not taken this step, despite its appealing features, because it would detract from the graphics and would make the book less accessible to students who are good programmers, but who are unfamiliar with object-oriented languages. Second, my experience has been that object-oriented approaches shield the user from what is going on inside (as they should), whereas, in an introduction to computer graphics, I want readers to be aware of what is happening at the lowest levels. Although the use of computer graphics is a wonderful way to introduce students to object-oriented programming, in my view, an object-oriented approach is not the most effective way to teach graphics to computer science and engineering students.

Intended Audience

This book is suitable for advanced undergraduates and first-year graduate students in computer science and engineering, and for students in other disciplines who have good programming skills. The book also will be useful to many professionals. I have taught approximately 100 short courses for professionals; my experiences with those students have had a great influence on what I have chosen to include in the book.

Prerequisites for the book are good programming skills in C, an understanding of basic data structures (linked list, trees), and a rudimentary knowledge of linear algebra and trigonometry. I have found that the mathematical backgrounds of computer-science students, whether of undergraduates or of graduates, vary considerably. Hence, I have chosen to integrate into the text much of the linear algebra and geometry that is required for fundamental computer graphics.

Organization of the Book

The book is organized as follows. Chapter 1 overviews the field and introduces image formation by optical devices; thus, we start with three-dimensional concepts immediately. Chapter 2 introduces programming using OpenGL. Although the example program that we develop—each chapter has one or more complete programming examples—is two dimensional, it is embedded in a three-dimensional setting. In Chapter 3, we discuss interactive graphics in a modern client–server setting, and develop event-driven graphics programs. Chapters 4 and 5 concentrate on three-dimensional concepts; Chapter 4 is concerned with defining and manipulating three-dimensional objects, whereas Chapter 5 is concerned with viewing them. Chapter 6 introduces light–material interactions and shading. These chapters should be covered in order, and can be done in about 10 weeks of a 15-week semester.

The last four chapters can be read in any order. All four are somewhat open ended, and can be covered at a survey level, or individual topics can be pursued in depth. Chapter 7 surveys implementation. It gives one or two major algorithms for each of the basic steps in the viewing pipeline. Chapter 8 contains a number of topics that fit loosely under the heading of modeling. These topics range from hierarchical models, such as are used in figure animation, to fractals, to models of surfaces built from data. Curves and surfaces are discussed in Chapter 9. Finally, Chapter 10 introduces many of the new capabilities that are now supported in graphics hardware and by OpenGL. All these techniques involve working with various buffers. We conclude with a short discussion of aliasing problems in computer graphics.

Programs from the book are included in Appendix A. They are also available electronically (see the next section).

Supplements

You will find current information about supplements to this book, and other information of interest, at Addison-Wesley's World Wide Web site:

http://www.aw.com/cseng

Materials available electronically include an instructor's guide, answers to selected exercises, links to other resources, and examples of student work.

Programs from the book, as well as alternative versions of these programs, are available over the Internet via anonymous ftp at:

ftp.cs.unm.edu under **pub/angel**

I welcome suggestions regarding other supplements that readers would find useful, as well as comments on the book itself:

angel@cs.unm.edu

Acknowledgments

I have been fortunate over the past few years to have worked with wonderful students at UNM. They were the first to get me interested in OpenGL, and I have learned much from them. They include Pat Crossno, Tommie Daniel, Lisa Desjarlais, Lee Ann Fisk, Maria Gallegos, Brian Jones, Thomas Keller, Pat McCormick, Martin Muller, Jim Pinkerton, Dave Rogers, and Dave Vick. Many of the examples in the Color Plates were created by these students.

This book was written during my sabbatical; various parts were written in five different countries. The experience speaks wonders for portable computers and the universality of the Internet. Nevertheless, the task would not have been accomplished without the help of a number of people and institutions that made their facilities available to me. I am greatly indebted to Jonas Montilva and Chris Birkbeck of the Universidad de los Andes (Venezuela), to Rodrigo

Gallegos and Aristides Novoa of the Universidad Tecnologica Equinoccial (Ecuador), to Long Wen Chang of the National Tsing Hua University (Taiwan), and to Kin Hong Wong and Pheng Ann Heng of the Chinese University of Hong Kong. John Brayer and Jason Stewart at the University of New Mexico, and Helen Goldstein at Addison-Wesley, somehow managed to get a variety of items to me, wherever I happened to be.

Silicon Graphics and Apple Computer were generous in making equipment available to me. John Schimpf at Silicon Graphics was a helpful resource with regard to my OpenGL needs. Portable Graphics, Template Graphics, and Metrowerks were kind enough to provide software so that I could test sample programs on a variety of platforms.

A number of other people provided significant help. I thank Gonzalo Cartagenova, Kathi Collins, Dave Klingler, Chuck Hansen, Mark Henne, Bernard Moret, Dick Nordhaus, Helena Saona, Gwen Sylvan, Carlton van Putten, and Mason Woo. I especially thank Ben Bederson and his class for class testing a draft of this manuscript. The sequence of images at the beginning of the Color Plates are from a project done by four students in that class.

Reviewers of my manuscript drafts provided a variety of viewpoints on what I should include, and on what level of presentation I should use. These reviewers included Hamid Arabnia (University of Georgia), Wayne Carlson (Ohio State University), Norman Chin (Silicon Graphics), Scott Grissom (University of Illinois, Springfield), Dick Phillips (formerly Los Alamos National Laboratories), Tom McReynolds (Silicon Graphics), and Jane Wilhelms (University of California, Santa Cruz). Although the final decisions may not reflect their views—which differed considerably from one another—each reviewer forced me to reflect on every page of the manuscript.

I acknowledge the whole production team at Addison-Wesley; these people, in addition to doing their usual great job, took on the additional burden of working with someone who was never in one place for long. My editor, Peter Gordon, was such a pleasure to work with that I am almost sorry the book is done. I am especially grateful to Lyn Dupré. I am not a natural writer. If the readers could see the original draft of this book, they would understand the wonders that Lyn does with a manuscript.

My wife, Rose Mary Molnar, did the figures for my previous book, many of which form the basis for the figures in this book. Wisely choosing not to fight over use of our only notebook computer, she was able to preserve our relationship and to contribute in a thousand other ways.

Edward Angel   *Kathmandu, Nepal*

Contents

Chapter 6   Shading   211

Figures

1

Graphics Systems and Models

As we approach the next millennium, the computer and communication technologies are becoming dominant forces in our lives. Activities as wide ranging as film making, publishing, banking, and education are undergoing revolutionary changes as these technologies alter how we conduct our daily activities. The combination of computers, networks, and the complex human visual system, through computer graphics, has led to new ways of displaying information, seeing virtual worlds, and communicating with both other people and machines.

Computer graphics is concerned with all aspects of producing pictures or images using a computer. The field began humbly over 40 years ago, with the display of a few lines on a cathode-ray tube (CRT); now, we can generate images that are nearly indistinguishable from photographs. We routinely train pilots with simulated airplanes, generating graphical displays of a virtual environment in real time. We can even make feature-length movies entirely by computer.

In this chapter, we shall start our journey with a short discussion of applications of computer graphics. Then, we shall overview graphics systems and imaging. Throughout this book, our approach will stress the relationships between computer graphics and image formation by familiar methods, such as drawing by hand and photography. We shall see that these relationships can help us to design application programs, graphics libraries, and architectures for graphics systems.

In this book, we shall introduce a particular graphics software system, **OpenGL**. OpenGL is becoming a widely accepted standard for developing graphics applications. Fortunately, it is easy to learn, and it possesses most of the characteristics of other popular graphics systems. Our approach is top down. We want you to start writing, as quickly as possible, application programs that will generate graphical output. After you begin writing simple programs, we shall discuss how the underlying graphics library and the hardware are implemented. This chapter should give you a sufficient overview to proceed to writing programs.

1.1   Applications of Computer Graphics

The development of computer graphics has been driven both by the needs of the user community and by advances in hardware and software. The applications of computer graphics are many and varied; we can, however, divide them into four major areas:

1. Display of information
2. Design
3. Simulation
4. User interfaces

Although many applications span two or more of these areas, the development of the field was based on separate work in each.

1.1.1 Display of Information

Classical graphics techniques arose as a medium to convey information among people. Although spoken and written languages serve a similar purpose, the human visual system is unrivaled both as a processor of data and as a pattern recognizer. Over 4000 years ago, the Babylonians displayed floor plans of buildings on stones. Over 2000 years ago, the Greeks were able to convey their architectural ideas graphically, even though the related mathematics were not developed until the Renaissance. Today, the same type of information is generated by architects, mechanical designers, and draftspeople using computer-based drafting systems.

For centuries, cartographers have developed maps to display celestial and geographical information. Such maps were crucial to navigators as these people explored the ends of the earth; maps are no less important today in fields such as geographic information systems.

Over the past 100 years, workers in the field of statistics have explored techniques for generating plots that aid the viewer in determining the information in a set of data. Now, we have computer plotting packages that provide a variety of plotting techniques and color tools, and that can handle multiple large data sets. Nevertheless, it is still the human's ability to recognize visual patterns that ultimately interprets what information is contained in the data.

Medicine poses interesting and important data-analysis problems. New imaging technologies—such as computerized tomography (CT), magnetic resonance imaging (MRI), ultrasound, and positron-emission tomography (PET)—generate three-dimensional data that must be subjected to computer-imaging techniques if these data are to produce useful information. Color

Plate 20 shows an image of a person's head in which the skin is displayed as transparent and the muscles are displayed as opaque. Although the data were generated by a medical imaging system, computer graphics produced the image that shows the structures.

Supercomputers now allow researchers in many areas to solve previously intractable problems. The field of scientific visualization provides graphical tools that help these researchers to interpret the vast quantity of data that they generate. In fields such as fluid flow, molecular biology, and mathematics, images generated by conversion of data to geometric entities that can be displayed have yielded new insights into complex processes. For example, Color Plate 19 shows fluid dynamics in the mantle of the Earth. A mathematical model was solved to generate the data; various visualization techniques that we shall discuss in Chapters 8 and 10 were used to produce the visualization.

1.1.2 Design

Professions such as engineering and architecture are concerned with design. Starting with a set of specifications, engineers and architects seek a cost-effective and esthetic solution satisfying the specifications. Design is an iterative process. Rarely in the real world is a problem specified such that there is a unique optimal solution. Design problems are either overdetermined, possessing no optimal solution, or underdetermined, having multiple solutions that satisfy the specifications. Thus, the designer works in an iterative manner. She generates a possible design, tests it, and then uses this solution as the basis for exploring other solutions.

The power of the paradigm of humans interacting with images on the screen of a CRT was recognized by Ivan Sutherland over 40 years ago. Today, the use of interactive graphical tools in computer-aided design (CAD) pervades fields such as architecture and the design of mechanical parts and of very-large-scale integrated (VLSI) circuits. In many such applications, the graphics is used in a number of distinct ways. For example, in a VLSI design, the graphics provides an interactive interface between the user and the design package, usually via tools such as menus and icons. In addition, once the user evolves a possible design, other tools analyze the design and display the analysis graphically. Color Plates 9 and 10 show two views of the same architectural design. Both images were generated with the same CAD system. They demonstrate the importance of having the tools available to generate different images of the same objects at different stages of the design process.

1.1.3 Simulation

Once graphics systems evolved to be capable of generating sophisticated images in real time, engineers and researchers began to use them as simulators. One of the most important uses has been in the training of pilots. Graphical flight simulators have proved both to increase safety and to reduce training expenses.

The use of special VLSI chips has led to a generation of arcade games that is as sophisticated as flight simulators. Games and educational software for home computers are almost as impressive. Color Plates 15 and 16 show two aspects of the use of computer graphics in robotic simulation. In Plate 15, we see a computer-simulated workcell. Plate 16 shows the physical robot and its graphical simulation. The simulator can be used for designing the robot, for planning its path, and for simulating its behavior in complex environments.

The television, motion picture, and advertising industries use computer graphics to generate the photorealistic images that we see on television, in movies, and in magazines. Often, these images are so realistic that we cannot distinguish computer-generated or computer-altered images from photographs. Entire animated movies can be made by computer at a cost comparable to that of movies made with traditional hand-animation techniques. In Chapters 6 and 10, we shall discuss many of the lighting effects that were used to produce computer animations. Color Plates 11–14 are four scenes from a computer-generated video. The artists and engineers who created these scenes used commercially available software (Color Plate 30 was made in the same way). The plates demonstrate our ability to generate realistic environments, such as the factory in Plate 11; to simulate robots, as shown in Plate 12; and to create special effects, such as the sparks in Plate 14. The images in Color Plate 31 show another example of the use of computer graphics to generate an effect that, although it looks realistic, could not have been created otherwise. The images in Color Plates 23 and 24 also are realistic renderings.

The field of virtual reality (VR) has opened up many new horizons. A human viewer can be equipped with a display headset (Color Plate 29) that allows her to see separate images with her right eye and her left eye. In addition, her body location and position, possibly including her head and finger positions, are tracked by the computer. She may have other interactive devices available, including force-sensing gloves and sound. She can then act as part of a computer-generated scene, limited by only the image-generation ability of the computer. For example, a surgical intern might be trained to do an operation in this way, or an astronaut might be trained to work in a weightless environment. Color Plate 22 shows one frame of a VR simulation of an airport used for situational training. The scene contains some figures that are controlled by human participants, and other figures that act autonomously, under program control.

1.1.4 User Interfaces

Our interaction with computers has become dominated by a visual paradigm that includes windows, icons, menus, and a pointing device, such as a mouse. From a user's perspective, windowing systems such as the X Window system, Microsoft Windows, and the Macintosh operating system differ in only details.

More recently, millions of people have become users of the Internet. Their access is through graphical network browsers such as Netscape that use these same interface tools. We have become so accustomed to this style of interface that we often forget that what we are doing is working with computer graphics.

Although we are familiar with the style of graphical user interface used on most workstations, advances in computer graphics have made possible other forms of interfaces. Color Plate 17 shows a network browser using the PAD++ interface. This interface allows the user to zoom in to any portion of the data using her mouse. Any object can appear at any location and at any size.

1.2   A Graphics System

A computer graphics system is a computer system; as such it must have all the components of a general-purpose computer system. Let's start with the block diagram in Figure 1.1. There are five major elements in our system:

1. Processor
2. Memory
3. Frame buffer
4. Output devices
5. Input devices

This model is general enough to include workstations, personal computers, graphics terminals attached to a central time-shared computer, and sophisticated image-generation systems. Although all the components, with the exception of the frame buffer, are present in a standard computer, it is the way each

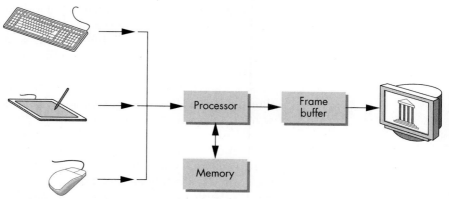

Figure 1.1 A graphics system.

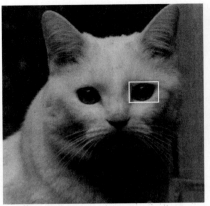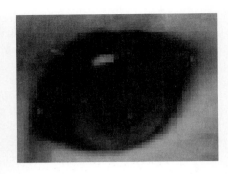

Figure 1.2 Pixels. (a) Image of a cat. (b) Detail of area around one eye showing individual pixels.

element is specialized for computer graphics that characterizes this diagram as a portrait of a graphics system.

1.2.1 Pixels and the Frame Buffer

At present, almost all graphics systems are raster based. A picture is produced as an array—the **raster**—of picture elements, or **pixels**, within the graphics system. As we can see from Figure 1.2, each pixel corresponds to a location, or small area, in the image. Collectively, the pixels are stored in a part of memory called the **frame buffer**. In high-end systems, the frame buffer is implemented with special types of memory chips—video random-access memory (VRAM) or dynamic random-access memory (DRAM)—that enable fast redisplay of the contents of the frame buffer. The **depth** of the frame buffer, defined as the number of bits that are used for each pixel, determines properties such as how many colors can be represented on a given system. For example, a 1-bit-deep frame buffer allows only two colors, whereas an 8-bit-deep frame buffer allows 2^8 (=256) colors. In **full-color** systems, there are 24 (or more) bits per pixel. Such systems can display sufficient colors to represent most images realistically. They are also called **true-color** systems, or **RGB-color** systems, because individual groups of bits in each pixel are assigned to each of the three primary colors—red, green, and blue—used in most displays. In simpler systems, the frame buffer is part of standard memory. The frame buffer can be viewed as the core element of a graphics system. Its **resolution**—the number of pixels in the frame buffer—determines the detail that you can see in the image.

In a simple system, there may be only one **processor,** which must do both the normal processing and the graphical processing. The main graphical function of the processor is to take specifications of graphical primitives (such as lines, circles, and polygons) specified by application programs, and to assign values to the pixels in the frame buffer that best represent these entities. The con-

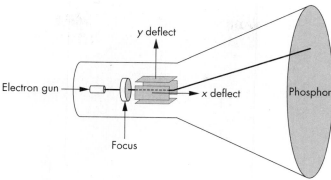

Figure 1.3 The cathode-ray tube.

verting of geometric entities to pixel assignments in the frame buffer is known as **rasterization**, or **scan conversion**. Sophisticated graphics systems are characterized by various special-purpose processors, each custom tailored to specific graphics functions.

1.2.2 Output Devices

The dominant type of display, and the one that we shall assume is used on our system, is the **cathode-ray tube** (**CRT**). A simplified picture of a CRT is shown in Figure 1.3 When electrons strike the phosphor coating on the tube, light is emitted. The direction of the beam is controlled by two pairs of deflection plates. The output of the computer is converted, by digital-to-analog converters, to voltages across the x and y deflection plates. Light appears on the surface of the CRT when a sufficiently intense beam of electrons is directed at the phosphor.

If the voltages steering the beam change at a constant rate, the beam will trace a straight line, visible to a viewer. This device is known as the **random-scan** or **calligraphic** CRT, because the beam can be moved directly from any position to any other position. If intensity of the beam is turned off, the beam can be moved to a new position without changing any visible display. This configuration was the basis of early graphics systems that predated the present raster technology.

A typical CRT will emit light for only a short time—usually, a few milliseconds—after the phosphor is excited by the electron beam. For a human to see a steady image on most CRT displays, the same path must be retraced, or **refreshed**, by the beam at least 50 times per second.

In a raster system, the graphics system takes pixels from the frame buffer and displays them as points on the surface of the display. The entire contents of the frame buffer are displayed on the CRT at a sufficiently high rate to avoid flicker. This rate is called the **refresh rate**. There are two fundamental ways that pixels are displayed on a CRT. In a **noninterlaced** system, the pixels are

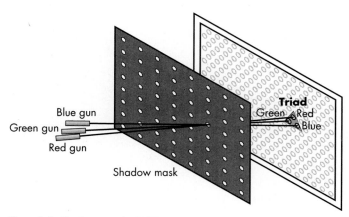

Figure 1.4 Shadow-mask CRT.

displayed row by row, or scan line by scan line, at the refresh rate, which is usually 50 to 75 times per second, or 50 to 75 Hertz (Hz). In an **interlaced** display, odd rows and even rows are refreshed alternately. Interlaced displays are used in commercial television. In an interlaced display operating at 60 Hz, the screen is redrawn in its entirety only 30 times per second, although the visual system is tricked into thinking the refresh rate is 60 Hz rather than 30 Hz. Viewers located near the screen, however, can tell the difference between the interlaced and noninterlaced displays. Noninterlaced displays are becoming more widespread, even though these displays process pixels at twice the rate of the interlaced display.

Color CRTs have three different colored phosphors (red, green, and blue), arranged in small groups. One common style arranges the phosphors in triangular groups called **triads**, each triad consisting of three phosphors, one of each primary. Most color CRTs have three electron beams, corresponding to the three types of phosphors. In the shadow-mask CRT (Figure 1.4), a metal screen with small holes—the **shadow mask**—ensures that an electron beam excites only phosphors of the proper color.

Although CRTs are the most common display device, they are not the only type. However, most other output technologies are also raster. Some, such as the liquid-crystal displays (LEDs) used in portable computers, must be refreshed, whereas hard-copy devices, such as printers, do not need to be refreshed, although they are raster based.

1.2.3 Input Devices

Most graphics systems provide a keyboard and at least one other input device. The most common input devices are the mouse, the lightpen, the joystick, and the data tablet. Each provides positional information to the system, and each usually is equipped with one or more buttons to provide signals to the processor. Often called **pointing devices**, these devices allow a user to indicate a particular location on the display. We shall study these devices in Chapter 3.

1.3   Images: Physical and Synthetic

The usual pedagogical approach to teaching computer graphics is to start with a discussion of how to construct raster images of simple two-dimensional geometric entities (for example, points, line segments, and polygons) in the frame buffer. Next, most textbooks discuss how to define mathematical objects in the computer based on the set of two-dimensional geometric entities. This approach works well for creating simple images of simple objects. In modern systems, however, we want to exploit the capabilities of the software and hardware to create realistic images of computer-generated three-dimensional objects—a task that involves many aspects of image formation, such as lighting, shading, and properties of materials. Because such functionality is supported by most present computer graphics systems, we prefer to set the stage for creating these images here, rather than to expand a limited model later.

Computer-generated images are synthetic or artificial, in the sense that the objects being imaged do not exist physically. In this chapter, we shall argue that the preferred method to form computer-generated images is similar to traditional imaging methods. Hence, before we discuss the mechanics of writing programs to generate images, we shall discuss the way images are formed by optical systems, such as cameras and the human visual system. We shall construct a model of the image-formation process that we can then use to understand and develop computer-generated imaging systems.

In this chapter, we shall make minimal use of mathematics. We want to establish a paradigm for creating images, and to present a computer architecture for implementing that paradigm. Details will be presented in subsequent chapters, where we discuss implementation. There, we shall generate the relevant equations.

1.3.1   Objects and Viewers

We live in a world of three-dimensional objects. We usually refer to the location of a point on an object in terms of some convenient reference coordinate system. We can measure the distance between points in space, and thus between various objects. The development of many branches of mathematics, including geometry and trigonometry, was in response to the desire to systematize conceptually simple ideas, such as measuring size and distance. Often, we seek to represent our understanding of such spatial relationships with pictures or images, such as maps, paintings, and photographs. Likewise, the development of many physical devices, including cameras, microscopes, and telescopes, was tied to the desire to visualize spatial relationships between objects. Hence,

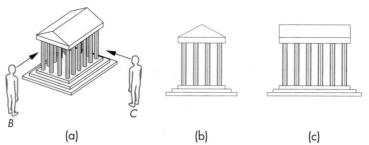

Figure 1.5 Image seen by three different viewers. (a) A's view. (b) B's view. (c) C's view.

there is a fundamental link between the physics and the mathematics of image formation—one that we shall exploit in our development of computer image formation.

Two basic entities must be part of any image-formation process, be it mathematical or physical: object and viewer. The object exists in space independent of any image-formation process, and of any viewer. In computer graphics, where we deal with synthetic objects, we form objects by specifying the positions in space of various geometric primitives, such as points, lines, and polygons. In most graphics systems, a set of locations in space, or **vertices**, is sufficient to define, or approximate, most objects. For example, two vertices define a line, a polygon can be defined by an ordered list of vertices, and a sphere can be specified by its center and any point on its circumference. One of the main functions of a CAD system is to provide an interface that makes it easy for a user to build a synthetic model of the world. In Chapter 2, we shall see how OpenGL allows us to build simple objects; in Chapter 8, we shall learn to define objects in a manner that incorporates relationships among objects.

Every imaging system must provide a means of forming images from objects. To form an image, we must have someone, or something, that is viewing our objects, be it a human, a camera, or a digitizer. It is the **viewer** that forms the image of our objects. In the human visual system, the image is formed on the back of the eye. In a camera, the image is formed in the film plane. It is easy to confuse images and objects. We usually see an object from our single perspective and forget that other viewers, located in other places, will see the same object differently. Figure 1.5(a) shows an image as seen by viewer A. In the scene are two other observers, B and C; they appear as objects to viewer A. Figures 1.5(b) and (c) show the images seen by B and C, respectively.

Figure 1.6 shows a camera system viewing a building. Here, we can observe that both the object and the viewer exist in a three-dimensional world. However, the image that they define—what we find on the film plane—is two-dimensional. The process by which the specification of the object is combined with the specification of the viewer to produce a two-dimensional image is the essence of image formation, and we shall study it in detail.

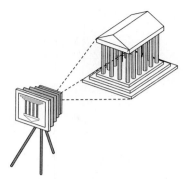

Figure 1.6 Camera system.

1.3.2 Light and Images

Much information is missing from the preceding description of image formation. For example, we have yet to mention light. If there were no light sources,
the objects would be dark and there would be nothing visible in our image.
We have not indicated how color enters the picture, or what are the effects of
different kinds of surfaces on the objects.

Taking a more physical approach, we can start with the arrangement in
Figure 1.7, which shows a simple physical imaging system. Again, we see a
physical object and a viewer (the camera); now, however, there is a light source
in the scene. Light from the source strikes various surfaces of the object, and
a portion of the reflected light enters the camera through the lens. The details
of the interaction between light and the surfaces of the object determine how
much light enters the camera.

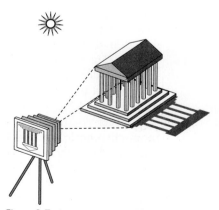

Figure 1.7 A camera system with a light
source.

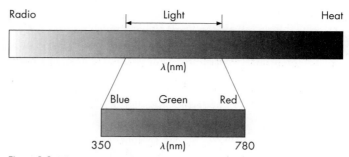

Figure 1.8 The electromagnetic spectrum.

Light is a form of electromagnetic radiation. Electromagnetic energy travels as waves that can be characterized by either their wavelengths or their frequencies.[1] The electromagnetic spectrum (Figure 1.8) includes radio waves, infrared (heat), and a portion that causes a response in our visual systems. This visible spectrum, which has wavelengths in the range of 350 to 780 nanometers (nm), is called **light**. A given light source has a color determined by the energy that it emits at various wavelengths. A laser, for example, emits light at a single wavelength, whereas an incandescent lamp emits energy over a range of wavelengths. Fortunately, except for recognizing that distinct frequencies are visible as distinct colors, we rarely need to deal with the wave nature of light in computer graphics.

Instead, we can follow a more traditional path that is correct when we are operating with sufficiently high light levels, and at a scale where the wave nature of light is not a significant factor. **Geometric optics** models light sources as emitters of light energy that have a fixed rate or intensity. Light travels in straight lines, from the sources to those objects with which it interacts. An ideal **point source** emits energy from a single location at one or more frequencies equally in all directions. More complex sources, such as a light bulb, can be characterized by emitting light over an area and by emitting more light in one direction than another. A particular source is characterized by the intensity of light that it emits at each frequency, and by that light's directionality. We shall consider only point sources for now. More complex sources often can be modeled by a number of carefully placed point sources. Modeling of light sources will be discussed in Chapter 6.

Another simplification that we will make, for now, is to consider purely **monochromatic** lighting—a source of a single frequency. Because we can add together the contributions of light at various frequencies, this assumption does

---

[1] The relationship between frequency f and wavelength λ is $f\lambda = c$, where c is the speed of light.

not restrict us, but it will make our development clearer. This assumption is equivalent to discussing only the brightness of a light, rather than the light's particular color or hue—an approach that is analogous to discussing black-and-white television before examining color television.

1.3.3 Ray Tracing

We can start building an imaging model by following light from a source. Consider the scene in Figure 1.9; it is illuminated by a single point source. We include the viewer in the figure because we are interested in the light that reaches her eye. The viewer can also be a camera as shown in Figure 1.10. A **ray** is a semi-infinite line that emanates from a point and travels to infinity in a particular direction. Because light travels in straight lines, we can think in terms of rays of light emanating in all directions from our point source. Of these infinite rays, some will contribute to forming an image on the film plane of our camera. For example, if the source is visible from the camera, some of the rays go directly from the source through the lens of the camera, and will strike the film plane. Most rays go off to infinity, neither entering the camera directly, nor striking any of the objects. These rays contribute nothing to the image, although they may be seen by some other viewer. The remaining rays strike and illuminate objects. These rays can interact with the objects' surfaces in a variety of ways. For example, if the surface is a mirror, a ray is reflected that might—depending on the orientation of the surface—enter the lens of the camera and contribute to the image. Other surfaces, known as **diffuse surfaces**, scatter light in all directions. If the surface is transparent, the light ray from the source can pass through it, perhaps being bent or **refracted**, and may interact with other objects, enter the camera, or travel to infinity without striking another surface. Figure 1.10 shows six of the possibilities.

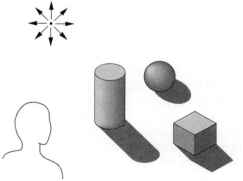

Figure 1.9 Scene with a single point source.

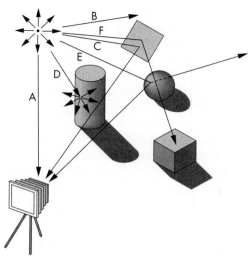

Figure 1.10 Ray tracing. Ray A goes directly through the lens, while ray B misses everything. Ray C bounces off a mirror and enters the camera. Ray D hits a diffuse surface and generates (infinite) new rays that, in principle, can contribute to the image. Ray E hits a surface that is partially transparent, and generates a transmitted ray and a reflected ray. Ray F is reflected from a surface, but strikes another surface that absorbs it.

Ray tracing is an image-formation technique that is based on these ideas and that can form the basis for producing computer-generated images. We can use the ray-tracing model to simulate physical effects as complex as we wish, as long as we are willing to carry out the requisite computing. Although the ray-tracing model is a close approximation to the physical world, it is not well suited for fast computation. We can, however, make one further simplification that will lead us to a more viable computational method. From a physical perspective, if an object emits light, we cannot tell whether we are looking at an object that is reflecting light, or whether the object is emitting light from internal energy sources. For example, a mirror that reflects light from a source toward the viewer looks like a light source. If we can see an object, it is illuminated by a source, is an emitter of light, or is both. We cannot tell by looking at the object which combination we are seeing.

Let's assume that all our objects are uniformly bright—a scenario that might be difficult to accomplish in practice, but often is a reasonable goal when we place lights in an environment. From the perspective of the viewer, a red triangle would appear to have the same shade of red at every point, and would be indistinguishable from a uniformly red emitter of light. Given this assumption, we can dispense with sources, and can use simple trigonometric methods to calculate the image. In Chapter 6, we shall relax this assumption and see how we can add light sources and more complex material properties, still without getting into the full complexity of the ray tracer.

We now introduce two imaging systems: the human visual system and the pinhole camera. The human visual system is extremely complex, but still obeys the physical principles of all imaging systems. We introduce it not only as an example of an imaging system, but also because understanding its properties will help us to exploit the capabilities of computer-graphics systems. The pinhole camera is a simple example of an imaging system that will enable us to understand the functioning of cameras and of other optical imagers. We shall emulate it to build a model of image formation.

1.4   The Human Visual System

Our extremely complex visual system has all the components of physical imaging system, such as a camera or a microscope. The major components of the visual system are shown in Figure 1.11. Light enters the eye through the lens and cornea, a transparent structure that protects the eye. The iris opens and closes to adjust the amount of light entering the eye. The lens forms an image on a two-dimensional structure called the retina at the back of the eye. The rods and cones (so named because of their appearance when magnified) are light sensors and are located on the retina. They are excited by electromagnetic energy in the range of 350 to 780 nm.

The rods are low-level-light sensors that account for our night vision; the cones are responsible for our day vision. The sizes of the rods and cones, coupled with the optical properties of the lens and cornea, determine the **resolution** of our visual systems, or our **visual acuity**. Resolution is a measure of what size objects we can see. More technically, it is a measure of how close we can place two points and still recognize that there are two distinct points.

The sensors in the human eye do not react uniformly to light energy at different wavelengths. There are three types of cones and a single type of rod.

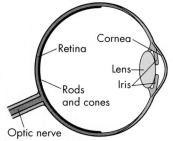

Figure 1.11 The human visual system.

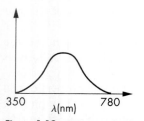

Figure 1.12 CIE standard observer curve.

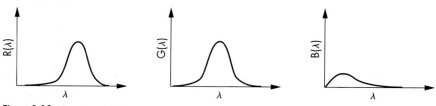

Figure 1.13 Cone sensitivity curves.

Whereas intensity is a physical measure of light energy, **brightness** is a measure of how intense we perceive the light emitted from an object to be. The human visual system does not have the same response to a monochromatic (single-frequency) red light as to a monochromatic green light. If these two lights were to emit energy with the same intensity, they would appear to us to have different brightness, due to the unequal response of the cones to red and green light. Relative brightness response at different frequencies is shown in Figure 1.12. This curve, which gives the relative sensitivity of the human visual system at visible-light frequencies, is known as the Commision Internationale de L'Eclairage **(CIE) standard observer curve.** It shows that we are most sensitive to green light, and least to red and blue. This curve also closely matches the sensitivity of the monochromatic sensors used in black-and-white film and in black-and-white video cameras.

Brightness is an overall measure of how we react to the intensity of light. Human color-vision capabilities are due to the different sensitivities of the three types of cones. Each type has its own sensitivity curve, as shown by Figure 1.13. Of the three curves, one is centered in the blue range, one in the green, and the third in the yellow.[2] The major consequence of having three types of cones is that most image-production systems, such as film and video, can work with three basic or **primary** colors. We can use standard primaries to approximate any color that we can perceive. We shall discuss color issues in Chapter 2.

The initial processing of light in the human visual system is based on the same principles as are used by most optical systems. However, the human visual system has a much more complex back end than does a camera or telescope. The optic nerves are connected to the rods and cones in an extremely complex arrangement that has many of the characteristics of a sophisticated signal processor. The final processing is done in a part of the brain called the visual cortex, where high-level functions, such as object recognition, are carried out. We shall

---

[2] The curve centered in the yellow is often referred to as the red curve to be compatible with other three-color systems used in film and video. The key point is that there are three types of sensors, rather than that the individual response curves are centered at a given frequency.

omit any discussion of high-level processing; instead we shall simply think in terms of an image that is conveyed from the rods and cones to the brain.

1.5   The Pinhole Camera

The pinhole camera in Figure 1.14 provides an example of image formation that we can understand with a simple geometric model. A **pinhole camera** is a box with a small hole in the center of one side of the box, and the film placed inside the box on the side opposite the pinhole. Suppose that we orient our camera along the z axis, with the pinhole at the origin of our coordinate system. We assume that the hole is so small that only a single ray of light, emanating from a point, can enter it. The film plane is located a distance d from the pinhole. A side view (Figure 1.15) allows us to calculate where the image of the point (x, y, z) is on the film plane $z = -d$. Using the fact that the two triangles in Figure 1.15 are similar, we find that the y coordinate of the image is at y_p, where

$$y_p = -\frac{y}{z/d}.$$

A similar calculation, using a top view, yields

$$x_p = -\frac{x}{z/d}.$$

The point $(x_p, y_p, -d)$ is called the **projection** of the point (x, y, z). In our idealized model, the color on the film plane at this point will be the color of the point (x, y, z). The **field** or **angle of view** of our camera is the angle made by the largest object that our camera can image on its film plane. We can calculate

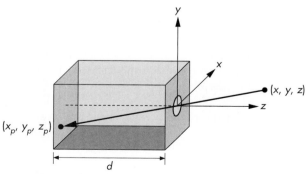

Figure 1.14 Pinhole camera.

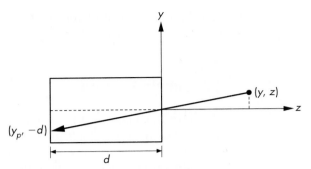

Figure 1.15 Side view of pinhole camera.

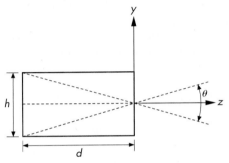

Figure 1.16 Angle of view.

the field of view with the aid of Figure 1.16.[3] If h is the height of the camera, the angle of view θ is

$$\theta = 2\tan^{-1}\frac{h}{2d}.$$

The ideal pinhole camera has an infinite **depth of field**: Every point within its field of view is in focus. The image of a point is a point. The pinhole camera has two disadvantages. First, because the pinhole is so small—it admits only a single ray from a point source—almost no light enters the camera. Second, the camera cannot be adjusted to have a different angle of view.

The jump to more sophisticated cameras and to other imaging systems that have lenses is a small one. By replacing the pinhole with a lens, we solve the two problems of the pinhole camera. First, the lens gathers more light than can pass through the pinhole. The larger the lens, the more light that lens can collect.

---

[3] If we consider the problem in three, rather than two, dimensions, then the diagonal length of the film will substitute for h. See Exercise 1.1.

Second, by picking a lens with the proper focal length—a selection equivalent to choosing d for the pinhole camera—we can achieve any desired angle of view (up to 180 degrees). Lenses, however, do not have an infinite depth of field; objects at different distances from the lens will not all be in focus.

For our purposes, in this chapter, we can work with a pinhole camera whose focal length is the distance d from the front of the camera to the film plane. Computer graphics will, like the pinhole camera, produce images in which all objects are in focus.

1.6 The Synthetic-Camera Model

Our models of optical imaging systems lead directly to the conceptual foundation for modern three-dimensional computer graphics. We look at creating a computer-generated image as being similar to forming an image using an optical system. This paradigm has become known as the **synthetic-camera model**. Consider the imaging system shown in Figure 1.17. We again see objects and a viewer. In this case, the viewer is a bellows camera.[4] The image is formed on the film plane at the back of the camera. So that we can emulate this process to create artificial images, we need to identify a few basic principles.

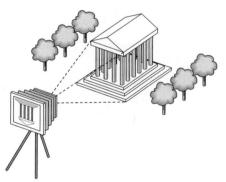

Figure 1.17 Imaging system.

First, the specification of the objects is independent of the specification of the viewer. Hence, we should expect that, within a graphics library, there will be separate functions for specifying the objects and the viewer.

---

[4] In a bellows camera, the front plane of the camera, where the lens is located, and the back of the camera, the film plane, are connected by flexible sides. Thus, we can move the back of the camera independently of the front of the camera, introducing additional flexibility in the image-formation process. We shall use this flexibility in Chapter 5.

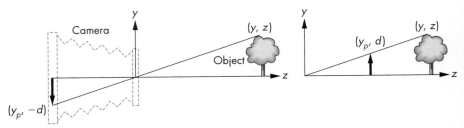

Figure 1.18 Equivalent views of image formation.

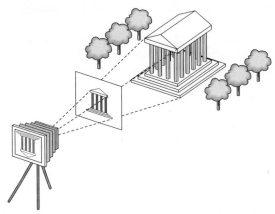

Figure 1.19 Imaging with the synthetic camera.

Second, we can compute the image using simple trigonometric calculations. We can derive these calculations in a straightforward manner. Consider the side view of the camera and a simple object in Figure 1.18. The view on the left is similar to that of the pinhole camera. We obtain the view on the right by noting the similarity of the two triangles: We move the image plane in front of lens, and, in three dimensions, work with the arrangement of Figure 1.19. We find the image of a point on the object by drawing a line, called a **projector**, from the point to the center of the lens, or the **center of projection.** Note that all projectors are rays emanating from the center of projection. In our synthetic camera, the film plane that we have moved in front of the lens is called the **projection plane.** The image of the point is located where the projector passes through the projection plane. In Chapter 5, we shall discuss this process in detail and derive the relevant mathematical formulas.

We must also consider the limited size of the image. As we saw, not all objects can be imaged onto the pinhole camera's film plane. The angle of view expresses this limitation. In the synthetic camera, we can move this limitation to the front by placing a **clipping rectangle**, or **clipping window**, in the projection plane (Figure 1.20). This rectangle acts as a window through which a viewer, located at the center of projection, sees the world. Given the location

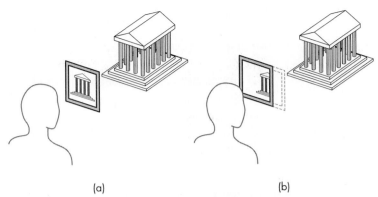

(a)   (b)

Figure 1.20 Clipping. (a) with window in initial position. (b) with window shifted.

of the center of projection, the location and orientation of the projection plane, and the size of the clipping rectangle, we can determine which objects will appear in the image.

1.7 The Programmer's Interface

There are numerous ways that a user can interact with a graphics system. With completely self-contained packages, such as are used in the CAD community, a user develops images through interactions with the display, using input devices, such as a mouse and a keyboard. In a typical application, such as the painting program in Figure 1.21, she sees menus and icons that represent possible actions. By clicking on these items, the user guides the software and produces images without having to write programs.

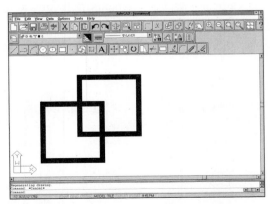

Figure 1.21 Interface for a painting program.

Of course, someone has to develop the code for these applications, and many of us, despite the sophistication of commercial products, still have to write our own graphics application programs (and even enjoy doing so).

1.7.1 Application Programmer's Interfaces

The interface between an application program and a graphics system can be specified through a set of functions that resides in a graphics library. These specifications are called the **application programmer's interface** (**API**). The application programmer's model of the system is as shown in Figure 1.22. The application programmer sees only the API, and is thus shielded from the details of both the hardware and the software implementation of the graphics library. From the perspective of the writer of an application program, the functions available through the API should match the conceptual model that the user wishes to employ to specify images. The synthetic-camera model is the basis for a number of popular APIs, including OpenGL, PHIGS, and GKS-3D.

If we are to follow the synthetic-camera model, we need functions in the API to specify

- Objects
- The viewer
- Light sources
- Material properties

Objects are usually defined by sets of vertices. For simple geometric objects—such as line segments, rectangles, and polygons—there is a simple relationship between a list of vertices and the object. For more complex objects, there may be multiple ways of defining the object from a set of vertices. A circle, for example, can be defined by three points on its circumference, or by its center and one point on the circumference.

Most APIs provide similar sets of primitive objects for the user. These primitives are usually those that can be displayed rapidly on the hardware. The usual sets include points, line segments, polygons, and, sometimes, text. OpenGL de-

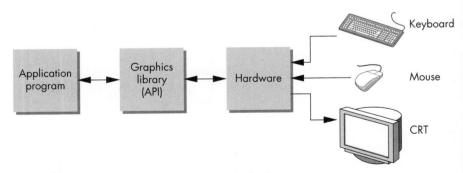

Figure 1.22 Application programmer's model of software.

fines primitives through lists of vertices. The following code fragment defines a triangular polygon in OpenGL through five function calls:

```
glBegin(GL_POLYGON);
    glVertex3f(0.0, 0.0, 0.0);
    glVertex3f(0.0, 1.0, 0.0);
    glVertex3f(0.0, 0.0, 1.0);
glEnd( );
```

Note that, by adding additional vertices, we can define an arbitrary polygon. If we change the type parameter, GL_POLYGON, we can use the same vertices to define a different geometric primitive. For example, the type GL_LINE_STRIP uses the vertices to define two connected line segments, whereas the type GL_POINTS uses the same vertices to define three points.

Some APIs let the user work directly in the frame buffer by providing functions that read and write pixels. Some APIs provide curves and surfaces as primitives; often, however, these types are approximated by a series of simpler primitives within the application program. OpenGL provides access to the frame buffer, curves, and surfaces.

We can define a viewer or camera in a variety of ways. Available APIs differ in both how much flexibility they provide in camera selection, and in how many different methods they allow. If we look at the camera in Figure 1.23, we can identify four types of necessary specifications:

1. **Position** The camera location usually is given by the position of the center of the lens (the center of projection).
2. **Orientation** Once we have positioned the camera, we can place a camera coordinate system with its origin at the center of projection. We can then rotate the camera independently around the three axes of this system.
3. **Focal length** The focal length of the lens determines the size of the image on the film plane or, equivalently, the portion of the world the camera sees.
4. **Film plane** The back of the camera has a height and a width. On the bellows camera, and in some APIs, the orientation of the back of the camera can be adjusted independently of the orientation of the lens.

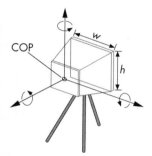

Figure 1.23 Camera specification.

These specifications can be satisfied in various ways. One way to develop the specifications for the camera location and orientation is with the aid of a series of coordinate-system transformations. These transformations convert object positions represented in the coordinate system that was used to specify object vertices to object positions in a coordinate system centered at the center of projection. This approach is useful, both for doing implementation and for getting the full set of views that a flexible camera can provide. We shall use this approach extensively, starting in Chapter 5.

Having many parameters to adjust, however, can also make it difficult to get a desired image. Part of the problem lies with the synthetic-camera model.

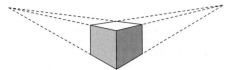

Figure 1.24 Two-point perspective of a cube.

Classical viewing techniques, such as are used in architecture, stress the *relationship* between the object and the viewer, rather than the *independence* that the synthetic-camera model emphasizes. Thus, the classical two-point perspective of a cube in Figure 1.24 is a two-point perspective because of a particular relationship between the viewer and the planes of the cube (see Exercise 1.6). Although the OpenGL API allows us to set transformations with complete freedom, it also provides helpful extra functions. For example, consider the two function calls

```
gluLookAt(cop_x, cop_y, cop_z, at_x, at_y, at_z, . . . );
glPerspective(field_of_view, . . . );
```

The first function call points the camera from a center of projection toward a desired point; the second selects a lens for a perspective view. However, none of the APIs built on the synthetic-camera model—OpenGL, PHIGS, GKS-3D—provide functions for specifying desired relationships between the camera and an object.

Light sources can be defined by their location, strength, color, and directionality. APIs provide a set of functions to specify these parameters for each source. Material properties are characteristics, or attributes, of the objects, and such properties are usually specified through a series of function calls at the time that each object is defined. Both light sources and material properties depend on the models of light–material interactions supported by the API. We shall discuss such models in Chapter 6.

1.7.2 A Sequence of Images

In Chapter 2, we begin our detailed discussion of the OpenGL API that we will use throughout this book. OpenGL will allow you to write graphical application programs. The images defined by your programs will be formed automatically by the hardware and software implementation of the image-formation process.

Here, we shall look at a sequence of images that shows what we can create using the OpenGL API. We shall present these images as an increasingly more complex series of renderings of the same objects. The sequence not only loosely follows the order in which we shall present related topics, but also reflects how graphics systems have developed over the past 20 years.

Color Plate 1 shows a scene rendered using only line segments. Although the scene consists of several objects, and although the programmer may have used sophisticated data structures to model each object and the relationships among the objects, the rendered scene shows only the outlines of the objects. This type of image is known as a **wireframe** image, because we can see only the edges of surfaces: Such an image would be produced if the objects were constructed with stiff wires that formed a frame with no solid material between the edges. Before raster-graphics systems became available, wireframe images were the only type of computer-generated images that we could produce.

In Color Plate 3, the same scene has been rendered with flat polygons. Certain surfaces are not visible because there is a solid surface between them and the viewer; these surfaces have been removed by a hidden-surface-removal (HSR) algorithm. Most raster systems can fill the interior of polygons with a solid color in the same time that they can render a wireframe image. Although the objects are three-dimensional, each surface is displayed in a single color, and the image fails to show the three-dimensional shapes of the objects. Early raster systems could produce images of this form.

In Chapters 2 and 3, we shall show you how to generate images composed of simple geometric objects—points, line segments, and polygons. In Chapters 4 and 5, you will learn how to transform objects in three dimensions, and how to obtain a desired three-dimensional view of a model, with hidden surfaces removed.

Color Plate 4 introduces a light source and a simple shading of the objects; it shows that the objects are three-dimensional. Color Plate 5 uses a more sophisticated shading model that we shall develop in Chapter 6, and that is supported in OpenGL. These shading models are also supported in the hardware of high-end graphics workstations; generating the shaded image on one of these systems takes the same amount of time as does generating a wireframe image.

In Color Plate 6, we add surface texture to our objects; texture is one of the effects that we shall discuss in Chapter 10. The most sophisticated workstations now support texture mapping in hardware, so that the rendering of a texture-mapped image requires no additional time. Color Plate 7 adds fractal objects, the mountains, to the scene. We shall learn to generate such objects in Chapter 8. Finally, in Color Plate 8, we have added fog to the rendering; fog is another effect that is supported in sophisticated hardware. We shall discuss implementation of this effect in Chapter 10.

Not only do these images show what is possible with available hardware and a good API, but also they are not difficult to generate, as we shall see in subsequent chapters. In addition, just as the images show incremental changes in the renderings, the programs are incrementally different from one another.

1.7.3 The Modeling–Rendering Paradigm

Another approach to image formation can also be pursued: In many situations—especially in CAD applications and in development of realistic images, such as for movies—we can separate the modeling of the scene from the

Figure 1.25 The modeling–rendering pipeline.

production of the image—the **rendering** of the scene. Hence, we can look at image formation as the two-step process shown in Figure 1.25. Although the tasks are the same as those that we have been discussing, this block diagram suggests that we might implement the modeler and the renderer with different software and hardware. For example, consider the production of a single frame in an animation. We first want to design and position our objects. This step is highly interactive, and we do not need to work with detailed images of the objects. Consequently, we prefer to carry out this step on a graphical workstation. Once we have designed the scene, we want to render it, adding light sources, material properties, and a variety of other detailed effects, to form a production-quality image. This step requires a tremendous amount of computation, so we prefer to use a number-cruncher machine. Not only is the optimal hardware different in the modeling and rendering steps, but also the software that we use may be different.

The interface between the modeler and renderer can be as simple as a file produced by the modeler that describes the objects, and that contains additional information important to only the renderer, such as light sources, viewer location, and material properties. PIXAR's Renderman Interface follows this approach. One of the other advantages of this approach is that it allows us to develop modelers that, although they use the same renderer, are custom-tailored to particular applications. Likewise, different renderers can take as input the same interface file. It is even possible, at least in principle, to dispense with the modeler completely, and to use a standard text editor to generate an interface file. For any but the simplest scenes, however, users cannot edit lists of information for a renderer. Rather, they use interactive modeling software. Because we must have at least a simple image of our objects to interact with a modeler, most modelers use the synthetic-camera model to produce these images in real time.

1.8   Graphics Architectures

On one side of the API is the application program. On the other is some combination of hardware and software that implements the functionality of the API. Researchers have taken various approaches to developing architectures to support graphics APIs.

Early graphics systems used general-purpose computers with the standard von Neumann architecture. Such computers are characterized by a single processing unit that processes a single instruction at a time. A simple model of these early graphics systems is shown in Figure 1.26. The display in these systems was based on a CRT display that included the necessary circuitry to generate a line segment connecting two points. The job of the host computer was to run the application program, and to compute the endpoints of the line segments in the image (in units of the display). This information had to be sent to the display at a rate high enough to avoid flicker on the display. In the early days of computer graphics, computers were so slow that refreshing even simple images, containing a few hundred line segments, would burden an expensive computer.

Figure 1.26 Early graphics system.

1.8.1 Display Processors

The earliest attempts to build special-purpose graphics systems were concerned primarily with relieving the general-purpose computer from the task of refreshing the display continuously. These **display processors** had conventional architectures (Figure 1.27), but included instructions to display primitives on the CRT. The main advantage of the display processor was that the instructions to generate the image could be assembled once in the host and sent to the display processor, where they were stored in the display processor's own memory as a **display list** or **display file**. The display processor would then execute repetitively the program in the display list, at a rate sufficient to avoid flicker, independently of the host, thus freeing the host for other tasks. This architecture has become closely associated with the client–server architectures that we shall discuss in Chapter 3.

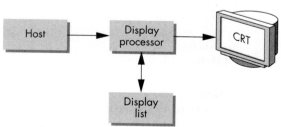

Figure 1.27 Display–processor architecture.

1.8.2 Pipeline Architectures

The major advances in graphics architectures parallel closely the advances in workstations. In both cases, the ability to create special-purpose VLSI circuits was the key enabling technology development. In addition, the availability of cheap solid-state memory led to the universality of raster displays.

For computer graphics applications, the most important use of custom VLSI circuits has been in creating **pipeline** architectures. The concept of pipelining is illustrated in Figure 1.28 for a simple arithmetic calculation.

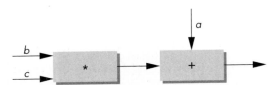

Figure 1.28 Arithmetic pipeline.

In our pipeline, there is an adder and a multiplier. If we use this configuration to compute $a + (b * c)$, the calculation takes one multiplication and one addition—the same amount of work required if we use a single processor to carry out both operations. However, suppose that we have to carry out the same computation with many values of a, b, and c. Now, the multiplier can pass on the results of its calculation to the adder, and can start its next multiplication while the adder carries out the second step of the calculation on the first set of data. Hence, whereas it takes the same amount of time to calculate the results for any one set of data, when we are working on two sets of data at one time, our total time for calculation is shortened markedly. Here, the rate at which data flows through the system, the **throughput** of the system, has been doubled.

We can construct pipelines for more complex arithmetic calculations that will afford even greater increases in throughput. Of course, there is no point in building a pipeline unless we will do the same operation on many data sets. But that is just what we do in computer graphics, where large sets of vertices must be processed in the same manner.

Suppose that we have a set of vertices that defines a set of primitives. Because our representation is given in terms of locations in space, we can refer to the set of primitive types and vertices as the **geometry** of the data. In a complex scene, there may be thousands—even millions—of vertices that define the objects. We must process all these vertices in a similar manner to form an image in the frame buffer. If we think in terms of processing the geometry of our objects to obtain an image, we can employ the block diagram in Figure 1.29, which shows the four major steps in the imaging process:

1. Transformation
2. Clipping
3. Projection
4. Rasterization

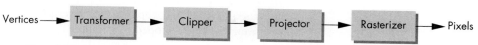

Figure 1.29 Geometric pipeline.

In subsequent chapters, we shall discuss the details of these steps. Here, we shall be content to show that these operations can be pipelined.

1.8.3 Transformations

Many of the steps in the imaging process can be viewed as transformations between representations of objects in different coordinate systems. For example, in our discussion of the synthetic camera, we observed that a major part of viewing is to convert to a representation of objects from the system in which they were defined to a representation in terms of the coordinate system of the camera. A further example of a transformation arises when we finally put our images onto a CRT display, or other output device. The internal representation of objects—whether in the camera coordinate system or perhaps in a system used by the graphics software—eventually must be represented in terms of the coordinate system of the display. We can represent each change of coordinate systems by a matrix. We can represent successive changes in coordinate systems by multiplying, or **concatenating**, the individual matrices into a single matrix. In Chapter 4, we shall examine these operations in detail. Because multiplying one matrix by another matrix yields a third matrix, a sequence of transformations is an obvious candidate for a pipeline architecture. In addition, because the matrices that we use in computer graphics will always be small (4×4), we have the opportunity to use parallelism within the transformation blocks in the pipeline.

1.8.4 Clipping

The second fundamental operation in the implementation of computer graphics is **clipping**. We do clipping because of the limitation that no imaging system can see the whole world at once. The human retina has a limited size corresponding to an approximately 90-degree field of view. Cameras have film of limited size, and we can adjust their fields of view by selecting a proper lens. We obtain the equivalent property in the synthetic camera by placing a **clipping rectangle** of limited size in the projection plane, as we saw in Figure 1.20. Objects whose projections are within the window appear in the image. Those that are outside do not, and are said to be clipped out. Objects whose projections straddle the edges of the window are partly visible in the image.

Clipping can occur at various stages in the imaging process. For simple geometric objects, we can determine whether or not an object is clipped out from its vertices. Because clippers work with vertices, clippers can be inserted with transformers into the pipeline. Clipping can even be subdivided further into a sequence of pipelined clippers (see Exercises 1.4 and 1.5). Efficient clipping algorithms will be developed in Chapter 7.

1.8.5 Projection

In general, three-dimensional objects are kept in three dimensions as long as possible, as they pass through the pipeline. Eventually, after multiple stages of transformation and clipping, the geometry of the remaining primitives (those that have not been clipped out and will appear the image) must be projected into two-dimensional objects. There are various projections that we can implement; we shall see in Chapter 5 that we can implement this step using 4×4 matrices, and, thus, also fit it in the pipeline.

1.8.6 Rasterization

Finally, our projected objects must be represented as pixels in the frame buffer. We shall discuss this scan-conversion or rasterization process in Chapter 7 for the standard primitives, such as line segments and polygons. Because the refreshing of the display is carried out automatically by the hardware, the details are of minor concern to the applications programmer. Thus, we can think of the rasterizer as being the end of the pipeline.

1.8.7 Performance Issues

There are two fundamentally different types of processing in our architecture. At the front end, there is geometric processing, based on processing vertices through the various clippers and transformers. This processing is ideally suited for pipelining, and usually involves floating-point calculations. The geometry engine developed by Silicon Graphics was a VLSI implementation for many of these operations in a special-purpose chip that became the basis for a series of fast graphics workstations. Later, floating-point accelerator chips, such as the Intel i860, put 4×4 matrix-transformation units on the chip, reducing a matrix multiplication to a single instruction.

Pipeline architectures are the dominant type of high-performance system. As we add more boxes to the pipeline, however, it takes more time for a single datum to pass through the system. This time is called the **latency** of the system; we must balance it against increased throughput in evaluating the performance of a pipeline.

Beginning with rasterization and including many features that we shall discuss later, processing involves a direct manipulation of bits in the frame buffer. This back-end processing is fundamentally different from front-end processing, and we implement it most effectively using architectures that have the ability to move blocks of bits quickly. The overall performance of a system is characterized by how fast we can move geometric entities through the pipeline, and by how many pixels per second we can alter in the frame buffer. Consequently, the fastest graphics workstations are characterized by pipeline front ends and parallel bit processors at the back ends.

Pipeline architectures dominate the graphics field, especially where real-time performance is of importance. Our presentation has made a case for using such an architecture to implement the hardware in a system. However, we can also make as strong a case for pipelining being the basis of a complete software implementation of an API. The power of the synthetic-camera paradigm is that the latter works well in both cases.

1.9   Summary

In this chapter, we have set the stage for our top-down development of computer graphics. We presented the overall picture so that you can proceed to writing graphics applications programs in the next chapter without feeling that you are working in a vacuum.

We have stressed that computer graphics is a method of image formation that should be related to classical methods of image formation—in particular, to image formation in optical systems, such as in cameras. We have also introduced the human visual system as an example of an imaging system. In Chapter 2, when we discuss color graphics, we shall see that understanding the perceptual aspects of the human visual system will help us to produce images that meet our expectations.

Along the way, we saw three distinct image-formation paradigms, each of which has applicability in computer graphics. The synthetic-camera model has two important consequences for computer graphics. First, it stresses the independence of the objects and the viewer—a distinction that leads to a good way of organizing the functions that will be in a graphics library. Second, it leads to the notion of a pipeline architecture, in which each of the various stages in the pipeline performs distinct operations on geometric entities, then passes the transformed objects on to the next stage.

We also introduced the idea of tracing rays of light to obtain an image. This paradigm is especially useful in understanding the interaction between light and materials that is essential to physical image formation. Ray tracing provides an alternative way to develop a computer graphics system. Were we to attempt such development, however, we would have to alter the paradigm, because, of all the rays leaving a source, only a small fraction enter the imaging system, and the time spent tracing most rays is wasted. In Chapter 6, we shall see a practical method that is based on casting rays from the center of projection. All such rays must contribute to the image.

The modeling–rendering paradigm is becoming increasingly important. A good graphics workstation can generate millions of line segments or polygons per second at the resolution of up to 1280×1024 pixels. Such a workstation can shade the polygons using a simple shading model, and can display only visible surfaces at this rate. However, realistic images may require a resolution of up to 4000×6000 pixels to match the capabilities of film, and may use light and material effects that cannot be implemented in real time. Even as the power of available hardware and software continues to grow, modeling and rendering have such different goals that we can expect the distinction between a modeling system and a rendering system to survive.

Our next step will be to explore the application side of graphics programming. We shall use the OpenGL API, which is powerful, is supported on most platforms, and has a distinct architecture that will allow us to use it to understand how computer graphics works, from an application program to a final image on a display.

1.10   Suggested Readings

There are many excellent graphics textbooks. The book by Newman and Sproull [New73] was the first to take the modern point of view of using the synthetic-camera model. The various versions of Foley et al. [Fol90, Fol94] have been the standard references for the past decade. Other good texts include Hearn and Baker [Hea94] and Hill [Hil90]. Foley, as well as Hearn and Baker, use PHIGS, whereas Angel [Ang90] uses GKS.

Good general references include *Computer Graphics*, the quarterly journal of SIGGRAPH (the Association for Computing Machinery's Special Interest Group on Graphics), *IEEE Computer Graphics and Applications*, and *Visual Computer*. The summer issue of *Computer Graphics* is the proceedings of the annual SIGGRAPH conference and includes the latest techniques. Of particular interest to newcomers to the field are the state-of-the-art videotapes available from SIGGRAPH, and the notes from tutorial courses taught at that conference. The latter are available on CD-ROM.

Sutherland's doctoral dissertation, "Project Sketchpad," published as *Sketchpad: A Man–Machine Graphical Communication System* [Sut63] was probably the seminal paper in the development of interactive computer graphics. Sutherland was the first to realize the power of the new paradigm in which humans interacted with images on a CRT display. Videotape copies of film of his original work are still available.

Tufte's books [Tuf83, Tuf90] show the importance of good visual design, and contain considerable historical information on the development of graphics. The article by Carlbom and Paciorek [Car78] gives a good discussion of some of the relationships between classical viewing, as used in fields such as architecture, and viewing by computer.

Many books describe the human visual system. Pratt [Pra78] gives a good short discussion for working with raster displays. Also see Glassner [Gla94], Wyszecki and Stiles [Wys82], and Hall [Hal89].

Exercises

1.1 The *focal length* of a camera lens is the distance from the center of the lens to the point at which parallel rays of light will all be focused. For a pinhole camera, the focal length is the distance from the pinhole to the film plane. The dimensions of a frame of 35-mm film are about 24 mm × 36 mm. Assuming that the human visual system has an angle of view of 90 degrees, what focal length should we use with 35-mm film to achieve a natural view?

1.2 In computer graphics, objects such as spheres are usually approximated by simpler objects constructed from flat polygons (polyhedra). Start with a regular tetrahedron, which is constructed from four triangles. Find its vertices, assuming that it is centered at the origin and has one vertex on the y axis. Derive an algorithm for obtaining increasingly closer approximations to a unit sphere, based on subdividing the faces of the tetrahedron.

1.3 Consider the clipping of a line segment defined by the latter's two endpoints. Show that you require only the endpoints to determine whether the line segment is not clipped, is partially visible, or is clipped out completely.

1.4 For a line segment, show that clipping against the top of the clipping rectangle can be done independently of the clipping against the other sides. Use this result to show that a clipper can be implemented as a pipeline of four simpler clippers.

1.5 Extend Exercises 1.3 and 1.4 to clipping against a three-dimensional right parallelepiped.

1.6 Consider the perspective views of the cube shown in Figure 1.30. The one on the left is called a *one-point perspective* because parallel lines in one direction of the cube—along the sides of the top—converge to a *vanishing point* in the image. In contrast, the image in the left is a *two-point perspective*. Characterize the particular relationship between the viewer, or a simple camera, and the cube that determines why one is a two-point perspective and the other a one-point perspective.

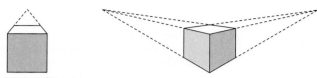

Figure 1.30 Perspectives of cube.

1.7 The memory in a frame buffer must be fast enough to allow the display to be refreshed at a rate sufficiently high to avoid flicker. A typical workstation display can have a resolution of 1280×1024 pixels. If it is refreshed 72 times per second, how fast must the memory be? That is, how much time can we take to read one pixel from memory? What is this number for a 480×640 display that operates at 60 Hz but is interlaced?

1.8 One second of a movie consists of 24 frames of film—a rate that appears to be too low to avoid visible flicker. How is the flicker problem handled by the projector?

1.9 Consider the design of a two-dimensional graphical API for a specific application, such as for VLSI design. List all the primitives and attributes that you would include in your system.

1.10 It is possible to design a color CRT that uses a single electron gun and does not have a shadow mask. The single beam is turned on and off at the appropriate times to excite the desired phosphors. Why might such a CRT be more difficult to design, as compared to the shadow-mask CRT?

1.11 In a typical shadow-mask CRT, if we want to have a smooth display, the width of a pixel must be about three times the width of a triad. Assume that a monitor displays 1280×1024 pixels, has a CRT diameter of 50 cm, and has a CRT depth of 25 cm. Estimate the spacing between holes in the shadow mask.

2 Graphics Programming

Our approach to computer graphics is programming oriented. Consequently, we want you to get started programming graphics as soon as possible. To this end, we shall introduce a minimal application programmer's interface (API). It will be sufficient to allow you to program many interesting two-dimensional problems and to familiarize you with the basic graphics concepts.

We shall regard two-dimensional graphics as a special case of three-dimensional graphics. This perspective will allow us to get started, even though we shall touch on three-dimensional concepts lightly in this chapter. Our code will be correct in the sense that it will execute without modification on a three-dimensional system.

Our development will use a simple but interesting problem: the Sierpinski gasket. It will show how we can generate an interesting and, to many people, unexpectedly sophisticated plot using only a handful of graphics functions. We shall use OpenGL as our API, but our discussion of the underlying concepts will be broad enough to encompass most modern systems, including the Programmer's Hierarchical Graphics System (PHIGS) and the Graphical Kernel System (GKS). The functionality that we shall introduce in this chapter will be sufficient for writing sophisticated two-dimensional programs that do not require user interaction.

2.1 The Sierpinski Gasket

We shall use as a sample problem the drawing of the Sierpinski gasket—an interesting shape that has a long history and that is of interest in areas such as fractal geometry. The Sierpinski gasket is an object that can be defined recursively and randomly, but, in the limit, has properties that are not at all random.

Suppose that we start with three vertices in the plane. Assume that their locations, as specified in some convenient coordinate system,[1] are (x_1, y_1), (x_2, y_2), and (x_3, y_3). The construction proceeds as follows:

1. Pick an initial point at random inside the triangle.
2. Select one of the three vertices at random.
3. Find the point halfway between the initial point and the randomly selected vertex.
4. Display this new point by putting some sort of marker, such as a small circle, at its location.
5. Replace the initial point with this new point.
6. Return to step 2.

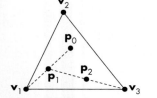

Figure 2.1 Generation of the Sierpinski gasket.

Thus, each time that we generate a point, we display it on the output device. This process is illustrated in Figure 2.1, where $\mathbf{p}_0$ is the initial point, and $\mathbf{p}_1$ and $\mathbf{p}_2$ are the first two points generated by our algorithm.

Before we develop the program, you might consider what you expect the resulting image to be. Try to construct it on paper; you might be surprised by your results.

Here is the form of our graphics program:

```
main( )
{
    initialize_the_system();

    for(some_number_of_points)
    {
        generate_a_point();
        display_the_point();
    }

    cleanup();
}
```

The corresponding OpenGL program is almost that simple. First, we shall concentrate on the core: generating and displaying points. Two questions that we must consider are how we represent points in space, and whether we use a two-dimensional, three-dimensional, or other representation.

---

[1] In Chapter 4, we shall expand the concept of a coordinate system to the more general formulation of a *frame*.

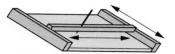

Figure 2.2 Pen plotter.

2.1.1 The Pen-Plotter Model

Historically, most early graphics systems were two-dimensional systems. The conceptual model that was used is now referred to as the pen-plotter model, referencing the output device that was available on these systems. A **pen plotter** (Figure 2.2) produces images by moving a pen held by a gantry, a structure that can move the pen in two orthogonal directions around the paper. The pen can be raised and lowered as required to create the desired image. Pen plotters are still in use; they are well suited for drawing large diagrams, such as blueprints. Various APIs—such as LOGO, GKS, and PostScript—all have their origins in this model. Although they differ from one another, what they have in common is that they view the process of creating an image as being similar to the process of drawing on a pad of paper. The user has a two-dimensional surface of some size. She moves a pen around on this surface, leaving an image on the paper.

We can describe such a graphics system with two drawing functions:

```
moveto(x,y);
lineto(x,y);
```

Execution of the moveto function moves the pen to the location (x, y) on the paper without leaving a mark. The lineto function moves the pen to (x, y), and draws a line from the old to the new location of the pen. We add a few initialization and termination procedures, and the ability to change pens to alter the drawing color or line thickness, and we have a simple—but complete—graphics system. Here is a fragment of a simple program in such a system:

```
moveto(0, 0);
lineto(1, 0);
lineto(1, 1);
lineto(0, 1);
lineto(0, 0);
```

This fragment would generate the output in Figure 2.3.

For certain applications, such as page layout in the printing industry, systems built on this model work well. For example, the PostScript page-description language, a sophisticated extension of these ideas, is a standard for controlling printers and typesetters.

We are much more interested, however, in the three-dimensional world. The pen-plotter model does not extend well to three-dimensional graphics systems. For example, if we wish to use the pen-plotter model to produce the image of a three-dimensional object on our two-dimensional pad, either by hand or by computer, we have to figure out where on the page to place two-dimensional points corresponding to points on our three-dimensional object. These two-dimensional points are, as we saw in Chapter 1, the projections of points in three-dimensional space. The mathematical process of determining projections is an application of trigonometry. We shall develop the mathematics of projection in Chapter 5, because projection is crucial for our understanding

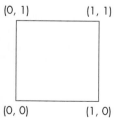

Figure 2.3 Output of pen–plotter program.

of three–dimensional graphics. We prefer, however, to use an API that allows users to work directly in the domain of their problems, and to use computers to carry out the details of the projection process automatically, without the users having any trigonometric calculations within the application program. That approach should be a boon to users who had difficulty learning to draw various projections on a drafting board, or sketching objects in perspective. More important, users can rely on hardware and software implementations of projection within the implementation of the API that are far more efficient than would be any possible implementation of projections within the user's program.

For two-dimensional applications, such as the Sierpinski gasket, we can start with a three-dimensional world and regard two-dimensional systems, such as our pad, as special cases. Mathematically, we view the two-dimensional plane, or a simple two-dimensional curved surface, as a subspace of a three-dimensional space. Hence, statements—both practical and abstract—about the bigger three-dimensional world will hold for the simpler two-dimensional one.

Suppose that we assume that our pad has infinite area (we shall limit its size later) and corresponds to the plane $z = 0$. We can represent a point in the plane as $\mathbf{p} = (x, y, 0)$ in the three-dimensional world, or as $\mathbf{p} = (x, y)$, in the two-dimensional subspace corresponding to our pad. OpenGL, like most three-dimensional graphics systems, allows us to use either representation, with the underlying internal representation being the same, regardless of which form the user chooses. We can implement representations of points in a number of ways, but the simplest is to think of a three-dimensional point as being represented by a triplet:

$$\mathbf{p} = \begin{bmatrix} x \\ y \\ z \end{bmatrix}.$$

Temporarily, we shall ignore the question of in what coordinate system $\mathbf{p}$ is represented.

We shall often use the term *vertex*, rather than *point*. A **vertex** is a location in space; we use two-, three-, and four-dimensional spaces in computer graphics. Vertices are used to define the atomic geometric objects that are recognized by our graphics system. The simplest geometric object is a point in space, which corresponds to a single vertex. Two vertices define a line segment, a second geometric object; three vertices can determine either a triangle or a circle; four determine a quadrilateral, and so on.

We specify a vertex in OpenGL using the general form

```
glVertex*()
```

There are numerous ways that a vertex can be specified by the user.[2] For example, if the user wants to work in two dimensions with integers, then the form

```
glVertex2i(GLint xi, GLint yi)
```

is appropriate, and

```
glVertex3f(GLfloat x, GLfloat y, GLfloat z)
```

describes a three-dimensional point using floating-point numbers. Finally if we use an array to store the information,

```
GLfloat vertex[3]
```

then we can use

```
glVertex3fv(vertex)
```

Regardless of which form a user chooses, the underlying representation is the same, just as our pad can be looked at as either a two-dimensional space or the subspace of three-dimensional space corresponding to the plane $z = 0$. In Chapter 4, we shall see that the underlying representation is four-dimensional, but we do not need to worry about that yet.

Vertices can define a variety of geometric objects, and, different numbers of vertices are required depending on the object. We can group as many vertices as desired, using the functions glBegin and glEnd. The argument of glBegin specifies the geometric type that we want our vertices to define. Hence, a line segment can be specified by

```
glBegin(GL_LINES);
    glVertex2f(x1,y1);
    glVertex2f(x2,y2);
glEnd();
```

We can use the same data to define a pair of points, by using the form

```
glBegin(GL_POINTS);
    glVertex2f(x1,y1);
    glVertex2f(x2,y2);
glEnd();
```

---

[2] OpenGL has multiple forms for many functions. The variety of forms allows the user to select the one best suited for her problem. The * can usually be interpreted as either two or three characters of the form nt or ntv, where n signifies the number of dimensions (2, 3, or 4); t denotes the data type, such as integer (i), float (f), or double(d); and v, if present, indicates the variables are specified through a pointer to an array, rather than through an argument list. We shall use whatever form is best suited for our discussion, leaving the details of the various other forms to the *OpenGL Reference Manual* [Ope93b].

We can now look at the heart of our Sierpinski gasket program. Suppose that we choose to generate all our points within the unit square whose lower-left-hand corner is at $(0, 0)$—a convenient, but easily altered, choice.

First, we must consider how we wish to represent geometric data in our program. We could employ the most basic representation of separate x, y, and z variables (in three dimensions). Many programmers prefer a more object-oriented approach, such as using a data type point for a three-dimensional vertex, or perhaps point2 for a two-dimensional point. In an object-oriented language, we could then have statements such as

```
new_point = old_point + random_number
```

Unfortunately, neither C nor OpenGL is oriented this way (at least at present). As a compromise between a truly low-level view and a high-level abstraction, we shall use a two-element array for two-dimensional points:

```
typedef GLfloat point2[2];
```

Note that we shall use the basic OpenGL types, such as GLfloat and GLint, rather than the C types, such as float and int, even though the two are almost always the same in practice.

We shall create a function, called display, that will generate a single point each time that it is called. We assume that an array of triangle vertices triangle[3] (of type point2) has been defined outside of display as a global array.

```
void display(void)
{
  static point2 p = {{.},{.}}; /* set to desired initial point */
  int i;
  long random(); /* standard random-number generator */

  /* pick a random vertex */

  i=random()%3;

  /* compute new point */

  p[0] = (p[0] + triangle[i][0])/2;
  p[1] = (p[1] + triangle[i][1])/2;

  /* display new point */

  glBegin(GL_POINTS);
      glVertex2fv(p);
  glEnd();

}
```

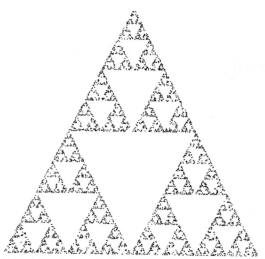

Figure 2.4 The Sierpinski gasket.

Although we still do not have a complete program, Figure 2.4 shows the output for a few thousand points.

We are done with the core of the program. But we still have to worry about issues such as

1. In what colors are we drawing?
2. Where on the screen does our image appear?
3. How large will the image be?
4. How do we create an area of the screen—a window—for our image?
5. How much of our infinite pad will appear on the screen?
6. How long will the image remain on the screen?

All these issues are important, even though, at first, they may appear to be peripheral to our major concerns. As we shall see, the basic code that we develop to answer these questions and to control the placement and appearance of our renderings will not change substantially across programs. Hence, the effort that we expend now to deal with these issues will be repaid later.

2.1.2 Coordinate Systems

At this point, you may be puzzled about how to interpret the values of x, y, and z in our specification of vertices. In what units are they? Are they in feet, meters, microns? Where is the origin? In each case, the simple answer is that it is up to you.

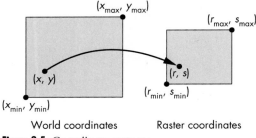

World coordinates   Raster coordinates

Figure 2.5 Coordinate systems.

Originally, graphics systems required the user to specify all information, such as vertex locations, directly in units of the display device.[3] If that were true for high-level application programs, we would have to talk about points in terms of screen locations in pixels or centimeters from a corner of the display. There are obvious problems with this method, not the least of which is the absurdity of using distances on the computer screen to describe phenomena where the natural unit might be light years (such as in displaying astronomical data) or microns (for integrated-circuit design). One of the major advances in graphics software systems occurred when the graphics systems allowed users to work in any coordinate system that the users desired. The advent of **device-independent graphics** freed application programmers from worrying about the details of input and output devices. The user's coordinate system became known as the **world coordinate system** or the **problem coordinate system**. Within the slight confines of the limitations of floating-point arithmetic on our computers, we can use any numbers that fit our problem.

Units on the display were first called **physical device coordinates** or just **device coordinates**. For raster devices, such as most CRT displays, we shall use the term **raster** or **screen coordinates**. Raster coordinates are always expressed in some integer type, because the center of any pixel in the frame buffer must be located on a fixed grid, or, equivalently, because pixels are inherently discrete and we can address them using integers.

At some point, the values in world coordinates must be mapped into device coordinates, as shown in Figure 2.5. The graphics system, rather than the user, is responsible for this task, and the mapping is performed automatically as part of the viewing process. As we shall see in the next few sections, the user needs only to specify a few parameters to define this mapping.

---

[3] Even today, the low-level commands to drive some CRT displays require locations to be specified in units of inches, where the range of allowable values corresponds to the physical dimensions of the screen.

2.2 The OpenGL API

We have the heart of a simple graphics program; now, we want to gain control over how our objects appear on the display. We also want to control the flow of the program, and we shall have to interact with the window system. Before completing our program, we shall describe the OpenGL API in more detail. Vertices, whether they are specified as two- or three-dimensional entities, are represented internally in the same manner. Thus, everything we do here will be equally valid in three dimensions. Of course, we can do much more in three dimensions, but we are only getting started. In this chapter, we shall concentrate on how we specify primitives to be displayed; we shall leave interaction to Chapter 3.

OpenGL's structure is similar to that of most modern APIs, including PHIGS and GKS. Hence, any effort you put into learning OpenGL will carry over to other software systems. Although, compared with other APIs, OpenGL is easy to learn, it is, nevertheless, powerful. It supports the simple two- and three-dimensional programs that we shall develop in Chapters 2 through 6; it also supports the advanced rendering techniques that we shall study in Chapters 8 through 10.

Our prime goal is to study computer graphics; we are using an API to help us attain that goal. Consequently, we shall not present all OpenGL functions, and we shall omit many details. However, our sample programs will be complete. More detailed information on OpenGL and on other APIs is given in the Suggested Readings section at the end of the chapter.

2.2.1 Graphics Functions

Our basic model of a graphics package is a **black box**, a term that engineers use to denote a system whose properties are described by only its inputs and outputs; nothing is known about its internal workings. We can think of the graphics system as a box whose inputs are function calls from a user program; measurements from input devices, such as the mouse and keyboard; and possibly other input, such as messages from the operating system. The outputs are primarily the graphics sent to our output devices. For now, we shall take the simplified view of inputs as function calls and outputs as primitives displayed on our CRT screen, as shown in Figure 2.6. Although OpenGL is the particular system that we shall use, all graphics APIs have a similar structure.

Figure 2.6 Graphics system as a black box.

We describe an API through the functions in its library. A good API may contain hundreds of functions, so we shall find it helpful to divide the functions into six groups by their functionality:

1. The **primitive functions** define the low-level objects or atomic entities that our system can display. Depending on the API, the primitives can include points, line segments, polygons, pixels, text, and various types of curves and surfaces.

2. If primitives are the *what* of an API—the objects that can be displayed— then attributes are the *how*. That is, the attributes govern the way that a primitive appears on the display. **Attribute functions** allow us to perform operations ranging from choosing the color with which we display a line segment, to picking a pattern with which to fill the inside of a polygon, to selecting a type face for the titles on a graph.

3. Our synthetic camera must be described if we are to create an image. As we saw in Chapter 1, we must describe its position and orientation in our world, and must select the equivalent of a lens. This process not only will fix the view, but also will allow us to clip out objects that are too close or too far away. The **viewing functions** allow us to specify various views, although APIs differ in the degree of flexibility in choosing a view that they provide.

4. One of the characteristics of a good API is that it provides the user a set of **transformation functions** that allow her to carry out transformations of objects, such as rotation, translation, and scaling. Our developments of viewing in Chapter 5 and modeling in Chapter 8 will make heavy use of matrix transformations.

5. For interactive applications, the API provides a set of **input functions** to allow us to deal with diverse forms of input that characterize modern graphics systems. We need functions to deal with devices such as keyboards, mice, and data tablets. In Chapter 3, we shall introduce functions for working with three different input modes and with a variety of input devices.

6. In any real application, we also have to worry about handling the complexities of working in a multiprocessing multiwindow environment— usually an environment where we are connected to a network and there are other users. The **control functions** enable us to communicate with the window system, to initialize our programs, and to deal with any errors that take place during the execution of our programs.

2.2.2 The OpenGL Interface

OpenGL function names begin with the letters gl and are stored in a library usually referred to as GL. There are a few related libraries that we shall also use. The first is the graphics utility library (GLU). This library uses only GL functions, but contains code for common objects, such as spheres, that users

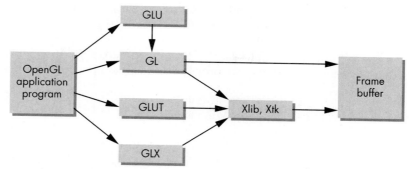

Figure 2.7 Library organization.

prefer not to have to write repeatedly. This library is available in all OpenGL implementations. The second library addresses the problems of interfacing with the window system. We shall use a readily available library called the *GL Utility Toolkit* (GLUT). It provides the minimum functionality that should be expected in any modern windowing system. We shall introduce a few of its functions in this chapter, and shall describe more of them in Chapter 3, where we consider input and interaction in detail. Figure 2.7 shows the organization of the libraries for an X Window system environment. Note that various other libraries are called from the OpenGL libraries, but that the application program does not need to refer to these libraries directly. A similar organization holds for other environments, such as Microsoft Windows.

2.3   Primitives and Attributes

Within the graphics community, there has been an ongoing debate over which primitives should be supported in an API. The debate is an old one and has never been fully resolved. On the minimalist side, the contention is that an API should contain a small set of primitives that all hardware can be expected to support. In addition, the primitives should be orthogonal, each giving a capability unobtainable from the others. Minimal systems typically support lines, polygons, and some form of text (strings of characters), all of which can be generated efficiently in hardware. On the other end are systems that can also support a variety of primitives, such as circles, curves, surfaces, and solids. The argument here is that users need more complex primitives to build sophisticated applications. However, because few hardware systems can be expected to support the large set of primitives that is the union of all the desires of the user community, a program developed with such a system probably would not be portable, because few implementations could be expected to support the entire set of primitives.

OpenGL takes an intermediate position. The basic library has a small set of primitives. An additional library, GLU, contains a richer set of objects derived from the basic library.

The basic OpenGL primitives are specified via points in space or vertices. Thus, the programmer defines her objects with sequences of the form

```
glBegin(type);
    glVertex*( . . . );
              .
              .
              .
    glVertex*( . . . );
glEnd();
```

The value of `type` specifies how OpenGL interprets the vertices to define geometric objects. Other code and OpenGL function calls can occur between `glBegin` and `glEnd`. For example, we can change attributes or perform calculations for the next vertex between `glBegin` and `glEnd`, or between two invocations of `glVertex`. A major conceptual difference between the basic geometric types is whether or not they have interiors. Aside from the point type, all the other basic types will be defined either in terms of vertices, or by finite pieces of lines, called **line segments**—in contrast to lines that are infinite in extent. Of course, a single line segment is itself specified by a pair of vertices, but the line segment is of such importance that we can consider it to be a basic graphical entity. You can use line segments to define approximations to curves, or you can use a sequence of line segments to connect data values for a graph. You can also use line segments for the edges of closed objects, such as polygons, that have interiors.

If we wish to display line segments, we have a few choices in OpenGL (Figure 2.8). The primitives and their `type` specifications include the following:

Line segments (`GL_LINES`**)**   The line-segment type causes successive pairs of vertices to be interpreted as the endpoints of individual segments. Note that, because the interpretation is done on a pairwise basis, successive segments usually are disconnected.

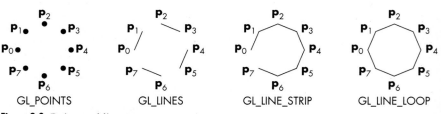

Figure 2.8 Point and line-segment types.

Polylines (`GL_LINE_STRIP`) If successive line segments are to be connected, we can use the line strip or **polyline** form. Many curves can be approximated via a suitable polyline. If we wish the polyline to be closed, we can locate the final vertex in the same place as the first, or can use the `GL_LINE_LOOP` type, which will draw a line segment from the final vertex to the first.

2.3.1 Polygon Basics

Line segments and polylines can model the edges of objects, but closed objects also may have interiors (Figure 2.9). We usually reserve the name **polygon** to refer to an object that is closed, as is a line loop, but that has an interior.[4] We can display a polygon in a variety of ways. We can display only its edges. We can fill its interior with a solid color, or a pattern, and can display or not display the edges, as shown in Figure 2.10. Although the outer edges of a polygon are easily defined by an ordered list of vertices, if the interior is not well-defined, then the polygon may be incorrectly rendered. Consequently, we shall investigate the mathematical aspects of how we can define the interior of a polygon.

In two dimensions, as long as no pair of edges of a polygon cross each other, we have a **simple** polygon. As we can see from Figure 2.11, simple polygons have well-defined interiors. Given that the locations of the vertices determine whether or not a polygon is simple, we can ask what a graphics system will do if it is given a nonsimple polygon to display. Fortunately, it is possible to define an interior for nonsimple polygons in a manner that the rendering algorithm can fill both simple and nonsimple polygons.

Polygon-fill algorithms are based on processing the points inside the polygon, assigning each interior point a desired color. There are two tests that we can use to determine whether a point is inside a polygon (or other closed object). The first, the **crossing** or **odd–even test**, is the most widely used. Suppose that **p** is a point inside a polygon. Any ray emanating from **p** and going off to infinity must cross an odd number of edges. Any ray emanating from a point outside the polygon crosses an even number of edges before reaching infinity. Hence, for the star-shaped polygon in Figure 2.12, we will get the inside coloring as shown.

Although the odd–even test is easy to implement and integrates well with the standard rendering process, we might want our fill algorithm to color the star polygon as shown in Figure 2.13(a). The **winding** test allows us to make that happen. This test considers the polygon as a knot being wrapped around a line. To implement the test, we consider traversing the edges of the polygon from any starting vertex and going around the edge in a particular direction (which

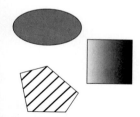

Figure 2.9 Filled objects.

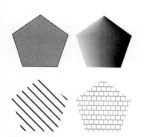

Figure 2.10 Methods of displaying a polygon.

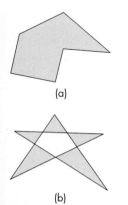

(a)

(b)

Figure 2.11 Polygons. (a) Simple. (b) Nonsimple.

---

[4] Certain systems, such as GKS, use the term *fill area* instead of *polygon*.

Figure 2.12 Filling with the odd–even test.

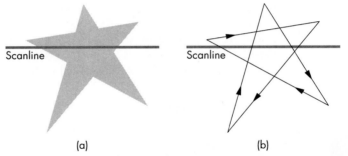

(a)   (b)

Figure 2.13 Winding-test fill. (a) Filled polygon. (b) Edge labeling.

direction does not matter) until we reach the starting point. We illustrate the path by labeling the edges, as shown in Figure 2.13(b). Next we consider any line through an interior point **p** that completely cuts through the polygon, as shown in the figure. The **winding number** for this point is the number of edges crossing our line in the downward direction, minus the number of edges crossing our line in the upward direction. If the winding number is not zero, the point is inside the polygon.

In both these tests, we can deal with edges parallel to the line (see Exercise 2.12). If the line passes through a vertex, we encounter the **singularity problem** shown in Figure 2.14. Here, we see that in one case, we must count the intersection with a vertex as an odd number of crossings; in the other, we must count it as an even number of crossings. In the rendering process, the line used in either test is usually a scan line. In Chapter 7, we shall see ways that renderers handle the singularity problem.

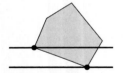

Figure 2.14 Singularities in inside-outside testing.

2.3.2 Convex Polygons

From the perspective of implementing a practical algorithm to fill the interior of a polygon, simplicity alone is often less than desired. Some APIs will guarantee a consistent fill from implementation to implementation only if the polygon is convex. An object is **convex** if all points on the line segment between any two points inside the object, or on its boundary, are inside the object (Figure 2.15). Although, so far, we have been dealing with only two-dimensional objects, this definition makes reference neither to the type of object nor to the number of dimensions. Convex objects include triangles, tetrahedra, rectangles, circles, spheres, and parallelepipeds (Figure 2.16). There are various tests for convexity. For two-dimensional polygons, we note that, if **p** is inside the polygon (Figure 2.17), and we trace the edges in a clockwise manner, the point is to the right of each line determined by an edge.

In three dimensions, polygons present a few more difficulties, because, unlike all two-dimensional objects, they are not necessarily flat. One property that most graphics systems exploit, and that we shall use, is that any three vertices

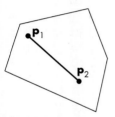

Figure 2.15 Convexity.

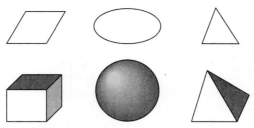

Figure 2.16 Convex objects.

that are not collinear determine both a triangle and the plane in which that triangle lies. Hence, if we always use triangles, we are safe and we can be sure that these objects will be rendered correctly. Often, we are almost forced to use triangles because typical rendering algorithms are guaranteed to be correct only if the vertices form a flat convex polygon. In addition, hardware and software will often support a triangle type that is rendered much faster than is a polygon with three vertices.

2.3.3 Polygon Types in OpenGL

Returning to the OpenGL types, for objects with interiors, we can specify the following types (Figure 2.18):

Polygons (GL_POLYGON**)**   The edges are the same as they would be if we used line loops. Successive vertices define line segments, and a line segment connects the final vertex to the first. The interior is filled according to the state of the relevant attributes. The state also determines whether and how the edge is displayed.

Triangles and Quadrilaterals (GL_TRIANGLES, GL_QUADS**)**   These objects are special cases of polygons. Successive groups of three and four vertices are interpreted as triangles and quadrilaterals, respectively. Using these types may lead to a more efficient rendering than will using polygons.

Strips and Fans (GL_TRIANGLE_STRIP, GL_QUAD_STRIP, GL_TRIANGLE_FAN**)**   These objects are based on groups of triangles or quadrilaterals that share vertices

Figure 2.17 Test for convexity.

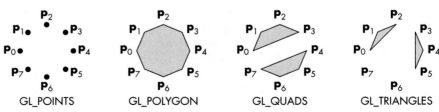

Figure 2.18 Polygon types.

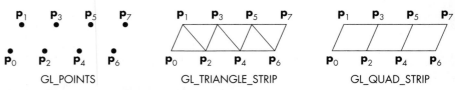

Figure 2.19 Triangle and quadrilateral strips.

and edges. In the triangle strip, for example, each additional vertex adds a new triangle (Figure 2.19).

2.3.4 Text

Graphical output in applications such as data analysis and display requires annotation, such as labels on graphs. Although, in nongraphical programs, textual output is the norm, text in computer graphics is problematic. In nongraphical applications, we are usually content with a simple set of characters, always displayed in the same manner. In computer graphics, however, we often wish to display text in a multitude of fashions by controlling type styles, sizes, colors, and other parameters. We also want to have available a choice of fonts. **Fonts** are families of type faces of a particular style, such as Times, Computer Modern, or Helvetica.

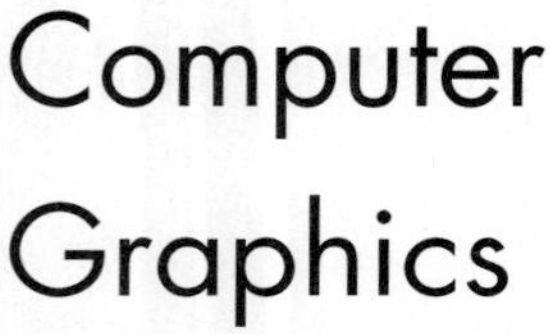

There are two forms of text: stroke and raster. **Stroke text** (Figure 2.20) is constructed as are other graphic primitives. We use vertices to define line segments or curves that outline each character. If the characters are defined by closed boundaries, we can fill them. The advantage of stroke text is that it can be defined to have all the detail of any other object, and, because it is defined in the same way as are other graphical objects, it can be manipulated by our standard transformations, and viewed as any other graphical primitive. An obvious advantage to stroke text is that, as we make a stroke character bigger or rotate it, it retains its detail and appearance. Consequently, we need to define a character only once, and can use transformations to generate it at the desired size and orientation.

Defining a full 128- or 256-character stroke font, however, can be complex, and the font can take up significant memory and processing time. The standard PostScript fonts are defined by polynomial curves, and they illustrate all the advantages and disadvantages of stroke text. The various PostScript fonts can be used for both high- and low-resolution applications. Often, developers mitigate the problems of slow rendering of such stroke characters by putting considerable processing power in the printer. This strategy is related to the client-server concepts that we shall discuss in Chapter 3.

Raster text (Figure 2.21) is simple and fast. Characters are defined as rectangles of bits called **bit blocks**. Each block defines a single character by the pattern of 0 and 1 bits in the block. A raster character can be placed in the frame buffer rapidly by a **bit-block-transfer** operation, **bitblt**, which moves the block

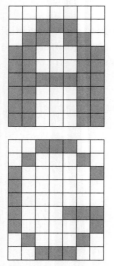

Figure 2.20 Stroke text (PostScript font).

Figure 2.21 Raster text.

Figure 2.22 Raster–character replication.

of bits using a single instruction. We shall discuss bitblt in Chapter 10; OpenGL allows the application program to use functions that allow direct manipulation of the contents of the frame buffer.

You can increase the size of raster characters only by replicating (duplicating) pixels, a process that gives larger characters a blocky appearance (Figure 2.22). Other transformations of raster characters, such as rotation, may not make sense, because the transformation may move the bits defining the character to locations that do not correspond to the location of pixels in the frame buffer. In addition, because raster characters often are stored in read-only memory (ROM) in the hardware, a particular font might be of limited portability.

We shall return to text in Chapter 3. There, we shall see that both stroke and raster text can be implemented most efficiently through display lists.

2.3.5 Curved Objects

The primitives in our basic set have all been defined through vertices. With the exception of the point type, all either consist of line segments or use line segments to define a boundary. We can take two approaches to creating a richer set of objects.

First, we can use the primitives that we have to approximate curves and surfaces. For example, if we want a circle, we can use a regular polygon of n sides. Likewise, we can approximate a sphere with a polyhedron.

The other approach, which we shall explore in Chapter 9, is to start with the mathematical definitions of curved objects, and then to build graphics functions to implement them. Objects such as quadric surfaces and parametric polynomial curves and surfaces are well understood mathematically, and we can specify them through sets of vertices. For example, we can define a sphere by its center and a point on its surface, or we can define a cubic polynomial curve by four points.

Most graphics systems give us aspects of both approaches. In OpenGL, we can use the utility library (GLU) for a collection of approximations to common curved surfaces, and can write functions to define more of our own. We can also use the advanced features of OpenGL to work with parametric polynomial curves and surfaces.

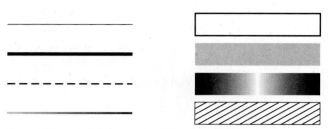

Figure 2.23 Attributes for lines and polygons.

2.3.6 Attributes

In a modern graphics system, there is a distinction between what the type of a primitive is and how that primitive is displayed. A red solid line and a green dashed line are the same geometric type, but each is displayed differently. An attribute is any property that determines how a geometric primitive is to be rendered. Color is an obvious attribute, as are the thickness of a line and the pattern used to fill a polygon. Several of these attributes are shown in Figure 2.23 for lines and polygons.

Attributes may be associated with, or **bound** to, primitives at various points in the modeling and rendering pipeline. Bindings may not be permanent. At this point, we are concerned with immediate-mode graphics. In **immediate mode**, primitives are not stored in the system and are passed through the system for possible display as soon as they are defined. The present values of attributes are part of the state of the graphics system. When a primitive is defined, the present attributes for that type are used, and it is displayed immediately. There is no memory of the primitive in the system. Only the primitive's image appears on the display; once erased from the display, it is lost. In Chapter 3, we shall introduce display lists, which will enable us to keep objects in memory, so that these objects can be redisplayed.[5]

Each geometric type has a set of attributes. For example, a point has a color attribute and a size attribute. Line segments can have color, thickness, and type (solid, dashed, or dotted). Filled primitives, such as polygons, have more attributes, because we must specify enough parameters to specify how the fill should be done. We can fill with a solid color or a pattern. We can decide not to fill the polygon and to display only its edges. If we fill the polygon, we might also display the edges in a color different from that of the interior.

In systems that support stroke text as a primitive, there is a variety of attributes. Some of these attributes are demonstrated in Figure 2.24; they include

---

[5] OpenGL's retention of primitives is a fundamental difference between it and systems such as PHIGS that use a database paradigm in which geometric entities reside in a central data store and can thus be recalled as desired.

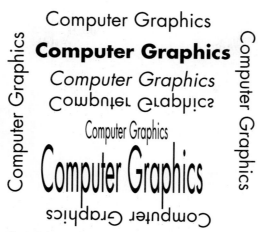

Figure 2.24 Stroke–text attributes.

the direction of the text string, the path followed by successive characters in the string, the height and width of the characters, the font, and the style (bold, italic, underlined).

2.4   Color

Color is one of the most interesting aspects of both human perception and computer graphics. Full exploitation of the capabilities of the human visual system with computer graphics requires a far deeper understanding of the anatomy, physiology, and psychophysics of the human than we can present here. We can, however, expand the model of the human visual system from Chapter 1 to obtain a useful color model.

Light is the part of the electromagnetic spectrum that occupies wavelengths from about 350 to 780 nm. The shorter wavelengths in the visible spectrum we see as blues; the longer wavelengths we see as reds, with greens in the middle. Other than those colors generated via pure spectral sources, such as lasers, or by passing light through extremely narrow filters, colors are combinations of wavelengths. A color can be characterized by a function $C(\lambda)$, as shown in Figure 2.25, whose value for a given wavelength λ in the visible spectrum gives the strength of that wavelength in the color.

Although this characterization is accurate in terms of a physical color whose properties we can measure, it does not take into account how we *perceive* color. To understand this distinction, let's consider one of the key tasks in using color in computer graphics: **color matching**. Suppose that we have a color characterized by a distribution $C(\lambda)$ that we would like to match on the screen of our CRT. Do we have to match C for every λ? A monitor that could do such

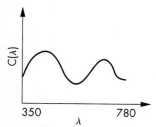

Figure 2.25 A color distribution.

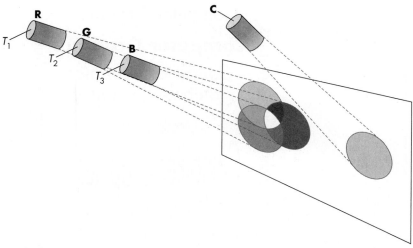

Figure 2.26 Additive color matching.

matching for all visible colors is beyond our ability to construct. Fortunately, we do not need such a monitor, because our visual systems are consistent with a three-primary-color model.

Color in computer graphics is based on what has become known as the **three-color theory**.[6] Using the **additive color model**, we think of a color as being formed from three primary colors that are mixed to form the desired color. A good analogy is to consider three colored spotlights (Figure 2.26) whose intensities can be varied. All three are focused on the same spot on a dark screen. Each of the three spotlights adds to the screen light that is reflected back to our eyes and that we see as a single color.

We can attempt to match a given color by adjusting the intensities of the individual spotlights. Although we might not be able to match all colors in this way with a particular set of primaries, if we use standard red, green, and blue spotlights, we can come close. We can represent this matching process abstractly as follows. We let C represent the color that we are trying to match, and R, G, and B represent the three spotlights. A color match is specified by the equation

$$\mathbf{C} = T_1\mathbf{R} + T_2\mathbf{G} + T_3\mathbf{B},$$

where T_1, T_2, and T_3 are the strengths, or intensities, of the three spotlights. These intensities are called the **tristimulus values**. We can characterize the

---

[6] The major exception is in the printing industry, which uses a four-color process for reasons that have more to do with the practical aspects of printing than with fundamental conceptual differences with three-color theory.

target color, relative to the particular set of primaries—our spotlights—by the triplet (T_1, T_2, T_3).

Obviously, most of the information about the distribution of $C(\lambda)$ cannot be in (T_1, T_2, T_3); we have reduced a continuous function to three numbers. That, however, is exactly what our visual systems do. The color receptors in our eyes—the cones—are of three different types. Type i, $i \in \{1, 2, 3\}$, has a sensitivity curve $S_i(\lambda)$, so, when it is exposed to a color distribution $C(\lambda)$, it measures and sends back to the brain a number

$$A_i = \int S_i(\lambda)C(\lambda)d\lambda,$$

where the integration is over the visible wavelengths. Thus, the brain perceives the color through a triplet (A_1, A_2, A_3), rather than as a continuous distribution $C(\lambda)$.

Putting it all together, we get the **basic tenet of three-color theory**: *If two colors produce the same tristimulus values they are visually indistinguishable*. Two colors that match visually are known as metameric pairs and have the same tristimulus values, although their distributions as a function of λ may be different. For a visual match, we need to match only a color's tristimulus values.

There are a number of issues that we are not exploring fully here. Most concern the differences among various sets of primaries, or limitations due to the physical constraints of real devices. The primaries that characterize the receptors in the eye neither are the same as the CRT primaries, nor are the same as the primaries for film, or for a printer. In addition, the tristimulus values that we use to match a color on our CRT screen must be positive, because we are adding light to the screen. We are also limited by the maximum intensity that we can produce with a device or perceive with our visual systems. Hence, although we can relate mathematically the tristimulus values in one set of primaries to the values in another, we may not always be able to produce the same color in both systems. The range of colors that we can produce on a given system with a given set of primaries is called that system's **color gamut**.

We have used an additive color model that is appropriate for CRT displays, transparencies, and slide (positive) film. In such systems, the primaries are usually red, green, and blue. We can view a color as a point in a **color solid**, as shown in Figure 2.27 and in Color Plate 21. The solid is drawn using a coordinate system corresponding to the three primaries. The distance along a coordinate axis represents the amount of the corresponding primary in the color. If we normalize the maximum value of each primary to be 1, then we can represent any color that we can produce with this set of primaries as a point in a unit cube. The vertices of the cube correspond to black (no primaries on); red, green, and blue (one primary fully on); the pairs of primaries, cyan (green and blue on), magenta (red and blue on), and yellow (red and green on); and white (all primaries fully on). The principal diagonal of the cube connects the origin (black) with white. All colors along this line have equal tristimulus values and

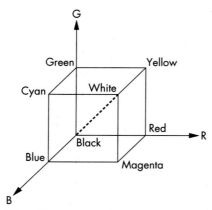

Figure 2.27 Color solid.

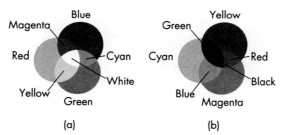

Figure 2.28 (a) Additive color. (b) Subtractive color.

appear as shades of gray. We can answer questions such as whether the color gamuts for two sets of primaries match by viewing them in terms of how the color cube for one set of primaries maps to the color space of another set.

With additive color, primaries add light to an initially black display, yielding the desired color. For processes such as commercial printing and painting, a **subtractive color model** is more appropriate. Here, we start with a white surface, such as a sheet of paper. Colored pigments remove color components from light that is striking the surface. If we assume that white light hits the surface, a particular point will be red if all components of the incoming light are absorbed by the surface except for wavelengths in the red part of the spectrum, which are reflected. In subtractive systems, the primaries are usually the **complementary** colors: cyan, magenta, and yellow (CMY; Figure 2.28). We shall not explore subtractive color here. You need to know only that an RGB additive system has a dual with a CMY subtractive system (see Exercise 2.9).

2.4.1 RGB Color

Now we can look at how color is handled in a graphics system from the programmer's perspective—that is, through the API. There are two different approaches. We shall stress the **RGB color model**, because understanding it will be crucial for our later discussion of lighting and shading. Compared to the indexed color model (Section 2.4.2), it is the more difficult model to support in hardware, due to higher memory requirements, but modern systems support it more easily now that memory is cheaper. It is also possible for a system to support true color in software through the API, and to have the hardware use approximate techniques to implement a display visually close to an RGB-color display.

In a three-primary-, additive-color RGB system, there are conceptually separate frame buffers for red, green, and blue images. Each pixel has separate red, green, and blue components that correspond to locations in memory (Figure 2.29). In a typical system, there might be a 1280×1024 array of pixels, and each pixel might consist of 24 bits (3 bytes): 1 byte for each of red, green, and blue. Such a frame buffer would have over 3 megabytes (MB) of memory that would have to be redisplayed at video rates. Until recently, this amount of memory was prohibitively expensive in all but the best systems.

As programmers, we would like to be able to specify any color that can be stored in the frame buffer. For our 24-bit example, there are 2^{24} possible colors, sometimes referred to as 16 M colors. where M denotes 1024^2. Other systems may have as many as 12 (or more) bits per color, or as few as 4 bits per color. Because our API should be independent of the particulars of the hardware, we would like to specify a color independently of the number of bits in the frame buffer, and to let the drivers and hardware match our specification as closely as possible to the available display. A natural technique is to use the color cube, and to specify color components as numbers between 0.0 and 1.0, where 1.0 denotes the maximum value of the corresponding primary, and 0.0 denotes a zero value of that primary. In OpenGL, we use the color cube as follows. To draw in red, we issue the function call

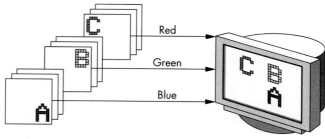

Figure 2.29 RGB color.

```
glColor3f(1.0, 0.0, 0.0);
```

The execution of this function will set the present drawing color to red. Because the color is part of the state, we continue to draw in red until the color is changed. The "3f" is used in a manner similar to the `glVertex` function; it conveys that the color is specified using a three-color (RGB) model, and that the values of the components are given as `floats` in C. If we use an integer or byte type to specify a color value, the maximum value of the chosen type corresponds to the primary fully on, and the minimum value corresponds to the primary fully off.

Later, we shall be interested in a four-color (RGBA) system. The fourth color (A) uses what is called the **alpha channel**, but is stored in the frame buffer, as are the RGB values and can be set with four-dimensional versions of the color functions. In Chapter 10, we shall see various uses of the alpha channel, such as for creating fog effects or for combining images. Here, we need the alpha value to aid in the initialization of an OpenGL program. The alpha value will be treated by OpenGL as an **opacity** or **transparency** value. Transparency and opacity are complements of each other. An opaque object passes no light through it; a transparent object passes all light. An object can range from fully transparent to fully opaque.

One of the first tasks that we must do in a program is to clear an area of the screen—a drawing window—in which to display our output. We also must clear this window whenever we want to draw a new frame. By using the four-dimensional (RGBA) color system, we can create effects where the drawing window interacts with other windows that may be beneath it, by manipulating the opacity assigned to the window when it is cleared. The function call

```
glClearColor(1.0, 1.0, 1.0, 1.0);
```

defines a four-color clearing color that is white, because the first three components are set to 1.0, and is opaque, because the alpha component is 1.0. We can then use the function `glClear` to make the window on the screen solid and white.

2.4.2 Indexed Color

Many systems have frame buffers that are limited in depth. For example, we might have a frame buffer that has a spatial resolution of 1280×1024, but each pixel is only 8 bits deep. Dividing these 8 bits into smaller groups of bits to assign to red, green, and blue is usually neither workable nor visually acceptable.

Rather, we can follow an analogy with an artist who paints in oils. The oil painter can produce an almost infinite number of colors by mixing together a limited number of pigments from tubes. We say that the painter has a potentially large color **palette**. At any one time, however, perhaps due to a limited number of brushes, the painter uses only a few colors. In this fashion, our

Input	Red	Green	Blue
0	0	0	0
1	$2^m - 1$	0	0
·	0	$2^m - 1$	0
·	·	·	·
·	·	·	·
$2^k - 1$	·	·	·

$\overbrace{\hspace{2cm}}^{m \text{ bits}}$ $\overbrace{\hspace{2cm}}^{m \text{ bits}}$ $\overbrace{\hspace{2cm}}^{m \text{ bits}}$

Figure 2.30 Color–lookup table.

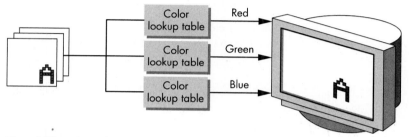

Figure 2.31 Indexed color.

painter can create an image that, although it contains a small number of colors, expresses the painter's desires because she can choose the few colors from a large palette.

Returning to the computer model, we can argue that, if we can choose, for each application, a limited number of colors from a large selection (our palette), we should be able to create good-quality images most of the time.

We can select colors by interpreting our limited-depth pixels as **indices**, rather than as color values. The indices point into a **color-lookup table**. Suppose that our frame buffer has k bits per pixel. Each pixel value or index is an integer between 0 and $2^k - 1$. Suppose that we can display colors with an accuracy of m bits; that is, we can choose from 2^m reds, 2^m greens, and 2^m blues. Hence, we can produce any of 2^{3m} colors on the display, but the frame buffer can specify only 2^k of them. We handle the specification through a user-defined color-lookup table that is of size $2^k \times 3m$ (Figure 2.30). The user program fills the 2^k entries (rows) of the table with the desired colors, using m bits for each of red, green, and blue. Once the user has constructed the table, she can specify a color by its index, which points to the appropriate entry in the color-lookup table (Figure 2.31). For $k = m = 8$, a common configuration, she can choose 256 out of 16 M colors. The 256 entries in the table constitute the user's color palette.

If we are in color-index mode, the present color is selected by a function such as

```
glIndexi(element);
```

that selects a particular color out of the table. Setting and changing the entries in the color-lookup table involves interacting with the window system, a topic discussed in Chapter 3. For the most part, we shall assume that we are using RGB color.

2.4.3 Setting of Color Attributes

For our simple example program, we shall use RGB color. We have three attributes to set. The first is the clear color, which is set via

```
glClearColor(1.0, 1.0, 1.0, 0.0);
```

We can select the rendering color for our points by setting the color state variable to red through the function call

```
glColor3f(1.0, 0.0, 0.0);
```

We can set the size of our rendered points to be two pixels wide, by using

```
glPointSize(2.0);
```

Note that attributes, such as the point size and line width, are specified in terms of the pixel size. Hence, if two displays have different-sized pixels (due to their particular screen dimensions and resolutions), the rendered images may appear slightly different. Certain graphics APIs, in an attempt to ensure that identical displays will be produced on all systems with the same user program, specify all attributes in a device-independent manner. Unfortunately, ensuring that two systems produce the same display has proved to be a difficult implementation problem. OpenGL has chosen a more practical balance between desired behavior and realistic constraints.

2.5   Viewing

We can now put a variety of graphical information into our two-dimensional world, and can describe how we would like these objects to appear, but we do not yet have a method for specifying exactly which of these objects should appear on the screen. Just as what we record in a photograph depends on where we point the camera and what lens we use, we have to make similar viewing decisions in our program.

A fundamental concept that emerges from the synthetic-camera model that we introduced in Chapter 1 is that the specification of the objects in our scene is completely independent of our specification of the camera. Once we have specified both the scene and the camera, we can compose an image. The camera forms an image by exposing the film, whereas the computer system forms an image by carrying out a sequence of operations in its viewing pipeline. The

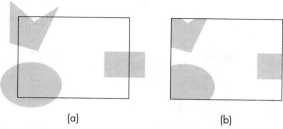

(a)   (b)

Figure 2.32 Two–dimensional viewing. (a) Objects before clipping. (b) Image after clipping.

application program needs to worry about only specification of the parameters for the objects and the camera, just as the casual photographer does not have to worry about how the shutter works or what are the details of the photochemical interaction of film with light.

There are default viewing conditions in computer image formation that are similar to the settings on a basic camera with a fixed lens. However, a camera that has a fixed lens and that sits in a fixed location forces us to distort our world to take a picture. We can create pictures of elephants only if we place the animals sufficiently far from the camera, or of ants if we put the insects relatively close to the lens. We prefer to have the flexibility to change the lens to make it easier to form an image of a collection of objects. The same is true when we use our graphics system.

Two-dimensional viewing is based on taking a rectangular area of our two-dimensional world and transferring its contents to the display, as shown in Figure 2.32. The area of the world that we image is known as the **viewing** or **clipping rectangle**. Objects inside the rectangle will be in the image; objects outside will be **clipped out** and will not be displayed. Objects that straddle the edges of the rectangle will be partially visible in the image. What the size of the window is on the display, and where this window is placed on the display, are independent decisions that we shall examine in Section 2.6.

Remember that, in our view, two-dimensional graphics is a special case of three-dimensional graphics. Our viewing rectangle is in the plane $z = 0$ within a three-dimensional **viewing volume**, as shown in Figure 2.33. If we do not specify a viewing volume, OpenGL uses its default, a $2 \times 2 \times 2$ cube, with the origin in the center. In terms of our two-dimensional plane, the bottom-left corner is at $(-1.0, -1.0)$, and the upper-right corner is at $(1.0, 1.0)$.

The two-dimensional view that we have described is a special case of the **orthographic projection** that we shall discuss in Chapter 5. This simple orthographic projection takes a point (x, y, z) and projects it into the point $(x, y, 0)$, as shown in Figure 2.34. Because our two-dimensional world consists of only the plane $z = 0$, the projection has no effect; however, we can employ the machinery of a three-dimensional graphics system to produce our image. In

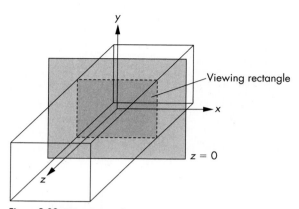

Figure 2.33 Viewing volume.

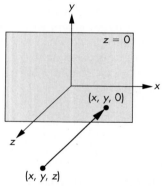

Figure 2.34 Orthographic projection.

OpenGL, an orthographic projection with a right-parallelepiped viewing volume is specified via

```
void glOrtho(GLdouble left, GLdouble right, GLdouble bottom,
    GLdouble top, GLdouble near, GLdouble far)
```

As long as the plane $z = 0$ is located between near and far, the two-dimensional plane will intersect the viewing volume. If using a three-dimensional volume seems strange in a two-dimensional application, the function

```
void gluOrtho2D(GLdouble left, GLdouble right,
    GLdouble bottom, GLdouble top)
```

in the utility library may make your program more readable. This function is equivalent to glOrtho, with near and far set to -1.0 and 1.0, respectively.

2.5.1 Matrix Modes

Pipeline graphics systems have an architecture that depends on multiplying together, or concatenating, a number of transformation matrices to achieve the desired image of a primitive. Like most other OpenGL variables, the values of these matrices are part of the state of the system and remain in effect until changed. The two most important matrices are the **model-view** and **projection** matrices. OpenGL provides functions to manipulate these matrices that we shall study in Chapter 4. Usually, we start with an identity matrix, which we update by applying a sequence of transformations. The matrix operations can be applied to any type of matrix; thus, we must first set the matrix mode that controls to which matrix operations are applied. The default mode is to have operations apply to the model-view matrix, so, to alter the projection matrix, we first switch modes. The following sequence is common for setting a two-dimensional viewing rectangle:

```
glMatrixMode(GL_PROJECTION);
glLoadIdentity();
gluOrtho2D(0.0, 500.0, 0.0, 500.0);
glMatrixMode(GL_MODELVIEW);
```

This sequence defines a 500×500 viewing rectangle with the lower-left corner of the rectangle at the origin of the two-dimensional system. It then switches the matrix mode back to model-view mode. It is a good idea, in complex programs, always to return to a given matrix mode, in this case model-view, to avoid problems caused by your losing track of which matrix mode the program is in at a given time.

2.6   Control Functions

We are almost done with our first program, but we still must discuss the minimal interactions with the window and operating systems. If we look at the details for a specific environment, such as the X Window system on a UNIX platform, we see that the interface between the graphics system and the operating and window systems can be complex. Exploitation of the possibilities open to the application programmer requires knowledge specific to these systems. In addition, the details can be different for two different environments, and discussing these differences will do little to enhance our understanding of computer graphics.

Rather than deal with these issues in detail, we shall look at a minimal set of operations that must take place from the perspective of the graphics application program. The OpenGL Utility Toolkit (GLUT) is a library of functions that provides a simple interface between the systems. Details specific to the underlying windowing or operating system are inside the implementation, rather than being part of its API. Operationally, we add another library to our standard library search path. Both here and in Chapter 3, GLUT will help us to understand the interactions that characterize modern interactive graphics systems, using a wide range of APIs, operating systems, and window systems. The application programs that we produce using GLUT should run under multiple window systems.

2.6.1 Interaction with the Window System

The term *window* is used in a number of different ways in the graphics and workstation literature. We shall use **window** to denote a rectangular area of our display that, by default, will be the screen of a CRT. We are concerned with only raster displays. A window has a height and width, and, because the window displays the contents of the frame buffer, positions in the window are measured in **window** or **screen coordinates**,[7] where the units are pixels.

In a modern environment, we can display many windows on the CRT screen. Each can have a different purpose, ranging from editing a file to monitoring our system. We shall use the term **window system** to refer to the multiwindow environment provided by systems such as the X Window system and Microsoft Windows. The window in which the graphics output appears will be one of the windows managed by the window system. Hence, to the window system, the graphics window is a particular type of window—one in which graphics can be displayed or rendered. References to positions in this window are relative to one corner of the window. We have to be careful about which corner is the origin. Usually, the lower-left corner will be the origin, and will have window coordinates (0,0). However, virtually all raster systems display their screens in the same way as commercial television systems do—from top to bottom, left to right. From this perspective, the top-left corner should be the origin. Our OpenGL commands will assume that the origin is bottom left, whereas information returned from the windowing system, such as the mouse position, will have the origin at top left.

Note also that, although our screen may have a resolution of, say, 1280 × 1024 pixels, the window that we use can have any size, up to the full screen size. Thus, the frame buffer must have a resolution equal to the screen size. Conceptually, if we use a window of 300 × 400 pixels, we can think of it as corresponding to a 300 × 400 frame buffer, even though it uses only a part of the real frame buffer.

Before we can open a window, there must be interaction between the windowing system and OpenGL. In GLUT, this interaction is initiated by the function call

---

[7] In OpenGL, window coordinates are three-dimensional, whereas screen coordinates are two-dimensional. Both systems use units measured in pixels, but window coooordinates retain depth information.

```
glutInit(int *argcp, char **argv)
```

The two arguments allow the user to pass command-line arguments, as in the standard C main function, and are usually the same as in main. We can now open an OpenGL window using the GLUT function:

```
glutCreateWindow(char *name)
```

where the title at top of the window is given by the string name.

The window that we create will have a default size, position on the screen, and characteristics such as use of RGB color. We can also use GLUT functions before window creation to specify these parameters. For example, the code

```
glutInitDisplayMode(GLUT_RGB | GLUT_DEPTH | GLUT_DOUBLE);
glutInitWindowSize(480, 640);
glutInitWindowPosition(0,0);
```

specifies a 480×640 window in the top-left corner of the display.[8] We specify RGB rather than indexed (GLUT_INDEX) color; a depth buffer for hidden-surface removal; and double rather than single (GLUT_SINGLE) buffering. The defaults, which are all we need for now, are RGB color, no hidden-surface removal, and single buffering. Thus, we do not need to request these options explicitly, but specifying them makes the code clearer. Note that parameters are logically OR-ed together in glutInitDisplayMode.

2.6.2 Aspect Ratio and Viewports

The **aspect ratio** of a rectangle is the ratio of the rectangle's width to its height. The independence of the object, viewing, and workstation window specifications can cause undesirable side effects if the aspect ratio of the viewing rectangle, specified by glOrtho, is not the same as the aspect ratio of the window specified by glutInitWindowSize. If they differ, as depicted in Figure 2.35, objects will be distorted on the screen. This distortion is a consequence of our default mode of operation, in which the entire clipping rectangle is mapped to the display window. The only way that we can map the entire contents of the clipping rectangle to the entire display window is to distort the contents of the former to fit inside the latter. We can avoid this distortion if we ensure that the clipping rectangle and display window have the same aspect ratio. Another, more flexible method is to use the concept of a viewport. A **viewport** is a rectangular area of the display window. By default, it is the entire window, but it can be set to any smaller size in pixels via the function

```
void glViewport(GLint x, GLint y, GLsizei w, GLsizei h)
```

---

[8] In systems such as the X Window system, we are requesting a window with certain properties. Our requests can be overridden by the window system, such as when the system does not support the requested modes.

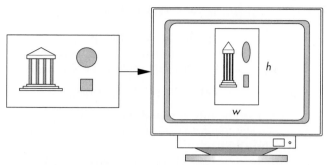

Figure 2.35 Aspect–ratio mismatch.

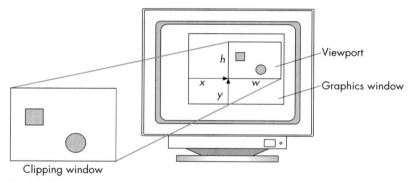

Figure 2.36 A mapping to the viewport.

where (x,y) is the lower-left corner of the viewport (measured relative to the lower-left corner of the window), and w and h give the height and width, respectively. The types are all integers that allow us to specify positions and distances in pixels. Primitives are displayed in the viewport, as shown in Figure 2.36. For a given window, we can adjust the height and width of the viewport to match the aspect ratio of the clipping rectangle, thus preventing any object distortion in the image. We can also use multiple viewports to put different images in different parts of the window. We shall see further uses of the viewport in Chapter 3, where we consider interactive changes in the size and shape of the window.

2.6.3 The main Function

In principle, we should be able to combine the simple initialization code with our code from Section 2.1, to form a complete OpenGL program to generate the Sierpinski gasket. Unfortunately, life in a modern system is not that simple. There are two problems: One is generic to all graphics systems; the second has more to do with problems of interacting with the underlying windowing system.

In immediate-mode graphics, a primitive is rendered to the screen as soon as it is defined; the system uses the present state to determine the primitive's appearance. Subsequently, the program goes on to the next statement. For an application such as our sample program, where we draw a few primitives and then are finished, as opposed to an interactive program, where we might continue to generate more graphics, our application may end, causing the screen to clear before we have even had a chance to see our output. A simple solution for our simple program might be to insert a delay, such as via a standard function such as `sleep(enough_time)`. For any but the most trivial applications, however, we need a more sophisticated mechanism. In Chapter 3, we shall discuss event processing, which will give us tremendous control in our programs. For now, we can use the GLUT function

```
void   glutMainLoop(void)
```

whose execution will cause the program to begin an event-processing loop. Here, we have no events to process, so that the execution of this function will have the effect of causing the program to sit in a wait state, with our graphics on the screen, until we terminate the program through some external means, such as by hitting the "kill" key.

The preceding calls will be almost identical in most programs. We can put them in a separate initialization routine, or in a short main function. If we use some other interface with the windowing system, we shall then have only to replace this function or to write a short `main`. One additional GLUT function

```
void glutDisplayFunc(void  (*func)(void))
```

can help us to organize our code. Here, `func` is the name of the function that will be called whenever the windowing system determines that the OpenGL window needs to be redisplayed. If we put all our graphics into this function (for our noninteractive example), `func` will be executed when the window is opened. Program 2.1 is a main program that can work for most noninteractive applications. The standard include (`.h`) files for OpenGL and GLUT are invoked before the beginning of the function definition. The macro definitions for our standard values, such as `GL_LINES` and `GL_RGB` are in these files.

We shall write the function `myinit()` in Section 2.7.[9] It will set the OpenGL state variables dealing with viewing and attributes—parameters that we prefer to set independently of the display function.

---

[9] We hope to avoid confusion by using the same function names as are used in the *OpenGL Programmer's Guide* [Ope93a] and in the GLUT documentation [Kil94a].

```
#include <GL/glut.h>

void main(int argc, char **argv)
{
    void myinit(), display();

    glutInit(&argc,argv);
    glutInitDisplayMode (GLUT_SINGLE | GLUT_RGB);
    glutInitWindowSize(500,500);
    glutInitWindowPosition(0,0);
    glutCreateWindow("simple  OpenGL example");
    glutDisplayFunc(display);
    myinit();
    glutMainLoop();
}
```

Program 2.1   The main function.

2.7   The Gasket Program

Using Program 2.1, we can write the myinit (Program 2.2) and display (Program 2.3) functions, and thus can complete our program that will generate the Sierpinski gasket. We shall draw red points on a white background. We shall also set up a two-dimensional coordinate system, so that our points will be defined within a 500×500 square with the origin in the lower-left corner.

```
void myinit(void)
{
/* attributes */

    glClearColor(1.0, 1.0, 1.0, 0.0); /* white background */
    glColor3f(1.0, 0.0, 0.0); /* draw in red */

/* set up viewing */

    glMatrixMode(GL_PROJECTION);
    gluLoadIdentity();
    gluOrtho2D(0.0, 500.0, 0.0, 500.0);
    glMatrixMode(GL_MODELVIEW);
}
```

Program 2.2   The initialization function.

```
void display( void )
{
    typedef GLfloat point2[2]; /* define a point data type */

    point2 vertices[3]={{0.0,0.0},{250.0,500.0},{500.0,0.0}};
        /*triangle */

    int i, j, k;
    long random(); /* standard random--number generator */
    point2 p ={75.0,50.0}; /* random point */

    glClear(GL_COLOR_BUFFER_BIT);  /*clear  the window */

/* computes and plots 5000 new points */

    for( k=0; k<5000; k++)
    {
        j=random()%3; /* pick a vertex at random */

/* Compute point halfway between vertex and old point */

        p[0] = (p[0]+vertices[j][0])/2.0;
        p[1] = (p[1]+vertices[j][1])/2.0;

    /* plot point */
        glBegin(GL_POINTS);
            glVertex2fv(p);
        glEnd();
    }

    glFlush();
}
```

Program 2.3 The display function.

Our display function has an arbitrary triangle (three vertices) defined in it, and an arbitrary initial point is defined within this triangle. It also has a loop that will generate a fixed number of 5000 points. A call to the OpenGL function glFlush has been included; it will force the system to plot the points on the display as soon as possible. You will probably not notice its effect unless you run this program over a network.

A complete listing of this program, and of the other example programs that we shall generate in subsequent chapters, is given in Appendix A.

2.8   The Three-Dimensional Gasket

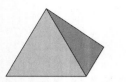

Figure 2.37 Tetrahedron.

We have seen that two-dimensional graphics is a special case of three-dimensional graphics, but we have not yet seen a true three-dimensional program. We shall conclude this chapter by observing how easy it is to convert our two-dimensional Sierpinski gasket program to a program that will generate a three-dimensional gasket.

We obtain three-dimensional version of the gasket by starting with a tetrahedron (Figure 2.37), instead of with a triangle. Because the tetrahedron is convex, the midpoint of any line segment between a vertex and any point inside the tetrahedron also is inside the tetrahedron. Hence, we can follow the same procedure as before, but this time we need four initial vertices to define the tetrahedron, instead of three required to define a triangle. Note that we can choose the four vertices of the tetrahedron at random without affecting the character of the result.

The required changes are primarily in the function `display.c`. We define a three-dimensional point data type

```
typedef GLfloat point[3];
```

and initialize the vertices of the tetrahedron; for instance, we can use the code

```
point vertices[4]={{0.0,0.0,0.0},{250.0,500.0,100.0},
                   {500.0,250.0,250.0},{250.0,100.0,250.0}};

point p ={250.0,100.0,250.0}; /* random initial point */
```

We now use the function `glPoint3fv` to display points. Here is the core of the display function:

```
/* computes and plots a single new point */

long random();
int i;
j=random()%4; /* pick a vertex at random */


/* Compute point halfway between vertex and old point */

p[0] = (p[0]+vertices[j][0])/2.0;
p[1] = (p[1]+vertices[j][1])/2.0;
p[2] = (p[2]+vertices[j][2])/2.0;

/* plot point */

glBegin(GL_POINTS);
```

```
glColor3f(p[0]/250.0,p[1]/250.0,p[2]/250.0);
glVertex3fv( p );
glEnd();
```

We are now working in three dimensions, so we define a three-dimensional clipping volume by

```
glOrtho(-500.0 , 500.0, -500.0, 500.0 ,-500.0, 500.0);
```

We also have added a color function that makes the color of each point depend on that point's location, so that we can understand the resulting image more easily. Figure 2.38 shows that if we generate enough points, the resulting figure will look like the initial tetrahedron with increasingly smaller tetrahedrons removed.

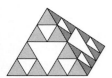

Figure 2.38 Three-dimensional Sierpinski gasket.

2.9 Summary

In this chapter, we introduced the OpenGL API and have applied the basic concepts that we introduced in Chapter 1. Although the application that we used to develop our first program was two-dimensional, we took the path of looking at two-dimensional graphics as a special case of three-dimensional graphics. This choice may make it slightly more difficult for you to understand the concepts. However, the effort you put in now will be rewarded later, as you become more comfortable with working in three dimensions.

The Sierpinski gasket provides a nontrivial beginning application. A few extensions and mathematical issues are presented in the exercises at the end of this chapter. We give a more detailed introduction to fractal geometry in Chapter 8, where we use these concepts to generate realistic-looking objects. The texts in the Suggested Readings section provide many other examples of interesting curves and surfaces that can be generated with simple programs.

The historical development of graphics APIs and graphical models illustrates the importance of starting in three dimensions. The pen-plotter model was used for many years and is the basis of many important APIs, such as Postscript. Work to define an international standard for graphics APIs began in the 1970s and culminated with the adoption of GKS by the International Standards Organization (ISO) in 1984. However, GKS had its basis in the pen-plotter model, and, being a two-dimensional API, was of limited utility in the CAD community. Although the standard was extended to three dimensions with GKS-3D, the limitations imposed by the original underlying model led to a standard that was lacking in many aspects. The PHIGS and PHIGS+ APIs, started in the CAD community, are inherently three-dimensional, and are based on the synthetic-camera model.

The modeling–rendering paradigm is illustrated by PIXAR's Renderman Interface. Although the specification is for interface between the modeler and the renderer, the interface is based on a high-quality renderer (Reyes) [Coo87]

that, among other applications, is used to create animated films. This interface makes use of the synthetic-camera model.

OpenGL is derived from the GL API, which is based on implementing the synthetic-camera model with a pipeline architecture. GL was developed for Silicon Graphics workstations that incorporated a pipeline architecture that originally was implemented with special-purpose VLSI chips. Hence, although PHIGS and GL have much in common, GL was designed specifically for high-speed real-time rendering. OpenGL was a result of application users realizing the advantages of GL programming and wanting to carry these advantages to other platforms. Because it removed input and windowing functions from GL and concentrated on the rendering aspects of the API, OpenGL emerged as a new API that is portable but that retains the features that make GL such a powerful API.

Our examples and simple programs have been concerned with how we describe and display geometric objects in a simple manner. In terms of the modeling–rendering paradigm that we presented in Chapter 1, we have focused on the modeling. However, our models are completely unstructured. Representations of objects are lists of vertices and attributes. In Chapter 8, we shall learn to construct hierarchical models that can represent relationships among objects. Nevertheless, at this point, you should be able to write interesting programs. Try to complete some of the exercises at the end of the chapter, and extend a few of the two-dimensional problems to three dimensions.

2.10   Suggested Readings

The Sierpinski gasket provides a good introduction to the mysteries of fractal geometry; see [Bar93, Hil90, Man82, Pru90] for discussions.

The pen-plotter API is used by Postscript [Ado85] and LOGO [Pap81]. LOGO provides turtle graphics, an API that is both simple to learn and capable of describing several of the two-dimensional mathematical curves that we shall use in Chapter 8; see Exercise 2.4.

GKS [ANSI85], GKS-3D [ISO88], PHIGS [ANSI88], and PHIGS+ [PHIG89] are both U.S. and international standards. Their formal descriptions can be obtained from the American National Standards Institute (ANSI) and from ISO. There are numerous textbooks that use these APIs; see [Ang90, End84, Fol94, Hea94, Hop83, Hop91].

The X Window system [Sch88] has become the standard on UNIX workstations, and has influenced the development of window systems on other platforms. Recent versions of the X Window system include the PHIGS extensions to X (PEX).

The Renderman interface is described in [Ups89].

The two standard references for OpenGL are the *OpenGL Programmer's Guide* [Ope93a] and the *OpenGL Reference Manual* [Ope93b]. There is also a formal specification of OpenGL [Seg92]. The *Programmer's Guide* uses a simple toolkit, aux, to interface to the window system. A more sophisticated toolkit, the GLUT library, was developed by Mark Kilgard [Kil94b]. The Programmer's Guide provides many more code examples using OpenGL. Conversion of programs written using aux to programs using GLUT is a trivial exercise. Much of this information and many of the example programs are available over the Internet. Some of these sites are listed at the beginning of Appendix A.

Exercises

Figure 2.39 Sierpinski gasket created via subdivision.

2.1 We defined the Sierpinski gasket by using points. An alternative is to use triangles. Start with an arbitrary triangle. Compute the midpoints of the three sides, and connect the midpoints with line segments, thus subdividing the original triangle into four triangles (Figure 2.39). Iterate on this procedure, each time subdividing all but the central triangle, to generate the gasket outlines. Then, add fill to the correct triangles to get the Sierpinski gasket.

2.2 A slight variation of Exercise 2.1 generates the *fractal mountains* used in computer-generated animations. After you find the midpoint of each side of the triangle, perturb this location before subdivision. Generate these triangles without fill. Later, you can do this exercise in three dimensions, and can add shading. After a few subdivisions, you should have generated enough detail that your triangles look like a mountain.

2.3 The Sierpinski gasket, as generated in Exercise 2.1, demonstrates many of the geometric complexities that are studied in fractal geometry (Chapter 8). Suppose that you construct the gasket with mathematical lines that have length but no width. In the limit, what percentage of the area of the original triangle remains after the central triangle has been removed after each subdivision? Consider the perimeters of the triangles remaining after each central triangle is removed. In the limit, what happens to the total perimeter length of all remaining triangles?

2.4 At the lowest level of processing, we manipulate bits in the frame buffer. OpenGL has pixel-oriented commands that allow users to access the frame buffer directly. You can experiment with simple raster algorithms, such as drawing lines or circles, by using the OpenGL function glPoint, as the basis of a simple virtual-frame-buffer library. Write a library that will allow you to work in a frame buffer that you create in memory. The core functions should be WritePixel and ReadPixel. Your library should allow you to set up and display your frame buffer, and allow you to run a user program that reads and writes pixels.

2.5   *Turtle graphics* is an alternative positioning system that is based on the concept of a turtle moving around the screen with a pen attached to the bottom of his shell. The turtle's position can be described by a triplet (x, y, θ), giving the location of the center and the orientation of the turtle. A typical API for such a system includes functions such as

```
init(x,y,theta); /* initialize position and orientation
                            of turtle */
forward(distance);
right(angle);
left(angle);
pen(up_down);
```

Implement a turtle-graphics library using OpenGL.

2.6   Use your turtle graphics library from Exercise 2.5 to generate the Sierpinski gasket and fractal mountains of Exercises 2.1 and 2.2.

2.7   Space-filling curves have interested mathematicians for centuries. In the limit, these curves have infinite length, but they are confined to a finite rectangle and never cross themselves. Many of these curves can be generated iteratively. Consider the "rule" pictured in Figure 2.40 that replaces a single line segment with four shorter segments. Write a program that starts with a triangle and iteratively applies the replacement rule to all the line segments. The object that you generate is called the Koch snowflake. For other examples of space-filling curves, see [Hil90, Bar93].

Figure 2.40 Generation of the Koch snowflake.

Figure 2.41 Maze.

2.8   You can generate a simple maze starting with a rectangular array of cells. Each cell has four sides. You remove the sides (except from the perimeter of all the cells), until all the cells are connected. Then you create an entrance and an exit by removing two sides from the perimeter. A simple example is shown in Figure 2.41. Write a program using OpenGL that takes as input the two integers N and M, and then draws an $N \times M$ maze.

2.9   Describe how you would adapt the RGB color model in OpenGL to allow you to work with a subtractive color model.

2.10   We saw that a fundamental operation in graphics systems is to map a point (x, y), which lies within a clipping rectangle, to a point (x_s, y_s), which lies in the viewport of a window on the screen. Assume that the two rectangles are defined by OpenGL function calls

```
glViewport(u, v, w , h);
gluOrtho2D(x_min, x_max, y_min, y_max);
```

Find the mathematical equations that map (x, y) into (x_s, y_s).

2.11 Many graphics APIs use relative positioning. In such a system, the API contains functions such as

```
move_rel(x,y);
line_rel(x,y);
```

for drawing lines and polygons. The move_rel function moves an internal position, or cursor, to a new position; the line_rel function moves the cursor, and defines a line segment between the old cursor position and the new position. What are advantages and disadvantages of relative positioning, as compared to the absolute positioning used in OpenGL? Describe how you would add relative positioning to OpenGL.

2.12 In Section 2.3, we ignored potential problems in determining whether or not a point is inside a polygon that might arise if one or more sides of the polygon are parallel to a scan line. How would you handle these difficulties?

2.13 In practice, testing each point in a polygon to determine whether it is inside or outside the polygon is extremely inefficient. Describe the general strategies that you might pursue to avoid point-by-point testing.

2.14 In Section 2.3, we saw that OpenGL defines polygons using lists of vertices. How could you use OpenGL to define polygons by their edges?

2.15 Devise a test to determine whether a simple two-dimensional polygon is convex.

2.16 Figure 2.42 shows a set of polygons called a *mesh*; these polygons share some edges and vertices. Find one or more simple data structures that represent the mesh. A good data structure should include information on shared vertices and edges. Using OpenGL, find an efficient method for displaying a mesh represented by your data structure.

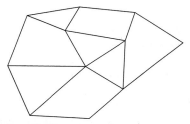

Figure 2.42 Polygonal mesh.

2.17 In OpenGL, we can associate a color with each vertex. If the endpoints of a line segment have different colors assigned to them, OpenGL will interpolate between the colors as it renders the line segment. It will do the same for polygons. Use this property to display the Maxwell triangle: an equilateral triangle whose vertices are red, green, and blue. What is the relationship between the Maxwell triangle and the color cube?

2.18 We can simulate many realistic effects using computer graphics by incorporating simple physics in the model. Simulate a bouncing ball in two dimensions, incorporating both gravity and elastic collisions with a surface. You can model the ball with a closed polygon that has a sufficient number of sides to look smooth.

2.19 An interesting, but difficult, extension of Exercise 2.18 is to simulate a game of pool or billiards. You will need to have multiple balls that can interact with the sides of the table and with one another. Hint: Start with two balls, and consider how to detect possible collisions.

2.20 A certain graphics system with a CRT display is advertised to display any four out of 64 colors. What does this statement tell you about the frame buffer, and about the quality of the CRT?

3 Input and Interaction

W̲e now turn to the development of interactive graphics programs. Interactive computer graphics opens up a myriad of applications, ranging from interactive design of buildings, to control of large systems through graphical interfaces, to virtual-reality systems, to computer games.

Our discussion has three main parts. First, we shall introduce the variety of devices available for interaction. We shall consider input devices from two different perspectives: first, the way the physical devices can be described by their real-world properties, and then, the way these devices appear to the application program. We shall then consider client–server networks and client–server graphics. We shall use these ideas to develop event-driven input for our graphics programs. Finally, we shall develop a paint program that demonstrates the important features of interactive graphics programming.

3.1 Interaction

One of the most important advances in computer technology was enabling users to interact with computer displays. More than any other event, Ivan Sutherland's Project Sketchpad launched the present era of *interactive* computer graphics. The basic paradigm that he introduced is deceptively simple. The user sees an image on the display. She reacts to this image via an interactive device, such as a mouse. The image changes in response to her input. She reacts to this change, and so on. Whether we are writing programs using the tools available in a modern window system, or are using the human–computer interface in an interactive museum exhibit, we are making use of this paradigm.

In the 30 years since Sutherland's work, there have been many advances in both hardware and software, but the viewpoint and ideas that he introduced still dominate interactive computer graphics. These influences range from how we conceptualize the human–computer interface, to how we can employ graphical data structures that allow for efficient implementations.

In this chapter, we shall take an approach slightly different from that in the rest of the book. Although rendering is the prime concern of most modern APIs, including OpenGL, interactivity is an important component of many applications. OpenGL, however, does not support interaction directly. The major reason for this omission is that many system architects wanted to increase OpenGL's portability by allowing it to work in a variety of environments. Consequently, windowing and input functions were left out of the API. Although this decision makes renderers portable, it makes more difficult discussions of interaction that do not include specifics of the windowing system. In addition, because any application program must have at least a minimal interface to the windowing environment, we cannot avoid such issues completely if we want to write complete, nontrivial programs. If interaction is omitted from the API, the application programmer is forced to worry about the often arcane details of her particular environment.

We can avoid such potential difficulties by using a simple library, or toolkit, as we did in Chapter 2. The toolkit can provide the minimal functionality that is expected on virtually all systems, such as opening of windows, use of the keyboard and mouse, and creation of pop-up menus through the toolkit's API. We shall adopt this approach, even though it may not provide all the features of any particular windowing system, and may produce code that neither makes use of the full capabilities of the window system, nor is as efficient as would be the code written in terms of the particular environment.

We are using the term *windowing system*, as in Chapter 2, to include the total environment provided by systems such as the X Window system, Microsoft Windows, and the Macintosh operating system. Graphics programs that we develop will render into a window within one of these environments. The terminology used in the windowing-system literature sometimes may confuse you as to the distinction between, for example, an X window and the OpenGL window into which our graphics are rendered. However, you will usually be safe if you regard the OpenGL window as a particular type of X window. Our use of the GLUT toolkit will enable us to avoid the complexities inherent in the interaction among the windowing system, the window manager, and the graphics system. Just as it did in Chapter 2, GLUT will allow our sample programs to be independent of any particular window system.

We shall start by describing several interactive devices and the variety of ways that we can interact with them. We shall then put these devices in the setting of a client–server network. Then, we shall introduce an API for minimal interaction. Finally, we shall generate sample programs.

3.2 Input Devices

We can think about input devices in two distinct ways. The obvious one is to look at them as physical devices, such as a keyboard or a mouse, and to discuss how they work. Certainly, we need to know something about the physical properties of our input devices, so such a discussion is necessary if we are to obtain a full understanding of input. However, from the perspective of an application programmer, we almost never want to use anything about the particular characteristics of a physical device in an application program. Rather, we prefer to treat input devices as *logical* devices whose properties are specified in terms of what they do from the perspective of the application program.

A **logical device** is characterized by its high-level interface with the user program, rather than by its physical characteristics. Logical devices are familiar to all writers of high-level programs. For example, data input and output in C are through functions such as the `printf`, `scanf`, `getchar`, and `putchar` functions, whose arguments use the standard C data types. When we wish to output a string via `printf`, the physical device on which the output appears could be a printer, a terminal, or a disk file. This output could even be the input to another program. The details of the format required by the destination device is of minor concern to the writer of the application program.

In computer graphics, the use of logical devices is slightly more complex, because the forms that input can take are more varied than the strings of bits or characters to which we are usually restricted in nongraphical applications. For example, we can use the mouse—a physical device—either to select a location on the screen of our CRT, or to indicate which item in a menu we wish to select. In the first case, an x, y pair (in some coordinate system) is returned to the user program; in the second, the application program may receive an integer as the identifier of a line in the menu. The separation of physical from logical devices allows us to use the same physical devices in two markedly different logical ways. It also allows the same program to work, without modification, if the mouse is replaced by another physical device, such as a data tablet or trackball.

3.2.1 Physical Input Devices

From the physical perspective, each device has properties that make it more suitable for certain tasks than for others. We shall take the view used in most of the workstation literature that there are two primary types of physical devices: pointing devices and keyboard devices. The **pointing device** allows the user to indicate a position on the screen, and almost always incorporates one or more buttons to allow the user to send signals or interrupts to the computer. The

Figure 3.1 Mouse.

Figure 3.2 Trackball.

keyboard device is almost always a physical keyboard but can be generalized to include any device that returns character codes[1] to a program.

The mouse (Figure 3.1) and trackball (Figure 3.2) are similar in use and, often, in construction. A typical mechanical mouse when turned over looks like a trackball. In both devices, the motion of the ball is converted to signals sent back to the computer by pairs of encoders inside the device that are turned by the motion of the ball. The encoders measure motion in two orthogonal directions.

There are many variants of these devices. Some use optical detectors, rather than mechanical detectors, to measure motion. Optical mice measure distance traveled by counting lines on a special pad. Small trackballs are popular with portable computers because they can be incorporated directly into the keyboard. There are also various pressure-sensitive devices used in keyboards that perform similar functions to the mouse and trackball, but do not move; their encoders measure the pressure exerted on a small knob that can be located between two keys in the middle of the keyboard.

We can view the output of the mouse or trackball as two independent values provided by the device. These values can be considered as positions and converted—either within the graphics system or by the user program—to a two-dimensional location in either screen or world coordinates. If configured in this manner, the device can be used to position a marker (cursor) automatically on the display; however, these devices are rarely used in this direct manner.

It is not necessary that the output of the mouse or trackball encoders be interpreted as a distance. Instead, either the device driver or a user program can interpret the information from the encoder as two independent velocities (see Exercise 3.4). The computer can then integrate these values to obtain a two-dimensional position. Thus, as a mouse moves across a surface, the integrals of the velocities yields x, y values that can be converted to the position for a cursor on the screen, as shown in Figure 3.3. By interpreting the distance traveled by the ball as a velocity, we can use the device as a variable-sensitivity input device. Small deviations from rest cause slow or small changes; large deviations cause rapid large changes. With either device, if the ball does not rotate, then there is no change in the integrals, and a cursor tracking the position of the mouse will not move. In this velocity mode, these devices are **relative-positioning** devices, because changes in the position of ball yield a position in the user program; the absolute location of the ball (or of the mouse) is not used by the application program.

Relative positioning, as provided by a mouse or trackball, is not always desirable. In particular, these devices are not suitable for an operation such as tracing

---

[1] We use the American Standard Code for Information Interchange (ASCII), although nothing we do restricts us to this particular choice, other than that ASCII is the prevailing code used.

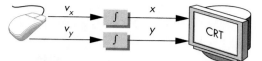

Figure 3.3 Cursor positioning.

Figure 3.4 Data tablet.

a diagram. If, while the user is attempting to follow a curve on the screen with a mouse, she lifts and moves the mouse, the absolute position on the curve being traced is lost. **Data tablets** provide absolute positioning. A typical data tablet (Figure 3.4) has rows and columns of wires embedded under its surface. The position of the stylus is determined through electromagnetic interactions between signals traveling through the wires and sensors in the stylus. There are also touch-sensitive transparent screens that can be placed over the face of a CRT which have many of the same properties as the data tablet. Small, rectangular pressure-sensitive touchpads are embedded in the keyboards of many portable computers. These touchpads can be configured as either relative- or absolute-positioning devices.

The **lightpen** has a long history in computer graphics. It was the device used in Sutherland's original Sketchpad. The lightpen contains a light-sensing device, such as a photocell (Figure 3.5). If the lightpen is positioned on the face of the CRT at a location opposite where the electron beam strikes the phosphor, the light emitted exceeds a threshold in the photodetector, and a signal is sent to the computer. Because each redisplay of the frame buffer starts at a precise time, we can use the time at which this signal occurs to determine a position on the CRT screen (see Exercise 3.19). Hence, we have a direct-positioning device. The lightpen is not as popular as are the mouse, data tablet, and trackball. One of its major deficiencies is the difficulty of obtaining the position corresponding to a dark area of the screen.

One other device, the **joystick** (Figure 3.6), is worthy of mention. The motion of the stick in two orthogonal directions is encoded, interpreted as two velocities, and integrated to identify a screen location. The integration implies that, if the stick is left in its resting position, there is no change in the cursor position, and the further the stick is moved from its resting position, the faster the screen location changes. Thus, the joystick is a variable-sensitivity device. The other advantage of the joystick is that the device can be constructed with

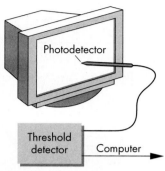

Figure 3.5 Lightpen.

Figure 3.6 Joystick.

mechanical elements, such as springs and dampers, that give resistance to a user who is pushing the stick. Such mechanical feel, not possible with the other devices, makes the joystick well-suited for applications such as flight simulators and games.

For three-dimensional graphics, we might prefer to use three-dimensional input devices. Although various such devices are available, none have yet the widespread acceptance of the popular two-dimensional input devices. A **spaceball** looks like a joystick with a ball on the end of the stick (Figure 3.7); however, the stick does not move. Rather, pressure sensors in the ball measure the forces applied by the user. The spaceball can measure not only the three direct forces (up–down, front–back, left–right), but also three independent twists. Thus, the device measures six independent values and has 6 **degrees of freedom**. Such an input device could be used, for example, both to position and to orient a camera.

Other three-dimensional devices, such as laser-based structured-lighting systems and laser-ranging systems, measure three-dimensional positions. Numerous tracking systems used in virtual-reality applications sense the position of the user. Virtual-reality and robotics applications often need more degrees of freedom than the two to six provided by the devices that we have described. Devices such as data gloves can sense motion of various parts of the human body, thus providing many additional input signals.

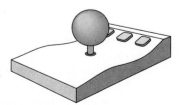

Figure 3.7 Spaceball.

We shall not use three-dimensional input in our code, although there is nothing in the API that restricts the input to two dimensions.

3.2.2 Logical Devices

We can now return to looking at input from inside the application program—that is, from the logical point of view. Two major characteristics describe the logical behavior of an input device: (1) what measurements the device returns to the user program, and (2) when the device returns those measurements.

Some APIs, such as PHIGS and GKS, consider six classes of logical input devices. Because input in a modern window system cannot always be disassociated completely from the properties of the physical devices, OpenGL does not take this approach. Nevertheless, we shall describe the six classes briefly, because they show the variety of input forms that a developer of graphical applications may want, and also show how OpenGL can provide similar functionality.

1. **String** A string device is a logical device that provides ASCII strings to the user program. Usually, this logical device is implemented via a physical keyboard. In this case, the terminology is consistent with the terminology used in most window systems and OpenGL, which do not distinguish between the logical string device and the keyboard.

2. **Locator** A locator device provides a position in world coordinates to the user program. It is usually implemented via a pointing device, such as a mouse or a trackball. In OpenGL, we shall usually use the pointing device in this manner, although we shall have to do the conversion from screen coordinates to world coordinates within our own programs.

3. **Pick** A pick device returns the identifier of an object to the user program. It is usually implemented with the same physical device as a locator, but has a separate software interface to the user program. In OpenGL, we can use a process called *selection* to accomplish picking.

4. **Choice** Choice devices allow the user to select one of a discrete number of options. In OpenGL, we can use various widgets provided by the window system. A **widget** is a graphical interactive device, provided by either the window system or a toolkit. Typical widgets include menus, scrollbars, and graphical buttons. Most widgets are implemented as special types of windows. For example, a menu with n selections acts as choice device, allowing us to select one of n alternatives.

5. **Dial** Dials provide analog input to the user program. Here again, widgets within various toolkits usually provide this facility through graphical devices, such as slidebars.

6. **Stroke** A stroke device returns an array of locations. Although we can think of a stroke as similar to multiple uses of a locator, it is often implemented such that an action, such as pushing down a mouse button, starts the transfer of data into the specified array, and a second action, such as releasing the button, ends this transfer.

3.2.3 Measure and Trigger

The manner by which physical and logical input devices provide input to an application program can be described in terms of two entities: a measure process and a device trigger. The **measure** of a device is what the device returns to the user program. The **trigger** of a device is a physical input on the device that the user can use to signal the computer. For example, the measure of a keyboard contains a string, and the trigger can be the "return" or "enter" key. For a locator, the measure includes the position, and the associated trigger can be a button on the pointing device.

In addition to its obvious parts, the measure can include other information, such as status. For example, a pick device will return in its measure the identifier of the object to which the user is pointing. If the physical device is a mouse, the trigger is a mouse button. However, problems can arise when we develop an application program if we have to account for the user triggering the device while she is not pointing to an object. If the measure consists of only an object identifier, we face problems in constructing code that takes care of this situation correctly. We can resolve the problem more easily if part of the measure is a status variable that indicates that the user was not pointing to an object, or that the cursor was outside the window, when the trigger occurred.

3.2.4 Input Modes

In addition to the multiple types of logical input devices, we can obtain the measure of a device in three distinct modes. Each mode is defined by the relationship between the measure process and the trigger. Normally, the initialization of the input device starts a measure process. The initialization may require an explicit function call in some APIs, or may occur automatically. In either case, once the measure process is started, the measure is taken and placed in a buffer, even though the contents of the buffer may not yet be available to the program. For example, the position of a mouse is tracked continuously by the underlying window system, regardless of whether the application program needs mouse input.

In **request mode**, the measure of the device is not returned to the program until the device is triggered. This input mode is standard in nongraphical applications, such as a typical C program that requires character input. When we use a function such as scanf, the program halts when it encounters this statement and waits while we type characters at our terminal. We can backspace to correct our typing, and can take as long as we like. The data are placed in a keyboard buffer whose contents are returned to our program only after a particular key, such as the "enter" key (the trigger), is depressed. For a logical device, such as a locator, we can move our pointing device to the desired location, and then trigger the device with its button; the trigger will cause the location to be returned to the application program. The relationship between measure and trigger for request mode is as shown in Figure 3.8.

Figure 3.8 Request mode.

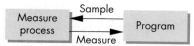

Figure 3.9 Sample mode.

Sample-mode input provides immediate input. As soon as the function call in the user program is encountered, the measure is returned. Hence, no trigger is needed (Figure 3.9). In sample mode, the user must have positioned the pointing device or entered data in the keyboard before the function call, because the measure is extracted immediately from the buffer.

One characteristic of both request- and sample-mode input in APIs that support them is that the user must identify which device is to provide the input. We usually interface with the devices through functions such as

```
request_locator(device_id, &measure);
sample_locator(device_id, &measure);
```

Consequently, any other information that becomes available from any other input device, other than the one specified in the function call, is ignored. Both request and sample modes are useful for situations where the program guides the user, but are not useful in applications where the user controls the flow of the program. For example, a flight simulator might have multiple input devices, such as a joystick, dials, buttons, and switches, most of which can be used at any time by the pilot. Writing programs to control the simulator with only sample- and request-mode input is nearly impossible, because we do not know what devices the pilot will use at any point in the simulation. More generally, sample- and request-mode input are not sufficient for handling the variety of possible human–computer interactions that arise in a modern computing environment.

Our third mode, **event mode**, can handle these other interactions. We introduce it in three steps. First, we show how event mode can be described as another mode within our measure–trigger paradigm. Second, we discuss the basics of client and servers where event mode is the preferred interaction mode. Third, we show the event-mode interface to OpenGL using GLUT.

Suppose that we are in an environment with multiple input devices, each with its own trigger and each running a measure process. Each time that a device is triggered, an **event** is generated. The device measure, with the identifier for the device, is placed in an **event queue**. This process of placing events in the event queue is completely independent of what the application program does with these events. One way that the application program can work with events

Figure 3.10 Event–mode model.

is shown in Figure 3.10. The user program can examine the top event in the queue, or can wait for an event to occur. If there is an event in the queue, the program can look at the event's type and then decide what to do. This method is used in the APIs for GKS and PHIGS.

Another approach is to associate a function called a **callback** with a specific type of event. We shall take this approach, because it is the one presently used with the major windowing systems and has proved to work well in client–server environments.

3.3   Clients and Servers

So far, our approach to input has been isolated from all other activities that might be happening in our computing environment. We have looked at our graphics system as a monolithic box that has limited connections to the outside world, other than through our carefully controlled input devices and a display. Networks and multiuser computing have changed this picture dramatically, and to such an extent that, even if we had a single-user isolated system, its software probably would be configured as a simple client–server network.

If computer graphics is to be useful for a variety of real applications, it must function well in a world of distributed computing and networks. In this world, our building blocks are entities called **servers** that can perform tasks for **clients**. Clients and servers can be distributed over a network (Figure 3.11) or contained entirely within a single computational unit. Familiar examples of servers include print servers, which can allow sharing of a high-speed printer among users; compute servers, such as remotely located supercomputers, accessible from user programs; and terminal servers that handle dial-in access. Users and user programs that make use of these services are clients or client programs.

It is less obvious what we should call a workstation connected to the network: It can be both a client and a server, or, perhaps more to the point, a workstation may run client programs and server programs concurrently.

The model that we shall use here was popularized by the X Window system. We shall use much of that system's terminology, which is now common to most window systems and fits well with graphical applications.

A workstation with a raster display, a keyboard, and a pointing device, such as mouse, is a **graphics server**. The server can provide output services on its display, and input services through the keyboard and pointing device. These services potentially are available to clients anywhere on the network.

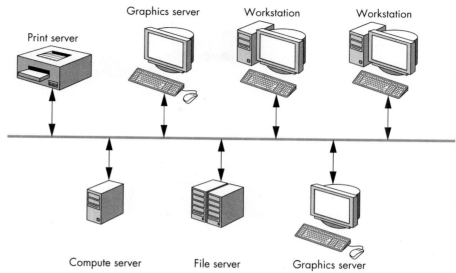

Figure 3.11 Network.

Our OpenGL application programs are clients that use the graphics server. Within an isolated system, this distinction may not be apparent as we write, compile, and run the software on a single machine. However, we shall be able to run the same application program using other graphics servers on the network.

3.4 Display Lists

Display lists illustrate how we can use clients and servers on a network to improve graphics performance. Display lists have their origins in the early days of computer graphics. As we saw in Chapter 1, the original architecture of a graphics system was based on a general-purpose computer (or host) connected, through digital-to-analog converters, to a CRT (Figure 3.12). The computer would send out the necessary information to redraw the display at a rate sufficient to avoid noticeable flicker.[2] At that time (circa 1960), computers were slow and expensive, so the cost of keeping even a simple display refreshed was prohibitive for all but a few applications.

The solution to this problem was to build a special-purpose computer, called a **display processor**, with an organization like that illustrated in Figure 3.13.

---

[2] This rate depends on the phosphors in the CRT, but we shall usually assume it to be in the range of 50 to 75 Hz, or one-half that rate if the display is interlaced.

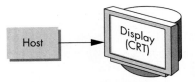

Figure 3.12 Simple graphics architecture

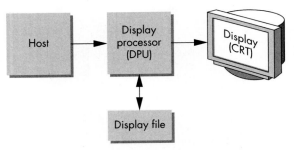

Figure 3.13 Display-processor architecture

The display processor had a limited instruction set, most of which was oriented toward drawing primitives on the CRT. The user program was executed in the host computer. A compiled list of instructions was then sent to the display processor, where the instructions were stored in a **display memory** as a **display file** or **display list**. For a simple noninteractive application, once the display list was sent to the display processor, the host was free for other tasks, and the display processor would execute its display list repeatedly at a rate sufficient to avoid flicker. In addition to resolving the bottleneck due to burdening the host, the display processor introduced the advantages of special-purpose rendering hardware.

Today, the display processor of old has become a graphics server, and the user program on the host computer has become a client. The major bottleneck is no longer the rate at which we have to refresh the display (although that is still a significant problem), but rather the amount of traffic that passes between the client and server. In addition, the use of special-purpose hardware now characterizes high-end systems.

We can send graphical entities to a display in one of two ways. We can send the complete description of our objects to the graphics server. For our typical geometric primitives, this transfer entails sending vertices, attributes, and primitive types, in addition to viewing information. In our fundamental mode of operation, **immediate mode**, as soon as the program executes a statement that defines a primitive, that primitive is sent to the server for display, and no memory of it is retained in the system.[3] To redisplay the primitive after a clearing of the screen, or in a new position after an interaction, the program must redefine the primitive and then must resend the primitive to the display. For complex objects in highly interactive applications, this process can cause a considerable quantity of data to pass from the client to the server.

Display lists offer an alternative to this method of operation. This second method is called **retained-mode** graphics. We can define the object once, then put its description in a display list. The display list can be stored in the server and redisplayed by a simple function call issued from the client to the server. In addition to conferring the obvious advantage of reduced network traffic, this model also allows the client to take advantage of any special-purpose graphics hardware that might be available in the graphics server. Thus, in many situations, the optimum configuration consists of a good numerical-processing computer that executes the client program, and a special-purpose graphics computer for the server—an old idea used with great efficiency in modern systems.

There are, of course, a few disadvantages to the use of display lists. Display lists require memory on the server, and there is the overhead of creating a display list. Although this overhead often is offset by the efficiency of the execution of the display list, such might not be the case if the data are changing.

3.4.1 Definition and Execution of Display Lists

Display lists have much in common with ordinary files. There must be a mechanism to define (create) and manipulate (place information in) them. The permissible contents of a display list should be flexible enough to allow considerable freedom to the user. OpenGL[4] has a small set of functions to manipulate display lists, and only a few restrictions on display-list contents. We shall develop several simple examples to show the functions' use.

Display lists are defined similarly to geometric primitives. There is a `glNewList` at the beginning and a `glEndList` at the end, with the contents between. Each display list must have a unique identifier—an integer that is usually macro-defined in the C program via a `#define` directive to an appropriate name for the object in the list. For example, the following code defines a red box. The code is similar to code from Chapter 2, but this time places the information in a display list:

```
glNewList(BOX,  GL_COMPILE);
    glBegin(GL_POLYGON);
        glColor3f(1.0,  0.0,  0.0);
```

---

[3] The *image* of the primitive is retained in the frame buffer, but objects and images are not the same.

[4] PHIGS contains *structures* and GKS contains *segments*, both of which provide many of the characteristics of OpenGL display files.

```
            glVertex2f(-1.0,  -1.0);
            glVertex2f( 1.0,  -1.0);
            glVertex2f( 1.0,   1.0);
            glVertex2f(-1.0,   1.0);
        glEnd();
    glEndList();
```

The flag GL_COMPILE tells the system to send the list to the server, but not to display its contents. If we want an immediate display of the contents, we can use the GL_COMPILE_AND_EXECUTE flag instead.

Each time that we wish to draw the box on the server, we execute the function

```
    glCallList(BOX);
```

Just as it does with other OpenGL functions, the present state determines which transformations are applied to the primitives in the display list. Thus, if we change the model-view or projection matrices between executions of the display list, the box will appear in different places or even will no longer appear, as the following code fragment demonstrates:

```
glMatrixMode(GL_PROJECTION);
for(i= 1 ; i<5; i++)
{
    glLoadIdentity();
    gluOrtho2D(-2.0*i  , 2.0*i , -2.0*i , 2.0*i );
    glCallList(BOX);
}
```

Each time that glCallList is executed, the box is redrawn, albeit with a different clipping rectangle.

In succeeding chapters, we shall introduce various transformation matrices that will enable us to use display lists for modeling. Note that, because we can change state from within a display list, we have to be careful to avoid these changes having undesirable, and often unexpected, effects later. For example, our box display list changes the drawing color. Each time that the display list is executed, the drawing color is set to red and, unless it is set to some other value, primitives defined subsequently in the program also will be colored red. The easiest safeguard is to use the matrix and attribute stacks provided by OpenGL. A **stack** is a data structure in which the last item placed in the structure is the first removed. We can save the present values of attributes and matrices by placing them on the top of the appropriate stack, or **pushing** them onto the stack; we can recover them later by removing, or **popping**, them from the stack. A standard, and safe, procedure is always to push both the attributes and matrices on their own stacks when we enter a display list, and to restore them when we exit. Thus, we usually see the function calls

```
glPushAttrib(GL_ALL_ATTRIB_BITS);
glPushMatrix();
```

at the beginning of a display list, and

```
glPopAttrib();
glPopMatrix();
```

at the end. We shall use matrix and attributes stacks extensively in Chapter 8 to build and display hierarchical models.

A few additional functions are available that make it easier to work with display lists. Often, we want to work with multiple display lists, as we shall demonstrate with the next example. Creation of multiple lists with consecutive identifiers can be made easier through the function `glGenLists(number)`, which returns the first integer (or base) of `number` consecutive integers that are unused labels. The function `glCallLists` allows us to execute multiple display lists with a single function call. Text generation is a good example of how we can make excellent use of the options available through display lists. Section 3.4.2 contains OpenGL details; you may want to skip it the first time that you read this chapter. It illustrates the flexibility that the API provides to the application programmer for dealing with troublesome issues that arise in working with text.

3.4.2 Text and Display Lists

In Chapter 2, we introduced both stroke and raster text. Regardless of which type we choose to use, we need a reasonable amount of code to describe a set of characters. For example, suppose that we use a raster font in which each character is stored as a 12×10 pattern of bits. It takes 15 bytes to store each character. If we want to display a string by the most straightforward method, we can send the character to the server each time that we want it displayed. This transfer will require the movement of at least 15 bytes per character. If we define a stroke font using only line segments, each character can require a different number of lines. If we use filled polygons for characters, as in Figure 3.14, we see that an "I" is fairly simple to define, but we may need many line segments to get a sufficiently smooth "O." On the average, we shall need many more than 15 bytes per character to represent a stroke font. For applications that display large quantities of text, sending each character to the display every time it is needed can place a significant burden on our graphics systems.

A more efficient strategy is to define the font once, using a display list for each character, and then to store the font on the server via these display lists. This solution is similar to what is done for bitmap fonts on standard alphanumeric display terminals. The patterns are stored in read-only memory (ROM) in the terminal, and each character is selected and displayed based on a single byte: its ASCII code. The difference here is one of both quantity and quality. We can define as many fonts as our display memory can hold, and we

(a) Input Output

(b)

Figure 3.14 Stroke characters (a) Filled strings. (b) Magnified outlines.

can treat stroke fonts like other graphical objects, allowing us to translate, scale, and rotate them as desired.

The basics of defining and displaying a character string (1 byte per character) using a stroke font and display lists provide a simple but important example of the use of display lists in OpenGL. The procedure is essentially the same for a raster font. We can define either the standard 96 printable ASCII characters or, we can define patterns for a 256-character extended ASCII character set.

First, we shall define a function OurFont(char c), which will draw any ASCII character c that can appear in our string. The function might have a form like

```
void OurFont(char c)
    {
        switch(c)
        {
            case 'a':
                .
                .
            break;
            case 'A':
                .
                .
            break;
                .
                .
        }
    }
```

Within each case, we have to be careful about the spacing; each character in the string must be displayed to the right of the previous character. We can use the translate function glTranslate to get the desired spacing. Suppose that we are defining the letter "O" and wish it to fit in a unit square. The corresponding part of OurFont might be

```
case 'O':
    glTranslatef(0.5, 0.5, 0.0); /* move to center */
    glBegin{GL_QUAD_STRIP);
    for (i=0; i<=12; i++)   /* 12 vertices */
    {
            angle = 3.14159 /6.0 * i; /* 30 degrees in radians */
            glVertex2f(0.4*cos(angle); 0.4*sin(angle));
            glVertex2f(0.5*cos(angle), 0.5*sin(angle));
    }
    glEnd();
    glTranslatef(0.5, -0.5, 0.0); /* move to lower right */
    break;
```

This code approximates the circle with 12 quadrilaterals. Each will be filled according to the present state. Although we shall not discuss the full power of transformations until Chapter 4, here we shall explain the use of the translation function in this code. We are working with two-dimensional characters. Hence, each character is defined in the plane $z = 0$. We can use whatever coordinate system we wish to define our characters. We shall assume that each character fits inside a box.[5] The usual strategy is to start at the lower-left corner of the first character in the string, and to draw one character at a time, drawing each character such that we end at the lower-right corner of that character's box, which is the lower-left corner of the successor's box.

The first translation moves us to the center of the "O" character's box, which we set to be a unit square. We then define our vertices using two concentric circles centered at this point (Figure 3.15). One way to envision the translation function is to say that it shifts the origin for all the drawing commands that follow. After the 12 quadrilaterals in the strip are defined, we move to the lower-right corner of the box. The two translations accumulate; as a result of the these translations, we are in the proper position to start the next character. Note that this is an example where we do not want to push and pop the matrices. Other characters can be defined in a similar manner.

Although our code is inelegant, its efficiency is of little consequence, because the characters are generated only once, and then are sent to the graphics server as a compiled display list.

Suppose that we want to generate a 256-character set. The required code, using the OurFont function, is as follows:

```
base = glGenLists(256); /* return index of first of 256
                            consecutive available ids */
for(i=0; i<256; i++)
{
        glNewList(base + i, GL_COMPILE);
        OurFont(i);
        glEndList();
}
```

When we wish to use these display lists to draw individual characters, rather than offsetting the identifier of the display lists by base each time, we can set an offset with

```
glListBase(base);
```

Finally, our drawing of a string is accomplished in the server by the function call

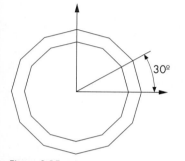

Figure 3.15 Drawing of the letter "O."

---

[5] Each character may have a different size and thus be in a box of its own unique dimension, or, if we are defining a fixed-width monotype font (such as the one used to set code in this book), all characters will have the same size box.

```
char *text_string;

glCallLists( (GLint) strlen(text_string), GL_BYTE, text_string);
```

that makes use of the standard UNIX function `strlen` to find the length of input string `text_string`. The first argument in the function `glCallLists` is the number of lists to be executed. The third is a pointer to an array of a type given by the second argument. The identifier of the kth display list executed is the sum of the list base (established by `glListBase`) and the value of the kth character in the array of characters.

3.4.3 Fonts in GLUT

In general, we prefer to use an existing font, rather than to define our own. GLUT provides a few raster and stroke fonts.[6] They do not make use of display lists; in the final example in this chapter, however, we shall create display lists to contain one of these GLUT fonts. We can access a single character from a **monotype**, or evenly spaced, font by the function call

```
glutStrokeCharacter(GLUT_STROKE_MONO_ROMAN, int  character)
```

`GLUT_STROKE_ROMAN` provides proportionally spaced characters. You should use these fonts with some caution. Their size (approximately 120 units maximum) may have little to do with the units of the rest of your program; thus, they may have to be scaled. We usually control the position of a character by using a translation before the character function is called. In addition, each invocation of `glutStrokeCharacter` includes a translation to the bottom right of the character's box, to prepare for the next character. Scaling and translation affect the OpenGL state, so here we should be careful to use `glPushMatrix` and `glPopMatrix` as necessary, to prevent undesirable positioning of objects defined later in the program.

Raster or bitmap characters are produced in a similar manner. For example, a single 8×13 character is obtained via

```
glutBitmapCharacter(GLUT_BITMAP_8_BY_13, int character)
```

Positioning of bitmap characters is considerably simpler than is that of stroke characters, because the characters are drawn directly in the frame buffer and are not subject to geometric transformations, whereas stroke characters are. OpenGL keeps, within its state, a **raster position**. This position identifies where the next raster primitive will be placed, and can be set via the function `glRasterPos*()`. The raster position is moved one character to the right each time that `glutBitmapCharacter` is invoked, but this change does not affect

---

[6] We can also access fonts that are provided by the windowing system.

subsequent rendering of geometric primitives. We shall use bitmap characters in our final example in this chapter, via display lists.

The case for always using display lists is strong, and we shall return to them when we discuss hierarchical modeling in Chapter 8. At this point, however, we are more interested in clarity and brevity than efficiency. Hence, we shall not use display lists in many of our examples. Most user code can be encapsulated between a glNewList and glEndList. Thus, you should be able to convert most code to using display lists with little effort.

3.5 Programming Event-Driven Input

We shall develop event-driven input through a number of simple examples that use the callback mechanism that we introduced in Section 3.2. We shall examine various events that are recognized by the window system and, for those of interest to our application, we shall write callback functions that will govern how the application program responds to these events.

3.5.1 Using the Pointing Device

We shall start by altering the main function in the gasket program from Chapter 2. In the original version, we used functions in the GLUT library to put a window on the screen, and then entered the event loop by executing the function glutMainLoop. In that chapter, we entered the loop but did nothing. We could not even terminate the program, except through an external mechanism. Our first example will remedy this omission by using the pointing device to terminate a program. We shall accomplish this task by having the program execute a standard termination function called, exit, when a particular mouse button is depressed.

We shall discuss only those events recognized by GLUT. A window system such as the X Window system recognizes many more events. However, the GLUT library will recognize a set of events that is common to most window systems, and is sufficient for developing basic interactive graphics programs that can be used with multiple window systems. Two types of events are associated with the pointing device, which is conventionally assumed to be a mouse. A **move event** is generated when the mouse is moved with one of the buttons depressed. If the mouse is moved without a button being held down, this event is classified as a **passive move event.** After a move event, the position of the mouse—its measure—is made available to the application program. A **mouse event** occurs when one of the mouse buttons is either depressed or released. A button being held down does not generate an event until the button is released.[7] The information returned—the measure—includes the button that

---

[7] Some systems count the pushing and the releasing of a button as only a single event.

generated the event, the state of the button after the event (up or down), and the position of the cursor tracking the mouse in screen coordinates. We specify the mouse callback function, usually in the `main` function, via the GLUT function

```
glutMouseFunc(mouse_callback_func)
```

The mouse callback must have the form

```
void mouse_callback_func(int button, int state, int x, int y)
```

Within the callback function, we define what actions we want to take place if the specified event occurs. There may be multiple actions defined in the mouse callback function corresponding to the many possible button and state combinations. For our simple example, we want the depression of the left mouse button to terminate the program. The required callback is the single-line function

```
void mouse_callback_function(int button, int state,
int x, int y)
{
    if(button == GLUT_LEFT_BUTTON && state == GLUT_DOWN)
            exit();
}
```

If any other mouse event—such as pushing of one of the other buttons or even releasing of the left-button—occurs, no action will occur, because no callback corresponding to these events has been defined, or **registered**, with the window system.

Our next example illustrates the benefits of the program structure that we introduced in the previous chapter. We shall write a program to draw a small box at each location on the screen where the mouse cursor is located at the time that the left button is pushed. A push of the middle button will terminate the program.

First, we look at the main program, which is much the same as our previous examples.[8]

```
int main(int argc, char **argv)
{

    glutInit(&argc,argv);
    glutInitDisplayMode(GLUT_SINGLE | GLUT_RGB);
    glutCreateWindow("square");
    myinit();
```

---

[8] We use naming conventions for callbacks similar to those in the *OpenGL Programmer's Guide* [Ope93a].

```
glutReshapeFunc(myReshape);
glutMouseFunc(mouse);
glutMainLoop();
}
```

The **reshape event** is generated whenever the window is resized, such as by a user interaction; we shall discuss it next. We do not use the required display callback in this example, because the only time that primitives will be generated is when a mouse event occurs. The mouse callbacks are again in the function mouse

```
void mouse(int btn, int state, int x, int y)
{
  if(btn==GLUT_LEFT_BUTTON && state==GLUT_DOWN) drawSquare(x,y);
  if(btn==GLUT_MIDDLE_BUTTON && state==GLUT_DOWN) exit();
}
```

Because only the primitives are generated in drawSquare, the desired attributes must have been set elsewhere, such as in our initialization function myinit.

We shall need three global variables. The size of the window may change dynamically, and its present size should be available, both to the reshape callback and to the drawing function drawSquare. If we want to change the size of the squares that we draw, we may find it beneficial also to make the square-size parameter global. Our initialization routine selects a clipping window that is the same size as the window created in main, and selects the viewport to correspond to the entire window. This window is cleared to black. Note that we could omit the setting of the window and viewport here; we are merely setting them to the default settings. However, it is illustrative to compare this code with what we shall do in the reshape callback in Section 3.5.2.

```
/* globals */

GLsizei wh = 500, ww = 500; /* initial window size */
GLfloat size = 3.0;    /*one--half of side length of square */

void myinit(void)
{
      glViewport(0,0,ww,wh);
      glMatrixMode(GL_PROJECTION);
      glLoadIdentity();
      gluOrtho2D(0.0, (GLdouble) ww , 0.0, (GLdouble) wh);
      glMatrixMode(GL_MODELVIEW);

      /* set clear color to black, and clear window */

      glClearColor (0.0, 0.0, 0.0, 0.0);
      glClear(GL_COLOR_BUFFER_BIT);
```

```
        glFlush();
    }
```

Our square-drawing routine has to take into account that the position re-turned from the mouse event is in the window system's coordinate system, which has its origin at the top left of the window. Hence, we have to flip the y value returned, using the present height of the window (the global wh). We pick a random color using the standard random-number generator random().

```
    void drawSquare(int x, int y)
    {

        y=wh-y;
        glColor3ub( (char) random()%256, (char) random()%256,
                                    (char) random()%256);
        glBegin(GL_POLYGON);
            glVertex2f(x+size, y+size);
            glVertex2f(x-size, y+size);
            glVertex2f(x-size, y-size);
            glVertex2f(x+size, y-size);
        glEnd();
        glFlush();
    }
```

Once we insert in the necessary include statements we shall have a program that works, as long as the window size remains unchanged.

3.5.2 Window Events

Most window systems allow a user to resize the window, usually by using the mouse to drag a corner of the window to a new location. This event is an example of a **window event**. If such an event occurs, the user program can decide what to do.[9] If the window size changes, we have to consider three questions:

1. Do we redraw all the objects that were in the window before it was resized?
2. What do we do if the aspect ratio of the new window is different from that of the old window?
3. Do we change the sizes or attributes of new primitives if the size of the new window is different from that of the old?

---

[9] There is a default reshape callback that might not do what the user desires.

There is no single answer to any of these questions. If we are displaying the image of a real-world scene, our reshape function probably should make sure that no shape distortions occur. But this choice may mean that part of the resized window is unused, or that part of the scene cannot be displayed in the window. If we want to redraw the objects that were in the window before it was resized, we need a mechanism for storing and recalling them. Often, we do this recall by encapsulating all drawing in a single function, such as the display function used in Chapter 2, which was registered as the display callback function. In the present example, however, that is probably not the best choice, because we decide what we draw interactively.

In our square-drawing example, we shall ensure that squares of the same size are drawn, regardless of the size or shape of the window. We clear the screen each time that it is resized, and use the entire new window as our drawing area. The reshape event returns in its measure the height and width of the new window. We use these values to create a new OpenGL clipping window using gluOrtho2D, and a new viewport with the same aspect ratio. We then clear the window to black. Thus, we have the callback

```
void myReshape(GLsizei w, GLsizei h)
{

    /* adjust clipping box */

    glMatrixMode(GL_PROJECTION);
    glLoadIdentity();
    gluOrtho2D(0.0, (GLdouble)w, 0.0, (GLdouble)h);
    glMatrixMode(GL_MODELVIEW);
    glLoadIdentity();

    /* adjust viewport and clear */

    glViewport(0,0,w,h);
    glClearColor (0.0, 0.0, 0.0, 0.0);
    glClear(GL_COLOR_BUFFER_BIT);
    glFlush();
}
```

The complete square-drawing program is given in Appendix A.

There are other possibilities here. We could change the size of the squares to match the increase or decrease of the window size. We have not considered other events, such as a window movement without resizing, an event that can be generated by the user dragging the window to a new location, and we do not know what to do if the window is hidden behind another window and then is exposed (brought to the front). There are callbacks for these events and we can write simple functions similar to MyReshape for them, or we can rely on the default behavior of GLUT. Another simple change that we can make to our program is to have new squares generated as long as one of the mouse buttons is held down. The relevant callback is the motion callback, which we set through the function

```
glutMotionFunc(drawSquare);
```

Each time the system senses the motion, a new square is drawn, an action that allows us to draw pictures using a brush with a square tip.

3.5.3 Keyboard Events

We can also use the keyboard as an input device. Keyboard events are generated when the mouse is in the window and one of the keys is depressed. Although in many window systems the release of a key generates a second event, GLUT does not have a callback for this event. The ASCII code for the key pressed and the location of the mouse are returned. All the keyboard callbacks are registered in a single callback function, such as

```
glutKeyboardFunc(keyboard);
```

For example if we wish to use the keyboard only to exit the program, we can use the callback function

```
void keyboard(unsigned char key, int x, int y)
{
    if(key=='q' || key == 'Q') exit( );
}
```

3.5.4 The Display and Idle Callbacks

Of the remaining callbacks, two merit special attention. We have already seen the display callback, which we used in Chapter 2. This function is specified in GLUT by the function

```
glutDisplayFunc(display);
```

It is invoked when GLUT determines that the window should be redisplayed. One such situation occurs when the window is opened initially. Because we know that a display event will be generated when the window is first opened, the display callback is a good place to put the code that generates most noninteractive output.

The **idle callback** is invoked when there are no other events. Its default is the null function.[10] A typical use of the idle callback is to continue to generate

---

[10] We can change most callbacks during program execution, or can disable them by setting a callback function to NULL. GLUT requires a display callback.

graphical primitives through a display function while nothing else is happening (see Exercise 3.2). We shall illustrate both the display and idle callbacks in the paint program we shall develop in Section 3.8.

3.6 Menus

Figure 3.16 Slidebar.

We could use our graphics primitives and our mouse callbacks to construct various graphical input devices. For example, we could construct a slidebar as shown in Figure 3.16, using filled rectangles for the device, text for the labels, and the mouse to get the position. Much of the code would be tedious to develop, however, especially if we tried to create visually appealing and effective graphical devices (widgets). Most window systems provide a toolkit that contains a set of widgets, but, because our philosophy is not to restrict our discussion to any particular window system, we shall not discuss the specifics of such widgets sets. Fortunately, GLUT provides one additional feature, **pop-up menus**, that we can use with the mouse to create sophisticated interactive applications.

Using menus involves taking a few simple steps. We must define the entries in the menu. We must link the menu to a particular mouse button. Finally, we must define a callback function corresponding to each menu entry. We can demonstrate simple menus with the example of a pop-up menu with three entries. The first selection will allow us to exit our program. The second and third will change the size of the squares in our drawSquare function. We will name the menu callback demo_menu. The function calls to set up the menu and to link it to the right mouse button should be placed in our main function. They are

```
glutCreateMenu(demo_menu);
glutAddMenuEntry("quit",1);
glutAddMenuEntry("increase square size", 2);
glutAddMenuEntry("decrease square size", 3);
glutAttachMenu(GLUT_RIGHT_BUTTON);
```

The second argument in each entry's definition is the identifier passed to the callback when the entry is selected. Hence, our callback function is

```
void demo_menu(int id)
{
    if(id == 1) exit( );
    else if (id == 2) size = 2 * size;
    else if (size > 1) size = size/2;
    glutPostRedisplay( );
}
```

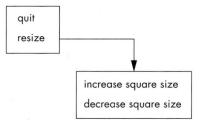

Figure 3.17 Hierarchical menus.

The call to `glutPostResdisplay` requests a redraw through the `glutDisplay-Func` callback, so that the screen is drawn again without the menu.

GLUT also supports hierarchical menus, as shown in Figure 3.17. For example, suppose that we want the main menu we create to have only two entries. The first will again cause the program to terminate, but now the second will cause a submenu to pop up. The submenu will contain the two entries for changing the size of the square in our square-drawing program. The following code for the menu (which will be in `main`) should be clear:

```
sub_menu = glutCreateMenu(size_menu);
glutAddMenuEntry("increase square size", 2);
glutAddMenuEntry("decrease square size", 3);
glutCreateMenu(top_menu);
glutAddMenuEntry("quit",1);
glutAddSubMenu("Resize", sub_menu);
glutAttachMenu(GLUT_RIGHT_BUTTON);
```

Writing the callback functions, `size_menu` and `top_menu`, should be a simple exercise for you (Exercise 3.5).

3.7   Picking

Picking is an input operation that allows the user to identify an object on the display. Although the action of picking uses the pointing device, the information that the user wants returned to the application program is not a position. A pick device is considerably more difficult to implement on a modern system than is a locator.

Such was not always the case. Old display processors with a lightpen could accomplish picking easily. Each redisplay of the screen would start at a precise time. The lightpen would generate an interrupt when the redisplay passed its sensor. By comparing the time of the interrupt with the time that the redisplay began, the processor could identify an exact place in the display list, and subsequently could determine which object was being displayed.

One reason for the difficulty of picking in modern systems is the forward nature of their rendering pipelines. Primitives are defined in an application program and move forward through a sequence of transformations and clippers until they are rasterized into the frame buffer. Although much of this process is reversible in a mathematical sense, the hardware is not reversible. Hence, converting from a location on the display to the corresponding primitive is not a direct calculation.[11]

There are two major ways to deal with this difficulty. One process, known as **selection**, involves adjusting the clipping region and viewport so that we can keep track of which primitives in a small clipping region are rendered into a region near the cursor. These primitives go into a **hit list** that can be examined later by the user program.

An alternative approach is to use **bounding rectangles**, or **extents**, for objects of interest. The extent of an object is the smallest rectangle, aligned with the coordinates axes, that contains the object. It is relatively easy to determine which rectangles in world coordinates correspond to a particular point in screen coordinates. If the application program maintains a simple data structure to relate objects and bounding rectangles, approximate picking can be done within the application program. We shall demonstrate a simple example of this approach in Section 3.8.

Picking presents a number of other difficulties for the implementor. One is that, if an object is defined hierarchically, like those we shall discuss in Chapter 8, then it is part of a set of objects. When the object is indicated by the pointing device, a list of all objects of which it is a part should be returned to the user program.

Graphics APIs usually do not specify how close to an object we must point for the object to be identified. One reason for this omission is to allow for multiple ways of picking. For example, if we use the bounding-rectangle strategy, we might not point to any point contained in the object. Another reason for this lack of preciseness is that humans are not accurate positioning devices. Although the display at which we point might have a high resolution, we may find it difficult to indicate reliably with our pointing device the location on the screen corresponding to a given pixel.

3.8 A Simple Paint Program

We shall illustrate the use of callbacks, display lists, and interactive program design by developing a simple paint program. Paint programs have most of the features of sophisticated CAD programs. Any paint program should demonstrate most of the following features:

---

[11] There are also potential uniqueness problems; see Exercises 3.11 and 3.12.

■ It should have the ability to work with geometric objects, such as line segments and polygons. Given that geometric objects are defined through vertices, the program should allow us to enter vertices interactively.

■ It should have the ability to manipulate pixels, and thus draw directly into the frame buffer.

■ It should provide control of attributes such as color, line type, and fill patterns.

■ It should include menus for controlling the application.

■ It should behave correctly when the window is moved or resized.

Our sample program will demonstrate these principles, and will incorporate many of the features that we introduced in the small examples that we have developed.

Figure 3.18 shows the initial display that a user will see. The four boxes are buttons that select from the four drawing modes: line segment, rectangle, triangle, and pixel. The left mouse button selects the mode. The left mouse button will have no effect until a mode is selected. If line-segment mode is selected, the next two clicks of the left mouse button while the cursor is outside the menu area give the locations of the endpoints. After the second endpoint is located, the line segment is drawn in the present color. Rectangle and triangle modes are similar: In rectangle mode, we select the diagonal corners; in triangle mode, we locate the three vertices. A new mode can be selected at any time. In pixel mode, successive mouse clicks give positions for randomly colored rectangles that can have a side length of two or more pixels.

The menus (Figure 3.19) are controlled by the middle and right mouse buttons. The right button allows us either to clear the screen or to terminate the program. The middle button allows us to change the drawing color, to

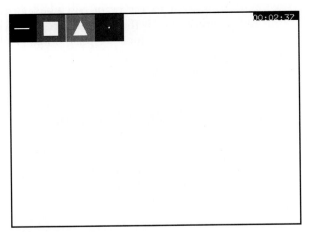

Figure 3.18 Initial display of paint program.

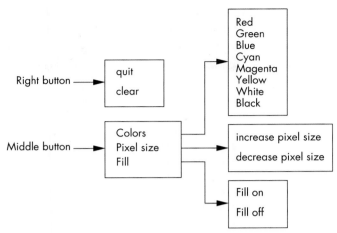

Figure 3.19 Menu structure of paint program.

select between fill and no fill for the triangles and rectangles, and to change the size of the pixel rectangles.

There is an elapsed-time clock in the top right of the display. It has no purpose other than to illustrate how we can integrate display lists and text into our programs.

Many of the functions in our program will be the same as those in our previous examples. The prototypes are the following:

```
void mouse(int btn, int state , int x, int y); /* mouse
                                                   callback */
void display(void);                /*display callback */
void idle(void);                   /* idle callback */
void drawSquare(int x, int y);  /* random--color square
                                   function*/
void myReshape(GLsizei, GLsizei);  /*reshape callback */
void myinit(void);              /* initialization function */
void screen_box(int x, int y, int s); /* box--drawing
                                         function */

void right_menu(int id);              /* menu callbacks */
void middle_menu(int id);
void color_menu(int id);
void pixel_menu(int id);
void fill_menu(int id);

long time(int t);          /* UNIX elapsed time function */
int pick(int x, int y);    /* mode--selection function */
```

We have used most of these functions in our previous examples; thus, the main function is similar to the main function in our other examples:

```
int main(int argc, char **argv)
{
    int c_menu, p_menu, f_menu;

    glutInit(&argc,argv);
    glutInitDisplayMode (GLUT_SINGLE | GLUT_RGB);
    glutCreateWindow("paint");
    glutDisplayFunc(display);
    c_menu = glutCreateMenu(color_menu);
    glutAddMenuEntry("Red",1);
    glutAddMenuEntry("Green",2);
    glutAddMenuEntry("Blue",3);
    glutAddMenuEntry("Cyan",4);
    glutAddMenuEntry("Magenta",5);
    glutAddMenuEntry("Yellow",6);
    glutAddMenuEntry("White",7);
    glutAddMenuEntry("Black",8);
    p_menu = glutCreateMenu(pixel_menu);
    glutAddMenuEntry("increase pixel size", 1);
    glutAddMenuEntry("decrease pixel size", 2);
    f_menu = glutCreateMenu(fill_menu);
    glutAddMenuEntry("fill on", 1);
    glutAddMenuEntry("fill off", 2);
    glutCreateMenu(right_menu);
    glutAddMenuEntry("quit",1);
    glutAddMenuEntry("clear",2);
    glutAttachMenu(GLUT_RIGHT_BUTTON);
    glutCreateMenu(middle_menu);
    glutAddSubMenu("Colors", c_menu);
    glutAddSubMenu("Pixel Size", p_menu);
    glutAddSubMenu("Fill", f_menu);
    glutAttachMenu(GLUT_MIDDLE_BUTTON);
    myinit ();
    glutReshapeFunc (myReshape);
    glutMouseFunc (mouse);
    glutIdleFunc(idle);
    glutMainLoop();

}
```

The most difficult part of the design is deciding what functionality to place in each of the functions. The decisions reflected in our code are consistent with our previous examples. We employ the following functions:

- ■ main sets up callbacks and the menus, and puts the program in an event loop.
- ■ display clears the window, sets the background to white, and then draws the buttons.
- ■ idle draws an elapsed-time clock on the top right of the window. It uses the UNIX elapsed-time function to determine the time elapsed in seconds since the program was initiated. We convert the time in seconds to the form hours:minutes:seconds; and we use display lists to show this time, using a raster font.
- ■ myReShape is the same reshape callback that we introduced earlier in Section 3.5.
- ■ myinit clears the window, sets up global variables, defines and compiles display lists for 128 characters, and initializes the elapsed-time clock.
- ■ mouse does most of the work of drawing. Once an area has been identified via pick, the code chooses a proper mode, and determines whether it needs to output a primitive or to store the mouse location.
- ■ pick determines which area of the screen corresponds to a given *x,y* pair. The options are 0 for the drawing area, and 1 to 4 for the buttons.
- ■ The menu callbacks should be clear from our previous examples.

A typical display from the middle of a drawing is shown in Figure 3.20. Although our paint program is simple and is limited in the facilities that it provides the user, it should allow us to add more functionality easily. Straightforward exercises are adding a text primitive, switching from raster to stroke text, adding

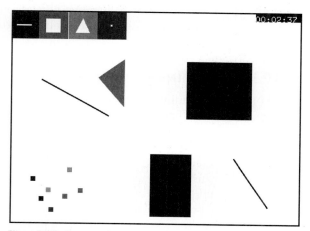

Figure 3.20 Output from painting program.

line attributes (width and type), allowing selection of fill methods (solid or patterns), and adding more objects (arbitrary polygons, circle approximations, and curves). However, making the paint program function as smoothly as commercial products do is much more difficult (although possible), for reasons that we shall discuss in the next section.

The complete program is given in Appendix A.

3.9   Design of Interactive Programs

What characterizes a good interactive program is difficult to define, but recognizing and appreciating a good interactive program is easy. Such programs include features such as these:

1. A smooth display, showing neither flicker nor any artifacts of the refresh process
2. A variety of interactive devices on the display
3. A variety of methods for entering and displaying information
4. An easy-to-use interface that does not require substantial effort to learn
5. Feedback to the user
6. Tolerance for user errors
7. A design incorporating consideration of both the visual and motor properties of the human

The importance of these features and the difficulty of designing a good interactive program should never be underestimated. The field of human–computer interaction (HCI) is an active one, and we shall not shortchange you by condensing it into a few pages. Our concern in this book is computer graphics; within this topic, our primary interest is rendering. However, there are a few topics common to computer graphics and HCI that we can pursue to improve our interactive programs.

3.9.1 Double Buffering

If you run our painting program, you will probably notice that the elapsed-time display flickers. What you are seeing is your system regenerating the display, first by clearing the area in the text box, and then by redrawing a new text string that gives the new elapsed time. Even though the rest of the display also is being refreshed, we do not notice any flicker. There is no need first to clear any other part of the window, because these areas are unchanged from refresh to refresh.

Backing up, we can examine why the clock appears this way. Our CRT display must be refreshed at a rate between 50 and 75 times per second, or we will notice the flicker. In a graphics system, this requirement means that the contents of the frame buffer must be redrawn at this refresh rate. As long as the contents of the frame buffer are unchanged and we refresh at the 50- to 75-Hz rate, we will not notice the refresh taking place.[12] If we change the contents of the frame buffer during a refresh, we may see undesirable artifacts of how we generate the display. One example is the repetitive clearing and redrawing of an area of the screen as in our paint program. Another can occur if the display being drawn is complex and cannot be drawn in a single refresh cycle. In this case, we see different parts of objects on successive refreshes. If the object is moving, its image may be distorted on the display.

Double buffering can provide a solution to these problems. Suppose that we have two frame buffers at our disposal, conventionally called the front and back buffers. The **front buffer** always is the one displayed, whereas the **back buffer** is the one into which we draw. We can swap the front and back buffers at will from the application program. When we swap buffers, a display callback is invoked. Hence, if we put our rendering into the display callback, the effect will be to update the back buffer automatically. We can set up **double buffering** by using the option GLUT_DOUBLE, instead of GLUT_SINGLE in glutInitDisplay-Mode. The buffer-swap function using GLUT is

```
glutSwapBuffers();
```

If we have a complex display to generate, we can draw it into the back buffer, using multiple refresh cycles, and swap buffers when done. Although this process will not generate the final display any faster than will single-buffer mode, the display will appear much smoother.

A more common use of double buffering is in animation, where the primitives, attributes, and viewing conditions can change continuously. We can generate a smooth display by using double buffering and putting the drawing functions into a display callback. Within this callback, the first step is to clear the front buffer through glClear, and the final step is to invoke glutSwapBuffers. Although it may take multiple refresh cycles to draw all the objects, the viewer will never see an incomplete frame.

Double buffering in such a simple manner does not provide a solution to the flicker problem in our paint program. The temptation is to alter the idle function so that there is a buffer swap after the text is specified:

```
        ⋮
glCallLists( strlen(out) , GL_BYTE, out);
glFlush();
glutSwapBuffers();
```

---

[12] If the display is interlaced, the odd and even lines in the frame buffer are displayed alternately, giving a true refresh rate of one-half of the specified rate. On such displays, you probably will notice the slight shifts of objects up and down on alternate refresh cycles.

Indeed, if we change to double buffering, the elapsed-time clock will no longer flicker, but the rest of the display will no longer look the same. A little thought should lead you to the conclusion that the problem is that we have rendered our other primitives into one of the buffers, but not into both. There are various solutions to this difficulty. You could go back to the paint program and make sure that each primitive is rendered into both buffers. A more elegant solution involves building up modes of writing into the frame buffers in a manner that accomplishes what we want by simply setting a state variable.

3.9.2 Toolkits, Widgets, and the Frame Buffer

In our paint program, we have used interactive tools, such as pop-up menus, that were provided by GLUT, and graphical buttons that we constructed in our programs. There are many more possibilities, such as slidebars, dials, hot areas of the screen, sound, and icons. Usually, these tools are supplied with various toolkits, although there is nothing to prevent us from writing our own. In general, these toolkits use callbacks to interface with application programs, and should be a simple extension of our development. Designing our own widget sets will be much easier after we introduce pixel operations in Chapter 10.

Two examples illustrate the limitations of geometric rendering and show why, at times, we need to work directly in the frame buffer. First, consider our pop-up menus. When a menu callback is invoked, the menu appears over whatever was on the display. After we make our selection, the menu disappears, and the screen is restored to the state that it was in before the menu was displayed. We cannot implement this sequence of operations using only what we have presented so far. One way to implement these operations is to store the part of the display under the menu, and to copy it back when the menu is no longer needed. Unfortunately, this description of what we want to do is in terms of what bits are on the display, or, equivalently, of what is contained in the frame buffer. The potential solution does not involve primitives in the application program; it involves only their scan-converted images. Consequently, a set of operations for implementing such operations should be described in terms of the contents of the frame buffer—that is, in terms of bit-block-transfer (bitblt) operations.

Our second example is **rubberbanding**, a technique for displaying line segments (and other primitives) in a changing manner as they are manipulated interactively. In our painting program, we indicated the endpoints of our desired line segment by two successive mouse locations. We did not have a mechanism for ensuring that any particular relationship would hold between these two locations, and we were not able to interact with the display to help us place the points. Suppose that, after we locate the first point, then, as we move the mouse, a line segment is drawn automatically (and is updated on each refresh), from the first location to the present position of the mouse, as shown in Figure 3.21. This process is called rubberbanding because the line segment that

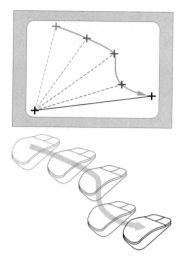

Figure 3.21 Rubberband line.

we see on the display appears to be an elastic band, with one end fixed to the first location and the second end stretched to wherever the cursor moves. Note that, before each new line segment appears, the previous line segment must be erased. Usually, the rubberbanding begins when a mouse button is depressed, and continues until the button is released, at which time a final line segment is drawn.

Rubberbanding is another operation that cannot be implemented without either bitblt operations or special hardware features such as overlay planes. The problem is similar to the menu problem in several ways. Each time that the mouse is moved to a new location, we must return the display to its original state before a new rubberband line can be drawn. Other objects that are drawn interactively using rubberbanding include rectangles and circles. Toolkits such as GLUT make use of bitblt operations; thus, menus and rubberbanding are often included, allowing the user to take advantage of these features, even if she is not able to program the equivalent functionality herself.

3.10 Summary

In this chapter, we have touched on a number of topics related to interactive computer graphics. These interactive aspects of computer graphics make the field exciting and fun. Although our API, OpenGL, is independent of any operating or window system, we recognize that any program must have at least minimal interaction with the rest of the computer system. We handled simple interactions by using a simple toolkit, GLUT, whose API provides the necessary additional functionality, without being dependent on a particular operating or window system.

We have been heavily influenced by the client–server perspective. Not only does it allow us to develop programs within a networked environment, but also it allows us to design programs that are portable yet can still take advantage of special features that might be available in the hardware.

From the application programmer's perspective, various characteristics of interactive graphics are shared by most systems. We see the graphics part of the system as a server, consisting of a raster display, a keyboard, and a pointing device. In almost all workstations, we have to work within a multiprocessing windowed environment. Most likely, many processes are executing concurrently with the execution of your graphics program. However, the window system allows us to write programs for a specific window that act as though this window is the display device of a single-user system.

The overhead of setting up a program to run in this environment is small. Each application program contains a set of function calls that is virtually the same in every program. The use of logical devices within the application program frees the programmer from worrying about the details of particular hardware.

Within the environment that we have described, event-mode input is the norm. Although the other forms are available—request-mode is the normal method used for keyboard input—event-mode input gives us far more flexibility in the design of interactive programs.

Interactive computer graphics is a powerful method with unlimited applications. At this point, you should be able to write fairly sophisticated interactive programs. Probably the most helpful exercise that you can do now is to write one. The exercises at the end of the chapter provide suggestions.

3.11   Suggested Readings

Sutherland's Project Sketchpad is described in [Sut63].

Many of the conceptual foundations for the windows-icons-menus-pointing interfaces that we now consider routine were developed at the Xerox Palo Alto Research Center (PARC) during the 1970s; see [Sch87]. The mouse also was developed there [Eng68]. The familiar interfaces of today—such as the Macintosh Operating System, the X Window system, and Microsoft Windows—all have their basis in this work.

Foley et al. [Fol94] contains a thorough description of the development of user interfaces, with an emphasis on the graphical aspects.

The X Window system [Sch88] was developed at the Massachusetts Institute of Technology and is the de facto standard in the UNIX workstation community. Recently the development of the LINUX version for PCs has allowed the X Window system to run on these platforms too.

The input and interaction modes that we discussed grew out of the standards that led to GKS [ANSI85] and PHIGS [ANSI88]. These standards were developed for both calligraphic and raster displays; thus, they do not take advantage of the possibilities available on raster-only systems; see [Pik84, Gol83].

Although we have used the GLUT toolkit [Kil94b] exclusively, we can also interface directly with the X Window system, with various X Window toolkits [Kil94a, OSF89], and with Microsoft Windows. Also of interest is the use of scripting languages, such as tcl/tk [Ous94], to develop user interfaces that work with OpenGL.

Exercises

3.1 Explain what problems you face in defining a stroke font. Create a simple data structure that will allow you to define a set of stroke characters using only line segments.

3.2 Rewrite the Sierpinski-gasket program from Chapter 2 such that the left mouse button will start the generation of points on the screen, the right mouse button will halt the generation of new points, and the middle mouse button will terminate the program. Include a reshape callback.

3.3 Construct slidebars to allow users to define colors in the paint program. Your interface should let the user see a color before that color is used.

3.4 We can construct a virtual trackball from a mouse by mapping the mouse pad onto a ball. A major use of such a device is to obtain velocities by using the mouse to "spin" the ball. Construct such a virtual device, and write a graphical application to demonstrate its use.

3.5 Alter the square-drawing program (Section 3.5) to incorporate menus like those described in Section 3.6.

3.6 Change the elapsed-time indicator in the paint program (Section 3.9) to a clock of your own design.

3.7 Creating simple games is a good way to become familiar with interactive graphics programming. Program the game of checkers. You can look at each square as an object that can be picked by the user. You can start with a program in which the user plays both sides.

3.8 Take a simple version of solitaire and write a program that allows a user to play it. First, design a simple set of cards, using only our basic primitives. Your program can be written in terms of picking rectangular objects.

3.9 Simulating a pool or billiards game presents interesting problems. Here, as in Exercise 2.19, you will have to compute trajectories and to detect collisions. The interactive aspects include initiating movement of the balls through a graphical cue stick, ensuring that the display is smooth, and creating a two-person game.

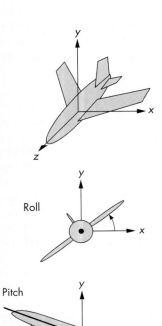

Figure 3.22 Airplane coordinate system.

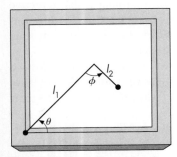

Figure 3.23 Two–dimensional sensing arm.

3.10 Rather than using buttons or menus to select options in an interactive program, we can make selections based on where in the window the mouse is located. Use this mechanism in the paint program (Section 3.9).

3.11 The mapping from a point in world coordinates to one in screen coordinates is well defined. It is not invertible because we go from three dimensions to two dimensions. Suppose, however, that we are working with a two-dimensional application. Is the mapping invertible? What problem can arise if you use a two-dimensional mapping to return a position in world coordinates by a locator device?

3.12 How do the results of Problem 3.11 apply to picking?

3.13 In a typical application program, the programmer must decide whether or not to use display lists. Consider a variety of applications. For each, list factors in favor and factors against the use of display lists. Using the fonts provided by GLUT, test whether what you wrote down is correct in practice.

3.14 Write an interactive program that will allow you to guide a graphical rat through the maze that you generated in Problem 2.8. You can use the left and right buttons to turn the rat, and the middle button to move him forward.

3.15 We observed in Section 3.9 that, even after adding double buffering to the paint program, we still have flickering of the display. Using only the rendering routines that we have described, can you fix this problem? Justify your answer.

3.16 Inexpensive joysticks, such as are used in toys and games, often lack encoders and contain only a pair of three-position switches. How might such a device function?

3.17 The orientation of an airplane is described by a coordinate system oriented as shown in Figure 3.22. The forward–backward motion of the joystick controls the up–down rotation with respect to the axis running along the length of the airplane, called the **pitch**. The right-left motion of the joystick controls the rotation about this axis, called the **roll**. Write a program that will use the mouse to control pitch and roll for the view seen by a pilot. You can do this problem in two dimensions by considering a set of objects to be located far from the airplane, and then having the mouse control the two-dimensional viewing of these objects.

3.18 Consider a table with a two-dimensional sensing device located at the end of two linked arms, as shown in Figure 3.23. Suppose that the lengths of the two arms are fixed, and the arms are connected by simple (1-degree-of-freedom) pivot joints. Determine the relationship between the joint angles θ and ϕ and the position of the sensor.

3.19 Suppose that a CRT has a square face of 40×40 centimeters and is refreshed in a noninterlaced manner at a rate of 60 Hz. Ten percent of the time to draw each scan line is used for the CRT beam to return from the right edge to the left edge of the screen–the horizontal-retrace time—and 10 percent of the total drawing time is allocated for the beam to return from the lower-right corner of the screen to the upper-left corner after each refresh is complete—the vertical-retrace time. Assume that the resolution of the display is 1024×1024 pixels. Find a relationship between the time at which a lightpen detects the beam and the lightpen's position. Give the result using both centimeters and screen coordinates for the location on the screen.

3.20 Circuit-layout programs are variants of paint programs. Consider the design of logical circuits using the AND, OR, and NOT functions. Each of these functions is provided by one of the three types of integrated circuits (gates), the symbols for which are shown in Figure 3.24. Write a program that will allow the user to design a logical circuit by selecting gates from a menu and positioning them on the screen. Consider methods for connecting the outputs of one gate to the inputs of others.

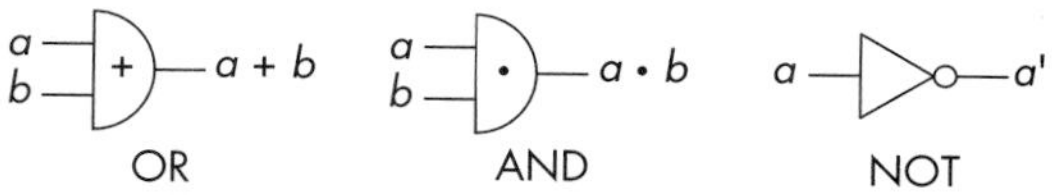

Figure 3.24 Symbols for logical circuits.

3.21 Extend Exercise 3.20 to allow the user to specify a sequence of input signals. Have the program display the resulting values at selected points in the circuit.

3.22 Extend Exercise 3.20 to have the user enter a logical expression. Have the program generate a logical diagram from that expression.

3.23 Use the methods of Exercise 3.20 to form flowcharts for programs or images of graphs that you have studied in a data-structures class.

3.24 Plotting packages offer a variety of methods for displaying data. Write an interactive plotting application for two-dimensional curves. Your application should allow the user to choose the mode (polyline display of the data, bar charts, and pie charts), colors, and line style.

3.25 The required refresh rate for CRT displays of 50 to 75 Hz is based on the use of short-persistence phosphors that emit light for extremely short intervals when excited. Long-persistence phosphors are available. Why are long-persistence phosphors not used in most workstation displays? In what types of applications might such phosphors be useful?

4 Geometric Objects and Transformations

We are now ready to concentrate on three-dimensional graphics. Much of this chapter is concerned with issues such as how to represent basic geometric types, how to convert between various representations, and what statements can we make about geometric objects, independent of a particular representation.

We begin with an examination of the mathematical underpinnings of computer graphics. This approach should avoid much of the confusion that arises from a lack of care in distinguishing among a geometric entity, its representation in a particular reference system, and a mathematical abstraction of it.

We shall use the notions of affine and Euclidean vector spaces to create the necessary mathematical foundation for later work. One of our goals is to establish a method for dealing with geometric problems that is independent of coordinate systems. The advantages of such an approach will be clear later on, when we worry about how to represent the geometric objects with which we would like to work. The coordinate-free approach will prove to be far more robust than one based on representing the objects in a particular coordinate system or frame. This approach will also lead to the use of homogeneous coordinates, a system that not only will enable us to explain this process, but also will lead to efficient implementation techniques.

We shall use the terminology of abstract data types to reinforce the distinction between objects and objects' representation. Our development will show that the mathematics arise naturally from our desire to manipulate a few basic geometric data types. Much of what we present here are applications of vector spaces, geometry, and linear algebra. Appendices B and C cover the formalities of vector spaces and matrix algebra, respectively.

In a similar vein to Chapters 2 and 3, we shall develop a simple application program to illustrate the basic principles and to see how the concepts are realized within an API. In this chapter, our example will focus on the representation and transformations of a cube.

4.1   Scalars, Points, and Vectors

In computer graphics, we work with a set of geometric objects, such as points, polygons, and polyhedra. But, as we discovered working in two dimensions, we can define most geometric objects using a limited set of simple entities. We shall need three basic types: scalars, points, and vectors.

There are many examples of mathematical scalars that satisfy the axioms of Appendix B. For our purposes, however, we can always use real numbers for scalars. Although scalars are not a geometric type, we need scalars as units of measurement. For example, the length of a line segment is scalar, as is the number of degrees by which we wish to rotate an object.

Our fundamental geometric object is a point. In a three-dimensional geometric system, a **point** is a location in space. The only attribute that the point possesses is the point's location; a mathematical point does not even have a size. Points exist in space regardless of any reference or coordinate system. Of course, we may find it inconvenient, at best, to refer to a specific point as "that point over there" or "the blue point to the right of the red one." Coordinate systems and frames (Section 4.5) will solve the reference problem, but for now we want to see just how far we can get without introducing an arbitrary reference system.

In computer graphics, we often draw vectors as directed line segments, as shown in Figure 4.1. Physicists use the term **vector** for any quantity with direction and magnitude. Physical quantities, such as velocity and force, are vectors. A vector does not, however, have a fixed position. Hence, the directed line segments shown in Figure 4.1 are vectors in that they have direction (orientation) and magnitude (length). They are also identical, because they have the same direction and magnitude, although their positions differ. In Appendix B, we define mathematical vectors that are consistent with the physicist's terminology. Directed line segments satisfy that definition, and we shall often use the terms *vector* and *directed line segment* synonymously.

Points and vectors are two distinct geometric types. Graphical representations that equate a point with a directed line segment drawn from the origin to that point (Figure 4.2) should be regarded with suspicion. We shall use directed line segments to represent vectors graphically. Note that a vector, like a point, exists regardless of the reference system, but, as we shall see with both points and vectors, we shall eventually have to work with their representation in a particular reference system.

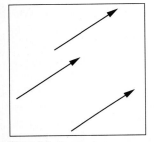

Figure 4.1 Vectors.

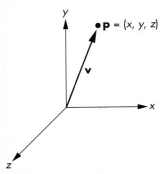

Figure 4.2 A dangerous representation.

4.1.1 Geometric Data Types

Our next step is to define a set of operations among our three types of objects. We can consider them to be both **abstract data types** (**ADTs**) and members of abstract mathematical spaces. The notion of data abstraction is fundamental to modern computer science. People familiar with this concept should have no trouble distinguishing between objects (and operations on objects), and objects' representations (or implementations) in a particular system. From a computational point of view, the code

```
vector u,v;
point p,q;
scalar a,b;
```

should make sense to them. The computer scientist sees these objects as ADTs. Operations on objects are defined independently of any internal representation or implementation of the objects on a particular system. In languages, such as C++, we can use language features, such as classes and overloading of operators, so we can write lines of code, such as

```
q = p+a*v;
```

using our geometric data types.[1] Of course, we have first to define functions that perform the necessary operations, and, to write these functions, we must look at the mathematical functions that we wish to implement. For this step, we look to certain abstract mathematical spaces.

4.1.2 Vector and Affine Spaces

Mathematicians have explored a number of abstract spaces for representing and manipulating sets of objects of interest in a variety of applied problems, ranging from the solution of differential equations to the approximation of mathematical functions. The formal definitions of the spaces of interest to us— vector spaces, affine spaces, and Euclidean spaces—are given in Appendix B. We shall be concerned with only the examples where the elements are geometric types.

Perhaps the most important mathematical space is the **(linear) vector space**. A vector space contains two distinct entities: vectors and scalars. An **affine space** is an extension of the vector space that includes an additional type of object: the point. A **Euclidean space** is an extension that adds a measure of size or distance. In these abstract spaces, objects are defined independently of any particular representation.

---

[1] Because we are using C rather than C++, and OpenGL is not object oriented, we shall have to be content with using `typedef` and `struct` constructions in our examples.

One of the major vector-space concepts is that of representing a vector in terms of one or more sets of basis vectors. Representation will provide the tie between the abstract objects and their implementation, and conversion between representations will lead us to geometric transformations.

4.1.3 Geometric ADTs

The only scalars that we shall use are the real numbers. Hence, the fundamental operations between two scalars are ordinary real addition and multiplication. The additive and multiplicative identities are the real numbers 0 and 1. Subtraction and division are defined through the additive and multiplicative inverses.

The vector and point data types are abstractions of the geometric entities of a directed line segment and a point in space. We shall let $\alpha, \beta, \gamma, \ldots$ denote scalars; $P, Q, R, \ldots$ define points; and $u, v, w, \ldots$ denote vectors. For vectors and points, this notation refers to the abstract objects, rather than to these objects' representations in a particular reference system. We shall use boldface letters for the latter. The **magnitude** of a vector v is a real number denoted by $|v|$. The operation of vector–scalar multiplication has the property that (see Appendix B)

$$|\alpha v| = |\alpha||v|,$$

and the direction of αv is the same as the direction of v if α is positive. Note that there must be a special vector, the **zero vector**, **0**, with zero magnitude.

There are two operations that relate points and vectors. First, there is the subtraction of two points, P and Q, an operation that yields a vector v denoted by

$$v = P - Q.$$

A consequence of this operation is that, given any point Q and vector v, there is a unique point, P, satisfying the preceding relationship. We can express this statement as follows: Given a Q and a v, there is a P such that

$$P = v + Q,$$

thus defining a point-vector addition operation. Figure 4.3 shows a visual interpretation of this operation. The **head-to-tail rule** gives us a convenient way of visualizing vector–vector addition. We obtain the sum $u + v$ as shown in Figure 4.4(a) by drawing the sum vector as connecting the tail of u to the head of v. However, we can also use this visualization, as demonstrated in Figure 4.4(b), to show that, for any three points P, Q, and R,

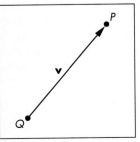

Figure 4.3 Point subtraction.

$$(P - Q) + (Q - R) = P - R.$$

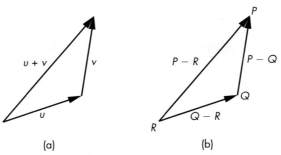

Figure 4.4 Use of the head-to-tail rule (a) for vectors, and (b) for points.

4.1.4 Lines

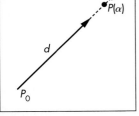

Figure 4.5 Line in an affine space.

The sum of a point and a vector (or the subtraction of two points) leads to the notion of a line in an affine space. Consider all points of the form

$$P(\alpha) = P_0 + \alpha d,$$

where P_0 is an arbitrary point, d is an arbitrary vector, and α is a scalar. Given the rules for combining points, vectors, and scalars in an affine space, $P(\alpha)$ is a point for any value of α. For geometric vectors, these points lie on a line, as shown in Figure 4.5. This form is sometimes called the **parametric form** of the line, because we generate points on the line by varying the parameter α. For $\alpha = 0$, the line passes through the point P_0 and, as α is increased, all the points generated lie in the direction of the vector d. If we restrict α to nonnegative values, we get the ray emanating from P_0 and going in the direction of d.

4.1.5 Affine Sums

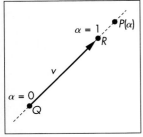

Figure 4.6 Affine addition.

Whereas in an affine space, the addition of two vectors, the multiplication of a vector by a scalar, and the addition of a vector and a point are defined, the addition of two arbitrary points and the multiplication of a point by a scalar are not. However, there is an operation called **affine addition** that has certain elements of these latter two operations. For any point Q, vector v, and positive scalar α,

$$P = Q + \alpha v$$

describes all points on the line from Q in the direction of v, as shown in Figure 4.6. However, we can always find a point R such that

$$v = R - Q;$$

thus

$$P = Q + \alpha(R - Q) = \alpha R + (1 - \alpha)Q.$$

This operation looks like the addition of two points and leads to the equivalent form

$$P = \alpha_1 R + \alpha_2 Q,$$

where

$$\alpha_1 + \alpha_2 = 1.$$

4.1.6 Convexity

A **convex** object is one for which any point lying on the line segment connecting any two points in the object is also in the object. We saw the importance of convexity for polygons in Chapter 2. We can use affine sums to help us achieve a deeper understanding of convexity. For $0 \le \alpha \le 1$, the affine sum defines the line segment connecting R and Q, as shown in Figure 4.7; thus, this line segment is a convex object. We can extend the affine sum to include objects defined by n points $P_1, P_2, \ldots, P_n$. Consider the form

$$P = \alpha_1 P_1 + \alpha_2 P_2 + \ldots + \alpha_n P_n.$$

We can show, by induction, that this sum is defined if and only if

$$\alpha_1 + \alpha_2 + \ldots + \alpha_n = 1.$$

The set of points formed by the affine sum of n points, under the additional restriction

$$\alpha_i \ge 0, i = 1, 2, \ldots, n,$$

is called the **convex hull** of the set of points (Figure 4.8). It is easy to verify that the convex hull includes all line segments connecting pairs of points in $\{P_1, P_2, \ldots, P_n\}$. Geometrically, the convex hull is the set of points that we form by stretching a tight-fitting surface over the given set of points—**shrink wrapping** the points. The notion of convexity is extremely important in the design of curves and surfaces; we shall return to it later, in Chapter 9.

4.1.7 Dot and Cross Products

Many of the geometric concepts relating the orientation between two vectors are given by the **dot (inner)** and **cross products** of two vectors. The dot product of u and v is written $u \cdot v$. If $u \cdot v = 0$, u and v are **orthogonal**. In a Euclidean space, the square of the magnitude of a vector is

$$|u|^2 = u \cdot u,$$

and the angle between two vectors is given by

$$\cos \theta = \frac{u \cdot v}{|u||v|}.$$

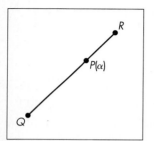

Figure 4.7 Line segment connecting two points.

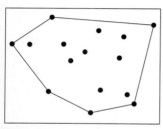

Figure 4.8 Convex hull.

Given three linearly independent vectors in a three-dimensional space, we can use the dot product to construct a set of vectors, the members of which are orthogonal to one another. This process is outlined in Appendix B. We can also use two nonparallel vectors, u and v, to determine a third vector n that is orthogonal to them. This vector is given by the cross product

$$n = u \times v,$$

derived in Appendix C. The magnitude of the cross product gives the sine of the angle θ between u and v

$$\sin \theta = \frac{|u \times v|}{|u||v|}.$$

Note that the vectors u, v and n form a **right-handed coordinate system**; that is, if u points in the direction of the thumb of the right hand, v points in the direction of the index finger, then n points in the direction of the middle finger.

4.1.8 Planes

A **plane** in an affine space can be defined as a direct extension of the parametric line. From simple geometry, we know that three points, not in a line, determine a unique plane. Suppose P, Q, and R are three such points in an affine space. The line segment joining P and Q is the set of points of the form

$$S(\alpha) = \alpha P + (1 - \alpha)Q, \qquad 0 \le \alpha \le 1.$$

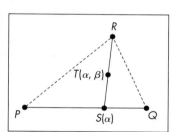

Figure 4.9 Formation of a plane.

Suppose that we take an arbitrary point on this line segment and form the line segment from this point to R, as shown in Figure 4.9. Using a second parameter β, we can describe points along this line segment as

$$T(\beta) = \beta S + (1 - \beta)R, \qquad 0 \le \beta \le 1.$$

Such points are determined by both α and β, and form the plane determined by P, Q, and R. Combining the preceding two equations, we obtain one form of the equation of a plane:

$$T(\alpha, \beta) = \beta[\alpha P + (1 - \alpha)Q] + (1 - \beta)R.$$

We can rearrange this equation in the form

$$T(\alpha, \beta) = P + \beta(1 - \alpha)(Q - P) + (1 - \beta)(R - P).$$

Noting that $Q - P$ and $R - P$ are arbitrary vectors, we have shown that a plane can also be determined from a point and two nonparallel vectors, and we can write the plane defined by P_0, u, and v as

$$T(\alpha, \beta) = P_0 + \alpha u + \beta v.$$

We can also observe that, for $0 \leq \alpha, \beta \leq 1$, all the points $T(\alpha, \beta)$ lie in the triangle formed by P, Q, and R. If a point P lies in the plane, then

$$P - P_0 = \alpha u + \beta v.$$

We can find a vector w that is orthogonal to both u and v. Using the cross product

$$n = u \times v,$$

the equation of the plane becomes

$$n \cdot (P - P_0) = 0.$$

The vector n is perpendicular, or orthogonal, to the plane, and is called the **normal** to the plane. The forms $P(\alpha)$, for the line, and $T(\alpha, \beta)$, for the plane, are known as **parametric forms**, because they give the value of a point in space for each value of the parameters α and β.

4.2   Three-Dimensional Primitives

In a three-dimensional world, we can have a far greater variety of geometric objects than we could in two dimensions. When we worked in a two-dimensional plane in Chapter 2, we considered objects that were simple curves, such as line segments, and objects that had interiors, such as polygons. In three dimensions, we retain these objects, but they are no longer restricted to lie in the same plane. Hence, curves become curves in space (Figure 4.10), and objects with interiors can become surfaces in space (Figure 4.11). In addition, we can have objects with volumes, such as parallelepipeds and ellipsoids (Figure 4.12).

We face two problems when we expand our graphics system to incorporate all these possibilities. First, the mathematical definitions of these objects can become complex. Second, we are interested in only those objects that lead to efficient implementations in graphics systems. The full range of three-dimensional objects cannot be supported on existing graphics systems, except by approximate methods.

If our three-dimensional objects are to fit well with existing graphics hardware and software, then three features should characterize those objects that we select:

1. The objects are described by their surfaces and can be thought of as being hollow.
2. The objects can be specified through a set of vertices in three dimensions.
3. The objects either are composed of or can be approximated by flat convex polygons.

We can understand these conditions if we consider what most modern graphics systems do best: They render triangular, or other flat, polygons. A high-end

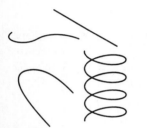

Figure 4.10 Curves in three dimensions.

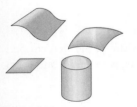

Figure 4.11 Surfaces in three dimensions.

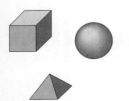

Figure 4.12 Volumetric objects.

system can render over 1 million small, flat polygons per second; boards in personal computers have rendering speeds in the hundreds of thousands of polygons per second. The first condition implies that we need only two-dimensional primitives to model three-dimensional objects; because a surface is a two- rather than a three-dimensional entity. The second condition is an extension of our observations in Chapters 1 and 2. If an object is defined by vertices, we can use a pipeline architecture to process these vertices at high rates, and we can use the hardware to generate the images of the objects only during rasterization. The final condition is an extension from our discussion of two-dimensional polygons. Most graphics systems are optimized for the processing of points and polygons. In three dimensions, a polygon can be defined by an ordered list of vertices. However, if there are more that three vertices, they do not have to be in the same plane; if they are not, there is no simple way to define the interior of the object. Consequently, most graphics systems require that the user specify simple planar polygons, or the results of rasterizing the polygon are not guaranteed to be what the programmer might desire. Because triangular polygons are always flat, either the modeling system is designed always to produce triangles, or the graphics system provides a method to divide, or **tessellate**, an arbitrary polygon into triangular polygons. If we apply this same argument to a curved object, such as to a sphere, we realize that we should use an approximation to the sphere composed of small flat polygons. Hence, even if our modeling system provides curved objects, we shall assume that a polygonal approximation is used for implementation.

The major exception to this approach is **constructive solid geometry** (**CSG**). In such systems, we build objects from a small set of volumetric objects through set operations such as union and intersection. Although this approach is an excellent one for modeling, rendering CSG models is more difficult than rendering surface-based polygonal models. Although this situation may not hold in the future, we shall discuss only surface rendering.

All the primitives with which we shall work can be specified through a set of vertices. As we move away from abstract objects to real objects, we must consider how we represent points in space in a manner that can be used within our graphics systems.

4.3   Coordinate Systems and Frames

So far, we have considered vectors and points as abstract objects, without representing them in an underlying coordinate system. In a three-dimensional vector space, we can represent any vector uniquely in terms of any three linearly independent vectors, v_1, v_2, and v_3 (see Appendix B), as

$$v = \alpha_1 v_1 + \alpha_2 v_2 + \alpha_3 v_3.$$

The scalars α_1, α_2, and α_3 are the **components** of v with respect to the **basis** v_1, v_2, and v_3. We can write the representation of v as the column matrix

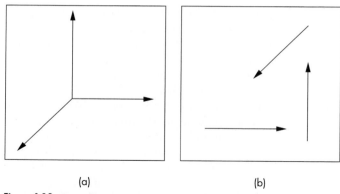

Figure 4.13 Coordinate system (a) with vectors emerging from a common point, and (b) with vectors moved.

$$\mathbf{v} = \begin{bmatrix} \alpha_1 \\ \alpha_2 \\ \alpha_3 \end{bmatrix}.$$

We usually think of the basis vectors, v_1, v_2, v_3, as defining a coordinate system. However, for dealing with problems using points, vectors and scalars, we need a more general method. Figure 4.13 shows the problem. The three vectors form a coordinate system that is shown in Figure 4.13(a) as we would usually draw it, with the three vectors emerging from a single point. Vectors, however, have direction and magnitude, but lack a position attribute. Hence, Figure 4.13(b) is equivalent, because we have moved the basis vectors, leaving their magnitudes and directions unchanged.

The affine space contains points in addition to vectors and scalars. Hence, once we fix a reference point—the origin—we can represent all points unambiguously. The usual convention for drawing coordinate axes in Figure 4.13(a) as emerging from the origin makes sense in the affine space where both points and vectors have representations.

In affine spaces, we obtain a more general representation by replacing a coordinate system with a frame. A **frame** is defined by a basis set of vectors and a particular point P_0. Loosely, this extension fixes the origin of the vector coordinate system at P_0. Within a given frame, every vector can be written uniquely as

$$v = \alpha_1 v_1 + \alpha_2 v_2 + \alpha_3 v_3,$$

just as in a vector space; in addition, every point can be written uniquely as

$$P = P_0 + \beta_1 v_1 + \beta_2 v_2 + \beta_3 v_3.$$

As we shall see in Section 4.3.3, by abandoning the more familiar notion of a coordinate system and a basis in that coordinate system, in favor of the less familiar notion of a frame, we avoid the difficulties caused by vectors having magnitude and direction but no fixed position. In addition, we are able to represent points and vectors in a manner that allows us to use matrix representations but maintains a distinction between the two different geometric objects.

4.3.1 Changes of Coordinate Systems

Frequently, we are required to find how the representation of a vector changes when we change the basis vectors. Suppose that $\{v_1, v_2, v_3\}$ and $\{u_1, u_2, u_3\}$ are two bases. Each basis vector in the second set can be represented in terms of the first basis (and vice versa). Hence, there exist scalar components, $\{\alpha_{ij}\}$, such that

$$u_1 = \alpha_{11}v_1 + \alpha_{12}v_2 + \alpha_{13}v_3,$$
$$u_2 = \alpha_{21}v_1 + \alpha_{22}v_2 + \alpha_{23}v_3,$$
$$u_3 = \alpha_{31}v_1 + \alpha_{32}v_2 + \alpha_{33}v_3.$$

The 3×3 matrix

$$\mathbf{M} = \begin{bmatrix} \alpha_{11} & \alpha_{12} & \alpha_{13} \\ \alpha_{21} & \alpha_{22} & \alpha_{23} \\ \alpha_{31} & \alpha_{32} & \alpha_{33} \end{bmatrix}$$

represents the change in basis; its inverse gives the matrix representation of the change from $\{u_1, u_2, u_3\}$ to $\{v_1, v_2, v_3\}$. If a vector v has the representation $\{\beta_1, \beta_2, \beta_3\}$ with respect to $\{v_1, v_2, v_3\}$, then we can use the column matrix

$$\mathbf{v} = \begin{bmatrix} \beta_1 \\ \beta_2 \\ \beta_3 \end{bmatrix}$$

for the representation. If $\mathbf{u}$ is the representation with respect to $\{u_1, u_2, u_3\}$, then

$$\mathbf{v} = \mathbf{M}^T\mathbf{u}.$$

Such changes in basis leave the origin unchanged. We can use them to represent rotation and scaling of a set of basis vectors to derive another basis set, as shown in Figure 4.14. However, a simple translation of the origin, or change of frame, as shown in Figure 4.15, cannot be represented in this way. After we complete a simple example, we shall introduce homogeneous coordinates, which will allow us to change frames and still to use matrices to represent the change.

4.3.2 Example of Change of Representation

Suppose that we have a vector whose representation in some basis is

$$\mathbf{v} = \begin{bmatrix} 1 \\ 2 \\ 3 \end{bmatrix}.$$

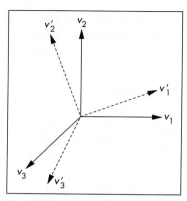

Figure 4.14 Rotation and scaling of a basis.

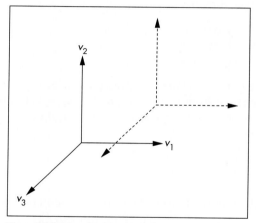

Figure 4.15 Translation of a basis.

We can denote the three basis vectors as e_1, e_2, and e_3.[2] Hence,

$$\mathbf{v} = 1\mathbf{e}_1 + 2\mathbf{e}_2 + 3\mathbf{e}_3.$$

---

[2] If we are working in the space of 3-tuples ($\mathbf{R}^3$), rather than in an abstract setting, then we can associate $\mathbf{e}_1$, $\mathbf{e}_2$, and $\mathbf{e}_3$ with the unit basis in $\mathbf{R}^3$:

$$\mathbf{e}_1 = \begin{bmatrix} 1 \\ 0 \\ 0 \end{bmatrix}, \qquad \mathbf{e}_2 = \begin{bmatrix} 0 \\ 1 \\ 0 \end{bmatrix}, \qquad \mathbf{e}_3 = \begin{bmatrix} 0 \\ 0 \\ 1 \end{bmatrix}.$$

Now suppose that we want to make a new basis from the three vectors whose representations, in terms of e_1, e_2, and e_3, are

$$v_1 = \begin{bmatrix} 1 \\ 0 \\ 0 \end{bmatrix}, \qquad v_2 = \begin{bmatrix} 1 \\ 1 \\ 0 \end{bmatrix}, \qquad v_3 = \begin{bmatrix} 1 \\ 1 \\ 1 \end{bmatrix},$$

or equivalently,

$$v_1 = e_1,$$
$$v_2 = e_1 + e_2,$$
$$v_3 = e_1 + e_2 + e_3.$$

The matrix that converts a representation in e_1, e_2, and e_3 to one in which the basis vectors have representations v_1, v_2, and v_3 is

$$\begin{aligned} A &= [\, v_1 \quad v_2 \quad v_3 \,]^{-1} \\ &= \begin{bmatrix} 1 & 1 & 1 \\ 0 & 1 & 1 \\ 0 & 0 & 1 \end{bmatrix}^{-1} \\ &= \begin{bmatrix} 1 & -1 & 0 \\ 0 & 1 & -1 \\ 0 & 0 & 1 \end{bmatrix}. \end{aligned}$$

In the new system, the representation of v is

$$u = Av = \begin{bmatrix} -1 \\ -1 \\ 3 \end{bmatrix};$$

that is,

$$u = -v_1 - v_2 + 3v_3.$$

Suppose that we now use as the basis in this second space the vectors that are represented as

$$u_1 = \begin{bmatrix} 1 \\ 0 \\ 0 \end{bmatrix}, \qquad u_2 = \begin{bmatrix} 1 \\ 1 \\ 0 \end{bmatrix}, \qquad u_3 = \begin{bmatrix} 1 \\ 1 \\ 1 \end{bmatrix}.$$

The matrix A will take vectors in the second space to the third, and the matrix

$$B = A^2 = \begin{bmatrix} 1 & -2 & 1 \\ 0 & 1 & -2 \\ 0 & 0 & 1 \end{bmatrix}$$

will take vectors from the first space to the third. Hence, the representation of our original vector becomes

$$\mathbf{w} = \mathbf{B} \begin{bmatrix} 1 \\ 2 \\ 3 \end{bmatrix} = \begin{bmatrix} 0 \\ -4 \\ 3 \end{bmatrix},$$

in the third basis. The matrix

$$\mathbf{B}^{-1} = \begin{bmatrix} 1 & 2 & 3 \\ 0 & 1 & 2 \\ 0 & 0 & 1 \end{bmatrix}$$

takes representations in the third space back to the first, and

$$\mathbf{B}^{-1} = \begin{bmatrix} 1 & 1 & 1 \\ 0 & 1 & 1 \\ 0 & 0 & 1 \end{bmatrix}^2 = (\mathbf{A}^{-1})^2.$$

4.3.3 Homogeneous Coordinates

If we represent a point P located at (x, y, z) in three-dimensional space with the column matrix

$$\mathbf{p} = \begin{bmatrix} x \\ y \\ z \end{bmatrix},$$

then its representation will be of the same form as the vector that we represented as

$$\mathbf{v} = \begin{bmatrix} \alpha_1 \\ \alpha_2 \\ \alpha_3 \end{bmatrix}.$$

This situation can cause confusion, and can make implementation more difficult. In addition, a matrix multiplication in three dimensions cannot represent changes in frames. We use homogeneous coordinates to avoid these difficulties by using four-dimensional column matrices to represent both points and vectors in three dimensions.

In the frame specified by (v_1, v_2, v_3, P_0), any point P can be written uniquely as

$$P = \alpha_1 v_1 + \alpha_2 v_2 + \alpha_3 v_3 + P_0.$$

We can express this relation formally, using a matrix product, as

$$P = \begin{bmatrix} \alpha_1 & \alpha_2 & \alpha_3 & 1 \end{bmatrix} \begin{bmatrix} v_1 \\ v_2 \\ v_3 \\ P_0 \end{bmatrix}.$$

Strictly speaking, this expression is not an inner or dot product, because the elements of the matrices are dissimilar; nonetheless, the expression is computed as though it were an inner product. The four-dimensional row matrix on the right side of the equation is the **homogeneous-coordinate representation** of the point P in the given frame. Equivalently, we can say that P is represented by the column matrix

$$\mathbf{p} = \begin{bmatrix} \alpha_1 \\ \alpha_2 \\ \alpha_3 \\ 1 \end{bmatrix}.$$

In the same frame, any vector v can be written

$$v = \beta_1 v_1 + \beta_2 v_2 + \beta_3 v_3,$$

$$= [\,\beta_1 \quad \beta_2 \quad \beta_3 \quad 0\,]^T \begin{bmatrix} v_1 \\ v_2 \\ v_3 \\ P_0 \end{bmatrix}.$$

Thus, v can be is represented by the column matrix

$$\mathbf{v} = \begin{bmatrix} \beta_1 \\ \beta_2 \\ \beta_3 \\ 0 \end{bmatrix}.$$

There are numerous ways to interpret this formulation geometrically. We simply note that we can carry out operations on points and vectors using their homogeneous-coordinate representations and ordinary matrix algebra. Consider, for example, a change of frames—a problem that caused difficulties when we used three-dimensional representations. If (v_1, v_2, v_3, P_0) and (u_1, u_2, u_3, Q_0) are two frames, we can express the basis vectors and reference point of the second frame in terms of the first as

$$u_1 = \alpha_{11} v_1 + \alpha_{12} v_2 + \alpha_{13} v_3,$$
$$u_2 = \alpha_{21} v_1 + \alpha_{22} v_2 + \alpha_{23} v_3,$$
$$u_3 = \alpha_{31} v_1 + \alpha_{32} v_2 + \alpha_{33} v_3,$$
$$Q_0 = \alpha_{41} v_1 + \alpha_{42} v_2 + \alpha_{43} v_3 + P_0.$$

These equations can be written in the form

$$\begin{bmatrix} u_1 \\ u_2 \\ u_3 \\ Q_0 \end{bmatrix} = \mathbf{M} \begin{bmatrix} v_1 \\ v_2 \\ v_3 \\ P_0 \end{bmatrix},$$

where $\mathbf{M}$ is the 4×4 matrix

$$\mathbf{M} = \begin{bmatrix} \alpha_{11} & \alpha_{12} & \alpha_{13} & 0 \\ \alpha_{21} & \alpha_{22} & \alpha_{23} & 0 \\ \alpha_{31} & \alpha_{32} & \alpha_{33} & 0 \\ \alpha_{41} & \alpha_{42} & \alpha_{43} & 1 \end{bmatrix}.$$

$\mathbf{M}$ is called the **matrix representation** of the change of frames.

We can also use $\mathbf{M}$ to compute the changes in the representations directly. Suppose that $\mathbf{u}$ and $\mathbf{v}$ are the homogeneous-coordinate representations either of a point or of a vector in the two frames. Then,

$$\mathbf{u}^T \begin{bmatrix} u_1 \\ u_2 \\ u_3 \\ Q_0 \end{bmatrix} = \mathbf{u}^T \mathbf{M} \begin{bmatrix} v_1 \\ v_2 \\ v_3 \\ P_0 \end{bmatrix} = \mathbf{v}^T \begin{bmatrix} v_1 \\ v_2 \\ v_3 \\ P_0 \end{bmatrix}.$$

Hence,

$$\mathbf{v} = \mathbf{M}^T \mathbf{u}.$$

There are other advantages to using homogeneous coordinates that we shall explore extensively in later chapters. Perhaps the most important is that all affine (line-preserving) transformations can be represented as matrix multiplications in homogeneous coordinates. Although we have to work in four dimensions to solve three-dimensional problems, when we use homogeneous-coordinate representations, less arithmetic work is involved. The uniform representation of all affine transformations makes carrying out successive transformations (concatenation) far easier than in three-dimensional space. In addition, modern hardware implements homogeneous-coordinate operations directly, using parallelism to achieve high-speed calculations.

4.3.4 Example of Change in Frames

Consider again the example of Section 4.3.2. If we again start with the basis vectors $\mathbf{e}_1$, $\mathbf{e}_2$, and $\mathbf{e}_3$, and convert to a basis determined by the same $\mathbf{v}_1$, $\mathbf{v}_2$, and $\mathbf{v}_3$, then the three equations are the same:

$$\mathbf{v}_1 = \mathbf{e}_1,$$
$$\mathbf{v}_2 = \mathbf{e}_1 + \mathbf{e}_2,$$
$$\mathbf{v}_3 = \mathbf{e}_1 + \mathbf{e}_2 + \mathbf{e}_3.$$

The reference point does not change, so we add the equation

$$Q_0 = P_0.$$

Thus, the matrices in which we are interested are the matrix

$$M = \begin{bmatrix} 1 & 1 & 1 & 0 \\ 0 & 1 & 1 & 0 \\ 0 & 0 & 1 & 0 \\ 0 & 0 & 0 & 1 \end{bmatrix},$$

and its inverse.

Suppose that, in addition to changing the basis vectors, we also want to move the reference point to the point that has the representation $(1, 2, 3, 1)$ in the original system. The first three components are the representations of a displacement vector $v = 1e_1 + 2e_2 + 3e_3$ that moves P_0 to Q_0. The fourth component identifies this entity as a point. Thus, we add to the three equations from the previous example the equation

$$Q_0 = P_0 + 1e_1 + 2e_2 + 3e_3,$$

and the matrix M becomes

$$M = \begin{bmatrix} 1 & 1 & 1 & 0 \\ 0 & 1 & 1 & 0 \\ 0 & 0 & 1 & 0 \\ 1 & 2 & 3 & 1 \end{bmatrix}.$$

Its inverse is

$$M^{-1} = \begin{bmatrix} 1 & -1 & 0 & 0 \\ 0 & 1 & -1 & 0 \\ 0 & 0 & 1 & 0 \\ -1 & -1 & -1 & 1 \end{bmatrix}.$$

This pair of matrices will allow us to move back and forth between representations in the two frames.

4.3.5 Data Types

Thus far, our discussion has been mathematical. You may be wondering what all the mathematics has to do with programming. In this section, we shall address such questions, starting with the notion of ADTs to which we alluded earlier.

We have introduced a few geometric objects—such as points, lines, and planes—that will be important, either as primitives in a graphics system, or as aids in defining other primitives. Thus, we would like to be able to write computer code such as

```
point_3 p,q;
line_segment_3 s;
```

and to expect to write programs that can be implemented in a number of ways. For example, C programmers might implement the `point_3` data type by using code like [3]

```
typedef struct {float x,y,z;} point_3
```

or

```
typedef float point_3[3];
```

This approach is taken in most graphics systems (GKS, PHIGS, and OpenGL). However, it does not solve certain difficulties. For example, consider the problem of initializing a point. In a standard C program, we might expect to see one of the two forms in the code fragments

```
point_3 p={1.0,2.0,3.0};
```

or

```
p.x=1.0;
p.y=2.0;
p.z=3.0;
```

There are two objections to this approach. First, we have mixed the implementation with the data type, and have subsequently created implementation-dependent code. Second, there is a question regarding what coordinate system or frame we are using.

We can solve the first problem by creating a set of functions that implements the abstract operations, rather than forcing a user to deal with implementation-dependent details. Hence, we would initialize a point through a function such as

```
p = new_point_3(1.0, 2.0, 3.0);
```

and all operations would be done through such functions, such as

```
point_3 p,q;
vector_3 v;
v = point_sub(p,q);
```

The second problem poses more difficulties in practice than in principle. As our discussion should have made clear, a representation of a point is with respect to a specific frame. Hence, one approach would be to have a type `frame` available as an additional graphical data type. The software would then allow the user

---

[3] Modern graphics systems provide one more layer of abstraction by using a data type for floating-point numbers: `GLfloat` in OpenGL, `Gfloat` in GKS, or `Pfloat` in PHIGS, instead of `float`. Each of these variables typically would be implemented by the type `float`, but could be implemented in other ways.

to use a default frame or to change frames. The graphical functions could then either require the frame to be included explicitly in function calls, such as

```
point_3 p,q;
vector_3 v;
frame f;
v = point_sub(p,q,f);
```

or have all coordinates be referenced to the present frame, as is done with attributes such as line type or color.

4.4   Drawing of a Rotating Cube

Figure 4.16 One frame of cube animation.

We now have the tools that we need to build three-dimensional graphical applications. Our tools are both conceptual and practical. We shall once again follow the pipeline approach that we pursued in our two-dimensional examples. Objects will again be defined in terms of sets of vertices. These vertices will pass through a number of transformations before the primitives that they define are rasterized in the frame buffer. The use of homogeneous coordinates not only will enable us to explain this process, but also will lead to efficient implementation techniques.

Consider the problem of drawing a rotating cube on the screen of our CRT. One frame of an animation is shown in Figure 4.16. We can identify a number of distinct tasks that we must perform to generate the image:

- Modeling
- Converting to the camera frame
- Clipping
- Projecting
- Removing hidden surfaces
- Rasterizing

We shall investigate each in turn. First, we shall see that three-dimensional objects can be represented, like two-dimensional objects, through a set of vertices. We shall also see that data structures will help us to incorporate the relationships among the vertices, edges, and faces of geometric objects.

Once we have modeled the cube, we shall be able to animate it using affine transformations. We shall introduce these transformations in Section 4.5. We shall use these transformations to alter OpenGL's model-view matrix. In Chapter 5, we shall use these transformations again as part of the viewing process. We shall see that our pipeline model will serve us well. Vertices will flow through a number of transformations in the pipeline, all of which will use our homogeneous-coordinate representation. At the end of the pipeline awaits the rasterizer. At this point, we can assume that it will do its job automatically, provided that we can perform the preliminary steps correctly.

4.4.1 Modeling of a Cube

The cube is as simple a three-dimensional object as we might expect to model and display. There are a number of ways, however, to model it. A CSG system would regard it as a single primitive. On the other extreme, the hardware will process the cube as an object consisting of eight vertices. Our decision to use surface-based models implies that we might regard a cube either as the intersection of six planes, or as the six polygons that define its faces, or **facets**. We shall start by assuming that the vertices of the cube are available through an array of vertices; for example, we could use

```
GLfloat vertices[][3] = {{-1.0,-1.0,-1.0},{1.0,-1.0,-1.0},
   {1.0,1.0,-1.0}, {-1.0,1.0,-1.0}, {-1.0,-1.0,1.0},
   {1.0,-1.0,1.0}, {1.0,1.0,1.0}, {-1.0,1.0,1.0}};
```

We can adopt a more object-oriented form if we first define a three-dimensional point type:[4]

```
typedef float point[3];
```

The vertices of the cube can then be defined as

```
point node[8] ={{-1.0,-1.0,-1.0},{1.0,-1.0,-1.0},
   {1.0,1.0,-1.0}, {-1.0,1.0,-1.0}, {-1.0,-1.0,1.0},
   {1.0,-1.0,1.0}, {1.0,1.0,1.0}, {-1.0,1.0,1.0}};
```

We can then use the list of points to define the faces of the cube. For example, one face is

```
glBegin{GL_POLYGON};
   glVertex3fv(node[0]);
   glVertex3fv(node[3]);
   glVertex3fv(node[2]);
   glVertex3fv(node[1]);
glEnd();
```

and we can define the other five faces in a similar manner. Note that we have defined three-dimensional polygons with exactly the same mechanism that we used to define two-dimensional polygons.

4.4.2 Inward- and Outward-Pointing Faces

We have to be careful about the order in which we specify our vertices when we are defining a three–dimensional polygon. We used the order 0, 3, 2, 1 for

---

[4] Remember that OpenGL implements all vertices in four-dimensional homogeneous coordinates. Function calls using a three-dimensional type, such as `glVertex3fv`, will have the values placed into four-dimensional form within the graphics system.

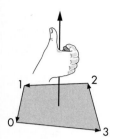

Figure 4.17 Traversal of the edges of a polygon.

the first face. The order 1, 0, 3, 2 would be the same, because the final vertex in a polygon definition is always linked back to the first. However, the order 0, 1, 2, 3 is different. Although it describes the same boundary, the edges of the polygon are traversed in the reverse order, from 0, 3 , 2 , 1, as shown in Figure 4.17. In addition, each polygon has two sides. We can display either or both of them. First, however, we need a consistent way of identifying the faces.

We call a face **outward facing** if the vertices are traversed in a counterclockwise order when the face is viewed from the outside. This method is also known as the **right-hand rule**, because, if you orient the fingers of your right hand in the direction the vertices are traversed, then the thumb points outward.

In our example, it was important to have defined the order as 0, 3, 2, 1, rather than as 0, 1, 2 , 3, so that we could define the outer side of the back of the cube correctly.[5]

4.4.3 Data Structures for Object Representation

We could now describe our cube through a set of vertex specifications. For example, we could use

    glBegin(GL_POLYGON)

six times, each time followed by four vertices (via glVertex) and a glEnd, or via

    glBegin(GL_QUADS)

followed by 24 vertices and a glEnd. Both of these methods will work, but both fail to capture the essence of the **topology** of the cube, as opposed to the cube's **geometry**. If we think of the cube as an example of a polyhedron, we have an object—the cube—that is composed of six faces. The faces are each quadrilaterals that meet at vertices; each vertex is shared by three faces. In addition, pairs of vertices define edges of the quadrilaterals; each edge is shared by two faces. These statements describe the topology of a six-sided polyhedron. All are true, regardless of the location of the vertices—that is, regardless of the geometry of the object.[6]

We shall see, throughout the rest of this book, that there are numerous advantages to building for our objects data structures that separate the topology from the geometry. In this example, we shall use a structure, the vertex list, that is simple, is useful, and can be expanded on later.

---

[5] *Back* here means as seen from the positive z direction. However, each face of an enclosed object, such as our cube, is an inside or outside face, regardless of from where we view it, as long as we view the face from outside the object.

[6] We are ignoring special cases (singularities) that arise such as when three or more vertices lie along the same line, or when the vertices are moved to where we no longer have nonintersecting faces.

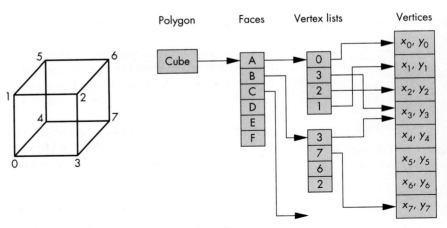

Figure 4.18 Vertex-list representation of a cube.

The data specifying the location of the vertices specify the geometry and can be stored as a simple list or array, as in node[8]—the **vertex list**. The top-level entity is a cube; we shall regard it as being composed of six faces. Each face consists of four ordered vertices. Each vertex can be specified indirectly through its index. This data structure is shown in Figure 4.18. One of the advantages of this structure is that, because each geometric location appears only once, instead of being repeated each time it is used for a facet. If, in an interactive application, the location of a vertex is changed, the application needs to change that location only once, rather than searching for multiple occurrences of the vertex.[7]

4.4.4 The Color Cube

We can use the vertex list to define a color cube. We assign the colors of the vertices of the color solid of Chapter 2 (black, white, red, green, blue, cyan, magenta, yellow) to the vertices. We define a function quad to draw quadrilateral polygons specified by pointers into the vertex list. Finally, the colorcube specifies the six faces, taking care to make them all outward facing.

```
typedef GLfloat point[3];

point node[8] ={{-1.0,-1.0,1.0},{1.0,-1.0,1.0},
    {1.0,1.0,1.0}, {-1.0,1.0,1.0}, {-1.0,-1.0,-1.0},
    {1.0,-1.0,-1.0}, {1.0,1.0,-1.0}, {-1.0,1.0,-1.0}};
```

---

[7] The latest version of OpenGL contains *vertex arrays* that can be used to support data structures, such as the one we have described.

```
GLfloat colors[][3] = {{0.0,0.0,0.0},{1.0,0.0,0.0},
    {1.0,1.0,0.0}, {0.0,1.0,0.0}, {0.0,0.0,1.0},
    {1.0,0.0,1.0}, {1.0,1.0,1.0}, {0.0,1.0,1.0}};

void quad(int a, int b, int c , int d)
{
  glBegin(GL_POLYGON);
    glColor3fv(colors[a]);
    glVertex3fv(node[a]);
    glColor3fv(colors[b]);
    glVertex3fv(node[b]);
    glColor3fv(colors[c]);
    glVertex3fv(node[c]);
    glColor3fv(colors[d]);
    glVertex3fv(node[d]);
  glEnd();
}

void colorcube()
{
    quad(0,3,2,1);
    quad(2,3,7,6);
    quad(0,4,7,3);
    quad(1,2,6,5);
    quad(4,5,6,7);
    quad(0,1,5,4);
}
```

4.4.5 Bilinear Interpolation

Although we have specified colors for the vertices of the cube, the graphics system must decide how to use this information to assign colors to points inside the polygon. There are many ways to use the colors of the vertices to fill in, or **interpolate**, colors across a polygon. Probably the most common method, and one that we shall use in other contexts, is **bilinear interpolation**. Consider the polygon in Figure 4.19. The colors C_0, C_1, C_2, and C_3 are the ones assigned to the vertices in the application program. We can use linear interpolation to interpolate colors[8] along the edges between vertices 0 and 1, and between 2 and 3, by using

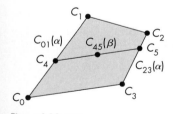

Figure 4.19 Bilinear interpolation.

---

[8] We are assuming we are using RGB color and that the interpolation is applied individually to each primary color.

$$C_{01}(\alpha) = (1 - \alpha)C_0 + \alpha C_1,$$

$$C_{23}(\alpha) = (1 - \alpha)C_2 + \alpha C_3.$$

As α goes from 0 to 1, we generate colors, $C_{01}(\alpha)$ and $C_{23}(\alpha)$, along these two edges. For a given value of α, we obtain two colors, C_4 and C_5, on these edges. We can now interpolate colors along the line connecting the two points on the edges corresponding to C_4 and C_5:

$$C_{45}(\beta) = (1 - \beta)C_4 + \beta C_5.$$

For a flat quadrilateral, each color generated by this method corresponds to a point on the polygon. If the four vertices are not all in the same plane, then although a color is generated, its location on a surface is not clearly defined.

A related algorithm, **scan-line interpolation**, avoids the flatness issue and can be made part of the scan-conversion process. A polygon is filled only when it is displayed. If we wait until rasterization, the polygon is first projected onto the two-dimensional plane (Figure 4.20). If we fill a quadrilateral scan line by scan line, as shown in Figure 4.21, then colors are assigned scan line by scan line on the basis of only two edges. OpenGL provides this method, not only for colors, but also, as we shall see in Chapter 6, for other values that can be assigned on a vertex-by-vertex basis.

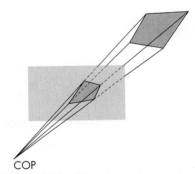

COP

Figure 4.20 Projection of polygon.

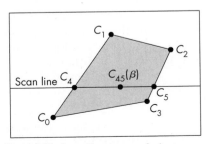

Figure 4.21 Scan-line interpolation.

We now have an object that we can display much as we did to the three-dimensional Sierpinski gasket in Section 2.8, using glOrtho to provide a basic orthographic projection. We shall first introduce transformations, so that we can animate the cube and also can construct more complex objects.

4.5 Affine Transformations

A **transformation** is a function that takes a point (or vector) and maps that point (or vector) into another point (or vector). We can picture such a function by looking at Figure 4.22 or by writing down the functional form

$$Q = T(P)$$

for points, or

$$v = R(u)$$

for vectors. If we can use homogeneous coordinates, then we can represent both vectors and points as four-dimensional column matrices, and can define the transformation with a single function

$$\mathbf{q} = f(\mathbf{p}),$$

$$\mathbf{v} = f(\mathbf{u}),$$

that transforms the representations of both points and vectors in a given frame. This formulation is too general to be useful, as it encompasses all single-valued mappings of points and vectors. In practice, even if we were to have a convenient description of the function $f()$, we would have to carry out the transformation on every point on a curve. For example, if we transform a line segment, a general transformation might require us to carry out the transformation for every point between the two endpoints.

We consider a restricted class of transformations. Let us assume that we are working in four-dimensional homogeneous coordinates. In this space, both

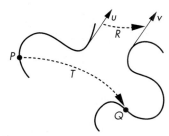

Figure 4.22 Transformation.

points and vectors are represented as vertices—that is, 4-tuples in a four-dimensional vector space.[9] We can obtain a useful class of transformations if we make restrictions on $f()$. The most important restriction is linearity. A function $f()$ is a **linear function** if and only if, for any scalars α and β, and any vertices p and q,

$$f(\alpha p + \beta q) = \alpha f(p) + \beta f(q).$$

The importance of such functions is that, if we know the transformations of vertices, we can obtain the transformations of linear combinations of vertices by linear combinations of transformations of the vertices. We do not have to recalculate the transformations for every linear combination.

In four-dimensional space, we work with the representations of points and vectors. A linear transformation then transforms the representation of a point (or vector) into the representation of a point (or vector), and can always be written in terms of the two representations, **u** and **v**, as a matrix multiplication:

$$\mathbf{v} = \mathbf{Mu},$$

where **M** is a square matrix. Comparing this expression with that we obtained in Section 4.3 for changes in frame, we can observe that, as long as **M** is nonsingular, each linear transformation corresponds to a change in frame. Hence, we can view a linear transformation in two equivalent ways: either as a change in the underlying representation, or frame, that yields a new representation of our vertices, or as a transformation of the vertices within the same frame.

When we work with homogeneous coordinates, **M** is a 4×4 matrix of the form

$$\mathbf{M} = \begin{bmatrix} \alpha_{11} & \alpha_{12} & \alpha_{13} & \alpha_{14} \\ \alpha_{21} & \alpha_{22} & \alpha_{23} & \alpha_{24} \\ \alpha_{31} & \alpha_{32} & \alpha_{33} & \alpha_{34} \\ 0 & 0 & 0 & 1 \end{bmatrix}.$$

The 12 values can be set arbitrarily, and we say this transformation has 12 **degrees of freedom**. However, points and vectors have slightly different representations in our affine space. Any vector is represented as

$$\mathbf{u} = \begin{bmatrix} \alpha_1 \\ \alpha_2 \\ \alpha_3 \\ 0 \end{bmatrix},$$

---

[9] We consider only those functions that map vertices to other vertices and that obey the rules for manipulating points and vectors that we have developed in this chapter and in Appendix B.

and any point can be written as

$$\mathbf{p} = \begin{bmatrix} \beta_1 \\ \beta_2 \\ \beta_3 \\ 1 \end{bmatrix}.$$

If we apply an arbitrary $\mathbf{M}$ to a vector,

$$\mathbf{v} = \mathbf{Mu},$$

we see that only nine of the elements of $\mathbf{M}$ affect $\mathbf{u}$, and, thus, there are only 9 degrees of freedom in the transformation of vectors. Affine transformations of points have the full 12 degrees of freedom.

We can also show that affine transformations preserve lines. Suppose that we write a line in the form

$$P(\alpha) = P_0 + \alpha d,$$

where P_0 is a point and d is a vector. In any frame, the line can be expressed as

$$\mathbf{p}(\alpha) = \mathbf{p}_0 + \alpha \mathbf{d},$$

where $\mathbf{p}_0$ and $\mathbf{d}$ are the representations of P_0 and d in that frame. For any affine transformation matrix $\mathbf{M}$,

$$\mathbf{Mp}(\alpha) = \mathbf{Mp}_0 + \alpha \mathbf{Md}.$$

Thus, we can construct the transformed line by first transforming $\mathbf{p}_0$ and $\mathbf{d}$, and using whatever line-generation algorithm we choose when the line segment must be displayed. If we use the two-point form of the line,

$$\mathbf{p}(\alpha) = \alpha \mathbf{p}_0 + (1 - \alpha)\mathbf{p}_1,$$

a similar result holds. We transform the representations of $\mathbf{p}_0$ and $\mathbf{p}_1$, and then construct the transformed line. Because there are only 12 elements in $\mathbf{M}$ that we can select arbitrarily, there are 12 degrees of freedom in the affine transformation of a line or line segment.

We have expressed these results in terms of abstract mathematical spaces. However, their importance in computer graphics is practical. We need only to transform the homogeneous-coordinate representation of the endpoints of a line segment to determine completely a transformed line. Thus, we can implement our graphics systems as a pipeline that passes endpoints through affine-transformation units, and can finally generate the line at the rasterization stage.

Fortunately, most of the transformations that we need in computer graphics are affine. These transformations include rotation, translation, and scaling. With slight modifications, we can also use these results to describe the standard parallel and perspective projections.

4.6   Rotation, Translation, and Scaling

We have been going back and forth between looking at geometric objects as abstract entities and working with their representation in a given frame. When we work with application programs, we have to work with representations. In this section, first we shall show how we can describe the most important affine transformations independently of any representation. Then, we shall find matrices that describe these transformations by acting on the representations of our points and vectors. In Section 4.8, we shall see how these transformations are implemented in OpenGL.

We shall look at transformations as ways of moving to new positions a group of points that describe one or more geometric objects. Although there are many ways to transform one point to a new position, there will almost always be only a single way to move a collection of points to new positions with a single transformation, preserving the relationships among the vertices of the object. Hence, although we can find both a rotation matrix and a translation that will move P_0 to Q_0, using these matrices on $\{P_0, P_1, P_2, \ldots\}$ will produce different results.

4.6.1 Translation

Translation is an operation that displaces points by a fixed distance in a given direction, as shown in Figure 4.23. To specify a translation, we need only to specify a displacement vector d, because the transformed points are given by

$$P' = P + d$$

for all points P on the object. Note that this definition of translation makes no reference to a frame or representation. Translation has 3 degrees of freedom, because we can specify the three components of the displacement vector arbitrarily.

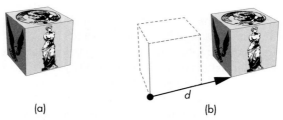

(a)   (b)

Figure 4.23 Translation. (a) Object in original position. (b) Object translated.

4.6.2 Rotation

Rotation is more difficult to specify, because more parameters are involved. We start with the simple example of rotating a point about the origin in a two-dimensional plane, as shown in Figure 4.24. Having specified a particular point—the origin—we are in a particular frame. A two-dimensional point at (x, y) in this frame is rotated about the origin by an angle θ to the position (x', y'). We can obtain the standard equations describing this rotation by representing (x, y) and (x', y') in polar form:

$$x = \rho \cos \phi,$$

$$y = \rho \sin \phi,$$

$$x' = \rho \cos(\theta + \phi),$$

$$y' = \rho \sin(\theta + \phi).$$

Expanding these terms using the trigonometric identities for the sine and cosine of the sum of two angles, we find

$$x' = \rho \cos \phi \cos \theta - \rho \sin \phi \sin \theta = x \cos \theta - y \sin \theta,$$

$$y' = \rho \cos \phi \sin \theta + \rho \sin \phi \cos \theta = x \sin \theta + y \cos \theta.$$

These equations can be written in matrix form as

$$\begin{bmatrix} x' \\ y' \end{bmatrix} = \begin{bmatrix} \cos \theta & -\sin \theta \\ \sin \theta & \cos \theta \end{bmatrix} \begin{bmatrix} x \\ y \end{bmatrix}.$$

We shall expand this form to three dimensions in Section 4.7.

Note three features of this transformation that extend to other rotations:

1. There is one point—the origin, in this case—that is unchanged by the rotation. We call this point the **fixed point** of the transformation. Figure 4.25 shows a two-dimensional rotation about a different fixed point.

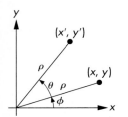

Figure 4.24 Two-dimensional rotation.

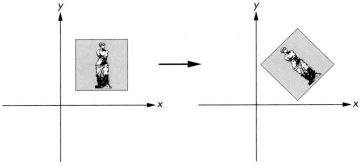

Figure 4.25 Rotation about a fixed point.

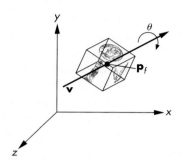

Figure 4.26 Three-dimensional rotation.

2. Knowing that the two-dimensional plane is part of three-dimensional space, we can reinterpret this rotation in three dimensions. In a right-handed system, when we draw the x and y axes in the standard way, the positive z axis comes out of the page. Our definition of a positive direction of rotation is counterclockwise when we look down the positive z axis toward the origin. We shall use this definition to define positive rotations about other axes.
3. Two-dimensional rotation in the plane is equivalent to three-dimensional rotation about the z axis. Points in planes of constant z all rotate in a similar manner, leaving their z values unchanged.

We can use these observations to define a general three-dimensional rotation that is independent of the frame. We must specify the three entities shown in Figure 4.26: a fixed point (P_f), a rotation angle (θ), and a line or vector about which to rotate. For a given fixed point, there are 3 degrees of freedom: the two angles necessary to specify the orientation of the vector and the angle that specifies the amount of rotation about the vector.

Rotation and translation are known as **rigid-body transformations**. No combination of rotations and translations can alter the shape of an object; they can alter only the object's location and orientation. Consequently, rotation and translation alone cannot give us all possible affine transformations. The transformations in Figure 4.27 are affine, but they are not rigid-body transformations.

4.6.3 Scaling

Scaling is an affine non–rigid-body transformation. We can combine a properly chosen sequence of scalings, translations, and rotations to form any affine transformation. Scaling can make an object bigger or smaller, as shown in Figure 4.28, which illustrates both uniform scaling in all directions and scaling in a single direction. We shall need nonuniform scaling to build up the full set of affine transformations that we shall use in modeling and viewing.

Figure 4.27 Non–rigid-body transformations

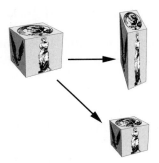

Figure 4.28 Uniform and nonuniform scaling

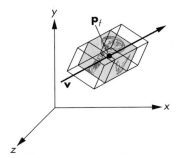

Figure 4.29 Effect of scale factor.

Scaling transformations have a fixed point, as we can see from Figure 4.29. Hence, to specify a scaling, we can specify the fixed point, a direction in which we wish to scale, and a scale factor (α). For $\alpha > 1$, the object gets longer in the specified direction; for $0 \leq \alpha < 1$, the object gets smaller in that direction. Negative values of α give us **reflection** (Figure 4.30), about the fixed point, in the scaling direction.

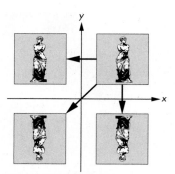

Figure 4.30 Reflection.

4.7   Transformations in Homogeneous Coordinates

Most graphics APIs force us to work within some reference system. Although we can alter this reference system—usually a frame—we cannot work with high-level representations, such as the expression

$$Q = P + \alpha v.$$

Instead, we work with representations in homogeneous coordinates, and with expressions such as

$$\mathbf{q} = \mathbf{p} + \alpha \mathbf{v}.$$

Within a frame, each affine transformation is represented by a 4×4 matrix of the form

$$\mathbf{M} = \begin{bmatrix} \alpha_{11} & \alpha_{12} & \alpha_{13} & \alpha_{14} \\ \alpha_{21} & \alpha_{22} & \alpha_{23} & \alpha_{24} \\ \alpha_{31} & \alpha_{32} & \alpha_{33} & \alpha_{34} \\ 0 & 0 & 0 & 1 \end{bmatrix}.$$

4.7.1   Translation

Translation displaces points to new positions defined by a displacement vector. If we move the point $\mathbf{p}$ to $\mathbf{p}'$ by displacing by $\mathbf{d}$, then

$$\mathbf{p}' = \mathbf{p} + \mathbf{d}.$$

Looking at their homogeneous-coordinate forms

$$\mathbf{p} = \begin{bmatrix} x \\ y \\ z \\ 1 \end{bmatrix}, \qquad \mathbf{p}' = \begin{bmatrix} x' \\ y' \\ z' \\ 1 \end{bmatrix}, \qquad \mathbf{d} = \begin{bmatrix} \alpha_x \\ \alpha_y \\ \alpha_z \\ 0 \end{bmatrix},$$

we see that these equations can be written component by component as

$$x' = x + \alpha_x,$$
$$y' = y + \alpha_y,$$
$$z' = z + \alpha_z.$$

This method of representing translation using the addition of column matrices will not combine well with our representations of other affine transformations. However, we can also get this result using the matrix multiplication:

$$\mathbf{p}' = \mathbf{T}\mathbf{p},$$

where

$$\mathbf{T} = \begin{bmatrix} 1 & 0 & 0 & \alpha_x \\ 0 & 1 & 0 & \alpha_y \\ 0 & 0 & 1 & \alpha_z \\ 0 & 0 & 0 & 1 \end{bmatrix}.$$

$\mathbf{T}$ is called the **translation matrix**. We shall sometimes write it as $\mathbf{T}(\alpha_x, \alpha_y, \alpha_z)$ to emphasize the three independent parameters.

It might appear that the fourth element of the column matrices is not necessary. However, it is not possible to get the same result using a three-dimensional version in the form $\mathbf{p}' = \mathbf{T}\mathbf{p}$. For this reason, the use of homogeneous coordinates is often seen as a clever trick that allows us to convert the addition of column matrices in three dimensions to matrix–matrix multiplication in four dimensions.

We can obtain the inverse of a translation matrix either by applying an inversion algorithm or by noting that, if we displace a point by the vector d, we can return to the original position by a displacement of $-d$. By either method, we find that

$$\mathbf{T}^{-1}(\alpha_x, \alpha_y, \alpha_z) = \mathbf{T}(-\alpha_x, -\alpha_y, -\alpha_z) = \begin{bmatrix} 1 & 0 & 0 & -\alpha_x \\ 0 & 1 & 0 & -\alpha_y \\ 0 & 0 & 1 & -\alpha_z \\ 0 & 0 & 0 & 1 \end{bmatrix}.$$

4.7.2 Scaling

For both scaling and rotation, there is a fixed point that is unchanged by the transformation. We shall let the fixed point be the origin, and shall show how we can concatenate transformations to obtain the transformation for an arbitrary fixed point.

A scaling matrix with a fixed point of the origin allows for independent scaling along the coordinate axes. The three equations are

$$x' = \beta_x x,$$
$$y' = \beta_y y,$$
$$z' = \beta_z z.$$

These three equations can be combined in homogeneous form as

$$\mathbf{p}' = \mathbf{S}\mathbf{p},$$

where

$$\mathbf{S} = \mathbf{S}(\beta_x, \beta_y, \beta_z) = \begin{bmatrix} \beta_x & 0 & 0 & 0 \\ 0 & \beta_y & 0 & 0 \\ 0 & 0 & \beta_z & 0 \\ 0 & 0 & 0 & 1 \end{bmatrix}.$$

Note that, as is true of the translation matrix and, indeed, of all homogeneous coordinate transformations, the final row of the matrix does not depend on the particular transformation, but rather forces the fourth component of the transformed point to retain the value 1.

We obtain the inverse of a scaling matrix by applying the reciprocals of the scale factors:

$$\mathbf{S}^{-1}(\beta_x, \beta_y, \beta_z) = \mathbf{S}(\frac{1}{\beta_x}, \frac{1}{\beta_y}, \frac{1}{\beta_z}).$$

4.7.3 Rotation

We shall first look at rotation with a fixed point at the origin. There are 3 degrees of freedom corresponding to our ability to rotate independently about the three coordinate axes. We shall have to be careful, however, as matrix multiplication is not a commutative operation (Appendix C). Rotation about the x axis by an angle θ followed by rotation about the y axis by an angle ϕ does not give us the same result if we reverse the order of the rotations.

We can find the matrices for rotation about the individual axes directly from the results of the two-dimensional rotation that we developed in Section 4.6. We saw that the two-dimensional rotation was actually a rotation in three dimensions about the z axis, and points remained in planes of constant z. Thus, in three dimensions, the equations for rotation about the z axis by an angle θ are

$$x' = x\cos\theta - y\sin\theta,$$
$$y' = x\sin\theta + y\cos\theta,$$
$$z' = z;$$

or, in matrix form,

$$\mathbf{p}' = \mathbf{R}_z \mathbf{p},$$

where

$$\mathbf{R}_z = \mathbf{R}_z(\theta) = \begin{bmatrix} \cos\theta & -\sin\theta & 0 & 0 \\ \sin\theta & \cos\theta & 0 & 0 \\ 0 & 0 & 1 & 0 \\ 0 & 0 & 0 & 1 \end{bmatrix}.$$

We can derive the matrices for rotation about the x and y axes through an identical argument. If we rotate about the x axis, x values are unchanged, and we have a two-dimensional rotation in which points rotate in planes of constant x; for rotation about the y axis, y values are unchanged. The matrices are

$$\mathbf{R}_x = \mathbf{R}_x(\theta) = \begin{bmatrix} 1 & 0 & 0 & 0 \\ 0 & \cos\theta & -\sin\theta & 0 \\ 0 & \sin\theta & \cos\theta & 0 \\ 0 & 0 & 0 & 1 \end{bmatrix},$$

$$\mathbf{R}_y = \mathbf{R}_y(\theta) = \begin{bmatrix} \cos\theta & 0 & \sin\theta & 0 \\ 0 & 1 & 0 & 0 \\ -\sin\theta & 0 & \cos\theta & 0 \\ 0 & 0 & 0 & 1 \end{bmatrix}.$$

The signs of the sine terms are consistent with our definition of a positive rotation in a right-handed system.

Suppose that we let $\mathbf{R}$ denote any of our three rotation matrices. A rotation by θ can always be undone by a subsequent rotation by $-\theta$; hence,

$$\mathbf{R}^{-1}(\theta) = \mathbf{R}(-\theta).$$

In addition, noting that all the cosine terms are on the diagonal and the sine terms are off-diagonal, we can use the trigonometric identities $\cos(-\theta) = \cos\theta$ and $\sin(-\theta) = -\sin\theta$ to find

$$\mathbf{R}^{-1}(\theta) = \mathbf{R}^T(\theta).$$

In Section 4.8, we shall show how to construct any desired rotation matrix, with a fixed point at the origin, as a product of individual rotations about the three axes

$$\mathbf{R} = \mathbf{R}_z \mathbf{R}_y \mathbf{R}_x.$$

Using the fact that the transpose of a product is the product of the transposes in the reverse order, we see that for any rotation matrix

$$\mathbf{R}^{-1} = \mathbf{R}^T.$$

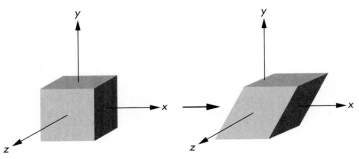

Figure 4.31 Shear.

A matrix whose inverse is equal to its transpose is called an **orthogonal matrix**, and all orthogonal matrices correspond to rotations about the origin.

4.7.4 Shear

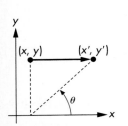

Figure 4.32 Computing the shear matrix.

Although we can construct any affine transformation from a sequence of rotations, translations, and scalings, there is one more affine transformation—the **shear** transformation—that is of such importance that we regard it as a basic type, rather than deriving it from the others. Consider a cube centered at the origin, aligned with the axes and viewed from the positive z axis, as shown in Figure 4.31. If we pull the top to the right and the bottom to the left, we **shear** the object in the x direction. Note that neither the y nor the z values are changed by the shear, so we can call this operation yz shear to distinguish it from other possible directions we can shear the cube. Using simple trigonometry on Figure 4.32, we see that each shear is characterized by a single angle θ; the equations for this shear are

$$x' = x + y \cot \theta,$$

$$y' = y,$$

$$z' = z,$$

leading to the shearing matrix

$$\mathbf{H}_{yz}(\theta) = \begin{bmatrix} 1 & \cot \theta & 0 & 0 \\ 0 & 1 & 0 & 0 \\ 0 & 0 & 1 & 0 \\ 0 & 0 & 0 & 1 \end{bmatrix}.$$

We can obtain the inverse by noting that we need only to shear in the opposite direction; hence,

$$\mathbf{H}_{yz}^{-1}(\theta) = \mathbf{H}_{yz}(-\theta).$$

4.8   Concatenation of Transformations

In this section, we shall create a number of affine transformations by multiplying together, or **concatenating**, sequences of the basic transformations that we just introduced. This strategy is preferable to attempting to define an arbitrary transformation directly. This approach fits well with our pipeline architectures for implementing graphics systems.

Suppose that we carry out three successive transformations on a point **p**, creating a new point **q**. Because the matrix product is associative, we can write the sequence as

$$\mathbf{q} = \mathbf{CBAp},$$

without parentheses. However, the order in which we carry out the transformations does affect the efficiency of the calculation. In one view, we can carry out **A**, followed by **B**, followed by **C**—an order that corresponds to the grouping (Figure 4.33)

$$\mathbf{q} = (\mathbf{C}(\mathbf{B}(\mathbf{Ap}))).$$

Figure 4.33 Application of transformations one at a time.

If we are to transform a single point, this order is the most efficient, because each matrix multiplication involves multiplying a column matrix by a square matrix. If we have many points to transform, then we can proceed in two steps. First, we calculate

$$\mathbf{M} = \mathbf{CBA}.$$

Then, we use this matrix on each point

$$\mathbf{q} = \mathbf{Mp}.$$

This order corresponds to the pipeline in Figure 4.34, where we compute **M** first, then load it into a pipeline transformation unit. If we simply count

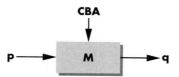

Figure 4.34 Pipeline transformation.

operations, we see that, although we do a little more work in computing $\mathbf{M}$ initially, because $\mathbf{M}$ may be applied to tens of thousands of points, this extra work is insignificant compared with the savings we obtain by using a single matrix multiplication for each point. We shall now derive a number of examples of computing $\mathbf{M}$.

4.8.1 Rotation About a Fixed Point

Our first example shows how we can alter the transformations that we defined with a fixed point at the origin (rotation, scaling, shear) to have an arbitrary fixed point. We shall demonstrate for rotation about the z axis; the technique will be the same for the other cases.

Consider a cube with its center at $\mathbf{p}_f$ and its sides aligned with the axes. We want to rotate the cube about the z axis, but this time about its center $\mathbf{p}_f$, which becomes the fixed point of the transformation, as shown in Figure 4.35. If $\mathbf{p}_f$ were the origin, we would know how to solve the problem: We would simply use $\mathbf{R}_z(\theta)$. This observation suggests the strategy of first moving the cube to the origin. We could then apply $\mathbf{R}_z(\theta)$, and finally move the object back such that its center is again at $\mathbf{p}_f$. This sequence is shown in Figure 4.36. In terms of our basic affine transformations, the first is $\mathbf{T}(-\mathbf{p}_f)$, the second is $\mathbf{R}_z(\theta)$, and the final is $\mathbf{T}(\mathbf{p}_f)$. Concatenating them together, we obtain the single matrix

$$\mathbf{M} = \mathbf{T}(\mathbf{p}_f)\mathbf{R}_z(\theta)\mathbf{T}(-\mathbf{p}_f).$$

If we multiply out the matrices, we find that

$$\mathbf{M} = \begin{bmatrix} \cos\theta & -\sin\theta & 0 & x_f - x_f\cos\theta + y_f\sin\theta \\ \sin\theta & \cos\theta & 0 & y_f - x_f\sin\theta - y_f\cos\theta \\ 0 & 0 & 1 & 0 \\ 0 & 0 & 0 & 1 \end{bmatrix}.$$

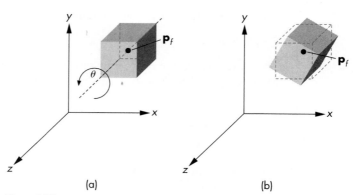

(a)   (b)

Figure 4.35 Rotating a cube about its center.

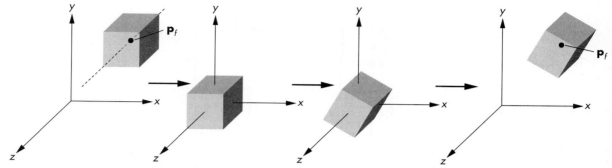

Figure 4.36 Sequence of transformations.

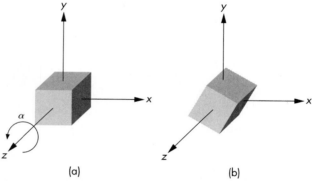

Figure 4.37 Rotation of a cube about the z axis. Cube (a) before rotation, and (b) after rotation.

4.8.2 General Rotation

We shall now show that an arbitrary rotation about the origin can be composed of three successive rotations about the three axes. The order is not unique (see Exercise 4.12), although the resulting rotation matrix is. We shall show how we can form the desired matrix by first doing a rotation about the z axis, followed by a rotation about the y axis, concluding with a rotation about the x axis.

Consider the cube, again centered at the origin with its sides aligned with the axes, as shown in Figure 4.37(a). We can rotate it about the z axis by an angle α to orient it as shown in Figure 4.37(b). We then rotate the cube by an angle β about the y axis, as shown in a top view in Figure 4.38. Finally, we rotate the cube by an angle γ about the x axis, as shown in a side view in Figure 4.39. Our final rotation matrix is

$$\mathbf{R} = \mathbf{R}_x \mathbf{R}_y \mathbf{R}_z.$$

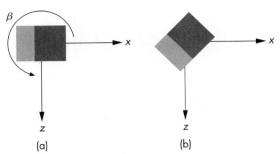

Figure 4.38 Rotation of a cube about y axis.

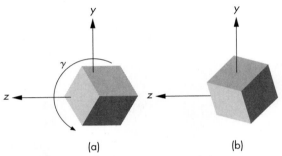

Figure 4.39 Rotation of a cube about x axis

A little experimentation should convince you that we can achieve any desired orientation by proper choice of α, β, and γ, although, as we shall see in the example of Section 4.8.4, finding these angles can be tricky.

4.8.3 The Instance Transformation

Our example of a cube that can be rotated to any desired orientation suggests a generalization appropriate for modeling. Consider a scene composed of many simple objects, such as that shown in Figure 4.40. One option is to define each of these objects, through its vertices, in the desired location with the desired orientation and size. An alternative is to define each of the object types once at a convenient size, in a convenient place, and with a convenient orientation. Each occurrence of an object in the scene is an **instance** of the object's proto-type, and we can obtain the desired size, orientation, and location by applying an affine transformation—the **instance transformation**—to the prototype. We can build a simple database to describe a scene from a list of object identifiers (such as 1 for a cube and 2 for a sphere), and of the instance transformation to be applied to each object.

The instance transformation is applied in the order shown in Figure 4.41. Objects are usually defined in their own frames, with the origin at the center of mass and the sides aligned with the axes. First, we scale the object to the

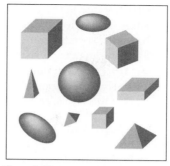

Figure 4.40 Scene of simple objects.

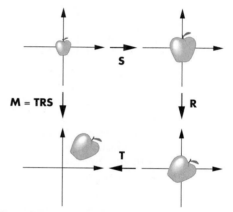

Figure 4.41 Instance transformation.

desired size. Then, we orient it with a rotation matrix. Finally, we translate it to the desired orientation. Hence, the instance transformation is of the form

$$\mathbf{M} = \mathbf{TRS}.$$

Modeling with the instance transformation works well not only with our pipeline architectures, but also with the display lists that we introduced in Chapter 3. A complex object that is used many times can be loaded into the server once as a display list. Displaying each instance of it requires only sending of the appropriate instance transformation to the server.

4.8.4 Rotation About an Arbitrary Axis

Our final rotation example illustrates not only how we can achieve a rotation about an arbitrary point and line in space, but also how we can use direction angles to specify orientations. Consider rotating a cube, as shown in Figure 4.42. We need three entities to specify this rotation. There is a fixed point $\mathbf{p}_0$ that we

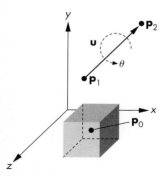

Figure 4.42 Rotation of a cube about an arbitrary axis.

shall assume is the center of the cube, a vector about which we rotate, and an angle of rotation. Note that none of these entities relies on a frame, and that we have just specified a rotation in a coordinate-free manner. Nonetheless, to find an affine matrix to represent this transformation, we shall have to assume that we are in some frame.

The vector about which we wish to rotate the cube can be specified in various ways. One way is to use two points, $\mathbf{p}_1$ and $\mathbf{p}_2$, defining the vector

$$\mathbf{u} = \mathbf{p}_2 - \mathbf{p}_1.$$

Note that the order of the points determines the positive direction of rotation for θ, and that, although we draw $\mathbf{u}$ as passing through $\mathbf{p}_0$, only the orientation of $\mathbf{u}$ matters. Replacing $\mathbf{u}$ with a unit-length vector

$$\mathbf{v} = \frac{\mathbf{u}}{|\mathbf{u}|} = \begin{bmatrix} \alpha_x \\ \alpha_y \\ \alpha_z \end{bmatrix}$$

in the same direction will simplify the subsequent steps. We have already seen that moving the fixed point to the origin is a helpful technique. Thus, our first transformation is the translation $\mathbf{T}(-\mathbf{p}_0)$, and the final one is $\mathbf{T}(\mathbf{p}_0)$. After the initial translation, the required rotation problem is as shown in Figure 4.43. Our previous example (Section 4.8.2) showed that we could get an arbitrary rotation from three rotations about the individual axes. This problem is more difficult, because we do not know what angles to use for the individual rotations. Our strategy will be to carry out two rotations to align the axis of rotation, $\mathbf{v}$, with the z axis. Then, we can rotate by θ about the z axis, and then we can undo the two rotations that did the aligning. Our rotation matrix will be of the form

$$\mathbf{R} = \mathbf{R}_x(-\theta_x)\mathbf{R}_y(-\theta_y)\mathbf{R}_z(\theta)\mathbf{R}_y(\theta_y)\mathbf{R}_x(\theta_x).$$

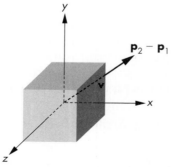

Figure 4.43 Movement of the fixed point to the origin.

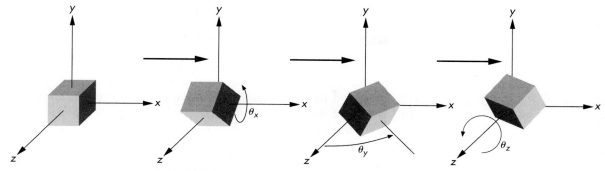

Figure 4.44 Sequence of rotations.

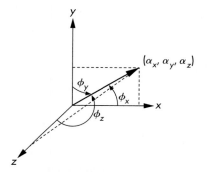

Figure 4.45 Direction angles.

This sequence of rotations is shown in Figure 4.44. The difficult part of the process will be determining θ_x and θ_y.

We proceed by looking at the components of $\mathbf{v}$. Because $\mathbf{v}$ is a unit-length vector,

$$\alpha_x^2 + \alpha_y^2 + \alpha_z^2 = 1.$$

We draw a line segment from the origin to the point $(\alpha_x, \alpha_y, \alpha_z)$. This line segment has unit length and the orientation of $\mathbf{v}$. Next, we draw the perpendiculars from the point $(\alpha_x, \alpha_y, \alpha_z)$ to the coordinate axes, as shown in Figure 4.45. The three **direction angles**—ϕ_x, ϕ_y, ϕ_z—are the angles between the line segment (or $\mathbf{v}$) and the axes. The **direction cosines** are given by

$$\cos \phi_x = \alpha_x,$$

$$\cos \phi_y = \alpha_y,$$

$$\cos \phi_z = \alpha_z.$$

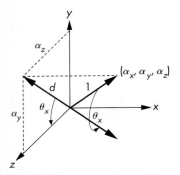

Figure 4.46 Computation of the x rotation.

Only two of the direction angles are independent, because

$$\cos^2 \phi_x + \cos^2 \phi_y + \cos^2 \phi_z = 1.$$

We can now compute θ_x and θ_y using these angles. Consider Figure 4.46. It shows that the effect of the desired rotation on the point $(\alpha_x, \alpha_y, \alpha_z)$ is to rotate the line segment into the plane $y = 0$. If we look at the projection of the line segment (before the rotation) on the plane $x = 0$, we see a line segment of length d on this plane. Another way to envision this figure is to think of the plane $x = 0$ as a wall, and to consider a distant light source located far down the positive x axis. The line that we see on the wall is the shadow of the line segment from the origin to $(\alpha_x, \alpha_y, \alpha_z)$. Note that the length of the shadow is less than the length of the line segment. We can say the line segment has been **foreshortened** to $d = \sqrt{\alpha_y^2 + \alpha_z^2}$. The desired angle of rotation is determined by the angle that this shadow makes with the z axis. However, the rotation matrix is determined by the sine and cosine of θ_x; thus, we need never to compute θ_x, but need only to compute

$$\mathbf{R}_x(\theta_x) = \begin{bmatrix} 1 & 0 & 0 & 0 \\ 0 & \alpha_z/d & -\alpha_y/d & 0 \\ 0 & \alpha_y/d & \alpha_z/d & 0 \\ 0 & 0 & 0 & 1 \end{bmatrix}.$$

We compute $\mathbf{R}_y$ in a similar manner. Figure 4.47 shows the rotation. Note that this angle is clockwise about the y axis, and we have to be careful of the sign of the sine terms in the matrix, which is

$$\mathbf{R}_y(\theta_y) = \begin{bmatrix} d & 0 & -\alpha_x & 0 \\ 0 & 1 & 0 & 0 \\ \alpha_x & 0 & d & 0 \\ 0 & 0 & 0 & 1 \end{bmatrix}.$$

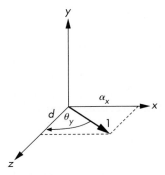

Figure 4.47 Computing the y rotation.

Finally, we concatenate together all the matrices to find

$$\mathbf{M} = \mathbf{T}(\mathbf{p}_0)\mathbf{R}_x(-\theta_x)\mathbf{R}_y(-\theta_y)\mathbf{R}_z(\theta)\mathbf{R}_y(\theta_y)\mathbf{R}_x(\theta_x)\mathbf{T}(-\mathbf{p}_0).$$

Let us look at a specific example. Suppose that we wish to rotate an object by 45 degrees about the line passing through the origin and the point $(1, 2, 3)$. We shall leave the fixed point at the origin. The first step is to find the point along the line that is a unit distance from the origin. We obtain it by normalizing $(1, 2, 3)$ to $(1/\sqrt{14}, 2/\sqrt{14}, 3/\sqrt{14})$, or $(1/\sqrt{14}, 2/\sqrt{14}, 3/\sqrt{14}, 1)$, in homogeneous coordinates. The first part of the rotation will take this point to $(0, 0, 1, 1)$. We first rotate about the x axis by the angle $\cos^{-1}\frac{3}{\sqrt{13}}$. This matrix carries $(1/\sqrt{14}, 2/\sqrt{14}, 3/\sqrt{14}, 1)$ to $(1/\sqrt{14}, 0, \sqrt{13/14}, 0)$, which is in the plane $y = 0$. The y rotation must be by the angle $\cos^{-1}(\sqrt{13/14})$. This rotation aligns the object with the z axis, and now we can rotate about the z axis by the desired 45 degrees. Finally, we undo the first two rotations. If we concatenate these five transformations into a single rotation matrix $\mathbf{R}$, we find that

$$\mathbf{R} = \mathbf{R}_x\left(-\cos^{-1}\frac{3}{\sqrt{14}}\right)\mathbf{R}_y\left(-\cos^{-1}\sqrt{\frac{13}{14}}\right)\mathbf{R}_z(45)\mathbf{R}_y\left(\cos^{-1}\sqrt{\frac{13}{14}}\right)$$

$$\mathbf{R}_x\left(\cos^{-1}\frac{3}{\sqrt{14}}\right)$$

$$= \begin{bmatrix} \dfrac{2 + 13\sqrt{2}}{28} & \dfrac{2 - \sqrt{2} - 3\sqrt{7}}{14} & \dfrac{6 - 3\sqrt{2} + 4\sqrt{7}}{28} & 0 \\[3mm] \dfrac{2 - \sqrt{2} + 3\sqrt{7}}{14} & \dfrac{4 + 5\sqrt{2}}{14} & \dfrac{6 - 3\sqrt{2} - \sqrt{7}}{14} & 0 \\[3mm] \dfrac{6 - 3\sqrt{2} - 4\sqrt{7}}{28} & \dfrac{6 - 3\sqrt{2} + \sqrt{7}}{14} & \dfrac{18 + 5\sqrt{2}}{28} & 0 \\[3mm] 0 & 0 & 0 & 1 \end{bmatrix}.$$

This matrix does not change any point on the line passing through the origin and the point $(1, 2, 3)$. If we want a fixed point other than the origin, we form the matrix

$$\mathbf{M} = \mathbf{T}(\mathbf{p}_f)\mathbf{R}\mathbf{T}(-\mathbf{p}_f).$$

This example is not simple. It illustrates the powerful technique of applying many simple transformations to get a complex one. The problem of rotation about an arbitrary point or axis arises in many applications. The major variants lie in the manner in which the axis of rotation is specified. However, we can usually employ techniques similar to the ones that we have used here to determine direction angles or direction cosines.

4.9   Implementation of Transformations

We can now focus on the implementation of a homogeneous-coordinate transformation package and of that package's interface to the user. In OpenGL, there are three matrices that are part of the state. We shall use only the model-view matrix in this chapter. All three types are manipulated by a common set of functions, and we use the `glMatrixMode` function to select the matrix to which the operations apply.

4.9.1 The Current Transformation Matrix

The generalization common to most graphics systems is the **current transformation matrix** (**CTM**). It is the matrix that is applied to any vertex that is defined subsequent to its setting. If we change the CTM, we change the state of the system. The CTM is part of the pipeline (Figure 4.48); thus, if **p** is a vertex, the pipeline produces **Cp**. The CTM is a 4×4 matrix; it can be altered by a set of functions provided by the graphics package.[10]

Figure 4.48 Current transformation matrix (CTM).

Let **C** denote the CTM. Initially, it is set to the 4×4 identity matrix; it can be reinitialized as needed. We can denote this operation as

$$\mathbf{C} \leftarrow \mathbf{I}.$$

The functions that alter **C** are of two forms: those that reset it to some matrix, and those that modify it by premultiplication or postmultiplication by a matrix.[11] The three transformations supported in most systems are translation, scaling with a fixed point of the origin, and rotation with a fixed point of the origin. Symbolically, we can write these operations in postmultiplication form as

$$\mathbf{C} \leftarrow \mathbf{CT},$$

$$\mathbf{C} \leftarrow \mathbf{CS},$$

$$\mathbf{C} \leftarrow \mathbf{CR},$$

---

[10] In OpenGL, the model-view matrix normally is an affine-transformation matrix and has only 12 degrees of freedom, as discussed in Section 4.5 The projection matrix, as we shall see in Chapter 5, is also 4×4 matrix, but it is not affine.

[11] OpenGL uses only postmultiplication. PHIGS allows both premultiplication and postmultiplication.

and in set form as

$$\mathbf{C} \leftarrow \mathbf{T},$$
$$\mathbf{C} \leftarrow \mathbf{S},$$
$$\mathbf{C} \leftarrow \mathbf{R}.$$

Most systems allow us to set directly, or to load, the CTM with an arbitrary matrix, or to postmultiply by an arbitrary matrix $\mathbf{M}$:

$$\mathbf{C} \leftarrow \mathbf{M},$$
$$\mathbf{C} \leftarrow \mathbf{CM}.$$

4.9.2 OpenGL Transformation Matrices

In OpenGL, the matrix that is applied to all primitives is the product of the model-view matrix (GL_MODELVIEW) and the projection matrix (GL_PROJECTION). We can think of the CTM as the product of these matrices (Figure 4.49), and we can manipulate each individually by selecting the desired matrix by glMatrixMode. We can load the selected matrix with either of the following functions:

```
glLoadIdentity();
glLoadMatrixf(pointer_to_matrix);
```

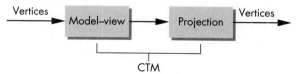

Figure 4.49 Model-view and projection matrices.

Arbitrary 4×4 matrices can be specified by a pointer to a one-dimensional array of 16 entries organized by the *columns* of the desired matrix. We can alter the selected matrix with glMultMatrixf(pointer_to_matrix). Rotation, translation, and scaling are provided through the three functions

```
glRotatef(angle, vx, vy, vz);
glTranslatef(dx, dy, dz);
glScalef(sx ,sy, sz);
```

All three alter the selected matrix by postmultiplication. For rotation, the angle is specified in degrees, and the variables vx, vy, and vz are the components of a vector about which we wish to rotate. In the translation function, the variables are the components of the displacement vector; for scaling, the variables determine the scale factors along the coordinate axes.

4.9.3 Rotation About a Fixed Point in OpenGL

In Section 4.8, we showed that we can perform a rotation about a fixed point, other than the origin, by first moving the fixed point to the origin, then rotating about the origin, and finally moving the fixed point back to its original location. The following sequence sets the matrix mode, then forms the required matrix for a 45-degree rotation about the line through the origin and the point $(1, 2, 3)$ with a fixed point of $(4, 5, 6)$:

```
glMatrixMode(GL_MODELVIEW)
glLoadIdentity();
glTranslatef(4.0, 5.0, 6.0);
glRotatef(45.0, 1.0, 2.0, 3.0);
glTranslatef(-4.0, -5.0, -6.0);
```

Note that we do not have to form the rotation matrix about an arbitrary axis, as we did in Section 4.8, although you might test your skill with transformations by doing so, forming the same matrix by concatenation of rotations about the three axes.

4.9.4 Order of Transformations

You might be bothered by the apparent reversal of the function calls. The rule in OpenGL is this: *The transformation specified most recently is the one applied first.* A little examination shows why this order is correct and is a consequence of multiplying the CTM on the right by the specified affine transformation. The sequence of operations that we specified was

$$\mathbf{C} \leftarrow \mathbf{I},$$
$$\mathbf{C} \leftarrow \mathbf{T}(4.0, 5.0, 6.0),$$
$$\mathbf{C} \leftarrow \mathbf{R}(45.0, 1.0, 2.0, 3.0),$$
$$\mathbf{C} \leftarrow \mathbf{T}(-4.0, -5.0, -6.0).$$

Each time, we postmultiply at the end of the existing CTM, forming the matrix

$$\mathbf{C} = \mathbf{T}(4.0, 5.0, 6.0)\mathbf{R}(45.0, 1.0, 2.0, 3.0)\mathbf{T}(-4.0, -5.0, -6.0),$$

which is the matrix that we expect from Section 4.8. Each vertex $\mathbf{p}$ that is specified *after* the model-view matrix has been set will be multiplied by $\mathbf{C}$, thus forming the new vertex

$$\mathbf{q} = \mathbf{C}\mathbf{p}.$$

There are other ways to think about the order of operations. One way is in terms of a stack. Altering the CTM is similar to pushing matrices onto a stack; when we apply the final transformation, the matrices are popped off the stack in the reverse of the order they were placed there. The analogy is conceptual, rather than exact, because, when we call a transformation function in OpenGL, the matrix is altered immediately. However, when we discuss hierarchical modeling in Chapter 8, we shall need the operations

```
glPushMatrix();
glPopMatrix();
```

to traverse our data structures. In addition, as we did when we used the pushing and popping attributes in Chapter 3, it is often helpful to bracket changes in state with a push and a pop of the matrix.

4.9.5 Spinning of the Cube

In this program, we shall take the cube that we defined in Section 4.4, and shall rotate it using the three buttons of the mouse. We shall define three callback functions:

```
glutDisplayFunc(display);
glutIdleFunc(spincube);
glutMouseFunc(mouse);
```

The display first sets a model-view matrix using the values of three angles determined by the mouse callback. It then draws a cube, using the colorcube function from Section 4.4. This example uses double buffering. Each time that display is called, it starts by clearing the frame buffer and the depth buffer—for hidden-surface removal—and finishes with a buffer swap.

```
void  display(void)
{
    glClear(GL_COLOR_BUFFER_BIT | GL_DEPTH_BUFFER_BIT);
    glLoadIdentity();
    glRotatef(theta[0], 1.0, 0.0, 0.0);
    glRotatef(theta[1], 0.0, 1.0, 0.0);
    glRotatef(theta[2], 0.0, 0.0, 1.0);
    colorcube();
    glFlush();
    glutSwapBuffers();
}
```

The mouse callback selects the axis for rotation:

```
void mouse(int btn, int state, int x, int y)
{
    if(btn==GLUT_LEFT_BUTTON && state == GLUT_DOWN) axis = 0;
    if(btn==GLUT_MIDDLE_BUTTON && state == GLUT_DOWN) axis = 1;
    if(btn==GLUT_RIGHT_BUTTON && state == GLUT_DOWN) axis = 2;
}
```

The idle callback increments the angle associated with the chosen axis by 2 degrees each time:

```
void spinCube()
{
    theta[axis] += 2.0;
    if( theta[axis] > 360.0 ) theta[axis] -= 360.0;
    display();
}
```

We shall not discuss hidden-surface removal until Chapter 5, but we note here that using it in OpenGL is almost trivial. We need only to clear the depth buffer and to enable the function by `glEnable(GL_DEPTH_TEST)`. For the complete program, see Appendix A.

4.10   Summary

In this chapter, we have presented two different—but ultimately complementary—points of view regarding the mathematics of computer graphics. One is that mathematical abstraction of the objects with which we work in computer graphics is necessary if we are to understand the operations that we carry out in our programs. The other is that transformations—and the techniques for carrying them out, such as the use of homogeneous coordinates—are the basis for implementations of graphics systems.

Our mathematical tools come from the study of vector analysis and linear algebra. For computer-graphics purposes, however, the order in which we have chosen to present these tools is the reverse of that most students learn. In particular, linear algebra is studied first, and vector space concepts are then linked to the study of n-tuples in $\mathbf{R}^n$. Our approach has been that the study of representation in mathematical spaces is what leads to our use of linear algebra as a tool for implementing abstract types.

We pursued a coordinate-free approach for two reasons. First, we wanted to show that all the basic concepts of geometric objects and of transformations are independent of the ways the latter are represented. Second, as object-oriented languages become more prevalent, application programmers will work directly with the objects, instead of with those objects' representations. The references in Section 4.11 contain examples of geometric programming systems that illustrate the potential of this approach.

Homogeneous coordinates provided a wonderful example of the power of mathematical abstraction. By going to an abstract mathematical space—the affine space—we were able to find a tool that led directly to efficient software and hardware methods.

Finally, we provided the set of affine transformations supported in OpenGL, and discussed ways that we could concatenate them to provide all affine transformations. The strategy of combining a few simple types of matrices to build a desired transformation is a powerful one; you should use it for a few of the exercises at the end of this chapter. In Chapter 5, we shall build on these techniques to develop viewing for three-dimensional graphics; in Chapter 8 we shall use our transformations to build hierarchical models.

4.11   Suggested Readings

There are many texts on vector analysis and linear algebra, although most treat the two topics separately. Within the geometric-design community the vector-space approach of coordinate-free descriptions of curves and surfaces has been popular; see [Fau80]. See [DeR89, DeR90] for an introduction to geometric programming.

Homogeneous coordinates arose in geometry [Max51], and were later discovered by the graphics community [Rie81]. Their use in hardware started with the Silicon Graphics Geometry Engine [Cla82], and extends to chips such as the Intel i860.

Software tools such as Mathematica [Wol91] and Matlab [Mat95] are excellent aides for learning to manipulate transformation matrices.

Exercises

4.1   Consider the solution of either constant coefficient linear differential or difference equations (recurrences). Show that the solutions of the homogeneous equations form a vector space. Relate the solution for a particular inhomogeneous equation to an affine space.

4.2   Show that the following sequences commute:

   a.   A rotation and a uniform scaling

   b.   Two rotations about the same axis

   c.   Two translations

4.3   Write a library of functions that will allow you to do geometric programming. Your library should contain functions for manipulating the basic geometric types (points, lines, vectors) and operations on those types, including dot and cross products. It should allow you to change frames. You can also create functions to interface with OpenGL, so that you can display the results of geometric calculations.

4.4   If we are interested in only two-dimensional graphics, we can use three-dimensional homogeneous coordinates by representing a point as $\mathbf{p} = [x\ y\ 1]^T$ and a vector as $\mathbf{v} = [a\ b\ 0]^T$. Find the 3×3 rotation, translation, scaling, and shear matrices. How many degrees of freedom are there in an affine transformation for transforming two-dimensional points?

4.5   We can specify an affine transformation by considering the location of a small number of points both before and after these points have been transformed. In three dimensions, how many points must we consider to specify the transformation uniquely? How does the required number of points change when we work in two dimensions?

4.6   How must we change the rotation matrices if we are working in a left-handed system and we retain our definition of a positive rotation?

4.7   Show that any sequence of rotations and translations can be replaced by a single rotation about the origin, followed by a translation.

4.8   Derive the shear transformation from the rotation, translation, and scaling transformations.

4.9   In two dimensions, we can write a line as $y = mx + h$. Find an affine transformation to reflect two-dimensional points about this line. Extend your result to reflection about a plane in three dimensions.

4.10 In Section 4.8, we showed that an arbitrary rotation matrix could be composed from successive rotations about the three axes. How many ways can we compose a given rotation if we can do only three simple rotations? Are all three of the simple rotation matrices necessary?

4.11 How would you add shear to the instance transformation? Show how to use this expanded instance transformation to generate parallelepipeds from a unit cube.

4.12 Find a homogeneous-coordinate representation of a plane.

4.13 Determine the rotation matrix formed by `glRotate`. That is, assume that the fixed point is the origin, and that the parameters are those of the function.

4.14 Write a program to generate a Sierpinski gasket as follows. Start with a white triangle. At each step, use transformations to generate three similar triangles that are drawn over the original triangle, leaving the center of triangle white and the three corners black.

4.15 Start with a cube centered at the origin and aligned with the coordinate axes. Find a rotation matrix that will orient the cube symmetrically, as shown in Figure 4.50.

Figure 4.50 Symmetric orientation of cube.

4.16 We have used vertices in three dimensions to define objects such as three-dimensional polygons. Given a set of vertices, find a test to determine whether the polygon that they determine is planar.

4.17 Three vertices determine a triangle if they do not lie in the same line. Devise a test for collinearity of three vertices.

4.18 We defined an instance transformation as the product of a translation, a rotation, and a scaling. Can we accomplish the same effect by applying these three types of transformations in a different order?

5 Viewing

W̶e have completed our discussion of the first half of the synthetic camera model—specifying objects in three dimensions. We shall now investigate the multitude of ways in which we can describe our virtual camera. Along the way, we shall investigate related topics, such as the relationship between classical viewing techniques and computer viewing.

We shall separate the viewing process into two parts. In the first, we shall use the model-view matrix to switch from the world frame in which we defined our objects to their representation in a frame in which the camera is at the origin. This representation of the geometry will allow us to use canonical viewing procedures. The second part of the process will deal with what type of projection we prefer (parallel or perspective), and what part of the world we wish to image (the clipping or view volume). These specifications will allow us to form a projection matrix that is concatenated with the model-view matrix.

Once more, we shall use a simple example program to demonstrate how the OpenGL API handles viewing. Finally, we shall derive the projection matrices that describe the most important parallel and perspective views.

5.1 Classical and Computer Viewing

Before looking at the interface between computer-graphics systems and application programmers for three-dimensional viewing, we shall take a slight diversion and consider classical viewing. There are two reasons for examining classical viewing. First, many of the jobs that were formerly done by hand drawing—such as animation in movies, architectural rendering, drafting, and mechanical-parts design—are now done routinely with the aid of computer graphics. Practitioners of these fields need to be able to produce classical views—such as isometrics, elevations, and various perspectives—and thus must be able to use

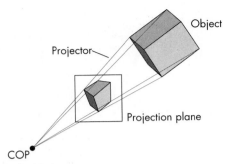

Figure 5.1 Viewing.

the computer system to produce such renderings. Second, the relationships between classical and computer viewing will show many advantages of, and a few difficulties with, the approach used by most APIs.

When we introduced the synthetic-camera model in Chapter 1, we pointed out the similarities between classical and computer viewing. The basic elements in both cases are the same. We have objects, a viewer, projectors, and a projection plane (Figure 5.1). The projectors meet at the **center of projection** (**COP**). The COP corresponds to the center of the lens in the camera or in the eye, and, in a computer-graphics systems, is the origin of the **camera frame**. All standard graphics systems follow the model that we described in Chapter 1, which is based on geometric optics. The projection surface is a plane, and the projectors are straight lines. This situation not only is the one usually encountered, but also is the one that is easiest to implement, especially with our pipeline model.

Both classical and computer graphics allow the viewer to be an infinite distance from the objects. Note that, as we move the COP to infinity, the projectors become parallel and the COP can be replaced by a **direction of projection** (**DOP**), as shown in Figure 5.2. Note also that, as the COP moves to infinity, the size of the image remains about the same, even though the viewer is infinitely far from the objects. Views with a finite COP are called **perspective views**; views with a COP at infinity are called **parallel views**.

Color Plates 9 and 10 show a parallel and perspective rendering, respectively. These plates illustrate the importance of having both types of views available in applications such as architecture, and, that in an API that supports both types of viewing, the user can switch between various viewing modes with little effort. Most modern APIs support both parallel and perspective viewing. The class of projections produced by these systems is known as **planar geometric projections**, because the projection surface is a plane, and the projectors are lines. Both perspective and parallel projections preserve lines; they do not, in general, preserve angles. Although the parallel views are the limiting case of perspective viewing, both classical and computer viewing usually treat them as separate cases. For classical views, the techniques used to con-

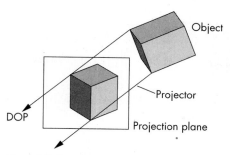

Figure 5.2 Movement of the center of projection to infinity.

struct the two types by hand are different, as anyone who has taken a drafting class surely knows. From the computer perspective, we shall find differences in how we specify the two types of views. In addition, parallel views are considerably easier to implement,[1] if, rather than looking at them as the limit of the perspective view, we derive the limiting equations and use those equations directly.

Although computer graphics systems have two fundamental types of viewing (parallel and perspective), classical graphics appears to have a host of different views, ranging from multiview orthographic projections to one-, two-, and three-point perspectives. This seeming discrepancy arises in classical graphics due to the desire to show a specific relationship among an object, the viewer, and the projection plane, as opposed to the computer graphics approach of complete independence of all specifications.

5.1.1 Classical Viewing

When an architect draws an image of a building, she knows which side she wishes to display, and thus where she should place the viewer in relationship to the building. Each classical view is determined by a specific relationship between the objects and the viewer.

In classical viewing, there is the underlying notion of a principal face. The types of objects viewed in real-world applications, such as architecture, tend to be composed of a number of planar faces, each of which can be thought of as a **principal face**. For a rectangular object, such as a building, there are natural notions of the front, back, top, bottom, right, and left faces. In addition, many real-world objects have faces that meet at right angles; thus such objects often have three orthogonal directions associated with them.

---

[1] In modern pipeline architectures, this statement may not always be true, because there may be only a single geometric pipeline that does both types of viewing. Software implementation of parallel viewing requires fewer operations than does that of perceptive viewing.

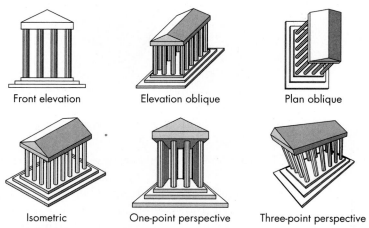

| Front elevation | Elevation oblique | Plan oblique |
| Isometric | One-point perspective | Three-point perspective |

Figure 5.3 Classical views.

Figure 5.3 shows some of the main types of views. We shall start with the most restrictive view for each of the parallel and perspective types, and shall move to the less restrictive conditions.

5.1.2 Orthographic Projections

Our first classical view is the **orthographic projection** shown in Figure 5.4. In all orthographic (or orthogonal) views, the projectors are perpendicular to the projection plane. In a **multiview orthographic projection**, the projection plane is parallel to one of the principal faces of the object. Usually, we display at least three views—such as the front, top, and right—to display the object. The reason that we produce multiple views should be clear from Figure 5.5. For a boxlike object, only the faces parallel to the projection plane appear in the image. A viewer usually needs more than two views to visualize what an object looks like from its multiview orthographic projections. Visualization from these

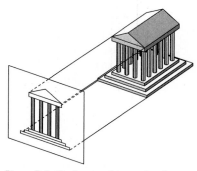

Figure 5.4 Orthographic projections.

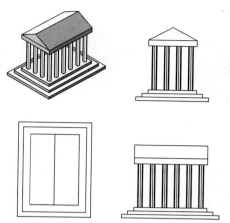

Figure 5.5 Temple and three multiview orthographic projections.

images can take skill on the part of the viewer. The importance of this type of view is that the view preserves both distances and angles, and, because there is no distortion of either distance or shape, multiview orthographic projections are well suited for working drawings.

5.1.3 Axonometric Projections

If we want to see more principal faces of our boxlike object in a single view, we must remove one of our restrictions. In **axonometric** views, the projectors are still orthogonal to the projection plane, as they are in Figure 5.6, but the projection plane can have any orientation with respect to the object. If

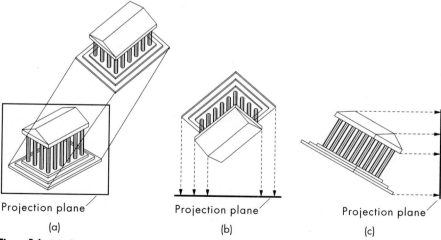

Projection plane

(a)

Projection plane

(b)

Projection plane

(c)

Figure 5.6 (a) Construction of an axonometric projection. (b) Top view. (c) Side view

Dimetric   Trimetric   Isometric

Figure 5.7 Axonometric views.

the projection plane is placed symmetrically with respect to the three principal faces that meet at a corner of our rectangular object, we have an **isometric** view. If the projection plane is placed symmetrically with respect to two of the principal faces, the view is **dimetric**. The general case is a **trimetric** view. These views are shown in Figure 5.7. Note that, in an isometric view, the length of a line segment in the image space is shorter than its length measured in the object space. This **foreshortening** of distances is the same in the three principal directions, and that allows us to make distance measurements. In the dimetric view, however, there are two different foreshortening ratios; in the trimetric view, there are three. We can also see that, although parallel lines are preserved in the image, angles are not. A circle will be projected into an ellipse. This distortion is the price that we pay for the ability to see more principal faces in a view that can be produced easily either by hand or by computer. Axonometric views are used extensively in architecture and in mechanical design.

5.1.4 Oblique Projections

The **oblique** views are the most general parallel views. We allow the projectors to make an arbitrary angle with the projection plane, as shown in Figure 5.8. In an oblique projection, angles in planes parallel to the projection plane are preserved. A circle in a plane parallel to the projection plane will be projected into a circle, and we will still be able to see more than one principal face of the object. Oblique views are the most difficult to construct by hand. They are also somewhat unnatural. Most physical viewing devices, including the human visual system, have a lens that has a fixed relationship with the image plane—usually, the lens is parallel to the plane. Although these devices produce perspective views, if the viewer is far from the object, the views are approximately parallel, but orthogonal, because the projection plane is parallel to the lens. The bellows camera that we used to develop the synthetic-camera model in Section 1.6 has the flexibility to produce approximations to parallel oblique views.

There is no significant difference, from the application programmer's point of view, among the different parallel views. The application programmer specifies a type of view—parallel or perspective—and a set of parameters that describe the camera. The problem for the application programmer is how to specify

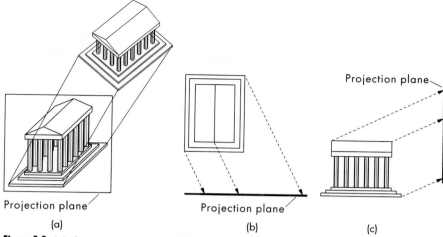

Figure 5.8 (a) Construction of an oblique view. (b) Top view. (c) Side view.

these parameters in the viewing procedures so as best to view an object or to produce a specific classical view.

5.1.5 Perspective Viewing

All perspective views are characterized by **diminution** of size. When objects are moved farther from the viewer, their images become smaller. This size change gives perspective views their natural appearance; however, because the amount by which a line is foreshortened depends on how far the line is from the viewer, we cannot make measurements from a perspective view. Hence, the major use of perspective views is in applications such as architecture and animation, where it is important to achieve real-looking images.

In the classical perspective views, the viewer is located symmetrically with respect to the projection plane, as shown in Figure 5.9. Thus, the pyramid determined by the window in the projection plane and the center of projection is a symmetric or right pyramid. This symmetry is caused by the fixed relationship between the back of the eye and its lens for human viewing, or between the back of a camera and its lens for standard cameras, and by similar fixed relationships in most physical situations. Some cameras, such as the bellows camera, have movable film backs and can produce general perspective views. The model used in computer graphics includes this general case.

The classical perspective views are usually known as **one-**, **two-**, and **three-point perspectives**. The difference among the three cases is based on how many of the three principal directions in the object are parallel to the projection plane. Consider the three perspective projections of the building in Figure 5.10. Any corner of the building includes the three principal directions. In the most general case—the three-point perspective—parallel lines in all three principal

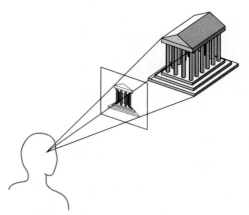

Figure 5.9 Perspective viewing.

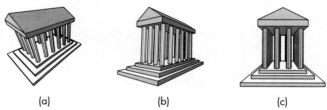

(a)   (b)   (c)

Figure 5.10 (a) Three, (b) Two, and (c) One-point perspective.

directions converge at three **vanishing points** (Figure 5.10a). If we allow one of the principal directions to become parallel to the projection plane, we have a two-point projection (Figure 5.10b), in which lines in only two of the principal directions converge. Finally, in the one-point perspective (Figure 5.10c), two of the principal directions are parallel to the projection plane, and we have only a single vanishing point. It should be apparent that, just as is true of parallel viewing, from the programmer's point of view, the three situations are merely special cases of general perspective viewing, which we shall implement in the Section 5.3.

5.2   Positioning of the Camera

We can now return to three-dimensional graphics from a computer perspective. We shall examine the API that OpenGL provides for three-dimensional graphics. We shall also see how other APIs, such as GKS-3D and PHIGS, differ from OpenGL. In this section, we shall deal with positioning the camera; in Section 5.4 we shall discuss how we specify the desired projection.

In OpenGL, the model-view and projection matrices are concatenated together to form the matrix that applies to geometric entities such as vertices. We have seen one use of the model-view matrix—to position objects in space. The other is to convert from the reference frame used for modeling to the frame of the camera.

5.2.1 Positioning of the Camera Frame

As we saw in Chapter 4, we can specify vertices in any units that we choose, and can define a model-view matrix by a sequence of affine transformations that repositions these vertices. We can also view this operation as changing the frame, and the result of applying the model-view transformation as giving the locations of the vertices in a different frame. In other words, we define objects in a reference frame, and the modeling part of the model-view matrix converts from the modeling frame to the world or user frame. In certain other APIs, objects are said to be modeled in **master** or **modeling coordinates**, and the instance transformation brings them into the world frame.

We model our objects independently from the viewing, and thus from the location of the viewer. OpenGL places a camera at the origin of the world frame pointing in the negative z direction (Figure 5.11). Hence, if the model-view matrix is an identity matrix, the camera frame and the world frame are identical. The model-view matrix can be looked at in one of two ways. It can be thought of as positioning the objects relative to the world frame, or as moving the world frame with respect to the camera frame.

If, as in most applications, we model our objects as being located around the origin, this default position of the camera will not capture all the objects in the scene; thus, either the camera must be repositioned, or the objects must be moved in front of the camera. These are equivalent operations, as either can be looked at as positioning the frame of the camera with respect to the frame of the objects.

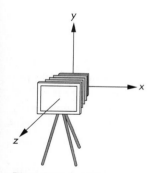

Figure 5.11 Initial camera position.

It might help to think of a scene in which we have defined several objects initially, with the model-view matrix as the identity, by specifying all vertices through glVertex. Subsequent changes to the model-view move the world frame relative to the camera, and affect the camera's view of all objects defined *afterward*, as their vertices are specified relative to the repositioned world frame.

Consider the sequence in Figure 5.12. In Figure 5.12(a), we have the initial configuration. A vertex specified at **p** has the same representation in both frames. In Figure 5.12(b), we have changed the model-view matrix to **C** by a sequence of transformations. The two frames are no longer the same, although **C** contains the information to move from the camera frame to the world frame, or, equivalently, contains the information that moves the camera away from its initial position at the origin of the world frame. A vertex specified at **q** through

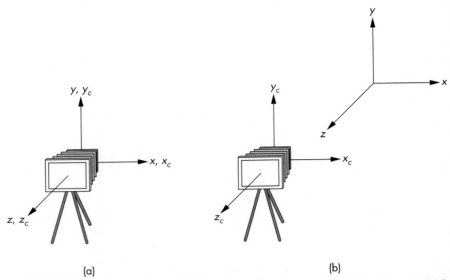

Figure 5.12 Movement of the camera and world frames. (a) Initial configuration. (b) After change in the model-view matrix.

glVertex, *after* the change to the model-view matrix, is at **q** in the world frame. However, its position in the camera frame is **Cq** and is known internally to OpenGL, where OpenGL will convert it to the camera frame by computing it in the viewing pipeline. The equivalent view is that the camera is still at the origin of its own frame, and the model-view matrix is applied to primitives specified in this system. In practice, you can use either view. But be sure to take great care regarding where in the program the primitives are specified relative to changes in the model-view matrix.

At any given time, the state of the model-view matrix gives the relation between the camera frame and the world frame. Although, initially, the combination of the modeling and viewing transformations into a single matrix may cause confusion, on closer examination, this approach is a good one. If we regard the camera as an object with geometric properties, then transformations that alter the position and orientation of objects should also affect the position and orientation of the camera relative to these objects.

The obvious next problem is how we specify the desired position of the camera. Here, we shall find it convenient to think in terms of moving the camera relative to the world frame. We shall outline two approaches; one is this section and one in Section 5.2.2. Two others will be given as exercises (Exercises 5.2 and 5.3). Our first approach is to specify the position indirectly by applying a sequence of rotations and translations to the model-view matrix. This approach is a direct application of the instance transformation that we presented in Chapter 4, but we must be careful for two reasons. First, we usually want to define the camera *before* we position any objects in the scene.[2] Second, transformations on the camera may appear to be backward from what you might expect.

Consider an object centered at the origin and the camera in its initial position, also at the origin pointing down the negative z axis. Suppose that we want an image of the face of the object that points in the positive x direction. We must move the camera *away* from the origin. If we allow the camera to remain pointing in the negative z direction, then we want to move the camera backward along the positive z axis, and the proper transformation is

```
glTranslatef(0.0, 0.0, -d);
```

where d is a positive number.

Many people find it helpful to interpret this operation as moving the camera frame relative to the world frame. This point of view has a basis in classical viewing. In computer graphics, we usually think of objects as being positioned in a fixed frame, and it is the viewer who must move himself to the right position to achieve the desired view. In classical viewing, the viewer dominates. Conceptually, we do viewing by picking up the object, orienting it as desired, and bringing it to the desired location. One consequence of this approach is that distances in classical viewing are measured from the viewer to the object, rather than—as in most physically based systems—from the object to the viewer. Classical viewing then results in a left-handed camera frame. Many graphics systems, including OpenGL, follow this view by having modeling in right-handed coordinates and viewing in left-handed coordinates, a decision that, although technically correct, can cause some confusion among users. Other APIs allow the user to choose the orientation of the coordinate systems.

Suppose that we want to look at the same object from the positive x axis. Now we not only have to move away from the object, but also have to rotate the camera about the y axis, as shown in Figure 5.13. We must do the translation after we rotate the camera by 90 degrees about the y axis. In the program, the calls must be in the reverse order, as we discussed in Section 4.8, so we expect to see code like the following:

```
glMatrixMode(GL_MODELVIEW);
glLoadIdentity();
glTranslatef(0.0, 0.0, -d);
glRotatef(-90.0, 0.0, 1.0, 0.0);
```

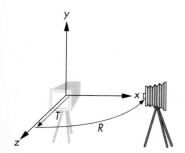

Figure 5.13 Positioning of the camera.

---

[2] In an animation, where in the program we define the position of the camera depends on whether we wish to attach the camera to a particular object or to place the camera in a fixed position in the scene; see Exercise 5.3.

In terms of the two frames, we first rotate the world frame relative to the camera frame; then, we move the two frames apart.

5.2.2 A Viewing API

We can take a different approach to positioning the camera—an approach that is similar to that used by PHIGS and GKS-3D, two of the standard APIs for three-dimensional graphics. Our starting point is again the world frame. We describe the camera's position and orientation in this frame. The precise type of image that we wish to obtain—perspective or parallel—is determined separately by the specification of the equivalent of the projection matrix in OpenGL. This part of the viewing process is often called the **normalization transformation**. We shall approach this problem as one of a change in frames. We again think of the camera as starting at the origin, pointed in the negative z direction. Its desired location is centered at a point called the **view reference point** (**VRP**; Figure 5.14), whose position is given in the world frame. The user executes a function such as

```
set_view_reference_point(x, y, z);
```

to specify this position. Next, we want to specify the orientation of the camera. We can divide this specification into two parts: specification of the **view-plane normal** (**VPN**), and specification of the **view-up vector** (**VUP**). The VPN (n in Figure 5.14) gives the orientation of the projection plane or back of the camera. The orientation of a plane is determined by that plane's normal, and thus part of the API is a function

```
set_view_plane_normal(nx, ny, nz);
```

The orientation of the plane does not specify what direction is up to the camera. Given only the VPN, we can rotate the camera with its back in this plane. The specification of the VUP fixes the camera and is evoked by

```
set_view_up(ux, uy, uz);
```

We project the VUP vector on the view plane to obtain the up-direction vector **v** (Figure 5.15). Use of the projection allows the user to specify any vector not parallel to **v**, rather than being forced to compute a vector lying in the projection plane. The vector **v** is orthogonal to **n**. We can use the cross product to obtain a third orthogonal direction **u**. This new orthogonal coordinate system usually is referred to as either the **viewing-coordinate system** or the **u-v-n system**. With the addition of the VRP, we have the desired camera frame. The matrix that does the change of frames is the **view-orientation matrix**. We leave its derivation for you to do as an exercise (Exercise 5.4).

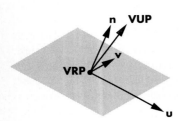

Figure 5.14 Camera frame.

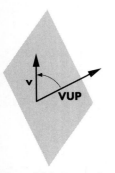

Figure 5.15 Determination of the view up vector.

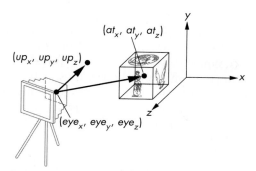

Figure 5.16 Look–at positioning

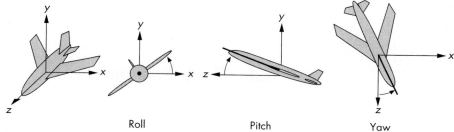

Roll   Pitch   Yaw

Figure 5.17 Roll, pitch, and yaw.

5.2.3 The Look-At Function

The use of the VRP, VPN, and VUP is but one way to provide an API for specifying the position of a camera. In many situations, a more direct method is appropriate. Consider the situation in Figure 5.16. Here, a camera is pointed at a point. The location of the camera is called the **eyepoint**, and it can be specified in the world frame, as can the point at which the camera is pointing. These points determine a VPN and a VRP. Hence, we need only to add the desired up direction for the camera. The OpenGL utility function

```
gluLookAt(eyex, eyey, eyez, atx, aty, atx, upx, upy, upz);
```

alters the model-view matrix for a camera pointed along this line. You can derive this matrix as another straightforward exercise (Exercise 5.5).

5.2.4 Other Viewing APIs

In many applications, neither of the viewing interfaces that we have presented is appropriate. Consider a flight-simulation application. The pilot using the simulator usually uses three angles—**roll**, **pitch**, and **yaw**—to specify position. These angles are specified relative to the center of mass of the vehicle and to a coordinate system aligned along the axes of the vehicle, as shown in Figure 5.17.

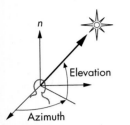

Figure 5.18 Elevation and azimuth.

Hence, the pilot sees an object in terms of the three angles, and of the distance from the object to the center of mass of her vehicle. A viewing transformation can be constructed (Exercise 5.2) from these specifications from a translation and three simple rotations.

Viewing in many applications is most naturally specified in polar, rather than rectilinear, coordinates. Applications involving objects that rotate about other objects fit this category. For example, consider the specification of a star in the sky. Its direction from a viewer is given by its elevation and azimuth (Figure 5.18). The **elevation** is the angle above the plane of the viewer at which the star appears. Note that, by defining a normal at the point that the viewer is located and using this normal to define a plane, we define the elevation, regardless of whether or not the viewer is actually standing on a plane. We can form two other axes in this plane, creating a viewing-coordinate system. The **azimuth** is the angle measured from an axis in this plane to the projection onto the plane of the line between the viewer and the star. The camera can still be rotated about the direction it is pointed by a **twist angle**.

5.3   Simple Projections

With a real camera, once we position it, we still must select a lens. As we saw in Chapter 1, it is the combination of the lens and the size of the film (or of the back of the camera) that determines how much of the world in front of a camera appears in the image. In computer graphics, we make an equivalent choice when we select the type of projection and the parameters.

With a physical camera, a wide-angle lens gives the most dramatic perspectives, with objects near the camera appearing large compared to objects far from the lens. A telephoto lens gives an image that appears flat and is close to a parallel view. Most APIs distinguish between parallel and perspective views by providing different functions for the two cases. OpenGL does the same, even though the implementation of the two can use the same pipeline, as we shall see in Sections 5.8 and 5.9.

Just as we did with the model-view matrix, we can set the projection matrix with glLoadMatrix function. Alternately, we can use OpenGL functions for the most common viewing conditions. First, we shall consider the mathematics of projection. We shall see that we can extend our use of homogeneous coordinates to the projection process, which will allow us to characterize a particular projection with a 4×4 matrix.

5.3.1 Perspective Projections

Suppose that we are in the camera frame with the camera located at the origin, pointed in the negative z direction. Figure 5.19 shows two possibilities. In Figure 5.19(a), the back of the camera is orthogonal to the z direction and is

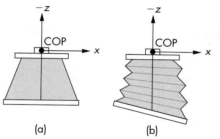

Figure 5.19 Two cameras.

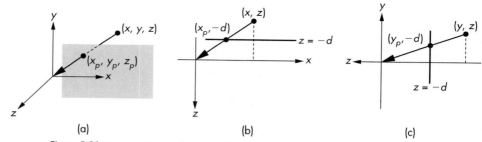

Figure 5.20 Three views of perspective projection. (a) Three-dimensional view. (b) Top view. (c) Side view.

parallel to the lens. This configuration corresponds to most physical situations, including those of the human visual system and of simple cameras. The situation in Figure 5.19(b) is more general; the back of the camera can have any orientation with respect to the front. We shall consider the first case in detail because it is simpler. However, the derivation of the general result follows the same steps and should be a direct exercise (Exercise 5.6).

As we saw in Chapter 2, we can place the projection plane in front of the center of projection. If we do so for the configuration of Figure 5.19(a), we get the views shown in Figure 5.20. A point in space (x, y, z) is projected along a projector into the point (x_p, y_p, z_p). All projectors pass through the origin and, because the projection plane is perpendicular to the z axis,

$$z_p = -d.$$

Here, the value of d is positive. Because the camera is pointing in the negative z direction, the projection plane is in the negative half-space $z < 0$.

From the top view of Figure 5.20(b), we see two similar triangles whose tangents must be same. Hence,

$$\frac{x}{z} = -\frac{x_p}{d},$$

and

$$x_p = -\frac{x}{z/d}.$$

Using the side view, we obtain a similar result for y_p,

$$y_p = -\frac{y}{z/d}.$$

These equations are nonlinear. The division by z describes **nonuniform fore-shortening**: The images of objects farther from the center of projection are reduced in size (diminution) compared to the images of objects closer to the COP.

We can look at the projection process as a transformation that takes points (x, y, z) to other points (x_p, y_p, z_p). Although this **perspective transformation** preserves lines, it is not affine. It is also irreversible: Because all points along a projector project into the same point, we cannot recover a point from its projection.[3] We can, however, modify our use of homogeneous coordinates slightly to handle projections.

When we introduced homogenous coordinates, we represented a point in three dimensions (x, y, z) by the point $(x, y, z, 1)$ in four dimensions. Suppose that, instead, we replace (x, y, z) by the four-dimensional point (wx, wy, wz, w). As long as $w \neq 0$, we can recover the three-dimensional point from its four-dimensional representation by dividing the first three components by w. In this new homogeneous-coordinate form, points in three dimensions become lines in four dimensions. Transformations are again represented by 4×4 matrices, but now the final row of the matrix can be altered, because we may not always be able to keep the w component unchanged.

Obviously, we would prefer to keep $w = 1$, so as to avoid the divisions otherwise necessary to recover the three-dimensional point. However, by allowing w to change, we can represent a broader class of transformations, including perspective projections. Consider the matrix

$$\mathbf{M} = \begin{bmatrix} 1 & 0 & 0 & 0 \\ 0 & 1 & 0 & 0 \\ 0 & 0 & 1 & 0 \\ 0 & 0 & -1/d & 0 \end{bmatrix}.$$

M transforms the point

---

[3] In Sections 5.7 and 5.8, we shall see the advantages of OpenGL's use of an invertible projection transformations.

$$\mathbf{p} = \begin{bmatrix} x \\ y \\ z \\ 1 \end{bmatrix}$$

to the point

$$\mathbf{q} = \begin{bmatrix} x \\ y \\ z \\ -z/d \end{bmatrix}.$$

At first glance, $\mathbf{q}$ may not seem sensible; but, when we remember that we have to divide the first three components by the fourth to return to our original three-dimensional space, we obtain the results

$$-\frac{x}{z/d} = x_p,$$

$$-\frac{y}{z/d} = y_p,$$

$$-\frac{z}{z/d} = -d = z_p,$$

which are the equations for a simple perspective projection. In homogenous coordinates, dividing $\mathbf{q}$ by its w component replaces $\mathbf{q}$ by the equivalent point

$$\mathbf{q}' = \begin{bmatrix} -\dfrac{x}{z/d} \\ -\dfrac{y}{z/d} \\ -d \\ 1 \end{bmatrix} = \begin{bmatrix} x_p \\ y_p \\ z_p \\ 1 \end{bmatrix}.$$

We have shown that we can do at least a simple perspective projection, by defining a 4×4 projection matrix that we apply after the model-view matrix. However, we must perform a **perspective division** at the end. This division can be made part of the pipeline, as shown in Figure 5.21.

Figure 5.21 Projection pipeline.

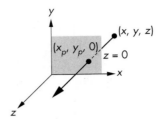

Figure 5.22 Orthogonal projection.

5.3.2 Orthogonal Projections

Orthogonal or **orthographic** projections are a special case of parallel projections, in which the projectors are perpendicular to the view plane. In terms of a camera, orthogonal projections correspond to a camera with a back plane parallel to the lens and a lens with an infinite focal length. However, rather than using limiting relations as the COP moves to infinity, we can derive the projection equations directly. Figure 5.22 shows an orthogonal projection with the projection plane as the plane $z = 0$. As points are projected into this plane, they retain their x and y values, and the equations of projection are

$$x_p = x,$$
$$y_p = y,$$
$$z_p = 0.$$

We can write this result using our original homogeneous coordinates:

$$\begin{bmatrix} x_p \\ y_p \\ z_p \\ 1 \end{bmatrix} = \begin{bmatrix} 1 & 0 & 0 & 0 \\ 0 & 1 & 0 & 0 \\ 0 & 0 & 0 & 0 \\ 0 & 0 & 0 & 1 \end{bmatrix} \begin{bmatrix} x \\ y \\ z \\ 1 \end{bmatrix}.$$

In this case, a division is unnecessary, although, in hardware implementations, we can use the same pipeline for both perspective and orthogonal transformations.

We can expand both our simple projections to general perspective and parallel projections by preceding the projection by a sequence of transformations that converts the general case to one of the two cases that we know how to apply. First, we shall examine the API that the application programmer uses in OpenGL to specify a projection.

5.4   Projections in OpenGL

The projections that we just developed did not take into account the size of the camera—the focal length of its lens or the size of the film plane. Figure 5.23 shows the **angle of view** for a simple pinhole camera, like the one that we discussed in Chapter 1. Only those objects that fit within the angle of view of the camera appear in the image. If the back of the camera is rectangular, only objects within a semi-infinite pyramid—the **view volume**— whose apex is at the COP can appear in the image. Objects not within the view volume are said to be **clipped** out of the scene. Hence, our description of simple projections has been incomplete; we did not include the effects of clipping.

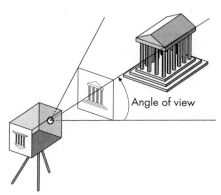

Figure 5.23 Definition of a view volume.

Most graphics APIs define clipping parameters through the specification of a projection. In a computer-graphics system, we allow a finite clipping volume by specifying, in addition to the angle of view, front and back clipping planes, as shown in Figure 5.24. The resulting viewing volume is a **frustum**—a truncated pyramid. The only parameter that we have fixed is that the COP is at the origin in the camera frame, and we should be able to define each of the six sides of the frustum to have almost any orientation and position. If we did so, however, we would make it difficult to specify a view, and rarely do we need this flexibility. We shall examine the OpenGL API. Other APIs differ in their function calls, but incorporate similar restrictions.

5.4.1 Perspective in OpenGL

In OpenGL, we have two functions for specifying perspective views and one for specifying parallel views. Alternatively, we can form the projection matrix directly, either by loading it, or by applying rotations, translations, and scalings to an initial identity matrix. The analogy of our camera view is the function

```
glFrustum(xmin, xmax, ymin, ymax, zmin, zmax)
```

These parameters are shown in Figure 5.25. The near and far distances must be positive and are measured from the COP to these planes, both of which are parallel to the plane $z = 0$. Note that, because the camera is pointing in the negative z direction, the front (near) clipping plane is the plane $z = -z_{min}$, and

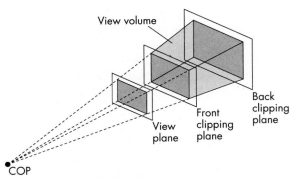

Figure 5.24 Front and back clipping planes.

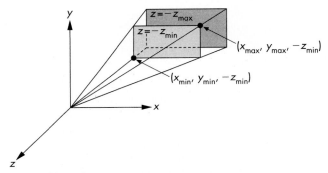

Figure 5.25 Specification of a frustum.

the back (far) clipping plane is the plane $z = -z_{max}$. This matrix multiplies the present matrix, so first we must select the mode. A typical sequence is

```
glMatrixMode(GL_PROJECTION);
glLoadIdentity();
glFrustum(xmin, xmax, ymin, ymax, zmin, zmax)
```

Note that neither the left (xmin) and right (xmax), nor the top (ymax) and bottom (ymin), specifications have to be symmetric with respect to the z axis, and the resulting frustum also does not have to be symmetric (a right frustum). In Section 5.13, we shall show how the projection matrix for this projection can be derived from the simple perspective-projection matrix of Section 5.7.

In many applications, it is natural to specify the angle or field of view. However, if the projection plane is rectangular, rather than square, then we see a different angle of view in the top and side views (Figure 5.26). The OpenGL utility function

```
gluPerspective(fovy, aspect, near, far)
```

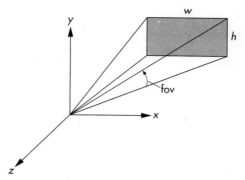

Figure 5.26 Specification using the field of view.

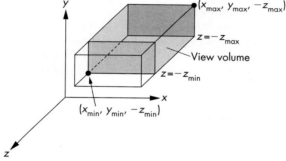

Figure 5.27 Orthographic viewing.

allows us to specify the field of view in the up (y) direction and the aspect ratio—width divided by height—of the projection plane. The near and far planes are specified as in glFrustum. This matrix also alters the present matrix, so we must again select the matrix mode, and usually must load an identity matrix, before evoking this function.

5.4.2 Parallel Viewing in OpenGL

The only parallel-viewing function provided by OpenGL is the orthogonal (orthographic) viewing function

```
gluOrtho2D(xmin, xmax, ymin, ymax, zmin, zmax)
```

Its parameters are identical to those of glFrustum. The view volume is a right parallelepiped, as shown in Figure 5.27. The near and far clipping planes are again at $z = -z_{min}$ and $z = -z_{max}$, respectively.

In perspective viewing, we require the distances to both the near and far planes to be positive, because all projectors pass through the COP at the origin, and objects behind the COP will be projected upside down, as compared with and objects behind the COP will be projected upside down, as compared with objects in front of the COP. Points in the plane $z = 0$ cannot be projected at all, and lead to division by zero. This problem does not exist in parallel viewing, and there are thus no restrictions on the sign of the near and far distances in glOrtho.

5.5 Hidden-Surface Removal

We can now return to our rotating-cube program of Section 4.9 and add perspective viewing and movement of the camera. First, we can use our development of viewing to understand the hidden-surface-removal process that we used in our first version of the program. When we look at a cube that has opaque sides, we see only its three front-facing sides. From the perspective of our basic viewing model, we can say that we see only these faces because they block the projectors from the COP from reaching any other surfaces.

From the perspective of computer graphics, however, all the faces of the cube have been specified and are part of the database; thus, the graphics systems must be careful about which surfaces it displays. Conceptually, we seek algorithms that either remove those surfaces that should not be visible to the viewer, called **hidden-surface-removal algorithms**, or find which surfaces are visible, called **visible-surface algorithms**. There are many approaches to the problem, several of which we shall investigate in Chapter 7. OpenGL has a particular algorithm associated with it, the **z-buffer algorithm**, to which we can interface through three function calls. Hence, we shall introduce the algorithm here, and shall return to the topic again in Chapter 7.

Hidden-surface-removal algorithms can be divided into two broad classes. **Object-space algorithms** attempt to order the surfaces of the objects in the scene such that drawing surfaces in a particular order provides the correct image. For example, for our cube, if we were to draw the back-facing surfaces first, we could "paint" over them with the front surfaces and would produce the correct image.[4] **Image-space algorithms** work as part of the projection process and seek to determine the relationship among object points on each projector. The z-buffer algorithm is of the latter type and fits in well with the rendering pipeline in most graphics systems.

The basic idea of the z-buffer algorithm is shown in Figure 5.28. A projector from the COP passes through two surfaces. If, as the polygons are rasterized, we can keep track of the distance from the COP to the closest point on each

---

[4] For a convex object, such as the cube, we could simply remove all the faces pointing away from the viewer, and could render only the ones facing the viewer. We shall consider this special case in Chapter 7.

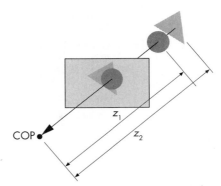

Figure 5.28 The z-buffer algorithm.

projector, then we can update this information as successive polygons are projected and filled. Ultimately, we display only the closest point on each projector.

The major advantages of this algorithm are that its worst-case complexity is proportional to the number of polygons, and that it can be implemented with a small number of additional calculations over what we have to do anyway to project and display polygons. The algorithm requires a **depth** or **z buffer** to store the necessary depth information as polygons are rasterized. This buffer can come from the standard memory in the system, or special memory can be added in at the end of a hardware pipeline.

From the application programmer's perspective, she must initialize the depth buffer and enable hidden-surface removal by using

```
glutInitDisplayMode(GLUT_DOUBLE | GLUT_RGB | GLUT_DEPTH);
glEnable(GL_DEPTH_TEST);
```

Here, we use the GLUT library for the initialization, and specify a depth buffer in addition to our usual RGB color and double buffering. The programmer can clear the buffer as necessary for a new rendering by using

```
glClear(GL_DEPTH_BUFFER_BIT);
```

5.6 Walking Through a Scene

The color-cube program in Chapter 4 had the cube rotating about the origin. We used an orthographic projection, and we did not have to worry about pointing the camera in any but the default direction, or about defining the relationship between the object and the center of projection.

In this version, we use perspective viewing, and we allow the viewer to move the camera by depressing the x, X, y, Y, z, and Z keys on the keyboard, but we have the camera always pointing at the center of the cube. The gluLookAt function provides a simple way to reposition and reorient the camera.

The changes that we have to make to our previous program (Section 4.9) are minor. We define an array viewer[3] to hold the camera position. Its contents are altered by the keyboard callback function keys

```
void keys(unsigned char key, int x, int y)
{
    if(key == 'x') viewer[0]-= 1.0;
    if(key == 'X') viewer[0]+= 1.0;
    if(key == 'y') viewer[1]-= 1.0;
    if(key == 'Y') viewer[1]+= 1.0;
    if(key == 'z') viewer[2]-= 1.0;
    if(key == 'Z') viewer[2]+= 1.0;
    display();
}
```

The display function calls LookAt using viewer for the camera position and uses the origin for the "at" position. The cube is rotated, as before, based on the mouse input. Note the order of the function calls in display that alter the model-view matrix:

```
void display(void)
{

    glClear(GL_COLOR_BUFFER_BIT | GL_DEPTH_BUFFER_BIT);
    glLoadIdentity();
    gluLookAt(viewer[0],viewer[1],viewer[2], 0.0, 0.0, 0.0,
                                              0.0, 1.0, 0.0);
    glRotatef(theta[0], 1.0, 0.0, 0.0);
    glRotatef(theta[1], 0.0, 1.0, 0.0);
    glRotatef(theta[2], 0.0, 0.0, 1.0);

    colorcube();

    glFlush();
    glutSwapBuffers();
}
```

We can use the reshape callback to specify the camera lens through glFrustum:

```
void myReshape(int w, int h)
{
    glViewport(0, 0, w, h);
    glMatrixMode(GL_PROJECTION);
    glLoadIdentity();
    if(w<=h) glFrustum(-2.0, 2.0, -2.0 * (GLfloat) h/ (GLfloat)
        w,2.0* (GLfloat) h / (GLfloat) w, 2.0, 20.0);
```

```
   else glFrustum(-2.0, 2.0, -2.0 * (GLfloat) w/ (GLfloat) h,
      2.0* (GLfloat) w / (GLfloat) h, 2.0, 20.0);
   glMatrixMode(GL_MODELVIEW);
}
```

Other than added specification of a keyboard callback function in main, the rest of the program is the same as the program in Section 4.9. The complete program is given in Appendix A. If you run this program, you should note the effects of moving the camera, the lens, and the sides of the viewing column. Note what happens as you move toward the cube. You should also consider the effect of always having the viewer look at the center of the cube as she is moving.

There are various ways to move around the scene using an interactive device. Suppose that we did not use the mouse to rotate the cube. Then, we could use the mouse buttons to move the user forward, or to turn her right or left (see Exercise 5.14). In this example, we are using direct positioning of the camera through gluLookAt. There are other possibilities. One is to use rotation and translation matrices to alter the model-view matrix incrementally. If we want to move the viewer through the scene without having her looking at a fixed point, this option may be more appealing. We could also keep a position variable in the program, and change it as the viewer moves. In this case, the model-view matrix would be computed from scratch, rather than changed incrementally. Which option we choose depends on the particular application, and often on other factors, such as the possibility that numerical errors might accumulate if we were to change the model-view matrix incrementally many times.

5.7   Parallel-Projection Matrices

From the application programmer's point of view, the projection functions that we introduced are sufficient for most viewing situations. However, views such as parallel-oblique views are not included; we can obtain them by setting up a projection matrix from scratch, or by modifying one of the standard views. In addition, you might be curious about the relationship between the two simple projection matrices that we introduced in Section 5.3 and the projection matrices provided by the OpenGL API. Understanding projections is crucial if you want to understand how three-dimensional graphics is implemented.

In this section and in Section 5.8, we shall show how we can go from the simple perspective and parallel-projection matrices that we introduced in Section 5.3 to the projection matrices provided in OpenGL, and to more general projection matrices.

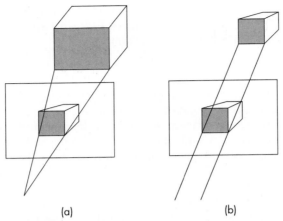

(a)   (b)

Figure 5.29 Predistortion of objects (a) perspective view. (b) Orthographic projection of distorted object.

5.7.1 Projection Normalization

Our approach is based on a technique called **projection normalization**, which converts all projections into orthogonal projections by first distorting the objects such that the orthogonal projection of the distorted objects is the same as the desired projection of the original objects. This technique is shown in Figure 5.29. However, because the distortion of the objects will be described by a homogeneous-coordinate matrix, we can, rather than distorting the objects, concatenate this matrix with a simple orthogonal-projection matrix to form the desired projection matrix, as shown in Figure 5.30.

Figure 5.30 Normalization transformation.

5.7.2 Orthogonal-Projection Matrices

Although parallel viewing is a special case of perspective viewing, we shall start with orthogonal parallel viewing, and shall extend the normalization technique to perspective viewing. We have shown that projection converts points in three-dimensional space to points on the projection plane, and that the transformation that does this operation is singular. All points along a projector project into the same point on the projection plane.

Our development will be clearer if we break projection into two parts. The first will convert the specified projection to an orthogonal projection with the same clipping volume by distorting objects, through the projection matrix, such that an orthogonal projection will yield the desired projection. This matrix will be nonsingular. The second step will carry out the orthogonal projection

$$x_p = x,$$
$$y_p = y,$$
$$z_p = 0.$$

Note that, in homogenous coordinates, carrying out this projection requires only setting the z value to zero, or neglecting it, because it is not needed. The reasons for separating the projection into two parts have to do with many of the other tasks that we do as part of the viewing pipeline. In particular, we shall see in Chapter 7 that clipping must be done in three dimensions, and that the use of the nonsingular projection matrix will allow us to retain depth information along projectors that is necessary for hidden-surface removal and shading (Chapter 6). The first part of the process defines what most systems, including OpenGL, call the **projection matrix**. OpenGL also distinguishes between *screen coordinates*, which are two-dimensional and lack depth information. and *window coordinates*, which are three-dimensional and retain the depth information. In OpenGL, the projection matrix and the subsequent perspective division, convert vertices to window coordinates.

For orthographic projections, the simplest clipping volume to deal with is a cube whose center is at the origin, whose sides are given by the six planes

$$x = \pm 1,$$
$$y = \pm 1,$$
$$z = \pm 1,$$

and which is the default OpenGL view volume; equivalently, we can use the function calls

```
glMatrixMode(GL_PROJECTION);
glLoadIdentity();
glOrtho(-1.0, 1.0, -1.0, 1.0, -1.0, 1.0);
```

We call this volume the **canonical view volume**.

Now suppose that, instead, we set the glOrtho parameters by the function call

```
glOrtho(xmin, xmax, ymax, ymin, zmin, zmax);
```

The projection matrix that OpenGL sets up will convert the vertices that specify our objects, such as through calls to glVertex, to vertices within the canonical view volume, by scaling and translating them. The vertices are transformed such that vertices within the specified view volume are transformed to vertices within the canonical view volume, and vertices outside the specified view volume are transformed to vertices outside the canonical view volume. Equivalently, the projection matrix is a 4×4 matrix that maps the specified view volume to the canonical view volume, as shown in Figure 5.31.

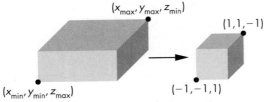

Figure 5.31 Mapping a view volume to the canonical view volume.

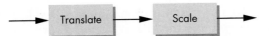

Figure 5.32 Affine transformations for normalization.

We can use our knowledge of affine transformations to find this projection matrix. There are two tasks that we need to do. First, we must move the center of the specified view volume to the center of the canonical view volume (the origin) by doing a translation. Second, we must scale the sides of the specified view volume to each have a length of 2 (Figure 5.32). Hence, the two transformations are $\mathbf{T}(-(x_{max} + x_{min})/2, -(y_{max} + y_{min})/2, -(z_{max} + z_{min})/2)$ and $\mathbf{S}(2/(x_{max} - x_{min}), 2/(y_{max} - y_{min}), 2/(z_{max} - z_{min}))$, and can be concatenated together to form the projection matrix

$$\mathbf{P} = \mathbf{ST} = \begin{bmatrix} \dfrac{2}{x_{max} - x_{min}} & 0 & 0 & -\dfrac{x_{max} + x_{min}}{x_{max} - x_{min}} \\ 0 & \dfrac{2}{y_{max} - y_{min}} & 0 & -\dfrac{y_{max} + y_{min}}{y_{max} - y_{min}} \\ 0 & 0 & \dfrac{2}{z_{max} - z_{min}} & -\dfrac{z_{max} + z_{min}}{z_{max} - z_{min}} \\ 0 & 0 & 0 & 1 \end{bmatrix}.$$

We started with the camera pointing in the negative z direction. Consequently, the projectors are directed from infinity on the negative z axis toward the origin. This choice can cause some confusion. For example, when we discussed the location of the projection plane for simple perspective, we defined it to be at $z = -d$, where d had to be positive. Some systems, including OpenGL, change from right-hand to left-hand coordinates as part of forming the projection matrix. Projectors then start at infinity on the positive z axis. This change is accomplished by use of a simple reflection in the z direction, through the scaling matrix $\mathbf{S}(1, 1, -1)$. The resulting projection matrix is

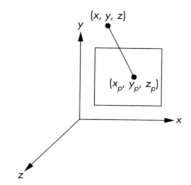

Figure 5.33 Oblique projection.

$$
\mathbf{P} =
\begin{bmatrix}
\dfrac{2}{x_{max} - x_{min}} & 0 & 0 & -\dfrac{x_{max} + x_{min}}{x_{max} - x_{min}} \\[2.5ex]
0 & \dfrac{2}{y_{max} - y_{min}} & 0 & -\dfrac{y_{max} + y_{min}}{y_{max} - y_{min}} \\[2.5ex]
0 & 0 & \dfrac{-2}{z_{max} - z_{min}} & -\dfrac{z_{max} + z_{min}}{z_{max} - z_{min}} \\[2.5ex]
0 & 0 & 0 & 1
\end{bmatrix}.
$$

5.7.3 Oblique Projections

OpenGL provides a limited class of parallel projections through glOrtho—namely, only those for which the projectors are orthogonal to the projection plane. As we saw earlier in this chapter, oblique parallel projections are useful in many fields.[5] We could develop an oblique projection matrix directly; instead, however, we shall follow the process that we used for the general orthogonal projection. We convert the desired projection to a canonical orthogonal projection of distorted objects.

An oblique projection can be characterized by the angle that the projectors make with the projection plane, as shown in Figure 5.33. In APIs that support general parallel viewing, the view volume for an oblique projection has the near and far clipping planes parallel to the view plane, and the right, left, top, and bottom planes parallel to the direction of projection, as shown in Figure 5.34. We can derive the equations for oblique projections by considering the top and side views in Figure 5.35, which shows a projector and the projection plane $z = 0$. The angles θ and ϕ characterize the degree of obliqueness. In

[5] Note that, without oblique projections, we cannot draw coordinate axes in the way that we have been doing in this book; see Exercise 5.15.

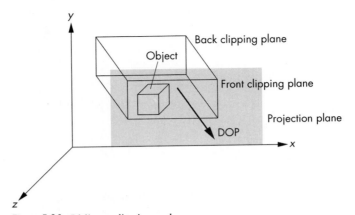

Figure 5.34 Oblique clipping volume.

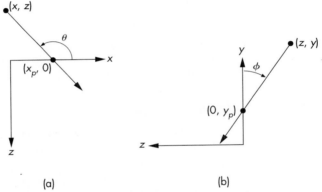

(a)   (b)

Figure 5.35 (a) Top view and (b) side view of oblique projection.

drafting, projections such as the cavalier and cabinet projections are specified by these angles. However, these angles are not the only possible interface (see Exercises 5.9 and 5.10).

If we consider the top view,[6] we can find x_p by noting that

$$\tan \theta = \frac{z}{x - x_p},$$

and thus

---

[6] Here, we are projecting from the negative z direction. Projection from the positive z direction can be done either by reflection about the plane $z = 0$ or by use of the negatives of the angles.

$$x_p = x - z \cot \theta.$$

Likewise

$$y_p = y - z \cot \phi.$$

Using the equation for the projection plane

$$z_p = 0,$$

we can write these results in terms of a homogeneous-coordinate matrix

$$\mathbf{P} = \begin{bmatrix} 1 & 0 & -\cot\theta & 0 \\ 0 & 1 & -\cot\phi & 0 \\ 0 & 0 & 0 & 0 \\ 0 & 0 & 0 & 1 \end{bmatrix}.$$

Following our strategy of the previous example, we can break $\mathbf{P}$ into the product

$$\mathbf{P} = \mathbf{P}_{\text{orth}} \mathbf{H}(\theta, \phi) = \begin{bmatrix} 1 & 0 & 0 & 0 \\ 0 & 1 & 0 & 0 \\ 0 & 0 & 0 & 0 \\ 0 & 0 & 0 & 1 \end{bmatrix} \begin{bmatrix} 1 & 0 & -\cot\theta & 0 \\ 0 & 1 & -\cot\phi & 0 \\ 0 & 0 & 1 & 0 \\ 0 & 0 & 0 & 1 \end{bmatrix},$$

where $\mathbf{H}(\theta, \phi)$ is a shearing matrix. Thus, we can implement an oblique projection by first doing a shear of the objects by $\mathbf{H}(\theta, \phi)$, and then doing an orthographic projection. Figure 5.36 shows the effect of $\mathbf{H}(\theta, \phi)$ on an object—a cube—inside an oblique view volume. The sides of the clipping volume become orthogonal to the view plane, but the sides of the cube become oblique as they are affected by the same shear transformation. However, the orthographic projection of the distorted cube is identical to the oblique projection of the undistorted cube.

We are not quite finished, because the view volume created by the shear is not our canonical view volume. We have to apply the transformation

$$\mathbf{P} = \begin{bmatrix} \dfrac{2}{x_{max} - x_{min}} & 0 & 0 & -\dfrac{x_{max} + x_{min}}{x_{max} - x_{min}} \\ 0 & \dfrac{2}{y_{max} - y_{min}} & 0 & -\dfrac{y_{max} + y_{min}}{y_{max} - y_{min}} \\ 0 & 0 & \dfrac{-2}{z_{max} - z_{min}} & -\dfrac{z_{max} + z_{min}}{z_{max} - z_{min}} \\ 0 & 0 & 0 & 1 \end{bmatrix}$$

after the shear and before the final orthographic projection. Depending on how the sides of the view volume are communicated through the API, the values of x_{min}, x_{max}, y_{min}, and y_{max} may have to be determined from the results of the shear.

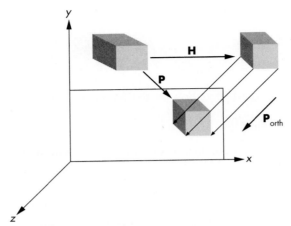

Figure 5.36 Effect of shear transformation.

5.8   Perspective-Projection Matrices

For perspective projections, we shall follow a path similar to the one that we used for parallel projections: Find a transformation that, by distorting the vertices of our objects, allows us to do a simple canonical projection to obtain the desired image. Our first step will be to decide what this canonical viewing volume should be. We shall then introduce a new transformation, the **perspective-normalization transformation**, that will convert a perspective projection to an orthogonal projection. Finally, we shall derive the perspective-projection matrix used in OpenGL.

5.8.1 Perspective Normalization

In Section 5.3, we introduced a simple projection matrix that, for the projection plane at $z = -1$, is

$$\mathbf{M} = \begin{bmatrix} 1 & 0 & 0 & 0 \\ 0 & 1 & 0 & 0 \\ 0 & 0 & 1 & 0 \\ 0 & 0 & -1 & 0 \end{bmatrix}.$$

Suppose that we fix the angle of view at 90 degrees by making the sides of the viewing volume intersect the projection plane at a 45-degree angle. The view volume is the semi-infinite view pyramid shown in Figure 5.37. We can make the volume finite by specifying the near plane to be $z = -1$ and the far plane to be $z = z_{\text{max}}$. Consider the matrix

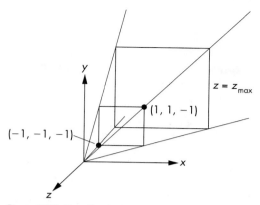

Figure 5.37 Simple perspective projection.

$$N = \begin{bmatrix} 1 & 0 & 0 & 0 \\ 0 & 1 & 0 & 0 \\ 0 & 0 & -2 & -2 \\ 0 & 0 & -1 & 0 \end{bmatrix},$$

which is similar to M but is nonsingular. If we apply it to the homogeneous coordinate point $p = [\, x \quad y \quad z \quad 1 \,]^T$, we obtain the new point $q = [\, x' \quad y' \quad z' \quad w' \,]^T$, where

$$x' = x,$$

$$y' = y,$$

$$z' = -2 - 2z,$$

$$w' = -z,$$

or, after dividing by w',

$$x'' = -\frac{x}{z},$$

$$y'' = -\frac{y}{z},$$

$$z'' = 2\left(1 + \frac{1}{z}\right).$$

If we apply an orthographic projection after transformation by N, we get

$$M_{\text{orth}}N = \begin{bmatrix} 1 & 0 & 0 & 0 \\ 0 & 1 & 0 & 0 \\ 0 & 0 & 0 & 0 \\ 0 & 0 & -1 & 0 \end{bmatrix},$$

which is a simple perspective-projection matrix, and the projection

$$\mathbf{p}_p = \mathbf{M}_{\text{orth}}\mathbf{N}\mathbf{p} = \begin{bmatrix} x \\ y \\ 0 \\ -z \end{bmatrix}.$$

After we do the perspective division, we obtain the expected values for x_p and y_p:

$$x_p = -\frac{x}{z},$$

$$y_p = -\frac{y}{z}.$$

The matrix $\mathbf{N}$ is nonsingular and transforms the viewing volume into a new volume. Consider the sides

$$x = \pm z.$$

They are transformed by $x'' = -x/z$ to the planes

$$x'' = \pm 1.$$

Likewise, the sides $y = \pm z$ are transformed to

$$y'' = \pm 1.$$

The front of the view volume $z = -1$ is transformed by

$$z'' = 2\left(1 + \frac{1}{z}\right)$$

to the plane

$$z'' = 0.$$

Finally, the far plane $z = z_{\max}$ is transformed to the plane

$$z'' = 2\left(1 + \frac{1}{z_{\max}}\right).$$

Figure 5.38 shows this transformation and the distortion to a cube within the volume. Note that, if we use the OpenGL convention of having the camera pointing in the negative z direction, $z_{\max}$ is negative and is less than -1. Thus, $\mathbf{N}$ has transformed the viewing frustum to a right parallelepiped, and an orthographic projection in the transformed volume yields the same image as does the perspective projection. $\mathbf{N}$ is called the **perspective-normalization matrix**.

Although we have shown that both perspective and parallel transformations can be converted to orthographic transformations, the effects of this result are greatest in implementation. As long as we can put a carefully chosen projection matrix in the pipeline before the vertices are defined, we need only one viewing pipeline for all possible views. In Chapter 7, where we discuss implementation

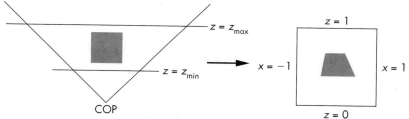

Figure 5.38 Perspective normalization of view volume.

in detail, we shall see how converting all view volumes to right parallelepipeds by our normalization process simplifies both clipping and hidden-surface removal.

5.8.2 OpenGL Perspective Transformations

The OpenGL function `gluPerspective` does not restrict the view volume to a symmetric (or right) frustum. The parameters are as shown in Figure 5.39. We can form the OpenGL perspective matrix by first converting this frustum to the symmetric frustum with 45-degree sides (Figure 5.37). The process is similar to the conversion of an oblique parallel view to an orthogonal view. First, we do a shear to convert the asymmetric frustum to a symmetric one. Figure 5.39 shows the desired transformation. The shear angle is determined by our desire to skew (shear) the point $((x_{min} + x_{max})/2, (y_{max} + y_{min})/2, z_{min})$ to $(0, 0, z_{min})$. The required shear is matrix is

$$\mathbf{H}(\cot\theta, \cot\phi) = \mathbf{H}\left(\frac{x_{min} + x_{max}}{2z_{min}}, \frac{y_{max} + y_{min}}{2z_{min}}\right).$$

The resulting frustum is described by the planes

$$x = \pm\frac{x_{max} - x_{min}}{2z_{min}},$$

$$y = \pm\frac{y_{max} - y_{min}}{2z_{min}},$$

$$z = z_{max},$$

$$z = z_{min}.$$

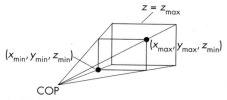

Figure 5.39 OpenGL perspective.

The next step is to scale the sides of this frustum to

$$x = \pm z,$$

$$y = \pm z,$$

and the near plane to

$$z_{min} = -1.$$

The required scaling matrix is $\mathbf{S}(2z_{min}/(x_{max} - x_{min}), 2z_{min}/(y_{max} - y_{min}), -1/z_{min})$. Note that this transformation is determined uniquely without reference to the location of the far plane $z = z_{max}$, because, in three dimensions, an affine transformation is determined by the results of the transformation on four points. In this case, these points are the four vertices where the sides of the frustum intersect the near plane.

To get the far plane to the plane $z = 1$ and the near plane to $z = 0$ after applying a projection normalization, we must make a slight change to the projection-normalization matrix $\mathbf{N}$. If we write $\mathbf{N}$ as

$$\mathbf{N} = \begin{bmatrix} 1 & 0 & 0 & 0 \\ 0 & 1 & 0 & 0 \\ 0 & 0 & \alpha & \beta \\ 0 & 0 & -1 & 0 \end{bmatrix},$$

we do not change the effect of this matrix on the x, y, and w components of a point $\mathbf{p}$ to which we might apply it. Consequently, we do not change the resulting projected image. However, the new z is given, after division by $w' = -z$, by

$$z' = -\frac{\alpha + \beta z}{z}.$$

We can determine α and β by requiring that plane $z = -1$ be moved to $z' = 0$, and the far plane at $z = -z_{max}/z_{min}$ (where it is after the scale) be moved to $z' = -1$. The selection of this far plane ensures that, whatever the choice of z_{min} and z_{max}, the same canonical view volume will be obtained.[7] The result is

$$z' = -\left(\frac{z_{max}}{z_{max} - z_{min}}\right)\frac{1 + z}{z}.$$

The projection normalization matrix is then

---

[7] One side effect of the nonlinear scaling of z is that the user must be careful in her specifications of the near and far clipping planes. Specifying these values carelessly can cause a loss of resolution in the z buffer, which usually has a depth resolution of between 24 and 32 bits.

$$N = \begin{bmatrix} 1 & 0 & 0 & 0 \\ 0 & 1 & 0 & 0 \\ 0 & 0 & -\dfrac{z_{max}}{z_{max} - z_{min}} & \dfrac{z_{max}}{z_{max} - z_{min}} \\ 0 & 0 & -1 & 0 \end{bmatrix}.$$

The resulting projection matrix is

$$P = NSH = \begin{bmatrix} \dfrac{2z_{min}}{x_{max} - x_{min}} & 0 & \dfrac{x_{max} + x_{min}}{x_{max} - x_{min}} & 0 \\ 0 & \dfrac{2z_{min}}{y_{max} - y_{min}} & \dfrac{y_{max} + y_{min}}{y_{max} - y_{min}} & 0 \\ 0 & 0 & -\dfrac{z_{max} + z_{min}}{z_{max} - z_{min}} & -\dfrac{2z_{max}z_{min}}{z_{max} - z_{min}} \\ 0 & 0 & -1 & 0 \end{bmatrix}.$$

5.9 Summary

We have come a long way. We can now write complete nontrivial three-dimensional applications. Probably the most instructive activity that you can do now is to write a three-dimensional application. Facility with manipulating the model-view and projection functions takes practice.

We have presented the mathematics of the standard projections. Although most APIs obviate the user from writing projection functions, understanding the mathematics leads to understanding a pipeline implementation based on concatenation of 4 × 4 matrices. Note that, until recently, user programs had to do the projections within the applications, and most hardware systems did not support perspective projections.

There are three major themes in the remainder of this book. One is to explore modeling further. We have introduced only a basic set of primitives. We shall expand this set in two ways. One will be to incorporate more complex relationships between simple objects through hierarchical models in Chapter 8. The second (Chapter 9) will be to leave the world of flat objects, and to add curves and curved surfaces. These objects will be defined by vertices, and we can implement them by breaking them into small flat primitives, allowing us to use the same viewing pipeline.

The second major theme is realism. Although more complex objects will allow us to build more realistic models, we shall also explore more complex rendering options. In Chapter 6, we shall consider the interaction of light with the materials that characterize our objects. We shall look more deeply at hidden-surface-removal methods, at shading models, and, in Chapter 10, at techniques such as texture mapping that allow us to create complex images from simple objects using advanced rendering techniques.

Third, we shall look more deeply at implementation in Chapter 7. At this point, we have introduced the major functional units of the graphics pipeline. We shall discuss the details of the algorithms used in each unit. We shall also see additional possibilities for creating images by working directly in the frame buffer.

After reading Chapter 6, you should be able to read the remaining chapters in any order.

5.10   Suggested Readings

Carlbom and Paciorek [Car78] discuss the relationships between classical and computer viewing. Rogers and Adams [Rog90] contains many examples of the projection matrices corresponding to the standard views using in drafting. Foley [Fol90], Watt [Wat93], Hearn and Baker [Hea94] derive canonical projection transformations. All follow a PHIGS orientation, so the API is slightly different from the one used here, although Foley derives the most general case. The references differ in whether they use column or row matrices, in where the COP is located, and in whether the projection is in the positive or negative z direction. See the *OpenGL Programmer's Guide* [Ope93a] for a further discussion of the use of the model-view and projection matrices in OpenGL.

Exercises

5.1   Not all projections are planar geometric projections. Give an example of a projection in which the projection surface is not a plane, and another in which the projectors are not lines.

5.2   Consider an airplane whose position is specified by the roll, pitch, and yaw, and by the distance from an object. Find a model-view matrix in terms of these parameters.

5.3   Consider a satellite rotating around the earth. Its position above the earth is specified in polar coordinates. Find a model-view matrix that keeps the viewer looking at the earth. Such a matrix could be used to show the earth as it rotates.

5.4   Use the VRP, VPN, and VUP to determine a model-view matrix

5.5   Find the matrix formed by `gluLookat`.

5.6   Derive the perspective-projection matrix when the COP can be at any point and the projection plane can be at any orientation.

5.7   Show that perspective projection preserves lines.

5.8   Any attempt to take the projection of a point in the same plane as the COP will lead to a division by zero. What is the projection of a line segment that has endpoints on either side of projection plane?

5.9 Define one or more APIs to specify oblique projections. You do not need write the functions; just decide which parameters the user must specify.

5.10 Derive an oblique-projection matrix from specification of front and back clipping planes, and top-right and bottom-left intersections of the sides of the clipping volume with the front clipping plane.

5.11 Our approach of normalizing all projections seems to imply that we could predistort all objects and support only orthographic projections. What problems would we face if we took this approach to building a graphics system?

5.12 How do the OpenGL projection matrices change if the COP is not at the origin? Assume that the COP is at $(0, 0, d)$ and the projection plane is $z = 0$.

5.13 We can create an interesting class of three-dimensional objects by extending two-dimensional objects into the third dimension by extrusion. For example, a circle becomes a cylinder, a line becomes a quadrilateral, and a quadrilateral in the plane becomes a parallelepiped. Use this technique to convert the two-dimensional maze from Exercise 2.8 to a three-dimensional maze.

5.14 Extend the maze program of Exercise 5.13 to allow the user to walk through the maze. A click on the middle mouse button should move the user forward; a click on the right or left buttons should turn the user 90 degrees to the right or left, respectively.

5.15 If we were to use orthogonal projections to draw the coordinate axes, the x and y axes would lie in the plane of the paper, but the z axis would point out of the page. Instead, we can draw the x and y axes as meeting at a 90-degree angle, with the z axis going off at -135 degrees from the x axis. Find the matrix that projects the original orthogonal-coordinate axes to this view.

6 Shading

We have learned to build three-dimensional graphical models and to display them. However, if you render one of our models, you might be disappointed to see images that look flat and thus fail to show the three-dimensional nature of the model. This appearance is a consequence of our unnatural assumption that each surface is lit such that it appears to a viewer in a single color. Under this assumption, the orthographic projection of a sphere is a uniformly colored circle, and a cube will appear as a flat hexagon. If we look at a photograph of a lit sphere, we see not a uniformly colored circle, but rather a circular shape with many gradations or **shades** of color. It is these gradations that give the two-dimensional images the appearance of being three-dimensional.

What we have left out is the interaction between light and the surfaces in our models. This chapter will fill that gap. We shall develop separate models of light sources and of the most common light–material interactions. Our aim is to add shading to a fast pipeline graphics architecture, so we shall develop only a local lighting model. Such models, as opposed to global lighting models, will allow us to compute the shade to assign to a point on a surface, independently of any other surfaces in the scene. The calculations will depend on only the material properties assigned to the surface, the local geometry of the surface, and the locations and properties of the light sources.

Following our previous development, we shall investigate how we can apply shading to polygonal models. We shall develop a recursive approximation to a sphere that will allow us to test our shading algorithms. We shall then see how light and material properties are specified in OpenGL and can be added to our sphere-approximating program.

We conclude the chapter with a short discussion of the two most important methods for handling global lighting effects: ray tracing and radiosity.

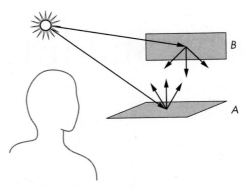

Figure 6.1 Reflecting surfaces.

6.1   Light and Matter

In Chapters 1 and 2, we presented the rudiments of human color vision, delaying until now any discussion of the interaction between light and surfaces. Perhaps the most general approach to rendering is based on physics, where we use principles such as conservation of energy to derive equations that describe how light is reflected from surfaces.

From a physical perspective, a surface can either emit light by self-emission, as a light bulb does, or reflect light from other surfaces that illuminate it. Some surfaces may both reflect light and emit light from internal physical processes. When we look at a point on an object, the color that we see is determined by multiple interactions among light sources and reflective surfaces. These interactions can be viewed as a recursive process. Consider the simple scene in Figure 6.1. Some light from the source that reaches surface A is reflected. Some of this reflected light reaches surface B, and some of it is then reflected back to A, where some of it is again reflected back to B, and so on. This recursive reflection of light between surfaces accounts for subtle shading effects. such as the bleeding of colors between adjacent surfaces. Mathematically, this recursive process results in an integral equation, the **rendering equation**, that, in principle, we could use to find the shading of all surfaces in a scene. Unfortunately, this equation cannot be solved in general, even by numerical methods. There are various approximate approaches, such as radiosity and ray tracing, each of which is an excellent approximation to the rendering equation for particular types of surfaces. Unfortunately, neither ray tracing nor radiosity can yet be used to render scenes at the rate at which we can pass polygons through the modeling-projection pipeline. Consequently, we shall focus on a simpler rendering model, based on the Phong reflection model, that provides a compromise between physical correctness and efficient calculation.

Rather than looking at a global energy balance, we shall follow rays of light from light-emitting (or self-luminous) surfaces, which we shall call **light**

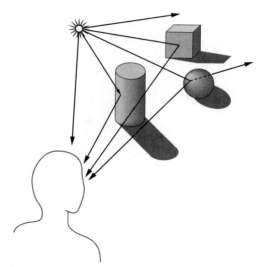

Figure 6.2 Light and surfaces.

sources. We shall then model what happens to these rays as they interact with reflecting surfaces in the scene. This approach is similar to ray tracing, but we shall consider only single interactions between light sources and surfaces. There are two independent parts of the problem. First, we must model the light sources in the scene. Then, we must build a reflection model that deals with the interactions between materials and light.

To get an overview of the process, we can start following rays of light from a point source, as shown in Figure 6.2. As we noted in Chapter 1, our viewer sees only the light that leaves the source and reaches her eyes—perhaps through a complex path and multiple interactions with objects in the scene. If a ray of light enters her eye directly from the source, she will see the color of the source. If the ray of light hits a surface that is visible to our viewer, the color she sees will be based on the interaction between the source and the surface material: She will see the color of the light reflected from the surface toward her eyes.

In terms of computer graphics, we replace the viewer by the projection plane, as shown in Figure 6.3. Conceptually, the clipping window in this plane is mapped to the screen; thus, we can think of the projection plane as ruled into rectangles, each corresponding to a pixel. The color of the light source and of the surfaces will determine the color of one or more pixels in the frame buffer.

We need to consider only those rays that leave the source and reach the viewer's eye, either directly or through interactions with objects. In the case of computer viewing, these are the rays that reach the COP after passing through the clipping rectangle. Note that most rays leaving a source do not contribute to the image and are thus of no interest to us. We shall make use of this observation in Section 6.10.

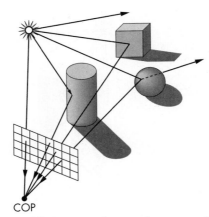

Figure 6.3 Light, surfaces, and computer imaging.

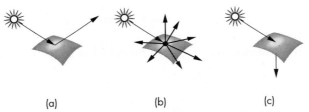

(a)   (b)   (c)

Figure 6.4 Light–material interactions. (a) Specular surface. (b) Diffuse surface.
(c) Translucent surface.

Figure 6.2 shows both single and multiple interactions between rays and objects. It is the nature of these interactions that determines whether an object appears red or brown, light or dark, dull or shiny. When light strikes a surface, some of it is absorbed, and some of it is reflected. If the surface is opaque, reflection and absorption will account for all the light striking the surface. If the surface is translucent, some of the light will be transmitted through the material and will emerge to interact with other objects. These interactions depend on wavelength. An object illuminated by white light appears red because it absorbs most of the incident light but reflects light in the red range of frequencies. A shiny object appears so because its surface is smooth. Conversely, a dull object has a rough surface. The shading of objects also depends on the orientation of their surfaces, a factor that, as we shall see, is characterized by the normal vector at each point. These interactions between light and materials can be classified into the three groups shown in Figure 6.4.

1. **Specular surfaces** appear shiny because most of the light that is reflected is **scattered** in a narrow range of angles close to the angle of reflection. Mirrors are **perfectly specular surfaces**. The light from an incoming

light ray may be partially absorbed, but all reflected light emerges at a single angle, obeying the rule that the angle of incidence is equal to the angle of reflection.

2. **Diffuse surfaces** are characterized by reflected light being scattered in all directions. Walls painted with matte or flat paint are diffuse reflectors, as are many natural materials, such as terrain viewed from an airplane or satellite. **Perfectly diffuse surfaces** scatter light equally in all directions and thus appear the same to all viewers.

3. **Translucent surfaces** allow some light to penetrate the surface and to emerge from another location on the object. This process of **refraction** characterizes glass and water. Some incident light may also be reflected at the surface.

We shall model all these surfaces in Section 6.3. First, we shall consider light sources.

6.2 Light Sources

Light can leave a surface through two fundamental processes: self-emission and reflection. We usually think of a light source as an object that emits light only through internal energy sources. However, a light source, such as light bulb, can also reflect some light that is incident on it from the surrounding environment. We shall neglect this term in our simple models. When we discuss OpenGL lighting in the Section 6.7, we shall see that we can easily simulate a self-emission term.

If we consider a source such as the one in Figure 6.5, we can look at it as an object with a surface. Each point (x, y, z) on the surface can emit light that is characterized by the direction of emission (θ, ϕ) and the intensity of energy emitted at each wavelength λ. Thus, a general light source can be characterized by a six-variable **illumination function** $I(x, y, z, \theta, \phi, \lambda)$. Note that we need

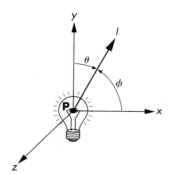

Figure 6.5 Light source.

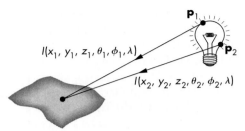

Figure 6.6 Adding the contribution from a source.

two angles to specify a direction, and that we are assuming that each frequency can be considered independently. From the perspective of a surface that is illuminated by this source, we can obtain the total contribution of the source (Figure 6.6) by integrating over the surface of the source, a process that accounts for the emission angles that reach the surface under consideration and that also must account for the distance between the source and the surface. For a distributed light source, such as a light bulb, the evaluation of this integral is difficult, whether we use analytic or numerical methods. Often, it is easier to model the distributed source with polygons, each of which is a simple source, or with an approximating set of point sources.

We shall consider four basic types of sources: ambient lighting, point sources, spotlights, and distant light. These four lighting types will be sufficient for rendering most simple scenes.

6.2.1 Color Sources

Not only do light sources emit different amounts of light at different frequencies, but also their directional properties vary with frequency. Consequently, a physically correct model can be complex. However, our model of the human visual system is based on three-color theory that says we perceive three primaries, rather than a full color distribution. For most applications, we can thus model light sources as having three components—red, green, and blue—and can use each of the three color sources to obtain the corresponding color component that a human observer will see.

We describe a source through a three-component intensity or **luminance** function

$$\mathbf{I} = \begin{bmatrix} I_r \\ I_g \\ I_b \end{bmatrix},$$

each of whose components is the intensity of the independent red, green, and blue components. Thus, we use the red component of a light source for the calculation of the red component of the image. Because color–light computations involve three similar but independent calculations, we shall tend to present a single scalar equation, with the understanding that it can represent any of the three color components.

6.2.2 Ambient Light

In some rooms, such as in some classrooms or kitchens, the lights have been designed and positioned to provide uniform illumination throughout the room. Often, such illumination is achieved through large sources with diffusers whose purpose is to scatter light in all directions. We could create an accurate simulation of such illumination, at least in principle, by modeling all the distributed sources, and then integrating the illumination from these sources at each point on a reflecting surface. Making such a model and rendering a scene with it would be a daunting task for a graphics system, especially one for which real-time performance is desirable. Alternatively, we can look at the desired effect of the sources: to achieve a uniform light level in the room. This uniform lighting is called **ambient light**. If we follow this second approach, we can postulate an ambient intensity at each point in the environment. Thus, ambient illumination is characterized by an intensity, $\mathbf{I}_a$, that is identical at every point in the scene.

Our ambient source has three color components:

$$\mathbf{I}_a = \begin{bmatrix} I_{ar} \\ I_{ag} \\ I_{ab} \end{bmatrix}.$$

We shall use the *scalar* I_a to denote any one of the red, green, or blue components of $\mathbf{I}_a$. Although every point in our scene receives the same illumination from $\mathbf{I}_a$, each surface can reflect this light differently.

6.2.3 Point Sources

An ideal **point source** emits light equally in all directions. We can characterize a point source located at a point $\mathbf{p}_0$ by a three-component color vector:

$$\mathbf{I}(\mathbf{p}_0) = \begin{bmatrix} I_r(\mathbf{p}_0) \\ I_g(\mathbf{p}_0) \\ I_b(\mathbf{p}_0) \end{bmatrix}.$$

The intensity of illumination received from a point source is proportional to the inverse square of the distance between the source and surface. Hence, at a point $\mathbf{p}$ (Figure 6.7), the intensity of light received from the point source is given by the vector

$$\mathbf{I}(\mathbf{p}, \mathbf{p}_0) = \frac{1}{|\mathbf{p} - \mathbf{p}_0|^2} \mathbf{I}(\mathbf{p}_0).$$

As we did with ambient light, we shall use $I(\mathbf{p}_0)$ to denote any of the components of $\mathbf{I}(\mathbf{p}_0)$.

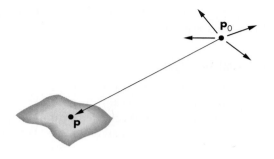

Figure 6.7 Point source illuminating surface.

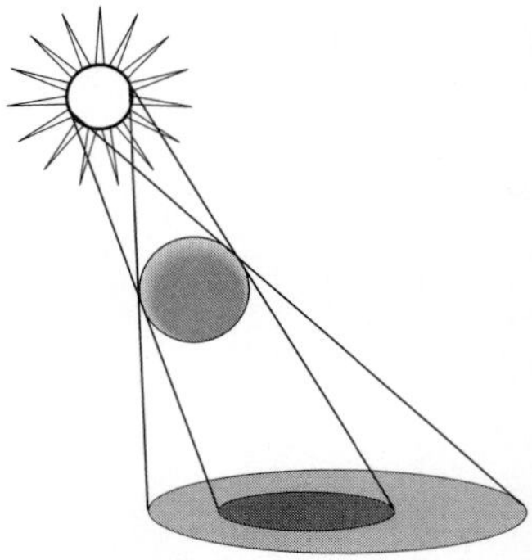

Figure 6.8 Shadows created by finite-size light source.

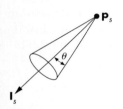

Figure 6.9 Spotlight.

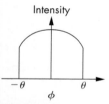

Figure 6.10 Attenuation of a spotlight.

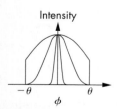

Figure 6.11 Spotlight exponent.

The use of point sources in most applications is determined more by their ease of use than by their resemblance to physical reality. Scenes rendered with only point sources tend to have high contrast; objects appear either bright or dark. In the real world, it is the large size of most light sources that contributes to softer scenes, as we can see from Figure 6.8, which shows the shadows created by a source of finite size. Some areas are fully in shadow, or in the **umbra**, whereas others are in partial shadow, or in the **penumbra**. We can mitigate the high-contrast effect by adding ambient light to a scene.

The distance term also contributes to the harsh renderings with point sources. Although the inverse-square distance term is correct for point sources, in practice it is usually replaced by a term of the form $(a + bd + cd^2)^{-1}$, where d is the distance and the constants a, b, and c can be chosen to soften the lighting. Note that, if the light source is far from the surfaces in the scene, the intensity of the light from the source will be sufficiently uniform that the distance term will be constant over the surfaces.

6.2.4 Spotlights

Spotlights are characterized by a narrow range of angles through which light is emitted. We can construct a simple spotlight from a point source by limiting the angles at which light from the source can be seen. We can use a cone whose apex is at $\mathbf{p}_s$, which points in the direction $\mathbf{l}_s$, and whose width is determined by an angle θ, as shown in Figure 6.9. Note that, if $\theta = 180$, the spotlight becomes a point source.

More realistic spotlights are characterized by the distribution of light within the cone—usually with most of the light concentrated in the center of the cone. Thus, the intensity is a function of the angle ϕ between the direction of the source and a vector $\mathbf{s}$ to a point on the surface (as long as this angle is less than θ; Figure 6.10). Although this function could be defined in many ways, it is usually defined by $\cos^e \phi$, where the exponent e (Figure 6.11) determines how rapidly the light intensity drops off. As we shall see throughout this chapter, cosines are convenient functions for lighting calculations. If both **s** and **l** are unit-length vectors, we can compute the cosine with the dot product

$$\cos \phi = \mathbf{s} \cdot \mathbf{l},$$

a calculation that requires only three multiplications and two additions.

6.2.5 Distant Light Sources

Figure 6.12 Parallel light source.

Most shading calculations require the direction from the point on the surface to the light source. As we move across a surface, calculating the intensity at each point, we should recompute this vector repeatedly—a computation that is a significant part of the shading calculation. However, if the light source is far from the surface, the vector will not change much as we move from point to point, just as the light from the sun strikes all objects that are in close proximity to one other at the same angle. Figure 6.12 illustrates that we are effectively replacing a point source of light with a source that illuminates objects with parallel rays of light—a parallel source. In practice, the calculations for distant light sources are similar to the calculations for parallel projections; they replace the *location* of the light source with the *direction* of the light source. Hence, in homogeneous coordinates, a point light source at **p**₀ will be represented internally as a four-dimensional column matrix

$$\mathbf{p}_0 = \begin{bmatrix} x \\ y \\ z \\ 1 \end{bmatrix},$$

whereas the distant light source will be represented by

$$\mathbf{p}_0 = \begin{bmatrix} x \\ y \\ z \\ 0 \end{bmatrix},$$

which is the representation of a vector. The graphics system can carry out rendering calculations more efficiently for distant light sources than for near ones. Of course, a scene rendered with distant light sources will look different from a scene rendered with near sources. Fortunately, OpenGL allows both types of sources.

6.3 The Phong Reflection Model

Although we could approach modeling light–material interactions through physical models, we have chosen to use a model that leads to efficient computations, especially when we use it with our pipeline rendering model. The

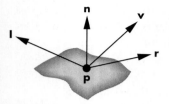

Figure 6.13 Vectors used by the Phong model.

reflection model that we shall develop was introduced by Phong. It has proved to be efficient, and to be a close enough approximation to physical reality to produce good renderings, under a variety of lighting conditions and material properties.

The model uses the four vectors shown in Figure 6.13 to calculate a color for an arbitrary point **p** on a surface. If the surface is curved, all four vectors can change as we move from point to point. The vector **n** is the normal at **p**; we shall discuss its calculation in Section 6.4. The vector **v** is in the direction from **p** to the viewer or COP. The vector **l** is in the direction of a line from **p** to an arbitrary point on the source for a distributed light source, or, as we are assuming for now, to the point light source. Finally, the vector **r** is in the direction that a perfectly reflected ray from **l** would take. Note that **r** is determined by **n** and **l**. We shall calculate it in Section 6.4.

The Phong model supports the three types of material–light interactions—ambient, diffuse, and specular—that we introduced in Section 6.1. Suppose that we have a set of point sources. We shall assume that each source can have separate ambient, diffuse, and specular components for each of the three primary colors. Although this assumption may appear unnatural, remember that our goal is to create realistic shading effects in as close to real time as possible. As we develop the model, we shall use a local model to simulate effects that can be global in nature. Thus, our light-source model has ambient, diffuse, and specular terms, and, at any point **p** on the surface, we can compute a 3×3 illumination matrix for the ith light source:

$$\mathbf{L}_i = \begin{bmatrix} L_{i\text{ra}} & L_{i\text{ga}} & L_{i\text{ba}} \\ L_{i\text{rd}} & L_{i\text{gd}} & L_{i\text{bd}} \\ L_{i\text{rs}} & L_{i\text{gs}} & L_{i\text{bs}} \end{bmatrix}.$$

The first row contains the ambient intensities for the red, green, and blue terms from source i. The second row contains the diffuse terms; the third contains the specular terms. We shall assume that any distance-attenuation terms have not yet been applied.

We construct the model by assuming that we can compute how much of each of the incident lights is reflected at the point of interest. For example, for the red diffuse term from source i, $L_{i\text{rd}}$, we can compute a reflection term $R_{i\text{rd}}$, and the latter's contribution to the intensity at **p** is $R_{i\text{rd}}L_{i\text{rd}}$. The value of $R_{i\text{rd}}$ will depend on the material properties, the orientation of the surface, the direction of the light source, and the distance between the light source and the viewer. Thus, for each point, we compute a matrix of reflection terms of the form

$$\mathbf{R}_i = \begin{bmatrix} R_{i\text{ra}} & R_{i\text{ga}} & R_{i\text{ba}} \\ R_{i\text{rd}} & R_{i\text{gd}} & R_{i\text{bd}} \\ R_{i\text{rs}} & R_{i\text{gs}} & R_{i\text{bs}} \end{bmatrix}.$$

We can then compute the contribution for each color source by adding the ambient, diffuse, and specular components. For example, the red intensity that we see at **p** from source i is

$$I_{ir} = R_{ira}L_{ira} + R_{ird}L_{ird} + R_{irs}L_{irs}$$
$$= I_{ira} + I_{ird} + I_{irs}.$$

We obtain the total intensity by adding the contributions of all sources and, possibly, a global ambient term. Thus, the red term is

$$I_r = \sum_i (I_{ira} + I_{ird} + I_{irs}) + I_{ar},$$

where I_{ar} is the red component of the global ambient light.

We can simplify our notation by noting that the necessary computations are the same for each source and for each primary color. They differ depending on whether we are considering the ambient, diffuse, or specular terms. Hence, we can omit the subscripts i, r, g and b. We shall write

$$I = I_a + I_d + I_s = L_a R_a + L_d R_d + L_s R_s,$$

with the understanding that the computation will be done for each of the primaries and each source, and the global ambient term can be added at the end.

6.3.1 Ambient Reflection

The intensity of ambient light L_a is the same at every point on the surface. Some of this light is absorbed, and some is reflected. The amount reflected is given by the ambient reflection coefficient, $R_a = k_a$. Because only a positive fraction of the light is reflected, we must have

$$0 \le k_a \le 1,$$

and thus

$$I_a = k_a L_a.$$

Here, L_a can be any of the individual light sources, or it can be a global ambient term.

A surface has, of course, three ambient coefficients—k_{ar}, k_{ag}, and k_{ab}—and they can differ. Hence, for example, a sphere will appear yellow under white ambient light if its blue ambient coefficient is small and its red and green coefficients are large.

6.3.2 Diffuse Reflection

A perfectly diffuse reflector scatters the light that it reflects equally in all directions. Hence, such a surface appears the same to all viewers. However, the

Figure 6.14 Rough surface.

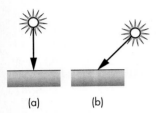

(a)   (b)

Figure 6.15 Illumination of a diffuse surface. (a) At noon. (b) In the afternoon.

amount of light reflected depends both on the material, because some of the incoming light is absorbed, and on the position of the light source relative to the surface. Diffuse reflections are characterized by rough surfaces. If we were to magnify a cross-section of a diffuse surface, we might see an image like that shown in Figure 6.14. Rays of light that hit the surface at only slightly different angles would be reflected back at markedly different angles. Perfectly diffuse surfaces are so rough that there is no preferred angle of reflection. Such surfaces, sometimes called **Lambertian surfaces**, can be modeled mathematically with Lambert's law.

Consider a diffuse planar surface, as shown in Figure 6.15, illuminated by the sun. The surface is brightest at noon, and dimmest at dawn and dusk, because, according to Lambert's law, we see only the vertical component of the incoming light. One way to understand this law is to consider a small parallel light source, as shown in Figure 6.16, striking a plane. As the source is lowered in the (artificial) sky, the same amount of light is spread over a larger areas, and the surface appears dimmer. Returning to the point source of Figure 6.15, we can characterize diffuse reflections mathematically. Lambert's law states that

$$R_d \propto \cos\theta,$$

where θ is the angle between the normal at the point of interest $\mathbf{n}$ and the direction of the light source $\mathbf{l}$. If both $\mathbf{l}$ and $\mathbf{n}$ are unit-length vectors,[1] then

$$\cos\theta = \mathbf{l} \cdot \mathbf{n}.$$

If we add in a reflection coefficient k_d that represents the fraction of incoming diffuse light that is reflected, we have the diffuse reflection term:

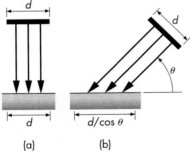

(a)   (b)

Figure 6.16 Lambert's law. (a) At noon. (b) In the afternoon.

----

[1] Direction vectors, such as $\mathbf{l}$ and $\mathbf{n}$, are used repeatedly in shading calculations through the dot product. In practice, both the programmer and the graphics software should seek to normalize all such vectors as soon as possible.

$$I_d = k_d(\mathbf{l} \cdot \mathbf{n})L_d.$$

If we wish to incorporate a distance term, to account for the attenuation of light as that light travels distance d from the source to the surface, we can again use the quadratic attenuation term:

$$I_d = \frac{k_d}{a + bd + cd^2}(\mathbf{l} \cdot \mathbf{n})L_d.$$

6.3.3 Specular Reflection

If we employ only ambient and diffuse reflections, our images will be shaded and will appear three-dimensional, but all the surfaces will look dull, somewhat like chalk. What we are missing is the highlights that we see reflected from shiny objects. These highlights usually show a color different from the color of the reflected ambient and diffuse light. A red ball will, under white light, have a white highlight that is the reflection of some of light from the source in the direction of the viewer (Figure 6.17).

Figure 6.17 Specular highlights.

Whereas a diffuse surface is rough, a specular surface is smooth. The smoother the surface is, the more it resembles a mirror, as shown in Figure 6.18. The figure shows that, as the surface gets smoother, the reflected light is concentrated in a smaller range of angles, centered about the angle of a perfect reflector—a mirror or a perfectly specular surface. Modeling specular surfaces realistically can be complex, because the pattern by which the light is scattered is not symmetric, depends on the wavelength of the incident light, and changes with the reflection angle.

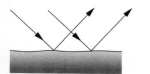

Figure 6.18 Specular surface.

Phong proposed an approximate model that can be computed with only a slight increase in work done for diffuse surfaces. The model adds a term for specular reflection. Hence, we consider the surface as being rough for the diffuse term and smooth for the specular term. The amount of light that the viewer sees depends on the angle ϕ between $\mathbf{r}$, the direction of a perfect reflector, and $\mathbf{v}$, the direction of the viewer. The Phong model uses the equation

$$I_s = k_s L_s \cos^\alpha \phi.$$

The coefficient k_s $(0 \le k_s \le 1)$ is the fraction of the incoming specular light that is reflected. The exponent α is a **shininess** coefficient. Figure 6.19 shows how, as α is increased, the reflected light is concentrated in a narrower region, centered on the angle of a perfect reflector. In the limit, as α goes to infinity, we get a mirror; values in the range 100 to 500 correspond to most metallic surfaces, and smaller values (< 100) correspond to materials that show broad highlights.

The computational advantage of the Phong model is that, if we have normalized $\mathbf{r}$ and $\mathbf{n}$ to unit length, we can again use the dot product, and the specular term becomes

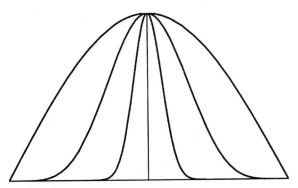

Figure 6.19 Effect of shininess coefficient.

$$I_s = k_s L_s (\mathbf{r} \cdot \mathbf{v})^\alpha.$$

We can add a distance term, as we did with diffuse reflections. What is referred to as the **Phong model**, including the distance term, is written

$$I = \frac{1}{a + bd + cd^2} (k_d L_d \mathbf{l} \cdot \mathbf{n} + k_s L_s (\mathbf{r} \cdot \mathbf{v})^\alpha) + k_a L_a.$$

This formula is computed for each light source and for each primary.

It might seem to make little sense either to associate a different amount of ambient light with each source, or to allow the components for specular and diffuse lighting to be different. Because we cannot solve the full rendering equation, we must use various tricks in an attempt to obtain realistic renderings. Consider, for example, an environment with many objects. When we turn on a light, some of that light will hit a surface directly. These contributions to the image can be modeled with specular and diffuse components of the source. However, much of the rest of the light from the source will be scattered from multiple reflections from other objects and will make a contribution to the light received at the surface under consideration. We can approximate this term by having an ambient component associated with the source. The shade that we should assign to this term depends on *both* the color of the source and the color of the objects in the room—an unfortunate consequence of our use of approximate models. To some extent, the same analysis holds for diffuse light. Diffuse light reflects among the surfaces, and the color that we see on a particular surface depends on other surfaces in the environment. Again, by using carefully separate diffuse and specular components with our light sources, we can attempt to approximate a global effect with local calculations.

Color Plate 25 shows a group of Utah teapots (Section 9.10) that have been rendered in OpenGL using the Phong model. Note that it is only our ability to control material properties that makes the teapots appear different from one another. The various teapots demonstrate how the Phong model can create a variety of surface effects, ranging from dull surfaces to highly reflective surfaces that look like metal.

We have developed the Phong model in object space. The actual shading, however, is not done until the objects have passed through the model-view and projection transformations. These transformations can affect the cosine terms in the model (see Exercise 6.22). Consequently, to make a correct shading calculation, we must either preserve the correct relationships as vertices and vectors pass through the pipeline, perhaps by sending additional information through the pipeline from object space, or go backward through the pipeline to obtain the required information when a shade needs to be determined.

6.4 Computation of Vectors

The illumination and reflection models that we have derived are sufficiently general that they can be applied to either curved or flat surfaces, to parallel or perspective views, and to distant or near surfaces. Most of the calculations for rendering a scene involve the determination of the required vectors and dot products. For each special case, simplifications are possible. For example, if the surface is a flat polygon, the normal is the same at all points on the surface. If the light source is far from the surface, the light direction is the same at all points.

In this section, we shall examine how the vectors are computed for the general case. In Section 6.5, we shall see what additional techniques can be applied when our objects are composed of flat polygons. This case is especially important, because most renderers, including OpenGL, render curved surfaces by approximating the surfaces with many small flat polygons.

6.4.1 Normal Vectors

For smooth surfaces, the vector normal to the surface exists at every point and gives the local orientation of the surface. Its calculation depends on how the surface is represented mathematically. Two simple cases—the plane and the sphere—will illustrate both how we compute normals and where the difficulties lie.

A plane can be described by the equation

$$ax + by + cz + d = 0.$$

As we saw in Chapter 4, this equation could also be written in terms of the normal to the plane $\mathbf{n}$, and a point $\mathbf{p}_0$, known to be on the plane, as

$$\mathbf{n} \cdot (\mathbf{p} - \mathbf{p}_0) = 0,$$

where $\mathbf{p}$ is any point (x, y, z) on the plane. Comparing the two forms, we see that the vector $\mathbf{n}$ is given by

$$\mathbf{n} = \begin{bmatrix} a \\ b \\ c \end{bmatrix},$$

or, in homogeneous coordinates,

$$\mathbf{n} = \begin{bmatrix} a \\ b \\ c \\ 0 \end{bmatrix}.$$

However, suppose that instead we are given three noncollinear points—$\mathbf{p}_0$, $\mathbf{p}_1$, $\mathbf{p}_2$—that are in this plane and thus are sufficient to determine it uniquely. The vectors $\mathbf{p}_2 - \mathbf{p}_0$ and $\mathbf{p}_1 - \mathbf{p}_0$ are parallel to the plane, and we can use their cross product to find the normal

$$\mathbf{n} = (\mathbf{p}_2 - \mathbf{p}_0) \times (\mathbf{p}_1 - \mathbf{p}_0).$$

We must be careful of the order of the vectors in the cross product. Reversing the order changes the surface from outward pointing to inward pointing, and that can affect the lighting calculations. Some graphics systems use the first three vertices in the specification of a polygon to determine the normal automatically. OpenGL does not do so, but, as we shall see in Section 6.5, forcing users to compute normals creates more flexibility in how we apply our lighting model.

For curved surfaces, how we compute normals depends on how we represent the surface. In Chapter 9, we shall discuss three different methods for representing curves and surfaces. We can see a few of the possibilities by considering how we represent a unit sphere centered at the origin. The usual equation for this sphere is the **implicit equation**

$$f(x, y, z) = x^2 + y^2 + z^2 - 1 = 0,$$

or, in vector form,

$$f(\mathbf{p}) = \mathbf{p} \cdot \mathbf{p} - 1 = 0.$$

The normal is given by the **gradient vector**, which is represented by the column matrix

$$\mathbf{n} = \begin{bmatrix} \dfrac{\partial f}{\partial x} \\[2mm] \dfrac{\partial f}{\partial y} \\[2mm] \dfrac{\partial f}{\partial z} \end{bmatrix} = \begin{bmatrix} 2x \\ 2y \\ 2z \end{bmatrix} = 2\mathbf{p}.$$

The sphere could also be represented in **parametric form**. In this form, the x, y, and z values of a point on the sphere are represented independently in terms of two parameters u and v:

$$x = x(u, v),$$
$$y = y(u, v),$$
$$z = z(u, v).$$

As we shall see in Chapter 9, this form is preferable in computer graphics, especially for representing curves and surfaces, although, for a particular surface, there may be multiple parametric representations. One parametric representation for the sphere is

$$x(u, v) = \cos u \sin v,$$
$$y(u, v) = \cos u \cos v,$$
$$z(u, v) = \sin u.$$

As u and v vary in the range $-\pi/2 < u < \pi/2$, $-\pi < v < \pi$, we get all the points on the sphere. When we are using the parametric form, we can obtain the normal from the **tangent plane**, shown in Figure 6.20, at a point $\mathbf{p}(u, v) = [\, x(u, v) \quad y(u, v) \quad z(u, v)\,]^T$ on the surface. The tangent plane gives the local orientation of the surface at a point; we can derive it by taking the linear terms of the Taylor series expansion of the surface at $\mathbf{p}$. The result is that, at $\mathbf{p}$, lines in the directions of the vectors represented by

Figure 6.20 Tangent plane to sphere.

$$\frac{\partial \mathbf{p}}{\partial u} = \begin{bmatrix} \dfrac{\partial x}{\partial u} \\[6pt] \dfrac{\partial y}{\partial u} \\[6pt] \dfrac{\partial z}{\partial u} \end{bmatrix}, \qquad \frac{\partial \mathbf{p}}{\partial v} = \begin{bmatrix} \dfrac{\partial x}{\partial v} \\[6pt] \dfrac{\partial y}{\partial v} \\[6pt] \dfrac{\partial z}{\partial v} \end{bmatrix}$$

lie in the tangent plane. We can use their cross product to obtain the normal

$$\mathbf{n} = \frac{\partial \mathbf{p}}{\partial u} \times \frac{\partial \mathbf{p}}{\partial v}.$$

For our sphere, we find that

$$\mathbf{n} = \cos u \begin{bmatrix} \cos u \sin v \\ \cos u \cos v \\ \sin u \end{bmatrix} = (\cos u)\mathbf{p}.$$

We are interested in only the direction of $\mathbf{n}$; thus, we can divide by $\cos u$ to obtain the unit normal to the sphere

$$\mathbf{n} = \mathbf{p}.$$

In Section 6.9, we shall use this result to shade a polygonal approximation to a sphere.

Within a graphics system, we usually work with a collection of vertices, and the normal vector is must be approximated from some set of points close to the point where the normal is needed. The pipeline architecture of real-time graphics systems makes this calculation difficult, because we process one vertex at a time, and thus the graphics system may not have the information available to compute the approximate normal at a given point. Consequently, graphics systems often leave the computation of normals to the user program.

In OpenGL, we can associate a normal with a vertex through functions such as

```
glNormal3f(nx, ny, nz);
glNormal3fv(pointer_to_normal);
```

Normals are modal variables. If we define a normal before a sequence of vertices through glVertex calls, this normal will be associated with all the vertices, and will be used for the lighting calculations at all the vertices. The problem remains, however, that we have to determine these normals ourselves.

6.4.2 Angle of Reflection

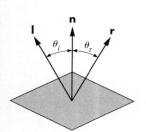

Figure 6.21 A mirror.

Once we have calculated the normal at a point, we can use this normal and the direction of the light source to compute the direction of a perfect reflection. An ideal mirror is characterized by the following statement: *The angle of incidence is equal to the angle of reflection.* These angles are as pictured in Figure 6.21. The **angle of incidence** is the angle between the normal and the light source (assumed to be a point source); the **angle of reflection** is the angle between the normal and the direction in which the light is reflected. In two dimensions, there is but a single angle satisfying the angle condition. In three dimensions, however, our statement is insufficient to compute the required angle; there is an infinite number of angles satisfying our condition. We must add the following statement: *At a point* **p** *on the surface, the incoming light ray, the reflected light ray, and the normal at the point must all lie in the same plane.* These two conditions are sufficient for us to determine **r** from **n** and **l**. Our primary interest is the direction rather than the magnitude of **r**. However, many of our rendering calculations will be easier if we deal with unit-length vectors. Hence, we shall assume that both **l** and **n** have been normalized such that

$$|\mathbf{l}| = |\mathbf{n}| = 1,$$

and we also want

$$|\mathbf{r}| = 1.$$

If $\theta_i = \theta_r$, then

$$\cos \theta_i = \cos \theta_r.$$

Using the dot product, the angle condition is

$$\cos \theta_i = \mathbf{l} \cdot \mathbf{n} = \cos \theta_r = \mathbf{n} \cdot \mathbf{r}.$$

The coplanar condition implies that we can write $\mathbf{r}$ as a linear combination of $\mathbf{l}$ and $\mathbf{n}$:

$$\mathbf{r} = \alpha \mathbf{l} + \beta \mathbf{n}.$$

Taking the dot product with $\mathbf{n}$, we find that

$$\mathbf{n} \cdot \mathbf{r} = \alpha \mathbf{l} \cdot \mathbf{n} + \beta = \mathbf{l} \cdot \mathbf{n}.$$

We can get a second condition between α and β from our requirement that $\mathbf{r}$ also be of unit length; thus,

$$1 = \mathbf{r} \cdot \mathbf{r} = \alpha^2 + 2\alpha\beta \mathbf{l} \cdot \mathbf{n} + \beta^2.$$

Solving these two equations, we find that

$$\mathbf{r} = 2(\mathbf{l} \cdot \mathbf{n})\mathbf{n} - \mathbf{l}.$$

6.4.3 Use of the Halfway Vector

If we use the Phong model with specular reflections in our rendering, the dot product $\mathbf{r} \cdot \mathbf{v}$ should be recalculated at every point on the surface. We can obtain an interesting approximation by using the unit vector halfway between the viewer vector and the light-source vector:

$$\mathbf{h} = \frac{\mathbf{l} + \mathbf{v}}{|\mathbf{l} + \mathbf{v}|}.$$

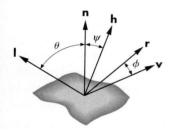

Figure 6.22 Determination of the halfway vector.

Figure 6.22 shows all five vectors. Here, we have defined ψ as the angle between $\mathbf{n}$ and $\mathbf{h}$, the **half-angle**. When $\mathbf{v}$ lies in the same plane as do $\mathbf{l}$, $\mathbf{n}$, and $\mathbf{r}$, we can show (Exercise 6.7) that

$$2\psi = \phi.$$

If we replace $\mathbf{r} \cdot \mathbf{v}$ with $\mathbf{n} \cdot \mathbf{h}$, we avoid calculation of $\mathbf{r}$. However, the halfway angle ψ is smaller that ϕ, and, if we use the same exponent e in $(\mathbf{n} \cdot \mathbf{h})^e$ that we used in $(\mathbf{r} \cdot \mathbf{v})^e$, the size of the specular highlights will be smaller. We can mitigate this problem by replacing the value of the exponent e with a value e', so that $(\mathbf{n} \cdot \mathbf{h})^{e'}$ is closer to $(\mathbf{r} \cdot \mathbf{v})^e$. It is clear that avoiding recalculation of $\mathbf{r}$ is desirable. However, to appreciate fully where savings can be made, you should consider all the cases of flat and curved surfaces, near and far light sources, and near and far viewers; see Exercise 6.8.

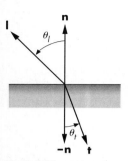

Figure 6.23 Perfect light transmission

6.4.4 Transmitted Light

Similar shading calculations apply if our model allows for transmitted light (as will our simple ray tracer in Section 6.10). Consider a surface that transmits all the light that strikes it, as shown in Figure 6.23. If the speed of light differs in the two materials, the light is bent at the surface. Let η_l and η_t be the **indices of refraction**—a measure of the relative speed of light in the two materials on the two sides of the surface. **Snell's law** (see Exercise 6.14) states that

$$\frac{\sin \theta_l}{\sin \theta_t} = \frac{\eta_t}{\eta_l}.$$

We can find the direction of the transmitted light **t** as follows. We know $\cos \theta_l$ from **n** and **l**; if they have been normalized, it is simply their dot product. Given $\cos \theta_t$, we can find $\sin \theta_t$, and from it $\sin \theta_l$. Letting $\eta = \eta_t/\eta_l$, we have

$$\cos \theta_t = \left(1 - \frac{1}{\eta^2}(1 - \cos^2 \theta_l)\right)^{\frac{1}{2}}.$$

Just as with reflected light, the three vectors must be coplanar; thus,

$$\mathbf{t} = \alpha \mathbf{n} + \beta \mathbf{l}.$$

If we further impose the condition that **t** have unit length, we can do a derivation, similar to that for the reflected vector, to find

$$\mathbf{t} = -\frac{1}{\eta}\mathbf{l} - \left(\cos \theta_t - \frac{1}{\eta} \cos \theta_l\right) \mathbf{n}.$$

The first two negative signs in this equation are a consequence of the fact that **t** points away from the back side of the surface. The angle for which the square-root term in the expression for $\cos \theta_t$ becomes zero ($\sin \theta_l = \eta$) is known as the **critical angle**. If light strikes the surface at this angle, the transmitted light is in a direction along the surface. If θ_l is increased further, all light is reflected, and none is transmitted.

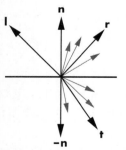

Figure 6.24 Light interaction at surface.

A more general expression for what happens at a transmitting surface corresponds to Figure 6.24. Some light is transmitted, some is reflected, and the rest is absorbed. Of the transmitted light, some is scattered in a manner similar to specular reflections, except that here the light is concentrated in the direction of **t**. Thus, a transmission model might include a term proportional to $\mathbf{t} \cdot \mathbf{v}$ for viewers on the transmitted side of the surface. We can also use the analogy of a half-angle to simplify calculation of this term (see Exercise 6.16).

6.5   Polygonal Shading

Assuming that we can compute normal vectors, given a set of light sources and a viewer, both the lighting and illumination models that we have devel-

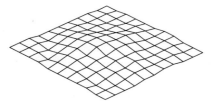

Figure 6.25 Polygonal mesh.

oped can be applied at every point on a surface. Unfortunately, even if we have simple equations to determine normal vectors, as we did in our example of a sphere (Section 6.4), the amount of computation required can be large. We have already seen the many of the advantages of using polygonal models for our objects. A further advantage is that, for flat polygons, we can significantly reduce the work required for shading. Most graphics systems, including OpenGL, exploit the efficiencies possible for rendering flat polygons by decomposing curved surfaces into many small flat polygons.

Consider a polygonal mesh, such as is shown in Figure 6.25, where each polygon is flat and thus has a well-defined normal vector. We shall consider three ways to shade the polygons: flat shading, interpolative or Gouraud shading, and Phong shading.

6.5.1 Flat Shading

The three vectors—l, n, and v—can vary as we move from point to point on a surface. For a flat polygon, however, n is constant. If we assume a distant viewer,[2] v is constant over the polygon. Finally, if the light source is distant, l is constant. Here, *distant* could be interpreted in the strict sense of meaning that the source is at infinity. The necessary adjustments, such as changing the *location* of the source to the *direction* of the source, could then be made to the shading equations and to their implementation. *Distant* could also be interpreted in terms of the size of the polygon relative to how far the polygon is from the source or viewer, as shown in Figure 6.26. Graphics systems or user programs can often exploit this latter definition.

If the three vectors are constant, then the shading calculation needs to be carried out only once for each polygon, and each point on the polygon will be assigned the same shade. This technique is known as **flat** or **constant shading**. In OpenGL, we specify flat shading through

```
glShadeModel(GL_FLAT);
```

---

[2] We can make this assumption in OpenGL by setting the near viewer flag to false.

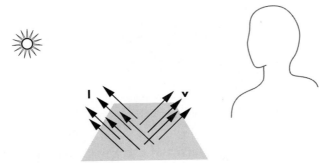

Figure 6.26 Distant source and viewer.

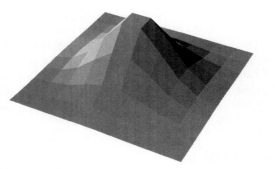

Figure 6.27 Flat shading of polygonal mesh.

If flat shading is in effect, OpenGL will use the normal associated with the first vertex of a single polygon for the shading calculation. For primitives such as a triangle strip, OpenGL uses the normal of the third vertex for the first triangle, the normal of the fourth for the second, and so on. Similar rules hold for other primitives, such as quadrilateral strips.

Flat shading will show differences in shading for the polygons in our mesh. If the light sources and viewer are near the polygon, the vectors $\mathbf{l}$ and $\mathbf{v}$ will be different for each polygon. However, if our polygonal mesh has been designed to model a smooth surface, flat shading will almost always be disappointing, because we shall see even small differences in shading between adjacent polygons, as shown in Figure 6.27. The human visual system has a remarkable sensitivity to small differences in light intensity, due to a property known as **lateral inhibition**. If we see an increasing sequence of intensities, as is shown in Figure 6.28, we perceive the increases in brightness as overshooting on one side of an intensity step and undershooting on the other, as shown in Figure 6.29. We see stripes, known as **Mach bands**, along the edges. This phenomenon is a consequence on how the cones in the eye are connected to the optic nerve, and there is little that we can do to avoid it, other than looking for smoother shad-

Figure 6.28 Step chart.

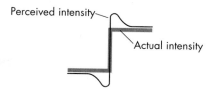

Figure 6.29 Perceived and actual intensities at an edge.

ing techniques that will not produce large differences in shades at the edges of polygons.

6.5.2 Interpolative and Gouraud Shading

In our rotating-cube example of Section 4.9, we saw that OpenGL will interpolate colors assigned to vertices across a polygon. If we set the shading model to be smooth via

```
glShadeModel(GL_SMOOTH);
```

then OpenGL will interpolate colors for other primitives such as lines. Suppose that we have enabled both smooth shading and lighting, and that we assign to each vertex the normal of the polygon being shaded. The lighting calculation will be made at each vertex, determining a vertex color, using the material properties and the vectors $\mathbf{v}$ and $\mathbf{l}$ computed for each vertex. Note that, if the light source is distant, and either the viewer is distant or there are no specular reflections, then interpolative shading will shade a polygon in a constant color.

If we consider our mesh, the idea of a normal existing at a vertex should cause concern to anyone worried about mathematical correctness. Because multiple polygons meet at interior vertices of the mesh, each of which has its own normal, the normal at the vertex is discontinuous. Although this situation might complicate the mathematics, Gouraud realized that the normal at the vertex could be *defined* in a way to achieve smoother shading through interpolation. Consider an interior vertex, as shown in Figure 6.30, where four polygons meet. Each has its own normal. In **Gouraud shading**, we define the normal at a vertex to be the normalized average of the normals of the polygons that share the vertex. For our example, the **vertex normal** is given by

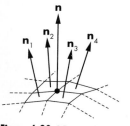

Figure 6.30 Normals near interior vertex.

$$\mathbf{n} = \frac{\mathbf{n}_1 + \mathbf{n}_2 + \mathbf{n}_3 + \mathbf{n}_4}{|\mathbf{n}_1 + \mathbf{n}_2 + \mathbf{n}_3 + \mathbf{n}_4|}.$$

From an OpenGL perspective, Gouraud shading is deceptively simple. We need only to set the vertex normals correctly. Often, the literature makes no distinction between interpolative and Gouraud shading. However, there is a problem. How do we find the normals that we should average together? If our program

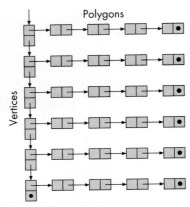

Figure 6.31 Mesh data structure.

is linear, specifying a list of vertices (and other properties), we do not have the necessary information about which polygons share a vertex. What we need, of course, is a data structure for representing the mesh. Traversing this data structure can generate the vertices with the averaged normals. Such a data structure should contain, minimally, polygons, vertices, normals, and material properties. One possible structure is the one shown in Figure 6.31. The key element that must be represented in the data structure is which polygons meet at each vertex.

Color Plates 3–5 show a progression of shading effects available in OpenGL. In Plate 3, there is no shading, and even though hidden surfaces have been removed, the image is flat. In Color Plate 4, there is a single light source, but each polygon has been rendered with a single shade (constant shading), computed using the Phong model. In Color Plate 5, normals have been assigned to all the vertices. OpenGL then computed shades for the vertices and interpolated these shades over the faces of the polygons.

Color Plate 22 contains another illustration of the smooth shading provided by OpenGL. We used this color cube as an example in both Chapter 2 and Chapter 3, and the programs are in Appendix A. The eight vertices are colored black, white, red, green, blue, cyan, magenta, and yellow. Once smooth shading is enabled, OpenGL interpolates the colors across the faces of the polygons automatically.

6.5.3 Phong Shading

Even the smoothness introduced by Gouraud shading may not prevent the appearance of Mach bands. Phong proposed that, instead of interpolating vertex intensities, as we do in Gouraud shading, we interpolate normals across each polygon. Consider a polygon that shares edges and vertices with other polygons in the mesh, as shown in Figure 6.32. We can compute vertex normals by interpolating over the normals of the polygons that share the vertex. Next, we

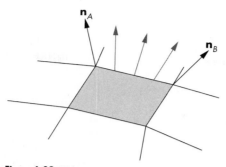

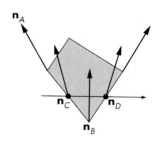

Figure 6.32 Edge normals.

Figure 6.33 Interpolation of normals in Phong shading.

can use bilinear interpolation, as we did in Chapter 4, to interpolate the normals over the polygon. Consider Figure 6.33. We can use the interpolated normals at vertices A and B to interpolate normals along the edge between them:

$$\mathbf{n}(\alpha) = (1 - \alpha)\mathbf{n}_A + \alpha\mathbf{n}_B.$$

We can do a similar interpolation on all the edges. The normal at any interior point can be obtained from points on the edges by

$$\mathbf{n}(\alpha, \beta) = (1 - \beta)\mathbf{n}_C + \beta\mathbf{n}_D.$$

Once we have the normal at each point, we can make an independent shading calculation. Usually, this process will be combined with the scan conversion of the polygon, so that the line between C and D projects to a scan line in the frame buffer. We shall examine such issues in Chapter 7.

Phong shading will produce renderings smoother than those of Gouraud shading, but at a significantly greater computational cost; see Exercise 6.23. Although there exist various hardware implementations for Gouraud shading, and the latter represents only a slight increase in the time required for rendering, the same cannot be said for Phong shading. Consequently, Phong shading is almost always done off-line.

6.6 Approximation of a Sphere by Recursive Subdivision

We have used the sphere as an example curved surface to illustrate shading calculations. However, the sphere is not an object that is supported within OpenGL. Both the GL utility library (GLU) and the GL Utility Toolkit (GLUT) contain spheres; the former by supporting quadric surfaces, a topic that we shall discuss in Chapter 9, and the latter through a polygonal approximation.

We shall develop our own polygonal approximation to a sphere. It will provide a basis for writing simple programs that illustrate the interactions between shading parameters and polygonal approximations to curved surfaces. Now, we shall introduce **recursive subdivision**, a powerful technique for generating approximations to curves and surfaces to any desired level of accuracy.

Our starting point is a tetrahedron, although we could start with any regular polygon whose facets could be divided initially into triangles.[3] The regular tetrahedron is composed of four equilateral triangles, determined by four vertices. We shall start with the four vertices $(0, 0, 1)$, $(0, 2\sqrt{2}/3, -1/3)$, $(-\sqrt{6}/3, -\sqrt{2}/3, -1/3)$, $(\sqrt{6}/3, -\sqrt{2}/3, -1/3)$. All four lie on the unit sphere, centered at the origin. Exercise 6.6 suggests one method for finding these points.

We get a first approximation by drawing a wireframe for the tetrahedron. We define the four vertices globally using our point type from Chapter 4,

```
point  v[4]={{0.0, 0.0, 1.0}, {0.0, 0.942809, -0.333333},
   {-0.816497, -0.471405, -0.333333},
   {0.816497, -0.471405, -0.333333}};
```

We can draw triangles via the function

```
void triangle( point a, point b, point c)
{
    glBegin(GL_LINE_LOOP);
        glVertex3fv(a);
        glVertex3fv(b);
        glVertex3fv(c);
    glEnd();
}
```

The tetrahedron can be drawn by

```
void tetrahedron(void)
{
    triangle(v[0], v[1], v[2] );
    triangle(v[3], v[2], v[1] );
    triangle(v[0], v[3], v[1] );
    triangle(v[0], v[2], v[3] );
}
```

The order of vertices obeys the right-hand rule, so we can convert the code to draw shaded polygons with little difficulty. If we add the usual code for initialization, our program will generate an image such as that in Figure 6.34: a simple regular polyhedron, but a poor approximation to a sphere.

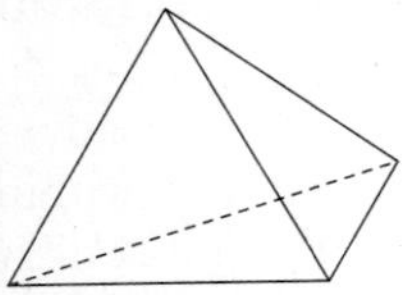

Figure 6.34 Tetrahedron.

---

[3] The regular icosahedron is composed of 12 equilateral triangles; it makes a nice starting point for generating spheres; see [Ope93a].

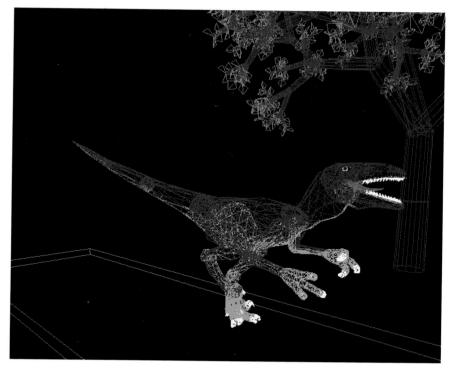

Plate 1 Wireframe model of dinosaur and environment. (Courtesy of Philip Eckenroth, Michael Tipping, Marilee Padilla, Joey Madrigal, University of New Mexico)

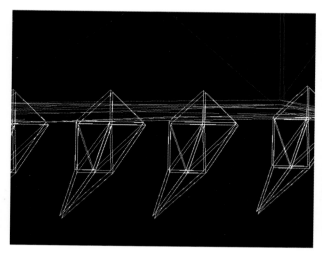

(a) No antialiasing.

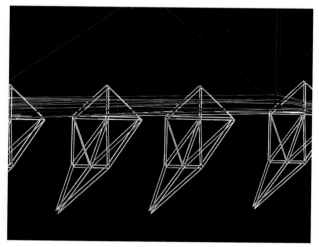

(b) With antialiasing.

Plate 2 Area of dinosaur teeth.
(Courtesy of Philip Eckenroth, Michael Tipping, Marilee Padilla, Joey Madrigal, University of New Mexico)

Plate 3 Flat shading (no light source) of dinosaur and environment. (Courtesy of Philip Eckenroth, Michael Tipping, Marilee Padilla, Joey Madrigal, University of New Mexico)

Plate 4 Constant shading of dinosaur and environment with one light source. (Courtesy of Philip Eckenroth, Michael Tipping, Marilee Padilla, Joey Madrigal, University of New Mexico)

Plate 5 Smooth shading of dinosaur and environment with one light source. (Courtesy of Philip Eckenroth, Michael Tipping, Marilee Padilla, Joey Madrigal, University of New Mexico)

Plate 6 Dinosaur and environment with texture mapping. (Courtesy of Philip Eckenroth, Michael Tipping, Marilee Padilla, Joey Madrigal, University of New Mexico)

Plate 7 Dinosaur and environment with fractal mountains. (Courtesy of Philip Eckenroth, Michael Tipping, Marilee Padilla, Joey Madrigal, University of New Mexico)

Plate 8 Dinosaur and environment with fog added. (Courtesy of Philip Eckenroth, Michael Tipping, Marilee Padilla, University of New Mexico)

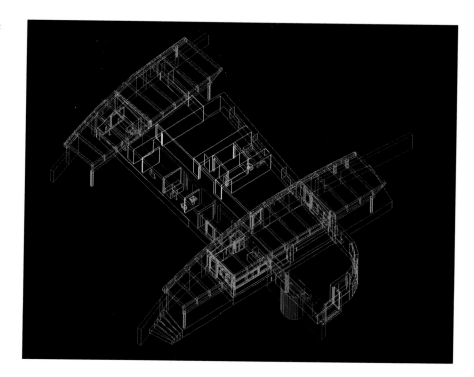

Plate 9 Axonometric wire frame of house design. (Courtesy of Richard Nordhaus, School of Architecture and Planning, University of New Mexico)

Plate 10 Perspective rendering of house design. (Courtesy of Richard Nordhaus, School of Architecture and Planning, University of New Mexico)

Plate 11 Factory environment from video "I thought, therefore I was." (Courtesy of James Pinkerton, Thomas Keller, Brian Jones, John Bell, University of New Mexico and Sandia National Laboratories)

Plate 12 Robot "Ed" from video "I thought, therefore I was." (Courtesy of James Pinkerton, Thomas Keller, Brian Jones, John Bell, University of New Mexico and Sandia National Laboratories)

Plate 13 Computer-modeled flower from video "I thought, therefore I was." (Courtesy of David Rogers, University of New Mexico)

Plate 14 Welding scene from video "I thought, therefore I was." (Courtesy of James Pinkerton, Thomas Keller, Brian Jones, John Bell, University of New Mexico and Sandia National Laboratories)

Plate 15 Graphical design of robotic workcell. Rendering uses texture mapping to simulate realistic environment.
(Courtesy of Sandia National Laboratories)

Plate 16 Physical robot and its graphical model. The graphical model is used for design, path planning, and simulation.
(Courtesy of Sandia National Laboratories)

Plate 17 Snapshot from the Pad++ World Wide Web browser with several pages loaded. Pad++ is a graphical user interface that eliminates some of the restrictions of typical window systems. The interface is based on zooming, so data can appear at any location at any size. (Courtesy of B. Bederson, J. Hollan, D. Vick, D. Rogers, J. Stewart, A. Druin, University of New Mexico)

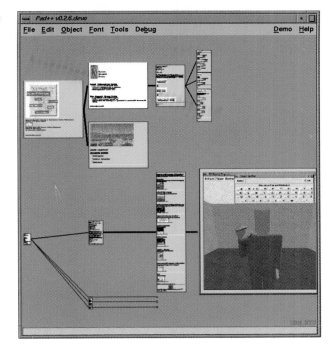

Plate 18 Scene from Nar: A study in using textures to define 3D space as opposed to using 3D perspective. (Courtesy of Thomas Keller, Director)

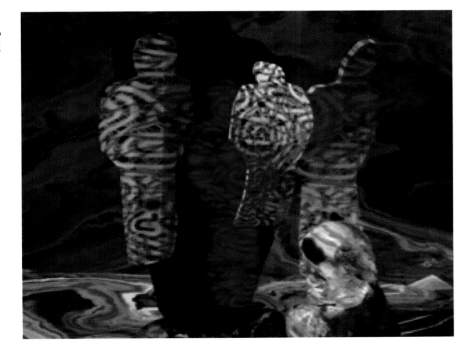

Plate 19 Fluid dynamics of the mantle of the Earth. Pseudocolor mapping of temperatures and iso-temperature surface. (Courtesy of Los Alamos National Laboratory)

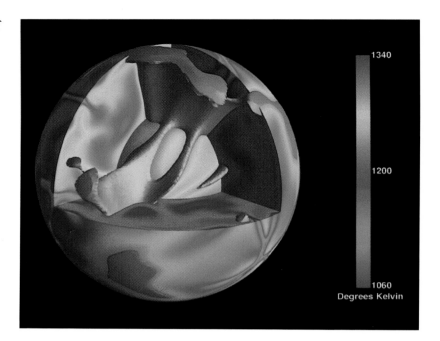

Plate 20 Volume-rendered image of head by parallel ray casting. Skin rendered as transparent, muscle rendered as opaque. (Courtesy of Los Alamos National Laboratory)

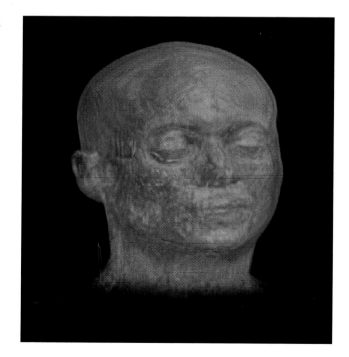

Plate 21 RGB color cube. (Courtesy of University of New Mexico)

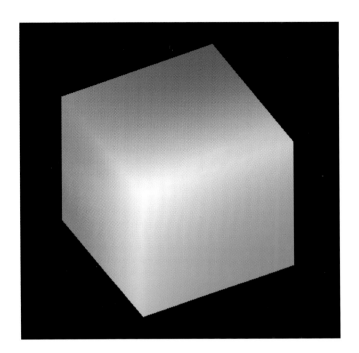

Plate 22 A VR system that allows interaction of partici-pants (represented by the Jack™ figure) and artificial agents (represented by the Improv™ dancer) in a fully texture-mapped environ-ment. A participant inter-acts with a computer-driven agent. Both Avatars and computer-controlled agents inhabit and interact with VR worlds such as this air-port, modeled after the building found in Albu-querque, New Mexico. (Courtesy of Sandia National Laboratories)

Plate 23 Rendering using ray tracer. (Courtesy of Patrick McCormick, University of New Mexico and Los Alamos National Laboratory)

Plate 24 Jerusalem City Hall. Radiosity-rendered image. (Courtesy of Lightscape Technologies, Inc.)

Plate 25 Array of Utah teapots with different material properties.
(Courtesy of Silicon Graphics, Inc.)

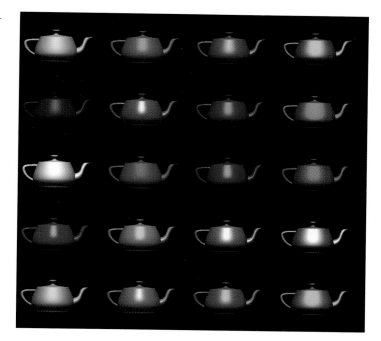

(Courtesy of Pat Crossno, University of New Mexico and Sandia National Laboratories)

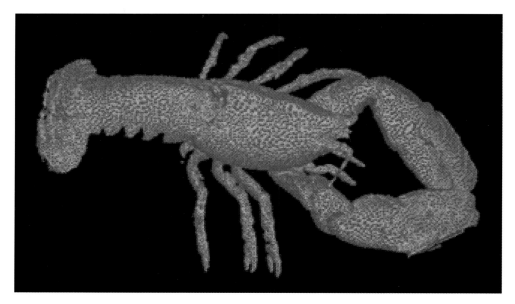

Plate 27 Volume rendering of lobster data set using a system of particles.
(Courtesy of Pat Crossno, University of New Mexico and Sandia National Laboratories)

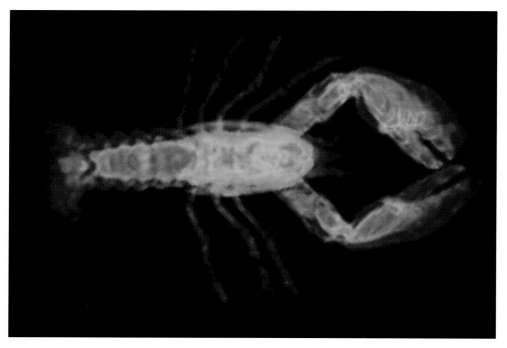

Plate 28 Volume rendering of lobster data set using splatting.
(Courtesy of Lee Ann Fisk, University of New Mexico and Sandia National Laboratories)

Plate 29 A variety of equipment is used to allow people to interact in a virtual world. This photo shows participants using headmounts with headphones to receive audio and visual output from the system. In addition, these participants are equipped with magnetic trackers which inform the VR system about locations of selected areas of their bodies, and pressure sensors (located in the palm straps), which inform the system about the state of the participants' hands. (Courtesy of Sandia National Laboratories)

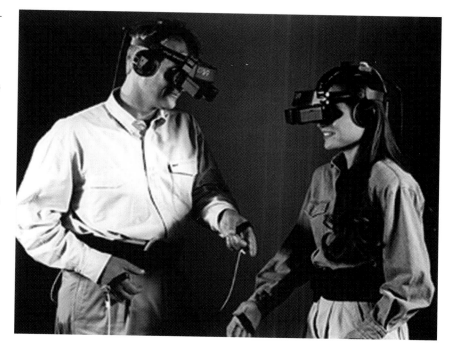

Plate 30 Finished frame from *Tin Toy* showing lighting, texture, and environmental maps. (Copyright Pixar Animation Studios)

(b) Model of Lexus with surface.

(d) Mesh blown away from Lexus.

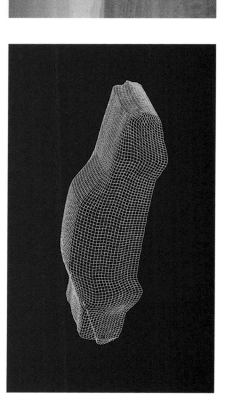

(a) Mesh of particles.

(c) Wind blowing mesh off Lexus.

Plate 31   Particle system. (Courtesy of Lexus and Rhythm and Hues)

We can get a closer approximation to the sphere by subdividing each facet of the tetrahedron into smaller triangles. Subdividing into triangles will ensure that all the new facets will be flat. There are at least three ways to do the subdivision, as shown in Figure 6.35. We can bisect each of the angles of the triangle, and draw the three bisectors, which meet at a common point, thus generating three new triangles. We can also compute the center of mass (centrum) of the vertices by simply averaging them, and then drawing lines from this point to the three vertices, again generating three triangles. However, these techniques do not preserve the equilateral triangles that make up the regular tetrahedron. Instead—recalling a possible construction for the Sierpinski gasket of Chapter 2—we can connect the bisectors of the sides of the triangle, forming four equilateral triangles, as shown in Figure 6.35(c). We shall use this technique for our example.

(a)   (b)   (c)

Figure 6.35 Subdivision of a triangle by (a) bisecting angles (b) computing the centrum (c) bisecting sides.

After we have subdivided a facet as was just described, the four new triangles will still be in the same plane as the original triangle. We can move the new vertices that we created by bisection to the unit sphere by normalizing each bisected vertex, using a simple normalization function, such as

```
void normal(point p)
{
    double d=0.0;
    int i;
    for(i=0; i<3; i++) d+=p[i]*p[i];
    d=sqrt(d);
    if(d > 0.0) for(i=0; i<2; i++) p[i]/=d;
}
```

We can now subdivide a single triangle, defined by the vertices numbered a, b, and c, by the code

```
point v1, v2, v3;
int j;
for(j=0; j<3; j++) v1[j]=v[a][j]+v[b][j];
normal(v1);
for(j=0; j<3; j++) v2[j]=v[a][j]+v[c][j];
normal(v2);
```

```
for(j=0; j<3; j++) v3[j]=v[c][j]+v[b][j];
normal(v3);
triangle(v[a], v2, v1);
triangle(v[c], v3, v2);
triangle(v[b], v1, v3);
triangle(v1, v2, v3);
```

We can use this code in our tetrahedron routine to generate 16 triangles rather than 4, but we would rather be able to repeat the subdivision process *n* times to generate successively closer approximations to the sphere. By calling the subdivision routine recursively, we can control the number of subdivisions.

First, we make the tetrahedron routine depend on the depth of recursion by adding an argument n:

```
void tetrahedron(int n)
{
      divide_triangle(v[0], v[1], v[2] , n);
      divide_triangle(v[3], v[2], v[1], n );
      divide_triangle(v[0], v[3], v[1], n );
      divide_triangle(v[0], v[2], v[3], n );
}
```

The divide_triangle function will call itself to subdivide further if n is greater than zero, but will generate triangles if n has been reduced to zero. Here is the code:

```
divide_triangle(point a, point b, point c, int n)
{
  point v1, v2, v3;
  int j;
  if(n>0)
  {
      for(j=0; j<3; j++) v1[j]=a[j]+b[j];
      normal(v1);
      for(j=0; j<3; j++) v2[j]=a[j]+c[j];
      normal(v2);
      for(j=0; j<3; j++) v3[j]=c[j]+b[j];
      normal(v3);
      divide_triangle(a ,v2, v1, n-1);
      divide_triangle(c ,v3, v2, n-1);
      divide_triangle(b ,v1, v3, n-1);
      divide_triangle(v1 ,v2, v3, n-1);
  }
  else triangle(a, b, c);
}
```

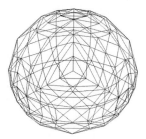

Figure 6.36 Sphere approximations using subdivision.

Figure 6.36 shows an approximation to the sphere drawn with this code. We now turn to adding lighting and shading to our sphere approximation. First, we must examine how lighting and shading are handled by the API.

6.7 Light Sources in OpenGL

OpenGL supports the four types of light sources that we just described, and allows at least eight light sources in a program. Each must be individually specified and enabled. Although there are many parameters that must be specified, they are exactly the parameters required by the Phong model. The OpenGL functions

```
glLightfv(source, parameter, pointer_to_array);
glLightf(source, parameter, value);
```

allow us to set the required vector and scalar parameters, respectively. There are four vector parameters that we can set: the position (or direction) of the light source, and the amount of ambient, diffuse, and specular light associated with the source.

For example, suppose that we wish to specify the first source GL_LIGHT0, and to locate it at the point $(1.0, 2.0, 3.0)$. We store its position as a point in homogeneous coordinates:

```
GLfloat light_0_pos[]={1.0, 2.0, 3.0, 1.0};
```

With the fourth component set to zero, the point source becomes a distant source with direction vector

```
GLfloat light_0_dir[]={1.0, 2.0, 3.0, 0.0};
```

For our single light source, if we want a white specular component, and red ambient and diffuse components, we can use the code

```
GLfloat light_0_dir[]={1.0, 2.0, 3.0, 0.0};
GLfloat diffuse_0[]={1.0, 0.0, 0.0, 1.0};
GLfloat ambient_0[]={1.0, 0.0, 0.0, 1.0};
GLfloat specular_0[]={1.0, 1.0, 1.0, 1.0};
```

```
glEnable{GL_LIGHTING};
glEnable{GL_LIGHT0);

glLightfv(GL_LIGHT0, GL_POSITION, light_0_pos);
glLightfv(GL_LIGHT0, GL_AMBIENT, ambient_0);
glLightfv(GL_LIGHT0, GL_DIFFUSE, diffuse_0);
glLightfv(GL_LIGHT0, GL_SPECULAR, specular_0);
```

Note that we must enable both lighting and the particular source.

We can also add a global ambient term that is independent of any of the sources. For example, if we want a small amount of white light, we can use the code

```
GLfloat global_ambient[]={0.1, 0.1, 0.1, 1.0};
```

```
glLightModelfv(GL_LIGHT_MODEL_AMBIENT, global_ambient);
```

The distance terms are based on the distance-attenuation model,

$$f(d) = \frac{1}{a + bd + cd^2},$$

which contains constant, linear, and quadratic terms. These terms are set via glLightf; for example,

```
glLightf(GL_LIGHT0, GL_CONSTANT_ATTENUATION, a);
```

We can convert a positional source to a spotlight by choosing the spotlight direction (GL_SPOT_DIRECTION), the exponent (GL_SPOT_EXPONENT), and the angle (GL_SPOT_CUTOFF). All three are specified by glLightf and glLightfv.

There are two other light parameters provided by OpenGL that we should mention: GL_LIGHT_MODEL_LOCAL_VIEWER and GL_LIGHT_MODEL_TWO_SIDE. Lighting calculations can be time consuming. If the viewer is assumed to be an infinite distance from the scene, then the calculation of reflections is easier, because the direction to the viewer from any point in the scene is unchanged. The default in OpenGL is to make this approximation, because its effect on many scenes is minimal. If you prefer that the full light calculation be made, using the true position of the viewer, you can change the model by using

Figure 6.37 Shading of convex objects.

```
glLightModeli(GL_LIGHT_MODEL_LOCAL_VIEWER, GL_TRUE);
```

In Chapter 4, we saw that a surface has both a front face and a back face. For polygons, front and back are determined by the order in which the vertices are specified, using the right-hand rule. For most objects, we see only the front faces, so we are not concerned with how OpenGL shades the back-facing surfaces. For example, for convex objects, such as a sphere or a parallelepiped (Figure 6.37), the viewer can never see a back face, regardless of where she is positioned. However, if we remove a side from a cube, or slice the sphere, as shown in Figure 6.38, a properly placed viewer may see a back face; thus, we

Figure 6.38 Visible back surfaces.

must shade both the front and back faces correctly. We can ensure that OpenGL handles both faces correctly by invoking the function

```
glLightModel(GL_LIGHT_MODEL_TWO_SIDED, GL_TRUE);
```

Light sources are objects, just like polygons and points. Hence, light sources are affected by the OpenGL model-view transformation. We can define them at the desired position, or define them in a convenient position and move them to the desired position by the model-view transformation. The basic rule governing object placement is that vertices are converted to eye coordinates by the model-view transformation that is in effect at the time the vertices are defined. Thus, by careful placement of the light-source specifications relative to the definition of other geometric objects, we can create light sources that remain stationary while the objects move, light sources that move while objects remain stationary, and light sources that move with the objects.

6.8 Specification of Materials in OpenGL

Material properties in OpenGL match up directly with the supported light sources and with the Phong reflection model. We can also specify different material properties for the front and back faces of a surface. All our reflection parameters are specified through the functions

```
glMaterialfv(face, type, pointer_to_array);
glMaterialf(face, value);
```

For example, we might define ambient, diffuse, and specular reflectivity coefficients (k_a, k_d, k_s) for each primary color through three arrays:

```
GLfloat ambient[] = {0.2, 0.2, 0.2, 1.0};
GLfloat diffuse[] = {1.0, 0.8, 0.0, 1.0};
GLfloat specular[]={1.0, 1.0, 1.0, 1.0};
```

Here, we have defined a small amount of white ambient reflectivity, yellow diffuse properties, and white specular reflections. We set the material properties for the front and back faces by the calls

```
glMaterialfv(GL_FRONT_AND_BACK, GL_AMBIENT, ambient);
glMaterialfv(GL_FRONT_AND_BACK, GL_DIFFUSE, diffuse);
glMaterialfv(GL_FRONT_AND_BACK, GL_SPECULAR, specular);
```

Note that, if both the specular and diffuse coefficients are the same (as is often the case), we can specify both by using GL_DIFFUSE_AND_SPECULAR for the type parameter. To specify different front- and back-face properties, we use GL_FRONT and GL_BACK. The shininess of a surface—the exponent in the specular-reflection term—is specified by glMaterialf; for example,

```
glMaterialf(GL_FRONT_AND_BACK, GL_SHININESS, 100.0);
```

Material properties are modal. Their values remain the same until changed, and, when changed, like other modal parameters, affect only surfaces defined after the change.[4]

OpenGL also allows us to define surfaces that have an emissive component that characterizes self-luminous sources. That method is useful if you want a light source to appear in your image. This term is unaffected by any of the light sources, and it does not affect any other surfaces. It adds a fixed color to the surfaces and is specified in a manner similar to other material properties. For example,

```
GLfloat emission[]={0.0, 0.3, 0.3, 1.0};

glMaterialfv(GL_FRONT_AND_BACK, GL_EMISSION, emission);
```

defines a small amount of blue–green (cyan) emission.

6.9   Shading of the Sphere Model

We can now shade our spheres. Here, we shall omit our standard OpenGL initialization; the complete programs are given in Appendix A.

If we are to shade our approximate spheres with OpenGL's shading model, we must assign normals. One simple, but illustrative, choice is to flat shade each triangle, using the three vertices to determine a normal, and then to assign this normal to the first vertex. Following our approach of Section 6.6, we use the cross product, and then normalize the result. A cross-product function is

```
cross(point a, point b, point c, point d);
{
    d[0]=(b[1]-a[1])*(c[2]-a[2])-(b[2]-a[2])*(c[1]-a[1]);
    d[1]=(b[2]-a[2])*(c[0]-a[0])-(b[0]-a[0])*(c[2]-a[2]);
    d[2]=(b[0]-a[0])*(c[1]-a[1])-(b[1]-a[1])*(c[0]-a[0]);
    normal(d);
}
```

Assuming that light sources have been defined and enabled, we can change the triangle routine to produce shaded spheres:

```
void triangle( point a, point b, point c)
{
    point n;
```

---

[4] OpenGL contains another method that you can use to change material properties; it uses the function glColorMaterial. It is more efficient for changing material properties, but is less general than the method using glMaterial.

```
    cross(a, b, c, n);
    glBegin(GL_POLYGON);
    glNormal3fv(n);
    glVertex3fv(a);
    glVertex3fv(b);
    glVertex3fv(c);
    glEnd();
}
```

The result of flat shading our spheres is shown in Figure 6.39. Note that, even as we increase the number of subdivisions so that the interior of the spheres appears smooth, we can still see edges of polygons around the outside of the sphere image. This type of outline is called a **silhouette edge**.

We can easily apply interpolative shading to the sphere models, because we know that the normal at each point **p** on the surface is in the direction from the origin to **p**. We can then assign the true normal to each vertex, and OpenGL will interpolate the shades at these vertices across each triangle. Thus, we change `triangle` to

Figure 6.39 Flat–shaded spheres.

```
void triangle( point a, point b, point c)
{
    point n;
    int i;
    glBegin(GL_POLYGON);
        for(i=0;i<3;i++) n[i]=a[i]:
        normal(n);
        glNormal3fv(n);
        glVertex3fv(a);
        for(i=0;i<3;i++) n[i]=b[i]:
        normal(n);
        glNormal3fv(n);
        glVertex3fv(b);
        for(i=0;i<3;i++) n[i]=c[i]:
        normal(n);
        glNormal3fv(n);
        glVertex3fv(c);
    glEnd();
}
```

The results of this definition of the normals are shown in Figure 6.40.

Although using the true normals produces a rendering more realistic than flat shading, the example is not general, because we have used normals that are known analytically. We also have not provided a true Gouraud-shaded image. Suppose that we want a Gouraud-shaded image of our approximate sphere. At each vertex, we need to know the normals of all polygons incident at the vertex.

Figure 6.40 Shading of the sphere with the true normals.

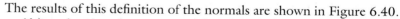

Our code does not have a data structure that contains the required information. Try Exercises 6.9 and 6.10, in which you construct such a structure. Note that six polygons meet at a vertex created by subdivision, whereas only three polygons meet at the original vertices of the tetrahedron.

6.10 Global Rendering

There are limitations imposed by the local lighting model that we have used. Consider, for example, an array of spheres illuminated by a distant source, as shown in Figure 6.41(a). The spheres close to the source will block some of the light from the source from reaching the other spheres. However, if we use our local model, each sphere will be shaded independently; all will appear the same to the viewer (Figure 6.41b). If these spheres are specular, in a real scene, some light will be scattered among spheres. Our lighting model cannot handle this situation. It also cannot produce shadows.[5]

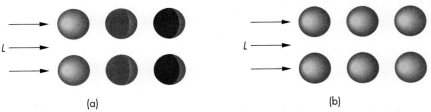

Figure 6.41 Array of shaded spheres. (a) Global lighting model. (b) Local lighting model.

If these effects are important, then we can use more sophisticated (and slower) rendering techniques, such as ray tracing and radiosity. We shall describe briefly these two complementary methods. Ray tracing works well for highly specular surfaces, such as in scenes composed of highly reflective and translucent objects such as glass balls. Radiosity is best suited for scenes with perfectly diffuse surfaces, such as interiors of buildings.

6.10.1 Ray Tracing

In many ways, ray tracing is an extension of our approach to rendering with a local lighting model. It is based on our previous observation that, of the rays of light leaving a source, the only ones that contribute to our image are those that enter the lens of our synthetic camera and pass through the center of projection.

---

[5] We can create shadows without global lighting by projecting objects onto surfaces and thus creating *shadow polygons*; see Exercise 6.19.

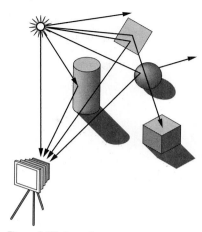

Figure 6.42 Rays leaving source.

Figure 6.42 shows several of the possible interactions with a single point source and perfectly specular surfaces. Rays can enter the lens of the camera directly from the source, from interactions with a surface visible to the camera, after multiple reflections from surfaces, or after transmission through one or more surfaces.

Most of the rays that leave a source will not enter the lens and will not contribute to our image. Hence, attempting to follow all rays from a light source is a hopeless endeavor. However, if we reverse the direction of the rays, and consider only those rays that start at the center of projection, we know that these **cast rays** must contribute to the image. Consequently, we start our ray tracer as shown in Figure 6.43. Here, we have included the image plane, and have ruled it into pixel-sized areas. Knowing that we must assign a color to every pixel, we must cast at least one ray through each pixel. Each cast ray either will intersect a surface or a light source, or will go off to infinity without striking anything. Pixels corresponding to this latter case can be assigned a background color. Rays that strike surfaces—for now, we can assume that all surfaces are opaque— require us to calculate a shade for the point of intersection. If we were simply to compute the shade at the point of intersection, using the Phong model, we would produce the same image as would our local renderer. However, we can do much more.

Note that the process that we have described thus far requires all the same steps as we use in our pipeline renderer: object modeling, projection, and visible-surface determination. However, the order in which the calculations are carried out is different. The pipeline renderer works on a vertex-by-vertex basis; the ray tracer works on a pixel-by-pixel basis. We shall consider the implications of this difference in Chapter 7.

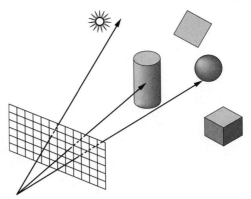

Figure 6.43 Ray-casting model.

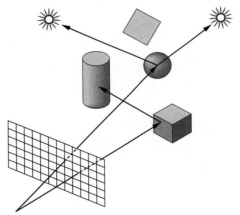

Figure 6.44 Shadow rays.

In ray tracing, rather than immediately applying our reflection model, we first check whether the point of intersection between the cast ray and the surface is illuminated. We compute **shadow** or **feeler rays** (Figure 6.44) from the point on the surface to each source. If a shadow ray intersects a surface before it meets the source, the light is blocked from reaching the point under consideration and this point is in shadow, at least from this source. No lighting calculation needs to be done for sources that are blocked from a point on the surface. If all surfaces are opaque and we do not consider light scattered from surface to surface, we have an image that has shadows added to what we have already done without ray tracing. The price that we pay is the cost of doing a type of hidden-surface calculation for each point of intersection between a cast ray and a surface.

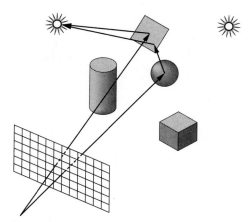

Figure 6.45 Ray tracing with mirrors.

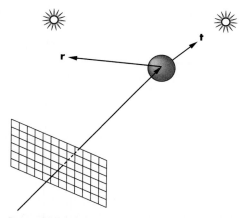

Figure 6.46 Ray tracing with reflection and transmission.

Suppose that some of our surfaces are highly reflective, like those shown in Figure 6.45. We can follow the shadow ray as it bounces from surface to surface, until it either goes off to infinity or intersects a source. Such calculations are usually done recursively, and take into account any absorption of light at surfaces.

Ray tracing is particularly good at handling surfaces that are both reflecting and transmitting. Using our basic paradigm, we follow a cast ray to a surface (Figure 6.46) with the property that, if a ray from a source strikes a point, then the light from the source is partially absorbed, and some of this light contributes to the diffuse reflection term. The rest of the incoming light is divided between a transmitted ray and a reflected ray. From the perspective of

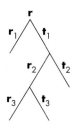
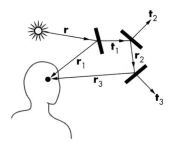
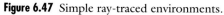

Figure 6.47 Simple ray-traced environments.

Figure 6.48 Ray tree corresponding to previous figure.

the cast ray, if a light source is visible at the intersection point, then we need to do three tasks. First, we must compute the contribution from the light source at the point, using our standard reflection model. Second, we must cast a ray in the direction of a perfect reflection. Third, we must cast a ray in the direction of the transmitted ray. These two rays are treated just like the original cast ray; that is, they are intersected (if possible) with other surfaces, end at a source, or go off to infinity. At each surface that these rays intersect, additional rays may be generated by reflection and transmission of light. Figure 6.47 shows a single cast ray and the path that it can follow through a simple environment. Figure 6.48 shows the **ray tree** generated. This tree shows which rays must be traced; it is constructed dynamically by the ray-tracing process.

The easiest way to describe a ray tracer is recursively, through a single function that traces a ray and calls itself for the reflected and transmitted rays (see Exercises 6.17 and 6.18). Most of the work in ray tracing goes into the calculation of intersections between rays and surfaces. It is difficult to implement a ray tracer that can handle a variety of objects, because, as we add more types of objects, computing intersections becomes problematic. Consequently, most basic ray tracers support only flat and quadric surfaces. In Chapter 9, we shall see a few of the complexities involved in computing these intersections.

Although our ray tracer uses the Phong model to include a diffuse term at the point of intersection between a ray and a surface, the light that is scattered diffusely at this point is ignored. If we were to attempt to follow such light, we would have so many rays to deal with that the ray tracer might never complete execution. Thus, ray tracers are best suited for highly reflective environments. Color Plate 23 was rendered with a public-domain ray tracer. Although the scene contains only a few objects, the reflective and transparent surfaces could not have been rendered correctly without the ray tracer. Also, note the complexity of the shadows in the scene, another effect that is created automatically by ray tracing.

Color Plate 20 was created by ray casting a three-dimensional data set. Here, shadow rays were not followed. However, by making the skin transparent and the muscle opaque, the ray-tracing paradigm was able to create an image of only the latter. This image was created on a parallel processor, making use of the fact that cast rays can be traced independently of one another.

6.10.2 Radiosity

Radiosity, on the other hand, is ideal for a scene consisting of only perfectly diffuse surfaces. Here, a global energy balance can be obtained that determines a color for each polygonal surface. Although even a modest treatment of radiosity is beyond the scope of this book, we can get an idea of the basic considerations through the following example.

Suppose that we have a simple scene, such as that shown in Figure 6.49, in which all the surfaces are perfectly diffuse. If we render this scene with a distant light source, each polygon surface will be rendered as a constant color. If this were a real scene, however, some of the diffuse reflections from the red wall would fall on the white wall, causing red light to be added to the white light reflecting from those parts of the white wall that are near the red wall. Diffuse light reflected from the white wall would have a similar effect on the red wall. Our simple shading model has not considered these **diffuse–diffuse interactions**.

The rendering equation, if we could solve it, would give the correct shading for all points on these surfaces. If we make the assumption that all surfaces are perfectly diffuse, we can simplify the rendering equation to a point where a numerical method for its solution, **radiosity**, exists.

The basic radiosity method breaks up the scene into small flat polygons, or **patches**, each of which can be assumed to be perfectly diffuse and will render in a constant shade (Figure 6.50). What we must do is to find these shades. There are two steps to the method. In the first step, we consider patches pairwise to determine **form factors** that describe how the light energy leaving one patch affects the other. Once the form factors are determined, the rendering equation, which starts as an integral equation, can be reduced to a set of linear equations for the radiosities—essentially the reflectivity—of the facets. Once we solve these equations, we can render the scene using any renderer with flat shading. Although the amount of calculation required to compute form factors is enormous—it is an $O(n^2)$ problem for n patches—once the patch radiosities are determined, they are independent of the location of the viewer, due to the assumption that all surfaces are perfectly diffuse. Hence, we can rerender the scene in a walkthrough as fast as we could render the same scene using our local lighting model.

The image in Color Plate 24 was rendered using radiosity; it shows the strength of radiosity for rendering interiors that are composed of diffuse reflectors. Note that distributed light sources have been modeled as emissive patches and appear in the rendering.

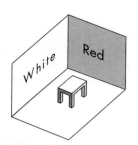

Figure 6.49 Simple scene with diffuse surfaces.

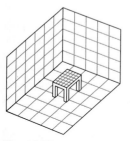

Figure 6.50 Division of surfaces into patches.

6.11   Summary

We have developed a lighting model that fits well with our pipeline approach to graphics. With it, we can create a variety of lighting effects, and can employ different types of light sources. Although we cannot create the global effects of a ray tracer, a good graphics workstation can render a polygonal scene using the Phong reflection model and interpolative shading in the same amount of time as it can render a scene without shading. From the perspective of a user program, adding shading requires only setting parameters that describe the light sources and materials. In spite of the limitations of the local lighting model that we have introduced, our simple renderer performs remarkably well; it is the basis of the reflection model supported by most APIs, including OpenGL.

The recursive-subdivision technique that we used to generate an approximation to a sphere is a powerful one that will reappear in various guises in Chapters 8 and 9. We shall use variants of this technique to render curves and surfaces. It will also arise when we introduce modeling techniques that rely on the self-similarity of many natural objects.

This chapter concludes our development of polygonal-based graphics. You should now be able to generate scenes with lighting and shading. Techniques for creating even more sophisticated images, such as texture mapping and compositing, involve using the pixel-level capabilities of graphics systems—topics that we shall consider in Chapter 10.

Now is a good time for you to write an application program. Experiment with various lighting and shading parameters. Try to create light sources that move, either independently or with the objects in the scene. You will probably face difficulties in producing shaded images that do not have small defects, such as cracks between polygons through which light can enter. Many of these problems are artifacts of small numerical errors in rendering calculations. There are many tricks of the trade for mitigating the effects of these errors. Some you will discover on your own; others are given in the suggested readings for this chapter.

We turn to implementation issues in the Chapter 7. Although we have seen pieces of how the different modules in the rendering pipeline function, we have not yet seen the details. As these details are developed in the next chapter, you will see how the pieces fit together such that each successive step in the pipeline requires only a small increment of work.

6.12   Suggested Readings

The use of lighting and reflection in computer graphics has followed two parallel paths: the physical and the computational. From the physical perspective, Kajiya's rendering equation [Kaj86] describes the overall energy balance in an environment, and requires knowledge of the reflectivity function for each surface. Reflection models, such as the Torrance–Sparrow model [Tor67] and Cook–Torrance model [Coo82], are based on modeling a surface with small planar facets. See [Hal89] and [Fol90] for discussions of such models.

Phong [Pho75] is credited with putting together a computational model that included ambient, diffuse, and specular terms. The use of the halfway vector was first suggested by Blinn [Bli77]. The basic model of transmitted light was used by Whitted [Whi80]. It was later modified by Heckbert and Hanrahan [Hec84]. Gouraud [Gou71] introduced interpolative shading.

Ray tracing was introduced to computer graphics by Appel [App68]. Many of the early papers on ray tracing are in Joy et al. [Joy88]. The book by Glassner [Gla89] is particularly helpful if you plan to write your own ray tracer. Radiosity is based on a method first used in heat transfer [Sie81]. It was first applied in computer graphics by Goral et al. [Gor84]. Since its introduction, researchers have done a great deal of work on increasing its efficiency [Coh85, Coh88] and incorporating specular terms [Sil89].

The *OpenGL Programmer's Guide* [Ope93a] contains many good hints on effective use of OpenGL's rendering capability.

Exercises

6.1 Most graphics systems and APIs use the simple lighting and reflection models that we introduced for polygon rendering. Describe the ways in which each of these models is incorrect. For each defect, give an example of a scene in which you would notice the problem.

6.2 Often, when a large polygon is shaded by OpenGL, it is rendered brightly in one area and dimmer in others. Explain why the image is uneven. Describe how you can avoid this problem.

6.3 In the development of the Phong reflection model, why do we not consider light sources being obscured from the surface by other surfaces in our reflection model?

6.4 How should the distance between the viewer and the surface enter the rendering calculations?

6.5 We have postulated an RGB model for the material properties of surfaces. Give an argument for using a subtractive color model instead.

6.6 Find four points equidistant from one another on a unit sphere. These points determine a tetrahedron. *Hint:* You can arbitrarily let one of the points be at $(0,1,0)$, and let the other three be in the plane $y = -d$ for some positive value of d.

6.7 Show that, if $\mathbf{v}$ lies in the same plane as $\mathbf{l}$, $\mathbf{n}$, and $\mathbf{r}$, then the half-angle satisfies

$$2\psi = \phi.$$

What relationship is there between the angles if **v** is not coplanar with the other vectors?

6.8   Consider all the combinations of near or far viewers, near or far light sources, flat or curved surfaces, and diffuse and specular reflections. For which cases can you simplify the shading calculations? In which cases does the use of the halfway vector help?

6.9   Construct a data structure for representing the subdivided tetrahedron. Traverse the data structure such that you can Gouraud shade the approximation to the sphere based on subdividing the tetrahedron.

6.10   Repeat Exercise 6.9, but start with an icosahedron instead of a tetrahedron.

6.11   Construct a data structure for representing meshes of quadrilaterals. Write a program to shade the meshes represented by your data structure.

6.12   Write a program that does recursive subdivisions on quadrilaterals and quadrilateral meshes.

6.13   Simple rendering models sometimes support only a single light source located behind the viewer, and are sometimes referred to as the *flashlight-in-the-eye* approach. Besides the reduced amount of calculation required, what is the principal advantage of this approach?

6.14   Consider two materials that meet along a planar boundary. Suppose that the speed of light in the two materials is v_1 and v_2. Show that Snell's law is a statement that light travels from a point in one material to a point in the second material in the minimum time.

6.15   Show that the halfway vector **h** is at the angle at which a surface must be oriented so that the maximum amount of reflected light reaches the viewer.

6.16   For transmitted light, find a vector **h'** such that, if the surface were oriented at this angle, the maximum amount of transmitted light would be in the direction of the viewer.

6.17   Although we have yet to discuss frame-buffer operations, you can start constructing a ray tracer using a single routine of the form `write_pixel(x, y, color)` that places the value of `color` (either an RGB color or an intensity) at the pixel located at `(x, y)` in the frame buffer. Write a pseudocode routine `ray` that recursively traces a cast ray. You can assume that you have a function available that will intersect a ray with an object. Consider how to limit how far the original ray will be traced.

6.18   If you have a pixel-writing routine available on your system, write a ray tracer that will ray trace a scene composed of only spheres. Use the mathematical equations for the spheres, rather than a polygonal approximation.

6.19   Create the shadow of a polygon on a flat surface by projecting the vertices onto the surface. Start with the surface $y = 0$; then, generalize your result. You should derive a projection matrix in homogeneous coordinates.

6.20 Add light sources and shading to the maze program in Exercise 5.13.

6.21 Using the sphere-generation program in Appendix A as a starting point, construct an interactive program that will allow you to position one or more light sources, and to alter material properties. Use your program to try to generate images of surfaces that match familiar materials, such as various metals, plastic, and carbon.

6.22 As geometric data passes through the viewing pipeline, a sequence of rotations, translations, scalings, and a projection transformation is applied to the vectors that determine the cosine terms in the Phong reflection model. Which, if any, of these operations preserve the angles between the vectors? What are the implications of your answer on implementation of shading?

6.23 Estimate the amount of extra work required for Phong shading as compared to Gouraud shading. Take into account the results of Exercise 6.22.

7

Implementation

W e now turn to implementation. There are three reasons for considering implementation at this point. First, you may be wondering how your programs are processed by the system that you are using: how lines are drawn on the screen, how polygons are filled, and what happens to primitives that lie outside the viewing volumes defined in your program. Second, our contention is that, if we are to use a graphics system efficiently, we need to have an understanding of the implementation process: which steps are easy, and which tax our hardware and software. Third, our discussion of implementation will open the door to new capabilities that employ the frame buffer, such as texture mapping and use of the alpha channel.

Learning implementation involves studying algorithms. As we must when we study other algorithms, we must be careful to consider issues such as theoretical versus practical performance, hardware versus software implementations, and the specific characteristics of an application. Although we can test whether an OpenGL implementation works correctly, in the sense that it produces the correct pixels on the screen, there are many choices for the algorithms employed. We shall focus on the basic operations that are necessary to implement a standard API, such as OpenGL, PHIGS, and Renderman, and are required, whether the rendering is done by a pipeline architecture, or via some other method, such as a ray tracer. Consequently, we shall present a variety of the basic algorithms for each of the principal tasks in an implementation.

7.1 Four Major Tasks

There are four major tasks that any implementation must perform to render a geometric entity, such as a three–dimensional polygon, as the latter passes from definition in a user program to possible display on an output device:

1. Modeling
2. Geometric processing
3. Rasterization
4. Display

Figure 7.1 shows how these tasks might be organized in a pipeline implementation. Regardless of the approach, all the tasks must be carried out.

Figure 7.1 Implementation tasks.

7.1.1 Modeling

The usual result of the modeling process is a set of vertices that specifies a set of geometric objects supported by the rest of the system. We have seen a few examples that required some modeling by the user, such as the approximation of spheres in Chapter 6. In Chapter 8, we shall explore a number of other modeling techniques.

We can look at the modeler as a black box that produces geometric objects and is usually a user program, yet there are other tasks that the modeler might perform. Consider, for example, clipping: the process of eliminating parts of objects that should not appear on the display. A user can generate geometric objects in her program, and can hope that the rest of the system can process these objects at the rate at which they are produced; or the modeler can attempt to ease the burden on the rest of the system by minimizing the number of objects that it passes on. This latter approach often means that the modeler may do some of the same jobs as the rest of the system, albeit with different algorithms. In the case of clipping, the modeler, knowing more about the specifics of the application, can often use a good heuristic to eliminate many, if not most, primitives before they are sent on through the standard viewing process.

7.1.2 Geometric Processing

The goals of the geometric processor are to determine which geometric objects appear on the display, and to assign shades or colors to these objects. Four related processes are required: normalization, clipping, hidden-surface removal, and shading. Once these processes have been carried out, the projection of the object from three to two dimensions can take place.

The first step in geometric processing usually is to change representations from user coordinates to either camera coordinates or screen coordinates. Regarding the geometric processor as a vertex processor, vertices, represented in homogeneous coordinates, are processed through a sequence of affine transformations so that the desired view is obtained. In most systems, a normalized view volume is created. Not only does the normalization allow us to support only orthographic projections, but in addition, by converting all views to equivalent orthographic views, we simplify the clipping process, as we shall see in Section 7.6.

Geometric objects are transformed by a sequence of transformations that may reshape and move them (modeling), or may change their representations (viewing). Eventually, only those primitives that fit within a specified volume, the **view volume**, will appear on the display after rasterization. We cannot, however, simply allow all objects to be rasterized, hoping that the hardware will take care of primitives that lie wholly or partially outside the view volume. The implementation must carry out this task.

Even though an object lies inside the view volume, it will not be displayed if it is obscured by another objects. Algorithms for **hidden-surface removal** (or **visible-surface determination**) are based on the three-dimensional spatial relationships among objects and must be carried out as part of our geometric processing. Our lighting model from Chapter 6 also requires geometric information, such as normals, to compute shading; thus, lighting calculations are another part of geometric processing.

Collectively, these operations constitute **front-end processing**. All involve three-dimensional calculations, and all require floating-point arithmetic. All generate similar hardware and software requirements.

7.1.3 Rasterization

Once projection takes places, we work with two-dimensional objects. Although we may have represented our primitives in screen coordinates, what we have is only a description of the object, such as the vertices. For example, after projection, a line segment that was defined in three dimensions by two vertices becomes a line segment in two dimensions defined by a pair of two-dimensional vertices. To display the object, we must use these vertices to generate a set of pixel values through a process called **rasterization** or **scan conversion**. We shall examine rasterization algorithms for line segments and polygons, assuming that we will rasterized other objects by approximating them with line segments and polygons.

From the perspective of the application program, the writing of pixels in the frame buffer is done automatically as part of rasterization, and the user program never needs to refer to individual pixels. However, many graphics systems, including OpenGL, allow programs to manipulate pixels directly, and to use other discrete buffers, a process that opens up new possibilities for creating images. We shall delay discussion of these operations until Chapter 10.

7.1.4 Display

In most displays, the process of taking the image from the frame buffer and displaying it on a CRT happens automatically and is not of concern to the application program. However, there are numerous problems with the quality of display such as the jaggedness associated with images on raster displays. We shall also introduce algorithms for reducing this jaggedness, or **aliasing**. We shall also discuss additional issues related to color reproduction on displays.

7.1.5 Basic Implementation Strategies

There are two major approaches to implementation. Each, of course, must perform the required steps; they differ in the order in which they perform the processing. We can think of the difference conceptually in terms of a single program that performs implementation. This program will take as input a set vertices specifying geometric objects, and will produce as output pixels in the frame buffer. If this program is to produce an image, it must assign every pixel. If it is to produce a correct image, it must process every geometric primitive and every light source. Hence, we expect this program to contain a number of loops that iterate over these basic variables.

If we wish to write such a program, then we must immediately address the following question: Which variable controls the outer loop? The answer we choose determines the flow of the entire implementation process. There are two fundamental answers. The two strategies that follow are often called the **image-oriented** and the **object-oriented** approaches, or the **sort first** and **sort last** approaches.

In the object-oriented approach, the outer loop is over the objects. We can think of the program as controlled by a loop of the form:

```
for(each_object) render(object);
```

A pipeline renderer fits this description. Vertices are defined by the program and flow through a series of modules that transforms them, colors them, and determines whether they are visible. A polygon might flow through the steps illustrated in Figure 7.2. Note that, after a polygon passes through the geometric processing, the rasterization of this polygon potentially can affect any pixels in the frame buffer. Most implementations that follow this approach are based on construction of a rendering pipeline that contains hardware or software modules for each of the tasks. Data (vertices) flow forward through the system.

The major limitations of the object-oriented approach are the large amount of memory required and the high cost of processing each object independently. Any geometric primitive that emerges from the geometric processing potentially can affect any set of pixels in the frame buffer; thus, the entire frame buffer—and various other buffers, such as the depth buffer used for hidden-surface removal—must be of the size of the display and must be available at

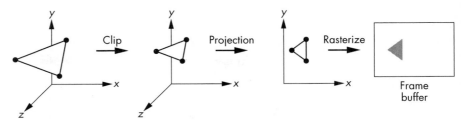

Figure 7.2 Object–oriented approach.

all times. Until recently, when memory became both cheap and dense, this requirement was considered to be a serious problem. Now various pipelined geometric processors are available that can process up to 1 million polygons per second. In fact, precisely because we are doing the same operations on every primitive, the hardware to build an object-based system is fast and relatively cheap, with many of the functions implemented with special-purpose chips.

Image-oriented approaches loop over pixels, or rows of pixels called **scan lines**, that constitute the frame buffer. In pseudocode, the outer loop of such a program is of the following form:

```
for(each_pixel) assign_a_color(pixel);
```

For each pixel (or scan line), we work backward, trying to determine which geometric primitives can contribute to its color. The advantages of this approach are that we need only limited display memory at any time, and that we can hope to generate pixels (or scan lines) at the rate and in the order required to refresh the display. Because the results of most calculations will not differ greatly from pixel to pixel (or scan line to scan line), we can use this coherence in our algorithms by developing incremental forms for many of the steps in the implementation. The main disadvantage of this approach is that, unless we first build a data structure from the geometric data, we do not know which primitives will affect which pixels. Such a data structure can be complex and may imply that all the geometric data must be available at all times during the rendering process.

We shall lean toward the object-based approach, although we shall look at examples of algorithms suited for both approaches.

7.2 Implementation of Transformations

The use of homogenous coordinates provides the basis for implementing geometric transformations. Our use of 4×4 matrices has allowed us to form arbitrary affine transformations by concatenating a sequence of matrices. In our discussions thus far, we have focused on the OpenGL use of model-view and projection matrices. Here, we take a slightly different, but equivalent, approach. We consider the transformations as performing a sequence of coordinate-system

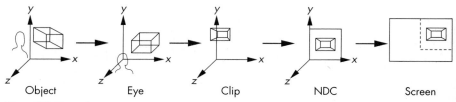

Figure 7.3 Transformation sequence.

changes, where each change can be represented by a homogeneous-coordinate matrix. There are five coordinate systems of interest:

1. Object (world) coordinates
2. Eye (camera) coordinates
3. Clip coordinates
4. Normalized device coordinates
5. Window (screen) coordinates

Figure 7.3 shows the sequence of transformations acting on a simple object. We first see the box and the viewer in the object coordinate system in which both their positions have been specified. The model-view matrix carries us to eye coordinates, where the viewer is at the origin. The next step in Figure 7.3 is the projection transformation. If our system uses this transformation, we stay in three dimensions, but we normalize the projection, as we did in Chapter 5, into an equivalent orthographic projection of distorted objects. The normalization process maps the view volume—a frustum for perspective views and parallelepiped for parallel views—to a centered cube with sides of length 2.[1] The points are now represented in **clip coordinates**.

Both the model-view and projection transformations are represented by 4×4 matrices in homogeneous coordinates. In hardware implementations, multiplication of four-dimensional vertices by 4×4 matrices is carried out by hardware, often with the matrix-multiplication units implemented at the chip level, allowing the entire matrix multiplication to be done in the same amount of time as a single multiplication. Examples include the Silicon Graphics geometry engine and the Intel i860 floating-point chip that is used by many graphics workstations.

In many implementations, the next stage is **clipping**, the process of determining which primitives, and parts of primitives, fit within the clipping volume defined by the application program. If the w component of a clipped vertex is not equal to 1, we will have to do a perspective division to convert back from homogenous coordinates to normal three-dimensional coordinates. The result

---

[1] In OpenGL, if the w component is not 1, the sides can be thought of as determined by the planes $x = \pm w$, $y = \pm w$, and $z = \pm w$.

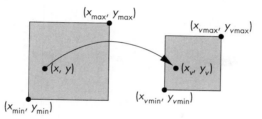

Figure 7.4 Viewport transformation.

of these steps is that all primitives that can possibly be displayed—we have yet to apply hidden-surface removal—lie within the cube

$$x = \pm 1,$$
$$y = \pm 1,$$
$$z = \pm 1.$$

This coordinate system is called **normalized device coordinates** because it depends on neither the original application units, nor the particulars of the display device, although the information to produce the correct image is retained in this coordinate system. Note also that projection has been carried out only partially. We still must do the final orthographic projection:

$$x_p = x,$$
$$y_p = y,$$
$$z_p = 0.$$

By retaining depth information, we have the necessary information for later hidden-surface removal.

The final transformation converts vertices to units of the display—**screen coordinates**. As we saw in Chapter 5, the projection of the clipping volume must appear in the assigned viewport. In OpenGL, this transformation is done after projection and is two dimensional. The preceding transformations have normalized the view volume such that its sides line up with the sides of the viewport (Figure 7.4), so this transformation is simply

$$x_v = x_{vmin} + (x - x_{max})\frac{x_{vmax} - x_{vmin}}{x_{max} - x_{min}},$$
$$y_v = y_{vmin} + (y - y_{max})\frac{y_{vmax} - y_{vmin}}{y_{max} - y_{min}}.$$

Some APIs allow for three-dimensional viewports, with the final projection being done after this transformation. In this case, we must add the equation

$$z_v = z_{vmin} + (z - z_{max})\frac{z_{vmax} - z_{vmin}}{z_{max} - z_{min}}.$$

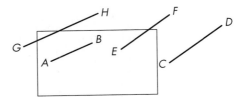

Figure 7.5 Two–dimensional clipping.

7.3   Line-Segment Clipping

A **clipper** decides decides which primitives, or parts of primitives, will appear on the display. Primitives that fit within the specified view volume pass through the clipper, or are **accepted**. Primitives that cannot appear on the display are eliminated, or **rejected** or **culled**. Primitives that are only partially within the view volume must be clipped so that any part lying outside the volume is removed.

Clipping can occur at one or more places in the viewing pipeline. The modeler may clip to limit the primitives that the hardware must handle. The primitives may be clipped after they have been projected from three- to two-dimensional objects. In OpenGL, at least conceptually, primitives are clipped against a three-dimensional view volume before projection and rasterization. We shall develop a sequence of clippers. For both pedagogic and historic reasons, we start with two two-dimensional line-segment clippers. Both extend directly to three dimensions and to clipping of polygons.

7.3.1 Cohen–Sutherland Clipping

The two-dimensional clipping problem for line segments is shown in Figure 7.5. We can assume for now that this problem arises after three-dimensional line segments have been projected onto the projection plane, and that the window is part of the projection plane that will be mapped to the viewport on the display. All values are specified as real numbers. We can see that the entire line segment AB will appear on the display, whereas none of CD will appear. EF and GH will have to be shortened before being displayed. Although a line segment is completely determined by its endpoints, GH shows that, even if both endpoints lie outside the clipping window, part of the line segment may still appear on the display.

We could compute the intersections of the lines of which the segments are parts with the sides of the window, and thus could determine the necessary information for clipping. However, we want to avoid intersection calculations, if possible, because each intersection requires a floating-point division. The Cohen–Sutherland algorithm was the first to seek to replace most of the expensive floating-point multiplications and divisions with a combination of floating-point subtractions and bit operations.

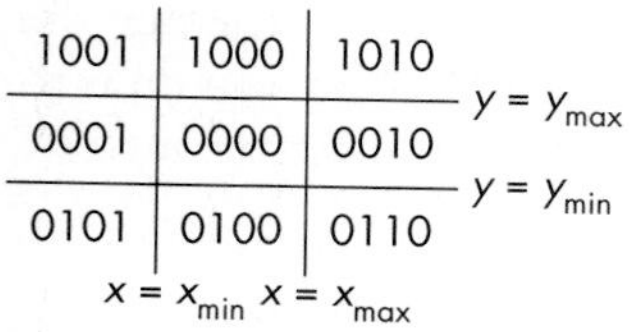

1001	1000	1010
0001	0000	0010
0101	0100	0110

$y = y_{max}$
$y = y_{min}$

$x = x_{min}$ $x = x_{max}$

Figure 7.6 Breaking up of space and outcodes.

The algorithm starts by extending the sides of the window to infinity, thus breaking up space into the nine regions shown in Figure 7.6. Each region can be assigned a unique 4-bit binary number, or **outcode**, $b_0 b_1 b_2 b_3$, as follows. Suppose that (x, y) is a point in the region; then,

$$b_0 = \begin{cases} 1 & \text{if } y > y_{max}, \\ 0 & \text{otherwise.} \end{cases}$$

Likewise, b_1 is 1 if $y < y_{min}$, and b_2 and b_3 are determined by the relationship between x and the left and right sides of the window. The resulting codes are indicated in Figure 7.6. For each endpoint of a line segment, we first compute the endpoint's outcode, a step that can require eight floating-point subtractions per line segment.

Consider a line segment whose outcodes are given by $o_1 = outcode(x_1, y_1)$ and $o_2 = outcode(x_2, y_2)$. We can now reason on the basis of these outcodes. There are four cases (Figure 7.7):

1. ($o_1 = o_2 = 0$.) Both endpoints are inside the clipping window, as is true for segment AB in Figure 7.7. The entire line segment is inside, and the segment can be sent on to be rasterized.
2. ($o_1 \neq 0, o_2 = 0$; or vice versa.) One endpoint is inside the clipping window; one is outside (see segment CD in Figure 7.7). The line segment must be shortened. The nonzero outcode indicates which edge, or edges, of the window are crossed by the segment. One or two intersections must be computed. Note that, after one intersection is computed, we can compute the outcode of the point of intersection to determine whether another intersection calculation is required.
3. ($o_1 \& o_2 \neq 0$) By taking the bitwise AND of the outcodes, we determine whether or not the two endpoints lie on the same outside side of the window. If so, the line segment can be discarded (see segment EF in Figure 7.7).
4. ($o_1 \& o_2 = 0$.) Both endpoints are outside, but they are on the outside of different edges of the window. As we can see from segments GH and

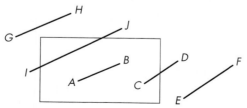

Figure 7.7 Cases of outcodes in Cohen–Sutherland algorithm.

IJ in Figure 7.7, we cannot tell from just the outcodes whether the segment can be discarded or must be shortened. The best we can do is to intersect with one of the sides of the window, and to check the outcode of the resulting point.

All our checking of outcodes requires only Boolean operations. We do intersection calculations only when they are needed, as in the second case, or as in the fourth case, where the outcodes did not contain enough information.

The Cohen–Sutherland algorithm works best when there is a large number of line segments, but few are actually displayed. In this case, most of the line segments will lie fully outside one or two of the extended sides of the clipping rectangle, and thus will be eliminated on the basis of their outcodes. The other advantage is that this algorithm can be extended to three dimensions.

We have not discussed how to compute any required intersections. The form that this calculation takes depends on how we choose to represent the line segment, although only a single division should be required in any case. If we use the standard explicit form of a line,

$$y = mx + h,$$

where m is the slope of the line and h is the line's y intercept, then we can compute m and h from the endpoints. However, vertical lines cannot be represented in this form—a critical weakness of the explicit form. If we were interested in only the Cohen–Sutherland algorithm, it would be fairly simple to program all cases directly because the sides of the clipping rectangle are parallel to the axes. However, we are interested in more than just clipping; consequently, other representations of the line and line segment are of importance. In particular, parametric representations are almost always used in computer graphics. We have already seen the parametric form of the line in Chapter 4; the parametric representation of other types of curves will be considered in Chapter 9.

7.3.2 Liang–Barsky Clipping

If we use the parametric form for lines, we can approach the clipping of line segments in a different—and ultimately more efficient—manner. Suppose that we have a line segment defined by the two endpoints $\mathbf{p}_1 = [x_1, y_1]^T$ and $\mathbf{p}_2 = [x_2, y_2]^T$. We can use these endpoints to define a unique line that we can express parametrically, either in matrix form

$$\mathbf{p}(\alpha) = (1 - \alpha)\mathbf{p}_1 + \alpha\mathbf{p}_2,$$

or as two scalar equations,

$$x(t) = (1 - \alpha)x_1 + \alpha x_2,$$
$$y(t) = (1 - \alpha)y_1 + \alpha y_2.$$

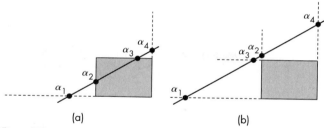

Figure 7.8 Two cases of a parametric line and a clipping window.

Note that this form is robust and needs no changes for horizontal or vertical lines. As the parameter α varies from 0 to 1, we move along the segment from $\mathbf{p}_1$ to $\mathbf{p}_2$. Negative values of α yield points on the line on the other side of $\mathbf{p}_1$ from $\mathbf{p}_2$. Similarly, values of $\alpha > 1$ give points on the line past $\mathbf{p}_2$ going off to infinity.

Consider the line segment and the line of which it is part, as shown in Figure 7.8(a). As long as the line is not parallel to a side of the window (if it is, we can handle that situation with ease), there are four points where the line intersects the extended sides of the window. These points correspond to the four values of the parameter: α_1, α_2, α_3, and α_4. One of these values corresponds to the line entering the window; another corresponds to the line leaving the window. Leaving aside, for the moment, how we compute these intersections, we can order them, and can determine which correspond to intersections that we need for clipping. For the given example,

$$1 > \alpha_4 > \alpha_3 > \alpha_2 > \alpha_1 > 0.$$

Hence, all four intersections are inside the original line segment, with the two innermost (α_2 and α_3) determining the clipped line segment. We can distinguish this case from the case in Figure 7.8(b), which also has the four intersections between the endpoints of the line segment, by noting that the order for this case is

$$1 > \alpha_4 > \alpha_2 > \alpha_3 > \alpha_1 > 0.$$

The line intersects both the top and the bottom of the window before it intersects either the left or the right; thus, the entire line segment must be rejected. Other cases of the ordering of the points of intersection can be argued in a similar way.

Efficient implementation of this strategy requires that we avoid computing intersections until they are needed. Many lines can be rejected before all four intersections are known. We also want to avoid floating-point divisions where possible. If we use the parametric form to determine the intersection with the top of the window, we find the intersection at the value

$$\alpha = \frac{y_{\max} - y_1}{y_2 - y_1}.$$

Similar equations hold for the other three sides of the window. Rather than computing these intersections, at the cost of a division for each, we instead write the equation as

$$\alpha(y_2 - y_1) = \alpha \Delta y = y_{\max} - y_1 = \Delta y_{\max}.$$

All the tests required by the algorithm can be restated in terms of Δy_{max}, Δy, and similar terms computed for the other sides of the windows. Thus, all decisions about clipping can be made without floating-point division. Only if an intersection is needed, because a segment has to be shortened, is the division done. The efficiency of this approach, compared to that of the Cohen–Sutherland algorithm, is that we avoid multiple shortening of line segments and the related reexecutions of the clipping algorithm. We shall forgo discussion of other efficient two-dimensional line-clipping algorithms because, unlike the Cohen–Sutherland and Liang–Barsky algorithms, these algorithms do not extend to three dimensions.

7.4   Polygon Clipping

Polygon clipping arises in a number of ways. Certainly, we want to be able to clip polygons against rectangular windows for display. We may at times want windows that are not rectangular. Other parts of an implementation, such as shadow generation and hidden-surface removal, can require clipping of polygons against other polygons. For example, Figure 7.9 shows the shadow of a polygon that we create by clipping a polygon that is closer to the light source against polygons that are farther away. Antialiasing and compositing methods that we shall consider in Chapter 10 rely on the ability to clip polygons against other polygons.

We can generate polygon-clipping algorithms directly from line-clipping algorithms by clipping the edges of the polygon successively. However, we must

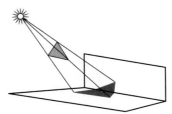

Figure 7.9 Shadow generation by clipping.

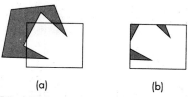

(a)   (b)

Figure 7.10 Clipping of a concave polygon. (a) Before clipping. (b) After clipping.

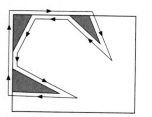

Figure 7.11 Creation of a single polygon.

be careful to remember that a polygon is an object, and, depending on the form of the polygon, we can generate more than one polygonal object by clipping. Consider the nonconvex (or **concave**) polygon in Figure 7.10(a). If we clip it against a rectangular window, we get the result shown in Figure 7.10(b). Most viewers looking at this figure would conclude that we have generated three polygons by clipping. Unfortunately, implementing a clipper that can increase the number of objects can be a problem. We could treat the result of the clipper as a single polygon, as shown in Figure 7.11, with edges that overlap along the sides of the window, but this choice might cause difficulties in other parts of the implementation.

Convex polygons do not present such problems. Clipping a convex polygon against a rectangular window can leave at most a single convex polygon (see Exercise 7.3) . A graphics system might then either forbid the use of concave polygons, or divide (**tessellate**) a given polygon into a set of convex polygons, as shown in Figure 7.12.[2]

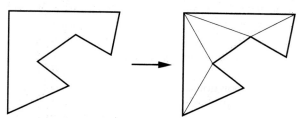

Figure 7.12 Tessellation of a concave polygon.

For rectangular clipping regions, both the Cohen–Sutherland and the Liang–Barsky algorithms can be applied to polygons on an edge-by-edge basis. There is another approach, developed by Sutherland and Hodgeman, that fits well with the pipeline architectures that we have discussed.

A line-segment clipper can be envisioned as a black box (Figure 7.13) whose input is the pair of vertices from the segment to be tested and clipped, and

---

[2] OpenGL includes tessellation functions in the utility library GLU.

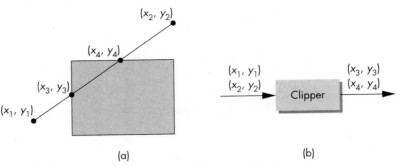

Figure 7.13 (a) Clipping problem. (b) Clipper as a black box.

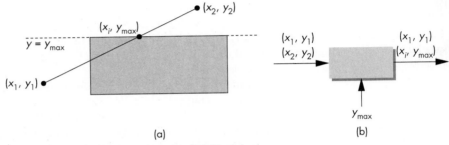

Figure 7.14 (a) Clipping against top. (b) Black box.

whose output is either a pair of vertices corresponding to the clipped line segment, or is nothing if the input line segment lies outside the window.

Rather than considering the clipping window as four line segments, we can consider it as the object created by the intersection of four infinite lines that determine the top, bottom, right, and left sides of the window. We can then subdivide our clipper into a pipeline of simpler clippers, each of which clips against a single edge of the window. We can use the black box view on each of the individual clippers.

Suppose that we consider clipping against only the top of the window. We can think of this operation as a black box (Figure 7.14) whose input and output are pairs of vertices, with the value of y_{max} as a parameter known to the clipper. Using the similar triangles in Figure 7.15, if there is an intersection, it lies at

$$x_3 = x_1 + (y_{max} - y_1)\frac{x_2 - x_1}{y_2 - y_1},$$

$$y_3 = y_{max}.$$

Thus, the clipper returns one of three pairs: $\{(x_1, y_1), (x_2, y_2)\}$, $\{(x_1, y_1), (x_i, y_{max})\}$, or $\{(x_i, y_{max}), (x_2, y_2)\}$. We can clip against the bottom, right, and left sides of the window independently, using the same equations with the roles

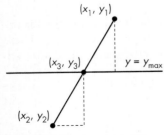

Figure 7.15 Intersection with the top of the window.

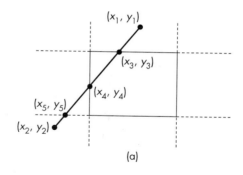

(a)

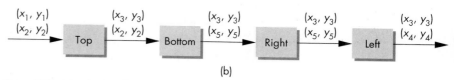

(b)

Figure 7.16 (a) Clipping problem. (b) Pipeline clippers.

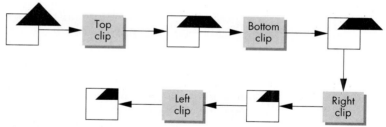

Figure 7.17 Example of pipeline clipping.

of x and y exchanged as necessary, and the values for the sides of the window inserted. The four clippers can now be arranged in the pipeline of Figure 7.16. If we build this configuration in hardware, we have a clipper that is working on four vertices concurrently. Figure 7.17 shows a simple example of the effect of successive clippers on a polygon.

7.5   Clipping of Other Primitives

Our emphasis in Chapters 1–6 was on writing programs in which the objects are built from line segments and flat polygons. We often render the curved objects that we shall discuss in Chapter 9 by subdividing them into small, approximately flat polygons. In pipeline architectures, we usually find some variant of the clippers we have presented. Nevertheless, there are situations in which we want

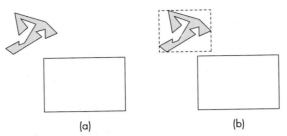

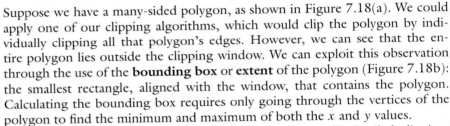

Figure 7.18 (a) Polygon and clipping window.
(b) Polygon, bounding box, and clipping window.

either to clip objects before they reach the hardware or to employ algorithms optimized for other primitives.

7.5.1 Bounding Boxes

Suppose we have a many-sided polygon, as shown in Figure 7.18(a). We could apply one of our clipping algorithms, which would clip the polygon by individually clipping all that polygon's edges. However, we can see that the entire polygon lies outside the clipping window. We can exploit this observation through the use of the **bounding box** or **extent** of the polygon (Figure 7.18b): the smallest rectangle, aligned with the window, that contains the polygon. Calculating the bounding box requires only going through the vertices of the polygon to find the minimum and maximum of both the x and y values.

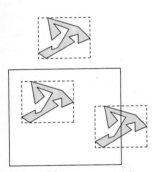

Figure 7.19 Clipping with bounding boxes.

Once we have the bounding box, we can often avoid detailed clipping. Consider the three cases in Figure 7.19. For the polygon above the window, no clipping is necessary, because the minimum y for the bounding box is above the top of the window. For the polygon inside the window, we can determine that it is inside by comparing the bounding box with the window. Only when we discover that the bounding box straddles the window do we have to carry out detailed clipping, using all the edges of the polygon. The use of extents is such a powerful technique—in both two and three dimensions—that modeling systems often compute a bounding box for each object, automatically, and store the bounding box with the object.

7.5.2 Curves, Surfaces, and Text

The variety of curves and surfaces that we can define mathematically makes it difficult to find general algorithms for processing these objects. The potential difficulties can be seen from the two-dimensional curves in Figure 7.20. For a simple curve, such as a quadratic, we can compute intersections, although at a cost higher than that for lines. For more complex curves, such as the spiral, not only must intersection calculations be computed using numerical techniques, but even determining how many intersections we must compute may be diffi-

Figure 7.20 Curve clipping.

cult. We can avoid such problems by approximating curves with line segments and surfaces with planar polygons. The use of bounding boxes can also prove helpful, especially in cases such as quadratics where we can compute intersections exactly, but would prefer to make sure that the calculation is necessary before carrying it out.

The handling of text differs from API to API, with many APIs allowing the user to specify how detailed a rendering of text is required. There are two extremes. On one end, text is stored as bit patterns and is rendered directly by the hardware without any geometric processing. Any required clipping is done in the frame buffer. At the other extreme, text is defined like any other geometric object, and is then processed through the standard viewing pipeline. OpenGL allows both these cases by not having a separate text primitive. The user can choose which mode she prefers by defining either bitmapped, using pixel operations, or stroke characters, using the standard primitives. Other APIs, such as PHIGS and GKS, add intermediate options, by having text primitives and a variety of text attributes. In addition to attributes that set the size and color of the text, there are others that allow the user to ask the system to use techniques such as bounding boxes to clip out strings of text that cross a clipping boundary.

7.5.3 Clipping in the Frame Buffer

We might also consider delaying clipping until after objects have been projected and converted into screen coordinates. Clipping can done in the frame buffer through a technique called scissoring. However, it is usually better to clip geometric entities before the vertices reach the frame buffer, and thus clipping within the frame buffer generally is required for only raster objects, such as blocks of pixels. We shall discuss such objects in Chapter 10.

7.6   Clipping in Three Dimensions

In three dimensions, we clip against a bounded volume, rather than against a bounded region in the plane. The simplest extension of two-dimensional clipping to three dimensions is for the right parallelepiped clipping region (Figure 7.21):

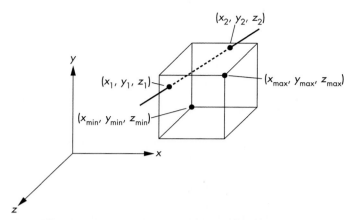

Figure 7.21 Three-dimensional clipping against a right parallelepiped.

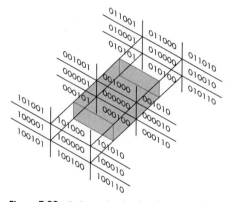

Figure 7.22 Cohen–Sutherland regions in three dimensions.

$$x_{min} \leq x \leq x_{max},$$
$$y_{min} \leq y \leq y_{max},$$
$$z_{min} \leq z \leq z_{max}$$

Our three clipping algorithms (Cohen–Sutherland, Liang–Barsky, and Sutherland–Hodgeman) and the use of extents can be extended to three dimensions. For the Cohen–Sutherland algorithm, we replace the 4-bit outcode with a 6-bit outcode. The additional 2 bits are set if the point lies either in front of or behind the clipping volume (Figure 7.22). The testing strategy is virtually identical for the two- and three-dimensional cases.

For the Liang–Barsky algorithm, we add the equation

$$z(\alpha) = (1 - \alpha)z_1 + \alpha z_2,$$

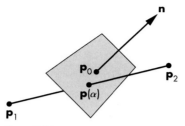

Figure 7.23 Plane–line intersection.

to obtain a three-dimensional parametric representation of the line segment. We will have to consider six intersections with the surfaces that form the clipping volume, but we can use the same logic as we did in the two-dimensional case. Pipeline clippers add two modules to clip against the front and back of the clipping volume.

The major difference between two- and three-dimensional clippers is that, instead of clipping lines against lines, as we do in two dimensions, in three dimensions, we are clipping either lines against surfaces or surfaces against surfaces. Consequently, our intersection calculations must be changed. A typical intersection calculation can be posed in terms of a parametric line in three dimensions intersecting a plane (Figure 7.23). If we write the line and plane equations in matrix form (where $\mathbf{n}$ is the normal to the plane and $\mathbf{p}_0$ is a point on the plane), we must solve the equations

$$\mathbf{p}(\alpha) = (1 - \alpha)\mathbf{p}_1 + \alpha\mathbf{p}_2,$$

$$\mathbf{n} \cdot (\mathbf{p}(\alpha) - \mathbf{p}_0) = 0,$$

for the α corresponding to the point of intersection. This value is

$$\alpha = \frac{\mathbf{n} \cdot (\mathbf{p}_0 - \mathbf{p}_1)}{\mathbf{n} \cdot (\mathbf{p}_2 - \mathbf{p}_1)},$$

and computation of an intersection requires six multiplications and a division. However, if we look at the standard viewing volumes, we see that simplifications are possible. For orthographic viewing (Figure 7.24), the view volume is a right parallelepiped, and each intersection calculation reduces to a single division, as it did for two-dimensional clipping.

When we consider an oblique view (Figure 7.25), we see that the clipping volume no longer is a right parallelepiped. Although you might think that we have to compute dot products to clip against the sides of the volume, here is where the normalization process that we introduced in Chapter 5 pays dividends. We showed that an oblique projection is equivalent to a shearing of the data followed by an orthographic projection. Although the shear transformation distorts objects, they are distorted such that they project correctly. The shear also distorts the clipping volume from a general parallelepiped to a right

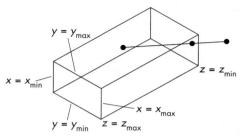

Figure 7.24 Clipping for orthographic viewing.

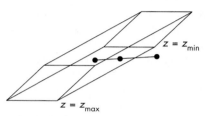

Figure 7.25 Clipping for oblique viewing.

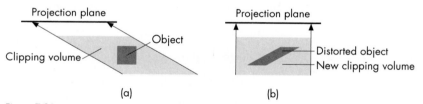

Figure 7.26 Distortion of view volume by shear. (a) Top view before shear. (b) After shear.

parallelepiped. Figure 7.26(a) shows a top view of an oblique volume with a cube inside the volume. Figure 7.26(b) shows the volume and object after they have been distorted by the shear. As far as projection is concerned, carrying out the oblique transformation directly or replacing it by a shear transformation and an orthographic projection requires the same amount of computation. When we add in clipping, it is clear that the second approach has a definite advantage, because we can clip against a right parallelepiped. This example illustrates the importance of considering the incremental nature of the steps in an implementation. Analysis of either projection or clipping, in isolation, fails to show the importance of the normalization process.

For perspective projections, the argument for normalization is just as strong. By carrying out the perspective-normalization transformation from Chapter 5, but not the orthographic projection, we again create a rectangular clipping volume and simplify all subsequent intersection calculations.

OpenGL supports additional clipping planes that can be oriented arbitrarily. Hence, if this feature is used in a user program, the implementation must carry out a general clipping routine, at a performance cost.

7.7 Hidden-Surface Removal

Once vertices have passed through the required geometric transformations, and the objects that they define have been assembled and clipped, we have a set of geometric entities—points, line segments, and polygons—any of which could appear on the display after final projection. But before we rasterize any of these objects, we must solve the problem of hidden-surface removal (or visible-surface determination) to discover whether each object is visible to the viewer, or is obscured from the viewer by other objects. We shall describe a number of techniques for a scene composed purely of planar polygons. This choice is appropriate, as most renderers will have subdivided surfaces into polygons at this point. Line segments can be handled by slight modifications (see Exercise 7.7).

7.7.1 Object-Space and Image-Space Approaches

The study of hidden-surface-removal algorithms clearly illustrates the variety of available algorithms, the differences between working with objects and working with images, and the importance of evaluating the incremental effects of successive algorithms in the implementation process.

Consider a scene composed of k three-dimensional opaque flat polygons, each of which we shall consider to be an individual object. We can derive a generic object-space approach by considering the objects pairwise, as seen from the center of projection. Consider two such polygons, A and B. There are four possibilities (Figure 7.27):

1. A completely obscures B from the camera; we display only A.
2. B obscures A; we display only B;
3. A and B both are completely visible; we display both A and B.

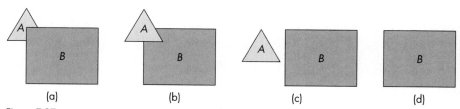

Figure 7.27 Two polygons. (a) B partially obscures A. (b) A partially obscures B. (c) A and B both are visible. (c) B totally obscures A.

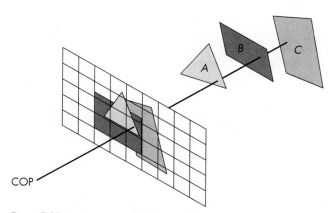

Figure 7.28 Image-space hidden-surface removal.

4. A and B partially obscure each other; we must calculate the visible parts of each polygon.

For complexity considerations, we can regard the determination of which case we have and any required calculation of the visible part of a polygon as a single operation. We then proceed inductively. We pick one of the k polygons and compare it pairwise with the remaining $k - 1$ polygons. At this point, we will know which part (if any) of this polygon is visible, and we can render the visible part. We are now done with this polygon, so we repeat the process with any of the other $k - 1$ polygons. Each step involves comparing one polygon, pairwise, with the other remaining polygons, until we have only two polygons remaining, and we compare them to each other. We can easily determine that the complexity of this calculation is $O(k^2)$. Thus, without deriving any of the details of any particular object-space algorithm, we should suspect that the object-space approach works best for scenes with relatively few polygons.

The image-space approach follows our viewing and ray-casting model, as shown in Figure 7.28. Consider a ray that leaves the center of projection and passes through a pixel. We can intersect this ray with each of the planes determined by our k polygons, determine for which planes the ray passes through a polygon, and finally, for those rays, find the intersection closest to the center of projection. We color this pixel with the shade of the polygon at the point of intersection. Our fundamental operation is the intersection of rays with polygons. For an $n \times m$ display, we have to carry out this operation nmk times, giving $O(k)$ complexity.[3] Again, without looking at the details of the operations, we

---

[3] We can use more than one ray for each pixel to increase the accuracy of the rendering.

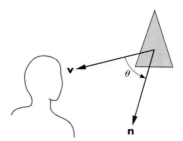

Figure 7.29 Back-face test.

were able to get an upper bound. In general, the $O(k)$ bound[4] accounts for the dominance of image-space methods. However, because image-space approaches work at the pixel level, they can create renderings more jagged than those of object-space algorithms.

7.7.2 Back-Face Removal

In Chapter 6, we noted that, in OpenGL, we can choose to render only front-facing polygons. For situations where we cannot see back faces, such as scenes composed of convex polyhedra, we can reduce the work required for hidden-surface removal by eliminating all back-facing polygons before we apply any other hidden-surface-removal algorithm. The test for **culling** a back-facing polygon can be derived from Figure 7.29. We see the front of a polygon if the normal, which comes out of the front face, is pointed toward the viewer. If θ is the angle between the normal and the viewer, then the polygon is facing forward if and only if

$$-90 \leq \theta \leq 90,$$

or, equivalently,

$$\cos \theta \geq 0.$$

The second condition is much easier to test, because, instead of computing the cosine, we can use the dot product:

$$\mathbf{n} \cdot \mathbf{v} \geq 0.$$

We can simplify this test even further if we note that usually it is applied after transformation to normalized device coordinates. In this system, all views are orthographic, with the direction of projection along the z axis. Hence, in

---

[4] The $O(k)$ bound is a worst-case bound. In practice, image space algorithms perform much better; see Exercise 7.9.

homogeneous coordinates,

$$\mathbf{n} = \begin{bmatrix} 0 \\ 0 \\ 1 \\ 0 \end{bmatrix}.$$

Thus, if the polygon is on the surface

$$ax + by + cz + d = 0$$

in normalized device coordinates, we need only to check the sign of c to determine whether we have a front- or back-facing polygon. This test can be implemented easily in either hardware or software; we must simply be careful to ensure that removing back-facing polygons is correct for our application. In OpenGL, the function glCullFace allows us to turn on back-face elimination.

7.7.3 The z-Buffer Algorithm

The **z-buffer algorithm** is the most widely used hidden-surface-removal algorithm. It has the advantages of being easy to implement, in either hardware or software, and of being compatible with pipeline architectures, where it can execute at the same speed as vertices are passing through the pipeline. Although the algorithm works in image space, it loops over the polygons, rather than over pixels, and can be regarded as part of the scan-conversion process that we shall discuss in Section 7.9.

Suppose that we are in the process of rasterizing one of the two polygons in Figure 7.30. We can compute a color for each point of intersection between a ray from the center of projection and a pixel, using our shading model. In addition, we must check whether this point is visible. It will be visible if it is the closest point of intersection along the ray. Hence, if we are rasterizing B, its shade will appear on the screen as the distance z_2 is less than the distance z_1 to

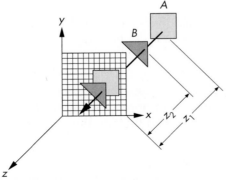

Figure 7.30 The z-buffer algorithm.

polygon A. Conversely, if we are rasterizing A, the pixel that corresponds to the point of intersection will not appear on the display. Because we are proceeding polygon by polygon, however, we do not have the information on all other polygons as we rasterize any given polygon. However, we can store and update the depth information as we do the scan conversion.

Suppose that we have a buffer, the z buffer, with the same resolution as the frame buffer and with depth consistent with the resolution that we wish to use for distance. For example, if we have a 1024×1280 display and we use single-precision floating-point numbers for the depth calculation, we could use a 1024×1280 z buffer with 32-bit elements. Initially, each element in the depth buffer is initialized to the maximum distance away from the center of projection.[5] The frame buffer is initialized to the background color. At any time during rasterization, each location in the z buffer contains the distance along the ray corresponding to this location of the closest intersection point on any polygon found so far.

The calculation proceeds as follows. We rasterize, polygon by polygon, using one of the methods from Section 7.9. For each point on the polygon corresponding to the intersection of the polygon with a ray through a pixel, we compute the distance from the center of projection. We compare this distance to the value in the z buffer corresponding to this point. If this distance is greater than the distance in the z buffer, then we have already processed a polygon closer to the viewer, and this point is not visible. If the distance is less than the distance in the z buffer,[6] then we have found a point closer to the viewer. We update the distance in the z buffer and place the shade computed for this point at the corresponding location in the frame buffer.

Unlike other aspects of rendering, where the particular implementation algorithms may not be known to the user, we have already seen that OpenGL uses the z-buffer algorithm for hidden-surface removal. This exception arises because the application program must initialize the z buffer explicitly every time that a new image is to be generated.

The z–buffer algorithm works well with the image-oriented approaches to implementation, because the amount of incremental work is small. Suppose that we are rasterizing a polygon, scan line by scan line—an option that we shall examine in Section 7.9. The polygon is part of a plane (Figure 7.31) that can be represented as

---

[5] If we have already done perspective normalization, we should replace the center of projection with the direction of projection, because all rays are parallel. However, this change will not affect the z-buffer algorithm, because we can measure distances from any arbitrary plane, such as the plane $z = 0$, rather than from the COP.

[6] In OpenGL, we can use the function `glDepthFunc` to decide what do when the distances are equal.

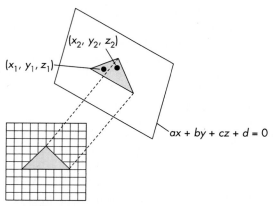

Figure 7.31 Incremental z-buffer algorithm.

$$ax + by + cz + d = 0.$$

Suppose that (x_1, y_1, z_1) and (x_2, y_2, z_2) are two points on the polygon (and the plane). If

$$\Delta x = x_2 - x_1,$$

$$\Delta y = y_2 - y_1,$$

$$\Delta z = z_2 - z_1,$$

then the equation for the plane can be written in differential form as

$$a\Delta x + b\Delta y + c\Delta z = 0.$$

This equation is in window coordinates, so each scan line corresponds to a line of constant y, and $\Delta y = 0$ as we move across a scan line. On a scan line, we increase x in unit steps, corresponding to moving one pixel in the frame buffer, and Δx is constant. Thus, as we move from point to point across a scan line,

$$\Delta z = -\frac{c}{a}\Delta x.$$

This value is a constant that needs to be computed only once for each polygon.

7.7.4 Depth Sort and the Painter's Algorithm

Depth sort is a direct implementation of the object-space approach to hidden–surface removal. We shall present the algorithm for a scene composed of planar polygons; extensions to other classes of objects are possible. Depth sort is a variant of an even simpler algorithm known as the **painter's algorithm**.

Suppose that we have a collection of polygons that is sorted based on how far the polygons are from the viewer. For the example in Figure 7.32(a), we have

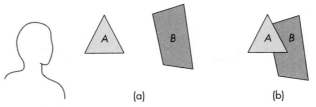

Figure 7.32 Painter's algorithm. (a) Two polygons and viewer. (b) *A* partially obscures *B* when viewed.

two polygons. When they are viewed by a viewer, they appear as shown in Figure 7.32(b), with the polygon in front partially obscuring the other. To render the scene correctly, we could find the part of the rear polygon that is visible, and could render that part into the frame buffer—a calculation that requires clipping one polygon against the other. Or we could use another approach, analogous to the way an oil painter might render the scene. She probably would paint the farther-back polygon in its entirety, and then would paint the front polygon, in the process painting over the part of the rear polygon not visible to the viewer. Both polygons would have be rendered completely, with the hidden-surface removal being done as a consequence of the **back-to-front rendering** of the polygons.[7] The two questions with this algorithm are how we do the sort, and what to do if polygons overlap. Depth sort addresses both, although in many applications more efficiencies can be found. See, for example, Exercise 7.10.

Suppose that we have already computed the extent of each polygon. The next step of depth sort is to order all the polygons by how far away from the viewer their maximum z value is. This step gives the algorithm the name **depth sort**. Suppose that the order is as shown in Figure 7.33, which depicts the z extents of the polygons after the sort. If the minimum depth—the z value—of each polygon is greater than the maximum depth of the polygon behind this one, we can paint the polygons back to front, and we are done. For example, polygon A in Figure 7.33 is behind all the other polygons and can be painted first. However, the others cannot be painted based solely on the z extents.

If the z extents of two polygons overlap, we still may be able to find an order to paint (render) the polygons individually and yield the correct image. The depth-sort algorithm goes through a number of increasingly more difficult tests, attempting to find such an ordering. Consider a pair of polygons

---

[7] Some application problems can be solved more efficiently with *front-to-back rendering* of polygons, a topic that we shall address in Chapter 10.

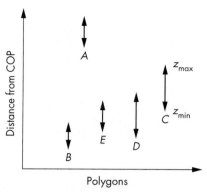

Figure 7.33 The z extents of sorted polygons.

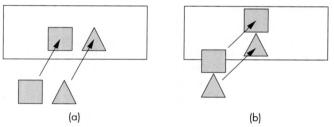

Figure 7.34 Test for overlap in x and y extents. (a) Nonoverlapping x extents. (b) Nonoverlapping y extents.

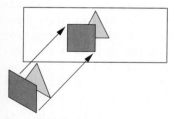

Figure 7.35 Polygons with overlapping extents.

whose z extents overlap. The simplest test is to check their x and y extents (Figure 7.34). If either of the x or y extents do not overlap,[8] neither polygon can obscure the other, and they can be painted in either order. Even if these tests fail, it may still be possible to find an order in which we can paint the polygons individually. Figure 7.35 shows such a case. All the vertices of one polygon lie on the same side of the plane determined by the other. We can process the vertices (see Exercise 7.12) of the two polygons to determine whether this case exists.

Two troublesome situations remain. If three or more polygons overlap cyclically, as shown in Figure 7.36, there is no correct order for painting. The best we can do is to divide at least one of the polygons into two parts, and to attempt to find an order to paint the new set of polygons. The second problematic

---

[8] The x- and y-extent tests apply to only a parallel view. Here is another example of the advantage of working in normalized device coordinates *after* perspective normalization.

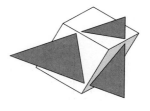

Figure 7.36 Cyclic overlap.

Figure 7.37 Piercing polygons.

case arises if a polygon can pierce another polygon, as shown in Figure 7.37. If we want to continue with depth sort, we must derive the details of the intersection—a calculation equivalent to clipping one polygon against the other. If the intersecting polygons have many vertices, you may want to try another algorithm that will require less computation. A performance analysis of depth sort is difficult because the particulars of the application determine how often the more difficult cases arise. For example, if we are working with polygons that describe the surfaces of solid objects, then no two polygons can intersect. Nevertheless, it should be clear that, due to the initial sort, the complexity must be greater than linear.

7.7.5 The Scan-Line Algorithm

Until the reduced cost of memory and the availability of special-purpose graphics chips made pipeline hardware implementations the dominant paradigm, the scan-line method was the most efficient hidden-surface-removal algorithm; it still influences many special-purpose systems. The algorithm combines polygon scan conversion with hidden-surface removal. Although we have yet to discuss the details of scan conversion, we can observe the salient features of the algorithm with the aid of Figure 7.38, which shows two intersecting polygons and their edges. If we rasterize the polygon scan line by scan line, we can use the incremental depth calculation that we derived in this section. However, if we look at the figure, we can observe some possibilities for even greater efficiency. As we

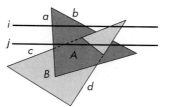

Figure 7.38 Scan-line algorithm.

go from left to right along scan line i, we cross edge a of polygon A. Because we have entered our first polygon on this scan line, there is no reason to carry out a depth calculation. No other polygon can yet affect the colors along this line. When we encounter the next edge, b, we are leaving polygon A, and we color the corresponding pixels with the background color. We next encounter edge c of polygon B; again having only a single polygon to consider, we can avoid depth calculations. Scan line j shows a more complex situation. First, we encounter edge a again and we can assign colors without a depth calculation. The second edge that we encounter is c; thus, we have two polygons to worry about. Until we pass edge d, we must carry out depth calculations, and we can make use of our incremental methods.

Although the strategy has elements in common with the z-buffer algorithm, it is fundamentally different because it is working one scan line at a time, rather than one polygon at a time. A good implementation of the algorithm requires a moderately sophisticated data structure for representing which edges are encountered on each scan line. The basic structure is an array of pointers, one for each scan line, each of which points to an incremental edge structure for the scan line.

7.8   Scan Conversion

We are about to take the final step in the journey from the specification of geometric entities in an application program to the setting of pixels in the frame buffer—rasterization of primitives. We shall be concerned with only line segments and polygons, both of which are defined by vertices. We can assume that we have clipped the primitives such that each primitive will appear on the display. To clarify the discussion, we shall neglect the effect of hidden-surface removal, and shall assume that we have objects that can be rasterized individually. We shall assume that we have projected all remaining (unclipped) vertices into two dimensions, and that we can work in screen coordinates.

We shall further assume that the frame buffer is an $n \times m$ array of pixels, with $(0, 0)$ corresponding to the lower-left corner. Pixels can be set to a given color by a single function inside the graphics implementation of the form

```
write_pixel(int ix,int iy, int value);
```

The argument `value` can be either an index, in color-index mode, or a pixel value, such as a 32-bit number in RGBA-color mode. A frame buffer is inherently discrete; it does not make sense to talk about pixels located at places other than integer values of ix and iy. On the other hand, screen coordinates, which range over the same values as do ix and iy, are real numbers. For example, we can compute a value such as $(63.4, 157.9)$ in screen coordinates, but must realize that the nearest pixel is centered at $(63, 158)$ or $(63.5, 157.5)$.

Pixels are numbers in the frame buffer. Pixels can be displayed in multiple shapes and sizes. We shall address this issue in Section 7.12. For now, we shall draw a displayed pixel as a square, whose center is at the location associated with the pixel,[9] and whose side is equal to the distance between pixels. We shall also assume that a concurrent process reads the contents of the frame buffer and creates the display at the required rate. This assumption, which holds in many systems that have dual-ported memory, allows us to treat the rasterization process independently of the display of the contents of the frame buffer.

The simplest scan-conversion algorithm for line segments has become known as the **DDA algorithm**, after the Digital Differential Analyzer, an early electromechanical device for digital simulation of differential equations. Because a line satisfies the differential equation $dy/dx = m$, where m is the slope, generating a line segment is equivalent to solving a simple differential equation numerically.

Suppose that we have a line segment defined by the endpoints (x_1, y_1) and (x_2, y_2). We assume that, because we are working in the frame buffer, these values have been rounded to have integer values, so the line segment starts and ends at a known pixel.[10] The slope is given by

$$m = \frac{y_2 - y_1}{x_2 - x_1} = \frac{\Delta y}{\Delta x}.$$

We assume that

$$0 \le m \le 1.$$

We can handle other values of m using symmetry. Our algorithm is based on writing a pixel for each value of ix in write_pixel as x goes from x_1 to x_2. If we are on the line segment, as shown in Figure 7.39, for any change in x equal to Δx, the corresponding changes in y must be

$$\Delta y = m \Delta x.$$

As we move from x_1 to x_2, we increase x by 1 each iteration; thus, we must increase y by

$$\Delta y = m.$$

Although each x is an integer, each y is not, because m is a floating-point number, and we must round it to find the appropriate pixel, as shown in Figure 7.40. Our algorithm, in pseudocode, is

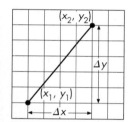

Figure 7.39 Line segment in window coordinates.

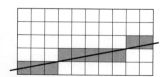

Figure 7.40 Pixels generated by DDA algorithm.

---

[9] In OpenGL, the centers of pixels are located at values halfway between integers. There are some advantages to this choice; see Exercise 7.19.

[10] This assumption is not necessary to derive an algorithm. If we use a fixed-point representation for the endpoints and do our calculations using fixed-point arithmetic, then we retain the computational advantages of the algorithm and produce a more accurate rasterization.

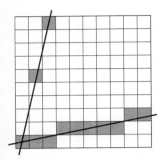

Figure 7.41 Pixels generated by high and low slope lines.

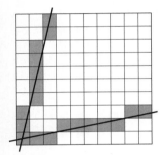

Figure 7.42 Pixels generated by revised DDA algorithm.

```
for(ix=x1, ix <= x2, ix++)
{
    y+=m;
    write_pixel(x, round(y) , line_color);
}
```

where `round` is a function that rounds a real to an integer. The reason that we limited the maximum slope to 1 can be seen from Figure 7.41. Our algorithm is of this form: For each x, find the best y. For large slopes, the separation between pixels that are colored can be large, generating an unacceptable approximation to the line segment. If, however, for slopes greater than 1, we swap the roles of x and y, the algorithm becomes this: For each y, find the best x. For the same line segments, we get the approximations in Figure 7.42. Note that the use of symmetry removes any potential problems from either vertical or horizontal line segments. You may want to derive the parts of the algorithm for negative slopes.

Because line segments are determined by vertices, we can use interpolation to assign different colors to each pixel that we generate. We can also generate various dash and dot patterns by changing the color that we use as we generate pixels. Neither of these effects has much to do with the basic rasterization algorithm, as the latter's job is to determine only which pixels to set, rather than to determine the color that is used.

7.9   Bresenham's Algorithm

The DDA algorithm appears efficient. Certainly it can be coded easily, but it requires a floating-point addition for each pixel generated. Bresenham derived a line-rasterization algorithm that, remarkably, avoids all floating-point calculations and has become the standard algorithm used in hardware and software rasterizers.

We assume, as we did with the DDA algorithm, that the line segment goes between the points (x_1, y_1) and (x_2, y_2), and that the slope satisfies

$$0 \leq m \leq 1.$$

This slope condition is crucial for the algorithm, as we can see with aid of Figure 7.43. Suppose that we are somewhere in the middle of the scan conversion of our line segment and have just placed a pixel at $(i + \frac{1}{2}, j + \frac{1}{2})$. If we look at only the pixel, we know that the line of which the segment is part can be represented as

$$y = mx + h.$$

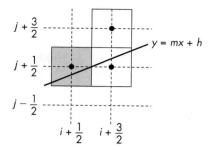

Figure 7.43 Conditions for Bresenham's algorithm.

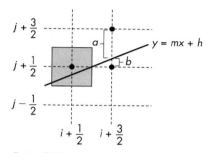

Figure 7.44 Decision variable for Bresenham's algorithm.

At $x = i + \frac{1}{2}$, this line must pass within one-half of a pixel of $(i + \frac{1}{2}, j + \frac{1}{2})$;[11] otherwise the rounding operation would not have generated this pixel. If we move ahead to $x = i + \frac{3}{2}$, the slope condition indicates that we must set one of only two possible pixels: either the pixel at $(i + \frac{3}{2}, j + \frac{1}{2})$, or the pixel at $(i + \frac{3}{2}, j + \frac{3}{2})$. Having reduced our choices to two pixels, we can re-pose the problem in terms of the **decision variable** $d = a - b$, where a and b are the distances between the line and, the upper and lower candidate pixels at $x = i + \frac{3}{2}$, respectively, as shown in Figure 7.44. If d is positive, the line passes closer to the lower pixel, so we choose the pixel at $(i + \frac{3}{2}, j + \frac{1}{2})$; otherwise, we choose the pixel at $(i + \frac{3}{2}, j + \frac{3}{2})$. Although we could compute d by computing $y = mx + b$, we hesitate to do so because m is a floating-point number.

We obtain the computational advantages of Bresenham's algorithm through two further steps. First, we replace floating-point operations with fixed-point operations. Second, we apply the algorithm incrementally. We start by replacing d with the new decision variable

---

[11] We are assuming pixels' centers are located halfway between integers.

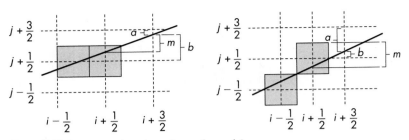

Figure 7.45 Incrementing the values of a and b.

$$d = (x_2 - x_1)(a - b) = \Delta x(a - b),$$

a change that cannot affect which pixels are drawn, because it is only the sign of the decision variable that matters. If we substitute for a and b, using the equation of the line, and noting that

$$m = \frac{y_2 - y_1}{x_2 - x_1} = \frac{\Delta y}{\Delta x},$$

$$h = y_2 - mx_2,$$

we can see that d is an integer. We have eliminated floating-point calculations, but the direct computation of d requires a fair amount of fixed-point arithmetic.

We shall take a slightly different approach. Suppose that d_k is the value of d at $x = k + \frac{1}{2}$. We would like to compute d_{k+1} incrementally from d_k. There are two situations, depending on whether or not we incremented the y location of the pixel at the previous step; these situations are shown in Figure 7.45. By observing that a is the distance between the location of the upper candidate location and the line, we see that a will increase by m only if x was increased by the previous decision; otherwise, it will decrease by $m - 1$. Likewise, b either decreases by $-m$ or increases by $1 - m$ when we increment x. Multiplying by Δx, we find that the possible changes in d are either $2\Delta y$ or $2(\Delta y - \Delta x)$. We can state this result in the form

$$d_{k+1} = d_k + \begin{cases} 2\Delta y & \text{if } d_k > 0; \\ 2(\Delta y - \Delta x) & \text{otherwise.} \end{cases}$$

The calculation of each successive pixel in the frame buffer requires only an addition and a sign test. This algorithm is so efficient that it has been incorporated as a single instruction on graphics chips. See Exercise 7.14 for calculation of the initial value d_0.

7.10   Scan-Conversion of Polygons

One of the major advantages that the first raster systems brought to users was the ability to display filled polygons. At that time, coloring each point

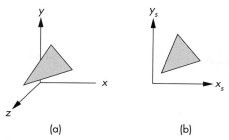

Figure 7.46 Dual representations of a polygon. (a) Normalized device coordinates. (b) Screen coordinates.

in the interior of a polygon with a different shade was not possible in real time, and the phrase *rasterization of polygons* came to mean filling a polygon with a single color. Unlike scan conversion of lines, where a single algorithm dominates, there are many viable methods for rasterizing polygons. The choice depends heavily on the implementation architecture. We shall concentrate on methods that fit with our pipeline approach and can also support shading. In Section 7.10.4, we shall survey a number of other approaches.

7.10.1 Scan Conversion with the z Buffer

We already have presented most of the essentials of polygon rasterization. In Chapter 2, we discussed the odd–even and winding tests for determining whether a point is inside a polygon. In Chapter 6, we learned to shade polygons by interpolation. Here, we have only to put together the pieces, and to consider efficiency.

Suppose that we follow the pipeline once more, concentrating on what happens to a single polygon. The vertices and normals pass through the geometric transformations one at a time. The vertices must be assembled into a polygon before the clipping stage. If our polygon is not clipped out, its vertices and normals can be passed on for shading and hidden-surface removal. At this point, although projection normalization has taken place, we still have depth information. If we wish to use an interpolative shading method, we can compute the lighting at each vertex.

Three tasks remain to be done: the final orthographic projection, hidden-surface removal, and shading. Careful use of the z-buffer algorithm can accomplish all three tasks simultaneously. Consider the dual representations of a polygon in Figure 7.46. On the left, the polygon is represented in three-dimensional normalized device coordinates; on the right, it is shown after projection in screen coordinates.

The strategy is to process each polygon, one scan line at a time. If we work in terms of the dual representations, we can see that a scan line, projected backward from screen coordinates, corresponds to a line of constant y in normalized

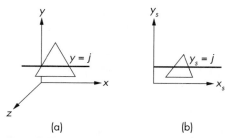

Figure 7.47 Scan line in (a) Normalized device coordinates. (b) Screen coordinates.

device coordinates (Figure 7.47). Suppose that we simultaneously march across this scan line and its back projection. For the scan line in screen coordinates, we move one pixel width each step. We use the normalized-device-coordinate line to determine depths incrementally, and to see whether or not the pixel in screen coordinates corresponds to a visible point on the polygon. Having computed shading for the vertices of the original polygon, we can use bilinear interpolation to obtain the correct color for visible pixels.[12] This process requires little extra effort over the individual steps that we have already discussed. It is controlled, and thus limited, by the rate at which we can send polygons through the pipeline. Modifications, such as applying bit patterns, called stipple patterns, or texture to polygons, require only slight modifications, several of which we shall discuss in Chapter 10.

7.10.2 Fill and Sort

A different approach to rasterization of polygons starts with the idea of a polygon processor, a black box whose inputs are the vertices for a set of two-dimensional polygons and whose output is a frame buffer with the correct pixels set. Suppose that we consider filling each polygon with a constant color—a choice that we make only to clarify the discussion. First, consider a single polygon. The basic rule for filling a polygon is as follows: *If a point is inside the polygon, color it with the inside (fill) color.* This conceptual algorithm indicates that polygon fill is a sorting problem, where we sort all the pixels in the frame buffer into those that are inside the polygon, and those that are not. From this perspective, we obtain different polygon-fill algorithms using different ways of sorting the points. We shall introduce three possibilities:

1. Flood fill
2. Scan-line fill
3. Odd–even fill.

---

[12] Note that carrying out interpolation of shades in normalized device coordinates will yield results different from those of interpolation after projection to screen coordinates.

7.10.3 Flood Fill

We can display an unfilled polygon by rasterizing its edges into the frame buffer using Bresenham's algorithm. Suppose that we have only two colors; a background color (white) and a foreground, or drawing, color (black). We can use the foreground color to rasterize the edges, resulting in a frame buffer colored, as shown in Figure 7.48, for a simple polygon. If we can find an initial point (x, y) inside the polygon—a **seed point**—then we can look at its neighbors recursively, coloring them with the foreground color if they are not edge points. The algorithm can be expressed in pseudocode, assuming that there is a function `read_pixel` that returns the color of a pixel:

```
flood_fill(int x, int y)
{
    if(read_pixel(x,y)==WHITE)
    {
        write_pixel(x,y,BLACK);
        flood_fill(x-1,y);
        flood_fill(x+1,y);
        flood_fill(x,y-1);
        flood_fill(x,y+1);
    }
}
```

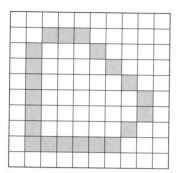

Figure 7.48 Polygon displayed by edges.

We can obtain a number of variants of flood fill by removing the recursion. One way to do so is to work one scan line at a time.

7.10.4 Scan-Line Algorithms

The attraction of a scan-line method is that such a method has the potential to generate pixels as they are displayed. Consider the polygon in Figure 7.49, with one scan line shown. If we use our odd–even rule for defining the inside of the polygon, we can see three groups of pixels, or **spans**, on this scan line that are inside the polygon. Note that each span can be processed independently for lighting or depth calculations, a strategy that has been employed in some hardware that has parallel span processors. For our simple example of constant fill, after we have identified the spans, we can color the interior pixels of each span with the fill color.

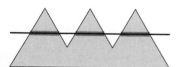

Figure 7.49 Polygon with spans.

The spans are determined by the set of intersections of polygons with scan lines. The vertices contain all the information necessary to determine these intersections, but the method that we use to represent the polygon determines the order in which these intersections are generated. For example, consider the polygon in Figure 7.50 that has been represented by an ordered list of vertices. The most obvious way to generate scan-line-edge intersections is to process edges defined by successive vertices. Figure 7.50 shows these intersections, indexed in the order in which this method would generate them. Note that this calculation can be done incrementally (see Exercise 7.18). However, as far

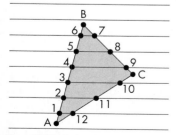

Figure 7.50 Polygon generated by vertex list.

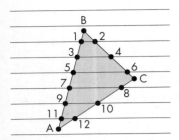

Figure 7.51 Desired order of vertices.

as fill is concerned, this order is far from the one we want. If we are to fill one scan line at a time, we would like the intersections sorted, first by scan lines, and then by order of x on each scan line, as shown in Figure 7.51. A brute-force approach might be to sort all the intersections into the desired order. However, a large or jagged polygon might intersect so many edges that the n intersections can be large enough—consider, for example, a polygon that spans one-half of the scan lines—that the $O(n \log n)$ complexity of the sort will make the calculation too slow for real-time implementations.

A number of methods avoid the general search. One, originally known as the **y-x algorithm**, creates a bucket for each scan line. As edges are processed, the intersections with scan lines are placed in the proper buckets. Within each bucket, an insertion sort orders the x values along each scan line. The data structure is shown in Figure 7.52. Once again, we see that a properly chosen data structure can speed up the algorithm. We can go even further by reconsidering how to represent polygons: We arrive at the scan-line method that was introduced in Section 7.7.

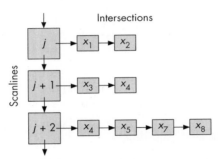

Figure 7.52 Data structure for y–x algorithm.

7.10.5 Singularities

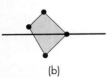

(a)

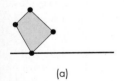

(b)

Figure 7.53 Singularities. (a) Zero or two edge crossings (b) One edge crossing.

We can extend most polygon-fill algorithms to other shapes if we use care (see Exercise 7.17). Polygons have the distinct advantage that the locations of their edges are known exactly. However, even polygons can present problems when vertices lie on scan lines. Consider the two cases in Figure 7.53. If we are using an odd–even fill definition, we have to treat these two cases differently. For part a, we can count the intersection of the scan line with the vertex as either zero or two edge crossings; for part b, the vertex–scan-line intersection must be counted as one edge crossing.

We can fix our algorithm in one of two ways. We can check to see which of the two situations we have, and can then count the edge crossings appropriately. Or we can prevent the special case of a vertex lying on an edge—a **singularity**—from ever arising. We rule it out by ensuring that no vertex has an integer y value. If we find one that does, we can perturb its location slightly. Another method, which is especially valuable if we are working in the frame buffer, is to consider a virtual frame buffer of twice the resolution of the real frame buffer. In the virtual frame buffer, pixels are located at only even values of y, and all vertices are located at only odd values of y. Placing pixel centers halfway between integers, as does OpenGL, is equivalent to this approach.

7.11 Antialiasing

Rasterized line segments and edges of polygons look jagged. Even on a CRT that has a resolution as high as 1024×1280, we can notice these defects in the display. This type of error arises whenever we attempt to go from the continuous representation of an object, which has infinite resolution, to a discrete approximation, which has limited resolution. The name **aliasing** has been given to this effect, because of the tie with aliasing in digital signal processing. We shall discuss this relationship further in Chapter 10.

The errors are caused by three related problems with the discrete nature of the frame buffer. First, if we have an $n \times m$ frame buffer, the number of pixels is fixed, and we can generate only certain patterns to approximate a line segment. Many different continuous line segments may be approximated by the same pattern of pixels. We can say that all these segment are **aliased** as the same sequence of pixels. Second, pixel locations are fixed on a uniform grid; regardless of where we would like to place pixels, we cannot place them at other than evenly spaced locations. Third, pixels have a fixed size and shape.

At first glance, it might appear that there is little we can do about such problems. Algorithms such as Bresenham's algorithm are optimal in that they choose the closest set of pixels to approximate lines and polygons. However, if we have a display that supports more than two shades of gray, there are other possibilities. Although mathematical lines are one-dimensional entities that have length but not width, rasterized lines must have a width in order to be visible. Suppose that each pixel is a square of width one unit, and can occupy a box of unit height and width on the display. Our basic frame buffer can work only in multiples of one pixel;[13] we can think of an idealized line segment in the frame buffer as being one pixel wide, as shown in Figure 7.54. Of course, we cannot draw this line, because it does not consist of our square pixels. We can view Bresenham's algorithm as a method for approximating the ideal one-pixel-wide line with our real pixels. If we look at the ideal one-pixel-wide line, we can see that it partially covers many pixel-sized boxes. It is our scan-conversion algorithm that forces us, for lines of slope less than 1, to choose exactly one

Figure 7.54 Ideal raster line.

---

[13] Some frame buffers permit operations in units of less than one pixel through supersampling, a topic we shall address in Chapter 10.

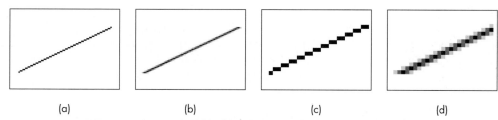

(a)   (b)   (c)   (d)

Figure 7.55 Aliased versus antialiased line segments: (a) Aliased line segment.
(b) Antialiased line segment. (c) Magnified aliased line segment.
(d) Magnified antialiased line segment.

pixel value for each value of x. If, instead, we shade each box by the percentage of the ideal line that crosses it, we get the smoother-appearing image shown in Figure 7.55(b). This technique is known as antialiasing by **area averaging**. The calculation is similar to polygon clipping. There are other approaches to antialiasing and antialiasing algorithms that can be applied to other primitives, such as polygons.

Color Plate 2 shows aliased and antialiased versions of a small area of one of the teeth of the dinosaur from the scene in Color Plate 1.

A related problem arises because of the simple way that we are using the z-buffer algorithm. As we have specified that algorithm, the color of a given pixel is determined by the shade of a single primitive. Consider the pixel shared by the three polygons shown in Figure 7.56. If each polygon has a different color, the color assigned to the pixel will be the one associated with the polygon closest to the viewer. We could obtain a much more accurate image if we could assign a color based on an area-weighted average of the colors of the three triangles. In Chapter 10, we shall introduce the accumulation buffer, which will allow us to implement such techniques.

We have discussed only one type of aliasing: **spatial-domain aliasing**. When we generate sequences of images, such as for animations, we also must be concerned with **time-domain aliasing**. Consider a small object that is moving in front of the projection plane and that has been ruled into pixel-sized units—as shown in Figure 7.57. If our rendering process sends a ray through the center of each pixel and determines what it hits, then sometimes we will intersect the object and sometimes, if the projection of the object is small, we will miss the object. The viewer will have the unpleasant experience of seeing the object flash on and off the display as the animation progresses. There are ways to deal with this problem. For example, we can use more than one ray per pixel–a technique common in ray tracing. What is common to all antialiasing techniques is that they require considerably more computation than does rendering without antialiasing. In practice, for high-resolution images, antialiasing is done off-line, and is done only when a final image is needed.

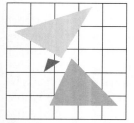

Figure 7.56 Polygons that share a pixel.

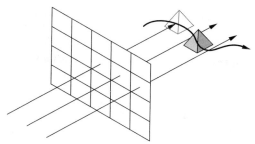

Figure 7.57 Time-domain aliasing.

7.12 Display Considerations

In most interactive applications, the application programmer does not have to worry about how the contents of the frame buffer are displayed. In scan-line-based systems, the display is generated directly by the rasterization algorithms. In the more common approach for workstations, the frame buffer consists of dual-ported memory; the process of writing into the frame buffer is completely independent of the process of reading the frame buffer's contents for display. Thus, the hardware redisplays the present contents of the frame buffer at a rate sufficient to avoid flicker—usually 60 to 75 Hz—and the application programmer worries about only whether or not her program can execute and fill the frame buffer fast enough. As we saw in Chapter 3, the use of double buffering allows the display to change smoothly, even if we cannot push our primitives through the system as fast as we would like.

Numerous other problems affect the quality of the display and often cause users to be unhappy with the output of their programs. For example, two CRT displays may have the same nominal resolution but may display pixels of different sizes (see Exercises 7.22 and 7.23).

7.12.1 Color Systems

Virtually all our discussion of color has been in terms of additive RGB color. Our basic assumption, supported by the three-color theory of human vision, is that the three color values that we determine for each pixel correspond to the tristimulus values that we introduced in Chapter 2. However, there are significant differences across RGB systems. For example, suppose that we have a yellow color that OpenGL has represented with the RGB triplet (0.8, 0.6, 0.0). If we use these values to drive both a CRT and a film-image recorder, we will see different colors, even though in both cases the red is 80 percent of maximum, the green is 60 percent of maximum, and the blue is off. The reason is that the film primaries and the CRT phosphors have different color distributions.

The emphasis in the graphics community has been on device-independent graphics; consequently, the real differences among display properties are not addressed by most APIs. Fortunately the colorimetry literature contains the information that we need. The standards for many of the common color systems exist. For example, CRTs are based on the National Television Systems Committee (NTSC) RGB system. We can look at differences in color systems as equivalent to different coordinate systems for representing our tristimulus values. If $\mathbf{C}_1 = [R_1, G_1, B_1]^T$ and $\mathbf{C}_2 = [R_2, G_2, B_2]^T$ are the representations of the same color in two different systems, there is a 3×3 color-conversion matrix $\mathbf{M}$ such that

$$\mathbf{C}_2 = \mathbf{MC}_1.$$

Whether we determine this matrix from the literature or by experimentation, it allows is to produce similar displays on different output devices.

There are numerous potential problems even with this approach. The color gamuts of the two systems may not be the same. Hence, even after the conversion of tristimulus, a color may not be producible on one of the systems. Second, the printing and graphic arts industries use a four-color subtractive system (CMYK) that adds black (K) as a fourth primary. Conversion between RGB and CMYK often requires a great deal of human expertise. Third, there are limitations to our linear color theory. The distance between colors in the color cube is not a measure of how far apart the colors are perceptually. For example, humans are particularly sensitive to color shifts in blue. Color systems such as YUV and Lab have been created to address such issues.

An additional defect of our development of color is that RGB color is based on how color is produced and measured, rather than on how we conceptualize a color. When we see a given color, we describe it not by three primaries, but rather based on other properties, such as the name that we give the color and how bright a shade we see. The hue-saturation-lightness (HLS) system is used by artists and some display manufacturers. The **hue** is the name that we give to a color: red, yellow, gold. The **lightness** is how bright the color appears. **Saturation** is the color attribute that distinguishes a pure shade of a color from the a shade of the same hue that has been mixed with white, forming a pastel shade. We can relate these attributes to a typical RGB color as shown in Figure 7.58(a). Given a color in the color cube, the lightness is a measure of how far the point is from the origin (black). If we note that all the colors on the principal diagonal of the cube, going from black to white, are shades of gray and are totally unsaturated, then the saturation is a measure of how far the given color is from this diagonal. Finally, the hue is a measure of where the color vector is pointing. HLS colors are usually described in terms of a color cone, as shown in Figure 7.58(b), or through a double cone that also converges at the top. From our perspective, we can look at the HLS system as providing a representation of an RGB color in polar coordinates.

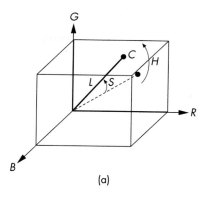

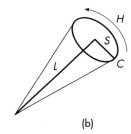

Figure 7.58 Hue-lightness-saturation color.
(a) In RGB color cube (b) Using single cone.

7.12.2 Gamma Correction

In Chapter 2, we defined brightness as perceived intensity, and observed that the human visual system perceives intensity in a logarithmic manner, as shown in Figure 7.59. One consequence of this property is that, if we want the brightness steps to appear to be uniformly spaced, the intensities that we assign to pixels should increase exponentially. These steps can be calculated from the measured minimum and maximum intensities that a display can generate (see Exercise 7.25).

In addition, the intensity I of a CRT is related to the voltage V applied by

$$\log I = c_0 + \gamma \log V,$$

where the constants γ and c_0 are properties of the particular CRT. One implication of these two results is that two monitors may generate different brightnesses for the same values in the frame buffer. One way to correct for this problem is to have a look-up table in the display whose values can be adjusted for the particular characteristics of the monitor—the gamma correction.

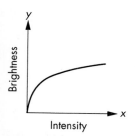

Figure 7.59 Logarithmic brightness.

7.12.3 Dithering and Halftoning

We have specified a frame buffer by its spatial resolution (the number of pixels), and by its depth (the number of colors that it can display). If we view these separate numbers as fixed, we say that a high-resolution black-and-white laser printer can display only 1-bit pixels. This argument also seems to imply that any black-and-white medium, such as a book, could not display images with multiple shades. We know from experience that that is not the case; the trick is to trade spatial resolution for gray-scale or color resolution. **Halftoning** techniques in the printing industry use photographic means to simulate gray levels by creating patterns of black dots of varying size. The human visual system tends to merge small dots together and sees, not the dots, but rather an intensity proportional to the percentage of black in a small area.

Digital halftones differ because the size and location of displayed pixels are fixed. Consider a 4×4 group of 1-bit pixels, as shown in Figure 7.60. If we look at this pattern from far away, we see not the individual pixels, but rather a gray level based on the number of black pixels. For our 4×4 example, although there are 2^{16} different patterns of black and white pixels, there are only 17 possible shades, corresponding to 0 to 16 black pixels in the array. There are many algorithms for generating halftone, or **dither**, patterns. The simplest picks 17 patterns (for our example), and uses them to create a display with 17 rather than two gray levels, although at the cost of decreasing the spatial resolution by a factor of 4.

The simple algorithm—always using the same array to simulate a shade—can generate beat or **moiré patterns** when displaying anything regular. Such patterns arise whenever we image two regular phenomena, as we see the sum and differences of their frequencies. Such effects are closely related to the aliasing problems to which we shall return in Chapter 10. More sophisticated dither algorithms use randomization to create patterns with the correct average properties, but avoid the repetition that can lead to moire effects (see Exercise 7.26).

Halftoning (or dithering) is often used with color, especially with hard-copy displays, such as ink-jet printers, that can produce only fully on or off colors. Each primary can be dithered to produce more visual colors. OpenGL supports such displays and allows the user to enable dithering (`glEnable(GL_DITHER)`).

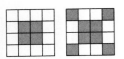

Figure 7.60 Digital halftone patterns.

7.13   Summary

We have presented an overview of the implementation process, including a sampling of the most important algorithms. Regardless of what the particulars are of an implementation, whether the tasks are done primarily in hardware or in software, whether we are working with a special-purpose graphics workstation or with a simple graphics terminal, and what the API is, the same tasks must be done. These tasks include implementation of geometric transformations, clipping, and rasterization. The relationship between hardware, software, and APIs is an interesting one.

The Geometry Engine that was the basis of many Silicon Graphics workstations is a VLSI chip that performed geometric transformations and clipping through a hardware pipeline. GL, the predecessor of OpenGL, was developed as an API for users of these workstations. Much of the OpenGL literature also follows the pipeline approach. However, we should keep in mind that OpenGL is an API: It does not say anything about the underlying implementation. In principle, an image defined by an OpenGL program could be obtained from a ray tracer. We should carry away two lessons from our emphasis on pipeline architectures. First, this architecture provides an aid to the applications programmer in understanding the process of creating images. Second, at present, the pipeline view can lead to efficient hardware and software implementations.

So what does the future hold? Certainly, graphics systems will get faster and cheaper. More than any other factor, advances in hardware probably will dictate what future graphics systems will look like.

The example of the z-buffer algorithm is illustrative of the relationship between hardware and software. A decade ago, many hidden-surface-removal algorithms were used, of which the z-buffer algorithm was only one. The availability of fast cheap memory has made the z-buffer algorithm the dominant algorithm for hidden-surface removal. A related example is that of workstation architectures, where many special-purpose graphics chips have been supplanted by standard floating-point and signal-processing chips.

Numerous advanced architectures under exploration use massive parallelism. How parallelism can be exploited most effectively for computer graphics is still an open issue. Our two approaches to rendering—object-oriented and image-oriented—lead to two entirely different ways to develop a parallel renderer.

We have barely scratched the surface of implementation. The literature is rich with algorithms for every aspect of the implementation process. The references should help you to explore this topic further. In Chapter 8, we shall turn to advanced techniques that are supported through APIs such as OpenGL.

7.14   References

The books by Rogers [Rog85] and Foley et al. [Fol90] contain many more algorithms than we can present here. Also see the series *Graphic Gems* [Gra90, Gra91, Gra92, Gra 94, Gra95].

The Cohen–Sutherland [Sut63] clipping algorithm goes back to the early years of computer graphics, as does Bresenham's algorithm [Bre63, Bre87], which was originally proposed for pen plotters. See [Lia84] and [Sut74a] for the Liang–Barsky and Sutherland–Hogman clippers.

The z-buffer algorithm was developed by Catmull [Cat75]. See [Sut74b] for a discussion of various approaches to hidden-surface removal.

Our decision to avoid details of the hardware does not imply that the hardware is either simple or uninteresting. The rate at which a modern graphics processor can display graphical entities requires sophisticated and clever hardware designs; see [Cla82, Ake88, Ake93]. The discussion by Molnar and Fuchs in [Fol90] shows a variety of approaches.

Pratt [Pra78] contains matrices to covert among various color systems. Halftone and dithering are discussing in Jarvis et al. [Jar76] and in Knuth [Knu87].

7.15   Exercises

7.1   Consider two line segments represented in parametric form:

$$\mathbf{p}(\alpha) = (1 - \alpha)\mathbf{p}_1 + \alpha\mathbf{p}_2,$$
$$\mathbf{q}(\beta) = (1 - \beta)\mathbf{q}_1 + \beta\mathbf{q}_2.$$

Find a procedure for determining whether the segments intersect, and, if they do, for finding the point of intersection.

7.2   Extend the argument of Exercise 7.1 to find a method for determining whether two flat polygons intersect.

7.3   Prove that clipping a convex object against another convex object results in at most one convex object.

7.4   In what ways can you parallelize the image- and object-oriented approaches to implementation?

7.5   Because normals and vertices can both be represented in homogenous coordinates, both can be operated on by the model-view transformation. Show that normals may not be preserved by the transformation.

7.6   Derive the viewport transformation. Express it in terms of the three-dimensional scaling and translation matrices used to represent affine transformations in two dimensions.

7.7   Pre–raster-graphics systems were able to display only lines. Three-dimensional images could be produced using hidden-line-removal techniques. Many current APIs allow us to produce wireframe images, composed of only lines, in which the hidden lines that define nonvisible surfaces have been removed. How does this problem differ from the polygon hidden-surface removal that we have considered? Derive a hidden-line-removal algorithm for objects consisting of the edges of planar polygons.

7.8   Often, we display functions of the form $y = f(x, z)$ by displaying a rectangular mesh generated by the set of values $\{f(x_i, z_j)\}$ evaluated at regular intervals in x and z. Hidden-surface removal should be applied, because parts of the surface can be obscured from view by other parts. Derive two algorithms, one using hidden-surface removal and the other using hidden-line removal, to display such a mesh.

7.9   Although we argued that the complexity of the image-space approach to hidden-surface removal is proportional to the number of polygons, performance studies have shown almost constant performance. How can you explain this result?

7.10   Consider a scene composed of only solid three-dimensional polyhedra. Can you devise an object-space hidden-surface-removal algorithm for this case? How much does it help if you know that all the polyhedra are convex?

7.11   We can look at object-space approaches to hidden-surface removal as analogous to sorting algorithms. However, we argued that the former's complexity is $O(k^2)$. We know that only the worst sorting algorithms have such poor performance, and most are $O(k \log k)$. Does it follow that object-space hidden-surface-removal algorithms should have similar complexity? Explain your answer.

7.12   Devise a method for testing whether one planar polygon is fully on one side of another planar polygon.

7.13   What are the differences between our image-space approaches to hidden-surface removal and to ray tracing? Can we use ray tracing as an alternate technique to hidden-surface removal? What are the advantages and disadvantages of such an approach?

7.14   Write a program to generate the locations of pixels along a rasterized line segment using Bresenham's algorithm. Check that your program works for all slopes and all possible locations of the endpoints. What is the initial value of the decision variable?

7.15   Bresenham's algorithm can be extended to circles. Convince yourself of this statement by considering a circle centered at the origin. Which parts of the circle must be generated by an algorithm, and which parts can be found by symmetry? Can you find a part of the circle such that, if we know a point generated by a scan-conversion algorithm, we can reduce the number of candidates for the next pixel?

7.16   Show how to use flood fill to generate a maze, like the one that you created in Exercise 2.8.

7.17   Suppose that you try to extend flood fill to arbitrary closed curves by scan converting the curve and then applying the same fill algorithm that we used for polygons. What problems can arise if you use this approach?

7.18   Consider the edge of a polygon between vertices at (x_1, y_1) and (x_2, y_2). Derive an efficient algorithm for computing the intersection of all scan lines with this edge. Assume that you are working in window coordinates.

7.19   Vertical and horizontal edges are potentially problematic for polygon-fill algorithms. How would you handle theses cases for the algorithms that we have presented?

7.20   In two-dimensional graphics, if two polygons overlap, we can ensure that they are rendered in the same order by all implementations by associating a priority attribute with each polygon. Polygons are rendered in reverse-priority order; that is, the highest-priority polygon is rendered last. How should we modify our polygon-fill algorithms to take priority into account?

7.21   A standard antialiasing technique used in ray tracing is to cast rays not only through the center of each pixel, but also through the pixel's four corners. What is the increase in work compared to casting a single ray through the center?

7.22   Although an ideal pixel is a square of 1 unit per side, most CRT systems generate round pixels that can be approximated as circles of uniform intensity. If a completely full unit square has intensity 1.0, and an empty square has intensity 0.0, how does the intensity of a displayed pixel vary with the radius of the circle?

7.23   Consider a bilevel display with round pixels. Do you think it is wiser to use small circles or large circles for foreground colored pixel? Explain your answer.

7.24   Why is defocusing the beam of a CRT sometimes called "the poor person's antialiasing"?

7.25   Suppose that a monochrome display has a minimum intensity output of I_{min}—a CRT display is never completely black—and a maximum output of I_{max}. Given that we perceive intensities in a logarithmic manner, how should we assign k intensity levels such that the steps appear uniform?

7.26   Generate a halftone algorithm based on the following idea. Suppose that gray levels vary from 0.0 to 1.0, and that we have a random-number generator that produces random numbers that are uniformly distributed over this interval. If we pick a gray level g, $g/100$ percent of the random numbers generated will be less than g.

7.27   Images produced on displays that support only a few colors or gray levels tend to show contour effects because the viewer can detect the differences between adjacent shades. One technique for avoiding this visual effect is to add a little noise (jitter) to the pixel values. Why does this technique work? How much noise should you add? Does it make sense to conclude that the degraded image created by the addition of noise is of quality higher than that of the original image?

8 Working with Models

Models are abstractions of the world—both of the real world in which we live, and of virtual worlds that we create through our programs. We are all familiar with mathematical models that are used in all areas of science and engineering. These models use equations to model the physical phenomena that we wish to study. In computer science, we use abstract data types to model organizations of objects; in computer graphics, we model our worlds with geometric objects. When we build a mathematical model, we choose carefully which type of mathematics will fit the phenomena that we wish to model. Although ordinary differential equations may be appropriate for modeling the dynamical behavior of a system of weights and pulleys, we would probably use partial differential equations to model turbulent fluid flow. We go through analogous processes in computer graphics, choosing which primitives to use in our models and how to show relationships among them. Often, as is true of choosing a mathematical model, there are multiple approaches, so we seek models that can take advantage of the capabilities of our graphics systems.

We shall explore four approaches to developing and working with models of geometric objects. You can study each approach independently. First, we consider models that use a set of simple geometric objects; either the primitives supported by our graphics systems, or a set of user-defined objects built from these primitives. We shall extend the use of transformations from Chapter 4 to include hierarchical relationships among the objects. The techniques that we shall develop will be appropriate for applications, such as robotics and figure animation, where the dynamic behavior of the objects is characterized by relationships among the parts of the model.

The second approach that we shall investigate is characterizing geometric models through language-based systems. These grammatical models not only will give us a second method for representing hierarchical structures, but also will allow us to control how much detail we generate when the model is rendered. This approach will lead us to consider models that possess a self-similarity, where one part of the model looks like a scaled version of the entire model. Here, we shall introduce elements of fractal geometry.

Third, we shall consider the related problems of imposing physical constraints on our models and using physical laws to govern the time behavior of geometric objects. We shall focus on particle systems, a method that has been applied in areas as diverse as animation and scientific visualization.

Finally, we shall consider two methods of building curves and surfaces from data. Although we shall not develop curves and surfaces systematically until Chapter 9, the focus here will be on generating geometric objects—models—from data sets, and on using the capabilities of the graphics system to display the resulting geometric objects such that humans can interpret the original data. We shall introduce a method of visualization for three-dimensional data sets—marching cubes—that will illustrate how scientific visualization can make use of the power of the geometric-processing capabilities in our graphics systems.

8.1   Symbols and Instances

Most APIs take a minimalist attitude toward primitives. They contain only a few primitives, leaving it to the user to construct more complex objects from these primitives. Sometimes, additional libraries, such as GLU and GLUT that we have used with OpenGL, provide additional objects, built on top of the basic primitives. We shall assume that we have available a collection of basic three-dimensional objects provided by these options.

We can take a nonhierarchical approach to modeling by regarding these objects as **symbols**, and modeling our world as a collection of symbols. Symbols can include geometric objects, fonts, and application-dependent sets of graphical objects, such as the standard symbols used in circuit design. Symbols are usually represented at a convenient size and orientation. For example, a cylinder is usually oriented parallel to one of the axes, as shown in Figure 8.1, often with a unit height and a unit radius, and with its bottom centered at the origin.

Various APIs, including PHIGS and GKS, make a distinction between the frame in which the symbol is defined, sometimes called the **model frame** or **model coordinates**, and the world frame. This distinction can be helpful when the symbols are purely shapes, such as the symbols that we might use for circuit elements in a CAD application, and have no physical units associated with them.

The instance transformation that we introduced in Chapter 4 allows us to place instances of each symbol in the model, with the desired size, and orientation, and at the desired location. Thus, the instance transformation

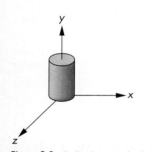

Figure 8.1 Cylinder symbol.

$$\mathbf{M} = \mathbf{TRS}$$

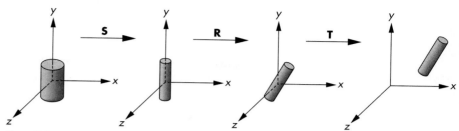

Figure 8.2 Instance transformation.

Symbol	Scale	Rotate	Translate
1	s_x, s_y, s_z	$\theta_x, \theta_y, \theta_z$	d_x, d_y, d_z
2			
3			
1			
1			
.			
.			

Figure 8.3 Symbol–instance transformation table.

is a concatenation of a translation, a rotation, and a scale (and possibly a shear), as shown in Figure 8.2. Consequently, OpenGL programs often contain repetitions of code in the form

```
glMatrixMode(GL_MODELVIEW);
glLoadIdentity();
glTranslatef( ... );
glRotatef( ... );
glScalef( ... );
glutSolidCylinder( ... ); /* or some other symbol */
```

We can also think of such a model in the form of a table, as shown in Figure 8.3. Here, each symbol is assumed to have a unique numerical identifier. The table shows that this modeling technique contains no information about relationships among objects. The table also shows, however, that we can use data structures to represent geometric models.

8.2 Hierarchical Models

Suppose that we wish to build a model of an automobile that we can animate. We can compose the model from five parts—the chassis and the four wheels (Figure 8.4)—each of which we can describe by using our standard graphics

Figure 8.4 Automobile model.

Figure 8.5 Two frames of animation.

primitives. Two frames of a simple animation of the model are shown in Figure 8.5. We could write a program to generate this animation by noting that, if each wheel has a radius r, then a 360-degree rotation of a wheel must correspond to the car moving forward (or backward) a distance of $2\pi r$. The program could then contain one function to generate each wheel, and another to generate the chassis. All these functions could use the same input, such as the desired speed and direction of the automobile. In pseudocode, our program might look like this:

```
main()
{
    float s= ...; /* speed */
    float d[3]={...}; /* direction */
    draw_right_front_wheel(s,d);
    draw_left_front_wheel(s,d);
    draw_right_rear_wheel(s,d);
    draw_left_rear_wheel(s,d);
    draw_chassis(s,d);
}
```

This program is just the kind that we do *not* want to write. It is linear, and it shows none of the relationships among the components of the automobile. There are two types of relationships that we would like to exploit. First, we cannot separate the movement of the car from the movement of the wheels. If the car moves forward, the wheels must turn.[1] We shall express this relationship graphically. Second, we would like to use the fact that all the wheels of the automobile are identical; they are merely located in different places, with different orientations.

We can represent the relationships among parts of the models, both abstractly and visually, with graphs. Mathematically, a **graph** consists of a set of **nodes** (or vertices) and a set of **edges**. Edges connect pairs of nodes, or possibly connect a node to itself. Edges can have a direction associated with them;

---

[1] It is not clear whether we should say the wheels move the chassis or the chassis moves the wheels. From a graphics perspective, the later view is probably more useful.

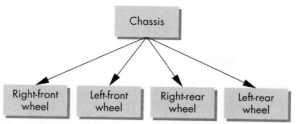

Figure 8.6 Tree structure for automobile.

the graphs we shall use here will all be **directed graphs**, graphs that have their edges leaving one node and entering another.

The most important type of graph with which we shall work is a tree. A (connected) **tree** is a directed graph without closed paths or loops. In addition, each node, except one—the **root node**—has one edge entering it. Thus, every node, except the root, has a **parent node**, the node from which an edge enters, and can have one or more **child nodes**, nodes to which edges are connected. A node without children is called a **terminal node**. Figure 8.6 shows a tree that represents the relationships in our car model. The chassis is the root node, and all four wheels are its children. Although the mathematical graph is a collection of set elements, in practice, both the edges and nodes can contain additional information. For our car example, the nodes can contain information on how to draw the various objects.

In most cars, the four wheels are identical, so storing the same information on how to draw each one at four nodes is inefficient. We can use the ideas behind the instance-transformation to allow us to use a single prototype wheel in our model. If we do so, we can replace the tree structure by the **directed acyclic graph (DAG)** in Figure 8.7. In a DAG, although there are loops, we cannot follow directed edges around the loop. Thus, if we follow any path of directed edges from a node, the path will terminate at another node. For our car, we can store the information that positions each instance of the single prototype wheel in the chassis node, in the wheel node, or with the edges.

Both forms—trees and DAGs—are **hierarchical** methods of expressing the relationships in the physical model. In each form, various elements of a model can be related to other parts—their parents and their children. We shall explore how to express these hierarchies in a graphics program.

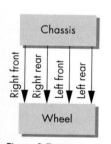

Figure 8.7 Directed-acyclic-graph model of automobile.

8.3   A Robot Arm

Robotics provides many opportunities for developing hierarchical models. Consider the simple robot arm in Figure 8.8(a). We can model it with three simple objects, or symbols, perhaps using only parallelepipeds and a cylinder. Each of the symbols can be built up from our basic primitives.

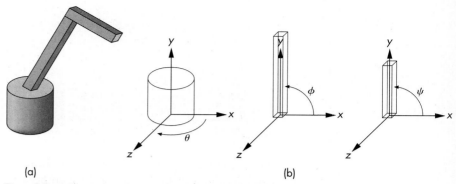

(a)   (b)

Figure 8.8 Robot arm. (a) Total model. (b) Components.

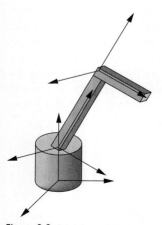

Figure 8.9 Moving robot components and frames.

The robot arm consists of the three parts shown in Figure 8.8(b). The mechanism has 3 degrees of freedom, each of which can be described by a **joint angle** that is measured in each component's own frame. We can rotate the base about its vertical axis by an angle θ. This angle is measured from the x axis to some fixed point on the bottom of the base. The lower arm of the robot is attached to the base by a joint that allows the arm to rotate in the plane $z = 0$ in the arm's frame. This rotation is specified by an angle ϕ that is measured from the x axis to the arm. The upper arm is attached to the lower arm by a similar joint, and it can rotate by an angle ψ, measured like that for the lower arm, in its own frame. As the angles vary, we can think of the frames of the upper and lower arms as moving relative to the base. By controlling the three angles, we can position the tip of the upper arm in three dimensions.

Suppose that we wish to write a program to animate our simple robot. Rather than defining each part of the robot, and its motion, independently, we shall take an incremental approach. The base of the robot can rotate about the y axis in its frame by the angle θ. Thus, we can describe the motion of any point **p** on the base by applying a rotation matrix $\mathbf{R}_y(\theta)$ to it.

The lower arm is rotated about the z axis in its own frame, but this frame must be shifted to the top of the base by a translation matrix $\mathbf{T}(0, h_1, 0)$, where h_1 is the height above the base, at the point where the joint between the base and the lower arm is located. However, if the base has rotated, then we must also rotate the lower arm, using $\mathbf{R}_y(\theta)$. We can accomplish the positioning of the lower arm by applying $\mathbf{R}_y(\theta)\mathbf{T}(0, h_1, 0)\mathbf{R}_z(\phi)$ to the arm's vertices. We can interpret the matrix $\mathbf{R}_y(\theta)\mathbf{T}(0, h_1, 0)$ as the matrix that positions the lower arm *relative* to the world frame, and $\mathbf{R}_z(\phi)$ as the matrix that positions the lower arm *relative* to the base. Equivalently, we can interpret these matrices as positioning the frames of the lower arm and base relative to some world frame, as shown in Figure 8.9.

When we apply similar reasoning to the upper arm, we find that this arm has to be translated by a matrix $\mathbf{T}(0, h_2, 0)$ relative to the lower arm, and then rotated by $\mathbf{R}_z(\psi)$. The matrix that controls the upper arm is thus $\mathbf{R}_y(\theta)\mathbf{T}(0, h_1, 0)\mathbf{R}_z(\phi)\mathbf{T}(0, h_2, 0)\mathbf{R}_z(\psi)$. The form of the display function for an OpenGL program to display the robot as a function of the joint angles shows how we can alter the model-view matrix incrementally to display the various parts of the model efficiently:

```
display()
{
    glRotatef(theta, 0.0, 1.0, 0.0);
    base();
    glTranslatef(0.0, h1, 0.0);
    glRotatef(phi, 0.0, 0.0, 1.0);
    lower_arm();
    glTranslatef(0.0, h2, 0.0);
    glRotatef(psi, 0.0, 0.0, 1.0);
    upper_arm();
}
```

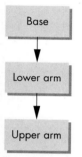

Figure 8.10 Tree structure for the robot arm in Figure 8.8.

Note that we have described the positioning of the arm independently of the details of the individual parts. As long as the positions of the joints do not change, we can alter the form of the robot by changing only the functions that draw the three parts. This separation makes it possible to write separate programs to describe the components and to animate the robot. Figure 8.10 shows the relationships among the parts of the robot arm as a tree. The program robot.c in Appendix A implements the structure, and allows you to animate the robot with the mouse through a menu. It uses a cylinder for the base and parallelepipeds for the arms.

Returning to the tree in Figure 8.10, we can look at it as a tree data structure of nodes and edges—as a graph. If we store all the necessary information in the nodes, rather than in the edges, then each node (Figure 8.11) must store at least three items:

1. A pointer to a function that draws the object represented by the node
2. A homogeneous-coordinate matrix that positions, scales, and orients this node (and its children) relative to the node's parent
3. Pointers to children of the node

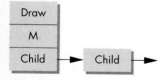

Figure 8.11 Node representation.

Certainly, we can include other information in a node, such as a set of attributes (color, fill pattern, material properties) that applies to the node. Drawing an object described by such a tree requires performing a tree **traversal**. That is, we must visit every node; at each node, we must compute the matrix that applies to the primitives pointed to by the node, and must display these primitives. Our OpenGL program shows an incremental approach to this traversal.

This example is a simple one: There is only a single child for each of the parent nodes in the tree. The next example will show how we handle more complex models.

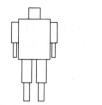

Figure 8.12 Figure representation.

8.4   Trees and Traversal

Figure 8.12 shows a boxlike representation of a human figure, or, possibly, of a robot. If we take the torso as the root element, we can represent this figure with a tree, as shown in Figure 8.13. Once we have positioned the torso, the position and orientation of the other parts of the model are determined by the set of joint angles. We can animate the figure by defining the motion of its joints. In a basic model, the knee and elbow joints might each have only a single degree of freedom, like the robot arm, whereas the joint at the neck might have 2 degrees of freedom.

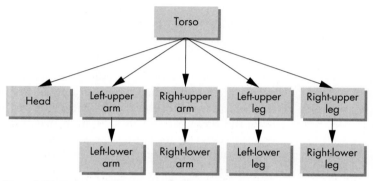

Figure 8.13 Tree representation of figure in Figure 8.12.

Let us assume that we have functions, such as head and left_upper_arm, that draw the individual parts (symbols) in their own frames. We can now build a set of nodes for our tree by defining matrices that position each part relative to its parent, exactly as we did for the robot arm. If we assume that each body part has been defined at the desired size, each of these matrices will be the concatenation of a translation matrix with a rotation matrix. We can show these matrices, as we do in Figure 8.14, by using the matrices to label the edges of the tree. Remember that each matrix represents the incremental change when we go from the parent to the child.

The interesting part of this example is how we do the traversal of the tree to draw the figure. In principle, we could use any tree-traversal algorithm, such as depth-first or breadth-first search. Although, in many applications, it is insignificant which traversal algorithm is used, we shall see that there are good reasons for always using the same algorithm for traversing our graphs. We shall always traverse our trees left to right, depth first. That is, we shall start with the left branch, follow it to the left as deep as we can go, then go back up to the first right branch, and proceed recursively.

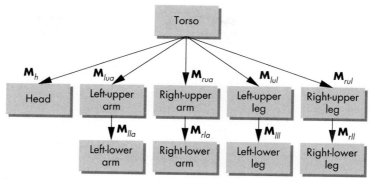

Figure 8.14 Tree with matrices.

Consider the drawing of the figure by a function figure. The model-view matrix, **M**, in effect when this function is invoked determines the position of the figure relative to the rest of the scene (and to the camera). The first node that we encounter results in the torso being drawn with **M** applied to all the torso's primitives.[2] We then trace the leftmost branch of the tree to the node for the head. There, we invoke the function head with the model-view matrix updated to $\mathbf{MM}_h$. Next, we back up to the torso node, then go down the subtree defining the left leg. This part looks just like the code for the robot arm; we draw the upper-left leg with the matrix $\mathbf{MM}_{lul}$, and the lower-left leg with matrix $\mathbf{MM}_{lul}\mathbf{M}_{lll}$. Then, we move on to the right leg, left arm, and left leg. Each time that we switch limbs, we must back up to the root and recover **M**.

It is probably easiest to think in terms of the current transformation matrix of Chapter 4—the model-view matrix **C** that is applied to the primitives defined at a node. **C** starts out as **M**, is updated to $\mathbf{MM}_h$ for the head, and later to $\mathbf{MM}_{lul}\mathbf{M}_{lll}$, and so on. The user program must manipulate **C** before each call to a function defining a part of the figure. In addition to the usual OpenGL functions for rotation, translation, and scaling, the functions glPushMatrix and glPopMatrix are particularly helpful for traversing our tree. Consider the code (without parameter values) for the beginning of the function figure

```
figure()
{
    glPushMatrix();
    torso();
```

---

[2] If there are modeling matrices within the function torso, they may be concatenated with **M** first, but this step probably will require a glPushMatrix and glPopMatrix, because we would then be traversing a subtree within the function torso.

```
glTranslate
glRotate3
head();
glPopMatrix();
glPushMatrix();
glTranslate
glRotate3
left_upper_leg();
glTranslate
glRotate3
left_lower_leg()
glPopMatrix();
glPushMatrix()
glTranslate
glRotate3
right_upper_leg();
glPopMatrix();
glPushMatrix()
           :
           :
```

The first `glPushMatrix` duplicates the current model-view matrix (assuming that we have done a previous `glMatrixMode(GL_MODELVIEW)`), putting the copy on the top of the model-view-matrix stack. This method of pushing allows us to work immediately with the other transformations that alter the model-view matrix, knowing that we have preserved a copy on the stack. The following calls to `glTranslate` and `glRotate` determine $\mathbf{M}_h$ *and* concatenate it with the initial model-view matrix. We can then generate the primitives for the head. The subsequent `glPopMatrix` recovers the original model-view matrix. Note that we must do another `glPushMatrix` to leave a copy of the original model-view matrix that we can recover when we come back to draw the right leg. You should be able to complete this function by continuing in a similar manner. The complete program is given in Appendix A.

We have not considered how attributes such as color and material properties are handled by our traversal of a hierarchical model. Attributes are modal variables: Once set, they remain in place until changed again. Hence, we must be careful as we traverse our tree. For example, suppose that, within the code for `torso`, we set the color to red; then, within the code for head, we set the color to blue. If there are no other color changes, the color will still be blue as we traverse the rest of the tree, and may remain blue after we leave the code for `figure`. Here is an example of where the particular traversal algorithm can make a difference, because what will be affected by a change in attributes depends on in what order the nodes are visited.

This situation may be disconcerting, but there is a solution. OpenGL has the functions `glPushAttrib` and `glPopAttrib` that allow us to deal with attributes in a manner similar to our use of the model-view matrix. If we push the attributes on the attribute stack on entrance to the function `figure`, and pop on exit, we will have restored the attributes to their original state. Moreover, we can use additional pushes and pops within `figure` to control how attributes are handled in greater detail. OpenGL divides its state into groups, and allows a user to push any set of these groups on the attribute stack. The user needs only to set the bits in a mask that is the parameter for `glPushAttrib`. Attribute groups include lighting, so we can push material properties and lights onto the stack, polygon, and line groups.

PHIGS provides a similar, but less powerful, method for working with trees and DAGs.[3] In PHIGS, the data are put in groups, called **structures**, that are roughly equivalent to our display lists. Structures can evoke other structures by an `execute_structure` function.[4] This mechanism allows us to create DAGs. PHIGS provides both local and global matrices that the application program can manipulate to achieve the functionality of OpenGL's pushing and popping of attributes and matrices.

Color Plates 12, 16, and 22 show hierarchical models of robots and figures used in simulations. These objects were created with high-level interactive software that relies on our ability to traverse hierarchical structures to render the models.

8.5 Animation

Our two examples—the robot and the figure–are **articulated**: The models consist of rigid parts connected by joints. We can make such models change their positions in time—animate them—by altering the values of a small set of parameters. Hierarchical models allow us to reflect correctly the compound motions incorporating the physical relationships among the parts of the model. What we have not discussed is how to alter the parameters over time so as to achieve the desired motion.

Of the many approaches to animation, a few basic techniques are of particular importance when we work with articulated figures. These techniques arise both from traditional hand animation and from robotics.

Consider the problem of moving from one position to another the tip of upper arm in our robot model. The model has 3 degrees of freedom—the three

---

[3] Although we have worked with trees, if two or more nodes call the same function, we really have a DAG.

[4] In OpenGL, display lists can call other display lists.

angles that we can specify. Although, for each set of angles, there is a unique position for the tip, the converse is not true. Given a desired position of the tip of the arm, there may be no set of angles that will place the tip as desired, a single set of angles that will yield the specified position, or multiple sets of angles that will place the tip at the desired position.

The study of **kinematics** involves describing the position of the parts of the model based on only the joint angles. We can use our hierarchical-modeling methods either to determine positions numerically, or to find explicit equations that give the position of any desired set of points in the model in terms of the joint angles. Thus, if θ is an array of the joint angles and $\mathbf{p}$ is an array whose elements are the vertices in our model, a kinematic model is of the form

$$\mathbf{p} = f(\theta).$$

Likewise, if we specify the rates of change of the joint angles—the joint velocities—then we can obtain velocities of points on the model.

The kinematic model neglects matters such as the effects of inertia and friction. We could derive more complex differential equations that describe the dynamical behavior of the model in terms of applied forces—a topic that is studied in robotics.

Whereas both kinematics and dynamics are ways of describing the forward behavior of the model, in animation, we are more concerned with **inverse kinematics** and **inverse dynamics**: Given a desired state of the model, how can we adjust the joint angles so as to achieve this position? There are two major concerns. First, given an environment including the robot and other objects, we must determine whether there exists a sequence of angles that will achieve the desired state. There may be no single-valued function of the form

$$\theta = g(\mathbf{p}).$$

Not only must we determine whether the final position corresponds to a set of joint angles, but also we must find a way to alter the joint angles so as not to hit any obstacles and not to violate any physical constraints. Although, for a model as simple as our robot, we might be able to find equations that give the joint angles in terms of the position, we cannot do so in general, because the forward equations do not have unique inverses. The figure model, with 11 degrees of freedom, should give you an idea of how difficult this problem is to solve.

A basic approach to overcoming these difficulties comes from traditional hand-animation techniques. In **key-frame animation**, the animator positions the objects at set of times—the key frames. In hand animation, animators then can fill in the remaining frames, a process called **inbetweening**. In computer graphics, we can automate inbetweening by interpolating the joint angles between the key frames, or equivalently, using simple approximations to obtain the required dynamic equations between key frames. We can also use the spline curves that we shall develop in Chapter 9 to give smooth methods of going between key frames. Although we can develop code for the interpolation, both a skillful (human) animator and good interactive methods are crucial to choosing the key frames and the positions of objects in these frames.

We can extend these ideas in many ways, as indicated by the suggested readings at the end of the chapter. For example, we can change the shape of an object by giving the shape, in terms of our standard primitives, at different key frames. We can then interpolate between these shapes with a technique known as morphing. Here, the major difficulties are to identify which vertices in the first frame correspond to which vertices in the second frame, and, to have automated methods that can generate new vertices or eliminate vertices when necessary to interpolate between objects with different numbers of vertices. Again, implementation involves interactive programs and skilled animators.

8.6   Scene Graphs

If we think about what goes into describing a scene, we can see that, in addition to our graphical primitives and geometric objects derived from these primitives, we have a number of other objects, such as lights and a camera. These objects may also be defined by vertices and vectors, and may have attributes, such as color, that are similar to the attributes associated with geometric primitives. It is the totality of these objects that describes a scene, and there may be hierarchical relationships among these objects. For example, when a primitive is defined in a program, the camera parameters that exist at that time are used to form the image. If we alter the camera lens between the definition of two geometric objects, we may produce an image in which each object is viewed differently. Although we cannot create such an image with a real camera, the example points out the power of our graphics systems. We can extend our use of tree data structures to describe these relationships among geometric objects, cameras, lights, and attributes.

Knowing that we can write a graphical application program to traverse a graph, we can expand our notion of the contents of a graph to describe an entire scene. One possibility is to use a tree data structure and to include at each node, in addition to the instance matrix and a pointer to the drawing function, various attributes. Another possibility is to allow new types of nodes, such as attribute-definition nodes and matrix-transformation nodes. Consider the tree in Figure 8.15. Here, we have set up separate nodes for the colors and for the model-view matrices and have added a separator node for clarity; the separator node does not change the state or cause any primitives to be drawn. Given that our traversal algorithm is left to right and depth first, the corresponding OpenGL code is of the form

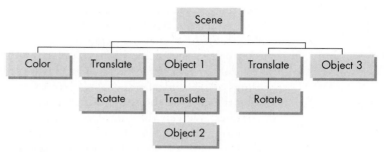

Figure 8.15 Scene tree.

```
glPushAttrib
glPushMatrix
glColor
glTranslate
glRotate
object1()
glTranslate
object2()
glPopMatrix
glPushMatrix
glTranslate
glRotate
object3()
glPopMatrix
glPopAttrib
```

This code preserves and restores both the attributes and the model-view matrix before exiting. It sets a drawing color that applies to the rest of the tree, and traverses the tree in a manner similar to the figure example.

We can go further and note that we can use the attribute and matrix stacks to store the viewing conditions; thus, we can create a camera node in the tree. Although we probably do not want individual objects viewed with different cameras, we may want to view the same set of objects with multiple cameras producing, for example, the multiview orthographic projections and the isometric view that are used by architects and engineers.

The scene tree that we have just described is equivalent to an OpenGL program in the sense that we can use the tree to generate the program in a totally mechanical fashion. This approach is taken by Open Inventor, an object-oriented API that is built on top of OpenGL. An Inventor program is a description of a scene tree. Execution of the program traverses the tree and executes graphics functions that are written in OpenGL.

The notion of scene graphs couples nicely with the object-oriented paradigm supported by languages such as C++. We can regard all primitives, attributes, and transformations as software objects, and can define classes to manipulate these entities. From this perspective, we can make use of concepts such as data encapsulation to build up scenes of great complexity with simple programs that use predefined software objects. We can even support animations through software objects that appear as nodes in the scene graph but cause parameters to change and the scene to be redisplayed. Although, in Open Inventor, the software objects are typically written in OpenGL, the scene graph itself is a database that includes all the elements of the scene. OpenGL enters as the rendering engine that allows the database to be converted to an image, but is not used in the specification of the scene. In this sense, Open Inventor resembles PHIGS: The job of the application program is to place elements in a database. Parts of a PHIGS database can be **posted** or sent to a workstations, and it is the job of the workstation to worry about how the rendering is accomplished.

8.7 Language-Based Models

Graphs such as trees and DAGs offer but one way of representing hierarchical relationships. In this section, we shall look at language-based models for representing relationships. Not only will these methods provide an alternate way of showing relationships, but also they will lead to procedural methods for defining objects.

Until now, we have defined geometrical objects in a fixed way; we process a model, and generate all the primitives regardless of whether or not they will be visible and, if they are visible, of whether they will make a significant contribution to the scene. Instead, we can define objects by the procedures or algorithms that generate the primitives, rather than by the primitives themselves. We can thus avoid generating the realization of the object—the geometric primitives—until the rendering stage, when we determine which primitives are necessary. These **procedural models** have the additional advantage that they can be used in conjunction with random-number generators, so that each execution of the procedure will generate a different geometric object; each object will be similar to the others, but will differ in detail. Such methods are particularly useful for generating images of real-world objects such as plants and terrain.

If we look at natural objects, such as plants, we see that, although no two trees are identical, we may have no difficulty telling the difference between two species of trees. Various methods have been proposed that give different realizations each time that the program is run, but that have clear rules for defining the structure. We shall look at the use of tree data structures for generating objects that look like plants.

In computer science, tree data structures are used for describing the parsing of sentences into constituent parts, in both computer and natural languages. For computer programs, doing this parsing is part of compiling the statements in a computer program. For natural languages, we parse sentences to determine whether they are grammatically correct. The tree that results from the parsing of a correct sentence gives the structure or syntax of that sentence. The interpretation of the individual elements in the tree—the words—give the meaning or semantics of the sentence.

If we look at only the syntax of a language, there is a direct correlation between the rules of the language and the form of the trees that represent the sentences. We can extend this idea to hierarchical objects in graphics, relating a set of rules and a tree-structured model. These systems are known as **tree grammars**. A grammar can be defined by a set of symbols and a set symbol-replacement rules, or **productions** that specify how to replace a symbol by one or more symbols. Typical rules will be written as

$A \to BC$,

$B \to ABA$.

Given a set of productions, we can generate an infinite number of strings. In general, there is more than one rule that we can apply to a given symbol at any time, and, if we select randomly which rule to apply, we can generate a different string each time that the program is executed. Programs can be written that not only generate such strings, but also take strings as input and test whether the strings are valid members of the set of strings generated by a given set of rules. Thus, we might have a set of rules for generating a certain type of object, such as a tree or a bush, and a separate program that can identify objects in a scene based on which grammar generates the shape.

The interpretation of the symbols in a string converts the string to a graphical object. There are numerous ways to generate rules and to interpret the resulting strings as graphical objects. One approach starts with the **turtle graphics** (Exercise 2.4) system. In turtle graphics, we have three basic ways of manipulating a graphics cursor, or **turtle**. The turtle can move forward 1 unit, turn right, or turn left. Suppose that the angle by which the turtle can turn is fixed. We can then denote our three operations as F, R, and L. Any string of these operations has a simple graphical interpretation. For example, if the angle is 120 degrees, the string $FRFRFR$ generates an equilateral triangle. We shall use the special symbols [and] to denote pushing and popping the state of the turtle (its position and orientation) onto a stack (an operation equivalent to using parentheses). Consider the production rule

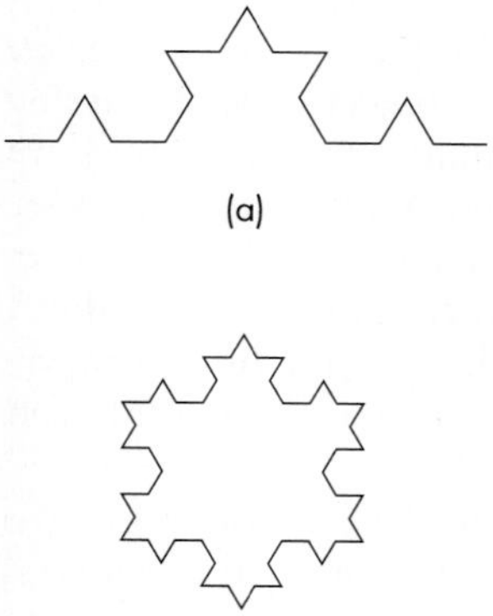

$F \to FLFRRFLF$,

Figure 8.16 Koch curve rule.

with an angle of 60 degrees. The graphical interpretation of this rule is shown in Figure 8.16. If we apply the rule again, in parallel to all instances of F, we get the curve in Figure 8.17(a); if we apply it to a triangle, we get the closed

Figure 8.17 Space-filling curves. (a) Koch curve. (b) Koch snowflake.

Figure 8.18 The rule $F \rightarrow F[RF]F[LF]F$.

Figure 8.19 Second iteration of rule in Figure 8.18.

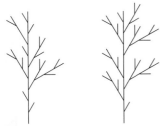

Figure 8.20 Results of applying the rule randomly from Figure 8.18.

curve in Figure 8.17(b). These curves are known as the **Koch curve** and **Koch snowflake**, respectively, and are both simple examples of **space-filling curves**: If we apply the rule recursively, the curves get longer and longer, without crossing themselves, but they still occupy a small region of two-dimensional space. If we scale the geometric interpretation of the curve each time that we execute the algorithm, so as to leave the original vertices in their original locations, we find we are generating a longer curve at each iteration, but this curve always fits inside the same box.

The push and pop operators allow us to develop side branches. Consider the rule

$$F \rightarrow F[RF]F[LF]F,$$

where the angle is 27 degrees (Figure 8.18). Note that we start at the bottom, and the angle is measured as a deviation from pointing forward.

If we start with a single line segment, Figure 8.18 is the resulting object. We can proceed in a number of ways. One method is to apply the rule again to each F in the sequence, resulting in the object in Figure 8.19. We can also adjust the length corresponding to a forward movement of the turtle so that branches get smaller on successive iterations. The object resembles a bush and will look more like a bush if we iterate a few more times. However, having only one rule and applying it in parallel results in every bush looking the same.

A more interesting strategy is to apply the rule *randomly* to occurrences of F. If we do, so our single rule can generate both of the objects in Figure 8.20. Adding a few more productions and controlling the probability function that determines which rule is to be applied next allows the user to generate a variety of types of trees. With only slight modifications, we can also draw leaves at the ends of the branches.

One of the attractions of this strategy is that we have defined a class of objects based on a handful of rules and a few parameters. Suppose that we wish to create a group of trees. The direct approach is to generate as many objects as needed, representing each one as a collection of geometric objects (lines, polygons, curves). In a complex scene, we might then be overwhelmed with the number of primitives generated. Depending on the viewing conditions, most of these primitives might not appear in the image, because they would be clipped out or would be too far from the viewer to be rendered at a visible size. In contrast, using our procedural method, we describe objects by simple algorithms and generate the geometric objects only when we need them and to only the level of detail that we need.

We can also describe a grammar directly in terms of shapes and affine transformations, creating a **shape grammar**. Consider our old friend the Sierpinski gasket. We can define a subdivision step in terms of three affine transformations, each of which scales the original triangle to one-half of the size, and places the small copy in a different position, as shown in Figure 8.21. We can apply these

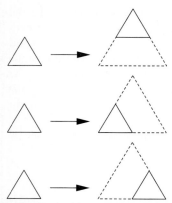

Figure 8.21 Three rules for the Sierpinski gasket.

rules randomly, or can apply all three in parallel. In either case, in the limit, we derive the gasket.

We now have three related procedural methods that can generate either models of natural objects, or models of interesting mathematical objects. The examples of the Koch curve and the Sierpinski gasket introduce a new aspect to the generation process—a method that can be applied recursively and that each time it is executed, generates detail similar in shape to the original object. Such phenomena can be explored through fractal geometry.

8.8   Recursive Methods and Fractals

The language-based procedural models are but one approach to generating complex objects with simple programs. Another approach, based on **fractal geometry**, uses the self-similarity of many real-world objects. Fractal geometry was developed by Mandelbrot, who was able to create a branch of mathematics that enables us to work with interesting phenomena that we cannot deal with using the tools of ordinary geometry. Workers in computer graphics have used the ideas of fractal geometry not only to create beautiful and complex objects, but also to model many real-world entities that are not easily modeled by other methods. Graphical objects generated by fractals have been called **graftals**.

8.8.1   Rulers and Length

There are two pillars to fractal geometry: the dependence of geometry on the scale, and self-similarity. We can examine both through the exploration of one of the questions that led to fractal geometry: What is the length of a coastline? Say that we have a map of a coastline. Because the coastline is wavy and irregular, we can take a string, lay it over the image of the coastline, and then measure the length of the string, using the scale of the map to convert distances. However, if we get a second map that shows a closer view of the coastline, we see more detail. The added detail looks much like the view of the first map, but with additional inlets and protrusions visible. If we take our string and measure the length on the second map, taking into account the difference in scale between the two maps, we will measure a greater distance. We can continue this experiment by going to the coast and trying to measure with even greater precision. We find new detail, perhaps even to the level of measuring individual pebbles along the shore. In principle, we could continue this process down to the molecular level, each time seeing a similar picture with more detail, and measuring a greater length.

If we want to get any useful information, or at least a measurement on which two people might agree, we must either limit the resolution of the map, or, equivalently, pick the minimum unit that we can measure. In computer

Figure 8.22 Lengthening of the Koch curve.

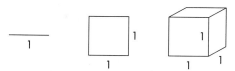

Figure 8.23 Line segment, square, and cube.

graphics, if we use perspective views, we have a similar problem, because what detail we see depends on how far we are from the object.

We can approach these problems mathematically by considering our recursion for the Koch snowflake in Section 8.7. Here, each line segment of length 1 was replaced by four line segments of length 1/3 (Figure 8.22). Hence, each time that we replace a segment, we span the distance between the same two endpoints with a curve four-thirds of the length of the original. If we consider the limit as we iterate an infinite number of times, the issue of dimension arises. The curve cannot be an ordinary one-dimensional curve because, in the limit, it has infinite length and its first derivative is discontinuous everywhere. It is not a two-dimensional object, however, because it does not fill a two-dimensional region of the plane. We can resolve this problem by defining a fractional dimension.

8.8.2 Fractal Dimension

Consider a line segment of length 1, a unit square, and a unit cube, as shown in Figure 8.23. Under any reasonable definition of *dimension*, the line segment, square, and cube are one-, two-, and three-dimensional objects, respectively. Suppose that we have a ruler, whose resolution is h, where $h = \frac{1}{n}$ is the smallest unit that we can measure. We assume that n is an integer. We can divide each of these objects into similar units in terms of h, as shown in Figure 8.24. We divide the line segment into $k = n$ identical segments, the square into $k = n^2$ small squares, and the cube into $k = n^3$ small cubes. In each case, we can say that we have scaled the original object by a factor of h. Suppose that d is the dimension of any one of these objects. What has remained constant in the subdivision is that the whole is the sum of the parts. Mathematically, for any of the objects, we have the equality

$$\frac{k}{n^d} = kn^{-d} = 1.$$

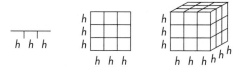

Figure 8.24 Subdivision of the objects $h = \frac{1}{3}$.

Solving for d, we can define the **fractal dimension** as

$$d = \frac{\ln k}{\ln n}.$$

In other words, the fractal dimension of an object is determined by how many similar objects we create by subdivision. Consider the Koch curve. We create four similar objects by the subdivision (scaling) of the original into thirds. The corresponding fractal dimensions is

Figure 8.25 Subdivision of the Sierpinski gasket

$$d = \frac{\ln 4}{\ln 3} = 1.26186.$$

Now consider the Sierpinski gasket. A scaling step is shown in Figure 8.25. Each time that we subdivide a side by a factor of 2, we keep three of the four triangles created, and

$$d = \frac{\ln 3}{\ln 2} = 1.58496.$$

In both examples, we can view the object created by the subdivision as occupying more space than a curve, but less space than a filled area. We can create a solid version of the gasket in a three-dimensional space by starting with a tetrahedron and subdividing each of the faces, as shown in Figure 8.26. We keep the four tetrahedrons at the original vertices, discarding the region in the middle. The object that we create has a fractal dimension of

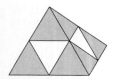

Figure 8.26 Solid gasket.

$$d = \frac{\ln 4}{\ln 2} = 2,$$

even though it does not lie in the plane. Also note that, although the volume is reduced by each subdivision, the surface area is increased. Suppose that we start with a cube and divide it into thirds, as shown in Figure 8.27. Next, we remove the center by pushing out the pieces in the middle of each face and the center, thus leaving 20 of the original 27 subcubes. This object has a fractal dimension of

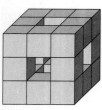

Figure 8.27 Subdivision of a cube.

$$d = \frac{\ln 20}{\ln 3} = 2.72683.$$

Although these constructions are interesting and are easy to generate graphically at any level of recursion, they are by themselves not useful for modeling

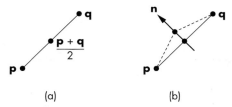

Figure 8.28 Midpoint displacement. (a) Original line segment. (b) Line segment after subdivision.

the world. However, if we add randomness, we get a powerful modeling technique.

8.8.3 Midpoint Division and Brownian Motion

A fractal curve has dimension $1 \leq d < 2$. Curves with lower fractal dimension appear smoother than curves with higher fractal dimension. A similar statement holds for surfaces that have fractal dimension $2 \leq d < 3$. In computer graphics, there are many situations where we would like to create a curve or surface that appears random, but that has a measurable amount of roughness. For example, the silhouette of a mountain range forms a curve that is rougher (has higher fractal dimension) than the skyline of the desert. Likewise, a surface model of mountain terrain should have a higher fractal dimension than the surface of farmland. We also often want to generate these objects in a resolution-dependent manner. For example, the detail that we generate for a terrain used in speed-critical application, such as in a flight simulator, should be generated at high resolution for only those areas near the aircraft.

The random movement of particles in fluids is known as **Brownian motion**. Simulating such motion provides an interesting approach to generating natural curves and surfaces. Physicists have modeled Brownian motion by forming polylines in which each successive point on the polyline is displaced by a random distance and in a random direction from its predecessor. True Brownian motion is based on a particular random-number distribution that generates paths that match actual particle paths. In computer graphics, we are more concerned with rapid computation, and with the ability to generate curves with a controllable amount of roughness; thus, we shall use the term *Brownian motion* in this broader sense.

Although we could attempt to generate Brownian motion through the direct generation of a polyline, a more efficient method is to use a simple recursive process. Consider the line segment in Figure 8.28(a). We find its midpoint; then, we displace the midpoint in the normal direction, by a random distance, as in Figure 8.28(b). We can repeat this process any number of times to produce curves like that in Figure 8.29. The variance of the random-number generator, or the average displacement, should be scaled by a factor, usually of $\frac{1}{2}$, each time, because the line segments are shortened at each stage. We can also allow

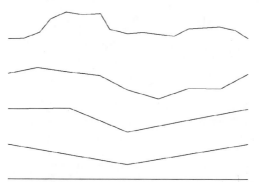

Figure 8.29 Fractal curves with 1, 2, 4, 8, and 16 segments.

the midpoint to be displaced in a random direction, rather than only along the normal. If the random numbers are always positive, we can create skylines. If we use a zero-mean Gaussian random-number generator, with variance proportional to $l^{2(2-d)}$, where l is the length of the segment to be subdivided, then d is the fractal dimension of the resulting curve. The value $d = 1.5$ corresponds to true Brownian motion.

8.8.4 Fractal Mountains

The best-known uses of fractals in computer graphics have been to generate mountains and terrain. We can generate a mountain with our tetrahedron–subdivision process, by adding in a midpoint displacement. Consider one facet of the tetrahedron, as shown in Figure 8.30. First, we find the midpoints of the sides; then, we displace each midpoint,[5] creating four new triangles. Once more, by controlling the variance of the random-number generator, we can control the roughness of the resulting object. Note that we must take great care in how the random numbers are generated if we are to create objects that are topologically correct and do not fold into themselves; see the suggested readings at the end of this chapter.

This algorithm can be applied equally well to any mesh. We can start with a flat mesh of rectangles in the x, z plane, and subdivide each rectangle into four smaller rectangles, displacing all vertices upward (in the y direction). Figure 8.31 shows one example of this process. Color Plate 7 contains fractal mountains.

---

[5] We can also displace the original vertices.

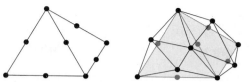

Figure 8.30 Midpoint subdivision of a tetrahedron facet.

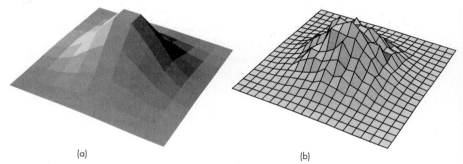

(a)   (b)

Figure 8.31 Fractal terrain. (a) Mesh. (b) Subdivided mesh with displaced vertices.

8.9   Physically Based Models and Particle Systems

One of the great strengths—and weaknesses—of modeling in computer graphics is that we can build models based on any principles we choose: The graphical objects of which we create images may have no connection with physical reality. This flexibility allows mathematicians to "see" shapes that do not exist in usual three-dimensional space and allows engineers to construct models of objects that are not limited by the properties of the materials of which the objects might eventually be built. However, when we wish to simulate objects in the real world, and to see the results of this simulation on our CRT, we can get into trouble. It is easy to make a model for a group of objects moving through space, but it is far more difficult to keep track of when two objects collide, and to have the graphics system react in a physically correct manner. Indeed, it is far easier in computer graphics to let a ball go directly through a wall than to model the ball bouncing off the surface, incorporating the correct elastic rebound.

Recently, researchers have become interested in **physically based modeling**, a style of modeling in which the graphical objects obey physical laws. Such modeling follows either of two related paths. In one, we model the physics of the underlying process, and use the physics to drive the graphics. For example, if we want a solid object to appear to tumble in space and to bounce from various surfaces, we can, at least in principle, use our knowledge of dynamics and continuum mechanics to derive the required equations. This approach is beyond the scope of a first course in computer graphics; we shall not pursue it. The other approach is to use a combination of basic physics and mathematical constraints to control the dynamical behavior of our objects. We shall follow this approach for a group of particles.

Particle systems are collections of particles, typically point masses, in which the dynamic behavior of the particles can be determined by the solution of sets of coupled differential equations. Particle systems have been used to generate a wide variety of behaviors in a number of fields. In fluid dynamics, particle systems are used to model turbulent behavior. Rather than solving partial differential equations, we can simulate various systems by following a group of particles that is subject to a variety of forces and constraints. In computer graphics, particles have been used to model such diverse phenomena as fireworks, the flocking behavior of birds, and wave action.

In each case, we work with a group of particles, each member of which we can regard as a point mass. We use physical laws to write differential equations that we can solve numerically to obtain the state of these particles at each time step. As a final step, we can render each particle as a graphical object—perhaps as a colored point for a fireworks application, or as a cartoon character in an animation.

We shall consider a set of particles that is subject to Newton's laws.[6] Any particle must obey Newton's second law, which states that the mass of the particle (m) times that particle's acceleration (a) is equal to the sum of the forces (f) acting on the particle, or, symbolically,

$$ma = f.$$

If the particle is a point, we can represent its state, within some frame, at any time by its position and velocity. Within this frame, the state of the ith particle is given by two three-element column matrices, a position matrix

$$\mathbf{p}_i = \begin{bmatrix} x_i \\ y_i \\ z_i \end{bmatrix},$$

and a velocity matrix

$$\mathbf{v}_i = \begin{bmatrix} \dot{x}_i \\ \dot{y}_i \\ \dot{z}_i \end{bmatrix}.$$

---

[6] There is no reason that we could not use other physical laws, or construct a set our own (virtual) physical laws.

Knowing that acceleration is the derivative of velocity, and velocity is the derivative of position, we can write Newton's second law for a particle as the six coupled first-order differential equations

$$\dot{\mathbf{p}}_i = \mathbf{v}_i,$$

$$\dot{\mathbf{v}}_i = \frac{1}{m_i}\mathbf{f}_i(t).$$

Hence, the dynamics of a system of n particles is governed by a set of $6n$ coupled differential equations.

In addition to its state, each particle may have a number of attributes, including its mass (m_i), and a set of properties that govern its behavior and display. For example, some attributes will govern how to render the particle and determine its color, shape, and surface properties. Note that, although the dynamics of a simple particle system are based on each particle being treated as a point mass, the user can specify how each particle should be rendered. For example, each particle may represent a person in a crowd scene, or a molecule in a chemical-synthesis application, or a portion of a cloth piece in the simulation of a flag blowing in the wind. In each case, the underlying particle system describes the location, the velocity, and the center of mass of the particle. Once we have the location of a particle, we can place the desired object at this location.

What governs the behavior of a system of particles is the set of forces $\{\mathbf{f}_i\}$. These forces are based on the state of the particle system and can change with time. We can base these forces on simple physical principles, such as spring forces, on physical constraints that we wish to impose on the system, or on external forces that we wish to apply to the system. If we think of the particle system as a system with $6n$ variables, a typical time step is based on computing the forces that apply at that time, through a user-defined function, and using these forces to update the state, through a numerical differential-equation solver. Thus, in pseudocode, we have a loop of the form

```
float time, delta;
float state[6n], force[3n];
state=get_intitial_state();
for(time=t0; time<time_final; time+=delta)
{
    force=force_function(state, time);
    state=ode(force, delta); /* standard differential equation
                                solver */
}
```

The main component that we must design in a given application is the function that computes the forces on each particle.

8.9.1 Independent Particles

There are numerous simple ways that we can describe those forces that are of interest. If the forces that act on a given particle are independent of other particles, the force on the ith particle can be described by the equation

$$\mathbf{f}_i = \mathbf{f}_i(\mathbf{p}_i, \mathbf{v}_i).$$

A simple case is when each particle is subject to only a constant gravitational force

$$\mathbf{f}_i = \mathbf{g}.$$

If this force points down, then

$$\mathbf{g} = \begin{bmatrix} 0 \\ -g \\ 0 \end{bmatrix},$$

where g is positive, and each particle will trace out a parabolic arc. By having some of the attributes change with time and giving each particle a (random) lifetime, we can simulate phenomena such as fireworks. More generally, external forces are applied independently to each point. If we allow the particles to drift randomly and render each as a large object, rather than as a point, we can model clouds or flows with independent particles.

Color Plate 14 shows the use of independent particles to model the sparks generated by welding. Each particle is independent of the others, is subject to gravity, and has a random lifetime.

8.9.2 Spring Forces

If, in a system of n particles, all particles are independent, the force calculation is $O(n)$. In the most general case, the computation of the forces on a given particle may involve contributions due to interactions with all the other particles, an $O(n^2)$ computation. Often, we can reduce this complexity by having a particle interact with only those particles that are close to it.

Consider the example of using particles to create a surface whose shape varies over time, such as a curtain or a flag blowing in the wind. We can use the location of each particle as a vertex for a rectangular mesh, as shown in Figure 8.32. The shape of the mesh changes over time, due both to external forces that act on each particle, such as gravity or wind, and to forces between particles that give the mesh the appearance of being a solid surface. We can approximate this second type of force by considering the forces between a particle and the latter's closest neighbors. Thus, if $\mathbf{p}_{ij}$ is the location of the particle at row i, column j of the mesh, the force calculation for $\mathbf{p}_{ij}$ needs to consider only the forces between $\mathbf{p}_{i,j}$ and $\mathbf{p}_{i+1,j}$, $\mathbf{p}_{i-1,j}$, $\mathbf{p}_{i,j+1}$, and $\mathbf{p}_{i,j-1}$—an $O(n)$ calculation.

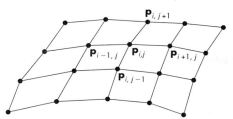

Figure 8.32 Mesh of particles.

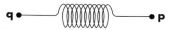

Figure 8.33 Particles connected by a spring.

One method to model the forces among particles is to consider adjacent particles as connected by springs. Consider two adjacent particles, located at $\mathbf{p}$ and $\mathbf{q}$, connected by a spring, as shown in Figure 8.33. Let $\mathbf{f}$ denote the force acting on $\mathbf{p}$ from $\mathbf{q}$.[7] The spring has a resting length s, which is the distance between particles if the system is not subject to external forces and is allowed to come to rest. When the spring is stretched, the force acts in the direction $\mathbf{d} = \mathbf{p} - \mathbf{q}$—that is, along the line between the points. It obeys **Hook's law**:

$$\mathbf{f} = -k_s(|\mathbf{d}| - s)\frac{\mathbf{d}}{|\mathbf{d}|},$$

where k_s is the spring constant. This law shows that, the farther apart the two particles are stretched, the stronger is the force attracting them back to the resting position. As we have stated Hook's law, however, there is no damping (or friction) in the system. A system of masses and springs defined in such a manner will oscillate forever when perturbed. We can include a drag term in Hook's law, and can use the force expression

$$\mathbf{f} = -\left(k_s(|\mathbf{d}| - s) + k_d\frac{\dot{\mathbf{d}} \cdot \mathbf{d}}{|\mathbf{d}|}\right)\frac{\mathbf{d}}{|\mathbf{d}|}.$$

Here, k_d is the damping constant, and

$$\dot{\mathbf{d}} = \dot{\mathbf{p}} - \dot{\mathbf{q}} = \mathbf{v_p} - \mathbf{v_q}.$$

The damping force operates in the same direction as the spring force, but is proportional to the velocity between the particles.

The four images in Color Plate 31 show a mesh that is generated from the locations of a set of particles. Each interior particle is connected to its four neighbors by springs. The particles are also subject to external forces—the wind. At each time step, once the positions of the particles are determined, the

---

[7] A force $-\mathbf{f}$ acts on $\mathbf{q}$ from $\mathbf{p}$.

mesh can be rendered using techniques such as texture mapping (Section 10.2) to create the detailed appearance of the surface.

8.9.3 Repulsive Forces

Whereas spring forces are used to keep a group of particles together, repulsive forces push particles away from one another. We could use such forces to distribute particles over a surface, or, if the particles represent locations of objects, to keep objects from hitting one another. For a pair of particles, located at $\mathbf{p}$ and $\mathbf{q}$, the repulsive force acts in the direction $\mathbf{d} = \mathbf{p} - \mathbf{q}$ and is inversely proportional to the particles' distance from each other. For example, we could use the expression

$$\mathbf{f} = -k_r \frac{\mathbf{d}}{|\mathbf{d}|^3}$$

for an inverse-square-law term. Unfortunately, unless the particles have known neighbors and we can neglect faraway terms, the computation of repulsive forces is $O(n^2)$.

8.9.4 Constraints

There are two types of constraints that we can impose on particles. **Hard constraints** are those that must be adhered to exactly. For example, a ball must bounce off a wall; it cannot penetrate the wall and emerge from the other side. Nor can we allow the ball just to come close, then let it bounce off in another direction. Such constraints are difficult to invoke, as we must first detect that a constraint is being violated, and then must respond in the appropriate manner. For a point mass, we can calculate its position and check for constraint violations for problems such as particles bouncing off simple surfaces. If, however, a particle represents, or is part of, a larger body, constraint detection becomes a difficult problem.

In many situations, we can work with **soft constraints**: constraints which we need only come close to satisfying. For example, if we want a particle, whose location is $\mathbf{p}$, always to be near the position $\mathbf{p}_0$, we can consider the **penalty function** $|\mathbf{p} - \mathbf{p}_0|^2$. The smaller this function is, the closer we are to obeying the constraint. This function is one example of an **energy function** whose value represents the amount of some type of energy stored in the system. In physics, such functions can represent quantities, such as the potential or kinetic energy in the system. Physical laws can be written either as differential equations, like those we used for our particles, or in terms of the minimization of expressions involving energy terms. One advantage of the latter form is that we can express constraints or desired behavior of a system directly in terms of potential or energy functions. Conversion of these expressions to force laws is a mechanical process, and is one whose mathematical details are beyond the scope of this book.

Color Plate 27 shows the use of a particle system for scientific visualization. The same data were also rendered by marching cubes (Section 8.10, Color Plate 26) and splatting (Section 10.8, Color Plate 28). In this example, particles were injected into a three-dimensional data set and each particle sought to find a surface of constant value, an isosurface. Constraints were used to make particles seek the desired surfaces, whereas repulsive forces kept the particles separated once they found a surface.

8.10 Models from Data

In most of our examples, the geometric objects that we display are the natural representations of the phenomena that we wish to represent. The robot model that we developed in Section 8.3 looks like a robot; the figure of Section 8.4, although simple, can be extended to a more human-looking figure with only a minimal effort. However, when we work with data, it is not clear how these data should be represented graphically. The numbers that we have to display have no natural visual representation. Basic plotting techniques—such as scatter plots, pie graphs, and bar charts—are well-established methods for displaying one-dimensional data, each generating different geometric objects to display the same data set. However, two-, three- and greater-dimensional data require more sophisticated methods. More important, the power of modern graphics systems allows us to create new methods to display data.

8.10.1 Scientific Visualization

Using advanced architectures—such as massively parallel processors and supercomputers—scientists can create enormous quantities of multidimensional data through simulations. New medical technologies, such as computed tomography and magnetic-resonance imaging in medicine, produce three-dimensional data sets of volume elements, or **voxels**. Both of these examples can produce three-dimensional arrays of voxels with more than $500 \times 500 \times 500$ elements, and can produce multiple frames of such data. Clearly, even just storing these data is a nontrivial task. **Scientific visualization** is a field that now seeks to display the information in such data sets using the capabilities of modern graphics hardware and software.

From the graphics perspective, what we can do well is to display simple geometric objects. Scientific visualization provides limitless possibilities for creating such displays by converting data into geometric objects. In this section, we shall introduce two related methods: contour plots for two-dimensional data and isosurface methods for three-dimensional data. The use of curves and surfaces that we shall discuss in Chapter 9, and compositing techniques that we shall introduce in Chapter 10, will provide alternate methods for displaying similar data sets.

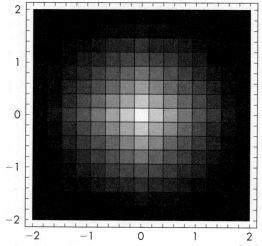

Figure 8.34 Gray-scale display of $f(x, y) = e^{-(x^2+y^2)}$.

8.10.2 Contour Plotting

Suppose that we have a two-dimensional set of data $\{f_{ij}\}$, where the integers i and j range over 0 to N and 0 to M, respectively. Each value can be thought of as a sample of a continuous function $f(x, y)$, where $f_{ij} = f(i \Delta x, j \Delta y)$, and Δx and Δy give the distances between samples on a rectilinear grid. We can display these data in a number of ways. For example, if we have a display that supports multiple shades, we can plot a small shaded rectangle whose gray level is determined by the value of f_{ij}. Figure 8.34 shows the values of the function $f(x, y) = e^{-(x^2+y^2)}$ displayed in this manner. Figure 8.35 shows another way of displaying these data. There, we convert each sample to a three-dimensional vertex $\mathbf{p}_{ij} = (i, f_{ij}, j)$. Each set of four adjacent vertices—$\mathbf{p}_{ij}$, $\mathbf{p}_{i+1,j}$, $\mathbf{p}_{i,j+1}$, and $\mathbf{p}_{i+1,j+1}$—defines a quadrilateral (or two triangles). We can display the data set as a mesh of these quadrilaterals (or triangles) with a simple OpenGL program, using our shading techniques from Chapter 6 to enhance the display.

Both of these techniques are commonly used, but neither extends well to three-dimensional (volumetric) data sets of the form $\{f_{ijk}\}$. There is, however, an older technique—**contour plotting**—that does extend to three dimensions. We shall develop the technique as a way of introducing the concepts important to the display of volumetric data sets.

Consider the equation

$$f(x, y) = c,$$

where c is a constant. The x, y pairs that satisfy this equation define the contours of the function. If f is a reasonably behaved function the contours are closed curves. Such curves are what we see on topographic maps, where f is a

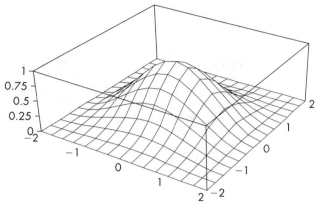

Figure 8.35   Mesh display of $f(x, y) = e^{-(x^2+y^2)}$.

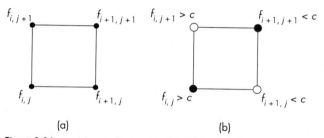

(a)   (b)

Figure 8.36   Vertex labeling with (a) function values, and (b) threshold values.

function that gives the altitude at each point. Each contour curve corresponds to a curve of constant altitude. In the early days of computer graphics, when we had neither raster displays nor the ability to display three-dimensional objects, contour plots were used routinely to display two-dimensional data sets.

Given only the data samples $\{f_{ij}\}$, it is unlikely that we will have many values that satisfy

$$f_{ij} = f(i\Delta x, j\Delta y) = c.$$

If, however, we consider the data at the corners of the rectangle, or **cell**, defined by the four adjacent points—(i, j), $(i + 1, j)$, $(i, j + 1)$, and $(i + 1, j + 1)$—we can make good estimates of the local behavior of a contour curve. Figure 8.36(a) shows a cell labeled with the function values. In Figure 8.36(b), the vertices are labeled (colored) black or white depending on whether the samples exceed (white) or are below (black) the chosen contour value c. If we always use the simplest possible explanation of the coloring of the vertices, we can make inferences based on only the colors of the vertices. For example, if all four vertices have the same color, the simplest interpretation is that the contour does

Figure 8.37 Interpretation of a cell.

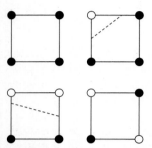

Figure 8.38 Four colorings of cell.

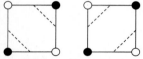

Figure 8.39 Ambiguous cell.

not pass through this cell. If the cell has one white vertex and three black vertices, as shown in Figure 8.37, we can assume that the contour cuts through the two edges that share the white vertex. We can then use the values of f_{ij} at the vertices to interpolate approximate locations for where the contour intersects these edges. We connect these intersection points with a line segment that will be part of a piecewise-linear approximation to the contour curve.

Although there are $16 = 2^4$ possible colorings for the vertices of the cells, once we account for the symmetries—rotations and swapping of black with white—we are left with only the four colorings in Figure 8.38. The first three cases contribute sections of the contour curves shown by the dotted lines in Figure 8.38, but the fourth case can be interpreted in the two ways shown in Figure 8.39. Lacking additional—usually unavailable—information, we have no reason to choose one interpretation over the other, although, as we can see from Figure 8.40, the resulting contours will be different. There are various approaches to dealing with the ambiguity. One approach is to choose one of the possible interpretations arbitrarily. Another is to look at adjacent cells before deciding on an interpretation. Another is to subdivide the ambiguous cell into four cells, then interpolate a center value that hopefully will generate unambiguous subcells. None of these approaches always works. The correct solution requires knowledge of the underlying function; just a set of its samples is insufficient. This difficulty is another manifestation of the sampling problem that we shall discuss further in Chapter 10.

One of the most appealing aspects of this approach is that each cell is processed independently and the algorithm can be parallelized easily. In addition, most of the algorithm can be reduced to a table lookup that maps the binary state of the four vertices of a cell into a one of the four cases. Although contour algorithms for two-dimensional data are less popular than other methods, their advantages are important when we move to three-dimensional data sets.

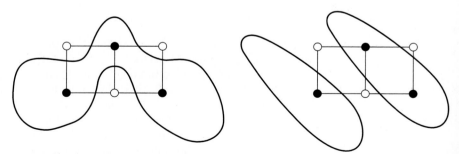

Figure 8.40 Two contour plots for the same data.

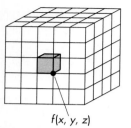

Figure 8.41 Volume of voxels.

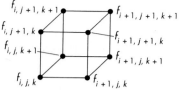

Figure 8.42 Voxel cell.

8.10.3 Isosurfaces for Volume Visualization

Now suppose that we have a volume of voxels $\{f_{ijk}\}$. We can think of each value f_{ijk} as a sample of a function $f(x, y, z)$ on a three-dimensional rectilinear grid. We can view each sample as the value of $f(x, y, z)$ at a point on the grid, or as the average value over a small parallelepiped centered at the grid point, as shown in Figure 8.41. Even more so than for two-dimensional data, there are multiple ways to display these data sets. There are two basic approaches: direct rendering and isosurfaces. **Direct-rendering** techniques make use of every voxel in producing an image. We shall consider such approaches in Chapter 10. **Isosurface techniques** create geometric objects from subsets of the data, and then use the graphics system to display these objects.

Isosurfaces are solutions of the equation

$$f(x, y, z) = c.$$

For a given value of c, there may be no such surface, one surface, or many surfaces. If we regard the data set $\{f_{ijk}\}$ as a set of samples of a function $f(x, y, z)$, we can use these data to build up approximations to isosurfaces in the form of polygonal meshes. Given how well we can display three-dimensional triangles, we shall describe a method, called **marching cubes**, that approximates a surface by generating a triangular mesh.

We have assumed that our voxel values $\{f_{ijk}\}$ are on a regular three-dimensional grid. If they are not, we can use an interpolation scheme (see Exercise 8.21) to obtain values on such a grid. Eight adjacent grid points define a three-dimensional cell, as shown in Figure 8.42. Vertex (i, j, k) of the cell is assigned the data value f_{ijk}. We can now look for parts of isosurfaces that pass through each of these cells, based on only the values at the vertices.

For a given isosurface value c, we can color the vertices of each cell black or white, depending on whether the value at the vertex is greater than or less than c. There are $256 = 2^8$ possible vertex colorings, but, once we account for symmetries, there are only the 14 unique cases shown in Figure 8.43.[8] Using the

---

[8] The original paper by Lorensen and Cline [Lor87] and many of the subsequent papers refer to 15 cases, but two of these cases are symmetric.

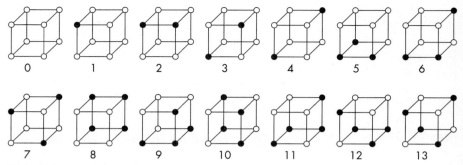

Figure 8.43 Vertex colorings.

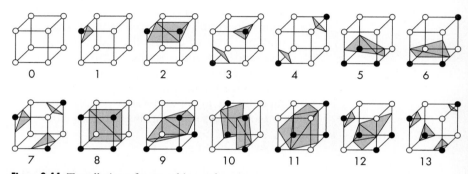

Figure 8.44 Tessellations for marching cubes.

simplest interpretation of the data, we can generate the points of intersection between the surface and the edges of the cubes by linear interpolation between the values at the vertices. Finally, we can use the triangular polygons to tessellate these intersections, forming pieces of a triangular mesh passing through the cell. These tessellations are shown in Figure 8.44.

Like the cells from our contour plots, each three-dimensional cell can be processed individually. In terms of the data, each interior voxel contributes to eight cells. We can go through the data, row by row, then plane by plane. As we do so, the location of the cell that we generate marches through the data set, giving the algorithm its name.

As each cell is processed, any triangles that it generates are sent off to be displayed through our graphics pipeline, where they can be lit, shaded, and rasterized. Because the algorithm is so easy to parallelize, and can be table driven, like the contour plot, marching cubes is a popular way of displaying three-dimensional data.

Marching cubes is both a data-reduction algorithm and a modeling algorithm. Both simulations and imaging systems can generate data sets containing from 10^7 to 10^9 voxels. With data sets this large, simple operations (such as

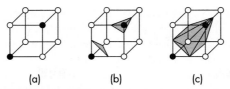

Figure 8.45 Ambiguity problem for marching cubes. (a) Cell. (b) One interpretation of cell. (c) Second interpretation.

reading in the data, rescaling the values, or rotating the data set) are time-consuming, memory-intensive tasks. In many of these applications, however, after executing the algorithm, we might have only $O(10^4)$ three-dimensional triangles—a number of geometric objects easily handled by a graphics system. We can rotate, color, and shade the surfaces in real time to interpret the data. Note that this method is but one way to display the data. In general, few voxels contribute to a particular isosurface; consequently, the information in the unused voxels is not in the image.

Color Plate 26 was generated using the marching cubes algorithm. Note the differences between this plate and the image in Color Plate 28 that was generated by splatting (Section 10.8). Plate 28 shows the effects of rendering three-dimensional objects through the shading of the surfaces, an effect lacking in Plate 28.

There is an ambiguity problem in marching cubes, analogous to the problem for contour maps. The problem can arise whenever we have different colors assigned to the diagonally opposite vertices of a side of a cell. Consider the cell coloring in Figure 8.45(a). Figures 8.45(b) and (c) show two ways to assign triangles to these data. If we compare two isosurface generated with the two different interpretations, areas where these cases arise will have completely different shapes and topologies. The "wrong" selection of an interpretation for a particular cell can leave holes in an otherwise smooth surface. Researchers have made many attempts to deal with this problem; no approach works all the time. As we saw with contour plots, an always correct solution requires more information than is in the data.

8.11 Summary

The speed at which modern hardware can render geometric objects has opened up the possibilities of a variety of modeling systems. As users of computer graphics, we need a large arsenal of techniques if we are to make full use of our graphics systems. We have introduced four forms of modeling. Not only are there many more, but also we can combine these techniques to generate new ones. The suggested readings will help you to explore modeling methods.

We have presented basic themes that apply to most approaches to modeling. One is the use of hierarchy to incorporate relationships among objects in a scene. We have seen that we can use fundamental data structures, such as trees and DAGs, to represent such relationships; traversing these data structures becomes part of the rendering process. The use of scene trees in Open Inventor allows the user to build complex animated scenes from a combination of predefined and user-defined software modules. Tree-structured models are also used in the Renderman Shading Language. Using this language, we can describe complex shaders that involve the interaction of light sources, material properties, atmospheric effects, and a variety of local reflection models. In a manner similar to the way multiple lights are used in the movie industry, a shader can be associated with a particular surface, an object, or collection of objects.

Recursion has appeared again; here we use it to generate procedural models that can generate primitives at different levels of detail. A unifying theme is that we can and should work with the basic tools of computer science—data structures, algorithms, graphs, recursion, languages. By interpreting the symbols as graphical objects, we create a toolkit of powerful modeling techniques.

Procedural methods have advantages in that we can control how many primitives we produce and at which point in the process these primitives are generated. Equally important is that procedural graphics provides an object-oriented approach to building models—an approach that should be of increasing importance in the future.

Combining physics with computer graphics provides a set of techniques that has the promise of generating physically correct animations and of providing new modeling techniques. Particle systems are but one example of physically based modeling, but a technique that has wide applicability. One of the most interesting and informative exercises that you can undertake at this point is to build a particle system.

In this chapter, we introduced animation and scientific visualization as applications of our modeling techniques. We shall see further examples of these applications when we discuss curves and surfaces in Chapter 9, and discrete techniques in Chapter 10. Both areas also are important in their own right. Several suggested readings include more systematic developments of these areas.

8.12   Suggested Readings

Hierarchical transformations through the use of a matrix stack were described in the graphics literature more than 20 years ago [New73]. However, the PHIGS API [ANSI88] was the first to incorporate them as part of a standard package. See [Wat93] for an introduction to the use of articulated figures in animation. The paper by Lassiter [Las87] shows the relationship between traditional animations techniques as practiced in the movie industry, and animation in computer graphics.

Scene graphs are the heart of Open Inventor [Wer94]. Trees are integral to the Renderman Shading Language [Ups89].

There is a wealth of literature on fractals and related methods. The paper by Fournier [Fou82] was the first to show the fractal mountain. For a deeper treatment of fractal mathematics, see [Man82, Pei88]. The use of graph grammars has appeared in number of forms; see [Pru90, Smi84, Lin68]. Both Hill [Hil90] and [Pru90] present interesting space-filling curves and surfaces. Barnsley's Iterated Function Systems [Bar93] provide another approach to using self-similarity; they have application in such areas as image compression.

Particle systems were introduced in computer graphics by Reeves [Ree83]. Since then, they have been used for a variety of phenomena, including flocking of birds [Rey87], fluid flow, modeling of grass, and display of surfaces [Wit94a]. Our approach follows [Wit94b].

The marching-cubes algorithm was developed by Lorensen and Cline [Lor87]. The ambiguity problem is discussed in [Van94].

Exercises

8.1 For our simple robot model, describe the set of points that can be reached by the tip of the upper arm.

8.2 Find equations for the position of any point on the simple robot in terms of the joint angles. Can you determine the joint angles from the position of the tip of the upper arm?

8.3 Given two points in space that are reachable by the robot, describe a path between them in terms of the joint angles.

8.4 Write a simple circuit-layout program in terms of a symbol–instance transformation table. Your symbols should include the shapes for circuit elements, such as resistors, capacitors, and inductors for electrical circuits, or the shapes for various gates (AND, OR, NOT) for logical circuits.

8.5 Find a set of productions to generate the Sierpinski gasket by starting with a single equilateral triangle.

8.6 How could you determine the fractal dimension of a coastline? How would you verify that the shape of a coastline is indeed a fractal?

8.7 Start with the tetrahedron-subdivision program that we used in Chapter 6 to approximate a sphere. Convert this program into one that will generate a fractal mountain.

8.8 We can write a description of a binary tree, such as we might use for search, as a list of nodes with pointers to its children. Write an OpenGL program that will take such a description and display the tree graphically.

8.9 Write a program for a simple particle systems of masses and springs. Render the particle system as a mesh of quadrilaterals. Include a form of interaction that allows a user to put particles in their initial positions.

8.10   Extend Exercise 8.9 by adding external forces to the particle system. Create an image of a flag blowing in the wind.

8.11   Write a program to fractalize a mesh. Try to use real elevation data for the initial positions of the mesh.

8.12   Robotics is only one example in which the parts of the scene show compound motion, where the movement of some objects depends on the movement of other objects. Other examples include bicycles (with wheels) , airplanes (with propellers), and merry-go-rounds (with horses). Pick an example of compound motion. Write a graphics program to simulate your selection.

8.13   Write a program that, given two polygons with the same number of vertices, will generate a sequence of images that converts one polygon into the other.

8.14   Write a particle system that simulates the sparks that are generated by welding or by fireworks.

8.15   Extend Exercise 8.14 to simulate the explosion of a polyhedron.

8.16   Write a program that will display a set of values $\{f_{ij}\}$ as

   a. a set of colored rectangles,
   b. a rectangular mesh
   c. a contour plot.

8.17   Generate a table that maps the 16 vertex colorings of a rectangular cell to the four ways that a contour curve can pass through the cell.

8.18   There are 256 ways to color the vertices of a cube with two colors; when we eliminate symmetries, however, there are only 14 unique cases. How many of the 256 colorings are included in each of these cases?

8.19   Implement the marching-cubes algorithm. Ignore the ambiguous case; you may use one of the possible interpretations.

8.20   You can display three-dimensional data by displaying local normals for each cell or for some collection of cells. Write a program that will display, for a given contour value, the approximate normal for the portion of the surface that passes through the cell.

8.21   Assume that you have values of a function at the eight vertices of a right parallelepiped. Develop a method of trilinear interpolation, similar to bilinear interpolation, to obtain interior values.

8.22   This chapter has emphasized tree-structured models. Identify applications where there are relationships among the parts, but tree–structured models cannot express all relationships. Describe types of problems that cannot be modeled with trees and DAGS, and require more general graphs.

9 Curves and Surfaces

That the world is not flat has been generally accepted since 1492. Nevertheless, in computer graphics, we continue to populate our virtual worlds with flat objects. We have a good reason for such persistence. Graphics systems can render flat three-dimensional polygons at high rates, including doing hidden-surface removal, shading, and even texture mapping. We could take the approach that we took with our sphere model, and define curved objects that are, in (virtual) reality, collections of flat polygons. Alternatively, as we shall do here, we can provide the user with the means to work with curved objects in her program, leaving the eventual rendering of these objects to the implementation.

We shall introduce three ways to model curves and surfaces, but shall expend most of our effort on the parametric polynomial forms. We shall also discuss how curves and surfaces can be rendered on present graphics systems, a process that usually involves subdividing the curved objects into collections of flat primitives. From the application programmer's perspective, this process will be transparent, because it is part of the implementation. However, it is important that we have an understanding of the work involved, so that we can appreciate the practical limitations that we face in using curves and surfaces.

9.1 Representation of Curves and Surfaces

Before proceeding to our development of parametric polynomial curves and surfaces, we pause to summarize our knowledge of the three major types of object representation—explicit, implicit, and parametric—and to observe the advantages and disadvantages of each form. We can illustrate the salient points using only lines, circles, planes, and spheres.

9.1.1 Explicit Representation

The **explicit form** of a curve in two dimensions gives the value of one variable, the **dependent variable**, in terms of the other, the **independent variable**. In x, y space, we might write

$$y = f(x),$$

or, if we are fortunate, we might be able to invert the relationship and express x as a function of y:

$$x = g(y).$$

We are not guaranteed that either form exists for a given curve. For the line, we usually write the equation

$$y = mx + h,$$

even though we know that this equation does not hold for vertical lines. This problem is one of many coordinate-system–dependent effects that cause problems for graphics systems, and more generally, for all fields where we work with design and manipulation of curves and surfaces. Lines and circles exist independently of any representation, and any representation that fails for certain orientations, such as vertical lines, has serious deficiencies.

Circles provide an even more illustrative example. A circle has constant **curvature**—a measure of how rapidly a curve is bending at a point. No closed two-dimensional curve can be more symmetric than the circle. However, the best we can do, using an explicit representation, is to write one equation for half of it,

$$y = \sqrt{r^2 - x^2},$$

and a second equation for the other half.

In three dimensions, the explicit representation of a curve requires two equations. For example, if x is again the independent variable, we have two dependent variables:

$$y = f(x),$$

$$z = g(x).$$

A surface requires two independent variables, and a representation might take the form

$$z = f(x, y).$$

As is true in two dimensions, a curve or surface may not have an explicit representation. For example, the equations

$$y = ax + b,$$
$$z = cx + d,$$

describe a line in three dimensions, but these equations cannot represent a line in a plane of constant x. Likewise, a surface represented by an equation of the form $z = f(x, y)$ cannot represent a sphere, because a given x and y will usually generate either zero or two points on the sphere.

9.1.2 Implicit Representations

Most of the curves and surfaces with which we shall work have implicit representations. In two dimensions, an **implicit curve** can be represented by the equation

$$f(x, y) = 0.$$

Our two examples—the line and the circle centered at the origin—have the respective representations

$$ax + by + c = 0,$$
$$x^2 + y^2 - r^2 = 0.$$

The function f, however, is really a testing, or **membership**, function that divides space into those points that belong to the curve and those that do not. It allows us to take an x, y pair and to evaluate f; in general, however, it gives us no analytic way to find a value y on the curve that corresponds to a given x, or vice versa. The implicit form is less coordinate-system–dependent than is the explicit form, however, in that it does represent all lines and circles.

In three dimensions, the implicit form

$$f(x, y, z) = 0$$

describes a surface. For example, any plane can be written as

$$ax + by + cz + d = 0,$$

and a sphere centered at the origin can be described by

$$x^2 + y^2 + z^2 - r^2 = 0.$$

Curves in three dimensions are not as easily represented in implicit form. We can represent a curve as the intersection, if it exists, of the two surfaces

$$f(x, y, z) = 0,$$
$$g(x, y, z) = 0.$$

Thus, if we test a point (x, y, z) and it is on both surfaces, then it must lie on their intersection curve.

Algebraic surfaces are those for which the function $f(x, y, z)$ is the sum of polynomials in the three variables. Of particular importance are the **quadric** surfaces, where each term in f can have degree up to 2.[1] Quadrics are of interest not only because they include useful objects (such as spheres, disks, and cones), but also because when we intersect these objects with lines, at most two intersection points are generated. We shall use this fact to render quadrics in Section 9.9.

9.1.3 Parametric Form

The **parametric form** of a curve expresses the value of each spatial variable for points on the curve in terms of an independent variable, u: the **parameter**. In three dimensions, we have three explicit functions:

$$x = x(u),$$
$$y = y(u),$$
$$z = z(u).$$

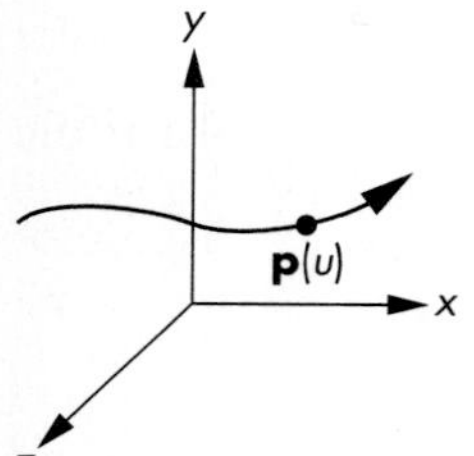

Figure 9.1 Parametric curve.

One of the advantages of the parametric form is that it is the same in two and three dimensions. In the former case, we simply drop the equation for z. A useful interpretation of the parametric form is to visualize the locus of points $\mathbf{p}(u) = [\, x(u) \quad y(u) \quad z(u) \,]^T$ being drawn as u varies, as shown in Figure 9.1. We can think of the derivative

$$\frac{d\mathbf{p}(u)}{du} = \begin{bmatrix} \dfrac{dx(u)}{du} \\ \dfrac{dy(u)}{du} \\ \dfrac{dz(u)}{du} \end{bmatrix}$$

as the velocity with which the curve is traced out and points in the direction tangent to the curve and is perpendicular to the normal at the point.

Parametric surfaces require two parameters. We can describe a surface by three equations of the form

$$x = x(u, v),$$
$$y = y(u, v),$$
$$z = z(u, v),$$

or through the column matrix $\mathbf{p}(u, v) = [\, x(u, v) \quad y(u, v) \quad z(u, v) \,]^T$. As u and v vary over some range, we generate all the points $\mathbf{p}(u, v)$ on the surface. As

---

[1] Degree is measured as the sum of the powers of the individual terms, so x, y, or z^2 can be in a quadric, but xy^2 cannot be.

we saw with our sphere example in Chapter 6, the column matrices $\partial \mathbf{p}/\partial u$ and $\partial \mathbf{p}/\partial v$ determine the tangent plane at each point on the surface.

The parametric form of curves and surfaces is the most flexible and robust for computer graphics. We could still argue that we have not fully removed all dependencies on a particular coordinate system or frame, because we are still using the x, y, and z for a particular representation. It is possible to develop a system solely on the basis of $\mathbf{p}(u)$ for curves and $\mathbf{p}(u, v)$ for surfaces. For example, the Frenet frame is often used for describing curves in three-dimensional space, and is defined using the tangent and the normal. However, this frame changes for each point on the curve. We shall find that the parametric form for x, y, z within a particular frame is sufficiently robust for our purposes.

9.1.4 Parametric Polynomial Curves

Parametric forms are not unique. A given curve or surface can be represented in many ways, but we shall find that parametric forms in which the functions are polynomials in u for curves, and polynomials in u and v for surfaces, are of most use in computer graphics. Many of the reasons will be summarized in the Section 9.2.

Consider a curve of the form[2]

$$\mathbf{p}(u) = \begin{bmatrix} x(u) \\ y(u) \\ z(u) \end{bmatrix}.$$

A polynomial parametric curve of degree[3] n is of the form

$$\mathbf{p}(u) = \sum_{k=0}^{n} u^k \mathbf{c}_k,$$

where each $\mathbf{c}_k$ has independent x, y, and z components; that is,

$$\mathbf{c}_k = \begin{bmatrix} c_{xk} \\ c_{yk} \\ c_{zk} \end{bmatrix}.$$

The $n + 1$ column matrices $\{\mathbf{c}_k\}$ are the coefficients of $\mathbf{p}$; they give us $3(n + 1)$ degrees of freedom in how we choose the coefficients of a particular $\mathbf{p}$. There is no coupling, however, among the x, y, and z components, so we can work with three independent equations, each of the form

---

[2] At this point there is no need to work in homogeneous coordinates; in Section 9.8 we shall work in them to derive NURBS curves.

[3] OpenGL often uses the term *order* to mean 1 greater than the degree.

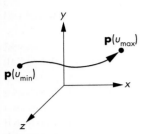

Figure 9.2 Curve segment.

$$p(u) = \sum_{k=0}^{n} u^k c_k,$$

and each with $n + 1$ degrees of freedom. We can define our curves for any range of u

$$u_{min} \le u \le u_{max},$$

but with no loss of generality (see Exercise 9.3), we can assume that $0 \le u \le 1$. As the value of u varies over its range, we define a **curve segment**, as shown in Figure 9.2.

9.1.5 Parametric Polynomial Surfaces

We can define a parametric polynomial surface as

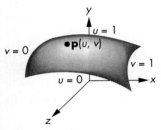

Figure 9.3 Surface patch.

$$\mathbf{p}(u, v) = \begin{bmatrix} x(u, v) \\ y(u, v) \\ z(u, v) \end{bmatrix} = \sum_{i=0}^{n} \sum_{j=0}^{m} \mathbf{c}_{ij} u^i v^j.$$

We must specify $3(n + 1)(m + 1)$ coefficients to determine a particular surface $\mathbf{p}(u, v)$. We shall always take $n = m$, and let u and v vary over the rectangle $0 \le u, v \le 1$, defining a **surface patch**, as shown in Figure 9.3. Note that any surface patch can be viewed as the limit of a collection of curves that we generate by holding either u or v constant, and varying the other. Our strategy shall be to define parametric polynomial curves, and to use the curves to generate surfaces with similar characteristics.

9.2   Design Criteria

The way curves and surfaces are used in computer graphics and computer-aided design is often different from the way they are used in other fields, and from the way you may have seen them used previously. There are many considerations that determine why we prefer to use parametric polynomials of low degree, including

- Local control of shape
- Smoothness and continuity
- Ability to evaluate derivatives
- Stability
- Ease of rendering

We can understand these criteria with the aid of a simple example. Suppose that we want to build a model airplane, using flexible strips of wood for the structure. We can build the body of the model by constructing a set of cross-sections, and then connecting them with longer pieces, as shown in Figure 9.4.

Figure 9.4 Model airplane.

Figure 9.5 Cross-section curve.

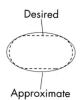

Figure 9.6 Approximation of cross-section curve.

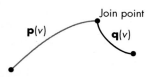

Figure 9.7 Derivative discontinuity at join point.

To design our cross-sections, we might start with a picture of a real airplane, or sketch a desired curve. One such cross-section might be like that shown in Figure 9.5. We could try to get a single global description of this cross-section, but that description probably would not be what we want. Each strip of wood can be bent to only a certain shape before breaking, and can bend in only a smooth way. Hence, we can regard the curve in Figure 9.5 as only an approximation to what we shall actually build, which might be more like Figure 9.6. In practice, we probably will make our cross-section out of a number of wood strips, each of which will become a curve segment for the cross-section. Thus, not only will each segment have to be smooth, but also we shall want a degree of smoothness where the segments meet at **join points**.

Note that, although we might be able ensure that a curve segment is smooth, we shall have to be particularly careful at the join points. Figure 9.7 shows an example in which, although the two curve segments are smooth, at the join point, the derivative is discontinuous. The usual definition of **smoothness** is given in terms of the derivatives along the curve. A curve with discontinuities is of little interest to us. A curve with a continuous first derivative is smoother than a curve whose first derivative has discontinuities (and so on for the higher derivatives). We shall make these notions more precise in the Section 9.3. However, it should be clear that, for a polynomial curve

$$p(u) = \sum_{k=0}^{n} c_k u^k,$$

all derivatives exist, and can be computed analytically. Consequently, the only places where we can encounter difficulties are at the join points.

We would like to design each segment individually, rather than designing all the segments by a single global calculation. One reason for this desire is that we would like to work interactively with the shape, carefully molding it to meet our specifications. When we make a change, this change will affect the shape in only the area where we are working. This sort of local control is but one aspect of a more general stability principle that can be stated: *Small changes in input should cause only small changes in output.*

Working with our piece of wood, we might be able to bend it to approximate the desired shape by comparing it to the entire curve. More likely, we would consider data at a small number of **control points**, and would use only these data to design our shape. Figure 9.8 shows a possible curve segment and a collection of control points. Note that the curve passes through, or **interpolates**, some of the control points, but only comes close to others. As we shall see throughout this chapter, in computer graphics and CAD, we are usually satisfied if the curve passes close to the control-point data, as long as it is smooth.

This example shows many of the reasons for working with polynomial parametric curves. In fact, the spline curves that we shall discuss in Sections 9.7 and 9.8 derive their name from a flexible wood or metal device that shipbuilders

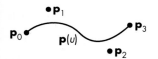

Figure 9.8 Curve segment and control points

used to design the shape of hulls. Each spline was held in place by pegs and the bending properties of the material gave the curve segment a polynomial shape.

Returning to computer graphics, remember that we need methods for rendering curves (and surfaces). A good mathematical representation may be of limited value if we cannot display the resulting curves and surfaces easily. We would like to display whatever curves and surfaces we choose with techniques similar to those used for flat objects, including color, shading, and the more advanced techniques that we shall consider in Chapter 10, such as texture mapping.

9.3   Parametric Cubic Polynomial Curves

Once we have decided to use parametric polynomial curves, we must choose the degree of the curve. If we choose a high degree, we will have many parameters that we can set to form the desired shape, but evaluation of points on the curve will be costly. In addition, as the degree of a polynomial curve becomes higher, there is more danger that the curve will become rougher. On the other hand, if we pick too low a degree, we may not have enough parameters with which to work. However, if we design each curve segment over a short interval, we can achieve many of our purposes with low-degree curves. Although there may be only a few degrees of freedom, these few may be sufficient to allow us to produce the desired shape in a small region. For this reason, most designers, at least initially, work with cubic polynomial curves.

We shall write a cubic parametric polynomial using a row and column matrix as[4]

$$\mathbf{p}(u) = \mathbf{c}_0 + \mathbf{c}_1 u + \mathbf{c}_2 u^2 + \mathbf{c}_3 u^3 = \sum_{k=0}^{3} \mathbf{c}_k u^k = \mathbf{u}^T \mathbf{c},$$

where

$$\mathbf{c} = \begin{bmatrix} \mathbf{c}_0 \\ \mathbf{c}_1 \\ \mathbf{c}_2 \\ \mathbf{c}_3 \end{bmatrix}, \qquad \mathbf{u} = \begin{bmatrix} 1 \\ u \\ u^2 \\ u^3 \end{bmatrix}, \qquad \mathbf{c}_k = \begin{bmatrix} c_{kx} \\ c_{ky} \\ c_{xz} \end{bmatrix}.$$

Thus, $\mathbf{c}$ is a column matrix containing the coefficients of the polynomial; it is what we wish to determine from the control-point data. We shall derive a number of types of cubic curves. The types will differ in how they use the control-point data. We shall seek to find 12 equations in 12 unknowns for each

---

[4] Most references use the order $p(u) = c_0 u^3 + c_1 u^2 + c_2 u + c_3$. If we did, however, we would then have to reverse the numbering of indices in our matrices.

type, but, because x, y, and z are independent, we can group these equations into three independent sets of four equations in four unknowns.

The design of a particular type of cubic will be based on data given at some values of the parameter u. These data might take the form of interpolating conditions in which the polynomial must agree with the data at some points. The data may also require the polynomial to interpolate some derivatives at certain values of the parameter. We might also have smoothness conditions that enforce various continuity conditions at the join points that are shared by two curve segments. Finally, we may have conditions that are not as strict, requiring only that the curve pass close to several known data. Each type of condition will define a different type of curve, and, depending how we use some given data, the same data can define more than a single curve.

9.4 Interpolation

Our first example of a cubic parametric polynomial is the cubic **interpolating polynomial**. Although we rarely use interpolating polynomials in computer graphics, the derivation of this familiar polynomial will illustrate the steps that we must follow for our other types, and the analysis of the interpolating polynomial will illustrate many of the important features by which we evaluate a particular curve or surface.

Suppose that we have four control points in three dimensions: $\mathbf{p}_0$, $\mathbf{p}_1$, $\mathbf{p}_2$, and $\mathbf{p}_3$. Each is of the form

$$\mathbf{p}_k = \begin{bmatrix} x_k \\ y_k \\ z_k \end{bmatrix}.$$

We seek the coefficients $\mathbf{c}$ such that the polynomial $\mathbf{p}(u) = \mathbf{u}^T \mathbf{c}$ passes through, or interpolates, the four control points. The derivation should be easy. We have four three-dimensional interpolating points; hence, we have 12 conditions and 12 unknowns. First, however, we have to decide at which values of the parameter u the interpolation takes place. Lacking any other information, we can take these values to be the equally spaced values $u = 0, \frac{1}{3}, \frac{2}{3}, 1$—remember that we have decided to let u always vary over the interval $[0, 1]$. The four conditions are thus

$$\mathbf{p}_0 = \mathbf{p}(0) = \mathbf{c}_0,$$

$$\mathbf{p}_1 = \mathbf{p}\left(\tfrac{1}{3}\right) = \mathbf{c}_0 + \tfrac{1}{3}\mathbf{c}_1 + \left(\tfrac{1}{3}\right)^2 \mathbf{c}_2 + \left(\tfrac{1}{3}\right)^3 \mathbf{c}_3,$$

$$\mathbf{p}_2 = \mathbf{p}\left(\tfrac{2}{3}\right) = \mathbf{c}_0 + \tfrac{2}{3}\mathbf{c}_1 + \left(\tfrac{2}{3}\right)^2 \mathbf{c}_2 + \left(\tfrac{2}{3}\right)^3 \mathbf{c}_3,$$

$$\mathbf{p}_3 = \mathbf{p}(1) = \mathbf{c}_0 + \mathbf{c}_1 + \mathbf{c}_2 + \mathbf{c}_3.$$

We can write these equations in matrix form as

$$\mathbf{p} = \mathbf{A}\mathbf{c},$$

where

$$\mathbf{p} = \begin{bmatrix} \mathbf{p}_0 \\ \mathbf{p}_1 \\ \mathbf{p}_2 \\ \mathbf{p}_3 \end{bmatrix},$$

and

$$\mathbf{A} = \begin{bmatrix} 1 & 0 & 0 & 0 \\ 1 & \frac{1}{3} & \left(\frac{1}{3}\right)^2 & \left(\frac{1}{3}\right)^3 \\ 1 & \frac{2}{3} & \left(\frac{2}{3}\right)^2 & \left(\frac{2}{3}\right)^3 \\ 1 & 1 & 1 & 1 \end{bmatrix}.$$

The matrix form here has to be interpreted carefully. If we interpret $\mathbf{p}$ and $\mathbf{c}$ as column matrices of 12 elements, the rules of matrix multiplication are violated. Instead, we view $\mathbf{p}$ and $\mathbf{c}$ each as a four-element column matrix whose elements are three-element row matrices. Hence, multiplication of an element of $\mathbf{A}$, a scalar, by an element of $\mathbf{c}$, a three-element column matrix, yields a three-element column matrix, which is the same type as an element of $\mathbf{p}$.[5] We can show that $\mathbf{A}$ is nonsingular, and can invert it to obtain the **interpolating geometry matrix**

$$\mathbf{M}_I = \mathbf{A}^{-1} = \begin{bmatrix} 1 & 0 & 0 & 0 \\ -5.5 & 9 & -4.5 & 1 \\ 9 & 22.5 & 18 & -4.5 \\ -4.5 & 13.5 & -13.5 & 4.5 \end{bmatrix},$$

and the desired coefficients

$$\mathbf{c} = \mathbf{M}_I \mathbf{p}.$$

Suppose that we have a sequence of control points $\mathbf{p}_0, \mathbf{p}_1, \ldots, \mathbf{p}_m$. Rather than defining a single interpolating curve of degree $m - 1$ for all the points— a calculation that we could do by following a similar derivation to the one for cubic polynomials—we can define a set of cubic interpolating curves, each defined by a group of four control points, and each valid over a short interval

---

[5] We could use row matrices for the elements of $\mathbf{p}$ and $\mathbf{c}$: in that case, ordinary matrix multiplications would work, because we would have a 4 × 4 matrix multiplying a 4 × 3 matrix. However, this method would fail for surfaces. The real difficulty is that we should be using *tensors* to carry out the mathematics—a topic beyond the scope of this book.

in u. We can achieve continuity at the join points by using the control point defining the right side of one segment as the first point for the next segment (Figure 9.9). Thus, we use $\mathbf{p}_0, \mathbf{p}_1, \mathbf{p}_2, \mathbf{p}_3$ to define the first segment; we use $\mathbf{p}_3, \mathbf{p}_4, \mathbf{p}_5, \mathbf{p}_6$, for the second; and so on. Note that, if each segment is defined for the parameter u varying over the interval $[0, 1]$, then the matrix $\mathbf{M}_I$ is the same for each segment. Although we have achieved continuity for the sequence of segments, derivatives at the join points will not be continuous.

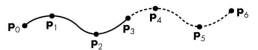

Figure 9.9 Joining of interpolating segments.

9.4.1 Blending Functions

We can obtain additional insights into the smoothness of the interpolating polynomial curves by reposing our equations in a slightly different form. We can substitute the interpolating coefficients into our polynomial; we obtain

$$\mathbf{p}(u) = \mathbf{u}^T \mathbf{c} = \mathbf{u}^T \mathbf{M}_I \mathbf{p},$$

which we can write as

$$\mathbf{p}(u) = \mathbf{b}(u)^T \mathbf{p},$$

where

$$\mathbf{b}(u) = \mathbf{M}_I^T \mathbf{u}$$

is a column matrix of the four **blending polynomials**

$$\mathbf{b}(u) = \begin{bmatrix} b_0(u) \\ b_1(u) \\ b_2(u) \\ b_3(u) \end{bmatrix}.$$

Each polynomial is a cubic. If we express $\mathbf{p}(u)$ in terms of these blending polynomials as

$$\mathbf{p}(u) = b_0(u)\mathbf{p}_0 + b_1(u)\mathbf{p}_1 + b_2(u)\mathbf{p}_2 + b_3(u)\mathbf{p}_3 = \sum_{i=0}^{3} b_i(u)\mathbf{p}_i,$$

we can see that the polynomials blend together the individual contributions of each control point and enable us to see the effect of a given control point on the entire curve. These blending functions for the cubic interpolating polynomial

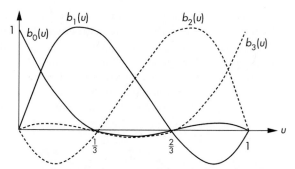

Figure 9.10 Blending polynomials for interpolation.

are shown in Figure 9.10 and are given by the equations

$$b_0(u) = -\tfrac{9}{2}\left(u - \tfrac{1}{3}\right)\left(u - \tfrac{2}{3}\right)(u - 1),$$

$$b_1(u) = \tfrac{27}{2}u\left(u - \tfrac{2}{3}\right)(u - 1),$$

$$b_2(u) = -\tfrac{27}{2}u(u - \tfrac{1}{3})(u - 1),$$

$$b_3(u) = \tfrac{9}{2}u\left(u - \tfrac{1}{3}\right)\left(u - \tfrac{2}{3}\right).$$

Because all the zeros of the blending functions lie in the closed interval $[0, 1]$, the blending functions must vary substantially over this interval and are not particularly smooth. This lack of smoothness is a consequence of the interpolating requirement that the curve must pass through the control points, rather than just come close to them. This characteristic is even more pronounced for interpolation polynomials of higher degree. This problem and the lack of derivative continuity at the join points account for limited use of the interpolating polynomial in computer graphics. However, the same derivation and analysis process will allow us to find smoother types of cubic curves.

9.4.2 The Cubic Interpolating Patch

There is a natural extension of the interpolating curve to an interpolating patch. A **bicubic surface patch** can be written in the form

$$\mathbf{p}(u, v) = \sum_{i=0}^{3} \sum_{j=0}^{3} u^i v^j \mathbf{c}_{ij},$$

where $\mathbf{c}_{ij}$ is a three-element column matrix of the x, y, and z coefficients for the ijth term in the polynomial. If we define a 4×4 matrix whose elements are three-element column matrices,

$$\mathbf{C} = [\, \mathbf{c}_{ij} \,],$$

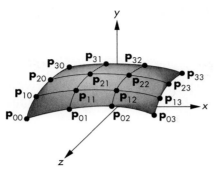

Figure 9.11 Interpolating surface patch.

we can write the surface patch as

$$\mathbf{p}(u, v) = \mathbf{u}^T \mathbf{C} \mathbf{v},$$

where

$$\mathbf{v} = \begin{bmatrix} 1 \\ v \\ v^2 \\ v^3 \end{bmatrix}.$$

A particular bicubic polynomial patch is defined by the 48 elements of $\mathbf{C}$—16 three-element vectors.

Suppose that we have 16 three-dimensional control points $\mathbf{p}_{ij}$, $i = 0, \ldots, 3$, $j = 0, \ldots, 3$. We can use these points to define an interpolating surface patch, as shown in Figure 9.11. If we assume that these data are used for interpolation at the equally spaced values of both u and v of $0, \frac{1}{3}, \frac{2}{3}$, and 1, then we get three sets of 16 equations in 16 unknowns. For example, for $u = v = 0$, we get the three independent equations

$$\mathbf{p}_{00} = \begin{bmatrix} 1 & 0 & 0 & 0 \end{bmatrix} \mathbf{C} \begin{bmatrix} 1 \\ 0 \\ 0 \\ 0 \end{bmatrix} = \mathbf{c}_{00}.$$

Rather than writing down and solving all these equations, we can proceed in a more direct fashion. If we consider $v = 0$, we get a curve in u that must interpolate $\mathbf{p}_{00}$, $\mathbf{p}_{10}$, $\mathbf{p}_{20}$, and $\mathbf{p}_{30}$. Using our results on interpolating curves, we write this curve as

$$\mathbf{p}(u, 0) = \mathbf{u}^T \mathbf{M}_I \begin{bmatrix} \mathbf{p}_{00} \\ \mathbf{p}_{10} \\ \mathbf{p}_{20} \\ \mathbf{p}_{30} \end{bmatrix} = \mathbf{u}^T \mathbf{C} \begin{bmatrix} 1 \\ 0 \\ 0 \\ 0 \end{bmatrix}.$$

Likewise, the values of $v = \frac{1}{3}, \frac{2}{3}, 1$ define three other interpolating curves, each of which has a similar form. Putting these curves together, we can write all 16 equations as

$$\mathbf{u}^T \mathbf{M}_I \mathbf{P} = \mathbf{u}^T \mathbf{C} \mathbf{A}^T,$$

where $\mathbf{A}$ is the inverse of $\mathbf{M}_I$. We can solve this equation for the desired coefficient matrix

$$\mathbf{C} = \mathbf{M}_I \mathbf{P} \mathbf{M}_I^T,$$

and, substituting into the equation for the surface, we have

$$\mathbf{p}(u, v) = \mathbf{u}^T \mathbf{M}_I \mathbf{P} \mathbf{M}_I^T \mathbf{v}.$$

We can interpret this result in a number of ways. First, the interpolating surface can be derived from our understanding of interpolating curves—a technique that will enable us to extend other types of curves to surfaces. Second, we can extend our use of blending polynomials to surfaces. By noting that $\mathbf{M}_I^T \mathbf{u}$ describes the interpolating blending functions, we can rewrite our surface patch as

$$\mathbf{p}(u, v) = \sum_{i=0}^{3} \sum_{j=0}^{3} b_i(u) b_j(v) \mathbf{p}_{ij}.$$

Each term $b_i(u) b_j(v)$ describes a **blending patch**. We form a surface by blending together 16 simple patches, each weighted by the data at a control point. The basic properties of the blending patches are determined by the same blending polynomials that arose for interpolating curves; thus, most of the characteristics of surfaces are similar to those of the curves. In particular, the blending patches are not particularly smooth, because the zeros of the functions $b_i(u) b_j(v)$ lie inside the unit square in u, v space. Surfaces formed from curves using this technique are known as tensor-product surfaces. Bicubic tensor-product surfaces are a subset of all surface patches that have up to cubic terms in both parameters. They are an example of separable surfaces, because they allow us to work with u and v independently.

9.5   Hermite Curves and Surfaces

We can use the techniques that we developed for interpolating curves and surfaces to generate a number of other types of curves and surfaces. The major difference will be in the way we use the data at control points.

9.5.1 The Hermite Form

Suppose that we start with only the control points $\mathbf{p}_0$ and $\mathbf{p}_3$,[6] and again insist that our curve interpolate these points at the parameter values $u = 0$ and $u = 1$, respectively. Using our previous notation, we have the two conditions

$$\mathbf{p}(0) = \mathbf{p}_0 = \mathbf{c}_0,$$

$$\mathbf{p}(1) = \mathbf{p}_3 = \mathbf{c}_0 + \mathbf{c}_1 + \mathbf{c}_2 + \mathbf{c}_3.$$

We can get two other conditions if we assume that we know the derivatives of the function at $u = 0$ and $u = 1$. The derivative of the polynomial is simply the parametric quadratic polynomial

$$\mathbf{p}'(u) = \begin{bmatrix} \dfrac{dx}{du} \\[6pt] \dfrac{dy}{du} \\[6pt] \dfrac{dz}{du} \end{bmatrix} = \mathbf{c}_1 + 2u\mathbf{c}_2 + 3u^2\mathbf{c}_3.$$

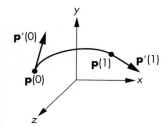

Figure 9.12 Definition of the Hermite cubic.

If we denote the given values of the two derivatives as $\mathbf{p}_0'$ and $\mathbf{p}_3'$, our two additional conditions are (Figure 9.12)

$$\mathbf{p}_0' = \mathbf{p}'(0) = \mathbf{c}_1,$$

$$\mathbf{p}_3' = \mathbf{p}'(1) = \mathbf{c}_1 + 2\mathbf{c}_2 + 3\mathbf{c}_3.$$

We can write these equations in matrix form as

$$\begin{bmatrix} \mathbf{p}_0 \\ \mathbf{p}_3 \\ \mathbf{p}_0' \\ \mathbf{p}_3' \end{bmatrix} = \begin{bmatrix} 1 & 0 & 0 & 0 \\ 1 & 1 & 1 & 1 \\ 0 & 1 & 0 & 0 \\ 0 & 1 & 2 & 3 \end{bmatrix} \mathbf{c}.$$

Letting $\mathbf{q}$ denote the data matrix

$$\mathbf{q} = \begin{bmatrix} \mathbf{p}_0 \\ \mathbf{p}_3 \\ \mathbf{p}_0' \\ \mathbf{p}_3' \end{bmatrix},$$

we can solve the equations to find

$$\mathbf{c} = \mathbf{M}_H \mathbf{q},$$

---

[6] We use this numbering to be consistent with our interpolation notation, and with the numbering that we shall use for Bezier curves in Section 9.6.

where $\mathbf{M}_H$ is the **Hermite geometry** matrix

$$\mathbf{M}_H = \begin{bmatrix} 1 & 0 & 0 & 0 \\ 0 & 0 & 1 & 0 \\ -3 & 3 & -2 & -1 \\ 2 & -2 & 1 & 1 \end{bmatrix}.$$

The resulting polynomial is given by

$$\mathbf{p}(u) = \mathbf{u}^T \mathbf{M}_H \mathbf{q}.$$

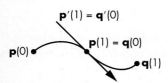

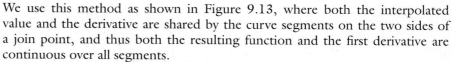

Figure 9.13 Hermite form at join point.

We use this method as shown in Figure 9.13, where both the interpolated value and the derivative are shared by the curve segments on the two sides of a join point, and thus both the resulting function and the first derivative are continuous over all segments.

We can get a more accurate idea of the increased smoothness of the Hermite form by rewriting the polynomial in the form

$$\mathbf{p}(u) = \mathbf{b}(u)^T \mathbf{q},$$

where the new blending functions are given by

$$\mathbf{b}(u) = \mathbf{M}_H^T \mathbf{u} = \begin{bmatrix} 2u^3 - 3u^2 + 1 \\ -2u^3 + 3u^2 \\ u^3 - 2u^2 + u \\ u^3 - u^2 \end{bmatrix}.$$

These four polynomials have none of their zeros inside the interval $(0,1)$ and are much smoother than are the interpolating polynomial blending functions (see Exercise 9.16).

We can go on and define a bicubic Hermite surface patch through these blending functions,

$$\mathbf{p}(u, v) = \sum_{i=0}^{3} \sum_{j=0}^{3} b_i(u) b_j(v) \mathbf{q}_{ij},$$

where $\mathbf{Q} = [\mathbf{q}_{ij}]$ is the extension of $\mathbf{q}$ to surface data. However, at this point, this equation is just a formal expression. It is not clear what the relationship is between the elements of $\mathbf{Q}$ and the derivatives of $\mathbf{p}(u, v)$. Four of the elements of $\mathbf{Q}$ are chosen to interpolate the corners of the patch, whereas the others are chosen to match certain derivatives at the corners of the patch. In most interactive applications, however, the user enters point data, rather than derivative data; consequently, unless we have analytic formulations for the data, usually we will not have these derivatives.

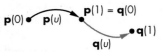

Figure 9.14 Continuity at join point.

9.5.2 Geometric and Parametric Continuity

Before we discuss the Bezier and spline forms, we shall examine a few issues concerning continuity and derivatives. Consider the join point in Figure 9.14. Suppose that the polynomial on the left is $\mathbf{p}(u)$, and that the one on the right is $\mathbf{q}(u)$. We enforce various continuity conditions by matching the polynomials and their derivatives at $u = 1$ for $\mathbf{p}(u)$, with the corresponding values for $\mathbf{q}(u)$ for $u = 0$. If we want the function to be continuous, we must have

$$\mathbf{p}(1) = \begin{bmatrix} p_x(1) \\ p_y(1) \\ p_z(1) \end{bmatrix} = \mathbf{q}(0) = \begin{bmatrix} q_x(0) \\ q_y(0) \\ q_z(0) \end{bmatrix}.$$

All three parametric components must be equal at the join point; we call this property C^0 **parametric continuity.**

When we consider derivatives, we can require, as we did with the Hermite curve, that

$$\mathbf{p}'(1) = \begin{bmatrix} p'_x(1) \\ p'_y(1) \\ p'_z(1) \end{bmatrix} = \mathbf{q}'(0) = \begin{bmatrix} q'_x(0) \\ q'_y(0) \\ q'_z(0) \end{bmatrix}.$$

If we match all three parametric equations and the first derivative, we have C^1 parametric continuity.

If we look at the geometry, however, we can take a different approach to continuity. In three dimensions, the derivative at a point on a curve defines the tangent line at that point. Suppose that, instead of requiring matching of the derivatives for the two segments at the join point, we require only that their derivatives be proportional,

$$\mathbf{p}'(1) = k\mathbf{q}'(0),$$

for some number k. If the tangents of the two curves are proportional, they point in the same direction, but they may have different magnitudes. We call this type of continuity G^1 **geometric continuity.**[7] If the two tangent vectors need only to be proportional, we have only two conditions to enforce, rather than three, leaving one extra degree of freedom that can potentially be used to satisfy some other criterion. We can extend this idea to higher derivatives, and can talk about both C^n and G^n continuity.

Although two curves that have only G^1 continuity at the join points will have a continuous tangent at the join points, the value of the constant of proportionality, or, equivalently, the relative magnitudes of the tangents on the two sides of the join point, does matter. Curves with the same tangent direction

---

[7] G^0 continuity is the same as C^0 continuity.

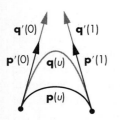

Figure 9.15 Change of magnitude in G^1 continuity.

but different magnitudes will differ, as shown in Figure 9.15. The curves $\mathbf{p}(u)$ and $\mathbf{q}(u)$ share the same endpoints, and the tangents at the endpoints point in the same direction, but the curves are different. This result is exploited in many painting programs, where the user can interactively change the magnitude, leaving the tangent direction unchanged. However, in other applications, such as animation, where a sequence of curve segments describes the path of an object, G^1 continuity may be insufficient; see Exercise 9.11.

9.6   Bezier Curves and Surfaces

Comparing the Hermite form to the interpolating form is like comparing apples to oranges. Both are cubic polynomial curves, but the forms do not use the same data, and thus, cannot be compared on equal terms. We can use the same control-point data that we used to derive the interpolating curves to approximate the derivatives in the Hermite curves. The resulting Bezier curves will be excellent approximations to the Hermite curves and will be comparable to the interpolating curves. In addition, because these curves do not need derivative information, they will be well suited for use in graphics and CAD.

9.6.1 Bezier Curves

Consider again the four control points: $\mathbf{p}_0$, $\mathbf{p}_1$, $\mathbf{p}_2$, and $\mathbf{p}_3$. Suppose that we still insist on the interpolation conditions at the endpoints for a cubic polynomial $\mathbf{p}(u)$:

$$\mathbf{p}_0 = \mathbf{p}(0),$$

$$\mathbf{p}_3 = \mathbf{p}(1).$$

Bezier proposed that, rather than using the other two control points, $\mathbf{p}_2$ and $\mathbf{p}_3$, for interpolation, we use them to approximate the tangents at $u = 0$ and $u = 1$. In parameter space, we can use the linear approximations

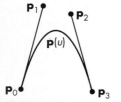

Figure 9.16 Approximating tangents.

$$\mathbf{p}'(0) = \frac{\mathbf{p}_1 - \mathbf{p}_0}{\frac{1}{3}} = 3(\mathbf{p}_1 - \mathbf{p}_0),$$

$$\mathbf{p}'(1) = \frac{\mathbf{p}_3 - \mathbf{p}_2}{\frac{1}{3}} = 3(\mathbf{p}_3 - \mathbf{p}_2),$$

as shown in Figure 9.16. Applying these approximations to the derivative of our parametric polynomial, $\mathbf{p}(u) = \mathbf{u}^T \mathbf{c}$, at the two endpoints, we have the two conditions

$$3\mathbf{p}_1 - 3\mathbf{p}_0 = \mathbf{c}_1,$$
$$3\mathbf{p}_3 - 3\mathbf{p}_2 = \mathbf{c}_1 + 2\mathbf{c}_2 + 3\mathbf{c}_3,$$

to add to our interpolation conditions

$$\mathbf{p}_0 = \mathbf{c}_0,$$

$$\mathbf{p}_3 = \mathbf{c}_0 + \mathbf{c}_1 + \mathbf{c}_2 + \mathbf{c}_3.$$

At this point, we again have three sets of four equations in four unknowns that we can solve, as before, to find

$$\mathbf{c} = \mathbf{M}_B \mathbf{p},$$

where $\mathbf{M}_B$ is the **Bezier geometry matrix**

$$\mathbf{M}_B = \begin{bmatrix} 1 & 0 & 0 & 0 \\ -3 & 3 & 0 & 0 \\ 3 & -6 & 3 & 0 \\ -1 & 3 & -3 & 1 \end{bmatrix}.$$

The cubic Bezier polynomial is thus

$$\mathbf{p}(u) = \mathbf{u}^T \mathbf{M}_B \mathbf{p}.$$

We use this formula exactly as we did for the interpolating polynomial. If we have a set of control points, $\mathbf{p}_0, \cdots, \mathbf{p}_n$, we use $\mathbf{p}_0, \mathbf{p}_1, \mathbf{p}_2,$ and $\mathbf{p}_3,$ for the first curve; $\mathbf{p}_3, \mathbf{p}_4, \mathbf{p}_5,$ and $\mathbf{p}_6$ for the second, and so on. It should be clear that we have C^0 continuity, but we have given up the C^1 continuity of the Hermite polynomial, because we use different approximations on the left and right of a join point.

We can see a number of important advantages to the Bezier curve by examining the blending functions in Figure 9.17. We write the curve as

$$\mathbf{p}(u) = \mathbf{b}(u)^T \mathbf{p},$$

where

$$\mathbf{b}(u) = \mathbf{M}_B^T \mathbf{u} = \begin{bmatrix} (1-u)^3 \\ 3u(1-u)^2 \\ 3u^2(1-u) \\ u^3 \end{bmatrix}.$$

These four polynomials are one case of the **Bernstein polynomials**,

$$b_{kd}(u) = \frac{d!}{k!(d-k)!} u^k (1-u)^{d-k},$$

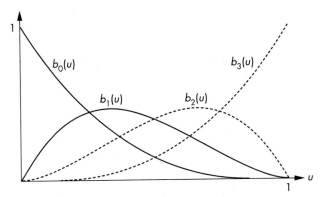

Figure 9.17 Blending polynomials for Bezier cubic.

which can be shown to have remarkable properties. First, all the zeros of the polynomials are either at $u = 0$ or at $u = 1$. Consequently, for each blending polynomial,

$$0 < b_{id}(u),$$

for $0 < u < 1$. Without any zeros in the interval, each blending polynomial must be smooth. We can also show that, in this interval (see Exercise 9.4),

$$b_{id}(u) \leq 1,$$

and

$$\sum_{i=0}^{d} b_{id}(u) = 1.$$

Under these conditions, the representation of our cubic Bezier polynomial,

$$\mathbf{p}(u) = \sum_{i=0}^{3} b_i(u)\mathbf{p}_i,$$

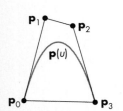

Figure 9.18 Convex hull and Bezier polynomial.

is a convex sum. Consequently, $\mathbf{p}(u)$ must lie in the convex hull of the four control points, as shown in Figure 9.18. Thus, even though the Bezier polynomial does not interpolate all the control points, it cannot be far from them. These two properties, combined with the fact that we are using control-point data, make it easy to work interactively with Bezier curves. A user can enter the four control points to define an initial curve, and then can manipulate the points to control the shape.

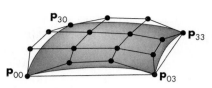
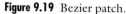

Figure 9.19 Bezier patch.

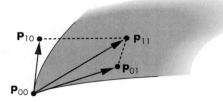

Figure 9.20 Twist at corner of Bezier patch.

9.6.2 Bezier Surface Patches

We can generate the **Bezier surface patches** through the blending functions. If **P** is a 4×4 array of control points,

$$\mathbf{P} = [\mathbf{p}_{ij}],$$

then the corresponding Bezier patch is

$$\mathbf{p}(u, v) = \sum_{i=0}^{3} \sum_{j=0}^{3} b_i(u) b_j(v) \mathbf{p}_{ij} = \mathbf{u}^T \mathbf{M}_B \mathbf{P} \mathbf{M}_B^T \mathbf{v}.$$

The patch is fully contained in the convex hull of the control points (Figure 9.19) and interpolates $\mathbf{p}_{00}$, $\mathbf{p}_{03}$, $\mathbf{p}_{30}$, and $\mathbf{p}_{33}$. We can interpret the other conditions as approximations to various derivatives at the corners of the patch.

Consider the corner for $u = v = 0$. We can evaluate $\mathbf{p}(u)$ and the first partial derivatives to find

$$\mathbf{p}(0, 0) = \mathbf{p}_{00},$$

$$\frac{\partial \mathbf{p}}{\partial u}(0, 0) = 3(\mathbf{p}_{10} - \mathbf{p}_{00}),$$

$$\frac{\partial \mathbf{p}}{\partial v}(0, 0) = 3(\mathbf{p}_{01} - \mathbf{p}_{00}),$$

$$\frac{\partial^2 \mathbf{p}}{\partial u \partial v}(0, 0) = 9(\mathbf{p}_{00} - \mathbf{p}_{01} + \mathbf{p}_{10} - \mathbf{p}_{11}).$$

The first three conditions are clearly extensions of our results for the Bezier curve. The fourth can be seen as a measure of the tendency of the patch to divert from being flat, or to **twist**, at the corner. If we consider the quadrilateral defined by these points (Figure 9.20), the points will lie in the same plane only if the twist is zero.

9.7   Cubic B-Splines

In practice, the cubic Bezier curves and surface patches are widely used. They have one fundamental limitation. At the join points (or patch edges, for surfaces), we have only C^0 continuity. If, for example, we were to use these curves to design our model-airplane cross-sections as shown in Section 9.2, and then were to attempt to build those cross-sections, we might be unhappy with the way that the pieces meet at the join points.

It might seem that we have reached the limit of what we can do with cubic parametric polynomials, and that, if we need more flexibility, we have either to go to high-degree polynomials or to shorten the interval and to use more polynomial segments. Both of these tactics are possible, but there is another possibility. We can use the same control-point data, but not require the polynomial to interpolate any of these points. If we can come close to the control points and get more smoothness at the join points, we might be content with the result.

9.7.1   The Cubic B-Spline Curve

In this section, we shall illustrate a particular example of a B-spline curve. We shall show how we can obtain C^2 continuity at the join points with a cubic. In Section 9.8, we shall give a short introduction to a more general approach to splines—an approach that is general enough to include the Bezier curves as a special case.

Figure 9.21 Four points defining a curve between the middle two.

Consider four control points in the middle of a sequence of control points: $\{\mathbf{p}_{i-2}, \mathbf{p}_{i-1}, \mathbf{p}_i, \mathbf{p}_{i+1}\}$. Our previous approach was to use these four points to define a cubic curve such that, as the parameter u varied from 0 to 1, the curve spanned the distance from $\mathbf{p}_{i-2}$ to $\mathbf{p}_{i+1}$, interpolating $\mathbf{p}_{i-2}$ and $\mathbf{p}_{i+1}$. Instead, suppose that, as u goes from 0 to 1, we span only the distance between the middle two control points, as shown in Figure 9.21. Likewise, we use $\{\mathbf{p}_{i-3}, \mathbf{p}_{i-2}, \mathbf{p}_{i-1}, \mathbf{p}_i\}$ between $\mathbf{p}_{i-2}$ and $\mathbf{p}_{i-1}$, and $\{\mathbf{p}_{i-1}, \mathbf{p}_i, \mathbf{p}_{i+1}, \mathbf{p}_{i+2}\}$ between $\mathbf{p}_i$ and $\mathbf{p}_{i+1}$. Suppose that $\mathbf{p}(u)$ is the curve that we use between $\mathbf{p}_{i-1}$ and $\mathbf{p}_i$, and $\mathbf{q}(u)$ is the curve to its left, used between $\mathbf{p}_{i-2}$ and $\mathbf{p}_{i-1}$. We can match conditions at $\mathbf{p}(0)$ with conditions at $\mathbf{q}(1)$. Using our standard formulation, we are looking for a matrix $\mathbf{M}$, such that the desired cubic polynomial is

$$\mathbf{p}(u) = \mathbf{u}^T \mathbf{M} \mathbf{p},$$

where $\mathbf{p}$ is the matrix of control points

$$\mathbf{p} = \begin{bmatrix} \mathbf{p}_{i-2} \\ \mathbf{p}_{i-1} \\ \mathbf{p}_i \\ \mathbf{p}_{i+1} \end{bmatrix}.$$

We can use the same matrix to write $\mathbf{q}(u)$ as

$$\mathbf{q}(u) = \mathbf{u}^T \mathbf{Mq},$$

where

$$\mathbf{q} = \begin{bmatrix} \mathbf{p}_{i-3} \\ \mathbf{p}_{i-2} \\ \mathbf{p}_{i-1} \\ \mathbf{p}_i \end{bmatrix}.$$

In principle, we could write down a set of conditions on $\mathbf{p}(0)$ that would match conditions for $\mathbf{q}(1)$, and could write equivalent conditions matching various derivatives of $\mathbf{p}(1)$ with conditions for another polynomial that starts there. For example, the condition

$$\mathbf{p}(0) = \mathbf{q}(1)$$

requires continuity at the join point, without requiring interpolation of any data. Enforcing this condition gives one equation for the coefficients of $\mathbf{M}$. There are clearly many sets of conditions that we can use; each set can define a different matrix.

We shall take a shortcut to deriving the most popular matrix, by noting that we must use symmetric approximations at the join point. Hence, any evaluation of conditions on $\mathbf{q}(1)$ cannot use $\mathbf{p}_{i-3}$, because this control point does not appear in the equation for $\mathbf{p}(u)$. Likewise, we cannot use $\mathbf{p}_{i+1}$ in any condition on $\mathbf{p}(0)$. Two conditions that satisfy this symmetry condition are

$$\mathbf{p}(0) = \mathbf{q}(1) = \tfrac{1}{6}(\mathbf{p}_{i-2} + 4\mathbf{p}_{i-1} + \mathbf{p}_i),$$

$$\mathbf{p}'(0) = \mathbf{q}'(1) = \tfrac{1}{2}(\mathbf{p}_i - \mathbf{p}_{i-2}).$$

Writing $\mathbf{p}(u)$ in terms of the coefficient array $\mathbf{c}$,

$$\mathbf{p}(u) = \mathbf{u}^T \mathbf{c},$$

these conditions are

$$\mathbf{c}_0 = \tfrac{1}{6}(\mathbf{p}_{i-2} + 4\mathbf{p}_{i-1} + \mathbf{p}_i),$$

$$\mathbf{c}_1 = \tfrac{1}{2}(\mathbf{p}_i - \mathbf{p}_{i-2}).$$

We can apply the symmetric conditions at $\mathbf{p}(1)$:

$$\mathbf{p}(1) = \mathbf{c}_0 + \mathbf{c}_1 + \mathbf{c}_2 + \mathbf{c}_3 = \tfrac{1}{6}(\mathbf{p}_{i-1} + 4\mathbf{p}_i + \mathbf{p}_{i+1}),$$

$$\mathbf{p}'(1) = \mathbf{c}_1 + 2\mathbf{c}_2 + 3\mathbf{c}_3 = \tfrac{1}{2}(\mathbf{p}_{i+1} - \mathbf{p}_{i-1}).$$

We now have four equations for the coefficients of $\mathbf{c}$, which we can solve for a matrix $\mathbf{M}_S$, the **B-spline geometry matrix**,

$$\mathbf{M}_S = \frac{1}{6} \begin{bmatrix} 1 & 4 & 1 & 0 \\ -3 & 0 & 3 & 0 \\ 3 & -6 & 3 & 0 \\ -1 & 3 & -3 & 1 \end{bmatrix}.$$

This particular matrix yields a polynomial with several important properties. We can see these properties by again examining the blending polynomials:

$$\mathbf{b}(u) = \mathbf{M}_S^T \mathbf{u} = \frac{1}{6} \begin{bmatrix} (1-u)^3 \\ 4 - 6u^2 + 3u^3 \\ 1 + 3u + 3u^2 - 3u^3 \\ u^3 \end{bmatrix}.$$

These polynomials are shown in Figure 9.22. We can show, as we did for the Bezier polynomials, that

$$\sum_{i=0}^{3} b_i(u) = 1,$$

and, in the interval $0 \le u \le 1$,

$$0 \le b_i(u) \le 1.$$

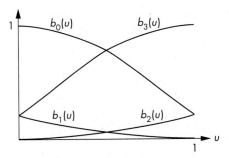

Figure 9.22 Spline-blending functions.

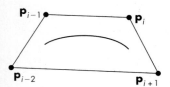

Figure 9.23 Convex hull for spline curve.

Thus, the curve must lie in the convex hull of the control points, as shown in Figure 9.23. Note that the curve is used for only part of the range of the convex hull. We defined the curve to have C^1 continuity; in fact, however, it has C^2 continuity,[8] as we can verify by computing $\mathbf{p}''(u)$ at $u = 0$ and $u = 1$, and seeing that the values are the same for the curves on the right and left. It is for this reason that spline curves are so important. From a physical point of view, metal will bend such that the second derivative is continuous. From a

---

[8] If we are concerned with only G^2, rather than with C^2, continuity, we can use the extra degrees of freedom to give additional flexibility in the design of the curves; see [Bar83].

visual perspective, a curve made of cubic segments with C^2 continuity will be seen as smooth, even at the join points.

Although we have used the same control-point data as those we used for the Bezier cubic to derive a smoother cubic curve, we must be aware that we are doing three times the work as compared with Bezier or interpolating cubics. The reason is that we are using the curve between only control point $i-1$ and control point i. A Bezier curve using the same data would be used from control point $i-2$ to control point $i+1$. Hence, each time we add a control point, a new spline curve must be computed, whereas for Bezier curves, we add the control points three at a time.

9.7.2 B-Splines and Basis

Instead of looking at the curve from the perspective of a single interval, we can gain additional insights by looking at the curve from the perspective of a single control point. Each control point contributes to the spline in four adjacent intervals. This property guarantees the locality of the spline; that is, if we change a single control point, we can affect the resulting curve in only four adjacent intervals. Consider the control point $\mathbf{p}_i$. In the interval between $u = 0$ and $u = 1$, it is multiplied by the blending polynomial $b_2(u)$. It also contributes to the interval on the left through $\mathbf{q}(u)$. In this interval, its contribution is $b_1(u + 1)$—we must shift the value of u by 1 to the left for this interval.

The total contribution of a single control point can be written as $B_i(u)\mathbf{p_i}$, where B_i is the function

$$B_i(u) = \begin{cases} 0 & u < i - 2, \\ b_0(u + 2) & i - 2 \leq u < i - 1, \\ b_1(u + 1) & i - 1 \leq u < i, \\ b_2(u) & i \leq u < i + 1, \\ b_3(u - 1) & i + 1 \leq u < i + 2, \\ 0 & u \geq i + 2. \end{cases}$$

This function is pictured in Figure 9.24. Given a set of control points $\mathbf{p}_0, \ldots, \mathbf{p}_m$, we can write the entire spline with the single expression[9]

$$\mathbf{p}(u) = \sum_{i=1}^{m-1} B_i(u - i)\mathbf{p}_i.$$

This expression shows that, for the set of functions $B(u - i)$, each is a shifted version of a single function, and the set forms a basis for all our cubic B-spline curves. Given a set of control points, we form a piecewise polynomial

---

[9] We shall worry about the proper conditions for the beginning and end of the spline in Section 9.8.

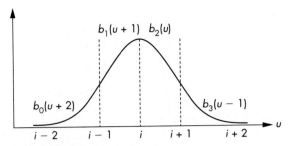

Figure 9.24 Spline basis function.

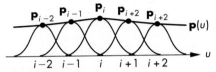

Figure 9.25 Approximating function over interval.

curve $\mathbf{p}(u)$ over the whole interval as a linear combination of basis functions. Figure 9.25 shows a function and the contributions from the individual basis functions. The general theory of splines that we shall develop in Section 9.8 will expand this view by allowing higher-degree polynomials in the intervals, and by allowing different polynomials in different intervals.

9.7.3 Spline Surfaces

B-spline surfaces can be defined in a similar way. If we start with the B-spline blending functions, the surface patch is given by

$$\mathbf{p}(u, v) = \sum_{i=0}^{3} \sum_{j=0}^{3} b_i(u) b_j(v) \mathbf{p}_{ij}.$$

This expression is of the same form as are those for our other surface patches, but, as we can see from Figure 9.26, we use the patch over only the central area, and we must do nine times the work as compared to the Bezier patch. However, because of inheritance of the convex hull property and the additional continuity at the edges from the B-spline curves, the B-spline patch is considerably smoother than a Bezier patch constructed from the same data would be.

Figure 9.26 Spline surface patch.

9.8 General B-Splines

Suppose that we have a set of control points, $p_0, \ldots, p_m$. The general approximation problem is to find a function $\mathbf{p}(u) = [\, x(u) \quad y(u) \quad z(u) \,]^T$, defined over an interval $u_{\min} \leq u \leq u_{\max}$, that is smooth and is close, in some sense, to the control points. Suppose that we have a set of values $\{u_k\}$, called **knots**, such that

$$u_{\min} = u_0 \leq u_1 \leq \ldots \leq u_n = u_{\max}.$$

We shall call sequence $u_0, u_1, \ldots, u_n$ the **knot array**.[10] In splines, the function $\mathbf{p}(u)$ is a polynomial of degree d between the knots,

$$\mathbf{p}(u) = \sum_{j=0}^{d} \mathbf{c}_{jk} u^j, \quad u_k < u < u_{k+1}.$$

Thus, to define a spline of degree d, we must define the $n(d + 1)$ three-dimensional coefficients $\mathbf{c}_{jk}$. We get the required conditions by applying various continuity and interpolation requirements at the knots.

For example, if $d = 3$, we have a cubic polynomial in each interval, and, for a given n, must define $4n$ conditions. There are $n - 1$ internal knots. If we want C^2 continuity at the knots, we have $3n - 3$ conditions. If, in addition, we want to interpolate the $n + 1$ control points, we have a total of $4n - 2$ conditions. We can pick the other two conditions in a number of ways, such as by fixing the slope at the ends of the curve. However, this particular spline is global; we must solve a set of $4n$ equations in $4n$ unknowns, and each coefficient will depend on all the control points. Thus, although such a spline provides a smooth curve that interpolates the control points, it is not well suited to computer graphics and CAD.

9.8.1 Recursively Defined B-splines

The approach taken in B-splines is to define the spline in terms of a set of basis or blending functions, each of which is nonzero over only the regions spanned by a few knots. Thus, we write the function $\mathbf{p}(u)$ as an expansion

$$\mathbf{p}(u) = \sum_{i=0}^{m} B_{id}(u) \mathbf{p}_i,$$

where each function $B_{id}(u)$ is a polynomial of degree d, except at the knots, and zero outside the interval $(u_{i_{\min}}, u_{i_{\max}})$. The name *B-splines* comes from the term *basis splines*, in recognition that the set of functions $\{B_{id}(u)\}$ forms a basis for the given knot sequence and degree. Although there are numerous ways to

---

[10] Most researchers call this sequence the *knot vector*, but this terminology violates our decision to use the term *vector* for only directed line segments.

define basis splines, of particular importance is the set of splines defined by the **Cox–deBoor** recursion[11]

$$B_{k0} = \begin{cases} 1, & u_k \leq u \leq u_{k+1}; \\ 0, & \text{otherwise.} \end{cases}$$

$$B_{kd} = \frac{u - u_k}{u_{k+d-1} - u_k} B_{k,d-1}(u) + \frac{u_{k+d} - u}{u_{k+d} - u_{k+1}} B_{k+1, d-1}(u).$$

Each of the first set of functions, B_{k0}, is constant over one interval and zero everywhere else; each of the second, B_{k1}, is linear over each of two intervals, and zero elsewhere; each of the third, B_{k2}, is quadratic over each of three intervals; and so on (Figure 9.27). In general, B_{kd} is nonzero over the $d + 1$ intervals between u_k and u_{k+d+1}, and is a polynomial of degree d in each of these intervals. At the knots, there is C^{d-1} continuity. The convex-hull property holds because

$$\sum_{i=0}^{m} B_{id}(u) = 1, \qquad \text{and} \qquad 0 \leq B_{id}(u) \leq 1.$$

However, because each B_{id} is nonzero in only $d + 1$ intervals, each control point can affect only $d + 1$ intervals, and each point on the resulting curve is within the convex hull defined by these $d + 1$ control points.

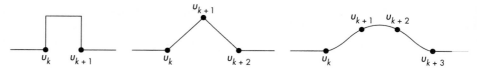

Figure 9.27 First three basis functions.

A set of spline basis functions is defined by the desired degree and the knot array. Note that we need what appears to be $d - 1$ "extra" knot values to define our spline, because the recursion requires u_0 through u_{n+d} to define splines from u_0 to u_{n+1}. These additional values are determined by conditions at the beginning and end of the whole spline.

Note that we have made no statement about the knot values, other than that $u_k \leq u_{k+1}$. If we define any $0/0$ term that arises in evaluating the recursion as equal to 1, then we can have repeated, or multiple, knots. If the knots are equally spaced, we have a **uniform spline**. However, we can achieve more flexibility by allowing not only nonuniform knot spacing, but also repeated ($u_k = u_{k+1}$) knots. We shall examine a few of the possibilities.

---

[11] This formula is also known as the *deCasteljau recursion*.

9.8.2 Uniform Splines

Consider the uniform knot sequence $\{0, 1, 2, \ldots, n\}$. The cubic B-spline that we discussed in Section 9.7 could be derived from the Cox–deBoor formula with equally spaced knots. Using the numbering we used there (which is shifted from the Cox–deBoor indexing), between knots k and $k + 1$ we use the control points $\mathbf{p}_{k-1}$, $\mathbf{p}_k$, $\mathbf{p}_{k+1}$, and $\mathbf{p}_{k+2}$. Thus, we have a curve defined for only the interval $u = 1$ to $u = n - 1$. For the data shown in Figure 9.28, we define a curve that does not span the knots. In certain situations, such as in Figure 9.29, we can use the periodic nature of the control-point data to define the spline over the entire knot sequence. These **uniform periodic B-splines** have the property that each spline basis function is a shifted version of a single function.

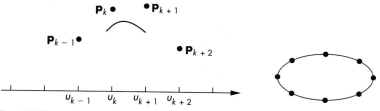

Figure 9.28 Uniform B-spline.

Figure 9.29 Periodic uniform B-spline.

9.8.3 Nonuniform B-Splines

Repeated knots have the effect of pulling the spline closer to the control point associated with the knot. If a knot has multiplicity $d + 1$, the B-spline of degree d must interpolate the point. Hence, one solution to the problem of the spline not having sufficient data to span the desired interval is to repeat knots at the ends, forcing interpolation at the endpoints, and using uniform knots everywhere else. Such splines are called **open splines**.

The knot sequence $\{0, 0, 0, 0, 1, 2, \ldots, n - 1, n, n, n, n\}$ is often used for cubic B-splines. The sequence $\{0, 0, 0, 0, 1, 1, 1, 1\}$ is of particular interest, because, in this case, the cubic B-spline becomes the cubic Bezier curve. In the general case, we can repeat internal knots, and can have any desired spacing of knots.

9.8.4 NURBS

In our development of B-splines, we have assumed that $\mathbf{p}(u)$ is the array $[\, x(u) \quad y(u) \quad z(u) \,]^T$. However, in two dimensions, we could have replaced it with simply $[\, x(u) \quad y(u) \,]^T$, and all our equations would be unchanged. Indeed, the equations remain unchanged if we go to four-dimensional B-splines. Consider a control point in three dimensions,

$$\mathbf{p}_i = [\, x_i \quad y_i \quad z_i \,],$$

and a weighted homogeneous-coordinate representation of this point:

$$\mathbf{q}_i = w_i \begin{bmatrix} x_i \\ y_i \\ z_i \\ 1 \end{bmatrix}.$$

The idea is to use the weights w_i to increase or decrease the importance of a particular control point. We can use these weighted points to form a four-dimensional B-spline. The first three components of the resulting spline are simply the B-spline representation of the weighted points,

$$\mathbf{q}(u) = \begin{bmatrix} x(u) \\ y(u) \\ z(u) \end{bmatrix} = \sum_{i=0}^{n} B_{i,d}(u) w_i \mathbf{p}_i,$$

whereas the w component is the scalar B-spline polynomial derived from the set of weights

$$w(u) = \sum_{i=0}^{n} B_{i,d}(u) w_i.$$

In homogenous coordinates, this representation has a w component that may not be equal to 1; thus, we must do a perspective division to derive the three-dimensional points:

$$\mathbf{p}(u) = \frac{1}{w(u)} \mathbf{q}(u) = \frac{\sum_{i=0}^{n} B_{i,d}(u) w_i \mathbf{p}_i}{\sum_{i=0}^{n} B_{i,d}(u) w_i}.$$

Each component of $\mathbf{p}(u)$ is now a rational function in u, and, because we have not restricted the knots in any way, we have derived a **nonuniform rational B-spline** curve or **NURBS** curve.

NURBS curves retain all the properties of our three-dimensional B-splines, such as the convex-hull and continuity properties. They have two other properties that make them of particular interest in computer graphics and CAD.

If we apply an affine transformation to a B-spline curve or surface, we get the same function as the B-spline derived from the transformed control points. Because perspective transformations are not affine, most splines will not be handled correctly in perspective viewing. However, the perspective division embedded in the construction of NURBS curves ensures that NURBS curves are handled correctly in perspective views.

Quadric surfaces are usually defined as algebraic implicit forms. If we are using nonrational splines, we can only approximate these surfaces. However, quadrics can be shown to be a special case of quadratic NURBS curve; thus, we can use a single modeling method, NURBS curves, for the most widely used curves and surfaces; see Exercises 9.14 and 9.15.

9.9 Rendering of Curves and Surfaces

Once we have defined a scene with curves and surfaces, we must find a way to render it. There are several approaches. In one, we compute points on the object that are the intersection of rays from the center of projection through pixels with the object. However, except for quadrics (Section 9.11), the intersection calculation requires the solution of nonlinear equations of too high a degree to be practical for real-time computation. A second approach involves evaluating the curve or surface at enough points that we can approximate the curve or surface with our standard flat objects. We shall focus on this approach for parametric polynomial curves and surfaces.

9.9.1 Polynomial Evaluation Methods

Suppose that we have a representation over our standard interval

$$\mathbf{p}(u) = \sum_{i=0}^{n} \mathbf{c}_i u^i, \quad 0 \le u \le 1.$$

We can evaluate $\mathbf{p}(u)$ at some set of values $\{u_k\}$, and can use a polyline (or GL_LINE_STRIP) to approximate the curve. Rather than evaluate each term u^k independently, we can group the terms as

$$\mathbf{p}(u) = \mathbf{c}_0 + u(\mathbf{c}_1 + u(\mathbf{c}_2 + u(\ldots + \mathbf{c}_n u))).$$

This grouping shows that we need only n multiplications to evaluate the $p(u_k)$; this algorithm is known as **Horner's method**. For our typical cubic $\mathbf{p}(u)$, the grouping becomes

$$\mathbf{p}(u) = \mathbf{c}_0 + u(\mathbf{c}_1 + u(\mathbf{c}_2 + u\mathbf{c}_3)).$$

If the points $\{u_i\}$ are uniformly spaced, we can use the method of **forward differences** to evaluate $\mathbf{p}(u_k)$ using $O(n)$ additions and no multiplications. The forward differences are defined recursively by the formulas

$$\Delta^{(0)}\mathbf{p}(u_k) = p(u_k),$$
$$\Delta^{(1)}\mathbf{p}(u_k) = \mathbf{p}(u_{k+1}) - \mathbf{p}(u_k),$$
$$\Delta^{(m+1)}\mathbf{p}(u_k) = \Delta^{(m)}\mathbf{p}(u_{k+1}) - \Delta^{(m)}\mathbf{p}(u_k).$$

If $u_{k+1} - u_k = h$ is constant, then we can show that, if $\mathbf{p}(u)$ is a polynomial of degree n, $\Delta^{(n)}\mathbf{p}(u_k)$ is constant for all k. This result suggests the strategy illustrated in Figure 9.30 for the scalar cubic polynomial

$$p(u) = 1 + 3u + 2u^2 + u^3.$$

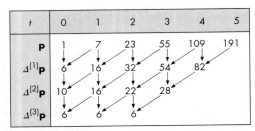

t	0	1	2	3	4	5
p	1	7	23	55	109	191
$\Delta^{(1)}$p	6	16	32	54	82	
$\Delta^{(2)}$p	10	16	22	28		
$\Delta^{(3)}$p	6	6	6			

Figure 9.30 Construction of a forward-difference table.

t	0	1	2	3	4	5
p	1	7	23	55	109	191
$\Delta^{(1)}$p	6	16	32	54	82	
$\Delta^{(2)}$p	10	16	22	28		
$\Delta^{(3)}$p	6	6	6			

Figure 9.31 Use of a forward-difference table.

We need the first $n + 1$ values of $p(u_k)$ to find $\Delta^{(n)}p(u_0)$. But, once we have $\Delta^{(n)}p(u_0)$, we can copy this value across the table and work upward, as shown in Figure 9.31, to compute successive values of $p(u_k)$, using the rearranged recurrence

$$\Delta^{(m-1)}(p_{k+1}) = \Delta^{(m)}p(u_k) + \Delta^{(m-1)}p(u_k).$$

This method is efficient, but is not without its faults: It applies to only a uniform grid, and it is prone to accumulation of numerical errors.

9.9.2 Recursive Subdivision of Bezier Polynomials

The most widely used rendering method is based on recursive subdivision of the Bezier curve. The method is based on the use of the convex hull, and never requires explicit evaluation of the polynomial. Suppose that we have a cubic Bezier polynomial, although the method applies to higher-degree Bezier curves. We know that the curve must lie within the convex hull of the control points. We can break the curve into two separate polynomials, $l(u)$ and $r(u)$, each valid over one-half of the original interval. Because the original polynomial is a cubic, each of these polynomials also is a cubic. Note that, because each is to be used over one-half of the original interval, we must rescale the parameter u for l and r, so that, as u varies over the range $(0, 1)$, $l(u)$ traces the left half of $p(u)$, and $r(u)$ traces the right half of $\mathbf{p}$. Each of our new polynomials has four control points that both define the polynomial and form its convex hull. We shall denote these two sets of points by $\{l_0, l_1, l_2, l_3\}$ and $\{r_0, r_1, r_2, r_3\}$; the original control points for $\mathbf{p}(u)$ are $\{p_0, p_1, p_2, p_3\}$. These points and the two convex hulls are shown in Figure 9.32. Note that the convex hulls for l and r must lie inside the convex hull for p, a fact known as the **variation-diminishing property** of the Bezier curve.

Consider the left polynomial. We can test the convex hull for flatness by measuring the deviation of l_1 and l_2 from the line segment connecting l_0 and l_3. If they are close, we can draw the line segment instead of the curve. If they are not close, we can divide l into two halves and test the two new convex hulls for flatness. Thus, we have a recursion that never requires us to evaluate points on a polynomial, but we have yet to discuss how to find $\{l_0, l_1, l_2, l_3\}$

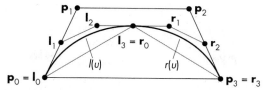

Figure 9.32 Convex hulls and control points.

and $\{r_0, r_1, r_2, r_3\}$. We shall find the hull for $l(u)$; the calculation for $r(u)$ is symmetric. We can start with

$$\mathbf{p}(u) = \mathbf{u}^T \mathbf{M}_B \begin{bmatrix} \mathbf{p}_0 \\ \mathbf{p}_1 \\ \mathbf{p}_2 \\ \mathbf{p}_3 \end{bmatrix},$$

where

$$\mathbf{M}_B = \begin{bmatrix} 1 & 0 & 0 & 0 \\ -3 & 3 & 0 & 0 \\ 3 & -6 & 3 & 0 \\ -1 & 3 & -3 & -1 \end{bmatrix}.$$

The polynomial $l(u)$ must interpolate $\mathbf{p}(0)$ and $\mathbf{p}\left(\frac{1}{2}\right)$; hence,

$$l(0) = l_0 = \mathbf{p}_0,$$

$$l(1) = l_3 = \mathbf{p}\left(\tfrac{1}{2}\right) = \tfrac{1}{8}(\mathbf{p}_0 + 3\mathbf{p}_1 + 3\mathbf{p}_2 + \mathbf{p}_3).$$

At $u = 0$, the slope of l must match the slope of $\mathbf{p}$, but, because the parameter for $\mathbf{p}$ covers only the range $\left(0, \frac{1}{2}\right)$ while u varies over $(0, 1)$, implicitly we have made the substitution $\bar{u} = 2u$. Consequently, derivatives for l and $\mathbf{p}$ are related by $d\bar{u} = 2du$, and

$$\tfrac{1}{2}l'(0) = \tfrac{3}{2}(l_1 - l_0) = \mathbf{p}'(0) = 3(\mathbf{p}_1 - \mathbf{p}_0).$$

Likewise, at the midpoint

$$\tfrac{1}{2}l'(1) = \tfrac{3}{2}(l_3 - l_2) = \mathbf{p}'\left(\tfrac{1}{2}\right) = \tfrac{3}{4}(-\mathbf{p}_0 - \mathbf{p}_1 + \mathbf{p}_2 + \mathbf{p}_3).$$

These four equations can be solved algebraically. Alternatively, a useful form of the solution can be obtained geometrically, with the aid of Figure 9.33. Here we construct both the left and right sets of control points concurrently. First, we note by interpolation that

$$l_0 = \mathbf{p}_0$$

$$r_3 = \mathbf{p}_3.$$

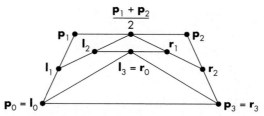

Figure 9.33 Construction of subdivision curves.

The slopes on the left and right give us

$$l_1 = \tfrac{1}{2}(p_0 + p_1),$$

$$r_2 = \tfrac{1}{2}(p_2 + p_3).$$

The interior slopes are given by

$$l_2 = \tfrac{1}{2}\left(l_1 + \tfrac{1}{2}(p_1 + p_2)\right),$$

$$r_1 = \tfrac{1}{2}\left(r_2 + \tfrac{1}{2}(p_1 + p_2)\right),$$

Finally, the shared middle point is

$$l_3 = r_0 = \tfrac{1}{2}(l_2 + r_1).$$

The advantage of this formulation is that we can determine both sets of control points using only shifts and adds. However, one of the advantages of the subdivision approach is that it can be made adaptive, and only one of the sides may require subdivision at some point in the rendering.

9.9.3 Rendering of Other Polynomial Curves by Subdivision

Just as any polynomial is a Bezier polynomial, it is also an interpolating polynomial, a B-spline polynomial, and any other type of polynomial for a properly selected set of control points. The efficiency of the Bezier subdivision algorithm is such that we usually are better off converting another curve form to Bezier form and then using the subdivision algorithm. A conversion algorithm can be obtained directly from our curve formulations. Consider a cubic Bezier curve. We can write it in terms of the Bezier matrix $\mathbf{M}_B$ as

$$\mathbf{p}(u) = \mathbf{u}^T \mathbf{M}_B \mathbf{p},$$

where $\mathbf{p}$ is the **geometry matrix** of control points. The same polynomial can be written as

$$\mathbf{p}(u) = \mathbf{u}^T \mathbf{M} \mathbf{q},$$

Figure 9.34 Cubic Bezier surface.

where $\mathbf{M}$ is the matrix for some other type of polynomial, and $\mathbf{q}$ is the matrix of control points for this type. We assume that both polynomials are defined over the same interval. The polynomials will be identical if we choose

$$\mathbf{q} = \mathbf{M}^{-1}\mathbf{M}_B\mathbf{p}.$$

For the conversion from interpolation to Bezier, the controlling matrix is

$$\mathbf{M}_I^{-B}\mathbf{M}_1 = \begin{bmatrix} 1 & 0 & 0 & 0 \\ -\frac{5}{6} & 3 & -\frac{3}{2} & \frac{1}{3} \\ \frac{1}{3} & -\frac{3}{2} & 3 & -\frac{5}{6} \\ 0 & 0 & 0 & 1 \end{bmatrix}.$$

For the conversion between cubic B-splines and cubic Bezier curves, it is

$$\mathbf{M}_B^{-1}\mathbf{M}_S = \frac{1}{6} \begin{bmatrix} 1 & 4 & 1 & 0 \\ 0 & 4 & 2 & 0 \\ 0 & 2 & 4 & 0 \\ 0 & 1 & 4 & 1 \end{bmatrix}.$$

9.9.4 Subdivision of Bezier Surfaces

We can extend our subdivision algorithm to Bezier surfaces. Consider the cubic surface in Figure 9.34, with the 16 control points shown. Each four points in a row or column determine a Bezier curve that can be subdivided. However, our subdivision algorithm should split the patch into four patches, and we have no control points along the center of the patch. We can proceed in two steps.

First, we apply our curve-subdivision technique to the four curves determined by the 16 control points in the u direction. Thus, for each of $u = 0, \frac{1}{3}, \frac{2}{3}, 1$, we create two groups of four control points, with the middle point shared by each group. There are then seven different points along each orginal curve; these points are indicated in Figure 9.35 by circles. We see there are three types of points: original control points that are kept after the subdivision (gray), original control points that are discarded after subdivision (white), and new points created by the subdivision. We now subdivide in the v direction using these points. Consider the rows of constant v, where v is one of $0, \frac{1}{3}, \frac{2}{3}, 1$. There are seven groups of four points. Each group defines a Bezier curve for a constant v. We can subdivide in the v direction, each time creating two groups

Figure 9.35 First subdivision of surface.

Figure 9.36 Points after second subdivision.

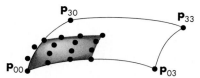

Figure 9.37 Subdivided quadrant.

of four points, again with the middle point shared. These points are indicated in Figure 9.36. If we divide these points in four groups of 16, with points on the edges shared (Figure 9.37), each quadrant contains 16 points that are the control points for a subdivided Bezier surface.

Compared to the calculation for curves, the test for whether the new convex hull is flat enough to stop a subdivision process is more difficult. Many renderers use a fixed number of subdivisions, often letting the user pick the number. If a high-quality rendering is desired, we can let the subdivision continue until the projected size of the convex hull is less than the size of one pixel.

9.10   The Utah Teapot

We conclude our discussion of parametric surfaces with an example of recursive subdivision of a set of cubic Bezier patches. The object that we show has become known as the **Utah teapot**. The data for the teapot were created at the University of Utah by M. Newell for testing various rendering algorithms. These data have been used in the graphics community for over 20 years. The teapot data consist of the control points for 32 bicubic Bezier patches. The data are given in terms of 306 vertices (numbered from 1 to 306). The first

12 patches define the body of the teapot; the next four define the handle; the next four define the spout; the following eight define the lid; and the final four define the bottom. These data are widely available.

For purposes of illustration let us assume that we want to subdivide each patch n times and, after these subdivisions, we will render the final vertices using either line segments or polygons passing through the four corners of each patch. Thus, our final drawing can be done with the function (for line segments)

```
void draw_patch(point p[4][4])
{
    glBegin(GL_QUADS);
    glVertex3fv(p[0][0]);
    glVertex3fv(p[3][0]);
    glVertex3fv(p[3][3]);
    glVertex3fv(p[0][3]);
    glEnd();
}
```

We build our patch subdivider from the curve subdivider for a cubic curve c, using our point type

```
void divide_curve(point c[4], point r[4], point l[4])
{
int i;
point t;
for(i=0;i<3;i++)
    {
    l[0][i]=c[0][i];
    r[3][i]=c[3][i];
    l[1][i]=(c[1][i]+c[0][i])/2;
    r[2][i]=(c[2][i]+c[3][i])/2;
    t[i]=(l[1][i]+r[2][i])/2;
    l[2][i]=(t[i]+l[1][i])/2;
    r[1][i]=(t[i]+r[2][i])/2;
    l[3][i]=r[0][i]=(l[2][i]+r[1][i])/2;
    }
}
```

The patch subdivider is easier to write—but is slightly less efficient—if we assume that we have a matrix-transpose function transpose. This code is then

```
void divide_patch(point p[4][4], int n)
{
point q[4][4], r[4][4], s[4][4], t[4][4];
point a[4][4], b[4][4];
```

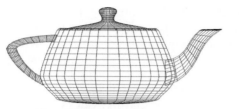

Figure 9.38 Rendered teapots.

```
int i,j, k;

if(n==0) draw_patch(p);
else
    {
    for(k=0; k<4; k++) divide_curve(p[k], a[k], b[k]);
    transpose(a);
    transpose(b);
    for(k=0; k<4; k++)
        {
        divide_curve(a[k], q[k], r[k]);
        divide_curve(b[k], s[k], t[k]);
        }
    divide_patch(q, n-1);
    divide_patch(r, n-1);
    divide_patch(s, n-1);
    divide_patch(t, n-1);
    }
}
```

A complete teapot-rendering program using shaded polygons is given in Appendix A. That program contains the teapot data.

The teapot is available as an object in both the GLUT and aux libraries. Here, we are interested in using it to demonstrate our recursive-subdivision algorithm. Figure 9.38 shows the teapot as a wire frame at three levels of subdivision, and a simple rendering with constant shading. Note that the various patches have different curvatures and sizes; thus, carrying out all subdivisions to the same depth can create many unnecessary small polygons.

The OpenGL Bezier curve functions that we shall introduce in Section 9.12 will allow us to render the patches through the API, using only a few function calls. These functions are usually implemented via recursive subdivision, but are more efficient than an implementation in the user program would be.

9.11 Algebraic Surfaces

Although quadrics can be generated as a special case of NURBS curves, this class of algebraic objects is of such importance that it merits independent discussion. Quadrics are the most important case of the algebraic surfaces that we introduced in Section 9.1.

9.11.1 Quadrics

Quadric surfaces are described by implicit algebraic equations in which each term is a polynomial of the form $x^i y^j z^k$, with $i + j + k \leq 2$. Any quadric can be written in the form

$$q(x, y, z) = a_{11}x^2 + 2a_{12}xy + a_{22}y^2 + a_{33}z^2 + 2a_{23}yz + 2a_{13}xz$$
$$+b_1 x + b_2 y + b_3 z + c = 0.$$

This class of surfaces includes ellipsoids, parabaloids, and hyperboloids. We can write the general equation in matrix form in terms of the three-dimensional column matrix $\mathbf{p} = [\begin{array}{ccc} x & y & z \end{array}]^T$ as the **quadratic form**

$$\mathbf{p}^T \mathbf{A} \mathbf{p} + \mathbf{b}^T \mathbf{p} + c = 0,$$

where

$$\mathbf{A} = \begin{bmatrix} a_{11} & a_{12} & a_{13} \\ a_{12} & a_{22} & a_{23} \\ a_{13} & a_{23} & a_{33} \end{bmatrix}, \qquad \mathbf{b} = \begin{bmatrix} b_1 \\ b_2 \\ b_3 \end{bmatrix}.$$

The 10 independent coefficients in $\mathbf{A}$, $\mathbf{b}$, and c determine a given quadric. However, for purpose of classification, we can apply a sequence of rotations and translations that reduces a quadric to a standard form without changing the type of surface. In three dimensions, we can write such a transformation as

$$\mathbf{p}' = \mathbf{M} \mathbf{p} + \mathbf{d}.$$

The matrix $\mathbf{M}$ is a rotation matrix that transforms $\mathbf{A}$ to a diagonal matrix $\mathbf{D} = \mathbf{M}^T \mathbf{A} \mathbf{M}$. If, for example, the equation is that of an ellipsoid, it can be put in the form

$$a'_{11}x'^2 + a'_{22}y'^2 + a_{33}z'^2 - c' = 0,$$

where all the coefficients are positive. Note that, because we can convert to a standard form by an affine transformation, quadrics are preserved by affine transformations, and thus fit well with our other primitives.

9.11.2 Rendering of Surfaces by Ray Casting

Quadrics are easy to render because we can find the intersection of a quadric with a ray by solving a scalar quadratic equation. We represent the ray from $\mathbf{p}_0$ in the direction $\mathbf{d}$ parametrically as

$$\mathbf{p} = \mathbf{p}_0 + \alpha\mathbf{d}.$$

Substituting into the equation for the quadric, we obtain the scalar equation for α:

$$\alpha^2\mathbf{d}^T\mathbf{A}\mathbf{d} + \alpha\mathbf{d}^T(\mathbf{b} + 2\mathbf{A}\mathbf{p}_0) + \mathbf{p}_0^T\mathbf{A}\mathbf{p}_0 + \mathbf{b}^T\mathbf{d} + c = 0.$$

As we may for any quadratic equation, we may find zero, one, or two real solutions. We can use this result to render a quadric into the frame buffer, or as part of a ray-tracing calculation. In addition, we can apply our standard shading model at every point on a quadric as we can compute the normal by taking the derivatives

$$\mathbf{n} = \begin{bmatrix} \dfrac{\partial q}{\partial x} \\[2mm] \dfrac{\partial q}{\partial y} \\[2mm] \dfrac{\partial q}{\partial z} \end{bmatrix} = 2\mathbf{A}\mathbf{p} - \mathbf{b}.$$

This method of rendering can be extended to any algebraic surface. Suppose that we have an algebraic surface

$$q(\mathbf{p}) = q(x, y, z) = 0.$$

As part of the rendering pipeline, we cast a ray from the center of projection through each pixel. Each of these rays can be written in the parametric form

$$\mathbf{p}(\alpha) = \mathbf{p}_0 + \alpha\mathbf{d}.$$

Substituting this expression into q yields an implicit polynomial equation in α:

$$q(\mathbf{p}(\alpha)) = 0.$$

We can find the points of intersection by numerical methods, or, for quadrics, by the quadratic formula. If we have terms up to $x^iy^jz^k$, we can have $i + j + k$ points of intersection, and the surface may require considerable time to render.

9.12   Curves and Surfaces in OpenGL

OpenGL supports Bezier curves and surfaces through mechanisms called **evaluators** that are used to compute values for the Bernstein polynomials of any order. Evaluators do not require uniform spacing of control points, and, because we can use Bezier curves and surfaces to generate other types of polynomial curves and surfaces by generating new control points, this mechanism is flexible. We can use evaluators to generate one-, two-, three-, and four-dimensional curves and surfaces. We might use one-dimensional curves to define color maps or paths in time for animations. The GLU library uses this mechanism in four dimensions to provide NURBS curves. In addition to defining curves and surfaces, the OpenGL evaluator functions can also provide colors, normals, and the texture coordinates that we shall use in Chapter 10.

9.12.1 Bezier Curves

For curves, we define a one-dimensional evaluator through the function

```
glMap1f(type, u_min, u_max, stride, order, point_array);
```

The `type` parameter specifies the type of objects we want to evaluate using Bezier polynomials. Options include three- and four-dimensional points, RGBA colors, normals, indexed colors, and one- through four-dimensional texture coordinates. The control-point data are in the array pointed to by `point_array`. The values u_min and u_max define the range of the parameter. The value of `stride` is the number of values of the parameter between curve segments. For example, in our cubic B-spline, we stride three points for each curve segment. The `order` parameter is 1 greater than the degree of the polynomial. Thus, for our cubic B-spline defined over $(0,1)$, we set up an evaluator for a three-dimensional curve by

```
point data[]={...
glMap1f(GL_MAP_VERTEX_3, 0.0, 1.0, 3, 4, data);
```

We can define multiple evaluators that are active at the same time, and can use them to evaluate, for example, curves and normals at the same time. Each evaluator must be enabled through

```
glEnable(type);
```

Once an evaluator has been set up, we use the function

```
glEvalCoord1f(u);
```

whenever we need a value from the active evaluators. Thus, `glEvalCoord1f` can replace any combination of `glVertex`, `glColor`, and `glNormal`, depending on which evaluators have been enabled. Suppose that we have defined evaluators for the cubic Bezier curve over $(0,10)$ and the array of control points. We can get 100 equally spaced points on the curve by the call

```
glBegin(GL_LINE_STRIP)
    for(i=0; i<100; i++) glEvalCoord1f( (float) i/100.0);
glEnd();
```

OpenGL provides an alternative if the values of u are equally spaced. In this case, we can use the functions

```
glMapGrid1f(100,0.0, 10.0);
glEvalMesh1(GL_LINE, 0, 100);
```

The first function sets up the uniform grid with 100 intervals; the second function generates the desired curve.

9.12.2 Bezier Surfaces

Bezier surfaces are generated in a manner similar to curves. We can use the functions `glMap2` and `glEvalCoord2`, but now there are two parameters, u and v, to specify. For example, a bicubic Bezier surface over the region $(0,1) \times (0,1)$ can be set up with the function calls

```
glMap2f(GL_MAP_VERTEX_3, 0.0, 1.0, 3, 4, 0.0, 1.0, 12, 4, data);
```

Note that we have to specify the order and stride for both parameters, allowing additional flexibility in defining the surface. The corresponding evaluator calls depend on whether we want to draw a mesh or to create a set of polygons for shading. For the mesh, we have to make sets of calls to the evaluator of the form

```
for(j=0; j<100; j++)
{
    glBegin(GL_LINE_STRIP);
        for(i=0; i<100; i++)
            glEvalCoord2f( (float) i/100.0, (float) j/100.0);
    glEnd();
    glBegin(GL_LINE_STRIP);
        for(i=0; i<100; i++)
            glEvalCoord2f( (float) j/100.0, (float) i/100.0);
    glEnd();
}
```

For quadrilaterals, the calls look like

```
for(j=0; j<99; j++)
{
    glBegin(GL_QUAD_STRIP);
    for(i=0; i<100; i++)
      glEvalCoord2f( (float) i/100.0, (float) j/100.0);
    for(i=0; i<100; i++)
      glEvalCoord2f( (float) (i+1)/100.0, (float) j/100.0);
    glEnd();
}
```

For uniform meshes, we can use `glMapGrid2` and `glEvalMesh2`.

9.12.3 NURBS Functions

We can use evaluators to generate nonuniform spacing of points and to generate four-dimensional curves and surfaces. If we recall our earlier observation that we can change any of the polynomial forms to a Bezier form by generating a proper set of control points, then we see that we have all the information necessary to define NURBS curves and surfaces. Rather than have the application programmer go through all these steps, the OpenGL Utility library, GLU, provides a set of NURBS functions. These functions also allow the user to specify various additional parameters that enable finer control of the rendering. There are five NURBS functions for surfaces:

```
gluNewNurbsRenderer
gluNurbsProperty
gluBeginNurbsSurface
gluNurbsSurface
gluEndNurbsSurface
```

The first two functions set up a new NURBS object and define how we would like it rendered. The final three are used to generate the surface. For NURBS curves, the final three are replaced by the functions `gluBeginNurbsCurve`, `gluNurbsCurve`, and `gluEndNurbsCurve`.

The GLU library provides an additional useful facility called trimming curves. **Trimming curves** are closed curves that we can use to render a surface with the areas defined by curves removed. Figure 9.39 illustrates a trimmed surface. The user can define a trimming curve either as a NURBS curve using `gluNurbsCurve`, or as a piecewise linear curve, through the `gluPwlCurve` function. The trimming curves are defined after the call to `glNurbsSurface`, and their vertices are specified between calls to `glBeginTrim` and `glEndTrim`.

9.12.4 Quadrics

OpenGL supports some quadric objects—disks, cylinders, and spheres—through GLU. These objects can be treated like other graphical objects: scaled, translated, and rotated, shaded, and texture mapped. The quadric routines allow for automatic generation of normals and texture coordinates (Chapter 10). We implement these objects, however, by approximating them with polygons,

Figure 9.39 Trimmed surface.

although we can specify how many polygons are to be used in the approximation.

Suppose that we want to use a cylinder for the base of the robot in Chapter 8 (see Appendix A). The first step is to define a new quadric object by

```
GLUquadricObj  *p;

p=gluNewQuadric();
```

We can then define how we would like the quadric to be rendered. For example, if we want a wire frame, using the present drawing color, we use the function call

```
gluQuadricDrawStyle(p, GLU_LINE);
```

We can now create the cylinder, centered at the origin, with its length along the *y* axis, by using

```
gluCylinder(p, BASE_RADIUS, BASE_RADIUS, BASE_HEIGHT, 5, 5);
```

The first three parameters specify the top and bottom radii, and the height. The final two parameters specify by how many slices we divide each circle of constant *y*, and into how many sections we slice the cylinder in the *y* direction.

9.13   Summary

Once again, we have only scratched the surface of a deep and important topic. Also once again, our focus has been on what we can do on a graphics system using a standard API such as OpenGL. From this perspective, there are huge advantages to using parametric Bezier curves and surfaces. The parametric form is robust and is easy to use interactively, because the required data are points that can be entered and manipulated interactively. The subdivision algorithm for Bezier curves and surfaces gives us the ability to render the resulting objects to any desired degree of accuracy.

Although Bezier surfaces are easy to render, we have seen that splines can provide additional smoothness and contol. The texts in the suggested readings discuss many variants of splines that are used in the CAD community.

Quadric surfaces are used extensively with ray tracers, because solving for the points of intersection between a ray with a quadric requires the solution of only a scalar quadratic equation. Deciding whether the point of intersection between a ray and the plane determined by a flat polygon is inside the polygon can be more difficult than solving the intersection problem for quadric surfaces. Hence, many ray tracers allow only infinite planes, quadrics, and, perhaps, convex polygons.

9.14   References

The book by Farin [Far88] provides an excellent introduction to curves and surfaces. It also has an interesting preface by Bezier discussing the almost simultaneous discovery by him and deCasteljau, of the surfaces that bear his name. Unfortunately, deCasteljau's work was described in unpublished technical reports, and so deCasteljau did not, until recently, receive the credit that he deserved for his work. Books such as Rogers [Rog90], Foley [Fol90], Bartels [Bar87], and Watt [Wat93] discuss a number of other forms of splines.

The book by Faux [Fau80] discusses the coordinate-free approach to curves and surfaces.

Although the book edited by Glassner [Gla89] is interested primarily in ray tracing, the section by Haines has considerable material on working with quadrics and other algebraic surfaces.

Exercises

9.1   Consider an algebraic surface $f(x, y, z) = 0$, where each term in f can have terms in x, y, and z of power up to m. How many terms can there be in f?

9.2   Consider the explicit equations $y = f(x)$ and $z = g(x)$. What types of curves do they describe?

9.3   Suppose that you have a polynomial $p(u) = \sum_{k=0}^{n} c_k u^k$. Find a polynomial $q(v) = \sum_{k=0}^{n} d_k v^k$ such that, for each point of p in the interval (a, b), there is a point v in the range $0 \leq v \leq 1$, such that $p(u) = q(v)$.

9.4   Show that, as long as the four control points for the cubic interpolating curve are defined at unique values of the parameter u, the interpolating geometry matrix always exists.

9.5   Show that, in the interval $(0,1)$, the Bernstein polynomials must be less than 1.

9.6   Verify the C^2 continuity of the cubic spline.

9.7   In Section 9.9, we showed that we can write a cubic polynomial as a cubic Bezier polynomial by choosing a proper set of control points, or equivalently, the proper convex hull. Using this fact, show how to render an interpolating curve using the Bezier renderer provided by OpenGL.

9.8   Find a homogeneous-coordinate representation for quadrics.

9.9   Suppose that we render Bezier patches by adaptive subdivision, so that each patch can be subdivided a different number of times. Do we maintain continuity along the edges of the patches? Explain your answer.

9.10 Write an OpenGL program that will take as input a set of control points, and that will produce the interpolating, B-spline, and Bezier curves for these data.

9.11 Suppose that you use a set of spline curves to describe a path in time that an object will take as part of an animation. How might you notice the difference between G^1 and C^1 continuity in this situation?

9.12 Extend the painting program from Chapter 3 to include Bezier curves. The user should be able to manipulate the control points interactively.

9.13 Derive a simple test for the flatness of a Bezier surface patch.

9.14 Derive the open rational quadratic B-spline with the knots $\{0,0,0,0, 1,1,1,1\}$ and the weights $w_0 = w_2 = 1$ and $w_1 = w$.

9.15 Using the result of Exercise 9.14, show that, if $w = \frac{r}{1-r}$, for $0 \le r \le 1$, you get all the conic sections. *Hint*: Consider $r < \frac{1}{2}$ and $r > \frac{1}{2}$.

9.16 Find the zeros of the Hermite blending functions. Why do these zeros imply that the Hermite curve is smooth in the interval $(0,1)$?

9.17 What is the relationship between the control-point data for a Hermite patch and the derivatives at the corners of the patch?

10 Discrete Techniques

For many years, computer graphics dealt exclusively with geometric objects, such as lines, polygons, and polyhedra. Raster systems have been in existence for over 20 years, but, until recently, application programmers have had only indirect access to the frame buffer. Although lines and polygons were rasterized into the frame buffer, application programmers had no functions in the API that would allow them to read or write individual pixels. Many of the most exciting methods that have evolved over the past decade rely on interactions either in the frame buffer or in some other discrete two-dimensional buffer. Texture mapping, antialiasing, compositing, and alpha blending are only a few of the techniques that become possible when the API allows us to work with discrete buffers. This chapter introduces these techniques, focusing on those that are supported by OpenGL and by similar APIs.

We shall start by considering mapping methods. These techniques are applied during the rendering process, and enable us to give the illusion of a surface of great complexity, although the surface might be a single polygon. All these techniques use arrays of pixels to define how the rendering process that we studied in Chapter 6 is modified to create these illusions. Next, we shall examine how we can modify the individual pixels in a buffer, and can define multiple ways of writing into a buffer. Then, we shall look at what buffers are supported by the OpenGL API, how an application program can modify these buffers, and how these buffers can be used for new applications. In particular, we shall examine techniques for combining or compositing images. Here we shall use the fourth "color" in RGBA mode, and shall see that we can use this channel to blend images and to create effects such as transparency. We shall conclude with a discussion of the aliasing problems that arise whenever we work with discrete elements.

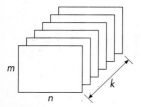

Figure 10.1 Buffer.

10.1   Buffers and Mappings

We have already used two of the standard buffers: the frame buffer and the depth buffer. Later, we shall introduce others. What all buffers have in common is that they are inherently discrete. They have limited resolution, both spatially and in depth. We can define a (two-dimensional)[1] **buffer** as a block of memory with a spatial resolution of $n \times m$ k bit elements (Figure 10.1). For the frame buffer, n and m match the resolution of the screen, and k is determined by how many colors the system can display. For the depth buffer, n and m also are determined by the resolution of the screen, but k is determined by the depth resolution that the system can support. We shall use the term **bitplane** to refer to any of the k $n \times m$ planes in a buffer, and **pixel** to refer to all k of the elements at a particular spatial location. With this definition, a pixel can be a byte, an integer, or even a floating-point number, depending on which buffer is used and how we choose to store the information.

One of the most powerful uses of buffers is for surface rendering. The process of modeling an object by a set of geometric primitives and then rendering these primitives has its limitations. Consider, for example, the task of creating a virtual orange by computer. Our first attempt might be to start with a sphere. From our discussion in Chapter 6, we know that we can build an approximate sphere out of triangles, and can render these triangles using material properties that match those of a real orange. Unfortunately, such a rendering would be far too regular to look much like an orange. We could instead follow the path that we used in Chapter 9: Try to model the orange with some sort of parametric surface, and to render the surface by subdivision. This procedure would give us more control over the shape of our virtual orange, but the image that we would produce still would not look right. Although it might have the correct overall properties, such as shape and color, it would lack the fine surface detail of the real orange. Some of the procedural modeling methods of Chapter 8 might be able to give us more detail, and might incorporate some of the randomness we see on the surface of a real orange, but they would do so at the cost of generating a model with more polygons than we would like to render.

An alternative is not to attempt to build increasingly more complex models, but rather to build a simple model and to add detail as part of the rendering process. As the implementation renders a surface, be it a polygon or a curved surface, it breaks the surface up into small pieces called **fragments**, each of which, when projected, is at most the size of one pixel. Fragments smaller than one pixel can be important because, in high-end systems, many surfaces may contribute to the color of a pixel. As part of the rendering process, we

---

[1] We can also have one-, three-, and four-dimensional buffers.

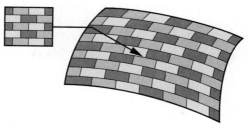

Figure 10.2 Texture mapping.

must assign a shade or color to each fragment. We start by choosing a shading model from the ones we studied in Chapter 6. The mapping algorithms can be thought of as either modifying the shading algorithm based on a two-dimensional array, the map, or as modifying the shading by using the map to alter surface parameters, such as material properties and normals. There are three major approaches:

1. Texture mapping
2. Bump mapping
3. Environmental mapping

Texture mapping uses a pattern (or texture) to determine the color of a fragment. These patterns could be determined by a fixed pattern, such as the regular patterns often used to fill polygons; by a procedural texture-generation method; or through a digitized image. In all cases, we can characterize the image produced by a mapping of a texture to the surface, as shown in Figure 10.2, as part of the rendering of the surface.

Whereas texture maps give detail by painting patterns onto smooth surfaces, **bump maps** distort the shape of the surface to create variations, such as the bumps on a real orange. **Reflection** or **environmental maps** allow us to create images with the appearance of ray-traced images without having to trace reflected rays. In this case, an image of the environment is painted onto the surface as the surface is being rendered.

The three methods have much in common. All three alter the shading of individual pixels and are implemented as part of the shading process. All rely on the map being stored as a one-, two-, or three-dimensional digital image. All are also subject to aliasing errors.

10.2   Texture Mapping

Textures are patterns. They can range from regular patterns, such as stripes and checkerboards, to the complex patterns that characterize natural materials. In the real world, we can distinguish among objects of similar size and shape by their textures. Thus, if we want to create detailed virtual objects, we can extend our present capabilities by placing, or mapping, a texture to the objects we create. We shall consider only two-dimensional textures, although the methods that we shall develop are applicable to one-, three-, and four-dimensional textures.

There are various examples of two-dimensional texture mapping among the color plates. Color Plate 6 was created using an OpenGL texture map and shows how a single texture map can add realism and complexity to an image. Color Plate 23 uses a texture map for the surface of the table; Color Plate 10 uses texture mapping to create a landscape around the house. In Color Plate 18, the artists have used texture maps as their fundamental method of creating objects. These texture maps were then subjected to three-dimensional geometric transformations. Much of the detail in Color Plates 15 and 22, is from texture maps. In these virtual reality and robotic simulations real-time performance is required. When these simulations are executed on workstations with hardware texture mapping, texture mapping allows the detail to be added without degrading the rendering time.

10.2.1 Two-Dimensional Texture Mapping

There is a sequence of steps involved in texture mapping. Our starting point is a two-dimensional texture pattern $T(s,t)$. The independent variables s and t are known as **texture coordinates**. At this point, we can think of T as continuous, although, in reality, it will be stored in texture memory as an $n \times m$ array of texture elements, **texels**.[2] With no loss of generality, we can scale our texture coordinates to vary over the interval $(0,1)$.

A **texture map** associates a unique point of T with each point on a geometric object that is itself mapped to screen coordinates for display. If the object is represented in spatial (geometric) coordinates ((x, y, z) or (x, y, z, w)), we can think in terms of a mathematical function that maps from texture coordinates to geometric coordinates and a projection function that maps from geometric coordinates to screen coordinates. If we define the geometric object using parametric (u, v) surfaces, there is an additional mapping function. For this case, we can think in terms of two concurrent mappings: the first from texture coordinates to geometric coordinates, and the second from parametric coordinates to geometric coordinates, as shown in Figure 10.3. A third mapping takes us to screen coordinates.

Conceptually, the texture-mapping process is simple. A small area of the texture pattern maps to the area of the geometric surface, corresponding to a pixel in the final image. If we assume that the values of T are RGB color values,

---

[2] In four dimensions, a value of T is a point in (s, t, r, q) space.

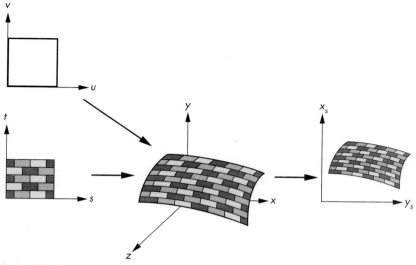

Figure 10.3 Texture maps for a parametric surface.

we use these values either to modify the color of the surface or to assign a color to the surface based on only the texture value. This color assignment is carried out as part of the shading calculation.

On closer examination, we face a number of difficulties. First, we must determine the map from texture coordinates to geometric coordinates. A two-dimensional texture usually is defined over a rectangular region in texture space. The mapping from this rectangle to an arbitrary region in three-dimensional space may be a complex function, or may have undesirable properties. For example, if we wish to map a rectangle to a sphere, we cannot do so without distortion of shapes and distances. Second, due to the nature of the rendering process, which works on a pixel-by-pixel basis, we are more interested in the inverse map from screen coordinates to texture coordinates. It is when we are determining the shade of a pixel that we must determine what point in the texture image to use—a calculation that requires us to go from screen coordinates to texture coordinates. Third, because we calculate the shade for pixels, each of which generates a color for a small rectangle on the display surface, we are interested in mapping not points to points, but rather areas to areas. Here again is a potential aliasing problem that we must treat carefully if we are to avoid artifacts, such as moiré patterns.

Figure 10.4 shows several of the difficulties. Suppose that we are computing a color for the square pixel centered at screen coordinates (x_s, y_s). The center (x_s, y_s) corresponds to a point (x, y, z) in object space, but, if the object is curved, the projection of the corners of the pixel backward into object space yields a curved **preimage** of the pixel. In terms of the texture image $T(s, t)$,

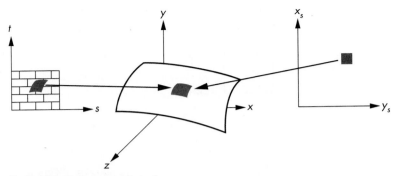

Figure 10.4 Preimages of pixel.

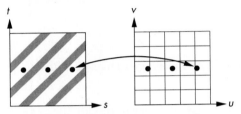

Figure 10.5 Aliasing in texture generation.

projecting the pixel back yields a preimage in texture space that is the area of the texture that should contribute to the shading of the pixel.

Let us put aside for a moment the problem of how we find the inverse map, and let us look at the assignment of shades. One possibility is to use the point that we get by back projection of the pixel center to find a texture value. Although this technique is simple, it is subject to serious aliasing problems, which will be especially visible if the texture is periodic. Figure 10.5 illustrates the aliasing problem. Here, we have a repeated texture and a flat surface. The back projection of the center of each pixel falls inbetween the dark lines, and the texture value is always the lighter color. More generally, not taking into account the finite size of a pixel can lead to moiré patterns in the image. A better strategy, but one more difficult to implement, is to assign a texture value based on averaging of the texture map over the preimage. Note that this method is imperfect too. For the example in Figure 10.5, we would assign an average shade, but we would still not get the striped pattern of the texture. Ultimately, we still have aliasing defects due to the limited resolution of both the frame buffer and the texture map. These problems are most visible when there is a regular texture.

Now we can turn to the mapping problem. For a parametric surface, we can often map a point in the texture map $T(s, t)$ to a point on the surface $\mathbf{p}(u, v)$ by a linear map of the form

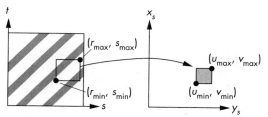

Figure 10.6 Linear texture mapping.

$$u = as + bt + c,$$
$$v = ds + et + f.$$

As long as $ae \neq bd$, this mapping is invertible. Linear mapping makes it easy to map a texture to a group of parametric surface patches. For example, if, as shown in Figure 10.6, the patch determined by the corners (s_{min}, t_{min}) and (s_{max}, t_{max}) corresponds to the surface patch with corners (u_{min}, v_{min}) and (u_{max}, v_{max}), the mapping is

$$u = u_{min} + \frac{s - s_{min}}{s_{max} - s_{min}}(u_{max} - u_{min}),$$

$$v = v_{min} + \frac{t - t_{min}}{t_{max} - t_{min}}(v_{max} - v_{min}).$$

This mapping is easy to apply, but it does not take into account the curvature of the surface. Equal-sized texture patches are stretched to fit over the surface patch.

Another approach to the mapping problem is to use a two-part mapping. The first step maps the texture to a simple three-dimensional intermediate surface, such as a sphere, cylinder, or cube. In the second step, the intermediate surface containing the mapped texture is mapped to the surface being rendered. This two-step mapping process can be applied to surfaces defined in either geometric or parametric coordinates. The following example is essentially the same in either system.

Suppose that our texture coordinates vary over the unit square, and that we use the surface of a cylinder of height h and radius r as our intermediate object, as shown in Figure 10.7. Points on the cylinder are given by the parametric equations

$$x = r\cos(2\pi u),$$
$$y = r\sin(2\pi u),$$
$$z = v/h,$$

as u and v vary over $(0,1)$. Hence, we can use the mapping

$$s = u,$$
$$t = v.$$

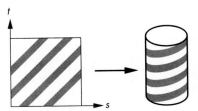

Figure 10.7 Texture mapping with a cylinder.

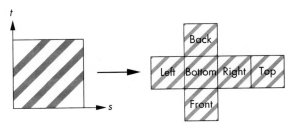

Figure 10.8 Texture mapping with box.

By using only the curved part of the cylinder, and not the top and bottom, we were able to map the texture without distorting its shape. However, if we map to a closed object, such as a sphere, we must introduce shape distortion. This problem is similar to the problem of creating a two-dimensional image of the earth for a map. If you look at the various maps of the earth in an atlas, all distort shapes and distances. Both texturing-mapping techniques and map-design techniques must choose among a variety of representations, based on where we wish to place the distortion. For example, the familiar Mercator projection puts most of the distortion at the poles. If we use a sphere of radius r as the intermediate surface, a possible mapping is

$$x = r\cos(2\pi u),$$
$$y = r\sin(2\pi u)\cos(2\pi v),$$
$$z = r\sin(2\pi u)\sin(2\pi v).$$

We can also use a rectangular box, as shown in Figure 10.8. Here, we map the texture to a box that can be unraveled, like a cardboard packing box. This mapping that is often used with environmental maps (Section 10.3).

The second step is to map the texture values on the intermediate object to the desired surface. Figure 10.9 shows three possible mapping strategies. In Figure 10.9(a), we take the texture value at a point on the intermediate object, go from this point in the direction of the normal until we intersect the object, and then place the texture value at the point of intersection. We could also reverse this method, starting at a point on the surface of the object and going in the direction of the normal at this point until we intersect the intermediate

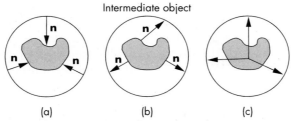

Figure 10.9 Second mapping. (a) Using the normal from the intermediate surface. (b) Using the normal from the object surface. (c) Using the center of the object.

object, where we obtain the texture value, as shown in Figure 10.9(b). A third option, if we know the center of the object, is to draw a line from the center through a point on the object, and to calculate the intersection of this line with the intermediate surface, as shown in Figure 10.9(c). The texture at the point of intersection with the intermediate object is assigned to the corresponding point on the desired object.

10.2.2 Texture Mapping in OpenGL

OpenGL gives the programmer considerable flexibility in how textures are mapped. We shall continue with two-dimensional textures, although we can use one- through four-dimensional texture maps. Here, we have to address issues that involve the discrete nature of the texture patterns. Two-dimensional textures are specified through the function

```
glTexImage2D(GL_TEXTURE_2D, level, components, width, height,
             border, format, type, image);
```

The texture pattern is stored in the `width` × `height` array `image`. The format of this image is described by the next two parameters. The value `components` is the number (1 through 4) of color components (RGBA) that we wish to affect with the map. The parameters `level` and `border` give us fine control over how texture is handled. OpenGL supports texture at multiple resolutions—a technique that can minimize the aliasing defects. We can also add a border of n pixels around the texture, so that we can match edges between multiple texture maps. We shall not discuss these options. Although there are numerous parameters involved in specifying a texture, a simple example is the function call

```
glTexImage2D(GL_TEXTURE_2D, 0, 3, 512, 512, 0,
             GL_RGB, GL_UNSIGNED_BYTE, image);
```

Here we have said that there is a 512 × 512 RGB array `image` whose components are bytes that should be interpreted as ranging from 0 to 255. We can define the elements of this array within the program, or this array might be a scanned array that is read from external memory.

The basic method of dealing with textures in OpenGL is to assign texture coordinates to each vertex, just as we assign colors and normal vectors. Texture coordinates are then mapped to fragments by interpolation. We use various forms of the function `glTexCoord` for this purpose. If we are using floating-point numbers and two-dimensional textures, the function call will be of the form

```
glTexCoord2f(s,t);
```

In general, the texture pattern defined in `glTexImage` corresponds to the unit square in (s, t) space. If we keep s and t in this range, then we have defined the map between the texture and the surface. Note that, like many other OpenGL features, texturing must be enabled explicitly.

OpenGL has a number of parameters that we can adjust to control the mapping in more detail. We can set parameters that define how we handle values of s and t outside the range $(0,1)$. We can specify how we wish to have the mapping deal with the problem of the area of a pixel not matching the area of a texel. We can also specify whether we want the texture to determine the color of a pixel totally, a technique called **decaling**, or to use the product of the texture color and the color associated with the vertex to determine the color of the pixel.

OpenGL can also generate texture coordinates automatically with the function `glTexGen`. This function allows a few interesting options. We can form linear maps from geometric coordinates to texture coordinates. One of the important applications of this technique is in terrain generation and mapping. We can map surface features (textures) directly onto a three-dimensional terrain. We can also use a spherical mapping, as we discussed for two-step texture generation. We can also specify the mapping in either eye or object coordinates, so we can fix the texture to the object, or, in the former case, we can have the texture remain fixed as the object moves, creating the illusion of the object moving through a texture field.

10.2.3 Texture Generation

One of the most powerful uses of texture mapping is to provide detail without generating numerous geometric objects. High-end graphics systems, such as SGI's Reality Engine, can do three-dimensional texture mapping in real time; for every frame, the texture is mapped to objects as part of the rendering process at the same rate as nontexture-mapped objects are processed. Hence, if we want to simulate grass in a scene, we can texture map an image of grass that we might have obtained by, say, scanning a photograph, faster than we can generate two- or three-dimensional objects that look like grass. In mapping applications, rather than generating realistic surface detail for terrain, we can digitize a real map, and can paint it on a three-dimensional surface model by texture mapping.

We can also look for procedural methods for determining texture patterns. Of particular interest are patterns that we see in nature, such as the texture of sand, grass, or minerals. These textures show both structure (regular patterns) and considerable randomness. Most approaches to generating such textures algorithmically start with a random-number generator and filter its output as shown in Figure 10.10. An ideal random-number generator produces a sequence of values that are statistically uncorrelated, or **white noise**. The filter correlates successive noise values, and, by controlling the filter, we can simulate various patterns. We can also design random-number generators to create samples of textures directly.

Figure 10.10 Texture generation.

Researchers have applied such random techniques successfully to create three-dimensional textures. Although the generation of a three-dimensional texture field $T(s,t,r)$ is a direct extension of two-dimensional texture-generation techniques, there are practical advantages to using three-dimensional textures. Most important is that, by associating each (s,t,r) value directly with an (x,y,z) point, we can avoid the mapping problem entirely. The user needs only to define a function $T(s,t,r)$ with the desired properties. Conceptually, this process is similar to sculpting the three-dimensional object from a solid block whose volume is colored by the specified texture.

10.3   Environmental Maps

Highly reflective surfaces are characterized by specular reflections that mirror the environment. Consider, for example, a shiny metal ball, that is in the middle of a room. We can see the contents of the room, in a distorted form, on the surface of the ball. Although a ray tracer can produce this kind of image, in practice, ray-tracing calculations can be too time consuming to be practical. We can extend our mapping techniques to obtain an image that approximates the desired reflection by extending texture maps to **environmental** or **reflection maps**.

The basic idea is simple. We note that a mirror maps its environment onto its surface. Consequently, if we start with the desired effect, rather than with the physics, we can execute a two-step procedure for mapping environments to the surfaces of objects. In the first step, we obtain an image of the environment on an intermediate projection surface such as one of those that we used in Section 10.2. The center of projection is located at the center of the reflective object, but the projections are computed with the object removed

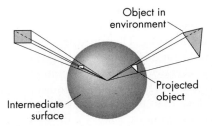

Figure 10.11 Mapping of the environment.

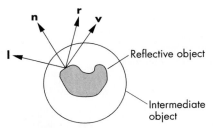

Figure 10.12 Mapping from the intermediate surface.

from the scene, as shown in Figure 10.11. Note that, because these images are projections, we can often use our graphics system to produce them. For an environment such as a room, the natural intermediate object is a box, and we compute six projections, corresponding to the walls, floor, and ceiling. At this point, we can treat the environmental map as a texture map. We place the object back in the scene, and transfer the texture map to its surface. However, because we are dealing with reflections, we must treat the object's surface as a mirror. Thus, the transfer of the image from the intermediate object to this surface uses the location of the viewer and the normal at the surface, as shown in Figure 10.12.

10.4 Bump Maps

Returning to our example of creating an image of an orange, we can take a picture of a real orange, and can apply it as a texture map to a surface. If we move the lights or rotate the object, however, we will immediately notice that we have the image of a model of an orange, rather than the image of a real orange. The problem is that a real orange is characterized primarily by small variations in its surface, rather than by variations in its color, and the former are not captured by texture mapping. The technique of **bump mapping** varies the apparent shape of the surface by perturbing the normal vectors as the surface is rendered; the colors that are generated by shading then show a variation in the surface properties.

We start with the observation that the normal at a point on the surface characterizes the shape of the surface at this point. If we perturb the normal at each point on the surface by a small amount, then we create a surface with small variations. If this perturbation can be applied during the rendering, we can use a smooth model of the surface, but can render it in a way that gives the appearance of a complex surface. Because the perturbations are to the normal vectors, the shading calculations will be correct for the altered surface.

We could perturb the normals in many ways; the following procedure for parametric surfaces is an efficient one. Let $\mathbf{p}(u, v)$ be a point on a parametric surface. The unit normal at that point is given by the cross-product of the partial derivative vectors:

$$\mathbf{n} = \frac{\mathbf{p}_u \times \mathbf{p}_v}{|\mathbf{p}_u \times \mathbf{p}_v|},$$

where

$$\mathbf{p}_u = \begin{bmatrix} \dfrac{\partial x}{\partial u} \\[2mm] \dfrac{\partial y}{\partial u} \\[2mm] \dfrac{\partial z}{\partial u} \end{bmatrix}, \qquad \mathbf{p}_v = \begin{bmatrix} \dfrac{\partial x}{\partial v} \\[2mm] \dfrac{\partial y}{\partial v} \\[2mm] \dfrac{\partial z}{\partial v} \end{bmatrix}.$$

Suppose that we displace the surface in the normal direction by a function called the **bump function**, $d(u, v)$, that is assumed known and small ($|d(u, v)| << 1$):

$$\mathbf{p}' = \mathbf{p} + d(u, v)\mathbf{n}.$$

We would prefer not to displace the surface; we just want to make it look as though we have displaced it. We can achieve the desired look by altering the normal $\mathbf{n}$, instead of $\mathbf{p}$, and using the perturbed normal in our shading calculations.

The normal at the perturbed point $\mathbf{p}'$ is given by the cross product

$$\mathbf{n}' = \mathbf{p}'_u \times \mathbf{p}'_v.$$

We can compute the two partial derivatives by differentiating the equation for $\mathbf{p}'$, obtaining

$$\mathbf{p}'_u = \mathbf{p}_u + \frac{\partial d}{\partial u}\mathbf{n} + d(u, v)\mathbf{n}_u,$$

$$\mathbf{p}'_v = \mathbf{p}_v + \frac{\partial d}{\partial v}\mathbf{n} + d(u, v)\mathbf{n}_v.$$

If d is small, we can neglect the term on the right of these two equations, and can take their cross product, noting that $\mathbf{n} \times \mathbf{n} = 0$, to obtain the perturbed normal:

$$\mathbf{n}' = \mathbf{n} + \frac{\partial d}{\partial u}\mathbf{n} \times \mathbf{p}_v + \frac{\partial d}{\partial v}\mathbf{n} \times \mathbf{p}_u.$$

This displacement must lie in the tangent plane at $\mathbf{p}$. To apply the bump map, we need two arrays that contain the values of $\partial d / \partial u$ and $\partial d / \partial v$. These arrays can be precomputed, by methods similar to those used for texture generation. The normal can then be perturbed during the shading process.

10.5   Writes into Buffers

In a modern graphics system, a user program can both write into and read from the buffers. There are two factors that make these operations different from the usual reading and writing into computer memory. First, we only occasionally want to read or write a single pixel or bit. Rather, we tend to read and write rectangular blocks of pixels (or bits). For example, we rasterize an entire scan line at a time when we fill a polygon; we write a small block of bits when we display a raster character; we change the values of all pixels in a buffer when we do a clear operation. Hence, it is of importance to have both the hardware and software support a set of operations that work on rectangular blocks of pixels, known as **bit-block transfer** (**bitblt**) operations, as efficiently as possible. These operations are also known as **raster operations** (**raster-ops**).

Suppose that we want to take an $n \times m$ block of pixels from one of our buffers, the **source buffer**, and to copy it into either the same buffer or another buffer, the **destination buffer**. This transfer is shown in Figure 10.13. A typical form for a bitblt write operation is

```
write_block(source, n, m, x, y, destination, u, v);
```

Although there are numerous details that we must consider, such as what happens if the source block goes over the boundary of the destination block,

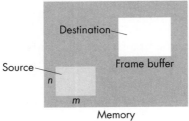

Figure 10.13 Writing of a block.

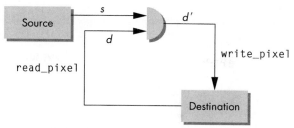

Figure 10.14 Writing modes.

the essence of bitblt is that a single function call alters the entire destination block. Note that, from the hardware perspective, the type of processing involved has none of the characteristics of the processing of geometric objects. Consequently, the hardware that optimizes bitblt operations has a completely different architecture from the pipeline hardware that we use for geometric operations.

10.5.1 Writing Modes

A second difference between normal writing into memory and bitblt operations is the variety of ways we can write into the buffers. The usual concept of a write to memory is replacement. The execution of statement in a C program such as

    y=x;

results in the value at the location where y is stored being replaced with the value at the location of x.

There are other possibilities. Suppose that we can work 1 bit at a time in our buffers. Consider the writing model in Figure 10.14. The bit that we wish to place in memory, perhaps in an altered form, is called the **source bit, s**; the place in memory where we want to put it is called the **destination bit, d**. If we are allowed to read before writing, as depicted in Figure 10.13, writing can be described by a replacement function f such that

$$d \leftarrow f(d, s).$$

For a 1-bit source and destination, there are only 16 possible ways to define the function f—namely, the 16 logical operations between 2 bits. These operations are shown in Figure 10.15, where each column in the table corresponds to one possible f. We can use the binary number represented by each column to denote a **writing mode**, or, equivalently, we can denote writing modes by the logical operation defined by the column. Suppose that we think of the logical value "1" as corresponding to a background color (say black) and "0" as corresponding to a foreground color (say white). We can examine the effects of various choices of f. Writing modes 0 and 15 are clear operations that change the value of the destination to either the foreground or the background color.

s	d	d'															
0	0	0	0	0	0	0	0	0	0	1	1	1	1	1	1	1	0
0	1	0	0	0	0	1	1	1	1	0	0	0	0	1	1	1	1
1	0	0	0	1	1	0	0	1	1	0	B	1	1	0	0	1	1
1	1	0	1	0	1	0	1	0	1	0	1	0	1	0	1	0	1

Figure 10.15 Logical operations between 2 bits.

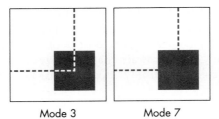

Mode 3   Mode 7

Figure 10.16 Writing in modes 3 and 7.

The new value of the destination bit is independent of both the source and the destination values. Modes 3 and 7 are the normal writing modes. Mode 3 is the function

$$d \leftarrow s;$$

it simply replaces the value of the destination bit with the source. Mode 7 is the logical OR operation:

$$d \leftarrow s + d.$$

Figure 10.16 shows that these two writing modes can have different effects on the contents of the frame buffer. Both modes will write the foreground color over the background color, but they will differ if we try to write the background color over the foreground color. Which mode should be used depends on what effect the application programmer wishes to create.

10.5.2 Writes with XOR

Mode 6 is the exclusive-or operation XOR, denoted by $\oplus$; it is the most interesting of the writing modes. Unlike modes 3 and 7, mode 6 cannot be implemented without a read of the destination bit. The power of the XOR write mode comes from the property that, if x and y are binary variables, then

$$x = (x \oplus y) \oplus y.$$

Thus, if we apply XOR twice to a bit, we return the bit to its original state.

The most important applications of this mode involve interaction. Consider what happens when we use menus in an interactive application, such as our painting program from Chapter 3. In response to a mouse click, a menu appears, covering some portion of the screen. After the user indicates an action from the menu, the menu disappears, and the area of the screen that it covered is returned to that area's original state. What has transpired involves the use of off-screen memory, known as backing store. Suppose that the menu has been stored off-screen as an array of bits, M, and that the area of the screen where the menu will appear is an array of bits, S. Consider the sequence of operations

$$S \leftarrow S \oplus M,$$

$$M \leftarrow S \oplus M,$$

$$S \leftarrow S \oplus M,$$

where we assume that the xor operation is applied to corresponding bits in S and M. If we substitute the result of the first equation in the second, and the result of the second in the third, we find that, at the end of three operations, the menu appears on the screen. The original contents of the screen, where the menu is now located, are now off-screen, where the menu was originally. We have swapped the menu with an area of the screen using three bitblt operations. This method of swapping is considerably different from the normal mode of swapping, which uses replacement-mode writing, but requires temporary storage to effect the swap.

There are numerous variants of this technique. One is to move a cursor around the screen without affecting the area under it. Another variant is to use xor to draw the rubber band lines, an option that as we pointed out in Chapter 3, is not provided in many APIs because the xor-write mode is not always available (see Exercises 10.1 and 10.2).

10.6 Bit and Pixel Operations in OpenGL

Digital images consist of k-bit pixels, where k can be any number from 1, for binary images, to 32, for RGBA images, to even greater numbers, for high-resolution color applications. Although, in principle, a 1-bit image, or **bitmap**, is the same type of entity as an 8-bit (1-byte) or 24-bit (3-byte) image, hardware and software often treat bitmaps differently. From the hardware perspective, bitmaps involve implementation of only logical operations, and work one plane at a time in a buffer. From the software perspective, bitmaps are used differently from multibit images, even though both use the same physical memory. Typically, bitmaps are used for fonts, masks, and patterns. OpenGL allows the user to work with either bitmaps or images of multibit pixels.

In addition to its geometry pipeline, OpenGL has a separate pipeline for pixels. The geometry and pixel pipelines eventually merge. Interactions between these two pipelines are used to implement many of the techniques that we have discussed, such as texture mapping, and open up the possibilities of many new techniques. In this section, however, we shall concentrate on how the buffers are seen from the application program.

10.6.1 OpenGL Buffers

OpenGL can support a number of buffers:

- Color buffers
- Depth buffer
- Accumulation buffer
- Stencil buffer

The color buffers include the frame buffer, but, as we saw in our discussion of double buffering in Chapter 3, there can be multiple color buffers. In double buffering, these color buffers are referred to as the front and back buffers. We may also want to produce stereo pairs of images, using right and left buffers, that contain the image as seen by the right and left eyes, respectively. For stereoscopic animations, we may want to employ four color buffers. Generally, we render geometric objects into the color buffers, but we can also write pixels directly into, and can read pixels from, the buffers. Only color buffers can be made visible.

The depth buffer is normally used for hidden-surface removal, but we can also read data from it and write data to it. In Section 10.8, we shall show how the accumulation buffer can be used for a variety of operations. The stencil buffer often is used for masking operations. For example, we can use the values in this buffer as a mask to determine whether a pixel in the color buffer should be written to the screen.

For now, we shall assume that we are working in a color buffer—typically the frame buffer—although many of these operations can be applied to other buffers. Note that a given implementation may support only some of these buffers, and that the depth of a buffer is implementation dependent.

OpenGL maintains a **raster position** independent of the position of geometric entities. We can think of this position as defining a cursor, in window coordinates, where writing of raster primitives will begin. The raster position can be set by the variants of the function glRasterPos. For example, the function

```
glRasterPos3f(x, y, z);
```

describes a position by three floats that is subject to both the model-view and projection transformations before conversion to screen coordinates. This position is stored, like any other geometric entity, in four-dimensional homogeneous coordinates. However, once this position is transformed by the viewing pipeline to a position in screen coordinates, writing of pixels or bits takes place in raster units (integers), with the pixel centers located halfway between integers.

10.6.2 Use of Bitmaps for Fonts

We can demonstrate the importance of maintaining a cursor for raster entities by considering the use of raster fonts for text. In Chapter 3, we observed that raster text is much faster to render than is stroke text. In general, a **font** or **typeface** defines a set of characters of a particular family, such as Times, Courier, or Computer Modern. Each font can have various sizes, such as 10 point or 24 point,[3] and styles, such as bold or italic. However, we shall use the term *font* with *raster* to denote a set of characters of a particular size and style. Hence, an 8 × 13 font, as provided by the GLUT library, is denoted by GLUT_BITMAP_8_BY_13; a 10-point proportional font[4] is GLUT_BITMAP_TIMES_ROMAN_10. A typical font has 128 or 256 characters. Each character in a raster font is defined by a pattern of bits, as shown in Figure 10.17. Note that, when we define a font as a pattern of bits, the size of text on the screen depends on the resolution of the screen—a relation that does not hold for the rendering of geometric objects.

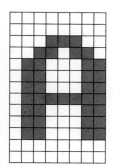

Figure 10.17 Definition of a character.

Bitmapped fonts are designed both to fit in a certain space and to be readable. Thus, as we can see from Figure 10.17, in all but the smallest fonts, we must allow for vertical and horizontal spacing between characters; for room for descenders, as in the lowercase letters g and y; and for the size differences between uppercase and lowercase letters. Once we have designed a font, we can store it in an array as bits. For example, if we wish to define a 128-character 8 × 13 font, we can use an array

```
GLubyte my_font[128][13];
```

We can place an array bitmap at the current raster position (assuming that this position is a valid location in the buffer) with the function

```
glBitmap(width, height, xo, yo, xi, yi, bitmap);
```

The width and height are in bits. The floating-point numbers xo and yo give an offset relative to the current raster position, and give the position where the lower-left corner of the bitmap is to start (Figure 10.18); xi and yi are floating-point numbers used to increment the raster position after the bitmap is drawn.

---

[3] There are 72 points to 1 inch.

[4] A *proportional font* is a font in which all characters do not have the same width. In a *monotype font*, all characters have the same width.

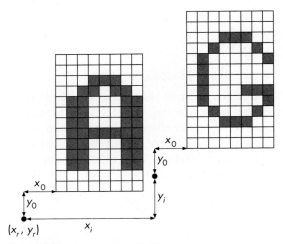

Figure 10.18 Outputting of a bitmap.

As we did in Chapter 3, we can define a font using a display list for each character. Assuming that the array my_font has been defined, these display lists can be generated by the code (see Section 3.4)[5]

```
base=glGenLists(128)
for(i=0, i<127, i++)
{
    glNewList(base+i, GL_COMPILE);
    glBitMap(8, 13, 0.0, 2.0, 10.0, 0.0, my_font[i];
    glEndList();
}
```

Note that, in this example, each character is started 2 bits up from the current raster position, and the raster position is shifted 2 additional bits after the character is drawn, leaving a 2-bit horizontal and vertical separation between characters.

10.6.3 Pixels and Images

In OpenGL, so that we can accommodate different types of images, pixels can be handled as groups of 8-bit bytes in a variety of formats. For example, we can work with RGB images, where the value of each color component is stored as

---

[5] We are, perhaps, wasting space by allocating memory for the first 32 ASCII characters. These characters are usually nonprinting characters, used only for control, and do not generate any visible output.

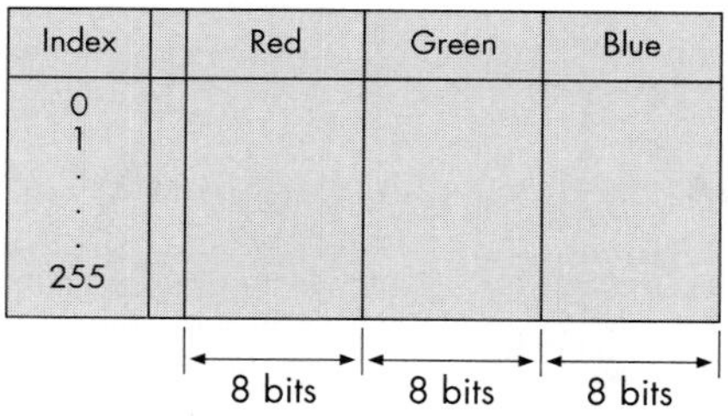

Figure 10.19 Lookup table for RGB.

a single byte, or we can work with a monochrome (luminance) image in which each pixel is a single floating-point number.

There are three functions for moving images in OpenGL:

```
glReadPixels(x, y, width, height, format, type, image);
glDrawPixels(width, height, format, type, image);
glCopyPixels(x,y, width, height,type);
```

The functions glReadPixels and glDrawPixels read and write rectangles of pixels between an OpenGL buffer and an array image, whereas glCopyPixels reads and writes from one area of the frame buffer to another area of the frame buffer. In glReadPixels, we can specify an offset (x, y) in the frame buffer where reading of the block of dimensions width and height should begin. Although, in most applications, we use the frame buffer, which is selected by default, we can use the functions glReadBuffer and glDrawBuffer to select any of OpenGL's buffers for reading and writing.

10.6.4 Lookup Tables

In OpenGL, all colors can be modified by lookup tables as they are placed into buffers. Suppose that all our buffers have 8-bit components. Then, each component has a 256-entry lookup table associated with it, as shown in Figure 10.19. We can regard each value in a buffer as determined by an index into the table that selects the value. The tables are defaulted to provide an identity mapping of input values to output values. The function glPixelMap allows us to load user-defined maps.

These maps are essentially the same as the color lookup tables that we introduced in Chapter 2. If we make a correspondence between the color indices and the gray levels of a monochromatic (luminance) image, we can use these maps to enhance a display by converting gray levels to colors. An image colored in such a manner is called a **pseudocolor** image. We shall demonstrate this technique to assign colors to points in the Mandlebrot set in Section 10.7.

The major problem for the user is how to select the palette of 256 colors from the (typically) 2^{24} available RGB colors. One popular choice is based on a thermal scale, using hot colors (red, white, and yellow) for important

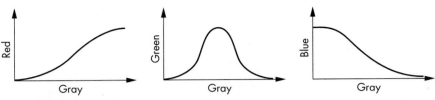

Figure 10.20 Thermal color map.

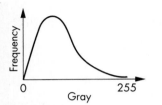

Figure 10.21 Histogram of dark image.

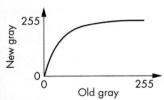

Figure 10.22 Lookup tables for lightening of an image.

values, and cool colors (blues and greens) for unimportant values. For example, suppose that our gray-scale image is such that the low values are least important and the high values are most important. Figure 10.20 shows a possible map of the gray levels to RGB that forms such a thermal scale. Color Plate 19 shows the use of a thermal scale in a scientific visualization. Here, the colors represent temperatures in the mantle of the Earth as generated by a computer model.

Another use of lookup tables is for color conversion and brightness adjustments. For example, the shading models that we use in computer graphics often generate images that are dark and lack contrast. If we were to plot the distribution of luminance values as a graph called a **histogram**, we might see a plot like the one shown in Figure 10.21, which shows that the majority of the values are in the lower ranges. If we apply the lookup table in Figure 10.22 to each color, we map lower gray levels to higher (brighter) values, and lighten the image. The distribution of levels for the resulting image is more uniform yet still spans the full range of luminance values, thus improving the contrast of the original image.

We can also use these tables for color conversion. In Chapter 7, we noted that the RGB values in most APIs, including OpenGL, do not refer to any particular system. Often, if we photograph the image that is on the screen of a CRT, the resulting photographic print may look noticeably different from the image on the screen, due to the differences in color properties among the film and the photographic paper, the CRT, and the perceptual characteristics of the viewer. We can use a lookup table for each of the R, G, and B components to make color adjustments (**color balancing**) before we take the photograph. The lookup tables thus provide a method of color conversion across different RGB systems.

10.6.5 Buffers for Picking

Buffers provide limitless opportunities for constructing and manipulating images. They can also be used interactively, in ways that might not be apparent at first. Consider the problem of picking. In picking, we return the identifier of an object to the user program. OpenGL includes a mechanism that uses feedback and hit lists to provide this information. This mechanism is dictated by the feed-forward nature of pipeline rendering, and requires an extra rendering of the data each time that a pick is needed. If there are not too many distinct object identifiers, we can use buffers to provide an alternate picking mechanism.

Suppose that we have no more than 256 identifiers (assuming 8-bit buffers). As we render primitives, we place the identifier of the fragment being rendered into an extra buffer at a location corresponding to the location in the frame buffer where the fragment will be rendered. Thus, the "colors" in this buffer are identifiers of objects located at corresponding pixels in the frame buffer. We can use OpenGL's pixel-reading functions to obtain these colors. Picking reduces to reading the value of this buffer at the pixel corresponding to the cursor location. If we combine this process with the z-buffer algorithm, then each pixel in this buffer will have the identifier of the closest object to the camera along the ray through the pixel.

10.7 The Mandelbrot Set

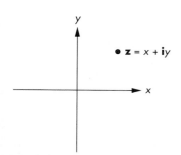

Figure 10.23 Complex plane.

We introduced fractals in Chapter 8. No discussion of fractals, no matter how elementary, would be complete without an introduction to the Mandelbrot set. The Mandelbrot set is easy to generate, but shows infinite complexity in the patterns it generates. It also provides a good example of generating images and using color lookup tables. In this discussion, we shall assume that you have a basic familiarity with complex arithmetic.

We denote a point in the complex plane as

$$\mathbf{z} = x + \mathbf{i}y,$$

where x is the real part and y is the imaginary part of $\mathbf{z}$ (Figure 10.23). If $\mathbf{z}_1 = x_1 + \mathbf{i}y_1$ and $\mathbf{z}_2 = x_2 + \mathbf{i}y_2$ are two complex numbers, complex addition and multiplication are defined by

$$\mathbf{z}_1 + \mathbf{z}_2 = x_1 + x_1 + \mathbf{i}(y_1 + y_2),$$

$$\mathbf{z}_1\mathbf{z}_2 = x_1x_2 - y_1y_2 + \mathbf{i}(x_1y_2 + x_2y_1).$$

The pure imaginary number $\mathbf{i}$ has the property that $\mathbf{i}^2 = -1$. A complex number $\mathbf{z}$ has magnitude such that

$$|\mathbf{z}|^2 = x^2 + y^2.$$

In the complex plane, a function

$$\mathbf{w} = F(\mathbf{z})$$

maps complex points into complex points. We can use such a function to define a complex recurrence of the form

$$\mathbf{z}_{k+1} = F(\mathbf{z}_k),$$

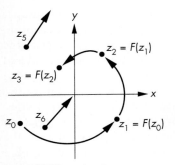

Figure 10.24 Paths from complex recurrence.

Figure 10.25 Mandelbrot set. (a) Black and white coloring. (b) Detail along edges.

where $\mathbf{z}_0 = \mathbf{c}$. If we plot the locations of $\mathbf{z}_k$ for particular starting points, we can see several of the possibilities in Figure 10.24. For a particular function F, some initial values will generate sequences that go off to infinity. Others may repeat periodically, and still other sequences will converge to points called attractors. For example, consider the function

$$\mathbf{z}_{k+1} = \mathbf{z}_k^2,$$

where $\mathbf{z}_0 = \mathbf{c}$. If $\mathbf{c}$ lies outside a unit circle, the sequence $\{\mathbf{z}_k\}$ diverges; if $\mathbf{c}$ is inside the unit circle, $\{\mathbf{z}_k\}$ converges to an attractor at the origin; if $|\mathbf{c}| = 1$, each $\mathbf{z}_k$ is on the unit circle. If we consider the points for which $|\mathbf{c}| = 1$, we can see that, depending on the value of $\mathbf{c}$, we can generate either a finite number of points, or all the points, on the unit circle.

A more interesting example is the function

$$\mathbf{z}_{k+1} = \mathbf{z}_k^2 + \mathbf{c},$$

with $\mathbf{z}_0 = 0 + \mathbf{i}0$. The point $\mathbf{c}$ is in the **Mandelbrot set** if and only if the points generated by this recurrence remain finite. Thus, we can break the plane into two groups of points: those that belong to the Mandelbrot set, and those that do not. Graphically, we can take a rectangular region of the plane, and color points black if they are in the set, and white if they are not (Figure 10.25a). However, it is the regions on the edges of the set that show the most complexity, so we often want to magnify these regions.

The computation of the Mandelbrot set can be time consuming; there are a few tricks to speed it up. The area centered around $\mathbf{c} = -0.5 + \mathbf{i}0.0$ is of the most interest, although we probably want to be able to change both the size and the center of our window.

We can usually tell after a few iterations whether a point will go off to infinity. For example, if $|z_k| > 4$, successive values will be larger, and we can stop the iteration. It is more difficult to tell whether a point near the boundary will converge. Consequently, an approximation to the set is usually generated as follows. We fix a maximum number of iterations. If, for a given **c**, we can determine that the point diverges, we color white the point corresponding to **c** in our image. If, after the maximum number of iterations, $|z_k|$ is less than some threshold, we decide that it is in the set, and we color it black. For other value of $|z_k|$, we assign a unique color to the point corresponding to **c**.

Appendix A contains a program that generates an approximation to the set. The user can set the size and center of the rectangle, and the number of iterations to be carried out. The magnitudes of the numbers z_k are scaled to be in the range of 0 to 255. We generate an n × m 1-byte array image by looping over all pixels up to the maximum number of iterations. The display consists of two parts. First, we define a color map in the initialization. The map shown uses a floating-point representation of the luminance values over the interval (0.0,1.0). We define an intensity-to-red map that assigns no red to black (0.0), assigns full red to white (1.0), and linearly interpolates between these values for the other intensities. For blue, we go from full blue for zero intensity to no blue for full intensity. We assign the intensity-to-green values randomly. This green assignment will enhance the detail in regions where there are slow changes in intensity (Figure 10.25b). The code is

```
for(i=0;i<256;i++)
{
    redmap[i]=i/255.;
    greenmap[i]=drand48();
    bluemap[i]=1.0-i/255.;
}

glPixelMapfv(GL_PIXEL_MAP_I_TO_R, 256, redmap);
glPixelMapfv(GL_PIXEL_MAP_I_TO_G, 256, greenmap);
glPixelMapfv(GL_PIXEL_MAP_I_TO_B, 256, bluemap);
```

You should be able to implement other color maps with no difficulty. The display function requires only clearing of the screen and sending of the pixels to the frame buffer:

```
void display()
{
    glClear(GL_COLOR_BUFFER_BIT);
    glDrawPixels(n,m,GL_COLOR_INDEX, GL_UNSIGNED_BYTE, image);
}
```

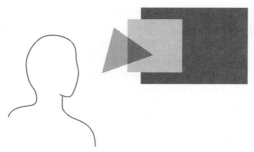

Figure 10.26 Translucent and opaque polygons.

10.8   Compositing Techniques

In Chapter 6, we developed a model for dealing with transparent objects. That model is most appropriate for use with ray tracing, which is a time-consuming rendering technique. OpenGL provides an alternate mechanism through alpha (α) blending, that can, among other effects, create images with transparent objects. The **alpha channel** is the fourth color in RGBA (or RGBα) color mode. Like the other colors, the application program can control the value of A (or α) for each pixel. However, in RGBA mode, if blending is enabled, the value of α controls how the RGB values are written into the frame buffer. Because fragments from multiple objects can contribute to the color of the same pixel, we can say these objects are **blended** or **composited** together.

10.8.1   Opacity and Blending

The **opacity** of an object is a measure of how much light penetrates through that object. An opacity of 1 ($\alpha = 1$) corresponds to a completely opaque surface that blocks all light incident on it. A surface with an opacity of 0 is transparent, and all light passes through it. The **transparency** or **translucency** of a surface with opacity α is given by $1 - \alpha$. Consider the three uniformly lit polygons shown in Figure 10.26. Assume that the middle polygon is opaque, and the front polygon, nearest to the viewer, is transparent. If the front polygon were perfectly transparent, the viewer would see only the back polygon. However, if the front polygon is only partially opaque (partially transparent), similar to colored glass, the color that viewer will see is a blending of the colors of the front and middle polygon. Because the middle polygon is opaque, the viewer will not see the back polygon. If the front polygon is red and the middle is blue, she will see magenta, due to the blending of the colors. If we let the middle polygon be only partially opaque, she will see the blending of the colors of all three polygons.

In computer graphics, we usually render polygons one at a time into the frame buffer. Consequently, if we want to use blending or compositing, we need a way to apply opacity as part of the rendering process. We can use the notion of source and destination pixels, just as we used source and destination bits in Section 10.1. As a polygon is processed, pixel-sized fragments are computed, and, if they are visible, are assigned colors based on the shading model in use. Until now, we have used the color of a fragment—as computed by the shading model and by any mapping techniques—to replace the color of the pixel in the frame buffer at the location in screen coordinates of the fragment. If we regard the fragment as the source pixel and the frame-buffer pixel as the destination, we can combine these values in various ways. The α channel is one way of controlling the blending on a pixel-by-pixel basis. Combining the colors of polygons is similar to joining two pieces of colored glass into a single piece of glass that will have a higher opacity and a color different from either of the original pieces.

If we represent the source and destination pixels with the four-element (RGBα) arrays

$$\mathbf{s} = [\, s_r \quad s_g \quad s_b \quad s_a \,],$$

$$\mathbf{d} = [\, d_r \quad d_g \quad d_b \quad d_a \,],$$

then a compositing operation replaces $\mathbf{d}$ with

$$\mathbf{d}' = [\, b_r s_r + c_r d_r \quad b_g s_g + c_g d_g \quad b_b s_b + c_b d_b \quad b_a s_a + c_a d_a \,].$$

The arrays of constants $\mathbf{b}$ and $\mathbf{c}$ are the **source** and **destination blending factors**, respectively. As occurs with RGB colors, a value of α over 1.0 will be limited (**clamped**) to the maximum of 1.0, and negative values will be clamped to 0.0. We can choose both the values of α and the method of combining source and destination values to achieve a variety of effects.

10.8.2 Image Compositing

The most straightforward use of α blending is to combine and display a number of images that exist as pixel maps, or equivalently, as sets of data that have been rendered independently. In this case, we can regard each image as a radiant object that contributes equally to the final image. Usually, we wish to keep our RGB colors between 0 and 1 in the final image, without having to clamp those values greater than 1. Hence, we can either scale the values of each image, or use the source and destination blending factors.

Suppose that we have n images that should contribute equally to the final display. At a given pixel, image i has components $\mathbf{C}_i \alpha_i$. Here, we are using $\mathbf{C}_i$ to denote the color triplet (R_i, B_i, G_i). If we replace $\mathbf{C}_i$ by $\frac{1}{n}\mathbf{C}_i$ and α_i by $\frac{1}{n}\alpha_i$, we can simply add each image into the frame buffer (assuming that the frame buffer is initialized to black with an $\alpha = 0$). Alternately, we can use a source blending factor of $\frac{1}{n}$ by setting the α value for each pixel in each image to be $\frac{1}{n}$, and using 1 for the destination blending factor and α for the source blending

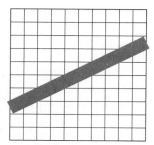

Figure 10.27 Raster line.

factor. Although these two methods produce the same image, if the hardware supports compositing, the second may be more efficient.

10.8.3 Antialiasing

One of the major uses of the α channel is for antialiasing. In Chapter 7, we noted that an ideal raster line should be one pixel wide, and that such a line will partially cover a number of pixels in the framer buffer, as shown in Figure 10.27. Suppose that, as part of the geometric-processing stage of the rendering process, as we process a fragment, we set the α value for the corresponding pixel to be a number between 0 and 1 that is the amount of that pixel covered by the fragment. We can then use this α value to modulate the color as we render the fragment to the frame buffer. We can use a destination blending factor of $1 - \alpha$, and a source destination factor of α. However, if there is overlap of fragments within a pixel, there are numerous possibilities, as we can see from Figure 10.28. In Figure 10.28(a), the fragments do not overlap; in Figure 10.28(b), they do overlap. Consider the problem from the perspective of a renderer that works one polygon a time. For our simple example, suppose that we start with an opaque background, and the frame buffer starts with the background color $\mathbf{C}_0$. We can set $\alpha_0 = 0$, because no part of the pixel has yet been covered with fragments from polygons. The first polygon is rendered. The color of the destination pixel is set to

$$\mathbf{C}_d = (1 - \alpha_1)\mathbf{C}_0 + \alpha_1\mathbf{C}_1,$$

and its α value is set to

$$\alpha_d = \alpha_1.$$

Thus, a fragment that covers the entire pixel ($\alpha_1 = 1$) will have its color assigned to the destination pixel and the destination pixel will be opaque. If the background is black, the destination color will be $\alpha_1\mathbf{C}_1$. Now consider the fragment from the second polygon that subtends the same pixel. How we add in its color and α value depends on how we wish to interpret the overlap. If there is no overlap, we can assign the new color by blending the color of the destination

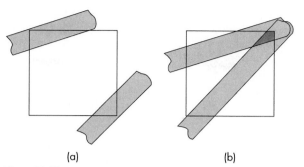

(a)   (b)

Figure 10.28 Fragments. (a) Nonoverlapping. (b) Overlapping.

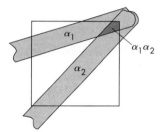

Figure 10.29 Average overlap.

with the color of fragment, resulting in the color and α:

$$\mathbf{C}_d = (1 - \alpha_2)((1 - \alpha_1)(\mathbf{C}_0 + \alpha_1\mathbf{C}_1) + \alpha_2\mathbf{C}_2,$$

$$\alpha_d = \alpha_1 + \alpha_2.$$

The color will be a blending of the two colors that will not need to be clamped, and the resulting value of α represents the new fraction of the pixel that is covered. However, the resulting color is affected by the order in which the polygons are rendered. The more difficult problems are what to do if the fragments overlap, and how to tell whether there is an overlap. One tactic is to take a probabilistic view. If fragment 1 occupies a fraction α_1 of the pixel, and fragment 2 occupies a fraction α_2 of the same pixel, and we have no other information about the location of the fragments within the pixel, then the average area of overlap will be $\alpha_1\alpha_2$. We can represent the average case as shown Figure 10.29. Hence, the new destination α should be

$$\alpha_d = \alpha_1 + \alpha_2 - \alpha_1\alpha_2.$$

How we should assign the color is a more complex problem, because we have to decide whether the second fragment is in front of the first, or the first is in front of the second, or even whether the two should be blended. We can define an appropriate blending for whichever assumption we wish to make. Note that, in a pipeline renderer, polygons can be generated in an order that has nothing to do with their distances from the viewer. However, if we couple α blending with hidden-surface removal, we can use the depth information to make front-versus-back decisions.

In OpenGL, we can invoke antialiasing without having the user program combine α values explicitly if we enable both blending and line or point smoothing; for example, we can use

```
glEnable(GL_POINT_SMOOTH);
glEnable(GL_LINE_SMOOTH);
glEnable(GL_SMOOTHING);
glBlendFunc(GL_SRC_ALPHA, GL_ONE_MINUS_SRC_ALPHA);
```

There may be a considerable time penalty associated with antialiasing.

10.8.4 Back-to-Front and Front-to-Back Rendering

Although using the α channel gives us a way of creating the appearance of translucency, it is difficult to handle transparency in a physically correct manner without taking into account how an object is lit and what happens to rays and projectors that pass through translucent objects. In Figure 10.30, we can see several of the difficulties. We shall ignore refraction of light through translucent surfaces—an effect than cannot be handled with a pipeline polygon renderer. Suppose that the rear polygon is opaque, but reflective, and that the two polygons closer to the viewer are translucent. By following various rays from the light source, we can see a number of possibilities. Some rays will strike the rear polygon, and the corresponding pixels can be colored with the shade at the intersection of the projector and the polygon. For these rays, we should also distinguish between points illuminated directly by the light source, and points for which the incident light passes through one or both translucent polygons. For rays that pass through only one translucent surface, we have to adjust the color based on the color and opacity of the polygon. We should also add a term that accounts for the light striking the front polygon that is reflected toward the viewer. For rays passing through both translucent polygons, we have to consider their combined effect. For a pipeline renderer, the task is even more difficult, if not impossible, because we have to determine the contribution of each polygon as it is passed through the pipeline, rather than considering the contributions of all polygons to a given pixel at the same time.

10.8.5 Splatting

There are numerous applications in which we have sufficient depth information to generate and render the polygons in either a front-to-back or back-to-front order. In such cases, the blending capabilities in OpenGL can work well. One

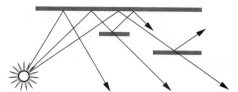

Figure 10.30 Scene with translucent objects.

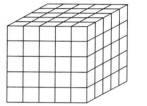

Figure 10.31 Volume of voxels.

such application area is **volume rendering**. Here, we start, as we did in Section 8.10, with a set of volume elements, or voxels, that we can view as located on a three-dimensional grid, as shown in Figure 10.31. We shall assume that each voxel is a single floating-point number. In Chapter 8, we developed an isosurface method—marching cubes—that did not use all the voxels in the data set.

Another group of techniques—direct methods—create a display in which all the voxels make a contribution. We start by assigning a color and transparency to each voxel. For example, if the data are from a computed tomography (CT) scan of a head, we might assign colors based on the X-ray density, and transparency based on what we want to see. Soft tissues (low densities) might be colored red, and hard tissues (high densities) might be colored white. If we want to show the brain, but not the skull, we can assign zero opacity to the values corresponding to the skull. The assignment of colors and opacities is a pattern-recognition problem that we shall not pursue. Often, a user interface allows the user to control these values interactively. Here, we are interested in how to construct a two-dimensional image after these assignments have been made.

One particularly simple way to generate an image is known as **splatting**. Each voxel is assigned a simple shape, and this shape is projected onto the image plane. Figure 10.32 shows a spherical voxel and the associated splat, or **footprint**. Note that, if we are using a parallel projection and each voxel is assigned the same shape, the splats will differ in only color and opacity. Thus, we do not need to carry out a projection for each voxel, but rather can save the footprint as a bitmap that can be bitblt into the frame buffer.

Color Plate 28 is a splatted image of a lobster that was created using the same data set as used for Color Plates 26 and 27. Although the image in Plate 28 lacks the three-dimensional character of Plates 26 and 27 (it looks like a color X-ray image), all voxels contributed to the image.

The key issue in creating a splatted image is how each splat is composited into the image. The data, being on a grid, are already sorted with respect to their distance from the viewer or the projection plane. We can go through the

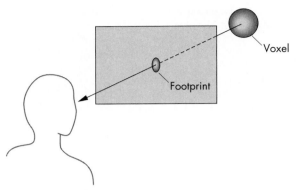

Figure 10.32 Splat, or footprint, of voxel.

data back to front,[6] adding the contributions of each voxel through its splat. We start with a background image, and blend in successive splats. We modify slightly our usual way of blending colors and opacities. Consider the formulas for combining source and destination pixels:

$$\mathbf{C}_{d'} = (1 - \alpha_s)\mathbf{C}_d + \alpha_s\mathbf{C}_s,$$

$$\alpha_{d'} = (1 - \alpha_s)\alpha_d + \alpha_s.$$

If we are compositing back to front, and, if the source is opaque ($\alpha_s = 1$), then so is $\alpha_{d'}$, and the new destination color is the same as the source color. If the source is transparent, we retain the original destination color and opacity. We can use OpenGL's blending functions if we first replace the color $\mathbf{C}$ of each voxel by $\alpha\mathbf{C}$, and use source and destination blending factors of 1 and $1 - \alpha_s$, respectively. The major advantage of this back-to-front compositing is that we can process the data in terms of slices of the volume data that correspond to viewing the voxel data as a stacked set of two-dimensional images. Not only are the data often generated in such a manner, but also we do not need to keep the entire data set in memory to do the rendering. However, our approach does not allow us to take advantage of data dependencies that potentially can speed up the processing. For example, if the front of the volume is opaque, a back-to-front renderer nevertheless will process all voxels, even though we shall see only the front voxels in the final image.

An alternative is front-to-back rendering by ray casting (Figure 10.33). Using the same compositing formulas that we used for splatting along a ray, we determine when an opaque voxel is reached, and we stop tracing this ray imme-

---

[6] The term *front* is defined relative to the viewer. For three-dimensional data sets, once we have positioned the viewer relative to the data set, *front* defines the order in which we process the array of voxels.

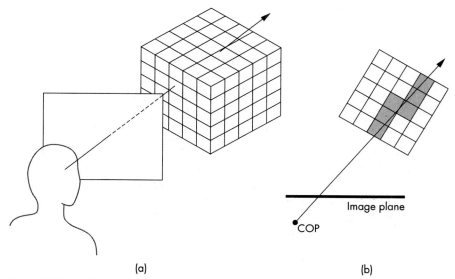

(a) (b)

Figure 10.33 (a) Ray casting for a volume. (b) Top view.

diately. The difficulty with this approach is that a given ray passes through many slices of the data, and thus we need to keep all the data available.

It should be clear that issues that govern the choice between a back-to-front and a front-to-back renderer are similar to the issues that arise when we choose between an image-oriented renderer and an object-oriented renderer. We have merely added opacity to the process.

10.8.6 Depth Cueing and Fog

Depth cueing is one the oldest techniques in three-dimensional graphics. Before raster systems became available, graphics systems could draw only lines. We created the illusion of depth by drawing lines farther from the viewer dimmer than lines closer to the viewer, a technique known as **depth cueing**. We can extend this idea to create the illusion of partially translucent space between the object and the viewer, by blending in a distance-dependent color as each fragment is processed.

Let f denote a **fog factor**, and let z be the distance between a fragment being rendered and the viewer. If the fragment has a color $\mathbf{C}_s$ and the fog is assigned a color $\mathbf{C}_f$, then we can use the color

$$\mathbf{C}_{s'} = f\mathbf{C}_s + (1 - f)\mathbf{C}_f$$

in the rendering. If f varies linearly between some minimum and maximum values, we have a depth-cueing effect. If this factor varies exponentially (Figure 10.34), then we get effects that look more like fog. OpenGL supports

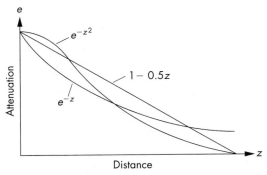

Figure 10.34 Fog density.

linear, exponential, and Gaussian fog densities. For example, in RGBA mode, we can set up a fog-density function $f = e^{-0.5z^2}$ by using the function calls

```
GLfloat fcolor[4] = { ... };
glEnable(GL_FOG);
glFogf(GL_FOG_MODE, GL_EXP);
glFogf(GL_FOG_DENSITY, 0.5);
glFogfv(GL_FOG_COLOR, fcolor);
```

Note that the value of z is given in eye coordinates. Color Plate 9 shows the use of fog in OpenGL. Color Plate 11 uses fog to give the factory environment a more realistic (but gloomy) feel.

10.9   Use of the Accumulation Buffer

There is one other buffer that, if present, is useful for a number of additional functions. The **accumulation buffer** has the same resolution as the frame buffer, but has greater depth resolution. We can use the additional resolution to render successive images into one location while retaining numerical accuracy. There are many possible applications.

In OpenGL, we can clear the accumulation buffer as we do any other buffer, and then can use the function `glAccum` either to add or to multiply values from the frame buffer into the accumulation buffer, or to copy the contents of the accumulation buffer back to the frame buffer. For example, the code

```
glClear(GL_ACUM_BUFFER_BIT)
for(i=0; i< num_mages; i++)
{
    glClear(GL_COLOR_BUFFER_BIT, GL_DEPTH_BUFFER_BIT);
    display_image(i);
    glAccum(GL_ACUUM, 1.0/ (float) num_images);
```

```
}
glAccum(GL_RETURN, 1.0);
```

uses the function `display_images` to generate a sequence of images into the frame buffer. Each is accumulated, with a scale factor, into the accumulation buffer. At the end, the accumulated image is copied back to the frame buffer. Note that we could have attempted the same task using blending, but we would have been forced to scale the colors in a lower-resolution buffer to avoid clamping.

One of the most important uses of the accumulation buffer is for antialiasing. Rather than antialias individual points and lines, we can antialias an entire scene into the accumulation buffer. The idea is that, if we regenerate the same scene with all the objects, or the viewer, shifted slightly (less than one pixel), then we will generate different aliasing artifacts. If we can average together the resulting images, the aliasing effects will be smoothed out. In general, it is easier to shift, or **jitter**, the viewer, as we have to change only the parameters in glPersective or glOrtho. However, we have to do some calculation in the program to determine how a small change in screen coordinates converts to a corresponding change in camera coordinates. In terms of sampling theory (Section 10.10), we have sampled the world at a finer resolution, or **supersampled** it, and then have used an averaging filter to reconstruct the world from the samples.

We can combine use of the accumulation buffer with pixel mapping to perform a number of digital-filtering operations. Suppose that we start with a discrete image. Perhaps this image was generated by a rendering, or perhaps we obtained it by digitizing a continuous image using a scanner. We can represent the image with an $N \times M$ matrix,

$$\mathbf{A} = [\, a_{ij} \,],$$

of scalar levels. If we process each color component of a color image independently, we can regard the entries in $\mathbf{A}$ as either individual color components, or gray (luminance) levels. A **linear filter H** produces a filtered matrix $\mathbf{B}$ whose elements are

$$b_{ij} = \sum_{k=-m}^{m} \sum_{l=-n}^{n} a_{kl} h_{i-k, j-l}.$$

We say that $\mathbf{B}$ is the result of **convolving A** with a filter matrix $\mathbf{H}$. In general, the values of m and n are small, and we can represent $\mathbf{H}$ by a small **convolution kernel** of its nonzero elements. We can view the filtering operation as shown in Figure 10.35. For each pixel in $\mathbf{A}$, we place the convolution kernel over a_{ij}, and take a weighted average of the surrounding points. The values in the kernel are the weights. For example, for $n = m = 1$, we can average each pixel with its four surrounding neighbors using the 3×3 kernel:

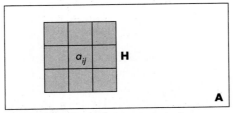

Figure 10.35 Filtering and convolution.

$$\mathbf{H} = \tfrac{1}{5} \begin{bmatrix} 0 & 1 & 0 \\ 1 & 1 & 1 \\ 0 & 1 & 0 \end{bmatrix}.$$

This filter can be used for antialiasing. We can use more points and weigh the center more heavily with

$$\mathbf{H} = \tfrac{1}{16} \begin{bmatrix} 1 & 2 & 1 \\ 2 & 4 & 2 \\ 1 & 2 & 1 \end{bmatrix}.$$

Note that we must define a border around **A** if we want **B** to have the same dimensions. Other operations are possible with small kernels. For example, we use the kernel

$$\mathbf{H} = \begin{bmatrix} 0 & -1 & 0 \\ -1 & 4 & -1 \\ 0 & -1 & 0 \end{bmatrix},$$

to detect changes in value or edges in the image. If a kernel is $k \times k$, we can implement a filter by accumulating k^2 images in the accumulation buffer, each time adding in a shifted version of **A** using a different filter coefficient in glAccum.

We can also use the accumulation buffer for filtering in time and depth. For example, if we jitter an object and render it multiple times, leaving the positions of the other objects unchanged, we get dimmer copies of the jittered object in the final image. If the object is moved along a path, rather than randomly jittered, we see the trail of the object. This **motion-blur** effect is similar to the result of taking a photograph of a moving object using a long exposure time. We can adjust the constant in glAccum so as to render the final position of the object with greater opacity, or to create the impression of speed differences. Note that, if we render the moving objects first in their final positions, and then successively in their previous positions, we will create a fading trail after the moving objects in the final image.

We can use filtering in depth to create focusing effects. A real camera cannot produce an image with all objects in focus. Objects within a certain distance from the camera, the camera's **depth of field**, are in focus: objects outside of it

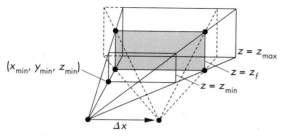

Figure 10.36 Depth-of-field jitter.

are out of focus and appear blurred. Computer graphics produces images with an infinite depth of field because we do not have to worry about the limitations of real lenses. Occasionally, however, we want to create an image that looks as though it were produced by a real camera, or to defocus part of a scene so as to emphasize the objects within a desired depth of field. Once more, we can use the accumulation buffer. This time, the trick is to move the viewer in a manner that leaves a plane fixed, as shown in Figure 10.36. Suppose that we wish to keep the plane at $z = z_f$ in focus, and to leave the near ($z = z_{min}$) and far ($z = z_{max}$) clipping distances unchanged. If we use glFrustum, we specify the near clipping rectangle ($x_{min}, x_{max}, y_{min}, y_{max}$). If we move the viewer from the origin in the x direction by Δx, we must change x_{min} to

$$x'_{min} = x_{min} + \frac{\Delta x}{z_f}(z_f - z_{near}).$$

Similar equations hold for x_{max}, y_{min}, and y_{max}. As we increase Δx and Δy, we create a narrower depth of field.

10.10 Sampling and Aliasing

We have seen a variety of applications in which the conversion from a continuous representation of an entity to a discrete approximation of that entity leads to visible errors in the display. We have used the term *aliasing* to characterize these errors. When we work with buffers, we are always working with digital images and, if we are not careful, these errors can be extreme. In this final section, we shall examine the nature of digital images, and shall gather facts that will help us to understand where aliasing errors arise and how the effects of these errors can be mitigated.

We start with a continuous two-dimensional image $f(x, y)$. We can regard the value of f as either a gray level in a monochromatic image, or the value of one of the primaries in a color image. In the computer, we work with a digital image that is an array of nm pixels arranged as n rows of m pixels. Each pixel has k bits. There are two processes involved in going from a continuous

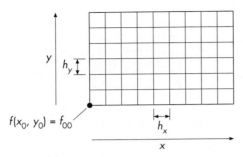

Figure 10.37 Sampling.

image to a discrete image. First, we must **sample** the continuous image at nm points on some grid to obtain a set of values $\{f_{ij}\}$. Each of these samples of the continuous image is the value of f measured over a small area in the continuous image. Then, we must convert each of these samples into a k-bit pixel by a process known as **quantization.**

10.10.1 Sampling Theory

Suppose that we have a rectangular grid of locations where we wish to obtain our samples of f, as in Figure 10.37. If we assume that the grid is equally spaced, then an ideal sampler would produce a value

$$f_{ij} = f(x_0 + ih_x, y_0 + jh_y),$$

where h_x and h_y are the distances between the grid points in the x and y directions, respectively. Leaving aside for now the fact that no real sampler can make such a precise measurement, there are two important issues. First, what errors have we made in this idealized sampling process? That is, how much of the information in the original image is included in the sampled image? Second, can we go back from the digital image to a continuous image without incurring additional errors? This latter step is called **reconstruction** and describes display processes such as are required in displaying the contents of a frame buffer on the screen of a CRT.

The mathematical analysis of these issues uses Fourier analysis, a branch of applied mathematics particularly well suited for explaining problems of digital signal processing. The essence of Fourier theory is that a function, of either space or time, can be decomposed into a set of sinusoids, at possibly an infinite number of frequencies. This concept is most familiar with sound, where we routinely think of a particular sound in terms of its frequency components or **spectrum**. For a two-dimensional image, we can think of it as being composed of sinusoidal patterns in two spatial frequencies that, when added together, produce the image. Figure 10.38(a) shows a one-dimensional function and (b) shows the two sinusoids that form it; Figure 10.39 shows two-dimensional

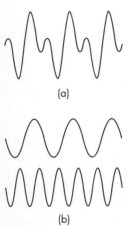

(a)

(b)

Figure 10.38 One-dimensional decomposition. (a) Function. (b) Components.

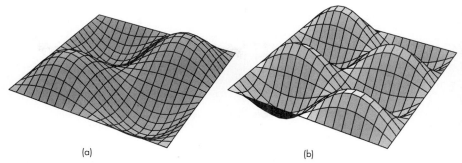

Figure 10.39 Two-dimensional periodic functions.

periodic functions. Thus, every two-dimensional spatial function $f(x, y)$ has two equivalent representations. One is its spatial form $f(x, y)$; the other is a representation in terms of its spectrum—the frequency-domain representation $g(\xi, \eta)$. By using these alternate representations of functions, we find that many phenomena, including sampling, can be explained much more easily in the frequency domain.

We can explain the consequences of sampling, without being overwhelmed by the mathematics, if we accept, without proof, the fundamental theorem known as the Nyquist sampling theorem. There are two parts to the theorem: the first will allow us to discuss sampling errors, whereas the second governs reconstruction. We shall examine the second in Section 10.10.2.

> **Nyquist sampling theorem (part 1):** The ideal samples of a continuous function contain all the information in the original function if and only if the continuous function is sampled at a frequency at least twice the highest frequency in the function.

Thus, if we are to have any chance of not losing information, we must restrict ourselves to functions that are zero in the frequency domain except in a window of width at least equal to the sampling frequency, centered at the origin. The highest frequency that can be in the data and avoid aliasing—one-half of the sampling frequency—is called the **Nyquist frequency**. Functions whose spectra are zero outside of some window are known as **band-limited** functions. For a two-dimensional image, the sampling frequencies are determined by the spacing of a two-dimensional grid with x and y spacing of $1/h_x$ and $1/h_y$, respectively. The theorem assumes an ideal sampling process that gathers an infinite number of samples, each of which is the exact value at the grid point. In practice, we can take only a finite number of samples—the number matching the resolution of our buffer. Consequently, we cannot produce a truly band-limited function. Although this result is a mathematical consequence of Fourier theory, we can observe that there will always be some ambiguity inherent in a

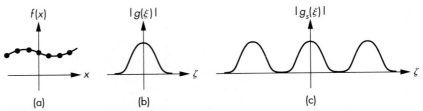

Figure 10.40 Band-limited function. (a) Function and its samples in the spatial domain. (b) Spectrum of the function. (c) Spectrum of the samples.

finite collection of sampled points, simply because we do not know the function outside the region from which we obtained the samples.[7]

The consequences of violating the Nyquist criteria are aliasing errors. We can see from where the name *aliasing* comes by considering an ideal sampling process. Both the original function and its set of samples have frequency-domain representations. The spectral components of the sampled function are replicas of the spectrum of the original function, with their centers separated by the sampling frequency. Consider the one-dimensional function in Figure 10.40(a), with the samples indicated. In Figure 10.40(b) is its spectrum; in Figure 10.40(c), we have the spectrum of the sampled function, showing the replications of the spectrum in Figure 10.40(b).[8] Because we have sampled at a rate higher than the Nyquist frequency, there is a separation between the replicas. Now consider the case in Figure 10.41. Here, we have violated the Nyquist criteria, and the replicas overlap. Consider the central part of the plot, which is magnified in Figure 10.42 and shows only the central replica, centered at the origin, and the replica to its right, centered at ξ_s. The frequency ξ_0 is above the Nyquist frequency $\xi_s/2$. There is, however, a replica of ξ_0, generated by the sampling process from the replica on the right, at $\xi_s - \xi_0$, a frequency less than the Nyquist frequency. The energy at this frequency can be heard, if we are dealing with digital sound, and seen, if we are considering two-dimensional images. We say that the frequency ξ_0 has an **alias** at $\xi_s - \xi_0$. Note that, once aliasing has occurred, we cannot distinguish between information that was at a frequency in the original data and information that was placed at this frequency by the sampling process.

We can demonstrate aliasing and ambiguity without using Fourier analysis by looking at a single sinusoid, as shown in Figure 10.43. If we sample this sinusoid at twice its frequency, we can recover it from two samples. However,

---

[7] This statement assumes no knowledge of the underlying function f, other than a set of its samples. If we have additional information, such as knowledge that the function is periodic, knowledge of the function over a finite interval can be sufficient to determine the entire function.

[8] We show the magnitude of the spectrum because the Fourier transform produces complex numbers for the frequency-domain components.

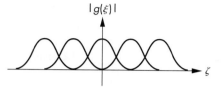

Figure 10.41 Overlapping replicas.

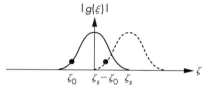

Figure 10.42 Aliasing.

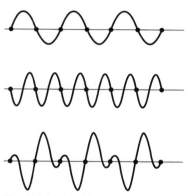

Figure 10.43 Aliasing of sinusoid.

these same two samples are samples of a sinusoid of twice this frequency, and can also be samples of sinusoids of other multiples of the basic frequency. All these frequencies are aliases of the same original frequency. However, if we know that the data were band limited, then the samples can only describe the original sinusoid.

If we were to do an analysis of the frequency content of real-world images, we would find that the spectral components of most images are concentrated in the lower frequencies. Consequently, although it is impossible to construct a finite-sized image that is band limited, the aliasing errors often will be minimal, because there is little content in frequencies above the Nyquist frequency, and little content is aliased into frequencies below the Nyquist frequency. The exceptions to this statement arise when there is regular (periodic) information in

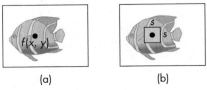

(a)   (b)

Figure 10.44 Scanning an image. (a) Point sampling. (b) Area averaging.

the continuous image. In the frequency representation, regularity places most of the information at a few frequencies. If any of these frequencies is above the Nyquist limit, the aliasing effect is noticeable as beat or moiré patterns. Some examples that you might have noticed include the patterns that appear on video displays from people wearing striped shirts or plaid ties, and wavy patterns that arise both in printed (halftoned) figures derived from computer displays and in digital images of farmland with plowed fields.

Often, we can minimize aliasing by prefiltering before we scan an image, or by controlling the area of the data that the scanner uses to measure a sample. Figure 10.44 shows two possible ways to scan an image. In Figure 10.44(a), we see an ideal scanner. It measures the value of a continuous image at a point, so the samples are given by

$$f_{ij} = f(x_i, y_i).$$

On the right, we have a more realistic scanner that obtains samples by taking a weighted average over a small interval to produce samples of the form

$$f_{ij} = \int_{x_i-s/2}^{x_i+s/2} \int_{y_i-s/2}^{y_i+s/2} f(x, y)w(x, y)dydx.$$

By selecting the size of the window, s, and the weighting function w, we can attenuate high-frequency components in the image, and thus can reduce aliasing. Fortunately, real scanners must take measurements over a finite region, called the **sampling aperture**; thus, some antialiasing takes place even if the user has no understanding of the aliasing problem.

10.10.2 Reconstruction

Suppose that we have an (infinite) set of samples, the members of which have been sampled at least at the Nyquist frequency. The reconstruction of a continuous function from the samples is based on part 2 of the Nyquist sampling theorem.

Nyquist sampling theorem (part 2): We can reconstruct a continuous function $f(x)$ from its samples $\{f_i\}$ by the formula

$$f(x, y) = \sum_{i=-\infty}^{\infty} f_i \mathrm{sinc}(x - x_i).$$

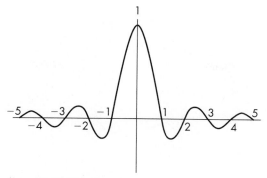

Figure 10.45 Sinc function.

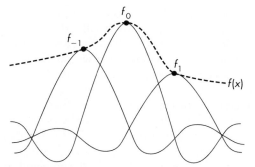

Figure 10.46 One-dimensional reconstruction.

The function sinc(x) is defined as (Figure 10.45)

$$\text{sinc}(x) = \frac{\sin \pi x}{\pi x}.$$

The two-dimensional version of the reconstruction formula for a function $f(x, y)$ with ideal samples $\{f_{ij}\}$ is

$$f(x, y) = \sum_{i=-\infty}^{\infty} \sum_{j=-\infty}^{\infty} f_{ij}\text{sinc}(x - x_i)\text{sinc}(y - y_j).$$

These formulas follow from the fact that we can recover an unaliased function in the frequency domain by using a filter that is zero except in the interval $(-\xi_s/2, \xi_s/2)$—a low-pass filter—to obtain a single replica from the infinite number of replicas generated by the sampling process shown in Figure 10.40. The reconstruction of a one-dimensional function appears as shown in Figure 10.46. In two dimensions, the reconstruction involves using a two-dimensional sinc, as shown in Figure 10.47. Unfortunately, the sinc function

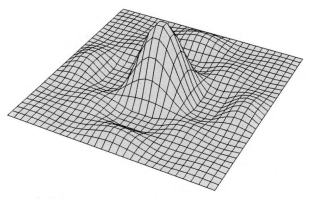

Figure 10.47 Two-dimensional sinc function.

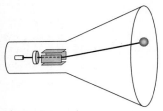

Figure 10.48 CRT display.

cannot be produced in a physical display, due to its negative side lobes. Consider the display problem for a CRT display. We start with a digital image that is a set of samples. For each sample, we can place a spot of light centered at a grid point on the display surface, as shown in Figure 10.48. The value of the sample controls the intensity of the spot, or modulates the beam. We can control the shape of the spot by using techniques such as focusing the beam. The reconstruction formula tells us that the beam should have the shape of a two-dimensional sinc, but because the beam puts out energy, the spot must be nonnegative at all points. Consequently, the display process must make errors. We can evaluate a real display by considering how well its spot approximates the desired sinc. Figure 10.49 shows the sinc and several one-dimensional approximations. The Gaussian-shaped spot corresponds to the shape of many CRT spots, whereas the rectangular spot might correspond to an LCD display with square pixels. Note that we can make either approximation wider or narrower. If we analyze the spot profiles in the frequency domain, we find that the wider spots are more accurate at low frequencies, but are less accurate at higher frequencies. In practice, the spot size that we choose is a compromise. Visible differences across monitors often can be traced to different spot profiles.

10.10.3 Quantization

The mathematical analysis of sampling explains a number of important effects. However, we have not included the effect of each sample being quantized into

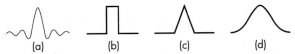

Figure 10.49 Display spots. (a) Ideal spot. (b) Rectangular approximation. (c) Piecewise-linear approximation. (d) Gaussian approximation.

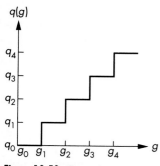

Figure 10.50 Quantizer.

k discrete levels. Given a scalar function g with values in the range

$$g_{min} \leq g \leq g_{max},$$

a **quantizer** is a function q such that, if $g_i \leq g \leq g_{i+1}$,

$$q(g) = q_i.$$

Thus, for each value of g, we assign it one of k values, as shown in Figure 10.50. In general, designing a quantizer involves choosing the $\{q_i\}$, the quantization levels, and the $\{g_i\}$, the threshold values. If we know the probability distribution for g, $p(g)$, we can solve for the values that minimize the mean square error:

$$e = \int (g - q(g))^2 p(g) dg.$$

However, we often design quantizers based on the perceptual issues that we discussed in Chapter 1. A simple rule of thumb is that we should not be able to detect one-level changes, but should be able to detect all two-level changes. Given the threshold for the visual system to detect a change in luminance, we usually need at least 7 or 8 bits (or 128 to 256 levels). We should also consider the logarithmic intensity-brightness response of humans. To do so, we usually distribute the levels exponentially, to give approximately equal perceptual errors as we go from one level to the next.

10.11   Summary

In the early days of computer graphics, people worked with only three-dimensional geometric objects, whereas those people who were involved with only two-dimensional images were considered to be working in image processing. Advances in hardware have made graphics and image-processing systems practically indistinguishable. For those people involved with synthesizing images—certainly a major part of computer graphics—this merging of fields has brought forth a plethora of new techniques. The idea that a two-dimensional image or texture can be mapped to a three-dimensional surface in no more time than it takes to render the surface with constant shading would have been unthinkable a few years ago. Now, these techniques are routine.

Techniques such as texture mapping have had an enormous impact on real-time graphics. In fields such as animation, virtual reality, and scientific visualization, we use hardware texture mappping to add detail to images without burdening the geometric pipeline. The use of compositing techniques, through the accumulation buffer and the alpha channel, allows the application programmer to perform tasks, such as antialiasing, and to create effects, such as fog and depth of field, that until recently were done on different types of architectures, after the graphics had been created.

In this chapter, we have concentrated on those techniques that are supported by recently available hardware and APIs. Not only are many of the techniques that we have introduced here new, but also many more are just appearing in the literature; even more remain to be discovered.

10.12   Suggested Readings

Bump mapping was first suggested by Blinn [Bli77]. Environmental mapping was developed by Blinn and Newell [Bli76]. Texture mapping was first used by Catmull; see the review by Heckbert [Hec86]. Hardware support for texture mapping came with the SGI Reality Engine; see Akeley [Ake93]. Perlin and Hoffert [Per89] designed a noise function to generate two- and three-dimensional texture maps.

The aliasing problem in computer graphics has been of importance since the advent of raster graphics; see Crow [Cro81]. The first concerns were with rasterization of lines, but later other forms of aliasing arose with animations [Mag85] and ray tracing [Gla89]. The image-processing books [Pra78, Gon87, Cas96] provide an introduction to signal processing and aliasing in two dimensions.

Direct methods for volume rendering are discussed in [Wat93, Lev88, Wes90]. See [Dre88] for a discussion of the color and opacity assignment problem.

Many of the compositing techniques, including use of the α channel, were suggested by Porter and Duff [Por84]. The *OpenGL Programmer's Guide* [Ope93a] contains many examples of how buffers can be used.

Exercises

10.1   Show how you can use the exclusive or writing mode to implement the odd–even fill algorithm.

10.2   What are the visual effects of using XOR to move a cursor around on the screen?

10.3   In what ways is an image produced with an environmental map different from a ray-traced image of the same scene?

10.4   In the movies and television, the wheels of cars and wagons often appear to be spinning in the wrong direction. What causes the effect? Can anything be done to fix this problem? Explain your answer.

10.5   We can attempt to display sampled data by simply plotting the points and letting the human visual system merge the points into shapes. Why is this technique dangerous if the data are close to the Nyquist limit?

10.6   Why do the patterns of striped shirts and ties change as an actor moves across the screen of your television?

10.7 Why should we do antialiasing by preprocessing the data, rather than by postprocessing them?

10.8 Suppose that we have two translucent surfaces characterized by opacities α_1 and α_2. What is the opacity of the translucent material that we create by using the two in series? Give an expression for the transparency of the combined material.

10.9 Assume that we view translucent surfaces as filters of light passing through them. Develop a blending model based on the complementary colors CMY.

10.10 In Section 10.8, we used $1 - \alpha$ and α for the destination and source blending factors, respectively. What would be the visual difference if we used 1 for the destination factor, and kept α for the source factor?

10.11 Add paintbrushes that add color gradually to image in the paint program in Chapter 3. Also use blending to add erasers that gradually remove images from the screen.

10.12 Devise a method of using texture mapping for the display of voxel data.

10.13 Show how to use the luminance histogram of an image to derive a lookup table that will make the altered image have a flat histogram.

10.14 When we supersample a scene using jitter, why should we use a random jitter pattern?

A Sample Programs

This appendix contains the complete programs that we developed in the text. These programs are also available via anonymous ftp from `ftp.cs.unm.edu` under the directory `/pub/angel`. A makefile that should work on most UNIX implementations is also available there, as are additional sample programs. Other examples, including those in the *OpenGL Programmer's Guide*, and GLUT can be obtained starting from the OpenGL World–Wide–Web home page (`http://www.sgi.com/Technology/OpenGL/`).

OpenGL is provided with all Silicon Graphics workstations and with Microsoft Windows NT. Sources of OpenGL for other systems are contained in the OpenGL home page. There are versions available for most UNIX workstations, Windows, OS/2, and the Macintosh—either through the manufacturers or through third-party suppliers, such as Portable Graphics and Template Graphics. There is a LINUX version available from Portable Graphics. There are two free versions available over the Internet: MESA, that can be run on most systems, and SGI's CosmoGL for Windows; see the OpenGL home page.

The programs that follow use the GLUT library for interfacing with the window system. The naming of the functions follow the *OpenGL Programmer's Guide* and the *GLUT Users Guide*. These programs share much of the same code. You should find functions, such as the reshape callback, the initialization function, and the `main` function, almost identical across the programs. Consequently, only the first instance of each function contains extensive comments.

In all these programs, illustration of graphical principles, other than efficiency, was the most important design criteria. You should find numerous ways both to extend these programs and to make them run more efficiently. In some instances, the same visual results can be generated in a completely different manner, using OpenGL capabilities other than the ones we used in the sample program.

The programs include:

1. A program that generates 5000 points on the Sierpinski gasket from Section 2.7
2. A program that illustrates the use of mouse with GLUT, as discussed in Section 3.5
3. The simple paint program that we developed in Section 3.8
4. The rotating-cube program from Section 4.9
5. The walk-through program from Section 5.6
6. The program that generates approximations to a sphere by recursive subdivision generation from Section 6.6
7. A program that moves the simple robot from Section 8.3
8. A program that moves the figure from Section 8.4
9. A program that generates approximations to the Utah teapot by recursive subdivision as discussed in Section 9.10
10. A program that generates approximations to the Mandelbrot set as discussed in Section 10.7

A.1   Sierpinski Gasket Program

```
/* The Sierpinski gasket is defined recursively as follows:
Start with three vertices in the plane that define a triangle.
Pick a  random point inside the triangle.
Select any of the vertices of the triangle.
Plot the point halfway between the random point and the
randomly chosen vertex.
Iterate with this point as the new starting point. */

/*This program computes 5000 points in response to display
callback issued when window opened
After computing points program sits in wait loop */

#include <GL/glut.h>


void myinit(void)
{

/* attributes */

    glClearColor(1.0, 1.0, 1.0, 1.0); /* white background */
    glColor3f(1.0, 0.0, 0.0); /* draw in red */
```

```
/* set up viewing */
/* 500 x 500 window with origin lower left */

    glMatrixMode(GL_PROJECTION);
    glLoadIdentity();
    gluOrtho2D(0.0, 500.0, 0.0, 500.0);
    glMatrixMode(GL_MODELVIEW);
}

void display( void )
{

/* define a point data type */

    typedef GLfloat point2[2];

    point2 vertices[3]={{0.0,.0},{25.0,50.00},{50.0,0.0}};
    /* Atriangle */

    int i, j, k;
    long random();          /* standard random number generator */
    point2 p ={75.0,50.0};  /* An arbitrary initial point */

    glClear(GL_COLOR_BUFFER_BIT);  /*clear the window */


/* computes and plots 5000 new points */

    for( k=0; k<5000; k++)
    {
       j=random()%3; /* pick a vertex at random */


       /* Compute point halfway between vertex and old point */

       p[0] = (p[0]+vertices[j][0])/2.0;
       p[1] = (p[1]+vertices[j][1])/2.0;

       /* plot new point */

         glBegin(GL_POINTS);
```

```
                    glVertex2fv(p);
               glEnd();


          }
          glFlush(); /* clear buffers */
     }

void main(int argc, char** argv)
{

/* Standard GLUT initialization */

     glutInit(&argc,argv);
     glutInitDisplayMode (GLUT_SINGLE | GLUT_RGB);
     /* default, not needed */
     glutInitWindowSize(500,500); /* 500 x 500 pixel window */
     glutInitWindowPosition(0,0); /* place window top left
                                     on display */
     glutCreateWindow("Sierpinski Gasket"); /* window title */
     glutDisplayFunc(display); /* display callback invoked
                                  when window opened */

     myinit(); /* set attributes */

     glutMainLoop(); /* enter event loop */
}
```

A.2   Square Drawing

```
/* This program illustrates the use of the glut library for
interfacing with a Window System */

/* The program opens a window, clears it to black,
then draws a box at the location of the mouse each time the
left button is clicked. The right button exits the program

The program also reacts correctly when the window is
moved or resized by clearing the new window to black */

#include <GL/glut.h>

/* globals */
```

```
GLsizei wh = 500, ww = 500; /* initial window size */
GLfloat size = 3.0;    /* half side length of square */


void drawSquare(int x, int y)
{

    y=wh-y;
    glColor3ub( (char) random()%256, (char) random()%256,
        (char) random()%256);
    glBegin(GL_POLYGON);
        glVertex2f(x+size, y+size);
        glVertex2f(x-size, y+size);
        glVertex2f(x-size, y-size);
        glVertex2f(x+size, y-size);
    glEnd();
    glFlush();
}


/* rehaping routine called whenever window is resized
or moved */

void myReshape(GLsizei w, GLsizei h)
{

/* adjust clipping box */

    glMatrixMode(GL_PROJECTION);
    glLoadIdentity();
    glOrtho(0.0, (GLdouble)w, 0.0, (GLdouble)h, -1.0, 1.0);
    glMatrixMode(GL_MODELVIEW);
    glLoadIdentity();

/* adjust viewport and clear */

    glViewport(0,0,w,h);
    glClearColor (0.0, 0.0, 0.0, 0.0);
    glClear(GL_COLOR_BUFFER_BIT);
    glFlush();

/* set global size for use by drawing routine */

    ww = w;
```

```
        wh = h;
}

void myinit(void)
{

    glViewport(0,0,ww,wh);

/* Pick 2D clipping window to match size of screen window
This choice avoids having to scale object coordinates
each time window is resized */

    glMatrixMode(GL_PROJECTION);
    glLoadIdentity();
    glOrtho(0.0, (GLdouble) ww, 0.0,
               (GLdouble) wh, -1.0, 1.0);

/* set clear color to black and clear window */

    glClearColor (0.0, 0.0, 0.0, 1.0);
    glClear(GL_COLOR_BUFFER_BIT);
    glFlush();



/* callback routine for reshape event */

    glutReshapeFunc(myReshape);

}

void mouse(int btn, int state, int x, int y)
{
    if(btn==GLUT_RIGHT_BUTTON && state==GLUT_DOWN)    exit();
}

void display(void) {}

int main(int argc, char** argv)
{

    glutInit(&argc,argv);
    glutInitDisplayMode (GLUT_SINGLE | GLUT_RGB);
    glutCreateWindow("square");
```

```
      myinit ();
      glutReshapeFunc (myReshape);
      glutMouseFunc (mouse);
      glutMotionFunc(drawSquare);
      glutDisplayFunc(display);

      glutMainLoop();

}
```

A.3   Paint Program

```
/* This program illustrates the use of the glut library for
interfacing with a window system */

/* Description of operation of program is in Chapter 3*/

#define NULL 0
#include <GL/glut.h>

void mouse(int, int, int, int);
void display(void);
void idle(void);
void drawSquare(int, int);
void myReshape(GLsizei, GLsizei);

void myinit(void);

void screen_box(int, int, int);
void right_menu(int);
void middle_menu(int);
void color_menu(int);
void pixel_menu(int);
void fill_menu(int);
long time(int);
int pick(int, int);

/* globals */

GLsizei wh = 500, ww = 500; /* initial window size */
GLfloat size = 3.0;    /* half side length of square */

int base; /* font list base */
```

```
long baset; /*time base */
GLfloat r = 1.0, g = 1.0, b = 1.0; /* drawing color */
int fill = 0; /* fill flag */



void drawSquare(int x, int y)
{

        y=wh-y;
        glColor3ub( (char) random()%256, (char) random()%256,
                    (char) random()%256);
        glBegin(GL_POLYGON);
                glVertex2f(x+size, y+size);
                glVertex2f(x-size, y+size);
                glVertex2f(x-size, y-size);
                glVertex2f(x+size, y-size);
        glEnd();
}


/* rehaping routine called whenever window is resized
or moved */

void myReshape(GLsizei w, GLsizei h)
{

/* adjust clipping box */

        glMatrixMode(GL_PROJECTION);
        glLoadIdentity();
        glOrtho(0.0, (GLdouble)w, 0.0, (GLdouble)h, -1.0, 1.0);
        glMatrixMode(GL_MODELVIEW);
        glLoadIdentity();

/* adjust viewport and  clear */

        glViewport(0,0,w,h);
    glClearColor (1.0, 1.0, 1.0, 1.0);
        glClear(GL_COLOR_BUFFER_BIT);
        display();
        glFlush();

/* set global size for use by drawing routine */
```

```
            ww = w;
            wh = h;
}

void myinit(void)
{

/* set up a font in display list */
    int i;
baset = time(0);
        base = glGenLists(128);
    for(i=0;i<128;i++)
                {
                glNewList(base+i, GL_COMPILE);
                glutBitmapCharacter(GLUT_BITMAP_9_BY_15, i);
                glEndList();
        }
        glListBase(base);

        glViewport(0,0,ww,wh);

/* Pick 2D clipping window to match size of X window
This choice avoids having to scale object coordinates
each time window is resized */

        glMatrixMode(GL_PROJECTION);
        glLoadIdentity();
        glOrtho(0.0, (GLdouble) ww, 0.0,
                    (GLdouble) wh, -1.0, 1.0);

/* set clear color to black and clear window */

        glClearColor (0.0, 0.0, 0.0, 1.0);
        glClear(GL_COLOR_BUFFER_BIT);
        glFlush();
}

void mouse(int btn, int state, int x, int y)
{
    static int draw_mode = 0; /* drawing mode */
    static int count;
    int where;
```

```
static int xp[2],yp[2];
if(btn==GLUT_LEFT_BUTTON && state==GLUT_DOWN)
{
    glPushAttrib(GL_ALL_ATTRIB_BITS);
    glutIdleFunc(NULL);

    where = pick(x,y);
    glColor3f(r, g, b);
    if(where != 0)
    {
        count = 0;
        draw_mode = where;
    }
    else if(draw_mode == 1 && count == 0)
    {
            count = 1;
            xp[0] = x;
            yp[0] = y;
    }
    else if(draw_mode == 1 && count != 0)
    {
            glBegin(GL_LINES);
                glVertex2i(x,wh-y);
                glVertex2i(xp[0],wh-yp[0]);
            glEnd();
            draw_mode=0;
            count=0;
    }
    else if(draw_mode == 2 && count == 0)
    {
            count = 1;
            xp[0] = x;
            yp[0] = y;
    }
    else if(draw_mode == 2 && count != 0)
    {
            if(fill) glBegin(GL_POLYGON);
            else glBegin(GL_LINE_LOOP);
                glVertex2i(x,wh-y);
                glVertex2i(x,wh-yp[0]);
                glVertex2i(xp[0],wh-yp[0]);
                glVertex2i(xp[0],wh-y);
            glEnd();
            draw_mode=0;
```

```
                                count=0;
                        }
                        else if(draw_mode == 3 && count == 0)
                        {
                                count = 1;
                                xp[0] = x;
                                yp[0] = y;
                        }
                        else if(draw_mode == 3 && count == 1)
                        {
                                count = 2;
                                xp[1] = x;
                                yp[1] = y;
                        }
                        else if(draw_mode == 3 && count == 2)
                        {
                                if(fill) glBegin(GL_POLYGON);
                                else glBegin(GL_LINE_LOOP);
                                    glVertex2i(xp[0],wh-yp[0]);
                                    glVertex2i(xp[1],wh-yp[1]);
                                    glVertex2i(x,wh-y);
                                glEnd();
                                draw_mode=0;
                                count=0;
                        }
                        else if(draw_mode == 4 )
                        {
                            drawSquare(x,y);
                            count++;
                        }

                        glutIdleFunc(idle);
                        glPopAttrib();
                        glFlush();
                }
        }

        int pick(int x, int y)
        {
            y = wh - y;
            if(y < wh-ww/10) return 0;
            else if(x < ww/10) return 1;
            else if(x < ww/5) return 2;
            else if(x < 3*ww/10) return 3;
```

```
        else if(x < 2*ww/5) return 4;
        else return 0;
}

void screen_box(int x, int y, int s )
{
    glBegin(GL_QUADS);
      glVertex2i(x, y);
      glVertex2i(x+s, y);
      glVertex2i(x+s, y+s);
      glVertex2i(x, y+s);
    glEnd();
}

void idle(void)
{

    char out[]="00:00:00";
    long t, time();
    int min, sec, hr;


    glPushAttrib(GL_ALL_ATTRIB_BITS);
    t=time(0)-baset;
    hr=t/3600;
    min = (t - 3600*hr) /60;
    sec = (t - 3600*hr - 60*min);
    hr = hr%24;
    out[0]='0'+hr/10;
    out[1]='0'+hr%10;
    out[3]='0'+min/10;
    out[4]='0'+min%10;
    out[6]='0'+sec/10;
    out[7]='0'+sec%10;
    glRasterPos2i(ww-80, wh-15);
    glColor3f(0.0,0.0,0.0);
    glBegin(GL_QUADS);
        glVertex2i(ww-80, wh-15);
        glVertex2i(ww, wh-15);
        glVertex2i(ww, wh);
        glVertex2i(ww-80, wh);
    glEnd();
    glColor3f(1.0,1.0,1.0);
    glCallLists( strlen(out) , GL_BYTE, out);
```

```
      glFlush();
      glPopAttrib();
}

void right_menu(int id)
{
   glutIdleFunc(NULL);
   if(id == 1) exit();
   else display();
   glutIdleFunc(idle);
}

void middle_menu(int id)
{
   glutIdleFunc(NULL);
   glutIdleFunc(idle);

}

void color_menu(int id)
{
   glutIdleFunc(NULL);
   if(id == 1) {r = 1.0; g = 0.0; b = 0.0;}
   else if(id == 2) {r = 0.0; g = 1.0; b = 0.0;}
   else if(id == 3) {r = 0.0; g = 0.0; b = 1.0;}
   else if(id == 4) {r = 0.0; g = 1.0; b = 1.0;}
   else if(id == 5) {r = 1.0; g = 0.0; b = 1.0;}
   else if(id == 6) {r = 1.0; g = 1.0; b = 0.0;}
   else if(id == 7) {r = 1.0; g = 1.0; b = 1.0;}
   else if(id == 8) {r = 0.0; g = 0.0; b = 0.0;}
   glutIdleFunc(idle);
}


void pixel_menu(int id)
{
   glutIdleFunc(NULL);
   if (id == 1) size = 2 * size;
   else if (size > 1) size = size/2;
   glutIdleFunc(idle);
}

void fill_menu(int id)
{
```

```
        glutIdleFunc(NULL);
        if (id == 1) fill = 1;
        else fill = 0;
        glutIdleFunc(idle);
    }

void display(void)
{
    glPushAttrib(GL_ALL_ATTRIB_BITS);
    glutIdleFunc(NULL);
    glClearColor (0.0, 0.0, 0.0, 1.0);
    glClear(GL_COLOR_BUFFER_BIT);
    glColor3f(1.0, 1.0, 1.0);
    screen_box(0,wh-ww/10,ww/10);
    glColor3f(1.0, 0.0, 0.0);
    screen_box(ww/10,wh-ww/10,ww/10);
    glColor3f(0.0, 1.0, 0.0);
    screen_box(ww/5,wh-ww/10,ww/10);
    glColor3f(0.0, 0.0, 1.0);
    screen_box(3*ww/10,wh-ww/10,ww/10);
    glColor3f(0.0, 0.0, 0.0);
    screen_box(ww/10+ww/40,wh-ww/10+ww/40,ww/20);
    glBegin(GL_LINES);
        glVertex2i(wh/40,wh-ww/20);
        glVertex2i(wh/40+ww/20,wh-ww/20);
    glEnd();
    glBegin(GL_TRIANGLES);
        glVertex2i(ww/5+ww/40,wh-ww/10+ww/40);
        glVertex2i(ww/5+ww/20,wh-ww/40);
        glVertex2i(ww/5+3*ww/40,wh-ww/10+ww/40);
    glEnd();
    glPointSize(3.0);
    glBegin(GL_POINTS);
        glVertex2i(3*ww/10+ww/20, wh-ww/20);
    glEnd();
    glutIdleFunc(idle);
    glFlush();
    glPopAttrib();
}


int main(int argc, char** argv)
{
    int c_menu, p_menu, f_menu;
```

```
    glutInit(&argc,argv);
    glutInitDisplayMode (GLUT_SINGLE | GLUT_RGB);
    glutCreateWindow("square");
    glutDisplayFunc(display);
    c_menu = glutCreateMenu(color_menu);
    glutAddMenuEntry("Red",1);
    glutAddMenuEntry("Green",2);
    glutAddMenuEntry("Blue",3);
    glutAddMenuEntry("Cyan",4);
    glutAddMenuEntry("Magenta",5);
    glutAddMenuEntry("Yellow",6);
    glutAddMenuEntry("White",7);
    glutAddMenuEntry("Black",8);
    p_menu = glutCreateMenu(pixel_menu);
    glutAddMenuEntry("increase pixel size", 1);
    glutAddMenuEntry("decrease pixel size", 2);
    f_menu = glutCreateMenu(fill_menu);
    glutAddMenuEntry("fill on", 1);
    glutAddMenuEntry("fill off", 2);
    glutCreateMenu(right_menu);
    glutAddMenuEntry("quit",1);
    glutAddMenuEntry("clear",2);
    glutAttachMenu(GLUT_RIGHT_BUTTON);
    glutCreateMenu(middle_menu);
    glutAddSubMenu("Colors", c_menu);
    glutAddSubMenu("Pixel Size", p_menu);
    glutAddSubMenu("Fill", f_menu);
    glutAttachMenu(GLUT_MIDDLE_BUTTON);
    myinit ();
    glutReshapeFunc (myReshape);
    glutMouseFunc (mouse);
    glutIdleFunc(idle);
    glutMainLoop();

}
```

A.4   **Rotating-Cube Program**

```
/* Rotating cube with color interpolation */

/* Demonstration of use of homogeneous coordinate
transformations and simple data structure for representing
cube from Chapter 4 */
```

```
/* Both normals and colors are assigned to the vertices */
/* Cube is centered at origin so (unnormalized) normals
are the same as the vertex values */

#include <stdlib.h>
#include <GL/glut.h>


GLfloat vertices[][3] = {{-1.0,-1.0,-1.0},{1.0,-1.0,-1.0},
{1.0,1.0,-1.0}, {-1.0,1.0,-1.0}, {-1.0,-1.0,1.0},
{1.0,-1.0,1.0}, {1.0,1.0,1.0}, {-1.0,1.0,1.0}};

GLfloat normals[][3] = {{-1.0,-1.0,-1.0},{1.0,-1.0,-1.0},
{1.0,1.0,-1.0}, {-1.0,1.0,-1.0}, {-1.0,-1.0,1.0},
{1.0,-1.0,1.0}, {1.0,1.0,1.0}, {-1.0,1.0,1.0}};

GLfloat colors[][3] = {{0.0,0.0,0.0},{1.0,0.0,0.0},
{1.0,1.0,0.0}, {0.0,1.0,0.0}, {0.0,0.0,1.0},
{1.0,0.0,1.0}, {1.0,1.0,1.0}, {0.0,1.0,1.0}};

void polygon(int a, int b, int c , int d)
{


/* draw a polygon via list of vertices */

  glBegin(GL_POLYGON);
  glColor3fv(colors[a]);
  glNormal3fv(normals[a]);
  glVertex3fv(vertices[a]);
  glColor3fv(colors[b]);
  glNormal3fv(normals[b]);
  glVertex3fv(vertices[b]);
  glColor3fv(colors[c]);
  glNormal3fv(normals[c]);
  glVertex3fv(vertices[c]);
  glColor3fv(colors[d]);
  glNormal3fv(normals[d]);
  glVertex3fv(vertices[d]);
 glEnd();
                                 }


void colorcube(void)
{
```

```
/* map vertices to faces */

 polygon(0,3,2,1);
 polygon(2,3,7,6);
 polygon(0,4,7,3);
 polygon(1,2,6,5);
 polygon(4,5,6,7);
 polygon(0,1,5,4);
}

static GLfloat theta[] = {0.0,0.0,0.0};
static GLint axis = 2;

void display(void)
{
/* display callback, clear frame buffer and z buffer,
   rotate cube and draw, swap buffers */

 glClear(GL_COLOR_BUFFER_BIT | GL_DEPTH_BUFFER_BIT);
 glLoadIdentity();
 glRotatef(theta[0], 1.0, 0.0, 0.0);
 glRotatef(theta[1], 0.0, 1.0, 0.0);
 glRotatef(theta[2], 0.0, 0.0, 1.0);

 colorcube();

 glFlush();
 glutSwapBuffers();
}

void spinCube()
{

/* Idle callback, spin cube 2 degrees about selected axis */

 theta[axis] += 2.0;
 if( theta[axis] > 360.0 ) theta[axis] -= 360.0;
 display();
}

void mouse(int btn, int state, int x, int y)
{

/* mouse callback, selects an axis about which to rotate */
```

```
    if(btn==GLUT_LEFT_BUTTON && state == GLUT_DOWN) axis = 0;
    if(btn==GLUT_MIDDLE_BUTTON && state == GLUT_DOWN) axis = 1;
    if(btn==GLUT_RIGHT_BUTTON && state == GLUT_DOWN) axis = 2;
}

void myReshape(int w, int h)
{
    glViewport(0, 0, w, h);
    glMatrixMode(GL_PROJECTION);
    glLoadIdentity();
    if (w <= h)
        glOrtho(-2.0, 2.0, -2.0 * (GLfloat) h / (GLfloat) w,
            2.0 * (GLfloat) h / (GLfloat) w, -10.0, 10.0);
    else
        glOrtho(-2.0 * (GLfloat) w / (GLfloat) h,
            2.0 * (GLfloat) w / (GLfloat) h, -2.0, 2.0, -10.0,
10.0);
    glMatrixMode(GL_MODELVIEW);
}

void
main(int argc, char **argv)
{
    glutInit(&argc, argv);

/* need both double buffering and z buffer */

    glutInitDisplayMode(GLUT_DOUBLE | GLUT_RGB | GLUT_DEPTH);
    glutInitWindowSize(500, 500);
    glutCreateWindow("colorcube");
    glutReshapeFunc(myReshape);
    glutDisplayFunc(display);
    glutIdleFunc(spinCube);
    glutMouseFunc(mouse);
    glEnable(GL_DEPTH_TEST); /* Enable hidden--surface--removal
*/
    glutMainLoop();
}
```

A.5   Moving Viewer

```
/* Rotating cube with viewer movement from Chapter 5 */
/* Cube definition and display similar to rotating-cube
program */
```

```
/* We use the Lookat function in the display callback to point
the viewer, whose position can be altered by the x, X, y, Y, z,
and Z keys.
The perspective view is set in the reshape callback */

#include <stdlib.h>
#include <GL/glut.h>


  GLfloat vertices[][3] = {{-1.0,-1.0,-1.0},{1.0,-1.0,-1.0},
  {1.0,1.0,-1.0}, {-1.0,1.0,-1.0}, {-1.0,-1.0,1.0},
  {1.0,-1.0,1.0}, {1.0,1.0,1.0}, {-1.0,1.0,1.0}};

  GLfloat normals[][3] = {{-1.0,-1.0,-1.0},{1.0,-1.0,-1.0},
  {1.0,1.0,-1.0}, {-1.0,1.0,-1.0}, {-1.0,-1.0,1.0},
  {1.0,-1.0,1.0}, {1.0,1.0,1.0}, {-1.0,1.0,1.0}};

  GLfloat colors[][3] = {{0.0,0.0,0.0},{1.0,0.0,0.0},
  {1.0,1.0,0.0}, {0.0,1.0,0.0}, {0.0,0.0,1.0},
  {1.0,0.0,1.0}, {1.0,1.0,1.0}, {0.0,1.0,1.0}};

void polygon(int a, int b, int c , int d)
{
 glBegin(GL_POLYGON);
  glColor3fv(colors[a]);
  glNormal3fv(normals[a]);
  glVertex3fv(vertices[a]);
  glColor3fv(colors[b]);
  glNormal3fv(normals[b]);
  glVertex3fv(vertices[b]);
  glColor3fv(colors[c]);
  glNormal3fv(normals[c]);
  glVertex3fv(vertices[c]);
  glColor3fv(colors[d]);
  glNormal3fv(normals[d]);
  glVertex3fv(vertices[d]);
 glEnd();
}

void colorcube()
{
 polygon(0,3,2,1);
 polygon(2,3,7,6);
 polygon(0,4,7,3);
 polygon(1,2,6,5);
```

```
  polygon(4,5,6,7);
  polygon(0,1,5,4);
}

static GLfloat theta[] = {0.0,0.0,0.0};
static GLint axis = 2;
static GLdouble viewer[]= {0.0, 0.0, 5.0}; /* initial viewer
                                                   location */

void display(void)
{

  glClear(GL_COLOR_BUFFER_BIT | GL_DEPTH_BUFFER_BIT);

/* Update viewer position in modelview matrix */

  glLoadIdentity();
  gluLookAt(viewer[0],viewer[1],viewer[2], 0.0, 0.0, 0.0,
                                          0.0, 1.0, 0.0);

/* rotate cube */

  glRotatef(theta[0], 1.0, 0.0, 0.0);
  glRotatef(theta[1], 0.0, 1.0, 0.0);
  glRotatef(theta[2], 0.0, 0.0, 1.0);

  colorcube();

  glFlush();
  glutSwapBuffers();
}

void mouse(int btn, int state, int x, int y)
{
  if(btn==GLUT_LEFT_BUTTON && state == GLUT_DOWN) axis = 0;
  if(btn==GLUT_MIDDLE_BUTTON && state == GLUT_DOWN) axis = 1;
  if(btn==GLUT_RIGHT_BUTTON && state == GLUT_DOWN) axis = 2;
  theta[axis] += 2.0;
  if( theta[axis] > 360.0 ) theta[axis] -= 360.0;
  display();
}

void keys(unsigned char key, int x, int y)
{
```

```
/* Use x, X, y, Y, z, and Z keys to move viewer */

    if(key == 'x') viewer[0]-= 1.0;
    if(key == 'X') viewer[0]+= 1.0;
    if(key == 'y') viewer[1]-= 1.0;
    if(key == 'Y') viewer[1]+= 1.0;
    if(key == 'z') viewer[2]-= 1.0;
    if(key == 'Z') viewer[2]+= 1.0;
    display();
}

void myReshape(int w, int h)
{
 glViewport(0, 0, w, h);

/* Use a perspective view */

 glMatrixMode(GL_PROJECTION);
 glLoadIdentity();
 if(w<=h) glFrustum(-2.0, 2.0, -2.0 * (GLfloat) h/ (GLfloat) w,
        2.0* (GLfloat) h / (GLfloat) w, 2.0, 20.0);
 else glFrustum(-2.0, 2.0, -2.0 * (GLfloat) w/ (GLfloat) h,
        2.0* (GLfloat) w / (GLfloat) h, 2.0, 20.0);

/* Or we can use gluPerspective */

 /* gluPerspective(45.0, w/h, 1.0, 10.0); */

 glMatrixMode(GL_MODELVIEW);
}


void
main(int argc, char **argv)
{
 glutInit(&argc, argv);
 glutInitDisplayMode(GLUT_DOUBLE | GLUT_RGB | GLUT_DEPTH);
 glutInitWindowSize(500, 500);
 glutCreateWindow("colorcube");
 glutReshapeFunc(myReshape);
 glutDisplayFunc(display);
 glutMouseFunc(mouse);
 glutKeyboardFunc(keys);
```

```
    glEnable(GL_DEPTH_TEST);
    glutMainLoop();
}
```

A.6   Sphere Program

```
/* Recursive subdivision of tetrahedron (Chapter 6). Three display
modes: wire frame, constant, and interpolative shading */

/* Program also illustrates defining materials and light sources
in myiit() */

/* mode 0 = wire frame, mode 1 = constant shading,
mode 3 = interpolative shading */

#include <stdlib.h>
#include <GL/glut.h>


typedef float point[3];

/* initial tetrahedron */

point v[]={{0.0, 0.0, 1.0}, {0.0, 0.942809, -0.33333},
        {-0.816497, -0.471405, -0.333333}, {0.816497,
          -0.471405, -0.333333}};

static GLfloat theta[] = {0.0,0.0,0.0};

int n;
int mode;


void triangle( point a, point b, point c)

/* display one triangle using a line loop for wire frame, a
single normal for constant shading, or three normals for
interpolative shading */
{
    if (mode==0) glBegin(GL_LINE_LOOP);
    else glBegin(GL_POLYGON);
        if(mode==1) glNormal3fv(a);
        if(mode==2) glNormal3fv(a);
```

```
            glVertex3fv(a);
            if(mode==2) glNormal3fv(b);
            glVertex3fv(b);
            if(mode==2) glNormal3fv(c);
            glVertex3fv(c);
        glEnd();
}


void normal(point p)
{

/* normalize a vector */

    double sqrt();
    float d =0.0;
    int i;
    for(i=0; i<3; i++) d+=p[i]*p[i];
    d=sqrt(d);
    if(d>0.0) for(i=0; i<3; i++) p[i]/=d;
}


void divide_triangle(point a, point b, point c, int m)
{

/* triangle subdivision using vertex numbers
righthand rule applied to create outward pointing faces */

    point v1, v2, v3;
    int j;
    if(m>0)
    {
        for(j=0; j<3; j++) v1[j]=a[j]+b[j];
        normal(v1);
        for(j=0; j<3; j++) v2[j]=a[j]+c[j];
        normal(v2);
        for(j=0; j<3; j++) v3[j]=b[j]+c[j];
         normal(v3);
        divide_triangle(a, v1, v2, m-1);
        divide_triangle(c, v2, v3, m-1);
        divide_triangle(b, v3, v1, m-1);
        divide_triangle(v1, v3, v2, m-1);
    }
    else(triangle(a,b,c)); /* draw triangle at end
                            of recursion */
}
```

```
void tetrahedron( int m)
{

/* Apply triangle subdivision to faces of tetrahedron */

    divide_triangle(v[0], v[1], v[2], m);
    divide_triangle(v[3], v[2], v[1], m);
    divide_triangle(v[0], v[3], v[1], m);
    divide_triangle(v[0], v[2], v[3], m);
}

void display(void)
{

/* Displays all three modes, side by side */

    glClear(GL_COLOR_BUFFER_BIT | GL_DEPTH_BUFFER_BIT);
    glLoadIdentity();
    mode=0;
    tetrahedron(n);
    mode=1;
    glTranslatef(-2.0, 0.0,0.0);
    tetrahedron(n);
    mode=2;
    glTranslatef( 4.0, 0.0,0.0);
    tetrahedron(n);


    glFlush();
}


void myReshape(int w, int h)
{
    glViewport(0, 0, w, h);
    glMatrixMode(GL_PROJECTION);
    glLoadIdentity();
    if (w <= h)
        glOrtho(-4.0, 4.0, -4.0 * (GLfloat) h / (GLfloat) w,
            4.0 * (GLfloat) h / (GLfloat) w, -10.0, 10.0);
    else
        glOrtho(-4.0 * (GLfloat) w / (GLfloat) h,
            4.0 * (GLfloat) w / (GLfloat) h, -4.0, 4.0, -10.0,
10.0);
```

```
        glMatrixMode(GL_MODELVIEW);
        display();
}


void myinit()
{
    GLfloat mat_specular[]={1.0, 1.0, 1.0, 1.0};
    GLfloat mat_diffuse[]={1.0, 1.0, 1.0, 1.0};
    GLfloat mat_ambient[]={1.0, 1.0, 1.0, 1.0};
    GLfloat mat_shininess={100.0};
    GLfloat light_ambient[]={0.0, 0.0, 0.0, 1.0};
    GLfloat light_diffuse[]={1.0, 1.0, 1.0, 1.0};
    GLfloat light_specular[]={1.0, 1.0, 1.0, 1.0};

/* set up ambient, diffuse, and specular components for light 0
*/

    glLightfv(GL_LIGHT0, GL_AMBIENT, light_ambient);
    glLightfv(GL_LIGHT0, GL_DIFFUSE, light_diffuse);
    glLightfv(GL_LIGHT0, GL_SPECULAR, light_specular);

/* define material proerties for front face of all polygons */

    glMaterialfv(GL_FRONT, GL_SPECULAR, mat_specular);
    glMaterialfv(GL_FRONT, GL_AMBIENT, mat_ambient);
    glMaterialfv(GL_FRONT, GL_DIFFUSE, mat_diffuse);
    glMaterialf(GL_FRONT, GL_SHININESS, mat_shininess);

    glEnable(GL_SMOOTH); /*enable smooth shading */
    glEnable(GL_LIGHTING); /* enable lighting */
    glEnable(GL_LIGHT0);  /* enable light 0 */
    glEnable(GL_DEPTH_TEST); /* enable z buffer */

    glClearColor (1.0, 1.0, 1.0, 1.0);
    glColor3f (0.0, 0.0, 0.0);
}


void
main(int argc, char **argv)
{
    n=atoi(argv[1]);
    glutInit(&argc, argv);
```

```
        glutInitDisplayMode(GLUT_SINGLE | GLUT_RGB | GLUT_DEPTH);
        glutInitWindowSize(500, 500);
        glutCreateWindow("sphere");
        myinit();
        glutReshapeFunc(myReshape);
        glutDisplayFunc(display);
        glutMainLoop();
    }
```

A.7   Robot Program

```
/* Robot program (Chapter 8). Cylinder for base, scaled cube
   for arms */
/* Shows use of instance transformation to define parts
   (symbols) */
/* The cylinder is a quadric object from the GLU library */
/* The cube is also obtained from GLU */

#include <GL/glut.h>

/* Let's start using #defines so we can better
interpret the constants (and change them) */

#define BASE_HEIGHT 2.0
#define BASE_RADIUS 1.0
#define LOWER_ARM_HEIGHT 5.0
#define LOWER_ARM_WIDTH 0.5
#define UPPER_ARM_HEIGHT 5.0
#define UPPER_ARM_WIDTH 0.5

typedef float point[3];

static GLfloat theta[] = {0.0,0.0,0.0};
static GLint axis = 0;
GLUquadricObj  *p; /* pointer to quadric object */


/* Define the three parts */
/* Note use of push/pop to return modelview matrix
to its state before functions were entered and use
rotation, translation, and scaling to create instances
of symbols (cube and cylinder) */
```

```
void base()
{
    glPushMatrix();

/* rotate cylinder to align with y axis */

    glRotatef(-90.0, 1.0, 0.0, 0.0);

/* cylinder aligned with z axis, render with
   5 slices for base and 5 along length */

    gluCylinder(p, BASE_RADIUS, BASE_RADIUS, BASE_HEIGHT, 5, 5);
    glPopMatrix();
}

void upper_arm()
{
    glPushMatrix();
    glTranslatef(0.0, 0.5*UPPER_ARM_HEIGHT, 0.0);
    glScalef(UPPER_ARM_WIDTH, UPPER_ARM_HEIGHT, UPPER_ARM_WIDTH);
    glutWireCube(1.0);
    glPopMatrix();
}

void lower_arm()
{
    glPushMatrix();
    glTranslatef(0.0, 0.5*LOWER_ARM_HEIGHT, 0.0);
    glScalef(LOWER_ARM_WIDTH, LOWER_ARM_HEIGHT, LOWER_ARM_WIDTH);
    glutWireCube(1.0);
    glPopMatrix();
}

void display(void)
{

/* Accumulate ModelView Matrix as we traverse tree */

    glClear(GL_COLOR_BUFFER_BIT);
    glLoadIdentity();
    glColor3f(1.0, 0.0, 0.0);
    glRotatef(theta[0], 0.0, 1.0, 0.0);
    base();
    glTranslatef(0.0, BASE_HEIGHT, 0.0);
```

```
        glRotatef(theta[1], 0.0, 0.0, 1.0);
        lower_arm();
        glTranslatef(0.0, LOWER_ARM_HEIGHT, 0.0);
        glRotatef(theta[2], 0.0, 0.0, 1.0);
        upper_arm();
        glFlush();
        glutSwapBuffers();
}



void mouse(int btn, int state, int x, int y)
{

/* left button increase joint angle, right button decreases it
*/

  if(btn==GLUT_LEFT_BUTTON && state == GLUT_DOWN)
        {
        theta[axis] += 5.0;
        if( theta[axis] > 360.0 ) theta[axis] -= 360.0;
        }
  if(btn==GLUT_RIGHT_BUTTON && state == GLUT_DOWN)
        {
        theta[axis] -= 5.0;
        if( theta[axis] < 360.0 ) theta[axis] += 360.0;
        }
        display();
}

void menu(int id)
{

/* menu selects which angle to change or whether to quit */

    if(id == 1) axis=0;
    if(id == 2) axis=1;
    if(id == 3) axis=2;
    if(id == 4) exit();
}

void
myReshape(int w, int h)
{
```

```
        glViewport(0, 0, w, h);
        glMatrixMode(GL_PROJECTION);
        glLoadIdentity();
        if (w <= h)
            glOrtho(-10.0, 10.0, -5.0 * (GLfloat) h / (GLfloat) w,
                15.0 * (GLfloat) h / (GLfloat) w, -10.0, 10.0);
        else
            glOrtho(-10.0 * (GLfloat) w / (GLfloat) h,
                10.0 * (GLfloat) w / (GLfloat) h, -5.0, 15.0, -10.0,
10.0);
        glMatrixMode(GL_MODELVIEW);
        glLoadIdentity();
}

void myinit()
{
    glClearColor(1.0, 1.0, 1.0, 1.0);
    glColor3f(1.0, 0.0, 0.0);

    p=gluNewQuadric(); /* allocate quadric object */
    gluQuadricDrawStyle(p, GLU_LINE); /* render it as wireframe
*/
}

void
main(int argc, char **argv)
{
    glutInit(&argc, argv);
    glutInitDisplayMode(GLUT_DOUBLE | GLUT_RGB | GLUT_DEPTH);
    glutInitWindowSize(500, 500);
    glutCreateWindow("robot");
    myinit();
    glutReshapeFunc(myReshape);
    glutDisplayFunc(display);
    glutMouseFunc(mouse);
    glutCreateMenu(menu);
    glutAddMenuEntry("base", 1);
    glutAddMenuEntry("lower arm", 2);
    glutAddMenuEntry("upper arm", 3);
    glutAddMenuEntry("quit", 4);
    glutAttachMenu(GLUT_MIDDLE_BUTTON);

    glutMainLoop();
}
```

A.8 Figure Program

```
/* Interactive Figure Program from Chapter 8 using cylinders
   (quadrics) */
/* Style similar to robot program but here we must traverse
   tree to display */
/* Cylinders are displayed as filled and light/material
   properties */
/* are set as in sphere approximation program */

#include <GL/glut.h>

#define TORSO_HEIGHT 5.0
#define UPPER_ARM_HEIGHT 3.0
#define LOWER_ARM_HEIGHT 2.0
#define UPPER_LEG_RADIUS  0.5
#define LOWER_LEG_RADIUS  0.5
#define LOWER_LEG_HEIGHT 2.0
#define UPPER_LEG_HEIGHT 3.0
#define UPPER_LEG_RADIUS  0.5
#define TORSO_RADIUS 1.0
#define UPPER_ARM_RADIUS  0.5
#define LOWER_ARM_RADIUS  0.5
#define HEAD_HEIGHT 1.5
#define HEAD_RADIUS 1.0

typedef float point[3];

static GLfloat theta[11] = {0.0,0.0,0.0,0.0,0.0,0.0,0.0,
            180.0,0.0,180.0,0.0}; /* initial joint angles */
static GLint angle = 2;

GLUquadricObj *t, *h, *lua, *lla, *rua, *rla, *lll, *rll, *rul,
*lul;

double size=1.0;


void torso()
{
   glPushMatrix();
   glRotatef(-90.0, 1.0, 0.0, 0.0);
```

```
        gluCylinder(t,TORSO_RADIUS, TORSO_RADIUS,
                    TORSO_HEIGHT,10,10);
     glPopMatrix();
}

void head()
{
   glPushMatrix();
   glTranslatef(0.0, 0.5*HEAD_HEIGHT,0.0);
   glScalef(HEAD_RADIUS, HEAD_HEIGHT, HEAD_RADIUS);
   gluSphere(h,1.0,10,10);
   glPopMatrix();
}

void left_upper_arm()
{
   glPushMatrix();
   glRotatef(-90.0, 1.0, 0.0, 0.0);
   gluCylinder(lua,UPPER_ARM_RADIUS, UPPER_ARM_RADIUS,
                   UPPER_ARM_HEIGHT,10,10);
   glPopMatrix();
}

void left_lower_arm()
{
   glPushMatrix();
   glRotatef(-90.0, 1.0, 0.0, 0.0);
   gluCylinder(lla,LOWER_ARM_RADIUS, LOWER_ARM_RADIUS,
                   LOWER_ARM_HEIGHT,10,10);
   glPopMatrix();
}

void right_upper_arm()
{
   glPushMatrix();
   glRotatef(-90.0, 1.0, 0.0, 0.0);
   gluCylinder(rua,UPPER_ARM_RADIUS, UPPER_ARM_RADIUS,
                   UPPER_ARM_HEIGHT,10,10);
   glPopMatrix();
}

void right_lower_arm()
{
   glPushMatrix();
```

```
      glRotatef(-90.0, 1.0, 0.0, 0.0);
      gluCylinder(rla,LOWER_ARM_RADIUS, LOWER_ARM_RADIUS,
                               LOWER_ARM_HEIGHT,10,10);
      glPopMatrix();
}

void left_upper_leg()
{
   glPushMatrix();
   glRotatef(-90.0, 1.0, 0.0, 0.0);
   gluCylinder(lul,UPPER_LEG_RADIUS, UPPER_LEG_RADIUS,
                               UPPER_LEG_HEIGHT,10,10);
   glPopMatrix();
}

void left_lower_leg()
{
   glPushMatrix();
   glRotatef(-90.0, 1.0, 0.0, 0.0);
   gluCylinder(lll,LOWER_LEG_RADIUS, LOWER_LEG_RADIUS,
                               LOWER_LEG_HEIGHT,10,10);
   glPopMatrix();
}

void right_upper_leg()
{
   glPushMatrix();
   glRotatef(-90.0, 1.0, 0.0, 0.0);
   gluCylinder(rul,UPPER_LEG_RADIUS, UPPER_LEG_RADIUS,
                               UPPER_LEG_HEIGHT,10,10);
   glPopMatrix();
}

void right_lower_leg()
{
   glPushMatrix();
   glRotatef(-90.0, 1.0, 0.0, 0.0);
   gluCylinder(rll,LOWER_LEG_RADIUS, LOWER_LEG_RADIUS,
                               LOWER_LEG_HEIGHT,10,10);
   glPopMatrix();
}

void
display(void)
```

```
{
    glClear(GL_COLOR_BUFFER_BIT|GL_DEPTH_BUFFER_BIT);
    glLoadIdentity();
    glColor3f(1.0, 0.0, 0.0);

    glRotatef(theta[0], 0.0, 1.0, 0.0);
    torso();
    glPushMatrix();

    glTranslatef(0.0, TORSO_HEIGHT+0.5*HEAD_HEIGHT, 0.0);
    glRotatef(theta[1], 1.0, 0.0, 0.0);
    glRotatef(theta[2], 0.0, 1.0, 0.0);
    glTranslatef(0.0, -0.5*HEAD_HEIGHT, 0.0);
    head();

    glPopMatrix();
    glPushMatrix();
    glTranslatef(-(TORSO_RADIUS+UPPER_ARM_RADIUS),
        0.9*TORSO_HEIGHT, 0.0);
    glRotatef(theta[3], 1.0, 0.0, 0.0);
    left_upper_arm();

    glTranslatef(0.0, UPPER_ARM_HEIGHT, 0.0);
    glRotatef(theta[4], 1.0, 0.0, 0.0);
    left_lower_arm();

    glPopMatrix();
    glPushMatrix();
    glTranslatef(TORSO_RADIUS+UPPER_ARM_RADIUS,
        0.9*TORSO_HEIGHT, 0.0);
    glRotatef(theta[5], 1.0, 0.0, 0.0);
    right_upper_arm();

    glTranslatef(0.0, UPPER_ARM_HEIGHT, 0.0);
    glRotatef(theta[6], 1.0, 0.0, 0.0);
    right_lower_arm();

    glPopMatrix();
    glPushMatrix();
    glTranslatef(-(TORSO_RADIUS+UPPER_LEG_RADIUS),
        0.1*UPPER_LEG_HEIGHT, 0.0);
    glRotatef(theta[7], 1.0, 0.0, 0.0);
    left_upper_leg();
```

```
        glTranslatef(0.0, UPPER_LEG_HEIGHT, 0.0);
        glRotatef(theta[8], 1.0, 0.0, 0.0);
        left_lower_leg();

        glPopMatrix();
        glPushMatrix();
        glTranslatef(TORSO_RADIUS+UPPER_LEG_RADIUS,
                  0.1*UPPER_LEG_HEIGHT, 0.0);
        glRotatef(theta[9], 1.0, 0.0, 0.0);
        right_upper_leg();

        glTranslatef(0.0, UPPER_LEG_HEIGHT, 0.0);
        glRotatef(theta[10], 1.0, 0.0, 0.0);
        right_lower_leg();

        glPopMatrix();
        glFlush();
        glutSwapBuffers();
}



void mouse(int btn, int state, int x, int y)
{
 if(btn==GLUT_LEFT_BUTTON && state == GLUT_DOWN)
        {
        theta[angle] += 5.0;
        if( theta[angle] > 360.0 ) theta[angle] -= 360.0;
        }
 if(btn==GLUT_RIGHT_BUTTON && state == GLUT_DOWN)
        {
        theta[angle] -= 5.0;
        if( theta[angle] < 360.0 ) theta[angle] += 360.0;
        }
        display();
}

void menu(int id)
{
   if(id <11 ) angle=id;
   if(id ==11 ) exit();
}
```

```
void
myReshape(int w, int h)
{
    glViewport(0, 0, w, h);
    glMatrixMode(GL_PROJECTION);
    glLoadIdentity();
    if (w <= h)
        glOrtho(-10.0, 10.0, -10.0 * (GLfloat) h / (GLfloat) w,
            10.0 * (GLfloat) h / (GLfloat) w, -10.0, 10.0);
    else
        glOrtho(-10.0 * (GLfloat) w / (GLfloat) h,
            10.0 * (GLfloat) w / (GLfloat) h, 0.0, 10.0, -10.0,
                                                           10.0);
    glMatrixMode(GL_MODELVIEW);
    glLoadIdentity();
}

void myinit()
{
        GLfloat mat_specular[]={1.0, 1.0, 1.0, 1.0};
        GLfloat mat_diffuse[]={1.0, 1.0, 1.0, 1.0};
        GLfloat mat_ambient[]={1.0, 1.0, 1.0, 1.0};
        GLfloat mat_shininess={100.0};
        GLfloat light_ambient[]={0.0, 0.0, 0.0, 1.0};
        GLfloat light_diffuse[]={1.0, 0.0, 0.0, 1.0};
        GLfloat light_specular[]={1.0, 1.0, 1.0, 1.0};
        GLfloat light_position[]={10.0, 10.0, 10.0, 0.0};

        glLightfv(GL_LIGHT0, GL_POSITION, light_position);
        glLightfv(GL_LIGHT0, GL_AMBIENT, light_ambient);
        glLightfv(GL_LIGHT0, GL_DIFFUSE, light_diffuse);
        glLightfv(GL_LIGHT0, GL_SPECULAR, light_specular);

        glMaterialfv(GL_FRONT, GL_SPECULAR, mat_specular);
        glMaterialfv(GL_FRONT, GL_AMBIENT, mat_ambient);
        glMaterialfv(GL_FRONT, GL_DIFFUSE, mat_diffuse);
        glMaterialf(GL_FRONT, GL_SHININESS, mat_shininess);

        glEnable(GL_SMOOTH);
        glEnable(GL_LIGHTING);
        glEnable(GL_LIGHT0);
        glDepthFunc(GL_LEQUAL);
        glEnable(GL_DEPTH_TEST);
```

```
                    glClearColor(1.0, 1.0, 1.0, 1.0);
                    glColor3f(1.0, 0.0, 0.0);

        /* allocate quadrics with filled drawing style */

                    h=gluNewQuadric();
                    gluQuadricDrawStyle(h, GLU_FILL);
                    t=gluNewQuadric();
                    gluQuadricDrawStyle(t, GLU_FILL);
                    lua=gluNewQuadric();
                    gluQuadricDrawStyle(lua, GLU_FILL);
                    lla=gluNewQuadric();
                    gluQuadricDrawStyle(lla, GLU_FILL);
                    rua=gluNewQuadric();
                    gluQuadricDrawStyle(rua, GLU_FILL);
                    rla=gluNewQuadric();
                    gluQuadricDrawStyle(rla, GLU_FILL);
                    lul=gluNewQuadric();
                    gluQuadricDrawStyle(lul, GLU_FILL);
                    lll=gluNewQuadric();
                    gluQuadricDrawStyle(lll, GLU_FILL);
                    rul=gluNewQuadric();
                    gluQuadricDrawStyle(rul, GLU_FILL);
                    rll=gluNewQuadric();
                    gluQuadricDrawStyle(rll, GLU_FILL);
        }

        void main(int argc, char **argv)
        {
            glutInit(&argc, argv);
            glutInitDisplayMode(GLUT_DOUBLE | GLUT_RGB | GLUT_DEPTH);
            glutInitWindowSize(500, 500);
            glutCreateWindow("robot");
            myinit();
            glutReshapeFunc(myReshape);
            glutDisplayFunc(display);
            glutMouseFunc(mouse);

            glutCreateMenu(menu);
            glutAddMenuEntry("torso", 0);
            glutAddMenuEntry("head1", 1);
            glutAddMenuEntry("head2", 2);
            glutAddMenuEntry("right_upper_arm", 3);
            glutAddMenuEntry("right_lower_arm", 4);
```

```
            glutAddMenuEntry("left_upper_arm", 5);
            glutAddMenuEntry("left_lower_arm", 6);
            glutAddMenuEntry("right_upper_leg", 7);
            glutAddMenuEntry("right_lower_leg", 8);
            glutAddMenuEntry("left_upper_leg", 9);
            glutAddMenuEntry("left_lower_leg", 10);
            glutAddMenuEntry("quit", 11);
            glutAttachMenu(GLUT_MIDDLE_BUTTON);

            glutMainLoop();
    }
```

A.9   Teapot Program

```
/* Shaded teapot using recursive subdivision of Bezier surfaces */
/* Depth of recursion entered as command line argument */

#include <stdlib.h>
#include <GL/glut.h>

typedef GLfloat point[3];

void draw_patch(point p[4][4]);
void divide_curve(point c[4], point *r, point *l);
void divide_patch(point p[4][4], int n);
void transpose(point p[4][4]);
void normal(point n, point p, point q, point r);

point data[32][4][4];

/* 306 vertices */

point vertices[306]={{1.4 , 0.0 , 2.4}, {1.4 , -0.784 , 2.4},
{0.784 , -1.4 , 2.4}, {0.0 , -1.4 , 2.4}, {1.3375 , 0.0 , 2.53125},
{1.3375 , -0.749 , 2.53125}, {0.749 , -1.3375 , 2.53125}, {0.0 , -1.3375 , 2.53125},
{1.4375 , 0.0 , 2.53125}, {1.4375 , -0.805 , 2.53125}, {0.805 , -1.4375 , 2.53125},
{0.0 , -1.4375 , 2.53125}, {1.5 , 0.0 , 2.4}, {1.5 , -0.84 , 2.4},
{0.84 , -1.5 , 2.4}, {0.0 , -1.5 , 2.4}, {-0.784 , -1.4 , 2.4},
{-1.4 , -0.784 , 2.4}, {-1.4 , 0.0 , 2.4}, {-0.749 , -1.3375 , 2.53125},
{-1.3375 , -0.749 , 2.53125}, {-1.3375 , 0.0 , 2.53125}, {-0.805 , -1.4375 , 2.53125},
{-1.4375 , -0.805 , 2.53125}, {-1.4375 , 0.0 , 2.53125}, {-0.84 , -1.5 , 2.4},
{-1.5 , -0.84 , 2.4}, {-1.5 , 0.0 , 2.4}, {-1.4 , 0.784 , 2.4},
```

```
{-0.784 , 1.4 , 2.4}, {0.0 , 1.4 , 2.4}, {-1.3375 , 0.749 , 2.53125},
{-0.749 , 1.3375 , 2.53125}, {0.0 , 1.3375 , 2.53125}, {-1.4375 , 0.805 , 2.53125},
{-0.805 , 1.4375 , 2.53125}, {0.0 , 1.4375 , 2.53125}, {-1.5 , 0.84 , 2.4},
{-0.84 , 1.5 , 2.4}, {0.0 , 1.5 , 2.4}, {0.784 , 1.4 , 2.4},
{1.4 , 0.784 , 2.4}, {0.749 , 1.3375 , 2.53125}, {1.3375 , 0.749 , 2.53125},
{0.805 , 1.4375 , 2.53125}, {1.4375 , 0.805 , 2.53125}, {0.84 , 1.5 , 2.4},
{1.5 , 0.84 , 2.4}, {1.75 , 0.0 , 1.875}, {1.75 , -0.98 , 1.875},
{0.98 , -1.75 , 1.875}, {0.0 , -1.75 , 1.875}, {2.0 , 0.0 , 1.35},
{2.0 , -1.12 , 1.35}, {1.12 , -2.0 , 1.35}, {0.0 , -2.0 , 1.35},
{2.0 , 0.0 , 0.9}, {2.0 , -1.12 , 0.9}, {1.12 , -2.0 , 0.9},
{0.0 , -2.0 , 0.9}, {-0.98 , -1.75 , 1.875}, {-1.75 , -0.98 , 1.875},
{-1.75 , 0.0 , 1.875}, {-1.12 , -2.0 , 1.35}, {-2.0 , -1.12 , 1.35},
{-2.0 , 0.0 , 1.35}, {-1.12 , -2.0 , 0.9}, {-2.0 , -1.12 , 0.9},
{-2.0 , 0.0 , 0.9}, {-1.75 , 0.98 , 1.875}, {-0.98 , 1.75 , 1.875},
{0.0 , 1.75 , 1.875}, {-2.0 , 1.12 , 1.35}, {-1.12 , 2.0 , 1.35},
{0.0 , 2.0 , 1.35}, {-2.0 , 1.12 , 0.9}, {-1.12 , 2.0 , 0.9},
{0.0 , 2.0 , 0.9}, {0.98 , 1.75 , 1.875}, {1.75 , 0.98 , 1.875},
{1.12 , 2.0 , 1.35}, {2.0 , 1.12 , 1.35}, {1.12 , 2.0 , 0.9},
{2.0 , 1.12 , 0.9}, {2.0 , 0.0 , 0.45}, {2.0 , -1.12 , 0.45},
{1.12 , -2.0 , 0.45}, {0.0 , -2.0 , 0.45}, {1.5 , 0.0 , 0.225},
{1.5 , -0.84 , 0.225}, {0.84 , -1.5 , 0.225}, {0.0 , -1.5 , 0.225},
{1.5 , 0.0 , 0.15}, {1.5 , -0.84 , 0.15}, {0.84 , -1.5 , 0.15},
{0.0 , -1.5 , 0.15}, {-1.12 , -2.0 , 0.45}, {-2.0 , -1.12 , 0.45},
{-2.0 , 0.0 , 0.45}, {-0.84 , -1.5 , 0.225}, {-1.5 , -0.84 , 0.225},
{-1.5 , 0.0 , 0.225}, {-0.84 , -1.5 , 0.15}, {-1.5 , -0.84 , 0.15},
{-1.5 , 0.0 , 0.15}, {-2.0 , 1.12 , 0.45}, {-1.12 , 2.0 , 0.45},
{0.0 , 2.0 , 0.45}, {-1.5 , 0.84 , 0.225}, {-0.84 , 1.5 , 0.225},
{0.0 , 1.5 , 0.225}, {-1.5 , 0.84 , 0.15}, {-0.84 , 1.5 , 0.15},
{0.0 , 1.5 , 0.15}, {1.12 , 2.0 , 0.45}, {2.0 , 1.12 , 0.45},
{0.84 , 1.5 , 0.225}, {1.5 , 0.84 , 0.225}, {0.84 , 1.5 , 0.15},
{1.5 , 0.84 , 0.15}, {-1.6 , 0.0 , 2.025}, {-1.6 , -0.3 , 2.025},
{-1.5 , -0.3 , 2.25}, {-1.5 , 0.0 , 2.25}, {-2.3 , 0.0 , 2.025},
{-2.3 , -0.3 , 2.025}, {-2.5 , -0.3 , 2.25}, {-2.5 , 0.0 , 2.25},
{-2.7 , 0.0 , 2.025}, {-2.7 , -0.3 , 2.025}, {-3.0 , -0.3 , 2.25},
{-3.0 , 0.0 , 2.25}, {-2.7 , 0.0 , 1.8}, {-2.7 , -0.3 , 1.8},
{-3.0 , -0.3 , 1.8}, {-3.0 , 0.0 , 1.8}, {-1.5 , 0.3 , 2.25},
{-1.6 , 0.3 , 2.025}, {-2.5 , 0.3 , 2.25}, {-2.3 , 0.3 , 2.025},
{-3.0 , 0.3 , 2.25}, {-2.7 , 0.3 , 2.025}, {-3.0 , 0.3 , 1.8},
{-2.7 , 0.3 , 1.8}, {-2.7 , 0.0 , 1.575}, {-2.7 , -0.3 , 1.575},
{-3.0 , -0.3 , 1.35}, {-3.0 , 0.0 , 1.35}, {-2.5 , 0.0 , 1.125},
{-2.5 , -0.3 , 1.125}, {-2.65 , -0.3 , 0.9375}, {-2.65 , 0.0 , 0.9375},
{-2.0 , -0.3 , 0.9}, {-1.9 , -0.3 , 0.6}, {-1.9 , 0.0 , 0.6},
{-3.0 , 0.3 , 1.35}, {-2.7 , 0.3 , 1.575}, {-2.65 , 0.3 , 0.9375},
{-2.5 , 0.3 , 1.125}, {-1.9 , 0.3 , 0.6}, {-2.0 , 0.3 , 0.9},
```

```
{1.7 , 0.0 , 1.425}, {1.7 , -0.66 , 1.425}, {1.7 , -0.66 , 0.6},
{1.7 , 0.0 , 0.6}, {2.6 , 0.0 , 1.425}, {2.6 , -0.66 , 1.425},
{3.1 , -0.66 , 0.825}, {3.1 , 0.0 , 0.825}, {2.3 , 0.0 , 2.1},
{2.3 , -0.25 , 2.1}, {2.4 , -0.25 , 2.025}, {2.4 , 0.0 , 2.025},
{2.7 , 0.0 , 2.4}, {2.7 , -0.25 , 2.4}, {3.3 , -0.25 , 2.4},
{3.3 , 0.0 , 2.4}, {1.7 , 0.66 , 0.6}, {1.7 , 0.66 , 1.425},
{3.1 , 0.66 , 0.825}, {2.6 , 0.66 , 1.425}, {2.4 , 0.25 , 2.025},
{2.3 , 0.25 , 2.1}, {3.3 , 0.25 , 2.4}, {2.7 , 0.25 , 2.4},
{2.8 , 0.0 , 2.475}, {2.8 , -0.25 , 2.475}, {3.525 , -0.25 , 2.49375},
{3.525 , 0.0 , 2.49375}, {2.9 , 0.0 , 2.475}, {2.9 , -0.15 , 2.475},
{3.45 , -0.15 , 2.5125}, {3.45 , 0.0 , 2.5125}, {2.8 , 0.0 , 2.4},
{2.8 , -0.15 , 2.4}, {3.2 , -0.15 , 2.4}, {3.2 , 0.0 , 2.4},
{3.525 , 0.25 , 2.49375}, {2.8 , 0.25 , 2.475}, {3.45 , 0.15 , 2.5125},
{2.9 , 0.15 , 2.475}, {3.2 , 0.15 , 2.4}, {2.8 , 0.15 , 2.4},
{0.0 , 0.0 , 3.15}, {0.0 , -0.002 , 3.15}, {0.002 , 0.0 , 3.15},
{0.8 , 0.0 , 3.15}, {0.8 , -0.45 , 3.15}, {0.45 , -0.8 , 3.15},
{0.0 , -0.8 , 3.15}, {0.0 , 0.0 , 2.85}, {0.2 , 0.0 , 2.7},
{0.2 , -0.112 , 2.7}, {0.112 , -0.2 , 2.7}, {0.0 , -0.2 , 2.7},
{-0.002 , 0.0 , 3.15}, {-0.45 , -0.8 , 3.15}, {-0.8 , -0.45 , 3.15},
{-0.8 , 0.0 , 3.15}, {-0.112 , -0.2 , 2.7}, {-0.2 , -0.112 , 2.7},
{-0.2 , 0.0 , 2.7}, {0.0 , 0.002 , 3.15}, {-0.8 , 0.45 , 3.15},
{-0.45 , 0.8 , 3.15}, {0.0 , 0.8 , 3.15}, {-0.2 , 0.112 , 2.7},
{-0.112 , 0.2 , 2.7}, {0.0 , 0.2 , 2.7}, {0.45 , 0.8 , 3.15},
{0.8 , 0.45 , 3.15}, {0.112 , 0.2 , 2.7}, {0.2 , 0.112 , 2.7},
{0.4 , 0.0 , 2.55}, {0.4 , -0.224 , 2.55}, {0.224 , -0.4 , 2.55},
{0.0 , -0.4 , 2.55}, {1.3 , 0.0 , 2.55}, {1.3 , -0.728 , 2.55},
{0.728 , -1.3 , 2.55}, {0.0 , -1.3 , 2.55}, {1.3 , 0.0 , 2.4},
{1.3 , -0.728 , 2.4}, {0.728 , -1.3 , 2.4}, {0.0 , -1.3 , 2.4},
{-0.224 , -0.4 , 2.55}, {-0.4 , -0.224 , 2.55}, {-0.4 , 0.0 , 2.55},
{-0.728 , -1.3 , 2.55}, {-1.3 , -0.728 , 2.55}, {-1.3 , 0.0 , 2.55},
{-0.728 , -1.3 , 2.4}, {-1.3 , -0.728 , 2.4}, {-1.3 , 0.0 , 2.4},
{-0.4 , 0.224 , 2.55}, {-0.224 , 0.4 , 2.55}, {0.0 , 0.4 , 2.55},
{-1.3 , 0.728 , 2.55}, {-0.728 , 1.3 , 2.55}, {0.0 , 1.3 , 2.55},
{-1.3 , 0.728 , 2.4}, {-0.728 , 1.3 , 2.4}, {0.0 , 1.3 , 2.4},
{0.224 , 0.4 , 2.55}, {0.4 , 0.224 , 2.55}, {0.728 , 1.3 , 2.55},
{1.3 , 0.728 , 2.55}, {0.728 , 1.3 , 2.4}, {1.3 , 0.728 , 2.4},
{0.0 , 0.0 , 0.0}, {1.5 , 0.0 , 0.15}, {1.5 , 0.84 , 0.15},
{0.84 , 1.5 , 0.15}, {0.0 , 1.5 , 0.15}, {1.5 , 0.0 , 0.075},
{1.5 , 0.84 , 0.075}, {0.84 , 1.5 , 0.075}, {0.0 , 1.5 , 0.075},
{1.425 , 0.0 , 0.0}, {1.425 , 0.798 , 0.0}, {0.798 , 1.425 , 0.0},
{0.0 , 1.425 , 0.0}, {-0.84 , 1.5 , 0.15}, {-1.5 , 0.84 , 0.15},
{-1.5 , 0.0 , 0.15}, {-0.84 , 1.5 , 0.075}, {-1.5 , 0.84 , 0.075},
{-1.5 , 0.0 , 0.075}, {-0.798 , 1.425 , 0.0}, {-1.425 , 0.798 , 0.0},
{-1.425 , 0.0 , 0.0}, {-1.5 , -0.84 , 0.15}, {-0.84 , -1.5 , 0.15},
```

```
{0.0 , -1.5 , 0.15}, {-1.5 , -0.84 , 0.075}, {-0.84 , -1.5 , 0.075},
{0.0 , -1.5 , 0.075}, {-1.425 , -0.798 , 0.0}, {-0.798 , -1.425 , 0.0},
{0.0 , -1.425 , 0.0}, {0.84 , -1.5 , 0.15}, {1.5 , -0.84 , 0.15},
{0.84 , -1.5 , 0.075}, {1.5 , -0.84 , 0.075}, {0.798 , -1.425 , 0.0},
{1.425 , -0.798 , 0.0}};

/* 32 patches each defined by 16 vertices, arranged in a 4 x 4 array */
/* NOTE: numbering scheme for teapot has vertices labeled from 1 to 306 */
/* remnant of the days of FORTRAN */

int indices[32][4][4]={{1, 2, 3, 4, 5, 6, 7, 8, 9, 10, 11, 12, 13, 14, 15, 16},
{4, 17, 18, 19, 8, 20, 21, 22, 12, 23, 24, 25, 16, 26, 27, 28},
{19, 29, 30, 31, 22, 32, 33, 34, 25, 35, 36, 37, 28, 38, 39, 40},
{31, 41, 42, 1, 34, 43, 44, 5, 37, 45, 46, 9, 40, 47, 48, 13},
{13, 14, 15, 16, 49, 50, 51, 52, 53, 54, 55, 56, 57, 58, 59, 60},
{16, 26, 27, 28, 52, 61, 62, 63, 56, 64, 65, 66, 60, 67, 68, 69},
{28, 38, 39, 40, 63, 70, 71, 72, 66, 73, 74, 75, 69, 76, 77, 78},
{40, 47, 48, 13, 72, 79, 80, 49, 75, 81, 82, 53, 78, 83, 84, 57},
{57, 58, 59, 60, 85, 86, 87, 88, 89, 90, 91, 92, 93, 94, 95, 96},
{60, 67, 68, 69, 88, 97, 98, 99, 92, 100, 101, 102, 96, 103, 104, 105},
{69, 76, 77, 78, 99, 106, 107, 108, 102, 109, 110, 111, 105, 112, 113, 114},
{78, 83, 84, 57, 108, 115, 116, 85, 111, 117, 118, 89, 114, 119, 120, 93},
{121, 122, 123, 124, 125, 126, 127, 128, 129, 130, 131, 132, 133, 134, 135, 136},
{124, 137, 138, 121, 128, 139, 140, 125, 132, 141, 142, 129, 136, 143, 144, 133},
{133, 134, 135, 136, 145, 146, 147, 148, 149, 150, 151, 152, 69, 153, 154, 155},
{136, 143, 144, 133, 148, 156, 157, 145, 152, 158, 159, 149, 155, 160, 161, 69},
{162, 163, 164, 165, 166, 167, 168, 169, 170, 171, 172, 173, 174, 175, 176, 177},
{165, 178, 179, 162, 169, 180, 181, 166, 173, 182, 183, 170, 177, 184, 185, 174},
{174, 175, 176, 177, 186, 187, 188, 189, 190, 191, 192, 193, 194, 195, 196, 197},
{177, 184, 185, 174, 189, 198, 199, 186, 193, 200, 201, 190, 197, 202, 203, 194},
{204, 204, 204, 204, 207, 208, 209, 210, 211, 211, 211, 211, 212, 213, 214, 215},
{204, 204, 204, 204, 210, 217, 218, 219, 211, 211, 211, 211, 215, 220, 221, 222},
{204, 204, 204, 204, 219, 224, 225, 226, 211, 211, 211, 211, 222, 227, 228, 229},
{204, 204, 204, 204, 226, 230, 231, 207, 211, 211, 211, 211, 229, 232, 233, 212},
{212, 213, 214, 215, 234, 235, 236, 237, 238, 239, 240, 241, 242, 243, 244, 245},
{215, 220, 221, 222, 237, 246, 247, 248, 241, 249, 250, 251, 245, 252, 253, 254},
{222, 227, 228, 229, 248, 255, 256, 257, 251, 258, 259, 260, 254, 261, 262, 263},
{229, 232, 233, 212, 257, 264, 265, 234, 260, 266, 267, 238, 263, 268, 269, 242},
{270, 270, 270, 270, 279, 280, 281, 282, 275, 276, 277, 278, 271, 272, 273, 274},
{270, 270, 270, 270, 282, 289, 290, 291, 278, 286, 287, 288, 274, 283, 284, 285},
{270, 270, 270, 270, 291, 298, 299, 300, 288, 295, 296, 297, 285, 292, 293, 294},
{270, 270, 270, 270, 300, 305, 306, 279, 297, 303, 304, 275, 294, 301, 302, 271}};

int level;
```

```
void normal(point n, point p, point q, point r)
{
n[0]=(q[1]-p[1])*(r[2]-p[2])-(q[2]-p[2])*(r[1]-p[1]);
n[1]=(q[2]-p[2])*(r[0]-p[0])-(q[0]-p[0])*(r[2]-p[2]);
n[2]=(q[0]-p[0])*(r[2]-p[2])-(q[2]-p[2])*(r[0]-p[0]);
}


void transpose(point a[4][4])
{

/* transpose wastes time but makes program more readable */

int i,j, k;
GLfloat tt;
for(i=0;i<4;i++) for(j=i;j<4; j++) for(k=0;k<3;k++)
    {
        tt=a[i][j][k];
        a[i][j][k]=a[j][i][k];
        a[j][i][k]=tt;
    }
}


void divide_patch(point p[4][4], int n)
    {
    point q[4][4], r[4][4], s[4][4], t[4][4];
    point a[4][4], b[4][4];
    int i,j, k;
    if(n==0) draw_patch(p); /* draw patch if recursion done */

/* subdivide curves in u direction, transpose results, divide
in u direction again (equivalent to subdivision in v) */

    else
        {
        for(k=0; k<4; k++) divide_curve(p[k], a[k], b[k]);
        transpose(a);
        transpose(b);
        for(k=0; k<4; k++)
            {
            divide_curve(a[k], q[k], r[k]);
            divide_curve(b[k], s[k], t[k]);
            }

/* recursive division of 4 resulting patches */
```

```
        divide_patch(q, n-1);
        divide_patch(r, n-1);
        divide_patch(s, n-1);
        divide_patch(t, n-1);
        }
}

void divide_curve(point c[4], point r[4], point l[4])
{

/* division of convex hull of Bezier curve */

    int i;
    point t;
    for(i=0;i<3;i++)
    {
        l[0][i]=c[0][i];
        r[3][i]=c[3][i];
        l[1][i]=(c[1][i]+c[0][i])/2;
        r[2][i]=(c[2][i]+c[3][i])/2;
        t[i]=(l[1][i]+r[2][i])/2;
        l[2][i]=(t[i]+l[1][i])/2;
        r[1][i]=(t[i]+r[2][i])/2;
        l[3][i]=r[0][i]=(l[2][i]+r[1][i])/2;
    }
}

void draw_patch(point p[4][4])
{
    point n;
    normal(n, p[0][0], p[3][0], p[3][3]);
    glBegin(GL_QUADS);
    glNormal3fv(n);
    glVertex3fv(p[0][0]);
    glVertex3fv(p[3][0]);
    glVertex3fv(p[3][3]);
    glVertex3fv(p[0][3]);
    glEnd();
}

void
display(void)
{
    int i;
```

```
    glClear(GL_COLOR_BUFFER_BIT | GL_DEPTH_BUFFER_BIT);
    glLoadIdentity();

/* data aligned along z axis, rotate to align with y axis */

    glRotatef(-90.0, 1.0,0.0, 0.0);
    for(i=0;i<32;i++) divide_patch(data[i], level); /* divide all 32 patches
*/

    glFlush();

}



void
myReshape(int w, int h)
{
    glViewport(0, 0, w, h);
    glMatrixMode(GL_PROJECTION);
    glLoadIdentity();
    if (w <= h)
        glOrtho(-4.0, 4.0, -4.0 * (GLfloat) h / (GLfloat) w,
            4.0 * (GLfloat) h / (GLfloat) w, -10.0, 10.0);
    else
        glOrtho(-4.0 * (GLfloat) w / (GLfloat) h,
            4.0 * (GLfloat) w / (GLfloat) h, -4.0, 4.0, -10.0, 10.0);
    glMatrixMode(GL_MODELVIEW);
    display();
}


void myinit()
{
    GLfloat mat_specular[]={1.0, 1.0, 1.0, 1.0};
    GLfloat mat_diffuse[]={1.0, 1.0, 1.0, 1.0};
    GLfloat mat_ambient[]={1.0, 1.0, 1.0, 1.0};
    GLfloat mat_shininess={100.0};
    GLfloat light_ambient[]={0.0, 0.0, 0.0, 1.0};
    GLfloat light_diffuse[]={1.0, 1.0, 1.0, 1.0};
    GLfloat light_specular[]={1.0, 1.0, 1.0, 1.0};
    GLfloat light_position[]={10.0, 10.0, 10.0, 0.0};

    glLightfv(GL_LIGHT0, GL_POSITION, light_position);
    glLightfv(GL_LIGHT0, GL_AMBIENT, light_ambient);
    glLightfv(GL_LIGHT0, GL_DIFFUSE, light_diffuse);
```

```
        glLightfv(GL_LIGHT0, GL_SPECULAR, light_specular);

        glMaterialfv(GL_FRONT, GL_SPECULAR, mat_specular);
        glMaterialfv(GL_FRONT, GL_AMBIENT, mat_ambient);
        glMaterialfv(GL_FRONT, GL_DIFFUSE, mat_diffuse);
        glMaterialf(GL_FRONT, GL_SHININESS, mat_shininess);

        glEnable(GL_SMOOTH);
        glEnable(GL_LIGHTING);
        glEnable(GL_LIGHT0);

        glEnable(GL_DEPTH_TEST);
        glClearColor (0.0, 0.0, 0.0, 1.0);
        glColor3f (1.0, 1.0, 1.0);
        glEnable(GL_NORMALIZE); /* automatic normalization of normals */
        glEnable(GL_CULL_FACE); /* eliminate backfacing polygons */
        glCullFace(GL_BACK);

}

main(int argc, char *argv[])
{
int i,j, k, m, n;


        level=atoi(argv[1]);

        for(i=0;i<32;i++) for(j=0;j<4;j++) for(k=0;k<4;k++) for(n=0;n<3;n++)
        {

/* put teapot data into single array for subdivision */

                m=indices[i][j][k];
                for(n=0;n<3;n++) data[i][j][k][n]=vertices[m-1][n];
        }
        glutInit(&argc, argv);
        glutInitDisplayMode(GLUT_SINGLE | GLUT_RGB | GLUT_DEPTH);
        glutInitWindowSize(500, 500);
        glutCreateWindow("teapot");
        myinit();
        glutReshapeFunc(myReshape);
        glutDisplayFunc(display);

        glutMainLoop();
}
```

A.10   Mandelbrot Set Progam

```c
#include <stdlib.h>
#include <GL/glut.h>

/* Default data via command line */
/* Can enter other values via command line arguments */

#define CENTERX -0.5
#define CENTERY 0.5
#define HEIGHT 0.5
#define WIDTH 0.5
#define MAX_ITER 100

/* N x M array to be generated */

#define N 500
#define M 500

float height = HEIGHT; /* size of window in complex plane */
float width = WIDTH;
float cx = CENTERX; /* center of window in complex plane */
float cy = CENTERY;
int max = MAX_ITER; /* number of iterations per point */

int n=N;
int m=M;


/* Use unsigned bytes for image */

GLubyte image[N][M];

/* Complex data type and complex add, mult,
   and magnitude functions */
/* Probably not worth overhead */

typedef float complex[2];

void add(complex a, complex b, complex p)
{
    p[0]=a[0]+b[0];
    p[1]=a[1]+b[1];
}
```

```
void mult(complex a, complex b, complex p)
{
    p[0]=a[0]*b[0]-a[1]*b[1];
    p[1]=a[0]*b[1]+a[1]*b[0];
}

float mag2(complex a)
{
    return(a[0]*a[0]+a[1]*a[1]);
}

void form(float a, float b, complex p)
{
    p[0]=a;
    p[1]=b;
}

void display()
{
    glClear(GL_COLOR_BUFFER_BIT);
    glDrawPixels(n,m,GL_COLOR_INDEX, GL_UNSIGNED_BYTE, image);
}

void myReshape(int w, int h)
{
    glViewport(0, 0, w, h);
    glMatrixMode(GL_PROJECTION);
    glLoadIdentity();
    if (w <= h)
    gluOrtho2D(0.0, 0.0, (GLfloat) n, (GLfloat) m* (GLfloat) h
/ (GLfloat) w);
    else
    gluOrtho2D(0.0, 0.0, (GLfloat) n * (GLfloat) w / (GLfloat)
h,(GLfloat) m);
    glMatrixMode(GL_MODELVIEW);
    display();
}

void myinit()
{
    float redmap[256], greenmap[256],bluemap[256];
    int i;

    glClearColor (1.0, 1.0, 1.0, 1.0);
```

```
            gluOrtho2D(0.0, 0.0, (GLfloat) n, (GLfloat) m);

    /* Define pseudocolor maps, ramps for red and blue,
       random for green */


        for(i=0;i<256;i++)
        {
            redmap[i]=i/255.;
            greenmap[i]=drand48();
            bluemap[i]=1.0-i/255.;
        }

        glPixelMapfv(GL_PIXEL_MAP_I_TO_R, 256, redmap);
        glPixelMapfv(GL_PIXEL_MAP_I_TO_G, 256, greenmap);
        glPixelMapfv(GL_PIXEL_MAP_I_TO_B, 256, bluemap);
    }


    main(int argc, char *argv[])
    {
        int i, j, k;
        float x, y, v;
        complex c0, c, d;

        if(argc>1) cx = atof(argv[1]); /* center x */
        if(argc>2) cy = atof(argv[2]);  /* center y */
        if(argc>3) height=width=atof(argv[3]); /* rectangle height
                                                    and width */
        if(argc>4) max=atoi(argv[4]); /* maximum iterations */

        for (i=0; i<n; i++) for(j=0; j<m; j++)
        {

    /* starting point */

        x= i *(width/(n-1)) + cx -width/2;
        y= j *(height/(m-1)) + cy -height/2;

        form(0,0,c);
        form(x,y,c0);

    /* complex iteration */
```

```
        for(k=0; k<max; k++)
            {
            mult(c,c,d);
            add(d,c0,c);
            v=mag2(c);
            if(v>4.0) break; /* assume not in set if mag > 4 */
            }

/* assign gray level to point based on its magnitude */
        if(v>1.0) v=1.0; /* clamp if > 1 */
        image[i][j]=255*v;
    }


    glutInit(&argc, argv);
    glutInitDisplayMode(GLUT_SINGLE | GLUT_RGB );
    glutInitWindowSize(N, M);
    glutCreateWindow("mandelbrot");
    myinit();
    glutReshapeFunc(myReshape);
    glutDisplayFunc(display);

    glutMainLoop();
}
```

B Spaces

Computer graphics is concerned with the representation and manipulation of sets of geometric elements, such as points and line segments. The necessary mathematics is found in the study of various types of abstract spaces. We shall review the rules governing three such spaces: the (linear) vector space, the affine space, and the Euclidean space. The **vector space** contains only two types of objects: scalars, such as real numbers, and vectors. The **affine space** adds a third element: the point. **Euclidean spaces** add the concept of distance.

The vectors of interest in computer graphics are directed line segments and the n-tuples of numbers are used to represent them. In Appendix C, we shall discuss matrix algebra as a tool for manipulating n-tuples. In this appendix, we are concerned with the underlying concepts and rules. It is probably helpful to think of these entities (scalars, vectors, points) as abstract data types, and the axioms as defining the valid operations on them.

B.1 Scalars

Ordinary real numbers and the operations on them are one example of a **scalar field**. Let S denote a set of elements called **scalars**, α, β, ... Scalars have two fundamental operations defined between pairs. These operations are often called addition and multiplication, and are symbolized by the operators $+$ and $\cdot$,[1] respectively. Hence, for $\forall \alpha, \beta \in S, \alpha + \beta \in S, \alpha \cdot \beta \in S$. These operations are

---

[1] Often, if there is no ambiguity, we write $\alpha\beta$ instead of $\alpha \cdot \beta$.

associative, commutative, and distributive, $\forall \alpha, \beta, \gamma \in S$

$$\alpha + \beta = \beta + \alpha,$$
$$\alpha \cdot \beta = \beta \cdot \alpha,$$
$$\alpha + (\beta + \gamma) = (\alpha + \beta) + \gamma,$$
$$\alpha \cdot (\beta \cdot \gamma) = (\alpha \cdot \beta) \cdot \gamma,$$
$$\alpha \cdot (\beta + \gamma) = (\alpha \cdot \beta) + (\alpha \cdot \gamma).$$

There are two special scalars—the additive inverse (0) and the multiplicative inverse (1)—such that $\forall \alpha \in S$

$$\alpha + 0 = 0 + \alpha = \alpha,$$
$$\alpha \cdot 1 = 1 \cdot \alpha = \alpha.$$

Each element α has an additive inverse, denoted $-\alpha$, and a multiplicative inverse, denoted $\alpha^{-1} \in S$, such that

$$\alpha + (-\alpha) = 0,$$
$$\alpha \cdot \alpha^{-1} = 1.$$

The real numbers using ordinary addition and multiplication form a scalar field, as do the complex numbers (under complex addition and multiplication) and rational functions (ratios of two polynomials).

B.2   Vector Spaces

A vector space, in addition to scalars, contains a second type of entity: **vectors**. Vectors have two operations defined: vector–vector addition and scalar–vector multiplication. Let u, v, w denote vectors in a vector space V. Vector addition is defined to be closed ($u + v \in V \ \forall u, v \in V$), commutative ($u + v = v + u$), and associative ($u + (v + w) = (u + v) + w$). There is a special vector (the **zero vector**) **0** defined such that $\forall u \in V$

$$u + \mathbf{0} = u.$$

Every vector u has an additive inverse denoted by $-u$ such that

$$u + (-u) = \mathbf{0}.$$

Scalar–vector multiplication is defined such that, for any scalar α and any vector u, αu is a vector in V. The scalar–vector operation is distributive. Hence,

$$\alpha(u + v) = \alpha u + \alpha v,$$
$$(\alpha + \beta)u = \alpha u + \beta u.$$

The two examples of vector spaces that we shall use are geometric vectors (directed line segments) and the n-tuples of real numbers. Consider a set of directed line segments that we can picture as shown in Figure B.1. If our

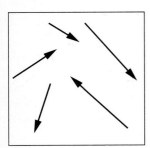

Figure B.1 Directed line segments.

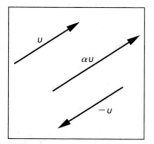

Figure B.2 Scalar–vector multiplication.

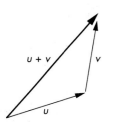

Figure B.3 Head-to-tail axiom for vectors.

scalars are real numbers, then scalar–vector multiplication changes the length of a vector, but not that vector's direction (Figure B.2).

Vector–vector addition can be defined by the **head-to-tail axiom**, which we can visualize easily for the example of directed line segments. We form the vector $u + v$ by connecting the head of u to the tail of v, as shown in Figure B.3. You should be able to verify that all the rules of a vector field are satisfied.

The second example of a vector space is n-tuples of scalars— usually, real or complex numbers. Hence, a vector can be written as

$$v = (v_1, v_2, \ldots, v_n).$$

Vector–vector addition and scalar–vector multiplication are given by

$$u + v = (u_1, u_2, \ldots, u_n) + (v_1, v_2, \ldots, v_n)$$
$$= (u_1 + v_1, u_2 + v_2, \ldots, u_n + v_n),$$
$$\alpha v = (\alpha v_1, \alpha v_2, \ldots, \alpha v_n).$$

This space is denoted $\mathbf{R}^n$, and is the vector space in which we can manipulate vectors using matrix algebra (Appendix C).

In a vector space, the concepts of linear independence and basis are crucial. A **linear combination** of n vectors $u_1, u_2, \ldots, u_n$ is a vector of the form

$$u = \alpha_1 u_1 + \alpha_2 u_2 + \ldots + \alpha_n u_n.$$

If the only set of scalars such that

$$\alpha_1 u_1 + \alpha_2 u_2 \ldots + \alpha_n u_n = 0$$

is

$$\alpha_1 = \alpha_2 = \ldots = \alpha_n = 0,$$

then the vectors are said to be **linearly independent**. The greatest number of linearly independent vectors that we can find in a space gives the **dimension** of the space. If a vector space has dimension n, any set of n linearly independent vectors form a **basis**. If $v_1, v_2, \ldots, v_n$ is a basis for V, any vector v can be expressed uniquely in terms of the basis vectors as

$$v = \beta_1 v_1 + \beta_2 v_2 + \ldots + \beta_n v_n.$$

The scalars $\{\beta_i\}$ give the **representation** of v with respect to the basis $v_1, v_2, \ldots,$ v_n. If $v_1', v_2', \ldots, v_n'$ is some other basis (the number of vectors in a basis is constant), there will be a representation of v with respect to this basis; that is,

$$v = \beta_1' v_1' + \beta_2' v_2' + \ldots + \beta_n' v_n'.$$

There exists an n x n matrix $\mathbf{M}$ such that

$$
\begin{bmatrix} \beta'_1 \\ \beta'_2 \\ \vdots \\ \beta'_N \end{bmatrix} = \mathbf{M} \begin{bmatrix} \beta_1 \\ \beta_2 \\ \vdots \\ \beta_N \end{bmatrix}.
$$

We shall derive $\mathbf{M}$ in Appendix C. This matrix gives a way of changing representations through a simple linear transformation involving only scalar operations for carrying out matrix multiplication. More generally, once we have a basis for a vector space, we can work only with representations. If the scalars are real numbers, then we can work with n-tuples of reals and use matrix algebra, instead of doing operations in the original abstract vector space

B.3   Affine Spaces

A vector space lacks any geometric concepts, such as location and distance. If we use the example of directed line segments as the natural vector space for our geometric problems, we get into difficulties, because these vectors, just like the physicist's vectors, have magnitude and direction, but have no position. The vectors in Figure B.4 are identical.

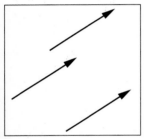

Figure B.4 Identical vectors.

If we think of this problem in terms of coordinate systems, we can express a vector in terms of a set of basis vectors that define a **coordinate system**. Figure B.5(a) shows three basis vectors emerging from a particular reference point, the **origin**. The location of the vectors in Figure B.5(b) is equally valid, however, because vectors have no position. In addition, we have no way to express this special point, because our vector space has only vectors and scalars as its members.

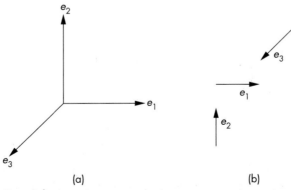

(a)   (b)

Figure B.5 Coordinate system. (a) Basis vectors located at the origin.
(b) Arbitrary placement of basis vectors.

We can resolve this difficulty by introducing an affine space that adds a third type of entity—points—to a vector space. The points $(P, Q, R, \ldots)$ form a set. There is a single new operation, **point–point subtraction**, that yields a vector. Hence, if P and Q are any two points, the subtraction

$$v = P - Q$$

always yields a vector in V. Conversely, for every v and every P, we can find a Q such that the preceding relation holds. We can thus write

$$Q = v + P,$$

defining a vector–point addition. A consequence of the head-to-tail axiom is that, for any three points $P, Q, R,$

$$(P - Q) + (Q - R) = (P - R).$$

If we visualize the vector $P - Q$ as the line segment from the point Q to the point P, using an arrow to denote direction, the head-to-tail axiom can be drawn as shown in Figure B.6.

Various properties follow from affine geometry. Perhaps the most important is that if we use a frame, rather than a coordinate system, we can specify both points and vectors in an affine space. A **frame** consists of a point P_0, and a set of vectors $v_1, v_2, \ldots, v_n$ that defines a basis for the vector space. Given a frame, an arbitrary vector can be written uniquely as

$$v = \alpha_1 v_1 + \alpha_2 v_2 + \ldots + \alpha_n v_n,$$

and an arbitrary point can be written uniquely as

$$P = P_0 + \beta_1 v_1 + \beta_2 v_2 + \ldots + \beta_n v_n.$$

The two sets of scalars, $\{\alpha_1, \ldots, \alpha_n\}$ and $\{\beta_1, \ldots, \beta_n\}$ give the representations of the vector and point, respectively, each representation consisting of n scalars. We can regard the point P_0 as the origin of the frame; all points are defined from this reference point.

If the origin never changes, we can worry about only those changes of frames corresponding to changes in coordinate systems. In computer graphics, however, we usually have to deal with making changes in frames and with representing objects in different frames. For example, we usually define our objects within a physical frame. The viewer, or camera, can be expressed in terms of this frame, but, as part of the image-creation process, we shall find it to our advantage to express object positions with respect to the camera frame—a frame whose origin usually is located at the center of projection.

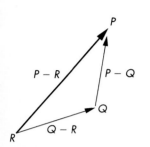

Figure B.6 Head-to-tail axiom for points.

B.4   Euclidean Spaces

Although affine spaces contain the necessary elements for building geometric models, there is no concept of how far apart two points are, or of what the length of a vector is. Euclidean spaces have such a concept. Strictly speaking, a Euclidean space needs to contain only vectors and scalars.

Suppose that E is a Euclidean space. It is a vector space containing scalars $(\alpha, \beta, \gamma, \ldots)$ and vectors $(u, v, w, \ldots)$. We shall assume the scalars are the ordinary real numbers. We add a new operation—the **inner (dot) product**—that combines two vectors to form a real. The inner product must satisfy the properties that, for any three vectors u, v, w and scalars α, β,

$$u \cdot v = v \cdot u,$$
$$(\alpha u + \beta v) \cdot w = \alpha u \cdot w + \beta v \cdot w,$$
$$v \cdot v > 0 (v \neq 0),$$
$$0 \cdot 0 = 0.$$

If

$$u \cdot v = 0,$$

then u and v are **orthogonal**. The magnitude (length) of a vector is usually measured as

$$|v| = \sqrt{v \cdot v}.$$

Once we add affine concepts, such as points, to the Euclidean space, we naturally get a measure of distance between points, because, for any two points P and Q, $P - Q$ is a vector, and hence

$$|P - Q| = \sqrt{(P - Q) \cdot (P - Q)}.$$

We can use the inner product to define a measure of the angle between two vectors:

$$u \cdot v = |u||v| \cos \theta.$$

It is easy to show that $\cos \theta$ as defined by this formula is 0 when the vectors are orthogonal, and lies between -1 and $+1$, and has magnitude 1 if the vectors are parallel $(u = \alpha v)$.

B.5   Projections

We can derive several of the important geometric concepts from the use of orthogonality. The concept of **projection** arises from the problem of finding the shortest distance from a point to a line or plane. It is equivalent to the

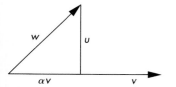

Figure B.7 Projection of one vector onto another.

following problem. Given two vectors, we can take one of them and divide it into two parts, one parallel, and one orthogonal to the other vector, as shown in Figure B.7 for directed line segments. Suppose that v is the first vector and w is the second. Then, w can be written as

$$w = \alpha v + u.$$

The parallel part is αv, but, for u to be orthogonal to v, we must have

$$u \cdot v = 0.$$

Because w and v are defined to be orthogonal,

$$w \cdot v = \alpha v \cdot v + u \cdot v = \alpha v \cdot v,$$

allowing us to find

$$\alpha = -\frac{w \cdot v}{v \cdot v}.$$

The vector αv is the projection of w onto v, and

$$u = w - \frac{w \cdot v}{v \cdot v} v.$$

We can extend this result to construct a set of orthogonal vectors from an arbitrary set of linearly independent vectors.

B.6   Gram–Schmidt Orthogonalization

Given a set of basis vectors, $a_1, a_2, \ldots, a_n$, in a space of dimension n, it is relatively straightforward to create another basis $b_1, b_2, \ldots, b_n$ that is **orthonormal** that is a basis in which each vector has unit length and is orthogonal to each other vector in the basis, or mathematically:

$$b_i \cdot b_j = \begin{cases} 0, & \text{if } i \neq j, \\ 1, & \text{otherwise.} \end{cases}$$

Hence, there is no real loss of generality in using orthogonal (Cartesian) coordinate systems.

We proceed iteratively. We look for a vector of the form

$$b_2 = a_2 + \alpha b_1,$$

that we can make orthogonal to b_1 by choosing α properly. Taking the dot product, we must have

$$b_2 \cdot b_1 = 0 = a_2 \cdot b_1 + \alpha b_1 \cdot b_1.$$

Solving, we have

$$\alpha = -\frac{a_2 \cdot b_1}{b_1 \cdot b_1},$$

and

$$b_2 = a_2 - \frac{a_2 \cdot b_1}{b_1 \cdot b_1} b_1.$$

We have constructed the orthogonal vector by removing the part parallel to b_1—that is, the projection of a_2 onto b_1.

The general iterative step is to find a

$$b_k = a_k + \sum_{i=1}^{k-1} \alpha_i b_i,$$

that is orthogonal to $b_1, \ldots, b_{k-1}$. There are $k-1$ orthogonality conditions that allow us to find

$$\alpha_i = -\frac{a_k \cdot b_i}{b_i \cdot b_i}.$$

We can normalize each vector, either at the end of the process, by replacing b_i by $b_i/|b_i|$, or, more efficiently, by normalizing each b_i as soon as possible.

B.7   Suggested Readings

There are many excellent books on linear algebra and vector spaces. For practitioners of computer graphics, the preferred approach is to start with vector-space ideas, and to see linear algebra as a tool for working with general vector spaces. Unfortunately, most of the linear-algebra textbooks are concerned with only the Euclidean spaces of n-tuples, $\mathbf{R}^n$. See [Bow83, Ban83].

Affine spaces can be approached in number of ways. See Foley [Fol90] for a more geometric development.

Exercises

B.1   Prove that the complex numbers form a scalar field. What are the additive and multiplicative identity elements?

B.2   Prove that the rational functions from a scalar field.

B.3   Prove that the rational functions with real coefficients form a vector space.

B.4   Prove that the number of elements in a basis is unique.

B.5 Consider a set of n real functions $\{f_i(x)\}, i = 1, \ldots, n$. Show how to form a vector space of functions with these elements. Define *basis* and *dimension* for this space?

B.6 Show that the set of polynomials of degree up to n form an n-dimensional vector space.

B.7 The most important Euclidean space is the space of n-tuples, $a_1, \ldots, a_n$: $\mathbf{R}^n$. Define the operations of vector addition and scalar-vector multiplication in this space. What is the dot product in $\mathbf{R}^n$?

B.8 Suppose that you are given three vectors in $\mathbf{R}^3$. How can you find whether they form a basis?

B.9 Consider the three vectors in $\mathbf{R}^3$: $(1,0,0)$, $(1,1,0)$ and $(1,1,1)$. Show that they are linearly independent. Derive an orthonormal basis from these vectors, starting with $(1,0,0)$.

C Matrices

In computer graphics, the major use of matrices is in the representation of changes in coordinate systems and frames. In the studies of vector analysis and linear algebra, the use of the term *vector* is somewhat different. Unfortunately, computer graphics relies on both of these fields, and the interpretation of *vector* has caused confusion. To remedy this situation, we shall use the terms *row matrix* and *column matrix*, rather than the linear-algebra terms of *row vector* and *column vector*. We reserve the *vector* to denote directed line segments, and occasionally, as in Appendix B, to denote the abstract-data-type vector that is an element of a vector space.

This appendix reviews the major results that you will need to manipulate matrices in computer graphics. We almost always use matrices that are 4 × 4. Hence, the parts of linear algebra that deal with manipulations of general matrices, such as the inversion of an arbitrary square matrix, are of limited interest. Most implementations will, instead, implement inversion of 4 × 4 matrices directly in the hardware or software.

C.1 Definitions

A **matrix** is an $n \times m$ array of scalars, arranged conceptually as n rows and m columns. Often, n and m are referred to as the row and column **dimensions** of the matrix, and, if $m = n$, we say that the matrix is a **square matrix** of dimension n. We shall use real numbers for scalars, almost exclusively, although most results will hold for complex numbers as well. The elements of a matrix **A** are the members of the set of scalars, $\{a_{ij}\}, i = 1, \ldots, n, j = 1, \ldots, m$. We write **A** in terms of its elements as

$$\mathbf{A} = [\, a_{ij} \,].$$

The **transpose** of an $n \times m$ matrix $\mathbf{A}$ is the $m \times n$ matrix that we obtain by interchanging the rows and columns of $\mathbf{A}$. We denote this matrix as $\mathbf{A}^T$, and it is given as

$$\mathbf{A}^T = [\, a_{ji} \,].$$

The special cases of matrices with one column ($n \times 1$ matrix) and one row ($1 \times m$ matrix) are called **column matrices** and **row matrices**. We shall denote column matrices with lowercase letters:

$$\mathbf{b} = [\, b_i \,].$$

The transpose of a row matrix is a column matrix; we shall write it as $\mathbf{b}^T$.

C.2   Matrix Operations

There are three basic matrix operations: scalar–matrix multiplication, matrix–matrix addition, and matrix–matrix multiplication. You can assume that the scalars are real numbers, although all these operations are defined in the same way when the elements of the matrices and the scalar multipliers are of the same type.

Scalar–matrix multiplication is defined for any size matrix $\mathbf{A}$; it is simply the element-by-element multiplication of the elements of the matrix by a scalar α. The operation is written as

$$\alpha\mathbf{A} = [\, \alpha a_{ij} \,].$$

We define **matrix–matrix addition**, the sum of two matrices, by adding the corresponding elements of the two matrices. The sum makes sense only if the two matrices have the same dimensions. The sum of two matrices of the same dimensions is given by the matrix

$$\mathbf{C} = \mathbf{A} + \mathbf{B} = [\, a_{ij} + b_{ij} \,].$$

For **matrix–matrix multiplication**, the product of an $n \times l$ matrix $\mathbf{A}$ by an $l \times m$ matrix $\mathbf{B}$ is the $n \times m$ matrix

$$\mathbf{C} = \mathbf{AB} = [\, c_{ij} \,],$$

where

$$c_{ij} = \sum_{k=1}^{l} a_{ik} b_{kj}.$$

The matrix–matrix product is thus defined only if the number of columns of $\mathbf{A}$ is the same as the number of rows of $\mathbf{B}$. We say that $\mathbf{A}$ premultiplies $\mathbf{B}$, or $\mathbf{B}$ postmultiplies $\mathbf{A}$.

Scalar–matrix multiplication obeys a number of simple rules that hold for any matrix **A**, and for scalars α and β, such as

$$\alpha(\beta\mathbf{A}) = (\alpha\beta)\mathbf{A},$$

$$\alpha\beta\mathbf{A} = \beta\alpha\mathbf{A},$$

all of which follow from the fact that our matrix operations reduce to scalar multiplications on the scalar elements of a matrix. For matrix–matrix addition, we have the **commutative** property. For any $n \times m$ matrices A and B:

$$\mathbf{A} + \mathbf{B} = \mathbf{B} + \mathbf{A}.$$

We also have the **associative** property, which states that for any three $n \times m$ matrices A, B, and C:

$$\mathbf{A} + (\mathbf{B} + \mathbf{C}) = (\mathbf{A} + \mathbf{B}) + \mathbf{C}.$$

Matrix–matrix multiplication, although associative,

$$\mathbf{A}(\mathbf{BC}) = (\mathbf{AB})\mathbf{C},$$

is almost never commutative. So not only is it almost always the case that $\mathbf{AB} \neq \mathbf{BA}$, but also one product may not even be defined when the other is. In graphics applications, where matrices represent transformations such as translation and rotation, these results express that the order in which you carry out a sequence of transformations is important. A rotation followed by a translation is not the same as a translation, followed by a rotation. However, if we do a rotation, followed by a translation, followed by a scaling, we get the same result if we first combine the scaling and translation, preserving the order, and applying the rotation to the combined transformation.

The identity matrix **I** is a square matrix with 1s on the diagonal and 0s elsewhere:

$$\mathbf{I} = [\, a_{ij} \,], \qquad a_{ij} = \begin{cases} 1 & \text{if } i = j; \\ 0 & \text{otherwise.} \end{cases}$$

Assuming that the dimensions make sense,

$$\mathbf{AI} = \mathbf{A},$$

$$\mathbf{IB} = \mathbf{B}.$$

C.3   Row and Column Matrices

The $1 \times n$ and $n \times 1$ row and column matrices are of particular interest to us. We can represent either a vector or a point in three-dimensional space,[1] with respect to some frame, as the column matrix

$$\mathbf{p} = \begin{bmatrix} x \\ y \\ z \end{bmatrix}.$$

We shall use lowercase letters for column matrices. The transpose of $\mathbf{p}$ is the row matrix

$$\mathbf{p}^T = [\, x \quad y \quad z \,].$$

Because the product of an $n \times l$ and a $l \times m$ matrix is an $n \times m$ matrix, the product of a square matrix of dimension n and a column matrix of dimension n is a new column matrix of dimension n. Our standard mode of representing transformations of points will be to use a column matrix of two, three, or four dimensions to represent a point (or vector), and a square matrix to represent a transformation of the point (or vector). Thus, the expression

$$\mathbf{p}' = \mathbf{A}\mathbf{p}$$

yields the representation of a transformed point (or vector), and expressions such as

$$\mathbf{p}' = \mathbf{A}\mathbf{B}\mathbf{C}\mathbf{p}$$

describe sequences, or **concatenations**, of transformations. Note that, because the matrix–matrix product is associative, we do not need parentheses in this expression.

Many graphics books prefer to use row matrices to represent points. If we do so, using the fact that the transpose of a product can be written as

$$(\mathbf{A}\mathbf{B})^T = \mathbf{B}^T \mathbf{A}^T,$$

then the concatenation of the three transformations can be written in row form as

$$\mathbf{p}'^T = \mathbf{p}^T \mathbf{C}^T \mathbf{B}^T \mathbf{A}^T.$$

The professed advantage of this form is that, in English, we read the transformations in the order in which they are performed; first $\mathbf{C}$, then $\mathbf{B}$, then $\mathbf{A}$.

---

[1] The homogeneous-coordinate representation introduced in Chapter 4 will distinguish between the representation of a point and the representation of a vector.

Almost all the scientific, mathematics, and engineering literature, however, uses column matrices, rather than row matrices. Consequently, we prefer the column form. Although the choice is conceptually simple, in practice, you have to be careful regarding which one your API is using, as not only is the order of transformations reversed, but also the transformation matrices themselves must be transposed.

C.4   Rank

In computer graphics, the primary use of matrices is as representations of points and of transformations. If a square matrix represents the transformation of a point or vector, we are often interested in whether or not the transformation is reversible or **invertible**. Thus, if

$$\mathbf{q} = \mathbf{Ap},$$

we want to know whether we can find a square matrix **B** such that

$$\mathbf{p} = \mathbf{Bq}.$$

Substituting for **q**,

$$\mathbf{p} = \mathbf{Bq} = \mathbf{BAp} = \mathbf{Ip} = \mathbf{p}$$

and

$$\mathbf{BA} = \mathbf{I}.$$

If such a **B** exists, it is the **inverse** of **A**, and **A** is said to be **nonsingular**. A noninvertible matrix is **singular**. The inverse of **A** is written as $\mathbf{A}^{-1}$.

The fundamental result about inverses is as follows: *The inverse of a square matrix exists if and only if the determinant of the matrix is nonzero.* Although the determinant of **A** is a scalar, denoted by $|\mathbf{A}|$, its computation, for anything but low-dimensional matrices, requires almost as much work as does computation of the inverse. These calculations are $O(n^3)$ for an *n*-dimensional matrix. For the two-, three-, and four-dimensional matrices of interest in computer graphics, we can compute determinants by Cramer's rule and inverses using determinants, or we can use geometric reasoning. For example, the inverse of a translation is a translation back, and thus the inverse of a translation matrix must be a translation matrix. We pursue this course in Chapter 4.

For general nonsquare matrices, the concept of rank is important. We can regard a square matrix as a row matrix whose elements are column matrices or, equivalently, as a column matrix whose elements are row matrices. In terms of the vector-space concepts of Appendix B, the rows of an $n \times m$ matrix are elements of the Euclidean space $\mathbf{R}^m$, whereas the columns are elements of $\mathbf{R}^n$. We can determine how many rows (or columns) are **linearly independent**.

The row (column) **rank** is the maximum number of linearly independent rows (columns), and thus *for an n × n matrix, the row rank and the column rank are the same and the matrix is nonsingular if and only if the rank is n.* Thus, a matrix is invertible if and only if its rows (and columns) are linearly independent.

C.5   Change of Representation

We can use matrices to represent changes in bases for any set of vectors satisfying the rules of Appendix B. Suppose that we have a vector space of dimension n. Let $\{u_1, u_2, \ldots, u_n\}$ and $\{v_1, v_2, \ldots, v_n\}$ be two bases for the vector space. Hence, a given vector v can be expressed as either

$$v = \alpha_1 u_1 + \alpha_2 u_2 + \ldots + \alpha_n u_n,$$

or

$$v = \beta_1 v_1 + \beta_2 v_2 + \ldots + \beta_n v_n.$$

Thus, $(\alpha_1, \alpha_2, \ldots, \alpha_n)$ and $(\beta_1, \beta_2, \ldots, \beta_n)$ are two different representations of v, and each can be expressed, equivalently, as a vector in the Euclidean space $\mathbf{R}^n$ or as a column matrix of dimension n. When we are working with representations, rather than with the vectors, we have to be careful to make sure that our notation reflects the difference. We shall write the representations of v as either

$$\mathbf{v} = [\, \alpha_1 \quad \alpha_2 \quad \ldots \quad \alpha_n \,]^T,$$

or

$$\mathbf{v}' = [\, \beta_1 \quad \beta_2 \quad \ldots \quad \beta_n \,]^T,$$

depending on which basis we use.

We can now address the problem of how we convert from the representation $\mathbf{v}$ to the representation $\mathbf{v}'$. The basis vectors $\{v_1, v_2, \ldots, v_n\}$ can be expressed as vectors in the basis $\{u_1, u_2, \ldots, u_n\}$. Thus, there exists a set of scalars γ_{ij} such that

$$u_i = \gamma_{i1} v_1 + \gamma_{i2} v_2 + \ldots + \gamma_{in} v_n, \quad i = 1, \ldots, n.$$

We can write the expression in matrix form for all u_i as

$$\begin{bmatrix} u_1 \\ u_2 \\ \vdots \\ u_n \end{bmatrix} = \mathbf{A} \begin{bmatrix} v_1 \\ v_2 \\ \vdots \\ v_n \end{bmatrix},$$

where $\mathbf{A}$ is the $n \times n$ matrix

$$\mathbf{A} = [\, \gamma_{ij} \,].$$

We can use column matrices to express both $\mathbf{v}$ and $\mathbf{v}'$ in terms of the vectors' representations as

$$\mathbf{v} = \mathbf{a}^T \begin{bmatrix} u_1 \\ u_2 \\ \vdots \\ u_n \end{bmatrix},$$

where

$$\mathbf{a} = [\, \alpha_i \,].$$

We can define $\mathbf{b}$ as

$$\mathbf{b} = [\, \beta_i \,],$$

and we can write $\mathbf{v}'$ as

$$\mathbf{v}' = \mathbf{b}^T \begin{bmatrix} v_1 \\ v_2 \\ \vdots \\ v_n \end{bmatrix}.$$

$\mathbf{A}$ relates the two bases, so we find by direct substitution that

$$\mathbf{b}^T = \mathbf{a}^T \mathbf{A}.$$

$\mathbf{A}$ is the **matrix representation** of the change between the two bases. It allows us to convert directly between the two representations. Equivalently, we can work with matrices of scalars rather than with abstract vectors. For geometric problems, although our vectors may be directed line segments, we can represent them by sets of scalars, and we can represent changes of bases or transformations by direct manipulation of these scalars.

C.6   The Cross Product

Given two nonparallel vectors, u and v, in a three-dimensional space, the cross product gives a third vector, w, that is orthogonal to both. Regardless of the representation, we must have

$$w \cdot u = w \cdot v = 0.$$

We can assign one component of w arbitrarily, because it is the direction of w, rather than the length, that is of importance, leaving us with three conditions for the three components of w. Within a particular coordinate system, if u has components $\alpha_1, \alpha_2, \alpha_3$, and v has components $\beta_1, \beta_2, \beta_3$, then, in this system, the **cross product** is defined as

$$\mathbf{w} = \mathbf{u} \times \mathbf{v} = \begin{bmatrix} \alpha_2\beta_3 - \alpha_3\beta_2 \\ \alpha_3\beta_1 - \alpha_1\beta_3 \\ \alpha_1\beta_2 - \alpha_2\beta_1 \end{bmatrix}.$$

Note that vector w is defined by u and v; we use their representation only when we wish to compute w in a particular coordinate system. The cross product gives a consistent orientation for $u \times v$. For example, consider the x, y, and z axes as three vectors that determine the three coordinate directions of a right-handed coordinate system.[2] If we use the usual x and y axes, the cross product $x \times y$ points in the direction of the positive z axis.

C.7   Suggested Readings

Some of the standard references on linear algebra and matrices, include Strang [Str93] and Banchoff and Werner [Ban83]. See also Rogers and Adams [Rog90] and the *Graphics Gems* series [Gra90, Gra91, Gra92, Gra94, Gra95].

The issue of row versus column matrices is an old one. Early graphics books [New73] used row matrices. The trend now is to use column matrices [Fol90], although a few books still use row representations [Wat93]. Within the API, it may not be clear which is being used, because the elements of a square matrix can be represented as a simple array of n^2 elements. Certain APIs, such as OpenGL, allow only postmultiplication of an internal matrix by a user-defined matrix; others, such as PHIGS, support both pre- and postmultiplication.

Exercises

C.1 In $\mathbf{R}^3$, consider the two bases $\{(1,0,0), (1,1,0), (1,1,1)\}$ and $\{(1,0,0), (0,1,0), (0,0,1)\}$. Find the two matrices that convert representations between the two bases. Show that they are inverses of each other.

C.2 Consider the vector space of polynomials of degree up to 2. Show that the sets of polynomials $\{1, x, x^2\}$ and $\{1, 1+x, 1+x+x^2\}$ are bases.

---

[2] A right-handed coordinate system has positive directions determined by the thumb, index, and middle fingers of the right hand used for the x, y, and z axes, respectively. Equivalently, on a piece of paper, if positive x points left to right, and positive y points bottom to top, then positive z points out of the page.

Give the representation of the polynomial $1 + 2x + 3x^2$ in each basis. Find the matrix that converts between representations in the two bases.

C.3 Suppose that $\mathbf{i}$, $\mathbf{j}$, and $\mathbf{k}$ represent the unit vectors in the x, y, and z directions, respectively, in $\mathbf{R}^3$. Show that the cross product $u \times v$ is given by the matrix

$$u \times v = \begin{bmatrix} \mathbf{i} & \mathbf{j} & \mathbf{k} \\ u_1 & u_2 & u_3 \\ v_1 & v_2 & v_3 \end{bmatrix}.$$

C.4 Show that, in $\mathbf{R}^3$,

$$|u \times v| = |u||v| \sin \theta,$$

where θ is the angle between u and v.

Bibliography

Ado85   Adobe Systems Incorporated, *PostScript Language Reference Manual*, Addison-Wesley, Reading, MA, 1985.

Ake88   Akeley, K., and T. Jermoluk, "High Performance Polygon Rendering," *Computer Graphics*, 22(4), 239–246, 1988.

Ake93   Akeley, K., "Reality Engine Graphics," *Computer Graphics*, 109–116, 1993.

Ang90   Angel, E., *Computer Graphics*, Addision-Wesley, Reading, MA, 1990.

ANSI85   American National Standards Institute (ANSI), *American National Standard for Information Processing Systems—Computer Graphics—Graphical Kernel System (GKS) Functional Description*, ANSI, X3.124-1985, ANSI, New York, 1985.

ANSI88   American National Standards Institute (ANSI), *American National Standard for Information Processing Systems—Programmer's Hierarchical Interactive Graphics System (PHIGS)*, ANSI, X3.144-1988, ANSI, New York, 1988.

App68   Appel, A., "Some Techniques for Shading Machine Renderings of Solids," *Spring Joint Computer Conference*, 37–45, 1968.

Ban83   Banchoff, T., and J. Werner, *Linear Algebra Through Geometry*, Springer-Verlag, New York, 1983.

Bar93   Barnsley, M., *Fractals Everywhere*, Second Edition, Academic Press, San Diego, CA, 1993.

Bar83   Barsky, B.A., and C. Beatty, "Local Control of Bias and Tension in Beta-Splines," *ACM Transactions on Graphics*, 2(2), 109–134, 1983.

Bar87   Bartels, C. Beatty and B.A. Barsky, *An Introduction to Splines for use in Computer Graphics and Geometric Modeling*, Morgan-Kaufman, Los Altos, CA, 1987.

Bli76   Blinn, J.F., and M.E. Newell, "Texture and Reflection in Computer Generated Images," CACM, 19(10), 542–547, 1976.

Bli77   Blinn, J.F., "Models of Light Reflection for Computer-Synthesized Pictures," *Computer Graphics*, 11(2), 192–198, 1977.

Bow83   Bowyer, A., and J. Woodwark, *A Programmer's Geometry*, Butterworth, 1983.

Bre63   Bresenham, J. E., "Algorithm for Computer Control of a Digital Plotter," *IBM Systems Journal*, January, 25–30, 1965.

Bre87   Bresenham, J. E., "Ambiguities in Incremental Line Rastering," *IEEE Computer Graphics and Applications*, May, 31–43, 1987.

Car78   Carlbom, I. and J. Paciorek, "Geometric Projection and Viewing Transformations," *Computing Surveys*, 1(4), 465–502, 1978.

Cas96   Castleman, K.C., *Digital Image Processing*, Prentice-Hall, Englewood Cliffs, NJ, 1996.

Cat75   Catmull, E., "A Hidden-Surface Algorithm with Antialiasing," *Computer Graphics*, 12(3), 6–11, 1975.

Cla82   Clark, J.E., "The Geometry Engine: A VLSI Geometry System for Graphics," *Computer Graphics*, 16, 127–133, 1982.

Coh85   Cohen, M.F., and D.P. Greenberg, "The Hemi-Cube: A Radiosity Solution for Complex Environments," *Computer Graphics*, 19(3), 31–40, 1985.

Coh88   Cohen, M.F., S.E. Chen, J.R. Wallace, and D.P. Greenberg, "A Progressive Refinement Approach to Fast Rasiosity Image Generation," *Computer Graphics*, 22(4), 75–84, 1988.

Coo82   Cook, R.L., and K.E. Torrance, "A Reflectance Model for Computer Graphics," *ACM Transactions on Graphics*, 1(1), 7–24, 1982.

Coo87   Cook, R.L., L. Carpenter, and E. Catmull, "The Reyes Image Rendering Architecture," *Computer Graphics*, 21(4), July, 95–102, 1987.

Cro81   Crow, F.C., "A Comparison of Antialiasing Techniques," *IEEE Computer Graphics and Applications*, 1(1), 40–48, 1981.

DeR88   DeRose, T.D., "A Coordinate Free Approach to Geometric Programming," SIGGRAPH Course Notes, *SIGGRAPH*, 1988.

DeR89   DeRose, T.D., "A Coordinate Free Approach to Geometric Programming," *Theory and Practice of Geometric Modeling*, W. Strasser and H.P. Seidel (Eds.), Springer-Verlag, Berlin, 1989.

Dre88   Drebin, R.A., L. Carpenter, and P. Hanrahan, "Volume Rendering," *Computer Graphics*, 22(4), 65–74, 1988.

End84   Enderle, G., K. Kansy, and G. Pfaff, *Computer Graphics Programming: GKS-The Graphics Standard*, Springer-Verlag, Berlin, 1984.

Eng68   Engelbart, D.C., and W.K. English, "A Research Center for Augmenting Human Intellect," *Fall Joint Computer Conference,*, Thompson Books, Washington, DC, 1968.

Far88   Farin, G., *Curves and Surfaces for Computer Aided Geometric Design*, Academic Press, New York, 1988.

Fau80   Faux, I.D., and M.J. Pratt, *Computational Geometry for Design and Manufacturing*, Halsted, Chichester, England, 1980.

Fol90   Foley, J.D., A. van Dam, S.K. Feiner, and J.F. Hughes, *Computer Graphics,* Second Edition, Addison-Wesley, Reading, MA, 1990 (C Version 1996).

Fol94   Foley, J.D., A. van Dam, S.K. Feiner, J. F. Hughes and R. Phillips, *Introduction to Computer Graphics,* Addison-Wesley, Reading, MA, 1994.

Fou82   Fournier, A., Fussell, D., and L. Carpenter, "Computer Rendering of Stochastic Models," *CACM*, 25(6), 371–384, 1982.

Gla89   Glassner, A.S. (Ed.), *An Introduction to Ray Tracing,* Academic Press, New York, 1989.

Gla94   Glassner, A.S., *Principles of Digital Image Synthesis,* Morgan-Kaufmann, New York, 1994.

Gol83   Goldberg, A., and D. Robson, *Smalltalk–80: The Language and Its Implementation,* Addison-Wesley, Reading, MA, 1983.

Gon87   Gonzalez, R., and P. Wintz, *Digital Image Processing*, Second Edition, Addison-Wesley, Reading, MA, 1987.

Gor84   Goral, C.M., K.E. Torrance, D.P. Greenberg, and B. Battaile, "Modeling the Interaction of Light Between Diffuse Surfaces," *Computer Graphics (SIGGRAPH 84)*, 18(3), 213–222, 1984.

Gou71   Gouraud, H., "Computer Display of Curved Surfaces," *IEEE Trans. Computers,* C-20, 623–628, 1971.

Gra90   *Graphics Gems I*, Glassner, A.S. (Ed.), Academic Press, San Diego, CA, 1990.

Gra91   *Graphics Gems II*, Arvo, J. (Ed.), Academic Press, San Diego, CA, 1991.

Gra92   *Graphics Gems III*, Kirk, D. (Ed.), Academic Press, San Diego, CA, 1992.

Gra94   *Graphics Gems IV*, Heckbert, P. (Ed.), Academic Press, San Diego, CA, 1994.

Gra95   *Graphics Gems V*, Paeth, A. (Ed.), Academic Press, San Diego, CA, 1995.

Hal89   Hall, R., *Illumination and Color in Computer Generated Imagery,* Springer-Verlag, New York, 1989.

Hea94   Hearn, D., and M.P. Baker, *Computer Graphics*, Second Edition, Prentice-Hall, Englewood Cliffs, NJ, 1994.

Hec84   Heckbert, P.S., and P. Hanrahan, "Beam Tracing Polygonal Objects," *Computer Graphics,* 18(3), 119–127, 1984.

Hek86   Heckbert, P.S., "Survey of Texture Mapping," *IEEE Computer Graphics and Applications,* 6(11), 56–67, 1986.

Hil90   Hill, F.S., *Computer Graphics*, MacMillan, New York, 1990.

Hop83   Hopgood, F.R.A., D.A. Duce, J.A. Gallop, and D.C. Sutcliffe, *Introduction to the Graphical Kernel System: GKS*, Academic Press, London, 1983.

Hop91   Hopgood, F.R.A., and D.A. Duce, *A Primer for PHIGS,* John Wiley & Sons, Chichester, England, 1991.

ISO88   International Standards Organization, *International Standard Information Processing Systems—Computer Graphics—Graphical Kernel System for Three Dimensions (GKS-3D),* ISO Document Number 8805:1988(E), American National Standards Institute, New York, 1988.

Jar76   Jarivs, J.F., C.N. Judice, and W.H. Ninke, "A Survey of Techniques for the Image Display of Continuous Tone Pictures on Bilevel Displays," *Computer Graphics and Image Processing,* 5(1), 13–40, 1976.

Joy88　Joy, K.I., C.W. Grant, N.L. Max, and L. Hatfield, *Computer Graphics: Image Synthesis*, Computer Society Press, Washington, DC, 1988.

Kaj86　Kajiya, J.T., "The Rendering Equation," *Computer Graphics,* 20(4), 143–150, 1986.

Kil94a　Kilgard, M.J., "OpenGL and X, Part 3: Integrated OpenGL with Motif," *The X Journal,* SIGS Publications, July/August 1994.

Kil94b　Kilgard, M.J., "An OpenGL Toolkit," *The X Journal,* SIGS Publications, November/December 1994.

Knu87　Knuth, D.E., "Digital Halftones by Dot Diffusion," *ACM Transactions on Graphics,* 6(40), 245–273, 1987.

Las87　Lasseter, J., "Principles of Traditional Animation Applied to 3D Computer Animation," *Computer Graphics*, 21(4), 33–44, 1987.

Lev88　Levoy, M., "Display of Surface from Volume Data," *IEEE Computer Graphics and Applications,* 8(3), 29–37, 1988.

Lia84　Liang, Y., and B. Barsky, "A New Concept and Method for Line Clipping," *ACM Transactions on Graphics*, 3(1), 1–22, 1984.

Lin68　Lindenmayer, A., "Mathematical Models for Cellular Interactions in Biology" *J. Theoretical Biology,* 18, 280–315, 1968.

Lor87　Lorensen, W.E., and H.E. Cline, "Marching Cubes: A High Resolution 3D Surface Construction Algorithm," *Computer Graphics,* 21(4), 163–169, 1987.

Mag85　Magnenat-Thalmann, N., and D. Thalmann, *Computer Animation: Theory and Practice,* Springer-Verlag, Tokyo, 1985.

Man82　Mandelbrot, B., *The Fractal Geometry of Nature,* Freeman Press, New York, 1982.

Mat95　The MathWorks, *Student Edition of MatLab Version 4 Users Guide,* Prentice-Hall, Englewood Cliffs, NJ, 1995.

Max51　Maxwell, E.A., General Homogeneous Coordinates in Space of Three Dimensions, Cambridge University Press, Cambridge, England, 1951.

New73　Newman, W.M. and R.F. Sproull, *Principles of Interactive Computer Graphics*, McGraw-Hill, New York, 1973.

Ope93a　OpenGL Architecture Review Board, *OpenGL Programming Guide,* Addison-Wesley, Reading, MA, 1993.

Ope93b　OpenGL Architecture Review Board, *OpenGL Reference Manual,* Addison-Wesley, Reading, MA, 1993.

OSF89　Open Software Foundation, *OSF/Motif Style Guide,* Prentice-Hall, Englewood Cliffs, NJ, 1989.

Ous94　Ousterhuat, J., *Tcl and the Tk Toolkit,* Addision-Wesley, Reading, MA, 1994.

Pap81　Papert, S., *LOGO: A Language for Learning*, Creative Computer Press, Middletown, NJ, 1981.

Per89　Perlin, K., and E. Hoffert, "Hypertexture," *Computer Graphics,* 23(3), 253–262, 1989.

PHI89　PHIGS+ Committee, "PHIGS+ Functional Description, Revision 3.0," *Computer Graphics,* 22(3), 1988, 125–218, July.

Pho75   Phong, B. T., "Illumination for Computer Generated Scenes," *Communications of the ACM*, 18(6), 311–317.

Pei88   Peitgen, H.O., and S. Saupe (Ed.), *The Science of Fractal Images,* Springer-Verlag, New York, 1988.

Pik84   Pike, R., L. Guibas, and D. Ingalls, "Bitmap Graphics," *Computer Graphics*, 18(3), 135–160, 1984.

Por84   Porter, T., and T. Duff, "Compositing Digital Images," *Computer Graphics,* 18(3), 253–259, 1984.

Pra78   Pratt, W.K., *Digital Image Processing*, Wiley, New York, 1978.

Pru90   Prusinkiewicz, P., and A. Lindenmayer, *The Algorithmic Beauty of Plants,*, Springer-Verlag, Berlin, 1990.

Rie81   Riesenfeld, R.F., "Homogeneous Coordinates and Projective Planes in Computer Graphics," *IEEE Computer Graphics and Applications*, 1(1), 50–56, 1981.

Ree83   Reeves, W.T., "Particle Systems—A Technique for Modeling a Class of Fuzzy Obejcts," *Computer Graphics*, 17(3), 359–376, 1983.

Rey87   Reynolds, C.W., "Flocks, Herds, and Schools: A Distributed Behavioral Model," *Computer Graphics*, 21(4), 25–34, 1987.

Rog85   Rogers, D.F., *Procedural Elements for Computer Graphics*, McGraw-Hill, New York, 1985.

Rog90   Rogers, D.F., and J.A. Adams, *Mathematical Elements for Computer Graphics,* McGraw-Hill, New York, 1990.

Sch88   Schiefler, R.W., J. Gettys, and R. Newman, *X Window System,* Digital Press, 1988.

Sch87   Schneiderman, B., *Designing the User Interface: Strategies for Effective Human–Computer Interaction*, Addison-Wesley, Reading, MA, 1987.

Seg92   Segal, M., and K. Akeley, *The OpenGL Graphics System: A Specification,* Version 1.0, Silicon Graphics, 1992.

Sie81   Siegel, R., and J. Howell, *Thermal Radiation Heat Transfer,* Hemisphere, Washington, DC, 1981.

Sil89   Sillion, F.X., and C. Puech, "A General Two-Pass Method Integrating Specular and Diffuse Reflection." *Computer Graphics,* 22(3), 335–344, 1989.

Smi84   Smith, A.R., "Plants, Fractals and Formal Languages," *Computer Graphics,* 18(3), 1–10, 1984.

Str93   Strang, G., *Introduction to Linear Algebra*, Wellesley-Cambridge Press, 1993.

Sut63   Sutherland, I. E., *Sketchpad, A Man–Machine Graphical Communication System, SJCC,* 329, Spartan Books, Baltimore, MD, 1963

Sut74a Sutherland, I.E. and G.W. Hodgeman, "Reentrant Polygon Clipping," *Communications of the ACM*, 17, 32–42, 1974.

Sut74b Sutherland, I.E., R.F. Sproull, and R.A. Schumacker, "A Characterization of Ten Hidden-Surface Algorithms," *Computer Surveys*, 6(1), 1–55, 1974.

Tor67   Torrance, K.E., and E.M. Sparrow, "Theory for Off–Specular Reflection from Roughened Surfaces," *J. Optical Society of America,* 57(9), 1105–1114, 1967.

Tuf83   Tufte, E.R., *The Visual Display of Quantitative Information*, Graphics Press, Cheshire, CN, 1983.

Tuf90   Tufte, E.R., *Envisioning Information*, Graphics Press, Cheshire, CN, 1990.

Ups89   Upstill, S., *The Renderman Companion: A Programmer's Guide to Realistic Computer Graphics,* Addison-Wesley, Reading, MA, 1989.

Van94   Van Gelder, A., and J. Wilhelms, "Topological Considerations in Isosurface Generation," *ACM Transactions on Graphics,* 13(4), 337–375, 1994.

Wat92   Watt, A., and Watt, M., *Advanced Animation and Rendering Techniques,* Addison-Wesley, Wokingham, England, 1992.

Wat93   Watt, A., *3D Computer Graphics*, Second Edition, Addison-Wesley, Wokingham, England, 1993.

Wer94   Wernecke, J., The Inventor Mentor, Addison-Wesley, Reading, MA, 1994.

Wes90   Westover, L., "Footprint Evaluation for Volume Rendering," *Computer Graphics*, 24(4), 367–376, 1990.

Whi80   Whitted, T., "An Improved Illumination Model for Shaded Display," *Communications of ACM*, 23(6), 343–348, 1980.

Wit94a Witkin, A.P., and P.S. Heckbert, "Using Particles to Sample and Control Implicit Surfaces," *Computer Graphics,* 28(3), 269–277, 1994.

Wit94b Witken, A. (Ed.), *An Introduction to Physically Based Modelling,* Course Notes, SIGGRAPH 94.

Wol91   Wolfram, S., *Mathematica*, Addison-Wesley, Reading, MA, 1991.

Wys82   Wyszecki, G., and W.S. Stiles, *Color Science*, Wiley, New York, 1982.

Function Index

This index includes only the first appearance of those functions that are used in the text. The complete list of OpenGL functions is contained in the *OpenGL Reference Manual* and the GLUT documentation. The function are grouped according to their inclusion in the GL, GLU, or GLUT libraries. Functions with multiple forms, such as glVertex, are listed once.

Index